FUNDAMENTALS OF INTERNATIONAL
BUSINESS TRANSACTIONS – DOCUMENTS

Fundamentals of International Business Transactions

Documents

edited by

Ronald A. Brand

KLUWER LAW INTERNATIONAL

The Hague • London • Boston

Published by Kluwer Law International,
P.O. Box 85889, 2508 CN The Hague, The Netherlands.

Sold and distributed in the U.S.A. and Canada
by Kluwer Law International,
675 Massachusetts Avenue, Cambridge, MA 02139, U.S.A.
tel: (617) 354-0140; fax: (617) 354-8595

In all other countries, sold and distributed
by Kluwer Law International,
P.O. Box 85889, 2508 CN The Hague, The Netherlands
tel: 31 70 308 1562; fax: 31 70 308 1555

ISBN 9041188576

Table of Contents

PART I. SELECTED INTERNATIONAL AGREEMENTS

A. United Nations Convention on Contracts for the International Sale of Goods

B. European Convention on Jurisdiction and the Enforcement of Judgments in Civil and Commercial Matters (Brussels Convention)

C. United Nations Convention on the Recognition and Enforcement of Foreign Arbitral Awards (New York Arbitration Convention)

D. Convention on Service Abroad of Judicial and Extrajudicial Documents in Civil or Commercial Matters (Hague Service Convention)

E. Convention on the Taking of Evidence Abroad in Civil or Commercial Matters (Hague Evidence Convention)

F. OECD Convention on Combating Bribery of Foreign Public Officials in International Business Transactions

G. Convention Establishing the Multilateral Investment Guarantee Agency (MIGA)

H. Convention on the Settlement of Disputes Between States and Nationals of Other States (ICSID)

I. United States Model Bilateral Investment Treaty

J. United States Model Income Tax Treaty

General website information:

http://www.state.gov/www/global/legal_affairs/tifindex.html
This website has a list of international agreements in force for the United States.

http://untreaty.un.org/
This website contains the United Nations Treaty Collection. Access may require a fee for certain types of use.

A. United Nations Convention on Contracts for the International Sale of Goods

Source: U.N. Document A/CONF.97/18, Annex I, *English version reprinted in* 52 Fed. Reg. 6264 (1987) and 19 I.L.M. 668 (1980)

Website information:

http://cisgw3.law.pace.edu
One of the most comprehensive Internet sources on the CISG, the Pace Law School website includes not only the CISG text (in English, French and Spanish) and ratification information, but also a table of Convention articles which allows users to search for bibliographic material, editorial analysis and cases. The site also provides CISG legislative history and "links" to related websites.

http://www.jura.uni-freiburg.de/ipr1/cisg
The University of Freiburg CISG Online Database contains texts of German case law on the CISG. It is sponsored by the Institute of Foreign and International Law (Dept. I).

http://www.uncitral.org/
This is the official website of the United Nations Commission on International Trade Law. It will (when complete) contain all current CISG case abstracts published by UNCITRAL as well as the various language versions of CLOUT documents. Also planned are postings of current Reports to and of Working Groups and the Commission.

http://www.unidroit.org/
The UNIDROIT site contains the full text of six UNIDROIT documents, including that of the *Principles of International Commercial Contracts,* with full comments.

http://www.state.gov/www/global/legal_affairs/private_intl_law.html
This database of the U.S. Department of State Office of Private International Law contains downloadable texts of international projects/conventions in the area of private international law to which the U.S. is a party or where the U.S. is considering accession/ratification. Also available are recent summaries of minutes of the Secretary of State's advisory committee meetings on private international law.

http://www.transworldlaw.com/
This is a private website that includes a useful comparison of provisions of the CISG and the Uniform Commercial Code (UCC).

Introduction

The United Nations Convention on Contracts for the International Sale of Goods (CISG) is a product of the United Nations Commission on International Trade Law (UNCITRAL). It was adopted at a diplomatic conference in Vienna in 1980, and is sometimes referred to as the "Vienna Sales Convention." It entered into force on January 1, 1988 for 11 countries ("Contracting States"), including the United States.[1] As of February 2000, there were 57 Contracting States. Notable exceptions are the United Kingdom, India and Japan.

The CISG provides the rules of contract formation and general contract rules for the sale of goods when the parties to a contract have their places of business in different Contracting States.[2] As a self-executing treaty, the CISG is the supreme law of the land pursuant to Article VI of the U.S. Constitution; it is the law in all state and federal courts applicable to contracts within its scope. Each of the six official languages of the United Nations in which the CISG has been adopted (Arabic, Chinese, English, French, Russian, and Spanish) has equal authenticity.

The 1978 draft of the Convention,[3] as well as the proceedings of the 1980 conference in Vienna, are of importance in interpreting of the CISG. Useful treatises on the Convention include the following:

JOHN O. HONNOLD, UNIFORM LAW FOR INTERNATIONAL SALES UNDER THE 1980 UNITED NATIONS CONVENTION ON CONTRACTS FOR THE INTERNATIONAL SALE OF GOODS (3d ed. 1999).

PETER SCHLECHTRIEM, UNIFORM SALES LAW: THE UN-CONVENTION ON CONTRACTS FOR THE INTERNATIONAL SALE OF GOODS (2d ed. 1998)

---

[1]The other original Contracting States were Argentina, China, Egypt, France, Hungary, Italy, Lesotho, Syrian Arab Republic, Yugoslavia and Zambia.

[2]Art. 1(1)(a). Art. 1(1)(b) provides that the CISG also applies "when the rules of private international law lead to the application of the law of a Contracting State." Article 95 allows Contracting States to opt out of this provision, and the U.S. has done so.

[3]*See* 18 I.L.M. 639 (1979).

UNITED NATIONS CONVENTION ON CONTRACTS FOR THE INTERNATIONAL SALE OF GOODS

THE STATES PARTIES TO THIS CONVENTION,

BEARING IN MIND the broad objectives in the resolutions adopted by the sixth special session of the General Assembly of the United Nations on the establishment of a New International Economic Order,

CONSIDERING that the development of international trade on the basis of equality and mutual benefit is an important element in promoting friendly relations among States,

BEING OF THE OPINION that the adoption of uniform rules which govern contracts for the international sale of goods and take into account the different social, economic and legal systems would contribute to the removal of legal barriers in international trade and promote the development of international trade,

HAVE AGREED as follows:

PART I
SPHERE OF APPLICATION AND GENERAL PROVISIONS

Chapter I
SPHERE OF APPLICATION

Article 1
(1) This Convention applies to contracts of sale of goods between parties whose places of business are in different States:

(a) when the States are Contracting States; or

(b) when the rules of private international law lead to the application of the law of a Contracting State.

(2) The fact that the parties have their places of business in different States is to be disregarded whenever this fact does not appear either from the contract or from any dealings between, or from information disclosed by, the parties at any time before or at the conclusion of the contract.

(3) Neither the nationality of the parties nor the civil or commercial character of the parties or of the contract is to be taken into consideration in determining the application of this Convention.

Article 2
This Convention does not apply to sales:

(a) of goods bought for personal, family or household use, unless the seller, at any time before or at the conclusion of the contract, neither knew nor ought to have known that the goods were bought for any such use;

(b) by auction;

(c) on execution or otherwise by authority of law;

(d) of stocks, shares, investment securities, negotiable instruments or money;

(e) of ships, vessels, hovercraft or aircraft;

(f) of electricity.

Article 3
(1) Contracts for the supply of goods to be manufactured or produced are to be considered sales unless the party who orders the goods undertakes to supply a substantial part of the materials necessary for such manufacture or production.

(2) This Convention does not apply to contracts in which the preponderant part of the obligations of the party who furnishes the goods consists in the supply of labour or other services.

Article 4
This Convention governs only the formation of the contract of sale and the rights and obligations of the seller and the buyer arising from such a contract. In particular, except as otherwise expressly provided in this Convention, it is not concerned with:

(a) the validity of the contract or of any of its provisions or of any usage;

(b) the effect which the contract may have on the property in the goods sold.

Article 5

This Convention does not apply to the liability of the seller for death or personal injury caused by the goods to any person.

Article 6

The parties may exclude the application of this Convention or, subject to article 12, derogate from or vary the effect of any of its provisions.

Chapter II
GENERAL PROVISIONS

Article 7

(1) In the interpretation of this Convention, regard is to be had to its international character and to the need to promote uniformity in its application and the observance of good faith in international trade.

(2) Questions concerning matters governed by this Convention which are not expressly settled in it are to be settled in conformity with the general principles on which it is based or, in the absence of such principles, in conformity with the law applicable by virtue of the rules of private international law.

Article 8

(1) For the purposes of this Convention statements made by and other conduct of a party are to be interpreted according to his intent where the other party knew or could not have been unaware what that intent was.

(2) If the preceding paragraph is not applicable, statements made by and other conduct of a party are to be interpreted according to the understanding that a reasonable person of the same kind as the other party would have had in the same circumstances.

(3) In determining the intent of a party or the understanding a reasonable person would have had, due consideration is to be given to all relevant circumstances of the case including the negotiations, any practices which the parties have established between themselves, usages and any subsequent conduct of the parties.

Article 9

(1) The parties are bound by any usage to which they have agreed and by any practices which they have established between themselves.

(2) The parties are considered, unless otherwise agreed, to have impliedly made applicable to their contract or its formation a usage of which the parties knew or ought to have known and which in international trade is widely known to, and regularly observed by, parties to contracts of the type involved in the particular trade concerned.

Article 10

For the purposes of this Convention:

(a) if a party has more than one place of business, the place of business is that which has the closest relationship to the contract and its performance, having regard to the circumstances known to or contemplated by the parties at any time before or at the conclusion of the contract;

(b) if a party does not have a place of business, reference is to be made to his habitual residence.

Article 11

A contract of sale need not be concluded in or evidence by writing and is not subject to any other requirements as to form. It may be proved by any means, including witnesses.

Article 12

Any provision of article 11, article 29 or Part II of this Convention that allows a contract of sale or its modification or termination by agreement or any offer, acceptance or other indication of intention to be made in any form other than in writing does not apply where any party has his place of business in a Contracting State which has made a declaration under article 96 of this Convention. The parties may not derogate from or vary the effect of this article.

Article 13

For the purposes of this Convention "writing" includes telegram and telex.

PART II
FORMATION OF THE CONTRACT

Article 14

(1) A proposal for concluding a contract addressed to one or more specific persons constitutes an offer if it is sufficiently definite and indicates the intention of the offeror to be bound in case of acceptance. A proposal is sufficiently definite if it indicates the goods and expressly or implicitly fixes or makes provision for determining the quantity and the price.

(2) A proposal other than one addressed to one or more specific persons is to be considered merely as an invitation to make offers, unless the contrary is clearly indicated by the person making the proposal.

Article 15

(1) An offer becomes effective when it reaches the offeree.

(2) An offer, even if it is irrevocable, may be withdrawn if the withdrawal reaches the offeree before or at the same time as the offer.

Article 16

(1) Until a contract is concluded an offer may be revoked if the revocation reaches the offeree before he has dispatched an acceptance.

(2) However, an offer cannot be revoked:

(a) if it indicates, whether by stating a fixed time for acceptance or otherwise, that it is irrevocable; or

(b) if it was reasonable for the offeree to rely on the offer as being irrevocable and the offeree has acted in reliance on the offer.

Article 17

An offer, even if it is irrevocable, is terminated when a rejection reaches the offeror.

Article 18

(1) A statement made by or other conduct of the offeree indicating assent to an offer is an acceptance. Silence or inactivity does not in itself amount to acceptance.

(2) An acceptance of an offer becomes effective at the moment the indication of assent reaches the offeror. An acceptance is not effective if the indication of assent does not reach the offeror within the time he has fixed or, if no time is fixed, within a reasonable time, due account being taken of the circumstances of the transaction, including the rapidity of the means of communication employed by the offeror. An oral offer must be accepted immediately unless the circumstances indicate otherwise.

(3) However, if, by virtue of the offer or as a result of practices which the parties have established between themselves or of usage, the offeree may indicate assent by performing an act, such as one relating to the dispatch of the goods or payment of the price, without notice to the offeror, the acceptance is effective at the moment the act is performed, provided that the act is performed within the period of time laid down in the preceding paragraph.

Article 19

(1) A reply to an offer which purports to be an acceptance but contains additions, limitations or other modifications is a rejection of the offer and constitutes a counter-offer.

(2) However, a reply to an offer which purports to be an acceptance but contains additional or different terms which do not materially alter the terms of the offer constitutes an acceptance, unless the offeror, without undue delay, objects orally to the discrepancy or dispatches a notice to that effect. If he does not so object, the terms of the contract are the terms of the offer with the modifications contained in the acceptance.

(3) Additional or different terms relating, among other things, to the price, payment, quality and quantity of the goods, place and time of delivery, extent of one party's liability to the other or the settlement of disputes are considered to alter the terms of the offer materially.

Article 20

(1) A period of time for acceptance fixed by the offeror in a telegram or a letter begins to run from the moment the telegram is handed in for dispatch or from the date shown on the letter or, if no such date is shown, from the date shown on the envelope. A period of time for acceptance fixed by the offeror by telephone, telex or other means of instantaneous communication, begins to run from the moment that the offer reaches the offeree.

(2) Official holidays or non-business days occurring during the period for acceptance are included in calculating the period. However, if a notice of acceptance cannot be delivered at the address of the offeror on the last day of the period because that day falls on an official holiday or a non-business day at the place of business of the offeror, the period is extended until the first business day which follows.

Article 21

(1) A late acceptance is nevertheless effective as an acceptance if without delay the offeror orally so informs the offeree or dispatches a notice to that effect.

(2) If a letter or other writing containing a late acceptance shows that it has been sent in such circumstances that if its transmission had been normal it would have reached the offeror in due time, the late acceptance is effective as an acceptance unless, without delay, the offeror orally informs the offeree that he considers his offer as having lapsed or dispatches a notice to that effect.

Article 22

An acceptance may be withdrawn if the withdrawal reaches the offeror before or at the same time as the acceptance would have become effective.

Article 23

A contract is concluded at the moment when an acceptance of an offer becomes effective in accordance with the provisions of this Convention.

Article 24

For the purposes of the Part of the Convention, an offer, declaration of acceptance or any other indication of intention "reaches" the addressee when it is made orally to him or delivered by any other means to him personally, to his place of business or mailing address or, if he does not have a place of business or mailing address, to his habitual residence.

PART III
SALE OF GOODS

Chapter I
GENERAL PROVISIONS

Article 25

A breach of contract committed by one of the parties is fundamental if it results in such detriment to the other party as substantially to deprive him of what he is entitled to expect under the contract, unless the party in breach did not foresee and a reasonable person of the same kind in the same circumstances would not have foreseen such a result.

Article 26

A declaration of avoidance of the contract is effective only if made by notice to the other party.

Article 27

Unless otherwise expressly provided in this Part of the Convention, if any notice, request or other communication is given or made by a party in accordance with this Part and by means appropriate in the circumstances, a delay of error in the transmission of the communication or its failure to arrive does not deprive that party of the right to rely on the communication.

Article 28

If, in accordance with the provisions of this Convention, one party is entitled to require performance of any obligation by the other party, a court is not bound to enter a judgement for specific performance unless the court would do so under its own law in respect of similar contracts of sale not governed by this Convention.

Article 29

(1) A contract may be modified or terminated by the mere agreement of the parties.

(2) A contract in writing which contains a provision requiring any modification or termination by agreement to be in writing may not be otherwise modified or terminated by agreement. However, a party may be precluded by his conduct from asserting such a provision to the extent that the other party has relied on that conduct.

Chapter II
OBLIGATIONS OF THE SELLER

Article 30

The seller must deliver the goods, hand over any documents relating to them and transfer the property in the goods, as required by the contract and this Convention.

Section I. Delivery of the goods and handing over of documents

Article 31

If the seller is not bound to deliver the goods at any other particular place, his obligation to deliver consists:

(a) if the contract of sale involves carriage of the goods—in handing the goods over to the first carrier for transmission to the buyer;

(b) if, in cases not within the preceding subparagraph, the contract relates to specific goods, or unidentified goods to be drawn from a specific stock or to be manufactured or produced, and at the time of the conclusion of the contract the parties knew that the goods were at, or were to be manufactured or produced at, a particular place—in placing the goods at the buyer's disposal at that place;

(c) in other cases—in placing the goods at the buyer's disposal at the place where the seller had his place of business at the time of the conclusion of the contract.

Article 32

(1) If the seller, in accordance with the contract or this Convention, hands the goods over to a carrier and if the goods are not clearly identified to the contract by markings on the goods, by shipping documents or otherwise, the seller must give the buyer notice of the consignment specifying the goods.

(2) If the seller is bound to arrange for carriage of the goods, he must make such contracts as are necessary for carriage to the place fixed by means of transportation appropriate in the circumstances and according to the usual terms for such transportation.

(3) If the seller is not bound to effect insurance in respect of the carriage of the goods, he must, at the buyer's request, provide him with all available information necessary to enable him to effect such insurance.

Article 33

The seller must deliver the goods:

(a) if a date is fixed by or determinable from the contract, on that date;

(b) if a period of time is fixed by or determinable from the contract, at any time within that period unless circumstances indicate that the buyer is to choose a date; or

(c) in any other case, within a reasonable time after the conclusion of the contract.

Article 34

If the seller is bound to hand over documents relating to the goods, he must hand them over at the time and place and in the form required by the contract. If the seller has handed over documents before that time, he may, up to that time, cure any lack of conformity in the documents, if the exercise of this right does not cause the buyer unreasonable inconvenience or unreasonable expense. However, the buyer retains any right to claim damages as provided for in this Convention.

Section II. Conformity of the goods and third party claims

Article 35

(1) The seller must deliver goods which are of the quantity, quality and description required by the contract and which are contained or packaged in the manner required by the contract.

(2) Except where the parties have agreed otherwise, the goods do not conform with the contract unless they:

(a) are fit for the purposes for which goods of the same description would ordinarily be used;

(b) are fit for any particular purpose expressly or impliedly made known to the seller at the time of the conclusion of the contract, except where the circumstances show that the buyer did not rely, or that it was unreasonable for

him to rely, on the seller's skill and judgement;

(c) possess the qualities of goods which the seller has held out to the buyer as a sample or model;

(d) are contained or packaged in the manner usual for such goods or, where there is no such manner, in a manner adequate to preserve and protect the goods.

(3) The seller is not liable under subparagraphs (a) to (d) of the preceding paragraph for any lack of conformity of the goods if at the time of the conclusion of the contract the buyer knew or could not have been unaware of such lack of conformity.

Article 36

(1) The seller is liable in accordance with the contract and this Convention for any lack of conformity which exists at the time when the risk passes to the buyer, even though the lack of conformity becomes apparent only after that time.

(2) The seller is also liable for any lack of conformity which occurs after the time indicated in the preceding paragraph and which is due to a breach of any of his obligations, including a breach of any guarantee that for a period of time the goods will remain fit for their ordinary purpose or for some particular purpose or will retain specified qualities or characteristics.

Article 37

If the seller has delivered goods before the date for delivery, he may, up to that date, deliver any missing part or make up any deficiency in the quantify of the goods delivered, or deliver goods in replacement of any non-conforming goods delivered or remedy any lack of conformity in the goods delivered, provided that the exercise of this right does not cause the buyer unreasonable inconvenience or unreasonable expense. However, the buyer retains any right to claim damages as provided for in this Convention.

Article 38

(1) The buyer must examine the goods, or cause them to be examined, within as short a period as is practicable in the circumstances.

(2) If the contract involves carriage of the goods, examination may be deferred until after the goods have arrived at their destination.

(3) If the goods are redirected in transit or redispatched by the buyer without a reasonable opportunity for examination by him and at the time of the conclusion of the contract the seller knew or ought to have known of the possibility of such redirection or redispatch, examination may be deferred until after the goods have arrived at the new destination.

Article 39

(1) The buyer loses the right to rely on a lack of conformity of the goods if he does not give notice to the seller specifying the nature of the lack of conformity within a reasonable time after he has discovered it or ought to have discovered it.

(2) In any event, the buyer loses the right to rely on a lack of conformity of the goods if he does not give the seller notice thereof at the latest within a period of two years from the date on which the goods were actually handed over to the buyer, unless this time-limit is inconsistent with a contractual period of guarantee.

Article 40

The seller is not entitled to rely on the provisions of articles 38 and 39 if the lack of conformity relates to facts of which he knew or could not have been unaware and which he did not disclose to the buyer.

Article 41

The seller must deliver goods which are free from any right or claim of a third party, unless the buyer agreed to take the goods subject to that right or claim. However, if such right or claim is based on industrial property or other intellectual property, the seller's obligation is governed by article 42.

Article 42

(1) The seller must deliver goods which are free from any right or claim of a third party based on industrial property or other intellectual property, of which at the time of the conclusion of the contract the seller knew or could not have been unaware, provided that the right or claim is based on industrial property or other intellectual property:

   (a) under the law of the State where the goods will be resold or otherwise used, if it was contemplated by the parties at the time of the conclusion of the contract that the goods would be resold or otherwise used in that State; or

   (b) in any other case, under the law of the State where the buyer has his place of business.

(2) The obligation of the seller under the preceding paragraph does not extend to cases where:

   (a) at the time of the conclusion of the contract the buyer knew or could not have been unaware of the right or claim; or

   (b) the right or claim results from the seller's compliance with technical drawings, designs, formulae or other such specifications furnished by the buyer.

Article 43

(1) The buyer loses the right to rely on the provisions of article 41 or article 42 if he does not give notice to the seller specifying the nature of the right or claim of the third party within a reasonable time after he has become aware or ought to have become aware of the right or claim.

(2) The seller is not entitled to rely on the provisions of the preceding paragraph if he knew of the right or claim of the third party and the nature of it.

Article 44

Notwithstanding the provisions of paragraph (1) of article 39 and paragraph (1) of article 43, the buyer may reduce the price in accordance with article 50 or claim damages, except for loss of profit, if he has a reasonable excuse for his failure to give the required notice.

Section III. Remedies for breach of contract by the seller

Article 45

(1) If the seller fails to perform any of his obligations under the contract or this Convention, the buyer may:

(a) exercise the rights provided in articles 46 to 52;

(b) claim damages as provided in articles 74 to 77.

(2) The buyer is not deprived of any right he may have to claim damages by exercising his right to other remedies.

(3) No period of grace may be granted to the seller by a court or arbitral tribunal when the buyer resorts to a remedy for breach of contract.

Article 46

(1) The buyer may require performance by the seller of his obligations unless the buyer has resorted to a remedy which is inconsistent with this requirement.

(2) If the goods do not conform with the contract, the buyer may require delivery of substitute goods only if the lack of conformity constitutes a fundamental breach of contract and a request for substitute goods is made either in conjunction with notice given under article 39 or within a reasonable time thereafter.

(3) If the goods do not conform with the contract, the buyer may require the seller to remedy the lack of conformity by repair, unless this is unreasonable having regard to all the circumstances. A request for repair must be made either in conjunction with notice given under article 39 or within a reasonable time thereafter.

Article 47

(1) The buyer may fix an additional period of time of reasonable length for performance by the seller of his obligations.

(2) Unless the buyer has received notice from the seller that he will not perform within the period so fixed, the buyer may not, during that period, resort to any remedy for breach of contract. However, the buyer is not deprived thereby of any right he may have to claim damages for delay in performance.

Article 48

(1) Subject to article 49, the seller may, even after the date for delivery, remedy at his own expense any failure to perform his obligations, if he can do so without unreasonable delay and without causing the buyer unreasonable inconvenience or uncertainty of reimbursement by the seller of expenses advanced by the buyer. However, the buyer retains any right to claim damages as provided for in this Convention.

(2) If the seller requests the buyer to make known whether he will accept performance and the buyer does not comply with the request within a reasonable time, the seller may perform within the time indicated in his request. The buyer may not, during that period of time, resort to any remedy which is inconsistent with performance by the seller.

(3) A notice by the seller that he will perform within a specified period of time is assumed to include a request, under the preceding paragraph, that the buyer make known his decision.

(4) A request or notice by the seller under paragraph (2) or (3) of this article is not effective unless received by the buyer.

Article 49

(1) The buyer may declare the contract avoided:

(a) if the failure by the seller to perform any of his obligations under the contract or this Convention amounts to a fundamental breach of contract; or

11

(b) in case of non-delivery, if the seller does not deliver the goods within the additional period of time fixed by the buyer in accordance with paragraph (1) or article 47 or declares that he will not deliver within the period so fixed.

(2) However, in cases where the seller has delivered the goods, the buyer loses the right to declare the contract avoided unless he does so:

(a) in respect of late delivery, within a reasonable time after he has become aware that delivery has been made;

(b) in respect of any breach other than late delivery, within a reasonable time:

(i) after he knew or ought to have known of the breach;

(ii) after the expiration of any additional period of time fixed by the buyer in accordance with paragraph (1) of article 47, or after the seller has declared that he will not perform his obligations within such an additional period; or

(iii) after the expiration of any additional period of time indicated by the seller in accordance with paragraph (2) of article 48, or after the buyer has declared that he will not accept performance.

Article 50

If the goods do not conform with the contract and whether or not the price has already been paid, the buyer may reduce the price in the same proportion as the value that the goods actually delivered had at the time of the delivery bears to the value that conforming goods would have had at that time. However, if the seller remedies any failure to perform his obligations in accordance with article 37 or article 48 or if the buyer refuses to accept performance by the seller in accordance with those articles, the buyer may not reduce the price.

Article 51

(1) If the seller delivers only a part of the goods or if only a part of the goods delivered is in conformity with the contract, articles 46 to 50 apply in respect of the part which is missing or which does not conform.

(2) The buyer may declare the contract avoided in its entirety only if the failure to make delivery completely or in conformity with the contract amounts to a fundamental breach of the contract.

Article 52

(1) If the seller delivers the goods before the date fixed, the buyer may take delivery or refuse to take delivery.

(2) If the seller delivers a quantity of goods greater than that provided for in the contract, the buyer may take delivery or refuse to take delivery of the excess quantity. If the buyer takes delivery of all or part of the excess quantity, he must pay for it at the contract rate.

Chapter III
OBLIGATIONS OF THE BUYER

Article 53

The buyer must pay the price for the goods and take delivery of them as required by the contract and this Convention.

Section I. Payment of the price

Article 54

The buyer's obligation to pay the price includes taking such steps and complying with such formalities as may be required under the contract or any laws and regulations to enable payment to be made.

Article 55

Where a contract has been validly concluded but does not expressly or implicitly fix or make provision for determining the price, the parties are considered, in the absence of any indication to the contrary, to have impliedly made reference to the price generally charged at the time of the conclusion of the contract for such goods sold under comparable circumstances in the trade concerned.

Article 56

If the price is fixed according to the weight of the goods, in case of doubt it is to be determined by the net weight.

Article 57

(1) If the buyer is not bound to pay the price at any other particular place, he must pay it to the seller:

    (a) at the seller's place of business; or

    (b) if the payment is to be made against the handing over of the goods or of documents, at the place where the handing over takes place.

(2) The seller must bear any increase in the expenses incidental to payment which is caused by a change in his place of business subsequent to the conclusion of the contract.

Article 58

(1) If the buyer is not bound to pay the price at any other specific time, he must pay it when the seller places either the goods or documents controlling their disposition at the buyer's disposal in accordance with the contract and this Convention. The seller may make such payment a condition for handing over the goods or documents.

(2) If the contract involves carriage of the goods, the seller may dispatch the goods on terms whereby the goods, or documents controlling their disposition, will not be handed over to the buyer except against payment of the price.

(3) The buyer is not bound to pay the price until he has had an opportunity to examine the goods, unless the procedures for delivery or payment agreed upon by the parties are inconsistent with his having such an opportunity.

Article 59

The buyer must pay the price on the date fixed by or determinable from the contract and this Convention without the need for any request or compliance with any formality on the part of the seller.

Section II. Taking delivery

Article 60

The buyer's obligation to take delivery consists:

    (a) in doing all the acts which could reasonably be expected of him in order to enable the seller to make delivery; and

    (b) in taking over the goods.

Section III. Remedies for breach of contract by the buyer

Article 61

(1) If the buyer fails to perform any of his obligations under the contract or this Convention, the seller may:

    (a) exercise the rights provided in articles 62 to 65;

    (b) claim damages as provided in articles 74 to 77.

(2) The seller is not deprived of any right he may have to claim damages by exercising his right to other remedies.

(3) No period of grace may be granted to the buyer by a court or arbitral tribunal when the seller resorts to a remedy for breach of contract.

Article 62

The seller may require the buyer to pay the price, take delivery or perform his other obligations, unless the seller has resorted to a remedy which is inconsistent with this requirement.

Article 63

(1) The seller may fix an additional period of time of reasonable length for performance by the buyer of his obligations.

(2) Unless the seller has received notice from the buyer that he will not perform within the period so fixed, the seller may not, during that period, resort to any remedy for breach of contract. However, the seller is not deprived thereby of any right he may have to claim damages for delay in performance.

Article 64

(1) The seller may declare the contract avoided:
- (a) if the failure by the buyer to perform any of his obligations under the contract or this Convention amounts to a fundamental breach of contract; or
- (b) if the buyer does not, within the additional period of time fixed by the seller in accordance with paragraph (1) of article 63, perform his obligation to pay the price or take delivery of the goods, or if he declares that he will not do so within the period so fixed.

(2) However, in cases where the buyer has paid the price, the seller loses the right to declare the contract avoided unless he does so:
- (a) in respect of late performance by the buyer, before the seller has become aware that performance has been rendered; or
- (b) in respect of any breach other than late performance by the buyer, within a reasonable time:
  - (i) after the seller knew or ought to have known of the breach; or
  - (ii) after the expiration of any additional period of time fixed by the seller in accordance with paragraph (1) of article 63, or after the buyer has declared that he will not perform his obligations within such an additional period.

Article 65

(1) If under the contract the buyer is to specify the form, measurement or other features of the goods and he fails to make such specification either on the date agreed upon or within a reasonable time after receipt of a request from the seller, the seller may, without prejudice to any other rights he may have, make the specification himself in accordance with the requirements of the buyer that may be known to him.

(2) If the seller makes the specification himself, he must inform the buyer of the details thereof and must fix a reasonable time within which the buyer may make a different specification. If, after receipt of such a communication, the buyer fails to do so within the time so fixed, the specification made by the seller is binding.

Chapter IV
PASSING OF RISK

Article 66

Loss of or damage to the goods after the risk has passed to the buyer does not discharge him from his obligation to pay the price, unless the loss or damage is due to an act or omission of the seller.

Article 67

(1) If the contract of sale involves carriage of the goods and the seller is not bound to hand them over at a particular place, the risk passes to the buyer when the goods are handed over to the first carrier for transmission to the buyer in accordance with the contract of sale. If the seller is bound to hand the goods over to a carrier at a particular place, the risk does not pass to the buyer until the goods are handed over to the carrier at that place. The fact that the seller is authorized to retain documents controlling the disposition of the goods does not affect the passage of the risk.

(2) Nevertheless, the risk does not pass to the buyer until the goods are clearly identified to

the contract, whether by markings on the goods, by shipping documents, by notice given to the buyer or otherwise.

Article 68

The risk in respect of goods sold in transit passes to the buyer from the time of the conclusion of the contract. However, if the circumstances so indicate, the risk is assumed by the buyer from the time the goods were handed over to the carrier who issued the documents embodying the contract of carriage. Nevertheless, if at the time of the conclusion of the contract of sale the seller knew or ought to have known that the goods had been lost or damaged and did not disclose this to the buyer, the loss or damage is at the risk of the seller.

Article 69

(1) In cases not within articles 67 and 68, the risk passes to the buyer when he takes over the goods or, if he does not do so in due time, from the time when the goods are placed at his disposal and he commits a breach of contract by failing to take delivery.

(2) However, if the buyer is bound to take over the goods at a place other than a place of business of the seller, the risk passes when delivery is due and the buyer is aware of the fact that the goods are placed at his disposal at that place.

(3) If the contract relates to goods not then identified, the goods are considered not to be placed at the disposal of the buyer until they are clearly identified to the contract.

Article 70

If the seller has committed a fundamental breach of contract, articles 67, 68 and 69 do not impair the remedies available to the buyer on account of the breach.

Chapter V
PROVISIONS COMMON TO THE OBLIGATIONS OF THE SELLER AND OF THE BUYER

Section I. Anticipatory breach and instalment contracts

Article 71

(1) A party may suspend the performance of his obligations if, after the conclusion of the contract, it becomes apparent that the other party will not perform a substantial part of his obligations as a result of:

   (a) a serious deficiency in his ability to perform or in his creditworthiness; or

   (b) his conduct in preparing to perform or in performing the contract.

(2) If the seller has already dispatched the goods before the grounds described in the preceding paragraph become evident, he may prevent the handing over of the goods to the buyer even though the buyer holds a document which entitles him to obtain them. The present paragraph relates only to the rights in the goods as between the buyer and the seller.

(3) A party suspending performance, whether before or after dispatch of the goods, must immediately give notice of the suspension to the other party and must continue with performance if the other party provides adequate assurance of his performance.

Article 72

(1) If prior to the date for performance of the contract it is clear that one of the parties will commit a fundamental breach of contract, the other party may declare the contract avoided.

(2) If time allows, the party intending to declare the contract avoided must give reasonable notice to the other party in order to permit him to provide adequate assurance of his performance.

(3) The requirements of the preceding paragraph do not apply if the other party has declared that he will not perform his obligations.

Article 73

(1) In the case of a contract for delivery of goods by instalments, if the failure of one party to perform any of his obligations in respect of any instalment constitutes a fundamental breach of contract with respect to that instalment, the other party may declare the contract avoided with respect to that instalment.

(2) If one party's failure to perform any of his obligations in respect of any instalment gives the other party good grounds to conclude that a fundamental breach of contract will occur with respect to future instalments, he may declare the contract avoided for the future, provided that he does so within a reasonable time.

(3) A buyer who declares the contract avoided in respect of any delivery may, at the same time, declare it avoided in respect of deliveries already made or of future deliveries if, by reason of their interdependence, those deliveries could not be used for the purpose contemplated by the parties at the time of the conclusion of the contract.

Section II. Damages

Article 74

Damages for breach of contract by one party consist of a sum equal to the loss, including loss of profit, suffered by the other party as a consequence of the breach. Such damages may not exceed the loss which the party in breach foresaw or ought to have foreseen at the time of the conclusion of the contract, in the light of the facts and matters of which he then knew or ought to have known, as a possible consequence of the breach of contract.

Article 75

If the contract is avoided and if, in a reasonable manner and within a reasonable time after avoidance, the buyer has bought goods in replacement or the seller has resold the goods, the party claiming damages may recover the difference between the contract price and the price in the substitute transaction as well as any further damages recoverable under article 74.

Article 76

(1) If the contract is avoided and there is a current price for the goods, the party claiming damages may, if he has not made a purchase or resale under article 75, recover the difference between the price fixed by the contract and the current price at the time of avoidance as well as any further damages recoverable under article 74. If, however, the party claiming damages has avoided the contract after taking over the goods, the current price at the time of such taking over shall be applied instead of the current price at the time of avoidance.

(2) For the purposes of the preceding paragraph, the current price is the price prevailing at the place where delivery of the goods should have been made or, if there is no current price at that place, the price at such other place as serves as a reasonable substitute, making due allowance for differences in the cost of transporting the goods.

Article 77

A party who relies on a breach of contract must take such measures as are reasonable in the circumstances to mitigate the loss, including loss of profit, resulting from the breach. If he fails to take such measures, the party in breach may claim a reduction in the damages in the amount by which the loss should have been mitigated.

Section III. Interest

Article 78

If a party fails to pay the price or any other sum that is in arrears, the other party is entitled to interest on it, without prejudice to any claim for damages recoverable under article 74.

Section IV. Exemptions

Section V. Effects of avoidance

Article 79

(1) A party is not liable for a failure to perform any of his obligations if he proves that the failure was due to an impediment beyond his control and that he could not reasonably be expected to have taken the impediment into account at the time of the conclusion of the contract or to have avoided or overcome it or its consequences.

(2) If the party's failure is due to the failure by a third person whom he has engaged to perform the whole or a part of the contract, that party is exempt from liability only if:

(a) he is exempt under the preceding paragraph; and

(b) the person whom he has so engaged would be so exempt if the provisions of that paragraph were applied to him.

(3) The exemption provided by this article has effect for the period during which the impediment exists.

(4) The party who fails to perform must give notice to the other party of the impediment and its effect on his ability to perform. If the notice is not received by the other party within a reasonable time after the party who fails to perform knew or ought to have known of the impediment, he is liable for damages resulting form such non-receipt.

(5) Nothing in this article prevents either party from exercising any right other than to claim damages under this Convention.

Article 80

A party may not rely on a failure of the other party to perform, to the extent that such failure was caused by the first party's act or omission.

Article 81

(1) Avoidance of the contract releases both parties from their obligations under it, subject to any damages which may be due. Avoidance does not affect any provision of the contract for the settlement of disputes or any other provision of the contract governing the rights and obligations of the parties consequent upon the avoidance of the contract.

(2) A party who has performed the contract either wholly or in part may claim restitution from the other party of whatever the first party has supplied or paid under the contract. If both parties are bound to make restitution, they must do so concurrently.

Article 82

(1) The buyer loses the right to declare the contract avoided or to require the seller to deliver substitute goods if it is impossible for him to make restitution of the goods substantially in the condition in which he received them.

(2) The preceding paragraph does not apply:

(a) if the impossibility of making restitution of the goods or of making restitution of the goods substantially in the condition in which the buyer received them is not due to his act or omission;

(b) if the goods or part of the goods have perished or deteriorated as a result of the examination provided for in article 38; or

(c) if the goods or part of the goods have been sold in the normal course of business or have been consumed or transformed by the buyer in the course of normal use before he discovered or ought to have discovered the lack of conformity.

17

Article 83

A buyer who has lost the right to declare the contract avoided or to require the seller to deliver substitute goods in accordance with article 82 retains all other remedies under the contract and this Convention.

Article 84

(1) If the seller is bound to refund the price, he must also pay interest on it, from the date on which the price was paid.

(2) The buyer must account to the seller for all benefits which he has derived from the goods or part of them:

(a) if he must make restitution of the goods or part of them; or

(b) if it is impossible for him to make restitution of all or part of the goods or to make restitution of all or part of the goods substantially in the condition in which he received them, but he has nevertheless declared the contract avoided or required the seller to deliver substitute goods.

Section VI. Preservation of the goods

Article 85

If the buyer is in delay in taking delivery of the goods or, where payment of the price and delivery of the goods are to be made concurrently, if he fails to pay the price, and the seller is either in possession of the goods or otherwise able to control their disposition, the seller must take such steps as are reasonable in the circumstances to preserve them. He is entitled to retain them until he has been reimbursed his reasonable expenses by the buyer.

Article 86

(1) If the buyer has received the goods and intends to exercise any right under the contract or this Convention to reject them, he must take such steps to preserve them as are reasonable in the circumstances. He is entitled to retain them until he has been reimbursed his reasonable expenses by the seller.

(2) If goods dispatched to the buyer have been placed at his disposal at their destination and he exercises the right to reject them, he must take possession of them on behalf of the seller, provided that this can be done without payment of the price and without unreasonable inconvenience or unreasonable expense. This provision does not apply if the seller or a person authorized to take charge of the goods on his behalf is present at the destination. If the buyer takes possession of the goods under this paragraph, his rights and obligations are governed by the preceding paragraph.

Article 87

A party who is bound to take steps to preserve the goods may deposit them in a warehouse of a third person at the expense of the other party provided that the expense incurred is not unreasonable.

Article 88

(1) A party who is bound to preserve the goods in accordance with article 85 or 86 may sell them by any appropriate means if there has been an unreasonable delay by the other party in taking possession of the goods or in taking them back or in paying the price or the cost of preservation, provided that reasonable notice of the intention to sell has been given to the other party.

(2) If the goods are subject to rapid deterioration or their preservation would involve unreasonable expense, a party who is bound to preserve the goods in accordance with article 85 or 86 must take reasonable measures to sell them. To the extent possible he must give notice to the other party of his intention to sell.

(3) A party selling the goods has the right to retain out of the proceeds of sale an amount equal to the reasonable expenses of preserving the goods and of selling them. He must account to the other party for the balance.

PART IV
FINAL PROVISIONS

Article 89

The Secretary-General of the United Nations is hereby designated as the depositary for this Convention.

Article 90

This Convention does not prevail over any international agreement which has already been or may be entered into and which contains provisions concerning the matters governed by this Convention, provided that the parties have their places of business in States parties to such agreement.

Article 91

(1) This Convention is open for signature at the concluding meeting of the United Nations Conference on Contracts for the International Sale of Goods and will remain open for signature by all States at the Headquarters of the United Nations, New York until 30 September 1981.

(2) This Convention is subject to ratification, acceptance or approval by the signatory States.

(3) This Convention is open for accession by all States which are not signatory States as from the date it is open for signature.

(4) Instruments of ratification, acceptance, approval and accession are to be deposited with the Secretary-General of the United Nations.

Article 92

(1) A Contracting State may declare at the time of signature, ratification, acceptance, approval or accession that it will not be bound by Part II of this Convention or that it will not be bound by Part III of this Convention.

(2) A Contracting State which makes a declaration in accordance with the preceding paragraph in respect of Part II or Part III of this Convention is not to be considered a Contracting State within paragraph (1) of article 1 of this Convention in respect of matters governed by the Part to which the declaration applies.

Article 93

(1) If a Contracting State has two or more territorial units in which, according to its constitution, different systems of law are applicable in relation to the matters dealt with in this Convention, it may, at the time of signature, ratification, acceptance, approval or accession, declare that this Convention is to extend to all its territorial units or only to one or more of them, and may amend its declaration by submitting another declaration at any time.

(2) These declarations are to be notified to the depositary and are to state expressly the territorial units to which the Convention extends.

(3) If, by virtue of a declaration under this article, this Convention extends to one or more but not all of the territorial units of a Contracting State, and if the place of business of a party is located in that State, this place of business, for the purposes of this Convention, is considered not to be in a Contracting State, unless it is in a territorial unit to which the Convention extends.

(4) If a Contracting State makes no declaration under paragraph (1) of this article, the Convention is to extend to all territorial units of that State.

Article 94

(1) Two or more Contracting States which have the same or closely related legal rules on matters governed by this Convention may at any time declare that the Convention is not to apply to contracts of sale or to their formation where the parties have their places of business in those States. Such declarations may be made jointly or by reciprocal unilateral declarations.

(2) A Contracting State which has the same or closely related legal rules on matters governed by this Convention as one or more non-Contracting States may at any time declare that the Convention is not to apply to contracts of sale or to their formation where the parties have their places of business in those States.

(3) If a State which is the object of a declaration under the preceding paragraph subsequently becomes a Contracting State, the declaration made will, as from the date on which

the Convention enters into force in respect of the new Contracting State, have the effect of a declaration made under paragraph (1), provided that the new Contracting State joins in such declaration or makes a reciprocal unilateral declaration.

Article 95

Any State may declare at the time of the deposit of its instrument of ratification, acceptance, approval or accession that it will not be bound by subparagraph (1)(b) of article 1 of this Convention.

Article 96

A Contracting State whose legislation requires contracts of sale to be concluded in or evidenced by writing may at any time make a declaration in accordance with article 12 that any provision of article 11, article 29, or Part II of this Convention, that allows a contract of sale or its modification or termination by agreement or any offer, acceptance, or other indication of intention to be made in any form other than in writing, does not apply where any party has his place of business in that State.

Article 97

(1) Declarations made under this Convention at the time of signature are subject to confirmation upon ratification, acceptance or approval.

(2) Declarations and confirmations of declarations are to be in writing and be formally notified to the depositary.

(3) A declaration takes effect simultaneously with the entry into force of this Convention in respect of the State concerned. However, a declaration of which the depositary receives formal notification after such entry into force takes effect on the first day of the month following the expiration of six months after the date of its receipt by the depositary. Reciprocal unilateral declarations under article 94 take effect on the first day of the month following the expiration of six months after the receipt of the latest declaration by the depositary.

(4) Any State which makes a declaration under this Convention may withdraw it at any time by a formal notification in writing addressed to the depositary. Such withdrawal is to take effect on the first day of the month following the expiration of six months after the date of the receipt of the notification by the depositary.

(5) A withdrawal of a declaration made under article 94 renders inoperative, as from the date on which the withdrawal takes effect, any reciprocal declaration made by another State under that article.

Article 98

No reservations are permitted except those expressly authorized in this Convention.

Article 99

(1) This Convention enters into force, subject to the provisions of paragraph (6) of this article, on the first day of the month following the expiration of twelve months after the date of deposit of the tenth instrument of ratification, acceptance, approval or accession, including an instrument which contains a declaration made under article 92.

(2) When a State ratifies, accepts, approves or accedes to this Convention after the deposit of the tenth instrument of ratification, acceptance, approval or accession, this Convention, with the exception of the Part excluded, enters into force in respect of that State, subject to the provisions of paragraph (6) of this article, on the first day of the month following the expiration of twelve months after the date of the deposit of its instrument of ratification, acceptance, approval or accession.

(3) A State which ratifies, accepts, approves or accedes to this Convention and is a party to either or both the Convention relating to a Uniform Law on the Formation of Contracts for the International Sale of Goods done at The Hague on 1 July 1964 (1964 Hague Formation Convention) and the Convention relating to a Uniform Law on the International Sale of Goods done at The Hague on 1 July 1964 (1964 Hague Sales Convention) shall at the same time denounce, as the case may be, either or both the

1964 Hague Sales Convention and the 1964 Hague Formation Convention by notifying the Government of the Netherlands to that effect.

(4) A State party to the 1964 Hague Sales Convention which ratifies, accepts, approves or accedes to the present Convention and declares or has declared under article 92 that it will not be bound by Part II of this Convention shall at the time of ratification, acceptance, approval or accession denounce the 1964 Hague Sales Convention by notifying the Government of the Netherlands to that effect.

(5) A State party to the 1964 Hague Formation Convention which ratifies, accepts, approves or accedes to the present Convention and declares or has declared under article 92 that it will not be bound by Part III of this Convention shall at the time of ratification, acceptance, approval or accession denounce the 1964 Hague Formation Convention by notifying the Government of the Netherlands to that effect.

(6) For the purpose of this article, ratifications, acceptances, approvals and accessions in respect of this Convention by States parties to the 1964 Hague Formation Convention or to the 1964 Hague Sales Convention shall not be effective until such denunciations as may be required on the part of those States in respect of the latter two Conventions have themselves become effective. The depositary of this Convention shall consult with the Government of the Netherlands, as the depositary of the 1964 Conventions, so as to ensure necessary co-ordination in this respect.

Article 100

(1) This Convention applies to the formation of a contract only when the proposal for concluding the contract is made on or after the date when the Convention enters into force in respect of the Contracting States referred to in subparagraph (1)(a) or the Contracting State referred to in subparagraph (1)(b) of article 1.

(2) This Convention applies only to contracts concluded on or after the date when the Convention enters into force in respect of the Contracting States referred to in subparagraph (1)(a) or the Contracting State referred to in subparagraph (1)(b) of article 1.

Article 101

(1) A Contracting State may denounce this Convention, or Part II or Part III of the Convention, by a formal notification in writing addressed to the depositary.

(2) The denunciation takes effect on the first day of the month following the expiration of twelve months after the notification is received by the depositary. Where a longer period for the denunciation to take effect is specified in the notification, the denunciation takes effect upon the expiration of such longer period after the notification is received by the depositary.

DONE at Vienna, this day of eleventh day of April, one thousand nine hundred and eighty, in a single original, of which the Arabic, Chinese, English, French, Russian and Spanish texts are equally authentic.

IN WITNESS WHEREOF the undersigned plenipotentiaries, being duly authorized by their respective Governments, have signed this Convention.

B. European Convention on Jurisdiction and the Enforcement of Judgments in Civil and Commercial Matters (Brussels Convention)

Source: European Convention on Jurisdiction and Enforcement of Judgments in Civil and Commercial Matters, done at Brussels, Sept. 27, 1968, 41 O.J. Eur. Comm. (C27/1) (Jan. 26, 1998) (consolidated and updated version of the 1968 Convention and the Protocol of 1971, following the 1996 accession of the Republic of Austria, the Republic of Finland and the Kingdom of Sweden).

Website information:

http://europa.eu.int/eur-lex/en/lif/dat/1998/en_498Y0126_01.html
The current text of the Brussels Convention can be found at this address on the EUR-Lex website.

Introduction

The six original Member States of the European Community signed the European Convention on Jurisdiction and Enforcement of Judgments in Civil and Commercial Matters in Brussels on September 27, 1968. By accession (as required by Art. 63), the Convention applies to all 15 present Member States of the European Community and must be agreed to by all future members.

The Convention grew out of Article 220 of the Treaty of Rome (now Article 293 of the Consolidated Version of the Treaty Establishing the European Community), which required that Member States enter into negotiations with the goal of developing treaties to simplify "formalities governing the reciprocal recognition and enforcement of judgements of courts or tribunals and of arbitration awards." The existence of the New York Arbitration Convention made application to arbitral awards unnecessary. Once negotiations began, it became clear that in order to deal adequately with enforcement of judgments it was best also to deal also with issues of jurisdiction. Thus, the Brussels Convention is a "double" convention, creating rules applicable to jurisdiction in the originating court, as well as rules for the recognition and enforcement of judgements rendered in another Member State.

The Article 2 general basis of jurisdiction under the Convention is the domicile of the defendant. Specific bases of jurisdiction are then provided for contract, tort and other matters. Article 17 specifically allows parties to agree to jurisdiction other than as provided in the Convention. Article 3 also protects defendants domiciled in Member States from being subject to certain "exorbitant" bases of jurisdiction otherwise available in other Member States.

Recognition rules are found in Articles 26 through 30. The control of jurisdiction in the originating court simplifies the recognition rules, with the general rule being recognition without barriers. A recognizing court is prohibited from revisiting the issue of jurisdiction decided in the originating court. Enforcement rules are found in Articles 31 through 49.

The Treaty of Amsterdam transferred competence for judicial cooperation issues from the Member States to the EC institutions effective May 1, 1999. Thus, the Brussels Convention is expected to be replaced with a regulation which was presented in draft form during the summer of 1999.

EUROPEAN CONVENTION ON JURISDICTION AND THE ENFORCEMENT OF JUDGMENTS IN CIVIL AND COMMERCIAL MATTERS (BRUSSELS CONVENTION)

THE HIGH CONTRACTING PARTIES TO THE TREATY ESTABLISHING THE EUROPEAN ECONOMIC COMMUNITY,

Desiring to implement the provisions of Article 220 of that Treaty by virtue of which they undertook to secure the simplification of formalities governing the reciprocal recognition and enforcement of judgments of courts or tribunals;

Anxious to strengthen in the Community the legal protection of persons therein established;

Considering that it is necessary for this purpose to determine the international jurisdiction of their courts, to facilitate recognition and to introduce an expeditious procedure for securing the enforcement of judgments, authentic instruments and court settlements;

Have decided to conclude this Convention and to this end have designated as their Plenipotentiaries:

HIS MAJESTY THE KING OF THE BELGIANS:

Mr Pierre HARMEL,

Minister for Foreign Affairs;

THE PRESIDENT OF THE FEDERAL REPUBLIC OF GERMANY:

Mr Willy BRANDT,

Vice-Chancellor, Minister for Foreign Affairs;

THE PRESIDENT OF THE FRENCH REPUBLIC:

Mr Michel DEBRE,

Minister for Foreign Affairs;

THE PRESIDENT OF THE ITALIAN REPUBLIC:

Mr Giuseppe MEDICI,

Minister for Foreign Affairs;

HIS ROYAL HIGHNESS THE GRAND DUKE OF LUXEMBOURG:

Mr Pierre GREGOIRE,

Minister for Foreign Affairs;

HER MAJESTY THE QUEEN OF THE NETHERLANDS:

Mr J.M.A.H. LUNS,

Minister for Foreign Affairs;

Who, meeting within the Council, having exchanged their Full Powers, found in good and due form,

Have agreed as follows:

Title I: Scope

Article 1

This Convention shall apply in civil and commercial matters whatever the nature of the court or tribunal. It shall not extend, in particular, to revenue, customs or administrative matters.

The Convention shall not apply to:

1. the status or legal capacity of natural persons, rights in property arising out of a matrimonial relationship, wills and succession;

2. bankruptcy, proceedings relating to the winding-up of insolvent companies or other legal persons, judicial arrangements, compositions and analogous proceedings;

3. social security;

4. arbitration.

Title II: Jurisdiction

Section 1. General Provisions

Article 2

Subject to the provisions of this Convention, persons domiciled in a Contracting State shall, whatever their nationality, be sued in the courts of that State.

Persons who are not nationals of the State in which they are domiciled shall be governed by the rules of jurisdiction applicable to nationals of that State.

Article 3

Persons domiciled in a Contracting State may be sued in the courts of another Contracting State only by virtue of the rules set out in Sections 2 to 6 of this Title.

In particular the following provisions shall not be applicable as against them:

—in Belgium: Article 15 of the civil code (Code civil—Burgerlijk Wetboek) and Article 638 of the judicial code (Code judiciaire—Gerechtelijk Wetboek),

—in Denmark: Article 248(2) of the law on civil procedure (Lov om rettens pleje) and Chapter 3, Article 3 of the Greenland law on civil procedure (Lov for Gronland om rettens pleje),

—in the Federal Republic of Germany: Article 23 of the code of civil procedure (Zivilprozessordnung),

—in Greece: Article 40 of the code of civil procedure

—in France: Articles 14 and 15 of the civil code (Code civil),

—in Ireland: the rules which enable jurisdiction to be founded on the document instituting the proceedings having been served on the defendant during his temporary presence in Ireland,

—in Italy: Articles 2 and 4, Nos. 1 and 2 of the code of civil procedure (Codice di procedura civile),

—in Luxembourg: Articles 14 and 15 of the civil code (Code civil),

—in the Netherlands: Articles 126(3) and 127 of the code of civil procedure (Wetboek van Burgerlijke Rechtsvordering),

—in the United Kingdom: the rules which enable jurisdiction to be founded on:

> (a) the document instituting the proceedings having been served on the defendant during his temporary presence in the United Kingdom; or

> (b) presence within the United Kingdom of property belonging to the defendant; or

(c) the seizure by the plaintiff of property situated in the United Kingdom.

Article 4

If the defendant is not domiciled in a Contracting State, the jurisdiction of the courts of each Contracting State shall, subject to the provisions of Article 16, be determined by the law of that State.

As against such a defendant, any person domiciled in a Contracting State may, whatever his nationality, avail himself in that State of the rules of jurisdiction there in force, and in particular those specified in the second paragraph of Article 3, in the same way as the nationals of that State.

Section 2. Special Jurisdiction

Article 5

A person domiciled in a Contracting State may, in another Contracting State, be sued:

1. in matters relating to a contract, in the courts for the place of performance of the obligation in question; in matters relating to individual contracts of employment, this place is that where the employee habitually carries out his work, or if the employee does not habitually carry out his work in any one country, the employer may also be sued in the courts for the place where the business which engaged the employee was or is now situated;

2. in matters relating to maintenance, in the courts for the place where the maintenance creditor is domiciled or habitually resident or, if the matter is ancillary to proceedings concerning the status of a person, in the court which, according to its own law, has jurisdiction to entertain those proceedings, unless that jurisdiction is based solely on the nationality of one of the parties;

3. in matters relating to tort, delict or quasi-delict, in the courts for the place where the harmful event occurred;

4. as regards a civil claim for damages or restitution which is based on an act giving rise to criminal proceedings, in the court seised of those proceedings, to the extent that that court has jurisdiction under its own law to entertain civil proceedings;

5. as regards a dispute arising out of the operations of a branch, agency or other establishment, in the courts for the place in which the branch, agency or other establishment is situated;

6. as settlor, trustee or beneficiary of a trust created by the operation of a statute, or by a written instrument, or created orally and evidenced in writing, in the courts of the Contracting State in which the trust is domiciled;

7. as regards a dispute concerning the payment of remuneration claimed in respect of the salvage of a cargo or freight, in the court under the authority of which the cargo or freight in question:

    (a) has been arrested to secure such payment, or

    (b) could have been so arrested, but bail or other security has been given;

    provided that this provision shall apply only if it is claimed that the defendant has an interest in the cargo or freight or had such an interest at the time of salvage;

Article 6

A person domiciled in a Contracting State may also be sued:

1. where he is one of a number of defendants, in the courts for the place where any one of them is domiciled;

2. as a third party in an action on a warranty or guarantee or in any other third party proceedings, in the court seised of the original proceedings, unless these were instituted solely with the object of removing him from the jurisdiction of the court which would be competent in his case;

3. on a counter-claim arising from the same contract or facts on which the original claim was based, in the court in which the original claim is pending.

4. in matters relating to a contract, if the action may be combined with an action against the same defendant in matters relating to rights *in rem* in immovable property, in the court of the Contracting State in which the property is situated.

Article 6a

Where by virtue of this Convention a court of a Contracting State has jurisdiction in actions relating to liability arising from the use or operation of a ship, that court, or any other court substitued [sic] for this purpose by the internal law of that State, shall also have jurisdiction over claims for limitation of such liability.

Section 3. Jurisdiction in Matters Relating to Insurance

Article 7

In matters relating to insurance, jurisdiction shall be determined by this Section, without prejudice to the provisions of Articles 4 and 5 point 5.

Article 8

An insurer domiciled in a Contracting State may be used:

1. the courts of the State where he is domiciled, or

2. in another Contracting State, in the courts for the place where the policy-holder is domiciled, or

3. if he is a co-insurer, in the courts of a Contracting State in which proceedings are brought against the leading insurer.

An insurer who is not domiciled in a Contracting State but has a branch, agency or other establishment in one of the Contracting States shall, in disputes arising out of the operations of the branch, agency or establishment, be deemed to be domiciled in that State.

Article 9

In respect of liability insurance or insurance of immovable property, the insurer may in addition be sued in the courts for the place where the harmful event occurred. The same applies if movable and immovable property are covered by the same insurance policy and both are adversely affected by the same contingency.

Article 10

In respect of liability insurance, the insurer may also, if the law of the court permits it, be joined in proceedings which the injured party had brought against the insured.

The provisions of Articles 7, 8 and 9 shall apply to actions brought by the injured party directly against the insurer, where such direct actions are permitted.

If the law governing such direct actions provides that the policy-holder or the insured may be joined as a party to the action, the same court shall have jurisdiction over them.

Article 11

Without prejudice to the provisions of the third paragraph of Article 10, an insurer may bring proceedings only in the courts of the Contracting State in which the defendant is domiciled, irrespective of whether he is the policy-holder, the insured or a beneficiary.

The provisions of this Section shall not affect the right to bring a counterclaim in the court in which, in accordance with this Section, the original claim is pending.

Article 12

The provisions of this Section may be departed from only by an agreement on jurisdiction:

1. which is entered into after the dispute has arisen, or

2. which allows the policy-holder, the insured or a beneficiary to bring proceedings in courts other than those indicated in this Section, or

3. which is concluded between a policy-holder and an insurer, both of whom are domiciled in the same Contracting State, and which has the effect of conferring jurisdiction on the courts of that State even if the harmful event were to occur abroad, provided that such an agreement is not contrary to the law of that State, or

4. which is concluded with a policy-holder who is not domiciled in a Contracting State, except insofar as the insurance is compulsory or relates to immovable property in a Contracting State, or

5. which relates to a contract of insurance insofar as it covers one or more of the risks set out in Article 12a.

Article 12a

The following are the risks referred to in point 5 of Article 12:

1. Any loss of or damage to

    (a) sea-going ships, installations situated off-shore or on the high seas, or aircraft, arising from perils which relate to their use for commercial purposes,

    (b) goods in transit other than passengers' baggage where the transit consists of or includes carriage by such ships or aircraft;

2. Any liability, other than for bodily injury to passengers or loss of or damage to their baggage,

    (a) arising out of the use or operation of ships, installations or aircraft as referred to in point 1(a) above insofar as the law of the Contracting State in which such aircraft are registered does not prohibit agreements on jurisdiction regarding insurance of such risks,

    (b) for loss or damage caused by goods in transit as described in point 1(b) above;

3. Any financial loss connected with the use or operation of ships, installations or aircraft as referred to in point 1(a) above, in particular loss of freight or charter-hire;

4. Any risk or interest connected with any of those referred to in points 1 to 3 above.

Section 4.   Jurisdiction over Consumer Contracts

Article 13

In proceedings concerning a contract concluded by a person for a purpose which can be regarded as being outside his trade or profession, hereinafter called "the consumer," jurisdiction shall be determined by this Section, without prejudice to the provisions of point 5 of Articles 4 and 5, if it is:

1. a contract for the sale of goods on instalment credit terms, or

2. a contract for a loan repayable by instalments, or for any other form of credit, made to finance the sale of goods, or

3. any other contract for the supply of goods or a contract for the supply of services, and

    (a) in the State of the consumer's domicile the conclusion of the contract was preceded by a specific invitation addressed to him or by advertising, and

    (b) the consumer took in that State the steps necessary for the conclusion of the contract.

Where a consumer enters into a contract with a party who is not domiciled in a Contracting State but has a branch, agency or other establishment in one of the Contracting States, that party shall, in disputes arising out of the operations of the branch, agency or establishment, be deemed to be domiciled in that State.

This Section shall not apply to contracts of transport.

Article 14

A consumer may bring proceedings against the other party to a contract either in the courts of the Contracting State in which that party is domiciled or in the courts of the Contracting State in which he is himself domiciled.

Proceedings may be brought against a consumer by the other party to the contract only in the courts of the Contracting State in which the consumer is domiciled.

These provisions shall not affect the right to bring a counter-claim in the court in which, in accordance with this Section, the original claim is pending.

Article 15

The provisions of this Section may be departed from only by an agreement:

1. which is entered into after the dispute has arisen, or

2. allows the consumer to bring proceedings in courts other than those indicated in this Section, or

3. which is entered into by the consumer and the other party to the contract, both of whom are at the time of conclusion of the contract domiciled or habitually resident in the same Contracting State, and which confers jurisdiction on the courts of that State, provided that such an agreement is not contrary to the law of that State.

Section 5. Exclusive Jurisdiction

Article 16

The following courts shall have exclusive jurisdiction, regardless of domicile:

1. in proceedings which have as their object rights in rem in, or tenancies of, immovable property, the courts of the Contracting State in which the property is situated;

2. in proceedings which have as their object the validity of the constitution, the nullity or the dissolution of companies or other legal persons or associations of natural or legal persons, or the decisions of their organs, the courts of the Contracting State in which the company, legal person or association has its seat;

3. in proceedings which have as their object the validity of entries in public registers, the courts of the Contracting State in which the register is kept;

4. in proceedings concerned with the registration or validity of patents, trade marks, designs, or other similar rights required to be deposited or registered, the courts of the Contracting State in which the deposit or registration has been applied for, has taken place or is under the terms of an international convention deemed to have taken place;

5. (5) in proceedings concerned with the enforcement of judgments, the courts of the Contracting State in which the judgment has been or is to be enforced.

Section 6. Prorogation of Jurisdiction

Article 17

If the parties, one or more of whom is domiciled in a Contracting State, have agreed that a court or the courts of a Contracting State are to have jurisdiction to settle any disputes which have arisen or which may arise in connection with a particular legal relationship, that court or those courts shall have exclusive jurisdiction. Such an agreement conferring jurisdiction shall be either:

(a) in writing or evidenced in writing; or

(b) in a form which accords with practices which the parties have established between themselves; or

(c) in international trade or commerce, in a form which accords with a usage of which the parties are or ought to have been aware and which in such trade or commerce is widely known to , and regularly observed by, parties to contracts of the type involved in the particular trade or commerce concerned.

Where such an agreement is concluded by parties, none of whom is domiciled in a Contracting State, the courts of other Contracting States shall have no jurisdiction over their disputes unless the court or courts chosen have declined jurisdiction.

The court or courts of a Contracting State on which a trust instrument has conferred jurisdiction shall have exclusive jurisdiction in any proceedings brought against a settlor, trustee or beneficiary, if relations between these persons or their rights or obligations under the trust are involved.

Agreements or provisions of a trust instrument conferring jurisdiction shall have no legal force if they are contrary to the provisions of Articles 12 or 15, or if the courts whose jurisdiction they purport to exclude have exclusive jurisdiction by virtue of Article 16.

If an agreement conferring jurisdiction was concluded for the benefit of only one of the parties, that party shall retain the right to bring proceedings in any other court which has jurisdiction by virtue of this Convention.

In matters relating to individual contracts of employment an agreement conferring jurisdiction shall have legal force only if it is entered into after the dispute has arisen or if the employee invokes it to seise courts other than those for the defendant's domicile or those specified in Article 5(1).

Article 18

Apart from jurisdiction derived from other provisions of this Convention, a court of a Contracting State before whom a defendant enters an appearance shall have jurisdiction. This rule shall not apply where appearance was entered solely to contest the jurisdiction, or where another court has exclusive jurisdiction by virtue of Article 16.

Section 7. Examination as to Jurisdiction [sic] and Admissibility

Article 19

Where a court of a Contracting State is seised of a claim which is principally concerned with a matter over which the courts of another Contracting State have exclusive jurisdiction by virtue of Article 16, it shall declare of its own motion that it has no jurisdiction.

Article 20

Where a defendant domiciled in one Contracting State is sued in a court of another Contracting State and does not enter an appearance, the court shall declare of its own motion that it has no jurisdiction unless its jurisdiction is derived from the provisions of this Convention.

The court shall stay the proceedings so long as it is not shown that the defendant has been able to receive the document instituting the proceedings or an equivalent document in sufficient time to enable him to arrange for his defence, or that all necessary steps have been taken to this end.

The provisions of the foregoing paragraph shall be replaced by those of Article 15 of the Hague Convention of 15 November 1965 on the service abroad of judicial and extrajudicial documents in civil or commercial matters, if the document instituting the proceedings or notice thereof had to be transmitted abroad in accordance with that Convention.

Section 8. Lis Pendens—Related Actions

Article 21
Where proceedings involving the same cause of action and between the same parties are brought in the courts of different Contracting States, any court other than the court first seised shall of its own motion stay its proceedings until such time as the jurisdiction of the court first seised is established.

Where the jurisdiction of the court first seised is established, any court other than the court first seised may, while the actions are pending at first instance, stay its proceedings.

Article 22
Where related actions are brought in the courts of different Contracting States, any court other than the court first seised may, while the actions are pending at first instance, stay its proceedings.

A court other than the court first seised may also, on the application of one of the parties, decline jurisdiction [sic] if the law of that court permits the consolidation of related actions and the court first seised has jurisdiction over both actions.

For the purposes of this article, actions are deemed to be related where they are so closely connected that it is expedient to hear and determine them together to avoid the risk of irreconcilable judgments resulting from separate proceedings.

Article 23
Where actions come within the exclusive jurisdiction of several courts, any court other than the court first seised shall decline jurisdiction in favour of that court.

Section 9. Provisional, Including Protective, Measures

Article 24
Application may be made to the courts of a Contracting State for such provisional, including protective, measures as may be available under the law of that State, even if, under this Convention, the courts of another Contracting State have jurisdiction as to the substance of the matter.

Title III: Recognition and Enforcement

Article 25
For the purposes of this Convention, "judgment" means any judgment given by a court or tribunal of a Contracting State, whatever the judgment may be called, including a decree, order, decision or writ of execution, as well as the determination of costs or expenses by an officer of the court.

Section 1. Recognition

Article 26
A judgment given in a Contracting State shall be recognized in the other Contracting States without any special procedure being required.

Any interested party who raises the recognition of a judgment as the principal issue in a dispute may, in accordance with the procedures provided for in Sections 2 and 3 of this Title, apply for a decision that the judgment be recognized.

If the outcome of proceedings in a court of a Contracting State depends on the determination of an incidental question of recognition that court shall have jurisdiction over that question.

Article 27

A judgment shall not be recognized:

1. if such recognition is contrary to public policy in the State in which recognition is sought;

2. where it was given in default of appearance, if the defendant was not duly served with the document which instituted the proceedings or with an equivalent document in sufficient time to enable him to arrange for his defence;

3. if the judgment is irreconcilable with a judgment given in a dispute between the same parties in the State in which recognition is sought;

4. if the court of the State of origin, in order to arrive at its judgment, has decided a preliminary question concerning the status or legal capacity of natural persons, rights in property arising out of a matrimonial relationship, wills or succession in a way that conflicts with a rule of the private international law of the State in which the recognition is sought, unless the same result would have been reached by the application of the rules of private international law of that State;

5. if the judgment is irreconcilable with an earlier judgment given in a non-Contracting State involving the same cause of action and

between the same parties, provided that this latter judgment fulfils the conditions necessary for its recognition in the State addressed.

Article 28

Moreover, a judgment shall not be recognized if it conflicts with the provisions of Sections 3, 4 or 5 of Title II, or in a case provided for in Article 59.

In its examination of the grounds of jurisdiction referred to in the foregoing paragraph, the court or authority applied to shall be bound by the findings of fact on which the court of the State of origin based its jurisdiction.

Subject to the provisions of the first paragraph, the jurisdiction of the court of the State of origin may not be reviewed; the test of public policy referred to in point 1 of Article 27, may not be applied to the rules relating to jurisdiction.

Article 29

Under no circumstances may a foreign judgment be reviewed as to its substance.

Article 30

A court of a Contracting State in which recognition is sought of a judgment given in another Contracting State may stay the proceedings if an ordinary appeal against the judgment has been lodged.

A court of a Contracting State in which recognition is sought of a judgment given in Ireland or the United Kingdom may stay the proceedings if enforcement is suspended in the State of origin by reason of an appeal.

Section 2. Enforcement

Article 31

A judgment given in a Contracting State and enforceable in that State shall be enforced in another Contracting State when, on the application of any interested party, it has been declared enforceable there.

However, in the United Kingdom, such a judgment shall be enforced in England and Wales, in Scotland, or in Northern Ireland when, on the application of any interested party, it has been registered for enforcement in that part of the United Kingdom.

Article 32

1. The application shall be submitted:

—in Belgium, to the tribunal de premier instance or rechtbank van eerste aanleg,

—in Denmark, to the byret,

—in the Federal Republic of Germany, to the presiding judge of a chamber of the Landgericht,

—in Greece, to the Movoueael Ipwtodikeio,

—in France, to the presiding judge of the tribunal de grande instance,

—in Ireland, to the High Court,

—in Italy, to the corte d'appello,

—in Luxembourg, to the presiding judge of the tribunal d'arrondissement,

—in the Netherlands, to the presiding judge of the arrondissementsrechtbank,

—in the United Kingdom:

    1. in England and Wales, to the High Court of Justice, or in the case of maintenance judgment to the Magistrates' Court on transmission by the Secretary of State;

    2. in Scotland, to the Court of Session, or in the case of a maintenance judgment to the Sheriff Court on transmission by the secretary of State;

    3. in Northern Ireland, to the High Court of Justice, or in the case of maintenance judgment to the Magistrates' Court on transmission by the Secretary of State.

The jurisdiction of local courts shall be determined by reference to the place of domicile of the party against whom enforcement is sought. If he is not domiciled in the State in which enforcement is sought, it shall be determined by reference to the place of enforcement.

Article 33

The procedure for making the application shall be governed by the law of the State in which enforcement is sought.

The applicant must give an address for service of process within the area of jurisdiction of the court applied to. However, if the law of the State in which enforcement is sought does not provide for the furnishing of such an address, the applicant shall appoint a representative ad litem.

The documents referred to in Articles 46 and 47 shall be attached to the application.

Article 34

The court applied to shall give its decision without delay; the party against whom enforcement is sought shall not at this stage of the proceedings be entitled to make any submissions on the application.

The application may be refused only for one of the reasons specified in Articles 27 and 28.

Under no circumstances may the foreign judgment be reviewed as to its substance.

Article 35

The appropriate officer of the court shall without delay bring the decision given on the application to the notice of the applicant in accordance with the procedure laid down by the law of the State in which enforcement is sought.

Article 36

If enforcement is authorized, the party against whom enforcement is sought may appeal against the decision within one month of service thereof.

If that party is domiciled in a Contracting State other than that in which the decision authorizing enforcement was given, the time for appealing shall be two months and shall run from the date of service, either on him in person or at his residence. No extension of time may be granted on account of distance.

Article 37

1. An appeal against the decision authorizing enforcement shall be lodged in accordance with the rules governing procedure in contentious matters:

—in Belgium, with the tribunal de premiere instance or rechtbank van eerste aanleg,

—in Denmark, with the landsret,

—in the Federal Republic of Germany, with the Oberlandesgericht,

—in Greece, with the Eoeteio

—in France, with the cour d'appel,

—in Ireland, with the High Court,

—in Italy, with the corte d'appello,

—in Luxembourg, with the Cour superieure de justice sitting as a court of civil appeal,

—in the Netherlands, with the arrondissementsrechtbank,

—in Portugal, with the Tribunal de Relação,

—in the United Kingdom:

(a) in England and Wales, with the High Court of Justice, or in the case of a maintenance judgment with the Magistrates' Court;

(b) in Scotland, with the Court of Session, or in the case of a maintenance judgment with the Sheriff Court;

(c) in Northern Ireland, with the High Court of Justice, or in the case of a maintenance judgment with the Magistrates' Court.

2. The judgment given on the appeal may be contested only:

—in Belgium, Greece, France, Italy, Luxembourg and in the Netherlands, by an appeal in cassation,

—in Denmark, by an appeal to the hojesteret, with the leave of the Minister of Justice,

—in the Federal Republic of Germany, by a Rechtsbeschwerde,

—in Ireland, by an appeal on a point of law to the Supreme Court,

—in Portugal, by an appeal on a point of law,

—in the United Kingdom, by a single further appeal on a point of law.

Article 38

The court with which the appeal under Article 37(1) is lodged may, on the application of the appellant, stay the proceedings if an ordinary appeal has been lodged against the judgment in the State of origin or if the time for such an appeal has not yet expired; in the latter case, the court may specify the time within which such an appeal is to be lodged.

Where the judgment was given in Ireland or the United Kingdom, any form of appeal available in the State of origin shall be treated as an ordinary appeal for the purposes of the first paragraph.

The court may also make enforcement conditional on the provision of such security as it shall determine.

Article 39

During the time specified for an appeal pursuant to Article 36 and until any such appeal has been determined, no measures of enforcement may be taken other than protective measures taken against the property of the party against whom enforcement is sought.

The decision authorizing enforcement shall carry with it the power to proceed to any such protective measures.

Article 40

1. If the application for enforcement is refused, the applicant may appeal:

—in Belgium, to the cour d'appel or hof van beroep,

—in Denmark, to the landsret,

—in the Federal Republic of Germany, to the Oberlandesgericht,

—in Greece, to the epsilon theta epsilon tau epsilon gamma omicron,

—in France, to the cour d'appel,

—in Ireland, to the High Court,

—in Italy, to the corte d'appello,

—in Luxembourg, to the Cour superieure de justice sitting as a court of civil appeal,

—in the Netherlands, to the gerechtshof,

—in Portugal, to the Tribunal da Relação,

—in the United Kingdom:

   (a) in England and Wales, to the High Court of Justice, or in the case of a maintenance judgment to the Magistrates' Court;

   (b) in Scotland, to the Court of Session, or in the case of a maintenance judgment to the Sheriff Court;

   (c) in Northern Ireland, to the High Court of Justice, or in the case of a maintenance judgment to the Magistrates' Court.

2. The party against whom enforcement is sought shall be summoned to appear before the appellate court. If he fails to appear, the provisions of the second and third paragraphs of Article 20 shall apply even where he is not domiciled in any of the Contracting States.

Article 41

A judgment given on an appeal provided for in Article 40 may be contested only:

—in Belgium, Greece, France, Italy, Luxembourg and in the Netherlands, by an appeal in cassation,

—in Denmark, by an appeal to the hojesteret, with the leave of the Minister of Justice,

—in the Federal Republic of Germany, by a Rechtsbeschwerde,

35

—in Ireland, by an appeal on a point of law to the Supreme Court,

—in Portugal, by an appeal on a point of law,

—in the United Kingdom, by a single further appeal on a point of law.

Article 42

Where a foreign judgment has been given in respect of several matters and enforcement cannot be authorized for all of them, the court shall authorize enforcement for one or more of them.

An applicant may request partial enforcement of a judgment.

Article 43

A foreign judgment which orders a periodic payment by way of a penalty shall be enforceable in the State in which enforcement is sought only if the amount of the payment has been finally determined by the courts of the State of origin.

Article 44

An applicant who, in the State of origin has benefited from complete or partial legal aid or exemption from costs or expenses, shall be entitled, in the procedures provided for in Articles 32 to 35, to benefit from the most favourable legal aid or the most extensive exemption from costs or expenses provided for by the law of the State addressed.

However, an applicant who requests the enforcement of a decision given by an administrative authority in Denmark in respect of a maintenance order may, in the State addressed, claim the benefits referred to in the first paragraph if he presents a statement from the Danish Ministry of Justice to the effect that he fulfils the economic requirements to qualify for the grant of complete or partial legal aid or exemption from costs or expenses.

Article 45

No security, bond or deposit, however described, shall be required of a party who in one Contracting State applies for enforcement of a judgment given in another Contracting State on the ground that he is a foreign national or that he is not domiciled or resident in the State in which enforcement is sought.

Section 3. Common Provisions

Article 46

A party seeking recognition or applying for enforcement of a judgment shall produce:

1. a copy of the judgment which satisfies the conditions necessary to establish its authenticity;

2. in the case of a judgment given in default, the original or a certified true copy of the document which establishes that the party in default was served with the document instituting the proceedings or with an equivalent document.

Article 47

A party applying for enforcement shall also produce:

1. documents which establish that, according to the law of the State in which it has been given, the judgment is enforceable and has been served;

2. where appropriate, a document showing that the applicant is in receipt of legal aid in the State of origin.

Article 48

If the documents specified in point 2 of Articles 46 and 47 are not produced, the court may specify a time for their production, accept equivalent documents or, if it considers that it has sufficient information before it, dispense with their production.

If the court so requires, a translation of the documents shall be produced; the translation shall be certified by a person qualified to do so in one of the Contracting States.

Article 49

No legalization or other similar formality shall be required in respect of the documents referred to in Articles 46 or 47 or the second paragraph of Article 48, or in respect of a document appointing a representative ad litem.

Title IV: Authentic Instruments and Court Settlements

Article 50

A document which has been formally drawn up or registered as an authentic instrument and is enforceable in one Contracting State shall, in another Contracting State, be declared enforceable there, on application made in accordance with the procedures provided for in Article 31 *et seq*. The application may be refused only if enforcement of the instrument is contrary to public policy in the State addressed.

The instrument produced must satisfy the conditions necessary to establish its authenticity in the State of origin.

The provisions of Section 3 of Title III shall apply as appropriate.

Article 51

A settlement which has been approved by a court in the course of proceedings and is enforceable in the State in which it was concluded shall be enforceable in the State addressed under the same conditions as authentic instruments.

Title V: General Provisions

Article 52

In order to determine whether a party is domiciled in the Contracting State whose courts are seised of a matter, the Court shall apply its internal law.

If a party is not domiciled in the State whose courts are seised of the matter, then, in order to determine whether the party is domiciled in another Contracting State, the court shall apply the law of that State.

Article 53

For the purposes of this Convention, the seat of a company or other legal person or association of natural or legal persons shall be treated as its domicile. However, in order to determine that seat, the court shall apply its rules of private international law.

In order to determine whether a trust is domiciled in the Contracting State whose courts are seised of the matter, the court shall apply its rules of private international law.

Title VI: Transitional Provisions

Article 54

The provisions of this Convention shall apply only to legal proceedings instituted and to documents formally drawn up or registered as authentic instruments after its entry into force in the State of origin and, where recognition or enforcement of a judgment or authentic instrument is sought, in the State addressed.

However, judgments given after the date of entry into force of this Convention between the State of origin and the State addressed in proceedings instituted before that date shall be recognized and enforced in accordance with the provisions of Title III if jurisdiction was founded upon rules which accorded with those provided for either in Title II of this Convention or in a convention concluded between the State of origin and the State addressed which was in force when the proceedings were instituted.

If the parties to a dispute concerning a contract had agreed in writing before 1 June 1988 for Ireland or before 1 January 1987 for the United Kingdom that the contract was to be governed by the law of Ireland or of a part of the United Kingdom, the courts of Ireland or of that part of the United Kingdom shall retain the right to exercise jurisdiction in the dispute.

Article 54a

For a period of three years from 1 November 1986 for Denmark and from 1 June 1988 for Ireland, jurisdiction in maritime matters shall be determined in these States not only in accordance with the provisions of Title II, but also in accordance with the provisions of paragraphs 1 to 6 following. However, upon the entry into force of the International Convention relating to the arrest of sea-going ships, signed at Brussels on 10 May 1952, for one of these States, these provisions shall cease to have effect for that State.

1. A person who is domiciled in a Contracting State may be sued in the courts of one of the States mentioned above in respect of a maritime claim if the ship to which the claim relates or any other ship owned by him has been arrested by judicial process within the territory of the latter State to secure the claim, or could have been so arrested there but bail or other security has been given, and either:

(a) the claimant is domiciled in the latter State; or

(b) the claim arose in the latter State; or

(c) the claim concerns the voyage during which the arrest was made or could have been made; or

(d) the claim arises out of a collision or out of damage caused by a ship to another ship or to goods or persons on board either ship, either by the execution or non-execution of a manoeuvre or by the non-observance of regulations; or

(e) the claim is for salvage; or

(f) the claim is in respect of a mortgage or hypothecation of the ship arrested.

2. A claimant may arrest either the particular ship to which the maritime claim relates, or any other ship which is owned by the person who was, at the time when the maritime claim arose, the owner of the particular ship. However, only the particular ship to which the maritime claim relates may be arrested in respect of the maritime claims set out in (5) (o), (p) or (q) of this Article.

3. Ships shall be deemed to be in the same ownership when all the shares therein are owned by the same person or persons.

4. When in the case of a charter by demise of a ship the charterer alone is liable in respect of a maritime claim relating to that ship, the claimant may arrest that ship or any other ship owned by the charterer, but no other ship owned by the owner may be arrested in respect of such claim. The same shall apply to any case in which a person other than the owner of a ship is liable in respect of a maritime claim relating to that ship.

5. The expression 'maritime claim' means a claim arising out of one or more of the following:

38

(a) damage caused by any ship either in collision or otherwise;

(b) loss of life or personal injury caused by any ship or occurring in connection with the operation on any ship;

(c) salvage;

(d) agreement relating to the use or hire of any ship whether by charterpartyor otherwise;

(e) agreement relating to the carriage of goods in any ship whether by charterparty or otherwise;

(f) loss of or damage to goods including baggage carried in any ship;

(g) general average;

(h) bottomry;

(i) towage;

(j) pilotage;

(k) goods or materials wherever supplied to a ship for her operation or maintenance;

(l) construction, repair or equipment of any ship or dock charges and dues;

(m) wages of masters, officers or crew;

(n) mater's disbursements, including disbursements made by shippers, charterers or agents on behalf of a ship or her owner;

(o) dispute as to the title to or ownership of any ship;

(p) disputes between co-owners of any ship as to the ownership, possession, employment or earnings of that ship;

(q) the mortgage or hypothecation of any ship.

6. In Denmark, the expression 'arrest' shall be deemed as regards the maritime claims referred to in 5(o) and (p) of this Article, to include a 'forbud', where that is the only procedure allowed in respect of such a claim under Articles 646to 653 of the law on civil procedure (lov om rettens pleje).

Title VII: Relationship to Other Conventions

Article 55

Subject to the provisions of the second sub-paragraph of Article 54, and of Article 56, this Convention shall, for the States which are parties to it, supersede the following conventions concluded between two or more of them:

—the Convention between Belgium and France on jurisdiction and the validity and enforcement of judgments, arbitration awards and authentic instruments, signed at Paris on 8 July 1899,

—the Convention between Belgium and the Netherlands on jurisdiction, bankruptcy, and the validity and enforcement of judgments, arbitration awards and authentic instruments, signed at Brussels on 28 March 1925,

—the Convention between France and Italy on the enforcement of judgments in civil and commercial matters, signed at Rome on 3 June 1930,

—the Convention between the United Kingdom and the French Republic providing for the reciprocal enforcement of judgments in civil and commercial matters, with Protocol, signed at Paris on 18 January 1934,

—the Convention between the United Kingdom and the Kingdom of Belgium providing for the reciprocal enforcement of judgments in civil and commercial matters, with Protocol, signed at Brussels on 2 May 1934,

—the Convention between Germany and Italy on the recognition and enforcement of judgments in civil and commercial matters, signed at Rome on 9 March 1936,

—the Convention between the Federal Republic of Germany and the Kingdom of Belgium on the mutual recognition and enforcement of judgments, arbitration awards and authentic instruments in civil and commercial matters, signed at Bonn on 30 June 1958,

—the Convention between the Kingdom of the Netherlands and the Italian Republic on the recognition and enforcement of judgments in civil and commercial matters, signed at Rome on 17 April 1959,

—the Convention between the United Kingdom and the Federal Republic of Germany for the reciprocal recognition and enforcement of judgments in civil and commercial matters, signed at Bonn on 14 July 1960,

—the Convention between the Kingdom of Greece and the Federal Republic of Germany for the reciprocal recognition and enforcement of judgments, settlements and authentic instruments in civil and commercial matters, signed in Athens on 4 November 1961,

—the Convention between the Kingdom of Belgium and the Italian Republic on the recognition and enforcement of judgments and other enforceable instruments in civil and commercial matters, signed at Rome on 6 April 1962,

—the Convention between the Kingdom of the Netherlands and the Federal Republic of Germany on the mutual recognition and enforcement of judgments and other enforceable instruments in civil and commercial matters, signed at The Hague on 30 August 1962,

—the Convention between the United Kingdom and the Republic of Italy for the reciprocal

recognition and enforcement of judgments in civil and commercial matters, signed at Rome on 7 February 1964, with amending Protocol signed at Rome on 14 July 1970,

—the Convention between the United Kingdom and the Kingdom of the Netherlands providing for the reciprocal recognition and enforcement of judgments in civil matters, signed at The Hague on 17 November 1967, and, insofar as it is in force:

—the Convention between Spain and France on the recognition and enforcement of judgment arbitration awards in civil and commercial matters, signed at Paris on 28 May 1969,

—the Convention between Spain and Italy regarding legal aid and the recognition and enforcement of judgments in civil and commercial matters, signed at Madrid on 22 May 1973,

—the Convention between Spain and the Federal Republic of Germany on the recognition and enforcement of judgments, settlements and enforceable authentic instruments in civil and commercial matters, signed at Bonn on 14 November 1983,

and, in so far as it is in force:

—the Treaty between Belgium, the Netherlands and Luxembourg on jurisdiction, bankruptcy, and the validity and enforcement of judgments, arbitration awards and authentic instruments, signed at Brussels on 24 November 1961.

Article 56
The Treaty and the conventions referred to in Article 55 shall continue to have effect in relation to matters to which this Convention does not apply.

They shall continue to have effect in respect of judgments given and documents formally drawn up or registered as authentic instruments before the entry into force of this Convention.

Article 57

1. This Convention shall not affect any conventions to which the Contracting States are or will be parties and which, in relation to particular matters, govern jurisdiction or the recognition or enforcement of judgments.

2. With a view to its uniform interpretation, paragraph 1 shall be applied in the following manner:

(a) this Convention shall not prevent a court of a Contracting State which is a party to a convention on a particular matter from assuming jurisdiction in accordance with that Convention, even where the defendant is domiciled in another Contracting State which is not a party to that Convention. The court hearing the action shall, in any event, apply Article 20 of this Convention;

(b) judgments given in a Contracting State by a court in the exercise of jurisdiction provided for in a convention on a particular matter shall be recognized and enforced in the other Contracting State in accordance with this Convention.

Where a convention on a particular matter to which both the State of origin and the State addressed are parties lays down conditions for the recognition or enforcement of judgments, those conditions shall apply. In any event, the provisions of this Convention which concern the procedure for recognition and enforcement of judgments may be applied.

3. This Convention shall not affect the application of provisions which, in relation to particular matters, govern jurisdiction or the recognition or enforcement of judgments and which are or will be contained in acts of the institutions of the European Communities or in national laws harmonized in implementation of such acts

Article 58

Until such time as the Convention on jurisdiction and the enforcement of judgments in civil and commercial matters, signed at Lugano on 16 September 1988, takes effect with regard to France and the Swiss Confederation, this Convention shall not affect the rights granted to Swiss nationals by the Convention between France and the Swiss Confederation on jurisdiction and enforcement of judgments in civil matters, signed at Paris on 15 June 1869.

Article 59

This Convention shall not prevent a Contracting State from assuming, in a convention on the recognition and enforcement of judgments, an obligation towards a third State not to recognize judgments given in other Contracting States against defendants domiciled or habitually resident in the third State where, in cases provided for in Article 4, the judgment could only be founded on a ground of jurisdiction specified in the second paragraph of Article 3.

However, a Contracting State may not assume an obligation towards a third State not to recognize a judgment given in another Contracting State by a court basing its jurisdiction on the presence within that State of property belonging to the defendant, or the seizure by the plaintiff of property situated there:

1. if the action is brought to assert or declare proprietary or possessory rights in that property, seeks to obtain authority to dispose of it, or arises from another issue relating to such property, or

2. if the property constitutes the security for a debt which is the subject-matter of the action.

41

Title VIII: Final Provisions

Article 60
[deleted]

Article 61
This Convention shall be ratified by the signatory States. The instruments of ratification shall be deposited with the Secretary-General of the Council of the European Communities.

Article 62
This Convention shall enter into force on the first day of the third month following the deposit of the instrument of ratification by the last signatory State to take this step.

Article 63
The Contracting States recognize that any State which becomes a member of the European Economic Community shall be required to accept this Convention as a basis for the negotiations between the Contracting States and that State necessary to ensure the implementation of the last paragraph of Article 220 of the Treaty establishing the European Economic Community.

The necessary adjustments may be the subject of a special convention between the Contracting States of one part and the new Member States of the other part.

Article 64
The Secretary-General of the Council of the European Communities shall notify the signatory States of:

(a) the deposit of each instrument of ratification;

(b) the date of entry into force of this Convention;

(c) [deleted]

(d) any declaration received pursuant to Article IV of the Protocol;

(e) any communication made pursuant to Article VI of the Protocol.

Article 65
The Protocol annexed to this Convention by common accord of the Contracting States shall form an integral part thereof.

Article 66
This Convention is concluded for an unlimited period.

Article 67
Any Contracting State may request the revision of this Convention. In this event, a revision conference shall be convened by the President of the Council of the European Communities.

Article 68
This Convention, drawn up in a single original in the Dutch, French, German and Italian languages, all four texts being equally authentic, shall be deposited in the archives of the Secretariat of the Council of the European Communities. The Secretary-General shall transmit a certified copy to the Government of each signatory State.[4]

---

[4]See also Article 41 of the 1978 Accession Convention, which provides that the Danish, English and Irish texts are equally authentic, Article 17 of the 1982 Accession Convention, which provides for equal authenticity of the Greek text, and Article 24 of the 1989 Accession Convention providing for equal authenticity of the Portuguese and Spanish languages.

In witness whereof, the undersigned Plenipotentiaries have signed this Convention.

Done at Brussels this twenty-seventh day of September in the year one thousand nine hundred and sixty-eight.

For His Majesty the King of the Belgians, Pierre HARMEL

For the President of the Federal Republic of Germany, Willy BRANDT

For the President of the French Republic, Michel DEBRE

For the President of the Italian Republic, Giuseppe MEDICI

For His Royal Highness the Grand Duke of Luxembourg, Pierre GREGOIRE

For Her Majesty the Queen of the Netherlands, J.M.A.H. LUNS

PROTOCOL
on the interpretation by the Court of Justice of the Convention of 27 September 1968 on jurisdiction and the enforcement of judgments in civil and commercial matters
(90/C 189/03)

THE HIGH CONTRACTING PARTIES TO THE TREATY ESTABLISHING THE EUROPEAN ECONOMIC COMMUNITY,

Having regard to the Declaration annexed to the Convention on jurisdiction and the enforcement of judgments in civil and commercial matters, signed at Brussels on 27 September 1968,

Have decided to conclude a Protocol conferring jurisdiction on the Court of Justice of the European Communities to interpret that Convention, and to this end have designated as their Plenipotentiaries:

HIS MAJESTY THE KING OF THE BELGIANS:
  Mr Alfons VRANCKX,
  Minister of Justice;

THE PRESIDENT OF THE FEDERAL REPUBLIC OF GERMANY:
  Mr Gerhard JAHN,
  Federal Minister of Justice;

THE PRESIDENT OF THE FRENCH REPUBLIC:
  Mr Rene PLEVEN,
  Keeper of the Seals,
  Minister of Justice;

THE PRESIDENT OF THE ITALIAN REPUBLIC:
  Mr Erminio PENNACCHINI,
  Under Secretary of State in the Ministry of Justice;

HIS ROYAL HIGHNESS THE GRAND DUKE OF LUXEMBOURG:
  Mr Eugene SCHAUS,
  Minister of Justice,
  Deputy Prime Minister;

HER MAJESTY THE QUEEN OF THE NETHERLANDS:
  Mr C. H. F. POLAK,
  Minister of Justice;

WHO, meeting within the Council, having exchanged their Full Powers, found in good and due form, HAVE AGREED AS FOLLOWS:

Brussels Convention on Jurisdiction and Judgments

Article 1

The Court of Justice of the European Communities shall have jurisdiction to give rulings on the interpretation of the Convention on jurisdiction and the enforcement of judgments in civil and commercial matters and of the Protocol annexed to that Convention, signed at Brussels on 27 September 1968, and also on the interpretation of the present Protocol.

The Court of Justice of the European Communities shall also have jurisdiction to give rulings on the interpretation of the Convention on the accession of the Kingdom of Denmark, Ireland and the United Kingdom of Great Britain and Northern Ireland to the Convention of 27 September 1968 and to this Protocol.

The Court of Justice of the European Communities shall also have jurisdiction to give rulings on the interpretation of the Convention on the accession of the Hellenic Republic to the Convention of 27 September 1968 and to this Protocol, as adjusted by the 1978 Convention.

The Court of Justice of the European Communities shall also have jurisdiction to give rulings on the interpretation of the Convention on the accession of the Kingdom of Spain and the Portuguese Republic to the Convention of 27 September 1968 and to this Protocol, as adjusted by the 1978 Convention and the 1982 Convention.

Article 2

The following courts may request the Court of Justice to give preliminary rulings on questions of interpretation:

1.   —in Belgium: la Cour de Cassation—het Hof van Cassatie and le Conseil d'Etat—de Raad van State,

   —in Denmark: hojesteret,

   —in the Federal Republic of Germany: die obersten Gerichtshofe des Bundes,

   —in Greece: the [FOREIGN LANGUAGE, UNKEYABLE],

   —in Spain: el Tribunal Supremo,

   —in France: la Cour de Cassation and le Conseil d'Etat,

   —in Ireland: the Supreme Court,

   —in Italy: la Corte Suprema di Cassazione,

   —in Luxembourg: la Cour superieure de Justice when sitting as Cour de Cassation,

   —in the Netherlands: de Hoge Raad,

   —in Portugal: o Supremo Tribunal de Justica and o Supremo Tribunal Administrativo,

   —in the United Kingdom: the House of Lords and courts to which application has been made under the second paragraph of Article 37 or under Article 41 of the Convention;

2.   the courts of the Contracting States when they are sitting in an appellate capacity;

3.   in the cases provided for in Article 37 of the Convention, the courts referred to in that Article.

Article 3

1.   Where a question of interpretation of the Convention or of one of the other instruments referred to in Article 1 is raised in a case pending before one of the courts listed in point 1 of Article 2, that court shall, if it considers that a decision on the question is necessary to enable it to give judgment, request the Court of Justice to give a ruling thereon.

2.   Where such a question is raised before any court referred to in point 2 or 3 of Article 2, that court may, under the conditions laid down in

45

paragraph 1, request the Court of Justice to give a ruling thereon.

Article 4

1. The competent authority of a Contracting State may request the Court of Justice to give a ruling on a question of interpretation of the Convention or of one of the other instruments referred to in Article 1 if judgments given by courts of that State conflict with the interpretation given either by the Court of Justice or in a judgment of one of the courts of another Contracting State referred to in point 1 or 2 of Article 2. The provisions of this paragraph shall apply only to judgments which have become res judicata.

2. The interpretation given by the Court of Justice in response to such a request shall not affect the judgments which gave rise to the request for interpretation.

3. The Procurators-General of the Courts of Cassation of the Contracting States, or any other authority designated by a Contracting State, shall be entitled to request the Court of Justice for a ruling on interpretation in accordance with paragraph 1.

4. The Registrar of the Court of Justice shall give notice of the request to the Contracting States, to the Commission and to the Council of the European Communities; they shall then be entitled within two months of the notification to submit statements of case or written observations to the Court.

5. No fees shall be levied or any costs or expenses awarded in respect of the proceedings provided for in this Article.

Article 5

1. Except where this Protocol otherwise provides, the provisions of the Treaty establishing the European Economic Community and those of the Protocol on the Statute of the Court of Justice annexed thereto, which are applicable when the Court is requested to give a preliminary ruling, shall also apply to any proceedings for the interpretation of the Convention and the other instruments referred to in Article 1.

2. The Rules of Procedure of the Court of Justice shall, if necessary, be adjusted and supplemented in accordance with Article 188 of the Treaty establishing the European Economic Community.

Article 6

[deleted]

Article 7

This Protocol shall be ratified by the signatory States. The instruments of ratification shall be deposited with the Secretary-General of the Council of the European Communities.

Article 8

This Protocol shall enter into force on the first day of the third month following the deposit of the instrument of ratification by the last signatory State to take this step; provided that it shall at the earliest enter into force at the same time as the Convention of 27 September 1968 on jurisdiction and the enforcement of judgments in civil and commercial matters.

Article 9

The Contracting States recognize that any State which becomes a member of the European Economic Community, and to which Article 63 of the Convention on jurisdiction and the enforcement of judgments in civil and commercial matters applies, must accept the provisions of this Protocol, subject to such adjustments as may be required.

Article 10

The Secretary-General of the Council of the European Communities shall notify the signatory States of:

(a) the deposit of each instrument of ratification;

(b) the date of entry into force of this Protocol;

(c) any designation received pursuant to Article 4 (3);

(d) [deleted]

Article 11
The Contracting States shall communicate to the Secretary-General of the Council of the European Communities the texts of any provisions of their laws which necessitate an amendment to the list of courts in point 1 of Article 2.

Article 12
This Protocol is concluded for an unlimited period.

Article 13
Any Contracting State may request the revision of this Protocol. In this event, a revision conference shall be convened by the President of the Council of the European Communities.

Article 14
This Protocol, drawn up in a single original in the Dutch, French, German and Italian languages, all four texts being equally authentic, shall be deposited in the archives of the Secretariat of the Council of the European Communities. The Secretary-General shall transmit a certified copy to the Government of each signatory State.

Zu Urkund dessen haben die unterzeichneten Bevollmachtigten ihre Unterschrift unter dieses Protokoll gesetzt.

En foi de quoi les plenipotentiaires soussignes ont appose leur signature au bas du present protocole.

In fede di che i plenipotenziari sottoscritti hanno apposto le loro firme in calce al presente protocollo.

Ten blijke waarvan de onderscheiden gevolmachtigden hun handtekening onder dit Protocol hebben gesteld.

Geschehen zu Luxembourg am dritten Juni neunzehnhunderteinundsiebzig.

Fait a Luxembourg, le trois juin mil neuf cent soixante et onze.

Fatto a Lussemburgo, addi tre giugno millenovencentosettantuno.

Gedaan te Luxemburg, de derde juni negentienhonderd eenenzeventig.

Pour Sa Majeste le roi des Belges
Voor Zijne Majesteit de Koning der Belgen
  Alfons VRANCKX

Fur den Prasidenten der Bundesrepublik Deutschland
  Gerhard JAHN

Pour le president de la Republique francaise
  Rene PLEVEN

Per il presidente delle Repubblica italiana
  Erminio PENNACCHINI

Pour Son Altesse Royale le grand-duc de Luxembourg
  Eugene SCHAUS

Voor Hare Majesteit de Koningin der Nederlanden
  C. H. F. POLAK

C. United Nations Convention on the Recognition and Enforcement of Foreign Arbitral Awards (New York Arbitration Convention)

Source: Done at New York, June 10, 1958, entered into force for the U.S. on June 7, 1959, 21 U.S.T. 2517, T.I.A.S. No. 6997, 330 U.N.T.S. 38.

Website information:

http://www.internationaladr.com/tc1.htm
This is the website of International Alternative Dispute Resolution, an electronic forum intended to serve as a resource for practitioners and others interested in learning more about the field of international alternative dispute resolution. The website contains the text of several international agreements relating to arbitration, as well as an updated list of member states to each agreement, and links to the individual arbitration laws of those states.

Introduction

The New York Arbitration Convention was adopted in 1953 in New York under the auspices of the United Nations Economic and Social Council and was based on a draft convention developed by the International Chamber of Commerce.[1] The New York Convention established a new legal regime that favors international arbitration through the facilitation of recognition and enforcement of arbitral agreements and awards. It has been an extremely successful treaty, with well over 100 contracting states.

The Convention facilitates the recognition and enforcement of both agreements to arbitrate (Art. II) and arbitral awards (Art. III). The general rule in the Convention is that arbitral awards made in any state are to be recognized and enforced (Art. I(1)). States are permitted, however, to make reservations limiting recognition and enforcement to awards made in the territory of another Contracting State, and to awards considered "commercial" under the national law of the Contracting State (Art. I(3)). The United States recognizes only awards from other Contracting States under the Convention.

Under the general rule, so long as there is a written agreement to arbitrate (Art. II(2)), the courts of Contracting States must enforce that agreement by referring the parties to arbitration, "unless it finds that the said agreement is null and void, inoperative or incapable of being performed." (Art. II(3)).

The party seeking recognition and/or enforcement must supply the authenticated original award or a certified copy thereof (Art. IV(1)(a)), along with a certified translation if the award was not rendered in an official language of the enforcing state (Art. IV(2)).

Article V(1) provides a limited list of grounds for refusal of recognition and enforcement of an arbitral award:

(1) incapacity of the parties or invalidity of the arbitration agreement,

(2) improper notice or other lack of due process,

(3) an award beyond the scope of the agreement to arbitrate,

---

[1] UN Doc. E/C.2/373.

49

(4) improper arbitral procedure or composition of the arbitral board, or

(5) that the award has been set aside or suspended or is otherwise not binding.

Recognition and enforcement may also be refused if the subject matter of the dispute is not capable of settlement by arbitration under the enforcing state's laws or if recognition or enforcement would be contrary to the public policy of that state (Art. V(2)).

UNITED NATIONS CONVENTION ON THE RECOGNITION AND ENFORCEMENT OF FOREIGN ARBITRAL AWARDS (NEW YORK ARBITRATION CONVENTION)

Article I

1. This Convention shall apply to the recognition and enforcement of arbitral awards made in the territory of a State other than the State where the recognition and enforcement of such awards are sought, and arising out of differences between persons, whether physical or legal. It shall also apply to arbitral awards not considered as domestic awards in the State where their recognition and enforcement are sought.

2. The term "arbitral awards" shall include not only awards made by arbitrators appointed for each case but also those made by permanent arbitral bodies to which the parties have submitted.

3. When signing, ratifying or acceding to this Convention, or notifying extension under Article X hereof, any State may on the basis of reciprocity declare that it will apply the Convention to the recognition and enforcement of awards made only in the territory of another Contracting State. It may also declare that it will apply the Convention only to differences arising out of legal relationships, whether contractual or not, which are considered as commercial under the national law of the State making such declaration.

Article II

1. Each Contracting State shall recognize an agreement in writing under which the parties undertake to submit to arbitration all or any differences which have arisen or which may arise between them in respect of a defined legal relationship, whether contractual or not, concerning a subject matter capable of settlement by arbitration.

2. The term "agreement in writing" shall include an arbitral clause in a contract or an arbitration agreement, signed by the parties or contained in an exchange of letters or telegrams.

3. The court of a Contracting State, when seized of an action in a matter in respect of which the parties have made an agreement within the meaning of this article, shall, at the request of one of the parties, refer the parties to arbitration, unless it finds that the said agreement is null and void, inoperative or incapable of being performed.

Article III

Each Contracting State shall recognize arbitral awards as binding and enforce them in accordance with the rules of procedure of the territory where the award is relied upon, under the conditions laid down in the following articles. There shall not be imposed substantially more onerous conditions or higher fees or charges on the recognition or enforcement of arbitral awards to which this Convention applies than are imposed on the recognition or enforcement of domestic arbitral awards.

Article IV

1. To obtain the recognition and enforcement mentioned in the preceding article, the party applying for recognition and enforcement shall, at the time of the application, supply:

(a) The duly authenticated original award or a duly certified copy thereof;

(b) The original agreement referred to in Article II or a duly certified copy thereof.

2. If the said award or agreement is not made in an official language of the country in which the award is relied upon, the party applying for recognition and enforcement of the award shall produce a translation of these documents into such

51

language. The translation shall be certified by an official or sworn translator or by a diplomatic or consular agent.

Article V

1. Recognition and enforcement of the award may be refused, at the request of the party against whom it is invoked, only if that party furnishes to the competent authority where the recognition and enforcement is sought, proof that:

(a) The parties to the agreement referred to in Article II were, under the law applicable to them, under some incapacity, or the said agreement is not valid under the law to which the parties have subjected it or, failing any indication thereon, under the law of the country where the award was made; or

(b) The party against whom the award is invoked was not given proper notice of the appointment of the arbitrator or of the arbitration proceedings or was otherwise unable to present his case; or

(c) The award deals with a difference not contemplated by or not falling within the terms of the submission to arbitration, or it contains decisions on matters beyond the scope of the submission to arbitration, provided that, if the decisions on matters submitted to arbitration can be separated from those not so submitted, that part of the award which contains decisions on matters submitted to arbitration may be recognized and enforced; or

(d) The composition of the arbitral authority or the arbitral procedure was not in accordance with the agreement of the parties, or, failing such agreement, was not in accordance with the law of the country where the arbitration took place; or

(e) The award has not yet become binding on the parties, or has been set aside or suspended by a competent authority of the country in which, or under the law of which, that award was made.

2. Recognition and enforcement of an arbitral award may also be refused if the competent authority in the country where recognition and enforcement is sought finds that:

(a) The subject matter of the difference is not capable of settlement by arbitration under the law of that country; or

(b) The recognition or enforcement of the award would be contrary to the public policy of that country.

Article VI

If an application for the setting aside or suspension of the award has been made to a competent authority referred to in Article V(1)(e), the authority before which the award is sought to be relied upon may, if it considers it proper, adjourn the decision on the enforcement of the award and may also, on the application of the party claiming enforcement of the award, order the other party to give suitable security.

Article VII

1. The provisions of the present Convention shall not affect the validity of multilateral or bilateral agreements concerning the recognition and enforcement of arbitral awards entered into by the Contracting States nor deprive any interested party of any right he may have to avail himself of an arbitral award in the manner and to the extent allowed by the law or the treaties of the country where such award is sought to be relied upon.

2. The Geneva Protocol on Arbitration Clauses of 1923 and the Geneva Convention on the

Execution of Foreign Arbitral Awards of 1927 shall cease to have effect between Contracting States on their becoming bound and to the extent that they become bound, by this Convention.

Article VIII

1. This Convention shall be open until 31 December 1958 for signature on behalf of any Member of the United Nations and also on behalf of any other State which is or hereafter becomes a member of any specialized agency of the United Nations, or which is or hereafter becomes a party to the Statute of the International Court of Justice, or any other State to which an invitation has been addressed by the General Assembly of the United Nations.

2. This Convention shall be ratified and the instrument of ratification shall be deposited with the Secretary-General of the United Nations.

Article IX

1. This Convention shall be open for accession to all States referred to in Article VIII.

2. Accession shall be effected by the deposit of an instrument of accession with the Secretary-General of the United Nations.

Article X

1. Any State may, at the time of signature, ratification or accession, declare that this Convention shall extend to all or any of the territories for the international relations of which it is responsible. Such a declaration shall take effect when the Convention enters into force for the State concerned.

2. At any time thereafter any such extension shall be made by notification addressed to the Secretary-General of the United Nations and shall take effect as from the 90th day after the day of receipt by the Secretary-General of the United Nations of this notification, or as from the date of entry into force of the Convention for the State concerned, whichever is the later.

3. With respect to those territories to which this Convention is not extended at the time of signature, ratification or accession, each State concerned shall consider the possibility of taking the necessary steps in order to extend the application of this Convention to such territories, subject, where necessary for constitutional reasons, to the consent of the Governments of such territories.

Article XI

In the case of a federal or non-unitary State the following provisions shall apply:

(a) With respect to those articles of this Convention that come within the legislative jurisdiction of the federal authority, the obligations of the federal Government shall to this extent be the same as those of Contracting States which are not federal States;

(b) With respect to those articles of this Convention that come within the legislative jurisdiction of constituent states or provinces which are not, under the constitutional system of the federation, bound to take legislative action, the federal Government shall bring such articles with a favourable recommendation to the notice of the appropriate authorities of constituent states or provinces at the earliest possible moment;

(c) A federal State Party to this Convention shall, at the request of any other Contracting State transmitted through the Secretary-General of the United Nations, supply a statement of the law and practice of the federation and its constituent units in regard to any particular provision of this Convention, showing the extent to which effect has been given to that provision by legislative or other action.

Article XII

1. This Convention shall come into force on the 90th day following the date of deposit of the third instrument of ratification or accession.

2. For each State ratifying or acceding to this Convention after the deposit of the third instrument of ratification or accession, this Convention shall enter into force on the 90th day after deposit by such State of its instrument of ratification or accession.

Article XIII

1. Any Contracting State may denounce this Convention by a written notification to the Secretary-General of the United Nations. Denunciation shall take effect one year after the date of receipt of the notification by the Secretary-General.

2. Any State which has made a declaration or notification under Article X may, at any time thereafter, by notification to the Secretary-General of the United Nations, declare that this Convention shall cease to extend to the territory concerned one year after the date of the receipt of the notification by the Secretary-General.

3. This Convention shall continue to be applicable to arbitral awards in respect of which recognition or enforcement proceedings have been instituted before the denunciation takes effect.

Article XIV

A Contracting State shall not be entitled to avail itself of the present Convention against other Contracting States except to the extent that it is itself bound to apply the Convention.

Article XV

The Secretary-General of the United Nations shall notify the States contemplated in Article VIII of the following:

(a) Signatures and ratifications in accordance with Article VIII;

(b) Accessions in accordance with Article IX;

(c) Declarations and notifications under Articles I, X and XI;

(d) The date upon which this Convention enters into force in accordance with Article XII;

(e) Denunciations and notifications in accordance with Article XIII.

Article XVI

1. This Convention, of which the Chinese, English, French, Russian and Spanish texts shall be equally authentic, shall be deposited in the archives of the United Nations.

2. The Secretary-General of the United Nations shall transmit a certified copy of this Convention to the States contemplated in Article VIII.

D. Convention on the Service Abroad of Judicial and Extrajudicial Documents in Civil or Commercial Matters (Hague Service Convention)

Source: 20 U.S.T. 361; T.I.A.S. 6638; 658 U.N.T.S. 163; *reprinted in* 4 I.L.M. 341 (1965) *and in* the Supplement to the U.S. Code Annotated following Rule 4 of the Federal Rules of Civil Procedure

Website information:

http://www.hcch.net/
This is the website of the Hague Conference on Private International Law. It contains both English and French language versions of all Hague conventions, including up-to-date status reports, current news, and a detailed database of convention proceedings and publications.

Introduction

The Hague Service Convention was adopted by the Hague conference on Private International Law in 1965, and entered into force for the United States on February 10, 1969. It is designed to facilitate service of "judicial and extrajudicial" documents from one country to another. It allows service:
(1) by methods prescribed by the law applicable to domestic service in the country in which service is to be performed,
(2) by voluntary delivery, and
(3) by a method requested by the applicant.
Each Contracting State designates a "Central Authority" to whom a foreign party may submit requests for service of process. The request is them submitted according to a form provided in an annex to the Convention (Art. 3), accompanied by the document to be served. Translation into the official language of the country of service may be required by reservation to the Convention.

CONVENTION ON THE SERVICE ABROAD
OF JUDICIAL AND EXTRAJUDICIAL DOCUMENTS
IN CIVIL OR COMMERCIAL MATTERS
(HAGUE SERVICE CONVENTION)

The States signatory to the present Convention,

Desiring to create appropriate means to ensure that judicial and extrajudicial documents to be served abroad shall be brought to the notice of the addressee in sufficient time,

Desiring to improve the organization of mutual judicial assistance for that purpose by simplifying and expediting the procedure,

Have resolved to conclude a Convention to this effect and have agreed upon the following provisions:

Article 1
The present Convention shall apply in all cases, in civil or commercial matters, where there is occasion to transmit a judicial or extrajudicial document for service abroad.

This Convention shall not apply where the address of the person to be served with the document is not known.

Chapter I: Judicial Documents

Article 2
Each contracting State shall designate a Central Authority which will undertake to receive requests for service coming from other contracting States and to proceed in conformity with the provisions of Articles 3 to 6.

Each State shall organise the Central Authority in conformity with its own law.

Article 3
The authority or judicial officer competent under the law of the State in which the documents originate shall forward to the Central Authority of the State addressed a request conforming to the model annexed to the present Convention, without

any requirement of legalisation or other equivalent formality.

The document to be served or a copy thereof shall be annexed to the request. The request and the document shall both be furnished in duplicate.

Article 4
If the Central Authority considers that the request does not comply with the provisions of the present Convention it shall promptly inform the applicant and specify its objections to the request.

Article 5
The Central Authority of the State addressed shall itself serve the document or shall arrange to have it served by an appropriate agency, either—

(a) by a method prescribed by its internal law for the service of documents in domestic actions upon persons who are within its territory, or

(b) by a particular method requested by the applicant, unless such a method is incompatible with the law of the State addressed.

Subject to sub-paragraph (b) of the first paragraph of this article, the document may

56

always be served by delivery to an addressee who accepts it voluntarily.

If the document is to be served under the first paragraph above, the Central Authority may require the document to be written in, or translated into, the official language or one of the official languages of the State addressed.

That part of the request, in the form attached to the present Convention, which contains a summary of the document to be served, shall be served with the document.

Article 6
The Central Authority of the State addressed or any authority which it may have designated for that purpose, shall complete a certificate in the form of the model annexed to the present Convention.

The certificate shall state that the document has been served and shall include the method, the place and the date of service and the person to whom the document was delivered. If the document has not been served, the certificate shall set out the reasons which have prevented service.

The applicant may require that a certificate not completed by a Central Authority or by a judicial authority shall be countersigned by one of these authorities.

The certificate shall be forwarded directly to the applicant.

Article 7
The standard terms in the model annexed to the present Convention shall in all cases be written either in French or in English. They may also be written in the official language, or in one of the official languages, of the State in which the documents originate.

The corresponding blanks shall be completed either in the language of the State addressed or in French or in English.

Article 8
Each contracting State shall be free to effect service of judicial documents upon persons abroad, without application of any compulsion, directly through its diplomatic or consular agents.

Any State may declare that it is opposed to such service within its territory, unless the document is to be served upon a national of the State in which the documents originate.

Article 9
Each contracting State shall be free, in addition, to use consular channels to forward documents, for the purpose of service, to those authorities of another contracting State which are designated by the latter for this purpose.

Each contracting State may, if exceptional circumstances so require, use diplomatic channels for the same purpose.

Article 10
Provided the State of destination does not object, the present Convention shall not interfere with—

(a) the freedom to send judicial documents, by postal channels, directly to persons abroad,

(b) the freedom of judicial officers, officials or other competent persons of the State of origin to effect service of judicial documents directly through the judicial officers, officials or other competent persons of the State of destination,

(c) the freedom of any person interested in a judicial proceeding to effect service of judicial documents directly through the judicial officers, officials or other competent persons of the State of destination.

Article 11

The present Convention shall not prevent two or more contracting States from agreeing to permit, for the purpose of service of judicial documents, channels of transmission other than those provided for in the preceding articles and, in particular, direct communication between their respective authorities.

Article 12

The service of judicial documents coming from a contracting State shall not give rise to any payment or reimbursement of taxes or costs for the services rendered by the State addressed.

The applicant shall pay or reimburse the costs occasioned by

(a) the employment of a judicial officer or of a person competent under the law of the State of destination,

(b) the use of a particular method of service.

Article 13

Where a request for service complies with the terms of the present Convention, the State addressed may refuse to comply therewith only if it deems that compliance would infringe its sovereignty or security.

It may not refuse to comply solely on the ground that, under its internal law, it claims exclusive jurisdiction over the subject-matter of the action or that its internal law would not permit the action upon which the application is based.

The Central Authority shall, in case of refusal, promptly inform the applicant and state the reasons for the refusal.

Article 14

Difficulties which may arise in connection with the transmission of judicial documents for service shall be settled through diplomatic channels.

Article 15

Where a writ of summons or an equivalent document had to be transmitted abroad for the purpose of service, under the provisions of the present Convention, and the defendant has not appeared, judgment shall not be given until it is established that

(a) the document was served by a method prescribed by the internal law of the State addressed for the service of documents in domestic actions upon persons who are within its territory, or

(b) the document was actually delivered to the defendant or to his residence by another method provided for by this Convention, and that in either of these cases the service or the delivery was effected in sufficient time to enable the defendant to defend.

Each contracting State shall be free to declare that the judge, notwithstanding the provisions of the first paragraph of this article, may give judgment even if no certificate of service or delivery has been received, if all the following conditions are fulfilled—

(a) the document was transmitted by one of the methods provided for in this Convention,

(b) a period of time of not less than six months, considered adequate by the judge in the particular case, has elapsed since the date of the transmission of the document,

(c) no certificate of any kind has been received, even though every reasonable effort has been made to obtain it through the competent authorities of the State addressed.

Notwithstanding the provisions of the preceding paragraphs the judge may order, in case of urgency, any provisional or protective measures.

Article 16
When a writ of summons or an equivalent document had to be transmitted abroad for the purpose of service, under the provisions of the present Convention, and a judgment has been entered against a defendant who has not appeared, the judge shall have the power to relieve the defendant from the effects of the expiration of the time for appeal from the judgment if the following conditions are fulfilled—

(a) the defendant, without any fault on his part, did not have knowledge of the document in sufficient time to defend, or knowledge of the judgment in sufficient time to appeal, and

(b) the defendant has disclosed a prima facie defence to the action on the merits.

An application for relief may be filed only within a reasonable time after the defendant has knowledge of the judgment.

Each contracting State may declare that the application will not be entertained if it is filed after the expiration of a time to be stated in the declaration, but which shall in no case be less than one year following the date of the judgment.

This article shall not apply to judgments concerning status or capacity of persons.

Chapter II: Extrajudicial Documents

Article 17
Extrajudicial documents emanating from authorities and judicial officers of a contracting State may be transmitted for the purpose of service in another contracting State by the methods and under the provisions of the present Convention.

Chapter III: General Clauses

Article 18
Each contracting State may designate other authorities in addition to the Central Authority and shall determine the extent of their competence.

The applicant shall, however, in all cases, have the right to address a request directly to the Central Authority.

Federal States shall be free to designate more than one Central Authority.

Article 19
To the extent that the internal law of a contracting State permits methods of transmission, other than those provided for in the preceding articles, of documents coming from abroad, for service within its territory, the present Convention shall not affect such provisions.

Article 20
The present Convention shall not prevent an agreement between any two or more contracting States to dispense with—

(a) the necessity for duplicate copies of transmitted documents as required by the second paragraph of Article 3,

(b) the language requirements of the third paragraph of Article 5 and Article 7,

(c) the provisions of the fourth paragraph of Article 5,

(d) the provisions of the second paragraph of Article 12.

Article 21

Each contracting State shall, at the time of the deposit of its instrument of ratification or accession, or at a later date, inform the Ministry of Foreign Affairs of the Netherlands of the following—

(a) the designation of authorities, pursuant to Articles 2 and 18,

(b) the designation of the authority competent to complete the certificate pursuant to Article 6,

(c) the designation of the authority competent to receive documents transmitted by consular channels, pursuant to Article 9.

Each contracting State shall similarly inform the Ministry, where appropriate, of -

(a) opposition to the use of methods of transmission pursuant to Articles 8 and 10,

(b) declarations pursuant to the second paragraph of Article 15 and the third paragraph of Article 16,

(c) all modifications of the above designations, oppositions and declarations.

Article 22

Where Parties to the present Convention are also parties to one or both of the Conventions on civil procedure signed at The Hague on 17th July 1905 [99 BFSP 990], and on 1st March 1954 [286 UNTS 265], this Convention shall replace as between them Articles 1 to 7 of the earlier Conventions.

Article 23

The present Convention shall not affect the application of Article 23 of the Convention on civil procedure signed at The Hague on 17th July 1905, or of Article 24 of the Convention on civil procedure signed at The Hague on 1st March 1954.

These articles shall, however, apply only if methods of communication, identical to those provided for in these Conventions, are used.

Article 24

Supplementary agreements between parties to the Conventions of 1905 and 1954 shall be considered as equally applicable to the present Convention, unless the Parties have otherwise agreed.

Article 25

Without prejudice to the provisions of Articles 22 and 24, the present Convention shall not derogate from Conventions containing provisions on the matters governed by this Convention to which the contracting States are, or shall become, Parties.

Article 26

The present Convention shall be open for signature by the States represented at the Tenth Session of the Hague Conference on Private International Law.

It shall be ratified, and the instruments of ratification shall be deposited with the Ministry of Foreign Affairs of the Netherlands.

Article 27

The present Convention shall enter into force on the 60th day after the deposit of the third instrument of ratification referred to in the second paragraph of Article 26.

The Convention shall enter into force for each signatory State which ratifies subsequently on the 60th day after the deposit of its instrument of ratification.

Article 28

Any State not represented at the Tenth Session of the Hague Conference on Private International Law may accede to the present Convention after it has entered into force in accordance with the first paragraph of Article 27. The instrument of accession shall be deposited with the Ministry of Foreign Affairs of the Netherlands.

The Convention shall enter into force for such a State in the absence of any objection from a State which has ratified the Convention before such deposit, notified to the Ministry of Foreign Affairs of the Netherlands within a period of six months after the date on which the said Ministry has notified it of such accession.

In the absence of any such objection, the Convention shall enter into force for the acceding State on the first day of the month following the expiration of the last of the periods referred to in the preceding paragraph.

Article 29

Any State may, at the time of signature, ratification or accession, declare that the present Convention shall extend to all the territories for the international relations of which it is responsible, or to one or more of them. Such a declaration shall take effect on the date of entry into force of the Convention for the State concerned.

At any time thereafter, such extensions shall be notified to the Ministry of Foreign Affairs of the Netherlands.

The Convention shall enter into force for the territories mentioned in such an extension on the 60th day after the notification referred to in the preceding paragraph.

Article 30

The present Convention shall remain in force for five years from the date of its entry into force in accordance with the first paragraph of Article 27, even for States which have ratified it or acceded to it subsequently.

If there has been no denunciation, it shall be renewed tacitly every five years.

Any denunciation shall be notified to the Ministry of Foreign Affairs of the Netherlands at least six months before the end of the five year period.

It may be limited to certain of the territories to which the Convention applies.

The denunciation shall have effect only as regards the State which has notified it. The Convention shall remain in force for the other contracting States.

Article 31

The Ministry of Foreign Affairs of the Netherlands shall give notice to the States referred to in Article 26, and to the States which have acceded in accordance with Article 28, of the following -

(a) the signatures and ratifications referred to in Article 26;

(b) the date on which the present Convention enters into force in accordance with the first paragraph of Article 27;

(c) the accessions referred to in Article 28 and the dates on which they take effect;

(d) the extensions referred to in Article 29 and the dates on which they take effect;

(e) the designations, oppositions and declarations referred to in Article 21;

(f) the denunciations referred to in the third paragraph of Article 30.

In witness whereof the undersigned, being duly authorised thereto, have signed the present Convention.

Done at The Hague, on the 15th day of November, 1965, in the English and French languages, both texts being equally authentic, in a single copy which shall be deposited in the archives of the Government of the Netherlands, and of which a certified copy shall be sent, through the diplomatic channel, to each of the States represented at the Tenth Session of the Hague Conference on Private International Law.

[Signatures omitted.]

Designations and Declarations Made on the Part of the United States in Connection with the Deposit of the United States Ratification:

1. In accordance with Article 2, the United States Department of State is designated as the Central Authority to receive requests for service from other Contracting States and to proceed in conformity with Articles 3 to 6.

2. In accordance with Article 6, in addition to the United States Department of State, the United States Department of Justice and the United States Marshal or Deputy Marshal for the judicial district in which service is made are designated for the purpose of completing the certificate in the form annexed to the Convention.

3. In accordance with the second paragraph of Article 15, it is declared that the judge may, notwithstanding the provisions of the first paragraph of Article 15, give judgment even if no certificate of service or delivery has been received, if all the conditions specified in

subdivisions (a), (b) and (c) of the second paragraph of Article 15 are fulfilled.

4. In accordance with the third paragraph of Article 16, it is declared that an application under Article 16 will not be entertained if it is filed

(a) after the expiration of the period within which the same may be filed under the procedural regulations of the court in which the judgment has been entered, or

(b) after the expiration of one year following the date of the judgment, whichever is later.

5. In accordance with Article 29, it is declared that the Convention shall extend to all the States of the United States, the District of Columbia, Guam, Puerto Rico, and the Virgin Islands.

FORMS (REQUEST AND CERTIFICATE)

SUMMARY OF THE DOCUMENT TO BE SERVED

(annexes provided for Articles 3, 5, 6 and 7)

ANNEX TO THE CONVENTION

Forms

REQUEST FOR SERVICE ABROAD OF JUDICIAL OR EXTRAJUDICIAL DOCUMENTS

Convention on the Service Abroad of Judicial and Extrajudicial Documents in Civil or
Commercial Matters,

signed at The Hague, the 15th of November 1965.

Identity and address of the applicant	Address of receiving authority

The undersigned applicant has the honour to transmit - in duplicate - the documents listed below
and, in conformity with Article 5 of the above-mentioned Convention, requests prompt service of
one copy thereof on the addressee, *i.e,*
(identity and address)

....

....

a) in accordance with the provisions of sub-paragraph *(a)* of the first paragraph of Article 5 of the Convention*.

b) in accordance with the following particular method (sub-paragraph *(b)* of the first paragraph of Article 5)*: ....

....

....

c) by delivery to the addressee, if he accepts it voluntarily (second paragraph of Article 5)*.

The authority is requested to return or to have returned to the applicant a copy of the documents—and of the annexes*—with a certificate as provided on the reverse side.

List of documents

....

....

....

....

....

....

....

....

....

Done at . . . . , the . . . .

Signature and/or stamp.

* Delete if inappropriate.

Reverse of the request

CERTIFICATE

The undersigned authority has the honour to certify, in conformity with Article 6 of the Convention,

1) that the document has been served*

- the (date)

....

- at (place, street, number)

....

....

- in one of the following methods authorised by Article 5:

a) in accordance with the provisions of sub-paragraph *(a)* of the first paragraph of Article 5 of the Convention*.

b) in accordance with the following particular method*:

....

....

c) by delivery to the addressee, who accepted it voluntarily* .

The documents referred to in the request have been delivered to:

- (identity and description of person)

- ....

....

- relationship to the addressee (family, business or other):

- ....

....

....

2) that the document has not been served, by reason of the following facts*:

....

....

....

In conformity with the second paragraph of Article 12 of the Convention, the applicant is requested to pay or reimburse the expenses detailed in the attached statement*.

Annexes

Documents returned:

....

....

....

In appropriate cases, documents establishing the service:

....

....

Done at . . . . , the . . . .

Signature and/or stamp.

* Delete if inappropriate.

SUMMARY OF THE DOCUMENT TO BE SERVED

Convention on the Service Abroad of Judicial and Extrajudicial Documents in Civil or Commercial Matters,

signed at The Hague, the 15th of November 1965.

(Article 5, fourth paragraph)

Name and address of the requesting authority:

....

....

Particulars of the parties*:

....

....

JUDICIAL DOCUMENT**

Nature and purpose of the document:

....

....

Nature and purpose of the proceedings and, where appropriate, the amount in dispute:

....

....

Date and place for entering appearance**:

....

....

Court which has given judgment**:

....

....

Date of judgment**:

....

Time-limits stated in the document**:

....

....

EXTRAJUDICIAL DOCUMENT**

Nature and purpose of the document:

....

....

Time-limits stated in the document**:

....

....

* If appropriate, identity and address of the person interested in the transmission of the document.

** Delete if inappropriate.

E. Convention on the Taking of Evidence Abroad in Civil or Commercial Matters (Hague Evidence Convention)

Source: 23 U.S.T. 2555; T.I.A.S. 7444; 847 U.N.T.S. 231, *reprinted in* 8 I.L.M. 37 (1969) *and in* United States Code Annotated (West), following 28 U.S.C.A. § 1781.

Website information:

http://www.hcch.net/
This is the website of the Hague Conference on Private International Law. It contains both English and French language versions of all Hague conventions, including up-to-date status reports, current news, and a detailed database of convention proceedings and publications. Information on the Evidence Convention includes the declarations of each Contracting State, including designation of Central Authority.

Introduction

The United States was one of the first states to ratify this convention, which came into effect on October 7, 1972. Over thirty states are now parties to the convention.

The Hague Evidence Convention is designed to ease certain procedural tensions that exist between civil and common law jurisdictions and, thereby, to facilitate the gathering of evidence for use in civil or commercial judicial proceedings that may be found in another member country (Art. 1). Whether or not a matter is to be defined as civil or commercial is left to the domestic law of each member State.

The method for the taking of evidence prescribed by the Convention is by "letter of request" directed to the "central authority" which is required to be established by each party state (Art. 3). The Convention governs, inter alia, the information required to be in the letter of request (Art. 3), language requirements (requests made in French or English must be accepted unless the state has made a reservation governing language), procedures for fulfilling the request, "special procedures" such as oaths, verbatim transcripts and cross-examination (Art. 9), grounds for refusal to execute a letter of request (Art. 12), and, fees and costs (Art. 14).

States may allow for methods for taking evidence other than those contemplated by the Convention and by Convention methods but under less restrictive terms than set up by the Convention (Art. 27).

CONVENTION ON THE TAKING OF EVIDENCE ABROAD IN CIVIL OR COMMERCIAL MATTERS (HAGUE EVIDENCE CONVENTION)

The States signatory to the present Convention.

Desiring to facilitate the transmission and execution of Letters of Request and to further the accommodation of the different methods which they use for this purpose,

Desiring to improve mutual judicial co-operation in civil or commercial matters, Have resolved to conclude a Convention to this effect and have agreed upon the following provisions—

Chapter I: Letters of Request

Article 1

In civil or commercial matters a judicial authority of a Contracting State may, in accordance with the provisions of the law of that State, request the competent authority of another Contracting State, by means of a Letter of Request, to obtain evidence, or to perform some other judicial act.

A Letter shall not be used to obtain evidence which is not intended for use in judicial proceedings, commenced or contemplated.

The expression "other judicial act" does not cover the service of judicial documents or the issuance of any process by which judgments or orders are executed or enforced, or orders for provisional or protective measures.

Article 2

A Contracting State shall designate a Central Authority which will undertake to receive Letters of Request coming from a judicial authority of another Contracting State and to transmit them to the authority competent to execute them. Each State shall organize the Central Authority in accordance with its own law.

Letters shall be sent to the Central Authority of the State of execution without being transmitted through any other authority of that State.

Article 3

A Letter of Request shall specify—

(a) the authority requesting its execution and the authority requested to execute it, if known to the requesting authority;

(b) the names and addresses of the parties to the proceedings and their representatives, if any;

(c) the nature of the proceedings for which the evidence is required, giving all necessary information in regard thereto;

(d) the evidence to be obtained or other judicial act to be performed. Where appropriate, the Letter shall specify, inter alia—

(e) the names and addresses of the persons to be examined;

(f) the questions to be put to the persons to be examined or a statement of the subject-matter about which they are to be examined;

(g) the documents or other property, real or personal, to be inspected;

(h) any requirement that the evidence is to be given on oath or affirmation, and any special form to be used;

(i) any special method or procedure to be followed under Article 9.

70

A Letter may also mention any information necessary for the application of Article 11.

No legalization or other like formality may be required.

Article 4
A Letter of Request shall be in the language of the authority requested to execute it or be accompanied by a translation into that language.

Nevertheless, a Contracting State shall accept a Letter in either English or French, or a translation into one of these languages, unless it has made the reservation authorized by Article 33.

A contracting State which has more than one official language and cannot, for reasons of internal law, accept Letters in one of these languages for the whole of its territory, shall, by declaration, specify the language in which the Letter or translation thereof shall be expressed for execution in the specified parts of its territory. In case of failure to comply with this declaration, without justifiable excuse, the costs of translation into the required language shall be borne by the State of origin.

A Contracting State may, by declaration, specify the language or languages other than those referred to in the preceding paragraphs, in which a Letter may be sent to its Central Authority.

Any translation accompanying a Letter shall be certified as correct, either by a diplomatic officer or consular agent or by a sworn translator or by any other person so authorized in either State.

Article 5
If the Central Authority considers that the request does not comply with the provisions of the present Convention, it shall promptly inform the authority of the State of origin which transmitted the Letter of Request, specifying the objections to the Letter.

Article 6
If the authority to whom a Letter of Request has been transmitted is not competent to execute it, the Letter shall be sent forthwith to the authority in the same State which is competent to execute it in accordance with the provisions of its own law.

Article 7
The requesting authority shall, if it so desires, be informed of the time when, and the place where, the proceedings will take place, in order that the parties concerned, and their representatives, if any, may be present. This information shall be sent directly to the parties or their representatives when the authority of the State of origin so requests.

Article 8
A Contracting State may declare that members of the judicial personnel of the requesting authority of another Contracting State may be present at the execution of a Letter of Request. Prior authorization by the competent authority designated by the declaring State may be required.

Article 9
The judicial authority which executes a Letter of Request shall apply its own law as to the methods and procedures to be followed.

However, it will follow a request of the requesting authority that a special method or procedure be followed, unless this is incompatible with the internal law of the State of execution or is impossible of performance by reason of its internal practice and procedure or by reason of practical difficulties.

A Letter of Request shall be executed expeditiously.

Article 10
In executing a Letter of Request the requested authority shall apply the appropriate measures of compulsion in the instances and to the same extent as are provided by its internal law for the execution of orders issued by the authorities of its own country or of requests made by parties in internal proceedings.

Article 11
In the execution of a Letter of Request the person concerned may refuse to give evidence insofar as he has a privilege or duty to refuse to give the evidence—

(a) under the law of the State of execution; or

(b) under the law of the State of origin, and the privilege or duty has been specified in the Letter, or, at the instance of the requested authority, has been otherwise confirmed to that authority by the requesting authority.

A Contracting State may declare that, in addition, it will respect privileges and duties existing under the law of States other than the State of origin and the State of execution, to the extent specified in that declaration.

Article 12
The execution of a Letter of Request may be refused only to the extent that—

(a) in the State of execution the execution of the Letter does not fall within the functions of the judiciary; or

(b) the State addressed considers that its sovereignty or security would be prejudiced thereby.

Execution may not be refused solely on the ground that under its internal law the State of execution claims exclusive jurisdiction over the subject-matter of the action or that its internal law would not admit a right of action on it.

Article 13
The documents establishing the execution of the Letter of Request shall be sent by the requested authority to the requesting authority by the same channel which was used by the latter.

In every instance where the Letter is not executed in whole or in part, the requesting authority shall be informed immediately through the same channel and advised of the reasons.

Article 14
The execution of the Letter of Request shall not give rise to any reimbursement of taxes or costs of any nature.

Nevertheless, the State of execution has the right to require the State of origin to reimburse the fees paid to experts and interpreters and the costs occasioned by the use of a special procedure requested by the State of origin under Article 9, paragraph 2.

The requested authority whose law obliges the parties themselves to secure evidence, and which is not able itself to execute the Letter, may, after having obtained the consent of the requesting authority, appoint a suitable person to do so. When seeking this consent the requested authority shall indicate the approximate costs which would result from this procedure. If the requesting authority gives its consent it shall reimburse any costs incurred; without such consent the requesting authority shall not be liable for the costs.

Chapter II: Taking of Evidence by Diplomatic Officers, Consular Agents and Commissioners

Article 15

In a civil or commercial matter, a diplomatic officer or consular agent of a Contracting State may, in the territory of another Contracting State and within the area where he exercises his functions, take the evidence without compulsion of nationals of a State which he represents in aid of proceedings commenced in the courts of a State which he represents.

A Contracting State may declare that evidence may be taken by a diplomatic officer or consular agent only if permission to that effect is given upon application made by him or on his behalf to the appropriate authority designated by the declaring State.

Article 16

A diplomatic officer or consular agent of a Contracting State may, in the territory of another Contracting State and within the area where he exercises his functions, also take the evidence, without compulsion, of nationals of the State in which he exercises his functions or of a third State, in aid of proceedings commenced in the courts of a State which he represents, if—

(a) a competent authority designated by the State in which he exercises his functions has given its permission either generally or in the particular case, and

(b) he complies with the conditions which the competent authority has specified in the permission.

A Contracting State may declare that evidence may be taken under this article without its prior permission.

Article 17

In a civil or commercial matter, a person duly appointed as a commissioner for the purpose may, without compulsion, take evidence in the territory of a Contracting State in aid of proceedings commenced in the courts of another Contracting State if—

(a) a competent authority designated by the State where the evidence is to be taken has given its permission either generally or in the particular case; and

(b) he complies with the conditions which the competent authority has specified in the permission.

A Contracting State may declare that evidence may be taken under this article without its prior permission.

Article 18

A Contracting State may declare that a diplomatic officer, consular agent or commissioner authorized to take evidence under Articles 15, 16 or 17, may apply to the competent authority designated by the declaring State for appropriate assistance to obtain the evidence by compulsion. The declaration may contain such conditions as the declaring State may see fit to impose.

If the authority grants the application it shall apply any measures of compulsion which are appropriate and are prescribed by its law for use in internal proceedings.

Article 19

The competent authority, in giving the permission referred to in Articles 15, 16 or 17, or in granting the application referred to in Article 18, may lay down such conditions as it deems fit, inter alia, as to the time and place of the taking of the evidence. Similarly it may require that it be given reasonable advance notice of the time, date and place of the taking of the evidence; in such a case a representative of the authority shall be entitled to be present at the taking of the evidence.

Article 20

In the taking of evidence under any article of this chapter persons concerned may be legally represented.

Article 21

Where a diplomatic officer, consular agent or commissioner is authorized under Articles 15, 16 or 17 to take evidence—

(a) he may take all kinds of evidence which are not incompatible with the law of the State where the evidence is taken or contrary to any permission granted pursuant to the above Articles, and shall have power within such limits to administer an oath or take an affirmation;

(b) a request to a person to appear or to give evidence shall, unless the recipient is a national of the State where the action is pending, be drawn up in the language of the place where the evidence is taken or be accompanied by a translation into such language;

(c) the request shall inform the person that he may be legally represented and, in any State that has not filed a declaration under Article 18, shall also inform him that he is not compelled to appear or to give evidence;

(d) the evidence may be taken in the manner provided by the law applicable to the court in which the action is pending provided that such manner is not forbidden by the law of the State where the evidence is taken;

(e) a person requested to give evidence may invoke the privileges and duties to refuse to give the evidence contained in Article 11.

Article 22

The fact that an attempt to take evidence under the procedure laid down in this chapter has failed, owing to the refusal of a person to give evidence, shall not prevent an application being subsequently made to take the evidence in accordance with Chapter I.

Chapter III: General Clauses

Article 23

A Contracting State may at the time of signature, ratification or accession, declare that it will not execute Letters of Request issued for the purpose of obtaining pre-trial discovery of documents as known in Common Law countries.

Article 24

A Contracting State may designate other authorities in addition to the Central Authority and shall determine the extent of their competence. However, Letters of Request may in all cases be sent to the Central Authority.

Federal States shall be free to designate more than one Central Authority.

Article 25

A Contracting State which has more than one legal system may designate the authorities of one of such systems, which shall have exclusive competence to execute Letters of Request pursuant to this Convention.

Article 26

A Contracting State, if required to do so because of constitutional limitations, may request the reimbursement by the State of origin of fees and costs, in connection with the execution of Letters of Request, for the service of process necessary to compel the appearance of a person to give evidence, the costs of attendance of such persons, and the cost of any transcript of the evidence.

Where a State has made a request pursuant to the above paragraph, any other Contracting State may request from that State the reimbursement of similar fees and costs.

Article 27

The provisions of the present Convention shall not prevent a Contracting State from—

(a) declaring that Letters of Request may be transmitted to its judicial authorities through channels other than those provided for in Article 2;

(b) permitting, by internal law or practice, any act provided for in this Convention to be performed upon less restrictive conditions;

(c) permitting, by internal law or practice, methods of taking evidence other than those provided for in this Convention.

Article 28

The present Convention shall not prevent an agreement between any two or more Contracting States to derogate from—

(a) the provisions of Article 2 with respect to methods of transmitting Letters of Request;

(b) the provisions of Article 4 with respect to the languages which may be used;

(c) the provisions of Article 8 with respect to the presence of judicial personnel at the execution of Letters;

(d) the provisions of Article 11 with respect to the privileges and duties of witnesses to refuse to give evidence;

(e) the provisions of Article 13 with respect to the methods of returning executed Letters to the requesting authority;

(f) the provisions of Article 14 with respect to fees and costs;

(g) the provisions of Chapter II.

Article 29

Between Parties to the present Convention who are also Parties to one or both of the Conventions on Civil Procedure signed at the Hague on the 17th of July 1905[2] and the 1st of March 1954,[3] this Convention shall replace Articles 8 to 16 of the earlier Conventions.

Article 30

The present Convention shall not affect the application of Article 23 of the Convention of 1905, or of Article 24 of the Convention of 1954.

Article 31

Supplementary Agreements between Parties to the Conventions of 1905 and 1954 shall be considered as equally applicable to the present Convention unless the Parties have otherwise agreed.

---

[2]99 British Foreign and State Papers 990.

[3]286 UNTS 265.

Article 32
Without prejudice to the provisions of Articles 29 and 31, the present Convention shall not derogate from conventions containing provisions on the matters covered by this Convention to which the Contracting States are, or shall become Parties.

Article 33
A State may, at the time of signature, ratification or accession exclude, in whole or in part, the application of the provisions of paragraph 2 of Article 4 and of Chapter II. No other reservation shall be permitted.

Each Contracting State may at any time withdraw a reservation it has made; the reservation shall cease to have effect on the 60th day after notification of the withdrawal.

When a State has made a reservation, any other State affected thereby may apply the same rule against the reserving State.

Article 34
A State may at any time withdraw or modify a declaration.

Article 35
A Contracting State shall, at the time of the deposit of its instrument of ratification or accession, or at a later date, inform the Ministry of Foreign Affairs of the Netherlands of the designation of authorities, pursuant to Articles 2, 8, 24 and 25.

A Contracting State shall likewise inform the Ministry, where appropriate, of the following—

(a) the designation of the authorities to whom notice must be given, whose permission may be required, and whose assistance may be invoked in the taking of evidence by diplomatic officers and consular agents, pursuant to Articles 15, 16 and 18 respectively;

(b) the designation of the authorities whose permission may be required in the taking of evidence by commissioners pursuant to Article 17 and of those who may grant the assistance provided for in Article 18;

(c) declarations pursuant to Articles 4, 8, 11, 15, 16, 17, 18, 23 and 27;

(d) any withdrawal or modification of the above designations and declarations;

(e) the withdrawal of any reservation.

Article 36
Any difficulties which may arise between Contracting States in connection with the operation of this Convention shall be settled through diplomatic channels.

Article 37
The present Convention shall be open for signature by the States represented at the Eleventh Session of the Hague Conference on Private International Law.

It shall be ratified, and the instruments of ratification shall be deposited with the Ministry of Foreign Affairs of the Netherlands.

Article 38
The present Convention shall enter into force on the 60th day after the deposit of the third instrument of ratification referred to in the second paragraph of Article 37.

The Convention shall enter into force for each signatory State which ratifies subsequently on the 60th day after the deposit of its instrument of ratification.

Article 39

Any State not represented at the Eleventh Session of the Hague Conference on Private International Law which is a Member of this Conference or of the United Nations or of a specialized agency of that Organization, or a Party to the Statute of the International Court of Justices[4] may accede to the present Convention after it has entered into force in accordance with the first paragraph of Article 38.

The instrument of accession shall be deposited with the Ministry of Foreign Affairs of the Netherlands.

The Convention shall enter into force for a State acceding to it on the 60 day after the deposit of its instrument of accession.

The accession will have effect only as regards the relations between the acceding State and such Contracting States as will have declared their acceptance of the accession. Such declaration shall be deposited at the Ministry of Foreign Affairs of the Netherlands; this Ministry shall forward, through diplomatic channels, a certified copy to each of the Contracting States.

The Convention will enter into force as between the acceding State and the State that has declared its acceptance of the accession on the 60th day after the deposit of the declaration of acceptance.

Article 40

Any State may, at the time of signature, ratification or accession, declare that the present Convention shall extend to all the territories for the international relations of which it is responsible, or to one or more of them. Such a declaration shall take effect on the date of entry into force of the Convention for the State concerned.

---

[4]TS 993; 59 Stat. 1055.

At any time thereafter, such extensions shall be notified to the Ministry of Foreign Affairs of the Netherlands.[5]

The Convention shall enter into force for the territories mentioned in such an extension on the 60th day after the notification indicated in the preceding paragraph.

Article 41

The present Convention shall remain in force for five years from the date of its entry into force in accordance with the first paragraph of Article 38, even for States which have ratified it or acceded to it subsequently.

If there has been no denunciation, it shall be renewed tacitly every five years.

Any denunciation shall be notified to the Ministry of Foreign Affairs of the Netherlands at least six months before the end of the five year period.

It may be limited to certain of the territories to which the Convention applies.

The denunciation shall have effect only as regards the State which has notified it. The Convention shall remain in force for the other Contracting States.

Article 42

The Ministry of Foreign Affairs of the Netherlands shall give notice to the States referred to in Article 37, and to the States which have acceded in accordance with Article 39, of the following—

---

[5]Extended to Guam, Puerto Rico, and the Virgin Islands pursuant to notification sent by the American Embassy at The Hague on Feb. 6, 1913.

(a) the signatures and ratifications referred to in Article 37;

(b) the date on which the present Convention enters into force in accordance with the first paragraph of Article 38;

(c) the accessions referred to in Article 39 and the dates on which they take effect;

(d) the extensions referred to in Article 40 and the dates on which they take effect;

(e) the designations, reservations and declarations referred to in Articles 33 and 35;

(f) the denunciations referred to in the third paragraph of Article 41.

In witness whereof the undersigned, being duly authorized thereto, have signed the present Convention.

Done at The Hague, on the 18th day of March 1970, in the English and French languages, both texts being equally authentic, in a single copy which shall be deposited in the archives of the Government of the Netherlands, and of which a certified copy shall be sent, through the diplomatic channel, to each of the States represented at the Eleventh Session of the Hague Conference on Private International Law.

[Signatures omitted.]

Hague Evidence Convention

Annex

**Model for Letters of Request Recommended for Use in Applying
the Hague Convention of 18 March 1970 on the Taking of Evidence
Abroad in Civil or Commercial Matters**

**Request for International Judicial Assistance Pursuant to the Hague Convention of 18 March
1970 on the Taking of Evidence Abroad in Civil or Commercial Matters**

N.B. Under the first paragraph of Article 4, the Letter of Request shall be in the language of the
authority requested to execute it or be accompanied by a translation into that language. However,
the provisions of the second and third paragraphs may permit use of other languages.

In order to avoid confusion, please spell out the name of the month in each date.

I. (Items to be included in all Letters of Request.)

    1.   Sender   _____(identity and address)_____

    2.   Central Authority of
          the Requested State   _____(identity and address)_____

    3.   Person to whom the   _____(identity and address)_____
          executed request is to
          be returned

II. (Items to be included in all Letters of Request.)

    4.   In conformity with Article 3 of the Convention, the undersigned applicant has
        the honour to submit the following request:

    5.   a.   Requesting   _____(identity and address)_____
             judicial authority
             (Article 3(a))

        b.   To the competent   _____(the requested State)_____
             authority of
             (Article 3(a))

6. Names and addresses
   of the parties and their
   representatives (Article
   3(b))

   (a) Plaintiff

   _____
   _____

   (b) Defendant

   _____
   _____

   (c) Other parties

   _____
   _____
   _____

7. Nature and purpose
   of the proceedings
   and summary of
   the facts (Article
   3(c))

   _____
   _____
   _____
   _____
   _____

8. Evidence to be
   obtained or other
   judicial act to be
   performed (Article
   3(d))

   _____
   _____
   _____
   _____
   _____

III. (Items to be completed where applicable.)

9. Identity and address
   of any person to be
   examined (Article
   3(e))

   _____
   _____
   _____
   _____

10. Questions to be
    put to the persons
    to be examined or
    statement of the
    subject-matter
    about which they
    are to be examined
    (Article 3(f))

    _____
    _____(or see attached list)_____
    _____
    _____
    _____
    _____
    _____
    _____

11. Documents or other property to be inspected (Article 3(g))

_____
_____(specify whether it is to be produced, copied, valued, etc.)_____
_____

12. Any requirement that the evidence be given on oath or affirmation and any special form to be used (Article 3(h))

_____
_____(In the event that the evidence cannot be taken in the manner requested, specify whether it is to be taken in such manner as provided by local law for the formal taking of evidence.)_____
_____
_____

13. Special methods or procedure to be followed (Article 3(i) and 9)

_____
_____
_____
_____

14. Request for notification of the time and place for the execution of the Request and identity and address of any person to be notified (Article 7)

_____
_____
_____
_____
_____
_____
_____
_____
_____

15. Request for attendance or participation of judicial personnel of the requesting authority at the execution of the letter of request

_____
_____
_____
_____
_____
_____
_____
_____

16. Specification of privilege or duty to refuse to give evidence under the law of the State of

_____
_____
_____
_____
_____

origin (Article
11(b))
_____
_____

17. The fees and costs _____(identity and address)_____
    incurred which are _____
    reimbursable _____
    under the second _____
    paragraph of _____
    Article 14 or under _____
    Article 26 of the _____
    Convention will _____
    be borne by _____

IV. (Items to be included in all Letters of Request.)

18. Date of request _____

19. Signature and seal _____
    of the requesting _____
    authority _____

F. OECD Convention on Combating Bribery of Foreign Public Officials in International Business Transactions

Source: Argentina-Brazil-Bulgaria-Chile-Slovak   Republic—Organization   for   Economic Cooperation and Development: Convention on Combating Bribery of Foreign Public Officials in International Business Transactions, done at Paris, December 18, 1997, *reprinted in* 37 I.L.M. 1 (1998).

Website information:

http://www.oecd.org/daf/nocorruption/instruments.htm
This site contains the text of the OECD Convention, the legislative measures undertaken by countries to ratify and implement the Convention, and links to national implementing legislation. It also contains other OECD instruments against corruption that relate to the Convention and help reinforce its aims.

http://usinfo.state.gov/topical/econ/bribes/homepage.htm
This website provides a comprehensive look at the effort to end bribery and corruption in international business practices by providing links to recent developments from the United States Government, the World Bank, OAS, the United Nations, and APEC.

http://www.ita.doc.gov/legal/
This website of the Office of the Chief Counsel for International Commerce at the U.S. Department of Commerce contains papers, memoranda, speeches and other materials on international trade and investment law with a focus on export and investment issues and transborder bribery.

http://www.state.gov/www/issues/economic/bribery.html
This website contains press releases from the Bureau of Economic and Business Affairs concerning bribery in international business transactions.

Introduction

The Organization for Economic Cooperation and Development (OECD) evolved out of the post-World War II Organization for European Economic Cooperation and is comprised of 29 member countries spanning North America, Europe and Asia, and accompanied by a host of non-member contacts in Latin America and the former Soviet Bloc. Membership in the OECD represents a nation's dedication to a pluralistic democracy and a market economy, and provides those nations with a forum in which to discuss economic and social policies.

The OECD's effort to combat bribery of public officials in international trade culminated in a multilateral convention signed on December 17, 1997. The Convention makes it a crime to offer, promise or give a bribe to a foreign public official in an effort to "obtain or retain business or any other improper advantage," and requires the OECD member states and other non-member states submitting to the Convention to implement domestic legislation in conformity with this policy.

OECD CONVENTION ON COMBATING BRIBERY
OF FOREIGN PUBLIC OFFICIALS
IN INTERNATIONAL BUSINESS TRANSACTIONS

Adopted by the Negotiating Conference on 20 November 1997

Preamble

The Parties,

Considering that bribery is a widespread phenomenon in international business transactions, including trade and investment, which raises serious moral and political concerns, undermines good governance and economic development, and distorts international competitive conditions;

Considering that all countries share a responsibility to combat bribery in international business transactions;

Having regard to the Revised Recommendation on Combating Bribery in International Business Transactions, adopted by the Council of the Organisation for Economic Co-operation and Development (OECD) on 23 May 1997, C(97)123/FINAL, which, inter alia, called for effective measures to deter, prevent and combat the bribery of foreign public officials in connection with international business transactions, in particular the prompt criminalisation of such bribery in an effective and co-ordinated manner and in conformity with the agreed common elements set out in that Recommendation and with the jurisdictional and other basic legal principles of each country;

Welcoming other recent developments which further advance international understanding and co-operation in combating bribery of public officials, including actions of the United Nations, the World Bank, the International Monetary Fund, the World Trade Organisation, the Organisation of American States, the Council of Europe and the European Union;

Welcoming the efforts of companies, business organisations and trade unions as well as other non-governmental organisations to combat bribery;

Recognising the role of governments in the prevention of solicitation of bribes from individuals and enterprises in international business transactions;

Recognising that achieving progress in this field requires not only efforts on a national level but also multilateral co-operation, monitoring and follow-up;

Recognising that achieving equivalence among the measures to be taken by the Parties is an essential object and purpose of the Convention, which requires that the Convention be ratified without derogations affecting this equivalence;

Have agreed as follows:

Article 1 - The Offence of
Bribery of Foreign Public Officials

1. Each Party shall take such measures as may be necessary to establish that it is a criminal offence under its law for any person intentionally to offer, promise or give any undue pecuniary or other advantage, whether directly or through intermediaries, to a foreign public official, for that official or for a third party, in order that the official act or refrain from acting in relation to the performance of official duties, in order to obtain or retain business or other improper advantage in the conduct of international business.

2. Each Party shall take any measures necessary to establish that complicity in, including incitement, aiding and abetting, or authorisation of an act of bribery of a foreign public official shall be a criminal offence. Attempt and conspiracy to bribe a foreign public official shall be criminal offences to the same extent as

attempt and conspiracy to bribe a public official of that Party.

3. The offences set out in paragraphs 1 and 2 above are hereinafter referred to as "bribery of a foreign public official".

4. For the purpose of this Convention:

a. "foreign public official" means any person holding a legislative, administrative or judicial office of a foreign country, whether appointed or elected; any person exercising a public function for a foreign country, including for a public agency or public enterprise; and any official or agent of a public international organisation;

b. "foreign country" includes all levels and subdivisions of government, from national to local;

c. "act or refrain from acting in relation to the performance of official duties" includes any use of the public official's position, whether or not within the official's authorised competence.

Article 2 - Responsibility of Legal Persons
Each Party shall take such measures as may be necessary, in accordance with its legal principles, to establish the liability of legal persons for the bribery of a foreign public official.

Article 3 - Sanctions
1. The bribery of a foreign public official shall be punishable by effective, proportionate and dissuasive criminal penalties. The range of penalties shall be comparable to that applicable to the bribery of the Party's own public officials and shall, in the case of natural persons, include deprivation of liberty sufficient to enable effective mutual legal assistance and extradition.

2. In the event that, under the legal system of a Party, criminal responsibility is not applicable to legal persons, that Party shall ensure that legal persons shall be subject to effective, proportionate

and dissuasive non-criminal sanctions, including monetary sanctions, for bribery of foreign public officials.

3. Each Party shall take such measures as may be necessary to provide that the bribe and the proceeds of the bribery of a foreign public official, or property the value of which corresponds to that of such proceeds, are subject to seizure and confiscation or that monetary sanctions of comparable effect are applicable.

4. Each Party shall consider the imposition of additional civil or administrative sanctions upon a person subject to sanctions for the bribery of a foreign public official.

Article 4 - Jurisdiction
1. Each Party shall take such measures as may be necessary to establish its jurisdiction over the bribery of a foreign public official when the offence is committed in whole or in part in its territory.

2. Each Party which has jurisdiction to prosecute its nationals for offences committed abroad shall take such measures as may be necessary to establish its jurisdiction to do so in respect of the bribery of a foreign public official, according to the same principles.

3. When more than one Party has jurisdiction over an alleged offence described in this Convention, the Parties involved shall, at the request of one of them, consult with a view to determining the most appropriate jurisdiction for prosecution.

4. Each Party shall review whether its current basis for jurisdiction is effective in the fight against the bribery of foreign public officials and, if it is not, shall take remedial steps.

Article 5 - Enforcement

Investigation and prosecution of the bribery of a foreign public official shall be subject to the applicable rules and principles of each Party. They shall not be influenced by considerations of national economic interest, the potential effect upon relations with another State or the identity of the natural or legal persons involved.

Article 6 - Statute of Limitations

Any statute of limitations applicable to the offence of bribery of a foreign public official shall allow an adequate period of time for the investigation and prosecution of this offence.

Article 7 - Money Laundering

Each Party which has made bribery of its own public official a predicate offence for the purpose of the application of its money laundering legislation shall do so on the same terms for the bribery of a foreign public official, without regard to the place where the bribery occurred.

Article 8 - Accounting

1. In order to combat bribery of foreign public officials effectively, each Party shall take such measures as may be necessary, within the framework of its laws and regulations regarding the maintenance of books and records, financial statement disclosures, and accounting and auditing standards, to prohibit the establishment of off-the-books accounts, the making of off-the-books or inadequately identified transactions, the recording of non-existent expenditures, the entry of liabilities with incorrect identification of their object, as well as the use of false documents, by companies subject to those laws and regulations, for the purpose of bribing foreign public officials or of hiding such bribery.

2. Each Party shall provide effective, proportionate and dissuasive civil, administrative or criminal penalties for such omissions and falsifications in respect of the books, records, accounts and financial statements of such companies.

Article 9 - Mutual Legal Assistance

1. Each Party shall, to the fullest extent possible under its laws and relevant treaties and arrangements, provide prompt and effective legal assistance to another Party for the purpose of criminal investigations and proceedings brought by a Party concerning offences within the scope of this Convention and for non-criminal proceedings within the scope of this Convention brought by a Party against a legal person. The requested Party shall inform the requesting Party, without delay, of any additional information or documents needed to support the request for assistance and, where requested, of the status and outcome of the request for assistance.

2. Where a Party makes mutual legal assistance conditional upon the existence of dual criminality, dual criminality shall be deemed to exist if the offence for which the assistance is sought is within the scope of this Convention.

3. A Party shall not decline to render mutual legal assistance for criminal matters within the scope of this Convention on the ground of bank secrecy.

Article 10 - Extradition

1. Bribery of a foreign public official shall be deemed to be included as an extraditable offence under the laws of the Parties and the extradition treaties between them.

2. If a Party which makes extradition conditional on the existence of an extradition treaty receives a request for extradition from another Party with which it has no extradition treaty, it may consider this Convention to be the legal basis for extradition in respect of the offence of bribery of a foreign public official.

3. Each Party shall take any measures necessary to assure either that it can extradite its nationals or that it can prosecute its nationals for the offence of bribery of a foreign public official. A Party which declines a request to extradite a person for bribery of a foreign public official solely on the ground that the person is its national shall submit

the case to its competent authorities for the purpose of prosecution.

4. Extradition for bribery of a foreign public official is subject to the conditions set out in the domestic law and applicable treaties and arrangements of each Party. Where a Party makes extradition conditional upon the existence of dual criminality, that condition shall be deemed to be fulfilled if the offence for which extradition is sought is within the scope of Article 1 of this Convention.

Article 11 - Responsible Authorities
For the purposes of Article 4, paragraph 3, on consultation, Article 9, on mutual legal assistance and Article 10, on extradition, each Party shall notify to the Secretary-General of the OECD an authority or authorities responsible for making and receiving requests, which shall serve as channel of communication for these matters for that Party, without prejudice to other arrangements between Parties.

Article 12 - Monitoring and Follow-up
The Parties shall co-operate in carrying out a programme of systematic follow-up to monitor and promote the full implementation of this Convention. Unless otherwise decided by consensus of the Parties, this shall be done in the framework of the OECD Working Group on Bribery in International Business Transactions and according to its terms of reference, or within the framework and terms of reference of any successor to its functions, and Parties shall bear the costs of the programme in accordance with the rules applicable to that body.

Article 13 - Signature and Accession
1. Until its entry into force, this Convention shall be open for signature by OECD members and by non-members which have been invited to become full participants in its Working Group on Bribery in International Business Transactions.

2. Subsequent to its entry into force, this Convention shall be open to accession by any non-signatory which is a member of the OECD or has become a full participant in the Working Group on Bribery in International Business Transactions or any successor to its functions. For each such non-signatory, the Convention shall enter into force on the sixtieth day following the date of deposit of its instrument of accession.

Article 14 - Ratification and Depositary
1. This Convention is subject to acceptance, approval or ratification by the Signatories, in accordance with their respective laws.

2. Instruments of acceptance, approval, ratification or accession shall be deposited with the Secretary-General of the OECD, who shall serve as Depositary of this Convention.

Article 15 - Entry into Force
1. This Convention shall enter into force on the sixtieth day following the date upon which five of the ten countries which have the ten largest export shares (see annex), and which represent by themselves at least sixty per cent of the combined total exports of those ten countries, have deposited their instruments of acceptance, approval, or ratification. For each signatory depositing its instrument after such entry into force, the Convention shall enter into force on the sixtieth day after deposit of its instrument.

2. If, after 31 December 1998, the Convention has not entered into force under paragraph 1 above, any signatory which has deposited its instrument of acceptance, approval or ratification may declare in writing to the Depositary its readiness to accept entry into force of this Convention under this paragraph 2. The Convention shall enter into force for such a signatory on the sixtieth day following the date upon which such declarations have been deposited by at least two signatories. For each signatory depositing its declaration after such entry into force, the Convention shall enter into force on the sixtieth day following the date of deposit.

Article 16 - Amendment

Any Party may propose the amendment of this Convention. A proposed amendment shall be submitted to the Depositary which shall communicate it to the other Parties at least sixty days before convening a meeting of the Parties to consider the proposed amendment. An amendment adopted by consensus of the Parties, or by such other means as the Parties may determine by consensus, shall enter into force sixty days after the deposit of an instrument of ratification, acceptance or approval by all of the Parties, or in such other circumstances as may be specified by the Parties at the time of adoption of the amendment.

Article 17 - Withdrawal

A Party may withdraw from this Convention by submitting written notification to the Depositary. Such withdrawal shall be effective one year after the date of the receipt of the notification. After withdrawal, co-operation shall continue between the Parties and the Party which has withdrawn on all requests for assistance or extradition made before the effective date of withdrawal which remain pending.

G. Convention Establishing the Multilateral Investment Guarantee Agency (MIGA)

Source: Multilateral Investment Guarantee Agency ('MIGA'), *reprinted in* 24 I.L.M. 1598 (1985).
For current status: Office of General Counsel, Multilateral Investment Guarantee Agency,
1818 H Street, N.W., Washington, DC 20433; Telephone: (202) 473-5245; Fax: (202)
477-0412.)

Website information:

http://www.miga.org/welcome.htm
This site contains the text and commentary for the MIGA convention, updated lists of member states,
and new developments and publications on multilateral investment.

http://www.ipanet.net/
IPAnet is an electronic clearinghouse for international investment information developed by the
Multilateral Investment Guarantee Agency (MIGA). It contains databases, directories, calendars of
events, and reference desk features which have been contributed by firms and institutions from over
160 countries.

Introduction

The Multilateral Investment Guarantee Agency (MIGA) was created with the entry into force
of the convention establishing it on April 12, 1988.[1] While MIGA is an autonomous institution, its
administration and purpose are closely related to the activities of its parent organization, the World
Bank. MIGA provides foreign investors in member countries with financial guarantees against non-
commercial risks, and offers technical advice to help developing member states secure foreign
investment. The Preamble states that it is the goal of MIGA to "strengthen international cooperation
for economic development," and "enhance the flow to developing countries of capital and
technology for productive purposes . . . on the basis of fair and stable standards for the treatment of
foreign investment."

Membership in MIGA is open to all member states of the World Bank and to Switzerland
(Article 5). Eligible investments in member states (Article 12) from eligible investors from other
member states (Article 13) may be guaranteed by MIGA against losses resulting from foreign
exchange restrictions, expropriation, breach of contract and war (Article 11). Such guarantees are
undertaken only upon approval of the investment by the host country government (Article 15), and
the satisfaction of the Agency of the soundness of the investment, the compliance with local laws
and regulations, consistency with local policy objectives, and the availability of local legal protection
(Article 12). Any disputes arising from a guarantee agreement, if not first resolved by negotiation,
are to be submitted to arbitration (Article 58) and are governed by the ICSID rules commonly
contained in MIGA's standard guarantee contracts.

---

[1]April 12, 1988 is also the date of the U.S. ratification of the Convention establishing MIGA. *See* Pub.
L. 100-202, § 10(e), Dec. 22, 1987, 101 Stat. 1329-134, 22 U.S.C. § 290k *et. seq.*

More than 20 industrialized countries and nearly 130 developing countries belong to MIGA, allowing the Agency to coinsure or reinsure political risks for which insurance may not otherwise be available.

CONVENTION ESTABLISHING THE
MULTILATERAL INVESTMENT GUARANTEE AGENCY
(MIGA)

PREAMBLE

The Contracting States

Considering the need to strengthen international cooperation for economic development and to foster the contribution to such development of foreign investment in general and private foreign investment in particular;

Recognizing that the flow of foreign investment to developing countries would be facilitated and further encouraged by alleviating concerns related to non-commercial risks;

Desiring to enhance the flow to developing countries of capital and technology for productive purposes under conditions consistent with their development needs, policies and objectives, on the basis of fair and stable standards for the treatment of foreign investment;

Convinced that the Multilateral Investment Guarantee Agency can play an important role in the encouragement of foreign investment complementing national and regional investment guarantee programs and private insurers of non-commercial risk; and

Realizing that such Agency should, to the extent possible, meet its obligations without resort to its callable capital and that such an objective would be served by continued improvement in investment conditions,

Have Agreed as follows:

Chapter I: ESTABLISHMENT, STATUS, PURPOSES AND DEFINITIONS

Article 1. Establishment and Status of the Agency

(a) There is hereby established the Multilateral Investment Guarantee Agency (hereinafter called the Agency).

(b) The Agency shall possess full juridical personality and, in particular, the capacity to:

(i) contract;

(ii) acquire and dispose of movable and immovable property; and

(iii) institute legal proceedings.

Article 2. Objective and Purposes

The objective of the Agency shall be to encourage the flow of investments for productive purposes among member countries, and in particular to developing member countries, thus supplementing the activities of the International Bank for Reconstruction and Development (hereinafter referred to as the Bank), the International Finance Corporation and other international development finance institutions.

To serve its objective, the Agency shall:

(a) issue guarantees, including coinsurance and reinsurance, against non-commercial risks in respect of investments in a member country which flow from other member countries;

(b) carry out appropriate complementary activities to promote the flow of investments to and among developing member countries; and

(c) exercise such other incidental powers as shall be necessary or desirable in the furtherance of its objective.

The Agency shall be guided in all its decisions by the provisions of this Article.

Article 3. Definitions

For the purposes of this Convention: (a) 'Member' means a State with respect to which this Convention has entered into force in accordance with Article 61.

(b) 'Host country' or 'host government' means a member, its government, or any public authority of a member in whose territories, as defined in Article 66, an investment which has been guaranteed or reinsured, or is considered for guarantee or reinsurance, by the Agency is to be located.

(c) A 'developing member country' means a member which is listed as such in Schedule A hereto as this Schedule may be amended from time to time by the Council of Governors referred to in Article 30 (hereinafter called the Council).

(d) A 'special majority' means an affirmative vote of not less than two-thirds of the total voting power representing not less than fifty-five percent of the subscribed shares of the capital stock of the Agency.

(e) A 'freely usable currency' means (i) any currency designated as such by the International Monetary Fund from time to time and (ii) any other freely available and effectively usable currency which the Board of Directors referred to in Article 30 (hereinafter called the Board) may designate for the purposes of this Convention after consultation with the International Monetary Fund and with the approval of the country of such currency.

Chapter II: MEMBERSHIP AND CAPITAL

Article 4. Membership

(a) Membership in the Agency shall be open to all members of the Bank and to Switzerland.

(b) Original members shall be the States which are listed in Schedule A hereto and become parties to this Convention on or before October 30, 1987.

Article 5. Capital

(a) The authorized capital stock of the Agency shall be one billion Special Drawing Rights (SDR1,000,000,000). The capital stock shall be divided into 100,000 shares having a par value of SDR10,000 each, which shall be available for subscription by members. All payment obligations of members with respect to capital stock shall be settled on the basis of the average value of the SDR in terms of United States dollars for the period January 1, 1981 to June 30, 1985, such value being 1.082 United States dollars per SDR.

(b) The capital stock shall increase on the admission of a new member to the extent that the then authorized shares are insufficient to provide the shares to be subscribed by such member pursuant to Article 6.

(c) The Council, by special majority, may at any time increase the capital stock of the Agency.

Article 6. Subscription of Shares

Each original member of the Agency shall subscribe at par to the number of shares of capital stock set forth opposite its name in Schedule A hereto. Each other member shall subscribe to such number of shares of capital stock on such terms and conditions as may be determined by the Council, but in no event at an issue price of less than par. No member shall subscribe to less than fifty shares. The Council may prescribe rules by which members may subscribe to additional shares of the authorized capital stock.

Article 7. Division and Calls of Subscribed Capital

The initial subscription of each member shall be paid as follows:

(i) Within ninety days from the date on which this Convention enters into force with respect to such member, ten percent of the price of each share shall be paid in cash as stipulated in Section (a) of Article 8 and an additional ten percent in the form of non-negotiable, non-interest-bearing promissory notes or similar obligations to be encashed pursuant to a decision of the Board in order to meet the Agency's obligations.

(ii) The remainder shall be subject to call by the Agency when required to meet its obligations.

Article 8. Payment of Subscription of Shares

(a) Payments of subscriptions shall be made in freely usable currencies except that payments by developing member countries may be made in their own currencies up to twenty-five percent of the paid-in cash portion of their subscriptions payable under Article 7(i).

(b) Calls on any portion of unpaid subscriptions shall be uniform on all shares.

(c) If the amount received by the Agency on a call shall be insufficient to meet the obligations which have necessitated the call, the Agency may make further successive calls on unpaid subscriptions until the aggregate amount received by it shall be sufficient to meet such obligations.

(d) Liability on shares shall be limited to the unpaid portion of the issue price.

Article 9. Valuation of Currencies

Whenever it shall be necessary for the purposes of this Convention to determine the value of one currency in terms of another, such value shall be as reasonably determined by the Agency, after consultation with the International Monetary Fund.

Article 10. Refunds

(a) The Agency shall, as soon as practicable, return to members amounts paid on calls on subscribed capital if and to the extent that:

(i) the call shall have been made to pay a claim resulting from a guarantee or reinsurance contract and thereafter the Agency shall have recovered its payment, in whole or in part, in a freely usable currency; or

(ii) the call shall have been made because of a default in payment by a member and thereafter such member shall have made good such default in whole or in part; or

(iii) the Council, by special majority, determines that the financial position of the Agency permits all or part of such amounts to be returned out of the Agency's revenues.

(b) Any refund effected under this Article to a member shall be made in freely usable currency in the proportion of the payments made by that member to the total amount paid pursuant to calls made prior to such refund.

(c) The equivalent of amounts refunded under this Article to a member shall become part of the callable capital obligations of the member under Article 7 (ii).

Chapter III: OPERATIONS

Article 11. Covered Risks

(a) Subject to the provisions of Sections (b) and (c) below, the Agency may guarantee eligible investments against a loss resulting from one or more of the following types of risk:

(i) Currency Transfer: any introduction attributable to the host government of restrictions on the transfer outside the host country of its currency into a freely usable currency or another currency acceptable to the holder of the guarantee, including a failure of the host government to act within a reasonable period of time on an application by such holder for such transfer;

(ii) Expropriation and Similar Measures: any legislative action or administrative action or omission attributable to the host government which has the effect of depriving the holder of a guarantee of his ownership or control of, or a substantial benefit from, his investment, with the exception of non-discriminatory measures of general application which governments normally take for the purpose of regulating economic activity in their territories;

(iii) Breach of Contract: any repudiation or breach by the host government of a contract with the holder of a guarantee, when (a) the holder of a guarantee does not have recourse to a judicial or arbitral forum to determine the claim of repudiation or breach, or (b) a decision by such forum is not rendered within such reasonable period of time as shall be prescribed in the contracts of guarantee pursuant to the Agency's regulations, or (c) such a decision cannot be enforced; and

(iv) War and Civil Disturbance: any military action or civil disturbance in any territory of the host country to which this Convention shall be applicable as provided in Article 66.

(b) Upon the joint application of the investor and the host country, the Board, by special majority, may approve the extension of coverage under this Article to specific non-commercial risks other than those referred to in Section (a) above, but in no case to the risk of devaluation or depreciation of currency.

(c) Losses resulting from the following shall not be covered:

(i) any host government action or omission to which the holder of the guarantee has agreed or for which he has been responsible; and

(ii) any host government action or omission or any other event occurring before the conclusion of the contract of guarantee.

Article 12. Eligible Investments

(a) Eligible investments shall include equity interests, including medium- or long-term loans made or guaranteed by holders of equity in the enterprise concerned, and such forms of direct investment as may be determined by the Board.

(b) The Board, by special majority, may extend eligibility to any other medium- or long-term form of investment, except that loans other than those mentioned in Section (a) above may be eligible only if they are related to a specific investment covered or to be covered by the Agency.

(c) Guarantees shall be restricted to investments the implementation of which begins subsequent to the registration of the application for the guarantee by the Agency. Such investments may include:

(i) any transfer of foreign exchange made to modernize, expand, or develop an existing investment; and

(ii) the use of earnings from existing investments which could otherwise be transferred outside the host country.

(d) In guaranteeing an investment, the Agency shall satisfy itself as to:

(i) the economic soundness of the investment and its contribution to the development of the host country;

(ii) compliance of the investment with the host country's laws and regulations;

(iii) consistency of the investment with the declared development objectives and priorities of the host country; and

(iv) the investment conditions in the host country, including the availability of fair and equitable treatment and legal protection for the investment.

Article 13. Eligible Investors

(a) Any natural person and any juridical person may be eligible to receive the Agency's guarantee provided that:

(i) such natural person is a national of a member other than the host country;

(ii) such juridical person is incorporated and has its principal place of business in a member or the majority of its capital is owned by a member or members or nationals thereof, provided that such member is not the host country in any of the above cases; and

(iii) such juridical person, whether or not it is privately owned, operates on a commercial basis.

(b) In case the investor has more than one nationality, for the purposes of Section (a) above the nationality of a member shall prevail over the nationality of a non-member, and the nationality of the host country shall prevail over the nationality of any other member.

(c) Upon the joint application of the investor and the host country, the Board, by special majority, may extend eligibility to a natural person who is a national of the host country or a juridical person which is incorporated in the host country or the majority of whose capital is owned by its nationals, provided that the assets invested are transferred from outside the host country.

Article 14. Eligible Host Countries

Investments shall be guaranteed under this Chapter only if they are to be made in the territory of a developing member country.

Article 15. Host Country Approval

The Agency shall not conclude any contract of guarantee before the host government has approved the issuance of the guarantee by the Agency against the risks designated for cover.

Article 16. Terms and Conditions

The terms and conditions of each contract of guarantee shall be determined by the Agency subject to such rules and regulations as the Board shall issue, provided that the Agency shall not cover the total loss of the guaranteed investment. Contracts of guarantee shall be approved by the President under the direction of the Board.

Article 17. Payment of Claims

The President under the direction of the Board shall decide on the payment of claims to a holder of a guarantee in accordance with the contract of guarantee and such policies as the Board may adopt. Contracts of guarantee shall require holders of guarantees to seek, before a payment is made by the Agency, such

administrative remedies as may be appropriate under the circumstances, provided that they are readily available to them under the laws of the host country. Such contracts may require the lapse of certain reasonable periods between the occurrence of events giving rise to claims and payments of claims.

Article 18. Subrogation

(a) Upon paying or agreeing to pay compensation to a holder of a guarantee, the Agency shall be subrogated to such rights or claims related to the guaranteed investment as the holder of a guarantee may have had against the host country and other obligors. The contract of guarantee shall provide the terms and conditions of such subrogation.

(b) The rights of the Agency pursuant to Section (a) above shall be recognized by all members.

(c) Amounts in the currency of the host country acquired by the Agency as subrogee pursuant to Section (a) above shall be accorded, with respect to use and conversion, treatment by the host country as favorable as the treatment to which such funds would be entitled in the hands of the holder of the guarantee. In any case, such amounts may be used by the Agency for the payment of its administrative expenditures and other costs. The Agency shall also seek to enter into arrangements with host countries on other uses of such currencies to the extent that they are not freely usable.

Article 19. Relationship to National and Regional Entities

The Agency shall cooperate with, and seek to complement the operations of, national entities of members and regional entities the majority of whose capital is owned by members, which carry out activities similar to those of the Agency, with a view to maximizing both the efficiency of their respective services and their contribution to increased flows of foreign investment. To this end, the Agency may enter into arrangements with such entities on the details of such cooperation, including in particular the modalities of reinsurance and coinsurance.

Article 20. Reinsurance of National and Regional Entities

(a) The Agency may issue reinsurance in respect of a specific investment against a loss resulting from one or more of the non-commercial risks underwritten by a member or agency thereof or by a regional investment guarantee agency the majority of whose capital is owned by members. The Board, by special majority, shall from time to time prescribe maximum amounts of contingent liability which may be assumed by the Agency with respect to reinsurance contracts. In respect of specific investments which have been completed more than twelve months prior to receipt of the application for reinsurance by the Agency, the maximum amount shall initially be set at ten percent of the aggregate contingent liability of the Agency under this Chapter. The conditions of eligibility specified in Articles 11 to 14 shall apply to reinsurance operations, except that the reinsured investments need not be implemented subsequent to the application for reinsurance.

(b) The mutual rights and obligations of the Agency and a reinsured member or agency shall be stated in contracts of reinsurance subject to such rules and regulations as the Board shall issue. The Board shall approve each contract for reinsurance covering an investment which has been made prior to receipt of the application for reinsurance by the Agency, with a view to minimizing risks, assuring that the Agency receives premiums commensurate with its risk, and assuring that the reinsured entity is appropriately committed toward promoting new investment in developing member countries.

(c) The Agency shall, to the extent possible, assure that it or the reinsured entity shall have the rights of subrogation and arbitration equivalent to those the Agency would have if it were the primary guarantor. The terms and conditions of reinsurance shall require that administrative remedies are sought in accordance with Article 17 before a payment is made by the Agency. Subrogation shall be effective with respect to the host country concerned only after its approval of the reinsurance by the Agency. The Agency shall include in the contracts of reinsurance provisions requiring the reinsured to pursue with due diligence the rights or claims related to the reinsured investment.

Article 21. Cooperation with Private Insurers and with Reinsurers

(a) The Agency may enter into arrangements with private insurers in member countries to enhance its own operations and encourage such insurers to provide coverage of non-commercial risks in developing member countries on conditions similar to those applied by the Agency. Such arrangements may include the provision of reinsurance by the Agency under the conditions and procedures specified in Article 20.

(b) The Agency may reinsure with any appropriate reinsurance entity, in whole or in part, any guarantee or guarantees issued by it.

(c) The Agency will in particular seek to guarantee investments for which comparable coverage on reasonable terms is not available from private insurers and reinsurers.

Article 22. Limits of Guarantee

(a) Unless determined otherwise by the Council by special majority, the aggregate amount of contingent liabilities which may be assumed by the Agency under this Chapter shall not exceed one hundred and fifty percent of the amount of the Agency's unimpaired subscribed capital and its reserves plus such portion of its reinsurance cover as the Board may determine. The Board shall from time to time review the risk profile of the Agency's portfolio in the light of its experience with claims, degree of risk diversification, reinsurance cover and other relevant factors with a view to ascertaining whether changes in the maximum aggregate amount of contingent liabilities should be recommended to the Council.

The maximum amount determined by the Council shall not under any circumstances exceed five times the amount of the Agency's unimpaired subscribed capital, its reserves and such portion of its reinsurance cover as may be deemed appropriate.

(b) Without prejudice to the general limit of guarantee referred to in Section (a) above, the Board may prescribe:

(i) maximum aggregate amounts of contingent liability which may be assumed by the Agency under this Chapter for all guarantees issued to investors of each individual member. In determining such maximum amounts, the Board shall give due consideration to the share of the respective member in the capital of the Agency and the need to apply more liberal limitations in respect of investments originating in developing member countries; and

(ii) maximum aggregate amounts of contingent liability which may be assumed by the Agency with respect to such risk diversification factors as individual projects, individual host countries and types of investment or risk.

Article 23. Investment Promotion

(a) The Agency shall carry out research, undertake activities to promote investment flows and disseminate information on investment opportunities in developing member countries, with a view to improving the environment for foreign investment flows to such countries. The Agency may, upon the request of a member, provide technical advice and assistance to improve the investment conditions in the territories of that member. In performing these activities, the Agency shall:

(i) be guided by relevant investment agreements among member countries;

(ii) seek to remove impediments, in both developed and developing member countries, to the flow of investment to developing member countries; and

(iii) coordinate with other agencies concerned with the promotion of foreign investment, and in particular the International Finance Corporation.

(b) The Agency also shall:

(i) encourage the amicable settlement of disputes between investors and host countries;

(ii) endeavor to conclude agreements with developing member countries, and in particular with prospective host countries, which will assure that the Agency, with respect to investment guaranteed by it, has treatment at least as favorable as that agreed by the member concerned for the most favored investment guarantee agency or State in an agreement relating to investment, such agreements to be approved by special majority of the Board; and

(iii) promote and facilitate the conclusion of agreements, among its members, on the promotion and protection of investments.

(c) The Agency shall give particular attention in its promotional efforts to the importance of increasing the flow of investments among developing member countries.

Article 24. Guarantees of Sponsored Investments

In addition to the guarantee operations undertaken by the Agency under this Chapter, the Agency may guarantee investments under the sponsorship arrangements provided for in Annex I to this Convention.

Chapter IV: FINANCIAL PROVISIONS

Article 25. Financial Management

The Agency shall carry out its activities in accordance with sound business and prudent financial management practices with a view to maintaining under all circumstances its ability to meet its financial obligations.

Article 26. Premiums and Fees

The Agency shall establish and periodically review the rates of premiums, fees and other charges, if any, applicable to each type of risk.

Article 27. Allocation of Net Income

(a) Without prejudice to the provisions of Section (a)(iii) of Article 10, the Agency shall allocate net income to reserves until such reserves reach five times the subscribed capital of the Agency.

(b) After the reserves of the Agency have reached the level prescribed in Section (a) above, the Council shall decide whether, and to what extent, the Agency's net income shall be allocated to reserves, be distributed to the Agency's members or be used otherwise. Any distribution of net income to the Agency's members shall be made in proportion to the share of each member in the capital of the Agency in accordance with a decision of the Council acting by special majority.

Article 28. Budget

The President shall prepare an annual budget of revenues and expenditures of the Agency for approval by the Board.

Article 29. Accounts

The Agency shall publish an Annual Report which shall include statements of its accounts and of the accounts of the Sponsorship Trust Fund referred to in Annex I to this Convention, as audited by independent auditors. The Agency shall circulate to members at appropriate intervals a summary statement of its financial position and a profit and loss statement showing the results of its operations.

Chapter V: ORGANIZATION AND MANAGEMENT

Article 30. Structure of the Agency

The Agency shall have a Council of Governors, a Board of Directors, a President and staff to perform such duties as the Agency may determine.

Article 31. The Council

(a) All the powers of the Agency shall be vested in the Council, except such powers as are, by the terms of this Convention, specifically conferred upon another organ of the Agency. The Council may delegate to the Board the exercise of any of its powers, except the power to:

(i) admit new members and determine the conditions of their admission;

(ii) suspend a member;

(iii) decide on any increase or decrease in capital;

(iv) increase the limit of the aggregate amount of contingent liabilities pursuant to Section (a) of Article 22;

(v) designate a member as a developing member country pursuant to Section (c) of Article 3;

(vi) classify a new member as belonging to Category One or Category Two for voting purposes pursuant to Section (a) of Article 39 or reclassify an existing member for the same purpose;

(vii) determine the compensation of Directors and their Alternates;

(viii) cease operations and liquidate the Agency;

(ix) distribute assets to members upon liquidation; and

(x) amend this Convention, its Annexes and Schedules.

(b) The Council shall be composed of one Governor and one Alternate appointed by each member in such manner as it may determine. No Alternate may vote except in the absence of his principal. The Council shall select one of the Governors as Chairman.

(c) The Council shall hold an annual meeting and such other meetings as may be determined by the Council or called by the Board. The Board shall call a meeting of the Council whenever requested by five members or by members having twenty-five percent of the total voting power.

Article 32. The Board

(a) The Board shall be responsible for the general operations of the Agency and shall take, in the fulfillment of this responsibility, any action required or permitted under this Convention.

(b) The Board shall consist of not less than twelve Directors. The number of Directors may be adjusted by the Council to take into account changes in membership. Each Director may appoint an Alternate with full power to act for him in case of the Director's absence or inability to act. The President of the Bank shall be ex officio Chairman of the Board, but shall have no vote except a deciding vote in case of an equal division.

(c) The Council shall determine the term of office of the Directors. The first Board shall be constituted by the Council at its inaugural meeting.

(d) The Board shall meet at the call of its Chairman acting on his own initiative or upon request of three Directors.

(e) Until such time as the Council may decide that the Agency shall have a resident Board which functions in continuous session, the Directors and Alternates shall receive compensation only for the cost of attendance at the meetings of the Board and the discharge of other official functions on behalf of the Agency. Upon the establishment of a Board in continuous session, the Directors and Alternates shall receive such remuneration as may be determined by the Council.

Article 33. President and Staff

(a) The President shall, under the general control of the Board, conduct the ordinary business of the Agency. He shall be responsible for the organization, appointment and dismissal of the staff.

(b) The President shall be appointed by the Board on the nomination of its Chairman. The Council shall determine the salary and terms of the contract of service of the President.

(c) In the discharge of their offices, the President and the staff owe their duty entirely to the Agency and to no other authority. Each member of the Agency shall respect the international character of this duty and shall refrain from all attempts to influence the President or the staff in the discharge of their duties.

(d) In appointing the staff, the President shall, subject to the paramount importance of securing the highest standards of efficiency and of technical competence, pay due regard to the importance of recruiting personnel on as wide a geographical basis as possible.

(e) The President and staff shall maintain at all times the confidentiality of information obtained in carrying out the Agency's operations.

Article 34. Political Activity Prohibited

The Agency, its President and staff shall not interfere in the political affairs of any member. Without prejudice to the right of the Agency to take into account all the circumstances surrounding an investment, they shall not be influenced in their decisions by the political character of the member or members concerned. Considerations relevant to their decisions shall be weighed impartially in order to achieve the purposes stated in Article 2.

Article 35. Relations with International Organizations

The Agency shall, within the terms of this Convention, cooperate with the United Nations and with other inter-governmental organizations having specialized responsibilities in related fields, including in particular the Bank and the International Finance Corporation.

Article 36. Location of Principal Office

(a) The principal office of the Agency shall be located in Washington, D.C., unless the Council, by special majority, decides to establish it in another location.

(b) The Agency may establish other offices as may be necessary for its work.

Article 37. Depositories for Assets

Each member shall designate its central bank as a depository in which the Agency may keep holdings of such member's currency or other assets of the Agency or, if it has no central bank, it shall designate for such purpose such other institution as may be acceptable to the Agency.

Article 38. Channel of Communication

(a) Each member shall designate an appropriate authority with which the Agency may communicate in connection with any matter arising under this Convention. The Agency may rely on statements of such authority as being statements of the member. The Agency, upon the request of a member, shall consult with that member with respect to matters dealt with in Articles 19 to 21 and related to entities or insurers of that member.

(b) Whenever the approval of any member is required before any act may be done by the Agency, approval shall be deemed to have been given unless the member presents an objection within such reasonable period as the Agency may fix in notifying the member of the proposed act.

Chapter VI: VOTING, ADJUSTMENTS OF SUBSCRIPTIONS AND REPRESENTATION

Article 39. Voting and Adjustments of Subscriptions

(a) In order to provide for voting arrangements that reflect the equal interest in the Agency of the two Categories of States listed in Schedule A of this Convention, as well as the importance of each member's financial participation, each member shall have 177 membership votes plus one subscription vote for each share of stock held by that member.

(b) If at any time within three years after the entry into force of this Convention the aggregate sum of membership and subscription votes of members which belong to either of the two Categories of States listed in Schedule A of this Convention is less than forty percent of the total voting power, members from such a Category shall have such number of supplementary votes as shall be necessary for the aggregate voting power of the Category to equal such a percentage of the total voting power. Such supplementary votes shall be distributed among the members of such Category in the proportion that the subscription votes of each bears to the aggregate of subscription votes of the Category. Such supplementary votes shall be subject to automatic adjustment to ensure that such percentage is maintained and shall be cancelled at the end of the above-mentioned three-year period.

(c) During the third year following the entry into force of this Convention, the Council shall review the allocation of shares and shall be guided in its decision by the following principles:

(i) the votes of members shall reflect actual subscriptions to the Agency's capital and the membership votes as set out in Section (a) of this Article;

(ii) shares allocated to countries which shall not have signed the Convention shall be made available for reallocation to such members and in such manner as to make possible voting parity between the above-mentioned Categories; and

(iii) the Council will take measures that will facilitate members' ability to subscribe to shares allocated to them.

(d) Within the three-year period provided for in Section (b) of this Article, all decisions of the Council and Board shall be taken by special majority, except that decisions requiring a higher majority under this Convention shall be taken by such higher majority.

(e) In case the capital stock of the Agency is increased pursuant to Section (c) of Article 5, each member which so requests shall be authorized to subscribe a proportion of the increase equivalent to the proportion which its stock theretofore subscribed bears to the total capital stock of the Agency, but no member shall be obligated to subscribe any part of the increased capital.

(f) The Council shall issue regulations regarding the making of additional subscriptions under Section (e) of this Article. Such regulations shall prescribe reasonable time limits for the submission by members of requests to make such subscriptions.

Article 40. Voting in the Council

(a) Each Governor shall be entitled to cast the votes of the member he represents. Except as otherwise specified in this Convention, decisions of the Council shall be taken by a majority of the votes cast.

(b) A quorum for any meeting of the Council shall be constituted by a majority of the Governors exercising not less than two-thirds of the total voting power.

(c) The Council may by regulation establish a procedure whereby the Board, when it deems such action to be in the best interests of the Agency, may request a decision of the Council on a specific question without calling a meeting of the Council.

Article 41. Election of Directors

(a) Directors shall be elected in accordance with Schedule B.

(b) Directors shall continue in office until their successors are elected. If the office of a Director becomes vacant more than ninety days before the end of his term, another Director shall be elected for the remainder of the term by the Governors who elected the former Director. A majority of the votes cast shall be required for election. While the office remains vacant, the Alternate of the former Director shall exercise his powers, except that of appointing an Alternate.

Article 42. Voting in the Board

(a) Each Director shall be entitled to cast the number of votes of the members whose votes counted towards his election. All the votes which a Director is entitled to cast shall be cast as a unit. Except as otherwise specified in this Convention, decisions of the Board shall be taken by a majority of the votes cast.

(b) A quorum for a meeting of the Board shall be constituted by a majority of the Directors exercising not less than one-half of the total voting power.

(c) The Board may by regulation establish a procedure whereby its Chairman, when he deems such action to be in the best interests of the Agency, may request a decision of the Board on a specific question without calling a meeting of the Board.

Chapter VII: PRIVILEGES AND IMMUNITIES

Article 43. Purposes of Chapter

To enable the Agency to fulfill its functions, the immunities and privileges set forth in this Chapter shall be accorded to the Agency in the territories of each member.

Article 44. Legal Process

Actions other than those within the scope of Articles 57 and 58 may be brought against the Agency only in a court of competent jurisdiction in the territories of a member in which the Agency has an office or has appointed an agent for the purpose of accepting service or notice of process. No such action against the Agency shall be brought (i) by members or persons acting for or deriving claims from members or (ii) in respect of personnel matters. The property and assets of the Agency shall, wherever located and by whomsoever held, be immune from all forms of seizure, attachment or execution before the delivery of the final judgment or award against the Agency.

Article 45. Assets

(a) The property and assets of the Agency, wherever located and by whomsoever held, shall be immune from search, requisition, confiscation, expropriation or any other form of seizure by executive or legislative action.

(b) To the extent necessary to carry out its operations under this Convention, all property and assets of the Agency shall be free from restrictions, regulations, controls and moratoria of any nature; provided that property and assets acquired by the Agency as successor to or subrogee of a holder of a guarantee, a reinsured entity or an investor insured by a reinsured entity shall be free from applicable foreign exchange restrictions, regulations and controls in force in the territories of the member concerned to the extent that the holder, entity or investor to whom the Agency was subrogated was entitled to such treatment.

(c) For purposes of this Chapter, the term 'assets' shall include the assets of the Sponsorship Trust Fund referred to in Annex I to this Convention and other assets administered by the Agency in furtherance of its objective.

Article 46. Archives and Communications

(a) The archives of the Agency shall be inviolable, wherever they may be.

(b) The official communications of the Agency shall be accorded by each member the same treatment that is accorded to the official communications of the Bank.

Article 47. Taxes

(a) The Agency, its assets, property and income, and its operations and transactions authorized by this Convention, shall be immune from all taxes and customs duties. The Agency shall also be immune from liability for the collection or payment of any tax or duty.

(b) Except in the case of local nationals, no tax shall be levied on or in respect of expense allowances paid by the Agency to Governors and their Alternates or on or in respect of salaries, expense allowances or other emoluments paid by the Agency to the Chairman of the Board, Directors, their Alternates, the President or staff of the Agency.

(c) No taxation of any kind shall be levied on any investment guaranteed or reinsured by the Agency (including any earnings therefrom) or any insurance policies reinsured by the Agency (including any premiums and other revenues therefrom) by whomsoever held: (i) which discriminates against such investment or insurance policy solely because it is guaranteed or reinsured by the Agency; or (ii) if the sole jurisdictional basis for such taxation is the location of any office or place of business maintained by the Agency.

Article 48. Officials of the Agency

All Governors, Directors, Alternates, the President and staff of the Agency:

(i) shall be immune from legal process with respect to acts performed by them in their official capacity;

(ii) not being local nationals, shall be accorded the same immunities from immigration restrictions, alien registration requirements and national service obligations, and the same facilities as regards exchange restrictions as are accorded by the members concerned to the representatives, officials and employees of comparable rank of other members; and

(iii) shall be granted the same treatment in respect of travelling facilities as is accorded by the members concerned to representatives, officials and employees of comparable rank of other members.

Article 49. Application of this Chapter

Each member shall take such action as is necessary in its own territories for the purpose of making effective in terms of its own law the principles set forth in this Chapter and shall inform the Agency of the detailed action which it has taken.

Article 50. Waiver

The immunities, exemptions and privileges provided in this Chapter are granted in the interests of the Agency and may be waived, to such extent and upon such conditions as the Agency may determine, in cases where such a waiver would not prejudice its interests. The Agency shall waive the immunity of any of its staff in cases where, in its opinion, the immunity would impede the course of justice and can be waived without prejudice to the interests of the Agency.

Chapter VIII: WITHDRAWAL, SUSPENSION OF MEMBERSHIP AND CESSATION OF OPERATIONS

Article 51. Withdrawal

Any member may, after the expiration of three years following the date upon which this Convention has entered into force with respect to such member, withdraw from the Agency at any time by giving notice in writing to the Agency at

its principal office. The Agency shall notify the Bank, as depository of this Convention, of the receipt of such notice. Any withdrawal shall become effective ninety days following the date of the receipt of such notice by the Agency. A member may revoke such notice as long as it has not become effective.

Article 52. Suspension of Membership

(a) If a member fails to fulfill any of its obligations under this Convention, the Council may, by a majority of its members exercising a majority of the total voting power, suspend its membership.

(b) While under suspension a member shall have no rights under this Convention, except for the right of withdrawal and other rights provided in this Chapter and Chapter IX, but shall remain subject to all its obligations.

(c) For purposes of determining eligibility for a guarantee or reinsurance to be issued under Chapter III or Annex I to this Convention, a suspended member shall not be treated as a member of the Agency.

(d) The suspended member shall automatically cease to be a member one year from the date of its suspension unless the Council decides to extend the period of suspension or to restore the member to good standing.

Article 53. Rights and Duties of States Ceasing to be Members

(a) When a State ceases to be a member, it shall remain liable for all its obligations, including its contingent obligations, under this Convention which shall have been in effect before the cessation of its membership.

(b) Without prejudice to Section (a) above, the Agency shall enter into an arrangement with such State for the settlement of their respective claims and obligations. Any such arrangement shall be approved by the Board.

Article 54. Suspension of Operations

(a) The Board may, whenever it deems it justified, suspend the issuance of new guarantees for a specified period.

(b) In an emergency, the Board may suspend all activities of the Agency for a period not exceeding the duration of such emergency, provided that necessary arrangements shall be made for the protection of the interests of the Agency and of third parties.

(c) The decision to suspend operations shall have no effect on the obligations of the members under this Convention or on the obligations of the Agency towards holders of a guarantee or reinsurance policy or towards third parties.

Article 55. Liquidation

(a) The Council, by special majority, may decide to cease operations and to liquidate the Agency. Thereupon the Agency shall forthwith cease all activities, except those incident to the orderly realization, conservation and preservation of assets and settlement of obligations. Until final settlement and distribution of assets, the Agency shall remain in existence and all rights and obligations of members under this Convention shall continue unimpaired.

(b) No distribution of assets shall be made to members until all liabilities to holders of guarantees and other creditors shall have been discharged or provided for and until the Council shall have decided to make such distribution.

(c) Subject to the foregoing, the Agency shall distribute its remaining assets to members in proportion to each member's share in the subscribed capital. The Agency shall also distribute any remaining assets of the Sponsorship Trust Fund referred to in Annex I to this Convention to sponsoring members in the proportion which the investments sponsored by each bears to the total of sponsored investments. No member shall be entitled to its share in the assets of the Agency or the Sponsorship Trust Fund unless that member has settled all outstanding claims by the Agency against it.

Every distribution of assets shall be made at such times as the Council shall determine and in such manner as it shall deem fair and equitable.

Chapter IX: SETTLEMENT OF DISPUTES

Article 56. Interpretation and Application of the Convention

(a) Any question of interpretation or application of the provisions of this Convention arising between any member of the Agency and the Agency or among members of the Agency shall be submitted to the Board for its decision. Any member which is particularly affected by the question and which is not otherwise represented by a national in the Board may send a representative to attend any meeting of the Board at which such question is considered.

(b) In any case where the Board has given a decision under Section (a) above, any member may require that the question be referred to the Council, whose decision shall be final. Pending the result of the referral to the Council, the Agency may, so far as it deems necessary, act on the basis of the decision of the Board.

Article 57. Disputes between the Agency and Members

(a) Without prejudice to the provisions of Article 56 and of Section (b) of this Article, any dispute between the Agency and a member or an agency thereof and any dispute between the Agency and a country (or agency thereof) which has ceased to be a member, shall be settled in accordance with the procedure set out in Annex II to this Convention.

(b) Disputes concerning claims of the Agency acting as subrogee of an investor shall be settled in accordance with either (i) the procedure set out in Annex II to this Convention, or (ii) an agreement to be entered into between the Agency and the member concerned on an alternative method or methods for the settlement of such disputes. In the latter case, Annex II to this Convention shall serve as a basis for such an agreement which shall, in each case, be approved by the Board by special majority prior to the undertaking by the Agency of operations in the territories of the member concerned.

Article 58. Disputes Involving Holders of a Guarantee or Reinsurance

Any dispute arising under a contract of guarantee or reinsurance between the parties thereto shall be submitted to arbitration for final determination in accordance with such rules as shall be provided for or referred to in the contract of guarantee or reinsurance.

Chapter X: AMENDMENTS

Article 59. Amendment by Council

(a) This Convention and its Annexes may be amended by vote of three-fifths of the Governors exercising four-fifths of the total voting power, provided that:

(i) any amendment modifying the right to withdraw from the Agency provided in Article 51 or the limitation on liability provided in Section (d) of Article 8 shall require the affirmative vote of all Governors; and

(ii) any amendment modifying the loss-sharing arrangement provided in Articles 1 and 3 of Annex I to this Convention which will result in an increase in any member's liability thereunder shall require the affirmative vote of the Governor of each such member.

(b) Schedules A and B to this Convention may be amended by the Council by special majority.

(c) If an amendment affects any provision of Annex I to this Convention, total votes shall include the additional votes alloted under Article 7 of such Annex to sponsoring members and countries hosting sponsored investments.

Article 60. Procedure

Any proposal to amend this Convention, whether emanating from a member or a Governor or a Director, shall be communicated to the Chairman of the Board who shall bring the proposal before the Board. If the proposed amendment is recommended by the Board, it shall be submitted to the Council for approval in accordance with Article 59. When an amendment has been duly approved by the Council, the Agency shall so certify by formal communication addressed to all members. Amendments shall enter into force for all members ninety days after the date of the formal communication unless the Council shall specify a different date.

Chapter XI: FINAL PROVISIONS

Article 61. Entry into Force

(a) This Convention shall be open for signature on behalf of all members of the Bank and Switzerland and shall be subject to ratification, acceptance or approval by the signatory States in accordance with their constitutional procedures.

(b) This Convention shall enter into force on the day when not less than five instruments of ratification, acceptance or approval shall have been deposited on behalf of signatory States in Category One, and not less than fifteen such instruments shall have been deposited on behalf of signatory States in Category Two; provided that total subscriptions of these States amount to not less than one-third of the authorized capital of the Agency as prescribed in Article 5.

(c) For each State which deposits its instrument of ratification, acceptance or approval after this Convention shall have entered into force, this Convention shall enter into force on the date of such deposit.

(d) If this Convention shall not have entered into force within two years after its opening for signature, the President of the Bank shall convene a conference of interested countries to determine the future course of action.

Article 62. Inaugural Meeting

Upon entry into force of this Convention, the President of the Bank shall call the inaugural meeting of the Council. This meeting shall be held at the principal office of the Agency within sixty days from the date on which this Convention has entered into force or as soon as practicable thereafter.

Article 63. Depository

Instruments of ratification, acceptance or approval of this Convention and amendments thereto shall be deposited with the Bank which shall act as the depository of this Convention. The depository shall transmit certified copies of this Convention to States members of the Bank and to Switzerland.

Article 64. Registration

The depository shall register this Convention with the Secretariat of the United Nations in accordance with Article 102 of the Charter of the United Nations and the Regulations thereunder adopted by the General Assembly.

Article 65. Notification

The depository shall notify all signatory States and, upon the entry into force of this Convention, the Agency of the following:

(a) signatures of this Convention;

(b) deposits of instruments of ratification, acceptance and approval in accordance with Article 63;

(c) the date on which this Convention enters into force in accordance with Article 61;

(d) exclusions from territorial application pursuant to Article 66; and

(e) withdrawal of a member from the Agency pursuant to Article 51.

Article 66. Territorial Application

This Convention shall apply to all territories under the jurisdiction of a member including the territories for whose international relations a member is responsible, except those which are excluded by such member by written notice to the depository of this Convention either at the time of ratification, acceptance or approval or subsequently.

Article 67. Periodic Reviews

(a) The Council shall periodically undertake comprehensive reviews of the activities of the Agency as well as the results achieved with a view to introducing any changes required to enhance the Agency's ability to serve its objectives.

(b) The first such review shall take place five years after the entry into force of this Convention. The dates of subsequent reviews shall be determined by the Council.

DONE at Seoul, in a single copy which shall remain deposited in the archives of the International Bank for Reconstruction and Development, which has indicated by its signature below its agreement to fulfill the functions with which it is charged under this Convention.

H. Convention on the Settlement of Investment Disputes Between States and Nationals of Other States (ICSID)

Source: Done at Washington, D.C., March 18, 1965, entered into force for the U.S., Oct. 14, 1966, 17 U.S.T. 1270, T.I.A.S. No. 6090, 575 U.N.T.S. 159, Doc. ICSID/15 (1985), *reprinted in* 4 I.L.M. 532 (1965). For current status: International Centre for Settlement of Investment Disputes, 1818 H Street, N.W., Washington, DC 20433; Telephone: (202) 477-1234.)

Website information:

http://www.worldbank.org/icsid/
This site contains the text and commentary for the ICSID convention, updated lists of member states, and cases applying the convention.

http://www.internationaladr.com/tc1.htm
This is the website of International Alternative Dispute Resolution, an electronic forum intended to serve as a resource for practitioners and others interested in learning more about the field of international alternative dispute resolution. The website contains the text of several international agreements relating to arbitration, as well as an updated list of member states to each agreement, and links to the individual arbitration laws of those states.

Introduction

The World Bank created the International Centre for the Settlement of Investment Disputes (ICSID) to promote the settlement of investment disputes between governments and foreign investors and to encourage the flow of international investment. The Convention on the Settlement of Investment Disputes between States and Nationals of Other States was signed on March 18, 1965, in Washington D.C. Since its entry entered into force on October 14, 1966, it has been ratified by over 130 developed and developing states in Asia, Africa, Europe, North America and South America. It provides an alternative to domestic litigation against a foreign or local sovereign and diplomatic negotiation of politically sensitive economic matters.

Any state that is a member of the World Bank may become a party to the Convention, and non-member states to the World Bank may join upon the invitation of a two-thirds majority of the ICSID Administrative Council if the new member state is a party to the Statute of the International Court of Justice (Article 67). Accession to the Convention does not bind the state to consent to arbitration of every dispute (Preamble). Consent to submission to ICSID dispute settlement must be in writing (Article 25), but may take the form of a written agreement between the contracting state and the private investor, national legislation, or a bilateral or multilateral treaty with the contracting state in which the investor is a national. Advance consent by governments to submit investment disputes to ICSID arbitration can be found in over twenty investment laws and over 700 bilateral investment treaties. Arbitration under the ICSID is also one of the primary mechanisms for the settlement of investment disputes under four recent multilateral investment treaties (the North American Free

Trade Agreement, the Cartagena Free Trade Agreement, the Energy Charter Treaty, and the Colonia Investment Protocol of Mercosur).

The Convention provides for the establishment and operation of the ICSID (Chapter I), its jurisdiction (Chapter II), the rules governing conciliation (Chapter III), arbitration (Chapter IV), enforcement (Chapter IV), replacement and disqualification of conciliators and arbitrators (Chapter V), costs and location of proceedings (Chapter VI and VII), settlement of disputes between contracting states (Chapter VIII), and amendment to the Convention (Chapter IX and X). Although the Centre itself does not arbitrate, it applies the Convention through the maintenance of panels of conciliators and arbitrators (Article 3). These panels appoint their members to consider specific disputes (Article 29 to 31, 37 to 40). The appointed arbitral tribunal then conducts arbitration in accordance with the procedural rules adopted by the ICSID Administrative Council (Article 6(1)(c) and Article 44) and either the law agreed to by the parties or that of the contracting state (Article 42). A final award is in writing, and includes the rationale for the decision (Article 48). Such an award cannot be annulled by a contracting state on the basis of public policy or nonarbitrability of the dispute, and must be recognized and enforced within each contracting state "as if it were a final judgment of a court in that state" (Article 54).

CONVENTION ON THE SETTLEMENT OF INVESTMENT DISPUTES BETWEEN STATES AND NATIONALS OF OTHER STATES

PREAMBLE

The Contracting States

Considering the need for international cooperation for economic development, and the role of private international investment therein;

Bearing in mind the possibility that from time to time disputes may arise in connection with such investment between Contracting States and nationals of other Contracting States;

Recognizing that while such disputes would usually be subject to national legal processes, international methods of settlement may be appropriate in certain cases;

Attaching particular importance to the availability of facilities for international conciliation or arbitration to which Contracting States and nationals of other Contracting States may submit such disputes if they so desire;

Desiring to establish such facilities under the auspices of the International Bank for Reconstruction and Development;

Recognizing that mutual consent by the parties to submit such disputes to conciliation or to arbitration through such facilities constitutes a binding agreement which requires in particular that due consideration be given to any recommendation of conciliators, and that any arbitral award be complied with; and

Declaring that no Contracting State shall by the mere fact of its ratification, acceptance or approval of this Convention and without its consent be deemed to be under any obligation to submit any particular dispute to conciliation or arbitration,

Have agreed as follows:

CHAPTER I

International Centre for Settlement of Investment Disputes

Section 1

Establishment and Organization

Article 1

(1) There is hereby established the International Centre for Settlement of Investment Disputes (hereinafter called the Centre).

(2) The purpose of the Centre shall be to provide facilities for conciliation and arbitration of investment disputes between Contracting States and nationals of other Contracting States in accordance with the provisions of this Convention.

Article 2

The seat of the Centre shall be at the principal office of the International Bank for Reconstruction and Development (hereinafter called the Bank). The seat may be moved to another place by decision of the Administrative Council adopted by a majority of two-thirds of its members.

Article 3

The Centre shall have an Administrative Council and a Secretariat and shall maintain a Panel of Conciliators and a Panel of Arbitrators.

Section 2

The Administrative Council

Article 4

(1) The Administrative Council shall be composed of one representative of each Contracting State. An alternate may act as representative in case of his principal's absence from a meeting or inability to act.

(2) In the absence of a contrary designation, each governor and alternate governor of the Bank appointed by a Contracting State shall be ex officio its representative and its alternate respectively.

Article 5

The President of the Bank shall be ex officio Chairman of the Administrative Council (hereinafter called the Chairman) but shall have no vote. During his absence or inability to act and during any vacancy in the office of President of the Bank, the person for the time being acting as President shall act as Chairman of the Administrative Council.

Article 6

(1) Without prejudice to the powers and functions vested in it by other provisions of this Convention, the Administrative Council shall

(a) adopt the administrative and financial regulations of the Centre;

(b) adopt the rules of procedure for the institution of conciliation and arbitration proceedings;

(c) adopt the rules of procedure for conciliation and arbitration proceedings (hereinafter called the Conciliation Rules and the Arbitration Rules);

(d) approve arrangements with the Bank for the use of the Bank's administrative facilities and services;

(e) determine the conditions of service of the Secretary-General and of any Deputy Secretary-General;

(f) adopt the annual budget of revenues and expenditures of the Centre;

(g) approve the annual report on the operation of the Centre.

The decisions referred to in sub-paragraphs (a), (b), (c) and (f) above shall be adopted by a majority of two-thirds of the members of the Administrative Council.

(2) The Administrative Council may appoint such committees as it considers necessary.

(3) The Administrative Council shall also exercise such other powers and perform such other functions as it shall determine to be necessary for the implementation of the provisions of this Convention.

Article 7

(1) The Administrative Council shall hold an annual meeting and such other meetings as may be determined by the Council, or convened by the Chairman, or convened by the Secretary-General at the request of not less than five members of the Council.

(2) Each member of the Administrative Council shall have one vote and, except as otherwise herein provided, all matters before the Council shall be decided by a majority of the votes cast.

(3) A quorum for any meeting of the Administrative Council shall be a majority of its members.

(4) The Administrative Council may establish, by a majority of two-thirds of its members, a procedure whereby the Chairman may seek a vote of the Council without convening a meeting of the Council. The vote shall be considered valid only if the majority of the

members of the Council cast their votes within the time limit fixed by the said procedure.

Article 8

Members of the Administrative Council and the Chairman shall serve without remuneration from the Centre.

Section 3

The Secretariat

Article 9

The Secretariat shall consist of a Secretary-General, one or more Deputy Secretaries-General and staff.

Article 10

(1) The Secretary-General and any Deputy Secretary-General shall be elected by the Administrative Council by a majority of two-thirds of its members upon the nomination of the Chairman for a term of service not exceeding six years and shall be eligible for re-election. After consulting the members of the Administrative Council, the Chairman shall propose one or more candidates for each such office.

(2) The offices of Secretary-General and Deputy Secretary-General shall be incompatible with the exercise of any political function. Neither the Secretary-General nor any Deputy Secretary-General may hold any other employment or engage in any other occupation except with the approval of the Administrative Council.

(3) During the Secretary-General's absence or inability to act, and during any vacancy of the office of Secretary-General, the Deputy Secretary-General shall act as Secretary-General. If there shall be more than one Deputy Secretary-General, the Administrative Council shall determine in advance the order in which they shall act as Secretary-General.

Article 11

The Secretary-General shall be the legal representative and the principal officer of the Centre and shall be responsible for its administration, including the appointment of staff, in accordance with the provisions of this Convention and the rules adopted by the Administrative Council. He shall perform the function of registrar and shall have the power to authenticate arbitral awards rendered pursuant to this Convention, and to certify copies thereof.

Section 4

The Panels

Article 12

The Panel of Conciliators and the Panel of Arbitrators shall each consist of qualified persons, designated as hereinafter provided, who are willing to serve thereon.

Article 13

(1) Each Contracting State may designate to each Panel four persons who may but need not be its nationals.

(2) The Chairman may designate ten persons to each Panel. The persons so designated to a Panel shall each have a different nationality.

Article 14

(1) Persons designated to serve on the Panels shall be persons of high moral character and recognized competence in the fields of law, commerce, industry or finance, who may be relied upon to exercise independent judgment. Competence in the field of law shall be of particular importance in the case of persons on the Panel of Arbitrators.

(2) The Chairman, in designating persons to serve on the Panels, shall in addition pay due regard to the importance of assuring representation on the Panels of the principal legal

systems of the world and of the main forms of economic activity.

Article 15

(1) Panel members shall serve for renewable periods of six years.

(2) In case of death or resignation of a member of a Panel, the authority which designated the member shall have the right to designate another person to serve for the remainder of that member's term.

(3) Panel members shall continue in office until their successors have been designated.

Article 16

(1) A person may serve on both Panels.

(2) If a person shall have been designated to serve on the same Panel by more than one Contracting State, or by one or more Contracting States and the Chairman, he shall be deemed to have been designated by the authority which first designated him or, if one such authority is the State of which he is a national, by that State.

(3) All designations shall be notified to the Secretary-General and shall take effect from the date on which the notification is received.

Section 5

Financing the Centre

Article 17

If the expenditure of the Centre cannot be met out of charges for the use of its facilities, or out of other receipts, the excess shall be borne by Contracting States which are members of the Bank in proportion to their respective subscriptions to the capital stock of the Bank, and by Contracting States which are not members of the Bank in accordance with rules adopted by the Administrative Council.

Section 6

Status, Immunities and Privileges

Article 18

The Centre shall have full international legal personality. The legal capacity of the Centre shall include the capacity

(a) to contract;

(b) to acquire and dispose of movable and immovable property;

(c) to institute legal proceedings.

Article 19

To enable the Centre to fulfil its functions, it shall enjoy in the territories of each Contracting State the immunities and privileges set forth in this Section.

Article 20

The Centre, its property and assets shall enjoy immunity from all legal process, except when the Centre waives this immunity.

Article 21

The Chairman, the members of the Administrative Council, persons acting as conciliators or arbitrators or members of a Committee appointed pursuant to paragraph (3) of Article 52, and the officers and employees of the Secretariat

(a) shall enjoy immunity from legal process with respect to acts performed by them in the exercise of their functions, except when the Centre waives this immunity;

(b) not being local nationals, shall enjoy the same immunities from immigration restrictions, alien registration requirements and national service obligations, the same facilities as regards exchange restrictions and the same treatment in respect of travelling facilities as are accorded by Contracting States to the representatives, officials and employees of comparable rank of other Contracting States.

Article 22

The provisions of Article 21 shall apply to persons appearing in proceedings under this Convention as parties, agents, counsel, advocates, witnesses or experts; provided, however, that sub-paragraph (b) thereof shall apply only in connection with their travel to and from, and their stay at, the place where the proceedings are held.

Article 23

(1) The archives of the Centre shall be inviolable, wherever they may be.

(2) With regard to its official communications, the Centre shall be accorded by each Contracting State treatment not less favourable than that accorded to other international organizations.

Article 24

(1) The Centre, its assets, property and income, and its operations and transactions authorized by this Convention shall be exempt from all taxation and customs duties. The Centre shall also be exempt from liability for the collection or payment of any taxes or customs duties.

(2) Except in the case of local nationals, no tax shall be levied on or in respect of expense allowances paid by the Centre to the Chairman or members of the Administrative Council, or on or in respect of salaries, expense allowances or other emoluments paid by the Centre to officials or employees of the Secretariat.

(3) No tax shall be levied on or in respect of fees or expense allowances received by persons acting as conciliators, or arbitrators, or members of a Committee appointed pursuant to paragraph (3) of Article 52, in proceedings under this Convention, if the sole jurisdictional basis for such tax is the location of the Centre or the place

where such proceedings are conducted or the place where such fees or allowances are paid.

CHAPTER II

Jurisdiction of the Centre

Article 25

(1) The jurisdiction of the Centre shall extend to any legal dispute arising directly out of an investment, between a Contracting State (or any constituent subdivision or agency of a Contracting State designated to the Centre by that State) and a national of another Contracting State, which the parties to the dispute consent in writing to submit to the Centre. When the parties have given their consent, no party may withdraw its consent unilaterally.

(2) 'National of another Contracting State' means:

(a) any natural person who had the nationality of a Contracting State other than the State party to the dispute on the date on which the parties consented to submit such dispute to conciliation or arbitration as well as on the date on which the request was registered pursuant to paragraph (3) of Article 28 or paragraph (3) of Article 36, but does not include any person who on either date also had the nationality of the Contracting State party to the dispute; and

(b) any juridical person which had the nationality of a Contracting State other than the State party to the dispute on the date on which the parties consented to submit such dispute to conciliation or arbitration and any juridical person which had the nationality of the Contracting State party to the dispute on that date and which, because of foreign control, the parties have agreed should be treated as a national of another Contracting State for the purposes of this Convention.

(3) Consent by a constituent subdivision or agency of a Contracting State shall require the approval of that State unless that State notifies the Centre that no such approval is required.

113

(4) Any Contracting State may, at the time of ratification, acceptance or approval of this Convention or at any time thereafter, notify the Centre of the class or classes of disputes which it would or would not consider submitting to the jurisdiction of the Centre. The Secretary-General shall forthwith transmit such notification to all Contracting States. Such notification shall not constitute the consent required by paragraph (1).

Article 26

Consent of the parties to arbitration under this Convention shall, unless otherwise stated, be deemed consent to such arbitration to the exclusion of any other remedy. A Contracting State may require the exhaustion of local administrative or judicial remedies as a condition of its consent to arbitration under this Convention.

Article 27

(1) No Contracting State shall give diplomatic protection, or bring an international claim, in respect of a dispute which one of its nationals and another Contracting State shall have consented to submit or shall have submitted to arbitration under this Convention, unless such other Contracting State shall have failed to abide by and comply with the award rendered in such dispute.

(2) Diplomatic protection, for the purposes of paragraph (1), shall not include informal diplomatic exchanges for the sole purpose of facilitating a settlement of the dispute.

CHAPTER III

Conciliation

Section 1

Request for Conciliation

Article 28

(1) Any Contracting State or any national of a Contracting State wishing to institute conciliation proceedings shall address a request to that effect in writing to the Secretary-General who shall send a copy of the request to the other party.

(2) The request shall contain information concerning the issues in dispute, the identity of the parties and their consent to conciliation in accordance with the rules of procedure for the institution of conciliation and arbitration proceedings.

(3) The Secretary-General shall register the request unless he finds, on the basis of the information contained in the request, that the dispute is manifestly outside the jurisdiction of the Centre. He shall forthwith notify the parties of registration or refusal to register.

Section 2

Constitution of the Conciliation Commission

Article 29

(1) The Conciliation Commission (hereinafter called the Commission) shall be constituted as soon as possible after registration of a request pursuant to Article 28.

(2)(a) The Commission shall consist of a sole conciliator or any uneven number of conciliators appointed as the parties shall agree.

(b) Where the parties do not agree upon the number of conciliators and the method of their appointment, the Commission shall consist of three conciliators, one conciliator appointed by each party and the third, who shall be the president of the Commission, appointed by agreement of the parties.

Article 30

If the Commission shall not have been constituted within 90 days after notice of registration of the request has been dispatched by the Secretary-General in accordance with paragraph (3) of Article 28, or such other period as the parties may agree, the Chairman shall, at the request of either party and after consulting both parties as far as possible, appoint the conciliator or conciliators not yet appointed.

Article 31

(1) Conciliators may be appointed from outside the Panel of Conciliators, except in the case of appointments by the Chairman pursuant to Article 30.

(2) Conciliators appointed from outside the Panel of Conciliators shall possess the qualities stated in paragraph (1) of Article 14.

Section 3

Conciliation Proceedings

Article 32

(1) The Commission shall be the judge of its own competence.

(2) Any objection by a party to the dispute that that dispute is not within the jurisdiction of the Centre, or for other reasons is not within the competence of the Commission, shall be considered by the Commission which shall determine whether to deal with it as a preliminary question or to join it to the merits of the dispute.

Article 33

Any conciliation proceeding shall be conducted in accordance with the provisions of this Section and, except as the parties otherwise agree, in accordance with the Conciliation Rules in effect on the date on which the parties consented to conciliation. If any question of procedure arises which is not covered by this Section or the Conciliation Rules or any rules agreed by the parties, the Commission shall decide the question.

Article 34

(1) It shall be the duty of the Commission to clarify the issues in dispute between the parties and to endeavour to bring about agreement between them upon mutually acceptable terms. To that end, the Commission may at any stage of the proceedings and from time to time recommend terms of settlement to the parties. The parties shall cooperate in good faith with the Commission in order to enable the Commission to carry out its functions, and shall give their most serious consideration to its recommendations.

(2) If the parties reach agreement, the Commission shall draw up a report noting the issues in dispute and recording that the parties have reached agreement. If, at any stage of the proceedings, it appears to the Commission that there is no likelihood of agreement between the parties, it shall close the proceedings and shall draw up a report noting the submission of the dispute and recording the failure of the parties to reach agreement. If one party fails to appear or participate in the proceedings, the Commission shall close the proceedings and shall draw up a report noting that party's failure to appear or participate.

Article 35

Except as the parties to the dispute shall otherwise agree, neither party to a conciliation proceeding shall be entitled in any other proceeding, whether before arbitrators or in a court of law or otherwise, to invoke or rely on any views expressed or statements or admissions or offers of settlement made by the other party in the conciliation proceedings, or the report or any recommendations made by the Commission.

CHAPTER IV

Arbitration

Section 1

Request for Arbitration

Article 36

(1) Any Contracting State or any national of a Contracting State wishing to institute arbitration proceedings shall address a request to that effect in writing to the Secretary-General who shall send a copy of the request to the other party.

(2) The request shall contain information concerning the issues in dispute, the identity of the parties and their consent to arbitration in accordance with the rules of procedure for the institution of conciliation and arbitration proceedings.

(3) The Secretary-General shall register the request unless he finds, on the basis of the information contained in the request, that the dispute is manifestly outside the jurisdiction of the Centre. He shall forthwith notify the parties of registration or refusal to register.

Section 2

Constitution of the Tribunal

Article 37

(1) The Arbitral Tribunal (hereinafter called the Tribunal) shall be constituted as soon as possible after registration of a request pursuant to Article 36.

(2)(a) The Tribunal shall consist of a sole arbitrator or any uneven number of arbitrators appointed as the parties shall agree.

(b) Where the parties do not agree upon the number of arbitrators and the method of their appointment, the Tribunal shall consist of three arbitrators, one arbitrator appointed by each party and the third, who shall be the president of the Tribunal, appointed by agreement of the parties.

Article 38

If the Tribunal shall not have been constituted within 90 days after notice of registration of the request has been dispatched by the Secretary-General in accordance with paragraph (3) of Article 36, or such other period as the parties may agree, the Chairman shall, at the request of either party and after consulting both parties as far as possible, appoint the arbitrator or arbitrators not yet appointed. Arbitrators appointed by the Chairman pursuant to this Article shall not be nationals of the Contracting State party to the dispute or of the Contracting State whose national is a party to the dispute.

Article 39

The majority of the arbitrators shall be nationals of States other than the Contracting State party to the dispute and the Contracting State whose national is a party to the dispute; provided, however, that the foregoing provisions of this Article shall not apply if the sole arbitrator or each individual member of the Tribunal has been appointed by agreement of the parties.

Article 40

(1) Arbitrators may be appointed from outside the Panel of Arbitrators, except in the case of appointments by the Chairman pursuant to Article 38.

(2) Arbitrators appointed from outside the Panel of Arbitrators shall possess the qualities stated in paragraph (1) of Article 14.

Section 3

Powers and Functions of the Tribunal

Article 41

(1) The Tribunal shall be the judge of its own competence.

(2) Any objection by a party to the dispute that that dispute is not within the jurisdiction of the Centre, or for other reasons is not within the competence of the Tribunal, shall be considered by the Tribunal which shall determine whether to deal with it as a preliminary question or to join it to the merits of the dispute.

Article 42

(1) The Tribunal shall decide a dispute in accordance with such rules of law as may be agreed by the parties. In the absence of such agreement, the Tribunal shall apply the law of the Contracting State party to the dispute (including its rules on the conflict of laws) and such rules of international law as may be applicable.

(2) The Tribunal may not bring in a finding of non liquet on the ground of silence or obscurity of the law.

(3) The provisions of paragraphs (1) and (2) shall not prejudice the power of the Tribunal to decide a dispute ex aequo et bono if the parties so agree.

Article 43

Except as the parties otherwise agree, the Tribunal may, if it deems it necessary at any stage of the proceedings,

(a) call upon the parties to produce documents or other evidence, and

(b) visit the scene connected with the dispute, and conduct such inquiries there as it may deem appropriate.

Article 44

Any arbitration proceeding shall be conducted in accordance with the provisions of this Section and, except as the parties otherwise agree, in accordance with the Arbitration Rules in effect on the date on which the parties consented to arbitration. If any question of procedure arises which is not covered by this Section or the Arbitration Rules or any rules agreed by the parties, the Tribunal shall decide the question.

Article 45

(1) Failure of a party to appear or to present his case shall not be deemed an admission of the other party's assertions.

(2) If a party fails to appear or to present his case at any stage of the proceedings the other party may request the Tribunal to deal with the questions submitted to it and to render an award. Before rendering an award, the Tribunal shall notify, and grant a period of grace to, the party failing to appear or to present its case, unless it is satisfied that that party does not intend to do so.

Article 46

Except as the parties otherwise agree, the Tribunal shall, if requested by a party, determine any incidental or additional claims or counter-claims arising directly out of the subject-matter of the dispute provided that they are within the scope of the consent of the parties and are otherwise within the jurisdiction of the Centre.

Article 47

Except as the parties otherwise agree, the Tribunal may, if it considers that the circumstances so require, recommend any provisional measures which should be taken to preserve the respective rights of either party.

117

Section 4

The Award

Article 48

(1) The Tribunal shall decide questions by a majority of the votes of all its members.

(2) The award of the Tribunal shall be in writing and shall be signed by the members of the Tribunal who voted for it.

(3) The award shall deal with every question submitted to the Tribunal, and shall state the reasons upon which it is based.

(4) Any member of the Tribunal may attach his individual opinion to the award, whether he dissents from the majority or not, or a statement of his dissent.

(5) The Centre shall not publish the award without the consent of the parties.

Article 49

(1) The Secretary-General shall promptly dispatch certified copies of the award to the parties. The award shall be deemed to have been rendered on the date on which the certified copies were dispatched.

(2) The Tribunal upon the request of a party made within 45 days after the date on which the award was rendered may after notice to the other party decide any question which it had omitted to decide in the award, and shall rectify any clerical, arithmetical or similar error in the award. Its decision shall become part of the award and shall be notified to the parties in the same manner as the award. The periods of time provided for under paragraph (2) of Article 51 and paragraph (2) and Article 52 shall run from the date on which the decision was rendered.

Section 5

Interpretation, Revision and Annulment of the Award

Article 50

(1) If any dispute shall arise between the parties as to the meaning or scope of an award, either party may request interpretation of the award by an application in writing addressed to the Secretary-General.

(2) The request shall, if possible, be submitted to the Tribunal which rendered the award. If this shall not be possible, a new Tribunal shall be constituted in accordance with Section 2 of this Chapter. The Tribunal may, if it considers that the circumstances so require, stay enforcement of the award pending its decision.

Article 51

(1) Either party may request revision of the award by an application in writing addressed to the Secretary-General on the ground of discovery of some fact of such a nature as decisively to affect the award, provided that when the award was rendered that fact was unknown to the Tribunal and to the applicant and that the applicant's ignorance of that fact was not due to negligence.

(2) The application shall be made within 90 days after the discovery of such fact and in any event within three years after the date on which the award was rendered.

(3) The request shall, if possible, be submitted to the Tribunal which rendered the award. If this shall not be possible, a new Tribunal shall be constituted in accordance with Section 2 of this Chapter.

(4) The Tribunal may, if it considers that the circumstances so require, stay enforcement of the award pending its decision. If the applicant requests a stay of enforcement of the award in his application, enforcement shall be stayed provisionally until the Tribunal rules on such request.

Article 52

(1) Either party may request annulment of the award by an application in writing addressed to the Secretary-General on one or more of the following grounds:

(a) that the Tribunal was not properly constituted;

(b) that the Tribunal has manifestly exceeded it powers;

(c) that there was corruption on the part of a member of the Tribunal;

(d) that there has been a serious departure from a fundamental rule of procedure; or

(e) that the award has failed to state the reasons on which it is based.

(2) The application shall be made within 120 days after the date on which the award was rendered except that when annulment is requested on the ground of corruption such application shall be made within 120 days after discovery of the corruption and in any event within three years after the date on which the award was rendered.

(3) On receipt of the request the Chairman shall forthwith appoint from the Panel of Arbitrators an ad hoc Committee of three persons. None of the members of the Committee shall have been a member of the Tribunal which rendered the award, shall be of the same nationality as any such member, shall be a national of the State party to the dispute or of the State whose national is a party to the dispute, shall have been designated to the Panel of Arbitrators by either of those States, or shall have acted as a conciliator in the same dispute. The Committee shall have the authority to annul the award or any part thereof on any of the grounds set forth in paragraph (1).

(4) The provisions of Articles 41-45, 48, 49, 53 and 54, and of Chapters VI and VII shall apply mutatis mutandis to proceedings before the Committee.

(5) The Committee may, if it considers that the circumstances so require, stay enforcement of the award pending its decision. If the applicant requests a stay of enforcement of the award in his application, enforcement shall be stayed provisionally until the Committee rules on such request.

(6) If the award is annulled the dispute shall, at the request of either party, be submitted to a new Tribunal constituted in accordance with Section 2 of this Chapter.

Section 6

Recognition and Enforcement of the Award

Article 53

(1) The award shall be binding on the parties and shall not be subject to any appeal or to any other remedy except those provided for in this Convention. Each party shall abide by and comply with the terms of the award except to the extent that enforcement shall have been stayed pursuant to the relevant provisions of this Convention.

(2) For the purposes of this Section, 'award' shall include any decision interpreting, revising or annulling such award pursuant to Articles 50, 51 or 52.

Article 54

(1) Each Contracting State shall recognize an award rendered pursuant to this Convention as binding and enforce the pecuniary obligations imposed by that award within its territories as if it were a final judgment of a court in that State. A Contracting State with a federal constitution may enforce such an award in or through its federal courts and may provide that such courts shall treat the award as if it were a final judgment of the courts of a constituent state.

(2) A party seeking recognition or enforcement in the territories of a Contracting State shall furnish to a competent court or other authority which such State shall have designated for this purpose a copy of the award certified by the Secretary-General. Each Contracting State shall notify the Secretary-General of the designation of the competent court or other

authority for this purpose and of any subsequent change in such designation.

(3) Execution of the award shall be governed by the laws concerning the execution of judgments in force in the State in whose territories such execution is sought.

Article 55

Nothing in Article 54 shall be construed as derogating from the law in force in any Contracting State relating to immunity of that State or of any foreign State from execution.

CHAPTER V

Replacement and Disqualification of Conciliators and Arbitrators

Article 56

(1) After a Commission or a Tribunal has been constituted and proceedings have begun, its composition shall remain unchanged; provided, however, that if a conciliator or an arbitrator should die, become incapacitated, or resign, the resulting vacancy shall be filled in accordance with the provisions of Section 2 of Chapter III or Section 2 of Chapter IV.

(2) A member of a Commission or Tribunal shall continue to serve in that capacity notwithstanding that he shall have ceased to be a member of the Panel.

(3) If a conciliator or arbitrator appointed by a party shall have resigned without the consent of the Commission or Tribunal of which he was a member, the Chairman shall appoint a person from the appropriate Panel to fill the resulting vacancy.

Article 57

A party may propose to a Commission or Tribunal the disqualification of any of its members on account of any fact indicating a manifest lack of the qualities required by paragraph (1) of Article 14. A party to arbitration proceedings may, in addition, propose the disqualification of an arbitrator on the ground that he was ineligible for appointment to the Tribunal under Section 2 of Chapter IV.

Article 58

The decision on any proposal to disqualify a conciliator or arbitrator shall be taken by the other members of the Commission or Tribunal as the case may be, provided that where those members are equally divided, or in the case of a proposal to disqualify a sole conciliator or arbitrator, or a majority of the conciliators or arbitrators, the Chairman shall take that decision. If it is decided that the proposal is well-founded the conciliator or arbitrator to whom the decision relates shall be replaced in accordance with the provisions of Section 2 of Chapter III or Section 2 of Chapter IV.

CHAPTER VI

Cost of Proceedings

Article 59

The charges payable by the parties for the use of the facilities of the Centre shall be determined by the Secretary-General in accordance with the regulations adopted by the Administrative Council.

Article 60

(1) Each Commission and each Tribunal shall determine the fees and expenses of its members within limits established from time to time by the Administrative Council and after consultation with the Secretary-General.

(2) Nothing in paragraph (1) of this Article shall preclude the parties from agreeing in advance with the Commission or Tribunal concerned upon the fees and expenses of its members.

Article 61

(1) In the case of conciliation proceedings the fees and expenses of members of the Commission as well as the charges for the use of the facilities of the Centre, shall be borne equally by the parties. Each party shall bear any other expenses it incurs in connection with the proceedings.

(2) In the case of arbitration proceedings the Tribunal shall, except as the parties otherwise agree, assess the expenses incurred by the parties in connection with the proceedings, and shall decide how and by whom those expenses, the fees and expenses of the members of the tribunal and the charges for the use of the facilities of the Centre shall be paid. Such decision shall form part of the award.

CHAPTER VII

Place of Proceedings

Article 62

Conciliation and arbitration proceedings shall be held at the seat of the Centre except as hereinafter provided.

Article 63

Conciliation and arbitration proceedings may be held, if the parties so agree,

(a) at the seat of the Permanent Court of Arbitration or of any other appropriate institution, whether private or public, with which the Centre may make arrangements for that purpose; or

(b) at any other place approved by the Commission or Tribunal after consultation with the Secretary-General.

CHAPTER VIII

Disputes between Contracting States

Article 64

Any dispute arising between Contracting States concerning the interpretation or application of this Convention which is not settled by negotiation shall be referred to the International Court of Justice by the application of any party to such dispute, unless the States concerned agree to another method of settlement.

CHAPTER IX

Amendment

Article 65

Any Contracting State may propose amendment of this Convention. The text of a proposed amendment shall be communicated to the Secretary-General not less than 90 days prior to the meeting of the Administrative Council at which such amendment is to be considered and shall forthwith be transmitted by him to all the members of the Administrative Council.

Article 66

(1) If the Administrative Council shall so decide by a majority of two-thirds of its members, the proposed amendment shall be circulated to all Contracting States for ratification, acceptance or approval. Each amendment shall enter into force 30 days after dispatch by the depositary of this Convention of a notification to Contracting States that all Contracting States have ratified, accepted or approved the amendment.

(2) No amendment shall affect the rights and obligations under this Convention of any Contracting State or of any of its constituent subdivisions or agencies, or of any national of such State arising out of consent to the jurisdiction of the Centre given before the date of entry into force of the amendment.

CHAPTER X

Final Provisions

Article 67

This Convention shall be open for signature on behalf of States members of the Bank. It shall also be open for signature on behalf of any other State which is a party to the Statute of the International Court of Justice and which the Administrative Council, by a vote of two-thirds of its members, shall have invited to sign the Convention.

Article 68

(1) This Convention shall be subject to ratification, acceptance or approval by the signatory States in accordance with their respective constitutional procedures.

(2) This Convention shall enter into force 30 days after the date of deposit of the twentieth instrument of ratification, acceptance or approval. It shall enter into force for each State which subsequently deposits its instrument of ratification, acceptance or approval 30 days after the date of such deposit.

Article 69

Each Contracting State shall take such legislative or other measures as may be necessary for making the provisions of this Convention effective in its territories.

Article 70

This Convention shall apply to all territories for whose international relations a Contracting State is responsible, except those which are excluded by such State by written notice to the depositary of this Convention either at the time of ratification, acceptance or approval or subsequently.

Article 71

Any Contracting State may denounce this Convention by written notice to the depositary of this Convention. The denunciation shall take effect six months after receipt of such notice.

Article 72

Notice by a Contracting State pursuant to Articles 70 or 71 shall not affect the rights or obligations under this Convention of that State or of any of its constituent subdivisions or agencies or of any national of that State arising out of consent to the jurisdiction of the Centre given by one of them before such notice was received by the depositary.

Article 73

Instruments of ratification, acceptance or approval of this Convention and of amendments thereto shall be deposited with the Bank which shall act as the depositary of this Convention. The depositary shall transmit certified copies of this Convention to States members of the Bank and to any other State invited to sign the Convention.

Article 74

The depositary shall register this Convention with the Secretariat of the United Nations in accordance with Article 102 of the Charter of the United Nations and the Regulations thereunder adopted by the General Assembly.

Article 75

The depositary shall notify all signatory States of the following:

(a) signatures in accordance with Article 67;

(b) deposits of instruments of ratification, acceptance and approval in accordance with Article 73;

(c) the date on which this Convention enters into force in accordance with Article 68;

(d) exclusions from territorial application pursuant to Article 70;

(e) the date on which any amendment of this Convention enters into force in accordance with Article 66; and

(f) denunciations in accordance with Article 71.

I. United States Model Bilateral Investment Treaty

Source: U.S. Department of State, Treaty Affairs Office.

Website information:

http://www.ita.doc.gov/legal/modelbit.html
This website contains the periodically updated text of the U.S. Model Bilateral Investment Treaty.

Introduction

The U.S. Bilateral Investment Treaty (BIT) Program was launched in 1982 out of concern for the lack of protection of United States direct foreign investment from host country regulation and interference. This program supplanted the outdated Treaties of Friendship, Commerce, and Navigation in investment issues. The BIT defines with greater specificity the substantive rights and duties of foreign investors and grants investors direct access to binding arbitration procedures provided through the International Centre for the Settlement of Investment Disputes (ICSID). In recent years, the BIT has become the standard form of agreement by which the United States attempts to define, on a reciprocal basis, the rights of U.S. investors in a foreign country and the rights of foreign investors in the United States.

The U.S. Model BIT covers five main subjects:
1) general principles for treatment of foreign investors;
2) conditions of expropriation and the measure of compensation payable;
3) the right to free transfer without delay of profits and other funds associated with investments;
4) the prohibition of inefficient and trade distorting practices; and
5) access to international arbitration for settlement of investment disputes.

Article I of the Model BIT introduces key definitions, setting forth the scope of activities falling under the treaty. The term "investment" is defined broadly so as to include not only equity and debt investment, but also contractual rights, legal rights, and interest in intellectual and industrial property. Article I also extends the scope of the treaty to include both indirect (i.e. through third country subsidiaries) and direct investment.

Article II sets forth the standard of "fair and equitable" treatment that a host country is to afford to the investments, judged by the current standards of international law. This requires that national and most-favored nation treatment be afforded to covered investments and similar activities, ensuring that investors are entitled to be treated as favorably as their competitors. This Article also places limitations on the host nation, precluding discriminatory measures associated with the management or operation of the investment, and requiring the provision of "effective means of asserting claims and enforcing rights with respect to covered investments."

Article III generally forbids expropriation of an investment covered by the treaty, but creates exceptions for non-discriminatory public purposes when there is payment of adequate compensation. Article IV deals with the issue of losses due to the actions of the host nation, affording national and most-favored nation status to covered investments disrupted by war, insurrection, and other civil

124

disturbances. Any restitution or other compensation in such events must conform with the general principles set forth in Article III.

Article V provides that all transfers, including interest, proceeds from liquidation, repatriated profits, and infusions of additional financial resources after the initial investment, are to be made "freely and without delay." Article VI limits the ability of host governments to require investors to adopt inefficient and trade distorting practices. Under the provisions of this article, local content quotas, export quotas, and technology transfers, are prohibited. Article VII gives investors the right to retain the managerial personnel of their choice, regardless of nationality, for the establishment, operation, development and administration of the investment.

Articles IX and X govern investment disputes under the BIT, and give investors the right to submit an investment dispute with the treaty partner's government to binding international arbitration. This access to the International Centre for the Settlement of Investment Disputes (ICSID) coexists with the investor's right to rely upon any contractually provided dispute resolution procedures, as well as with access to national judicial and administrative tribunals.

The United States has over 40 BITs in effect with developing nations and new market economies around the world.

UNITED STATES: 1994 MODEL BILATERAL INVESTMENT TREATY

TREATY BETWEEN THE GOVERNMENT OF THE UNITED STATES OF AMERICA AND THE GOVERNMENT OF _____ CONCERNING THE ENCOURAGEMENT AND RECIPROCAL PROTECTION OF INVESTMENT

The Government of the United States of America and the Government of _____ (hereinafter the "Parties");

Desiring to promote greater economic cooperation between them, with respect to investment by nationals and companies of one Party in the territory of the other Party;

Recognizing that agreement upon the treatment to be accorded such investment will stimulate the flow of private capital and the economic development of the Parties;

Agreeing that a stable framework for investment will maximize effective utilization of economic resources and improve living standards;

Recognizing that the development of economic and business ties can promote respect for internationally recognized worker rights;

Agreeing that these objectives can be achieved without relaxing health, safety and environmental measures of general application; and

Having resolved to conclude a treaty concerning the encouragement and reciprocal protection of investment;

Have agreed as follows:

ARTICLE I

For the purposes of this Treaty,

(a) "company" means any entity constituted or organized under applicable law, whether or not for profit, and whether privately or governmentally owned or controlled, and includes a corporation, trust, partnership, sole proprietorship, branch, joint venture, association, or other organization;

(b) "company of a Party" means a company constituted or organized under the laws of that Party;

(c) "national" of a Party means a natural person who is a national of that Party under its applicable law;

(d) "investment" of a national or company means every kind of investment owned or controlled directly or indirectly by that national or company, and includes investment consisting or taking the form of:

(i) a company;

(ii) shares, stock, and other forms of equity participation, and bonds, debentures, and other forms of debt interests, in a company;

(iii) contractual rights, such as under turnkey, construction or management contracts, production or revenue-sharing contracts, concessions, or other similar contracts;

(iv) tangible property, including real property; and intangible property, including rights, such as leases, mortgages, liens and pledges;

(v) intellectual property, including:
copyrights and related rights,
patents,
rights in plant varieties,
industrial designs,
rights in semiconductor layout designs,
trade secrets, including know-how and confidential business information,
trade and service marks, and trade names; and

(vi) rights conferred pursuant to law, such as licenses and permits;

(e) "covered investment" means an investment of a national or company of a Party in the territory of the other Party;

(f) "state enterprise" means a company owned, or controlled through ownership interests, by a Party;

(g) "investment authorization" means an authorization granted by the foreign investment authority of a Party to a covered investment or a national or company of the other Party;

(h) "investment agreement" means a written agreement between the national authorities of a Party and a covered investment or a national or company of the other Party that (i) grants rights with respect to natural resources or other assets controlled by the national authorities and (ii) the investment, national or company relies upon in establishing or acquiring a covered investment.

(i) "ICSID Convention" means the Convention on the Settlement of Investment Disputes between States and Nationals of Other States, done at Washington, March 18, 1965;

(j) "Centre" means the International Centre for Settlement of Investment Disputes established by the ICSID Convention; and

(k) "UNCITRAL Arbitration Rules" means the arbitration rules of the United Nations Commission on International Trade Law.

ARTICLE II

1. With respect to the establishment, acquisition, expansion, management, conduct, operation and sale or other disposition of covered investments, each Party shall accord treatment no less favorable than that it accords, in like situations, to investments in its territory of its own nationals or companies (hereinafter "national treatment") or to investments in its territory of nationals or companies of a third country (hereinafter "most favored nation treatment"), whichever is most favorable (hereinafter "national and most favored nation treatment"). Each Party shall ensure that its state enterprises, in the provision of their goods or services, accord national and most favored nation treatment to covered investments.

2. (a) A Party may adopt or maintain exceptions to the obligations of paragraph 1 in the sectors or with respect to the matters specified in the Annex to this Treaty. In adopting such an exception, a Party may not require the divestment, in whole or in part, of covered investments existing at the time the exception becomes effective.

(b) The obligations of paragraph 1 do not apply to procedures provided in multilateral agreements concluded under the auspices of the World Intellectual Property Organization relating to the acquisition or maintenance of intellectual property rights.

3. (a) Each Party shall at all times accord to covered investments fair and equitable treatment and full protection and security, and shall in no case accord treatment less favorable than that required by international law.

(b) Neither Party shall in any way impair by unreasonable and discriminatory measures the management, conduct, operation, and sale or other disposition of covered investments.

4. Each Party shall provide effective means of asserting claims and enforcing rights with respect to covered investments.

5. Each Party shall ensure that its laws, regulations, administrative practices and procedures of general application, and adjudicatory decisions, that pertain to or affect covered investments are promptly published or otherwise made publicly available.

ARTICLE III

1. Neither Party shall expropriate or nationalize a covered investment either directly or indirectly through measures tantamount to expropriation or nationalization ("expropriation") except for a public purpose; in a non-discriminatory manner; upon payment of prompt, adequate and effective compensation; and in accordance with due process of law and the

general principles of treatment provided for in Article II(3).

2. Compensation shall be paid without delay; be equivalent to the fair market value of the expropriated investment immediately before the expropriatory action was taken ("the date of expropriation"); and be fully realizable and freely transferable. The fair market value shall not reflect any change in value occurring because the expropriatory action had become known before the date of expropriation.

3. If the fair market value is denominated in a freely usable currency, the compensation paid shall be no less than the fair market value on the date of expropriation, plus interest at a commercially reasonable rate for that currency, accrued from the date of expropriation until the date of payment.

4. If the fair market value is denominated in a currency that is not freely usable, the compensation paid—converted into the currency of payment at the market rate of exchange prevailing on the date of payment—shall be no less than:

(a) the fair market value on the date of expropriation, converted into a freely usable currency at the market rate of exchange prevailing on that date, plus

(b) interest, at a commercially reasonable rate for that freely usable currency, accrued from the date of expropriation until the date of payment.

ARTICLE IV

1. Each Party shall accord national and most favored nation treatment to covered investments as regards any measure relating to losses that investments suffer in its territory owing to war or other armed conflict, revolution, state of national emergency, insurrection, civil disturbance, or similar events.

2. Each Party shall accord restitution, or pay compensation in accordance with paragraphs 2 through 4 of Article III, in the event that covered investments suffer losses in its territory, owing to war or other armed conflict, revolution, state of national emergency, insurrection, civil disturbance, or similar events, that result from:

(a) requisitioning of all or part of such investments by the Party's forces or authorities, or

(b) destruction of all or part of such investments by the Party's forces or authorities that was not required by the necessity of the situation.

ARTICLE V

1. Each Party shall permit all transfers relating to a covered investment to be made freely and without delay into and out of its territory. Such transfers include:

(a) contributions to capital;

(b) profits, dividends, capital gains, and proceeds from the sale of all or any part of the investment or from the partial or complete liquidation of the investment;

(c) interest, royalty payments, management fees, and technical assistance and other fees;

(d) payments made under a contract, including a loan agreement; and

(e) compensation pursuant to Articles III and IV, and payments arising out of an investment dispute.

2. Each Party shall permit transfers to be made in a freely usable currency at the market rate of exchange prevailing on the date of transfer.

3. Each Party shall permit returns in kind to be made as authorized or specified in an investment authorization, investment agreement, or other written agreement between the Party and a covered investment or a national or company of the other Party.

4. Notwithstanding paragraphs 1 through 3, a Party may prevent a transfer through the equitable, non-discriminatory and good faith application of its laws relating to:

(a) bankruptcy, insolvency or the protection of the rights of creditors;

(b) issuing, trading or dealing in securities;

(c) criminal or penal offenses; or

(d) ensuring compliance with orders or judgments in adjudicatory proceedings.

ARTICLE VI

Neither Party shall mandate or enforce, as a condition for the establishment, acquisition, expansion, management, conduct or operation of a covered investment, any requirement (including any commitment or undertaking in connection with the receipt of a governmental permission or authorization):

(a) to achieve a particular level or percentage of local content, or to purchase, use or otherwise give a preference to products or services of domestic origin or from any domestic source;

(b) to limit imports by the investment of products or services in relation to a particular volume or value of production, exports or foreign exchange earnings;

(c) to export a particular type, level or percentage of products or services, either generally or to a specific market region;

(d) to limit sales by the investment of products or services in the Party's territory in relation to a particular volume or value of production, exports or foreign exchange earnings;

(e) to transfer technology, a production process or other proprietary knowledge to a national or company in the Party's territory, except pursuant to an order, commitment or undertaking that is enforced by a court, administrative tribunal or competition authority to remedy an alleged or adjudicated violation of competition laws; or

(f) to carry out a particular type, level or percentage of research and development in the Party's territory.

Such requirements do not include conditions for the receipt or continued receipt of an advantage.

ARTICLE VII

1.   (a) Subject to its laws relating to the entry and sojourn of aliens, each Party shall permit to enter and to remain in its territory nationals of the other Party for the purpose of establishing, developing, administering or advising on the operation of an investment to which they, or a company of the other Party that employs them, have committed or are in the process of committing a substantial amount of capital or other resources.

(b) Neither Party shall, in granting entry under paragraph 1(a), require a labor certification test or other procedures of similar effect, or apply any numerical restriction.

2.   Each Party shall permit covered investments to engage top managerial personnel of their choice, regardless of nationality.

ARTICLE VIII

The Parties agree to consult promptly, on the request of either, to resolve any disputes in connection with the Treaty, or to discuss any matter relating to the interpretation or application of the Treaty or to the realization of the objectives of the Treaty.

ARTICLE IX

1.   For purposes of this Treaty, an investment dispute is a dispute between a Party and a national or company of the other Party arising out of or relating to an investment authorization, an investment agreement or an alleged breach of any right conferred, created or recognized by this Treaty with respect to a covered investment.

2. A national or company that is a party to an investment dispute may submit the dispute for resolution under one of the following alternatives:

(a) to the courts or administrative tribunals of the Party that is a party to the dispute; or

(b) in accordance with any applicable, previously agreed dispute-settlement procedures; or

(c) in accordance with the terms of paragraph 3.

3. (a) Provided that the national or company concerned has not submitted the dispute for resolution under paragraph 2(a) or (b), and that three months have elapsed from the date on which the dispute arose, the national or company concerned may submit the dispute for settlement by binding arbitration:

(i) to the Centre, if the Centre is available; or

(ii) to the Additional Facility of the Centre, if the Centre is not available; or

(iii) in accordance with the UNCITRAL Arbitration Rules; or

(iv) if agreed by both parties to the dispute, to any other arbitration institution or in accordance with any other arbitration rules.

(b) A national or company, notwithstanding that it may have submitted a dispute to binding arbitration under paragraph 3(a), may seek interim injunctive relief, not involving the payment of damages, before the judicial or administrative tribunals of the Party that is a party to the dispute, prior to the institution of the arbitral proceeding or during the proceeding, for the preservation of its rights and interests.

4. Each Party hereby consents to the submission of any investment dispute for settlement by binding arbitration in accordance with the choice of the national or company under paragraph 3(a)(i), (ii), and (iii) or the mutual agreement of both parties to the dispute under paragraph 3(a)(iv). This consent and the submission of the dispute by a national or company under paragraph 3(a) shall satisfy the requirement of:

(a) Chapter II of the ICSID Convention (Jurisdiction of the Centre) and the Additional Facility Rules for written consent of the parties to the dispute; and

(b) Article II of the United Nations Convention on the Recognition and Enforcement of Foreign Arbitral Awards, done at New York, June 10, 1958, for an "agreement in writing".

5. Any arbitration under paragraph 3(a)(ii), (iii) or (iv) shall be held in a state that is a party to the United Nations Convention on the Recognition and Enforcement of Foreign Arbitral Awards, done at New York, June 10, 1958.

6. Any arbitral award rendered pursuant to this Article shall be final and binding on the parties to the dispute. Each Party shall carry out without delay the provisions of any such award and provide in its territory for the enforcement of such award.

7. In any proceeding involving an investment dispute, a Party shall not assert, as a defense, counterclaim, right of set-off or for any other reason, that indemnification or other compensation for all or part of the alleged damages has been received or will be received pursuant to an insurance or guarantee contract.

8. For purposes of Article 25(2)(b) of the ICSID Convention and this Article, a company of a Party that, immediately before the occurrence of the event or events giving rise to an investment dispute, was a covered investment, shall be treated as a company of the other Party.

ARTICLE X

1. Any dispute between the Parties concerning the interpretation or application of the Treaty, that is not resolved through consultations or other diplomatic channels, shall be submitted upon the request of either Party to an arbitral tribunal for binding decision in accordance with the applicable rules of international law. In the absence of an agreement by the Parties to the contrary, the UNCITRAL Arbitration Rules shall govern, except to the extent these rules are (a) modified by the Parties or (b) modified by the arbitrators unless either Party objects to the proposed modification.

2. Within two months of receipt of a request, each Party shall appoint an arbitrator. The two arbitrators shall select a third arbitrator as Chairman, who shall be a national of a third State. The UNCITRAL Arbitration Rules applicable to

appointing members of three member panels shall apply mutatis mutandis to the appointment of the arbitral panel except that the appointing authority referenced in those rules shall be the Secretary General of the Centre.

3. Unless otherwise agreed, all submissions shall be made and all hearings shall be completed within six months of the date of selection of the third arbitrator, and the arbitral panel shall render its decisions within two months of the date of the final submissions or the date of the closing of the hearings, whichever is later.

4. Expenses incurred by the Chairman and other arbitrators, and other costs of the proceedings, shall be paid for equally by the Parties. However, the arbitral panel may, at its discretion, direct that a higher proportion of the costs be paid by one of the Parties.

ARTICLE XI

This Treaty shall not derogate from any of the following that entitle covered investments to treatment more favorable than that accorded by this Treaty:

(a) laws and regulations, administrative practices or procedures, or administrative or adjudicatory decisions of a Party;

(b) international legal obligations; or

(c) obligations assumed by a Party, including those contained in an investment authorization or an investment agreement.

ARTICLE XII

Each Party reserves the right to deny to a company of the other Party the benefits of this Treaty if nationals of a third country own or control the company and

(a) the denying Party does not maintain normal economic relations with the third country; or

(b) the company has no substantial business activities in the territory of the Party under whose laws it is constituted or organized.

ARTICLE XIII

1. No provision of this Treaty shall impose obligations with respect to tax matters, except that:

(a) Articles III, IX and X will apply with respect to expropriation; and

(b) Article IX will apply with respect to an investment agreement or an investment authorization.

2. A national or company, that asserts in an investment dispute that a tax matter involves an expropriation, may submit that dispute to arbitration pursuant to Article IX(3) only if:

(a) the national or company concerned has first referred to the competent tax authorities of both Parties the issue of whether the tax matter involves an expropriation; and

(b) the competent tax authorities have not both determined, within nine months from the time the national or company referred the issue, that the matter does not involve an expropriation.

ARTICLE XIV

1. This Treaty shall not preclude a Party from applying measures necessary for the fulfillment of its obligations with respect to the maintenance or restoration of international peace or security, or the protection of its own essential security interests.

2. This Treaty shall not preclude a Party from prescribing special formalities in connection with covered investments, such as a requirement that such investments be legally constituted under the laws and regulations of that Party, or a requirement that transfers of currency or other monetary instruments be reported, provided that such formalities shall not impair the substance of any of the rights set forth in this Treaty.

ARTICLE XV

1. (a) The obligations of this Treaty shall apply to the political subdivisions of the Parties.

(b) With respect to the treatment accorded by a State, Territory or possession of the

United States of America, national treatment means treatment no less favorable than the treatment accorded thereby, in like situations, to investments of nationals of the United States of America resident in, and companies legally constituted under the laws and regulations of, other States, Territories or possessions of the United States of America.

2. A Party's obligations under this Treaty shall apply to a state enterprise in the exercise of any regulatory, administrative or other governmental authority delegated to it by that Party.

ARTICLE XVI

1. This Treaty shall enter into force thirty days after the date of exchange of instruments of ratification. It shall remain in force for a period of ten years and shall continue in force unless terminated in accordance with paragraph 2. It shall apply to covered investments existing at the time of entry into force as well as to those established or acquired thereafter.

2. A Party may terminate this Treaty at the end of the initial ten year period or at any time thereafter by giving one year's written notice to the other Party.

3. For ten years from the date of termination, all other Articles shall continue to apply to covered investments established or acquired prior to the date of termination, except insofar as those Articles extend to the establishment or acquisition of covered investments.

4. The Annex [AND PROTOCOL (if any)] shall form an integral part of the Treaty.

IN WITNESS WHEREOF, the respective plenipotentiaries have signed this Treaty.
DONE in duplicate at [CITY] this [NUMBER] day of [MONTH], [YEAR], in the English and _____ languages, each text being equally authentic.
FOR THE GOVERNMENT OF THE UNITED STATES OF AMERICA:
FOR THE GOVERNMENT OF _____:

Annex

1. The Government of the United States of America may adopt or maintain exceptions to the obligation to accord national treatment to covered investments in the sectors or with respect to the matters specified below:

atomic energy; custom house brokers; licenses for broadcast, common carrier, or aeronautical radio stations; COMSAT; subsidies or grants, including government-supported loans, guarantees and insurance; state and local measures exempt from Article 1102 of the North American Free Trade Agreement pursuant to Article 1108 thereof; landing of submarine cables.

Most favored nation treatment shall be accorded in the sectors and matters indicated above.

2. The Government of the United States of America may adopt or maintain exceptions to the obligation to accord national and most favored nation treatment to covered investments in the sectors or with respect to the matters specified below: fisheries; air and maritime transport, and related activities; banking* insurance* securities* and other financial services*.

*Note: If the treaty partner undertakes acceptable commitments with respect to all or certain financial services, the Government of the United States of America will consider limiting these exceptions accordingly, so that, for example, particular obligations as to treatment would apply on no less favorable terms than in the North American Free Trade Agreement.

3. The Government of _____ may adopt or maintain exceptions . . .

4. Notwithstanding paragraph 3, each Party agrees to accord national treatment to covered investments in the following sectors:

leasing of minerals or pipeline rights-of-way on Government lands.

I.E.L.-III-0083

J. United States Model Income Tax Treaty

Source: United States Treasury Department

Website information:

http://www.ustreas.gov/taxpolicy/t0txmod1.html
This website provides the text of the U.S. Model Income Tax Treaty, with a link to the Model Treaty Technical Explanation.

http://www.taxresources.com/html/taxsites/treaty.html
This website provides texts of the U.S. Model Income Tax Treaty, related publications and additional information.

Introduction

The primary purpose of an income tax treaty is to minimize tax barriers such as double taxation in the exchange of goods and services across national boundaries, thus increasing international trade and investment. The current U.S. Model Income Tax Treaty, completed on September 20, 1996, builds on the U.S. Treasury Department's 1981 draft Model Income Tax Convention, and the 1995 updated OECD Model Double Taxation Convention on Income and Capital. Like its predecessors, the current Model Treaty is intended to be an evolving document, and is subject to amendments over time. The Model Treaty facilitates bilateral tax treaty negotiations by helping the negotiators identify differences between income tax policies in the two countries.

The Model Treaty changes the application of status and source rules contained in the U.S. Internal Revenue Code by focusing on the concept of "permanent establishment." (Article 5) Article 7(1) provides that "[t]he business profits of an enterprise of a Contracting State shall be taxable only in that State unless the enterprise carries on a business in the other Contracting State through a permanent establishment situated therein." Thus, the general rule is that an enterprise is taxed only by its home government unless it has a permanent establishment in the other treaty state. The treaty also contains specific rules for the taxation of dividends (Article 10), interest (Article 11), royalties (Article 12), gains from the sale of real property (Article 13), personal services income (Articles 14 and 15), directors' fees (Article 16), income of artists and sportsmen (Article 17), pensions, annuities, alimony and child support (Article 18), government service income (Article 19) and student and trainee compensation (Article 20). The convention provides a general rule of non-discrimination (Article 24), and establishes a mutual agreement procedure for dispute resolution (Article 25).

UNITED STATES MODEL
INCOME TAX CONVENTION OF
SEPTEMBER 20, 1996

CONVENTION BETWEEN
THE UNITED STATES OF AMERICA
AND ————
FOR THE AVOIDANCE OF DOUBLE TAXATION AND THE
PREVENTION OF FISCAL EVASION
WITH RESPECT TO TAXES ON INCOME

The United States of America and—, desiring to conclude a Convention for the avoidance of double taxation and the prevention of fiscal evasion with respect to taxes on income, have agreed as follows:

Article 1
GENERAL SCOPE

1. This Convention shall apply only to persons who are residents of one or both of the Contracting States, except as otherwise provided in the Convention.

2. The Convention shall not restrict in any manner any benefit now or hereafter accorded:

    a) by the laws of either Contracting State; or

    b) by any other agreement between the Contracting States.

3. Notwithstanding the provisions of subparagraph 2(b):

    (a) the provisions of Article 26 (Mutual Agreement Procedure) of this Convention exclusively shall apply to any dispute concerning whether a measure is within the scope of this Convention, and the procedures under this Convention exclusively shall apply to that dispute; and

    (b) unless the competent authorities determine that a taxation measure is not within the scope of this Convention, the nondiscrimination obligations of this Convention exclusively shall apply with respect to that measure, except for such national treatment or most-favored-nation obligations as may apply to trade in goods under the General Agreement on Tariffs and Trade. No national treatment or most-favored-nation obligation under any other agreement shall apply with respect to that measure.

    (c) For the purpose of this paragraph, a "measure" is a law, regulation, rule, procedure, decision, administrative action, or any similar provision or action.

4. Notwithstanding any provision of the Convention except paragraph 5 of this Article, a Contracting State may tax its residents (as determined under Article 4 (Residence)), and by reason of citizenship may tax its citizens, as if the Convention had not come into effect. For this purpose, the term "citizen" shall include a former citizen or long-term resident whose loss of such status had as one of its principal purposes the avoidance of tax (as defined under the laws of the Contracting State of which the person was a

citizen or long-term resident), but only for a period of 10 years following such loss.

5. The provisions of paragraph 4 shall not affect:

a) the benefits conferred by a Contracting State under paragraph 2 of Article 9 (Associated Enterprises), paragraphs 2 and 5 of Article 18 (Pensions, Social Security, Annuities, Alimony, and Child Support), and Articles 23 (Relief From Double Taxation), 24 (Non-Discrimination), and 25 (Mutual Agreement Procedure); and

b) the benefits conferred by a Contracting State under paragraph 6 of Article 18 (Pensions, Social Security, Annuities, Alimony, and Child Support), Articles 19 (Government Service), 20 (Students and Trainees), and 27 (Diplomatic Agents and Consular Officers), upon individuals who are neither citizens of, nor have been admitted for permanent residence in, that State.

Article 2
TAXES COVERED

1. The existing taxes to which this Convention shall apply are:

a) in the United States: the Federal income taxes imposed by the Internal Revenue Code (but excluding social security taxes), and the Federal excise taxes imposed with respect to private foundations.

b)   in   _ _ _ _ _ _ _ _ _   :
_____
_____
_____
_____ .

2. The Convention shall apply also to any identical or substantially similar taxes that are imposed after the date of signature of the Convention in addition to, or in place of, the existing taxes. The competent authorities of the Contracting States shall notify each other of any significant changes that have been made in their respective taxation laws or other laws affecting their obligations under the Convention, and of any official published material concerning the application of the Convention, including explanations, regulations, rulings, or judicial decisions.

Article 3
GENERAL DEFINITIONS

1. For the purposes of this Convention, unless the context otherwise requires:

a) the term "person" includes an individual, an estate, a trust, a partnership, a company, and any other body of persons;

b) the term "company" means any body corporate or any entity that is treated as a body corporate for tax purposes according to the laws of the state in which it is organized;

c) the terms "enterprise of a Contracting State" and "enterprise of the other Contracting State" mean respectively an enterprise carried on by a resident of a Contracting State, and an enterprise carried on by a resident of the other Contracting State; the terms also include an enterprise carried on by a resident of a Contracting State through an entity that is treated as fiscally transparent in that Contracting State;

d) the term "international traffic" means any transport by a ship or aircraft, except when such transport is solely between places in a Contracting State;

e) the term "competent authority" means:

(i) in the United States: the Secretary of the Treasury or his delegate; and

(ii) in _____:
_____;

f) the term "United States" means the United States of America, and includes the states thereof and the District of Columbia; such term also includes the territorial sea thereof and the sea bed and subsoil of the submarine areas adjacent to that territorial sea, over which the United States exercises sovereign rights in accordance with international law; the term, however, does not include Puerto Rico, the Virgin Islands, Guam or any other United States possession or territory;

g) the term _____ means
_____;

h) the term "national" of a Contracting State, means:

(i) any individual possessing the nationality or citizenship of that State; and

(ii) any legal person, partnership or association deriving its status as such from the laws in force in that State;

i) the term "qualified governmental entity" means:

(i) any person or body of persons that constitutes a governing body of a Contracting State, or of a political subdivision or local authority of a Contracting State;

(ii) a person that is wholly owned, directly or indirectly, by a Contracting State or a political subdivision or local authority of a Contracting State, provided (A) it is organized under the laws of the Contracting State, (B) its earnings are credited to its own account with no portion of its income inuring to the benefit of any private person, and (C) its assets vest in the Contracting State, political subdivision or local authority upon dissolution; and

(iii) a pension trust or fund of a person described in subparagraph (i) or (ii) that is constituted and operated exclusively to administer or provide pension benefits described in Article 19;

provided that an entity described in subparagraph (ii) or (iii) does not carry on commercial activities.

2. As regards the application of the Convention at any time by a Contracting State any term not defined therein shall, unless the context otherwise requires, or the competent authorities agree to a common meaning pursuant to the provisions of Article 25 (Mutual Agreement Procedure), have the meaning which it has at that time under the law of that State for the purposes of the taxes to which the Convention applies, any meaning under the applicable tax laws of that State prevailing over a meaning given to the term under other laws of that State

Article 4
RESIDENCE

1. Except as provided in this paragraph, for the purposes of this Convention, the term "resident of a Contracting State" means any person who, under the laws of that State, is liable to tax therein by reason of his domicile, residence, citizenship, place of management, place of incorporation, or any other criterion of a similar nature.

a) The term "resident of a Contracting State" does not include any person who is liable to tax in that State in respect only of income from sources in that State or of profits attributable to a permanent establishment in that State.

b) A legal person organized under the laws of a Contracting State and that is generally exempt from tax in that State and is established and maintained in that State either:

i) exclusively for a religious, charitable, educational, scientific, or other similar purpose; or

ii) to provide pensions or other similar benefits to employees pursuant to a plan

is to be treated for purposes of this paragraph as a resident of that Contracting State.

c) A qualified governmental entity is to be treated as a resident of the Contracting State where it is established.

d) An item of income, profit or gain derived through an entity that is fiscally transparent under the laws of either Contracting State shall be considered to be derived by a resident of a State to the extent that the item is treated for purposes of the taxation law of such Contracting State as the income, profit or gain of a resident.

2. Where by reason of the provisions of paragraph 1, an individual is a resident of both Contracting States, then his status shall be determined as follows:

a) he shall be deemed to be a resident of the State in which he has a permanent home available to him; if he has a permanent home available to him in both States, he shall be deemed to be a resident of the State with which his personal and economic relations are closer (center of vital interests);

b) if the State in which he has his center of vital interests cannot be determined, or if he does not have a permanent home available to him in either State, he shall be deemed to be a resident of the State in which he has an habitual abode;

c) if he has an habitual abode in both States or in neither of them, he shall be deemed to be a resident of the State of which he is a national;

d) if he is a national of both States or of neither of them, the competent authorities of the Contracting States shall endeavor to settle the question by mutual agreement.

3. Where by reason of the provisions of paragraph 1 a company is a resident of both Contracting States, then if it is created under the laws of one of the Contracting States or a political subdivision thereof, it shall be deemed to be a resident of that State.

4. Where by reason of the provisions of paragraph 1 a person other than an individual or a company is a resident of both Contracting States, the competent authorities of the Contracting States shall endeavor to settle the question by mutual agreement and determine the mode of application of the Convention to such person.

Article 5
PERMANENT ESTABLISHMENT

1. For the purposes of this Convention, the term "permanent establishment" means a fixed place of business through which the business of an enterprise is wholly or partly carried on.

2. The term "permanent establishment" includes especially:

a) a place of management;

b) a branch;

c) an office;

d) a factory;

e) a workshop; and

f) a mine, an oil or gas well, a quarry, or any other place of extraction of natural resources.

3.   A building site or construction or installation project, or an installation or drilling rig or ship used for the exploration of natural resources, constitutes a permanent establishment only if it lasts or the activity continues for more than twelve months.

4. Notwithstanding the preceding provisions of this Article, the term "permanent establishment" shall be deemed not to include:

a) the use of facilities solely for the purpose of storage, display or delivery of goods or merchandise belonging to the enterprise;

b) the maintenance of a stock of goods or merchandise belonging to the enterprise solely for the purpose of storage, display or delivery;

c) the maintenance of a stock of goods or merchandise belonging to the enterprise solely for the purpose of processing by another enterprise;

d) the maintenance of a fixed place of business solely for the purpose of purchasing goods or merchandise, or of collecting information, for the enterprise;

e) the maintenance of a fixed place of business solely for the purpose of carrying

on, for the enterprise, any other activity of a preparatory or auxiliary character;

f) the maintenance of a fixed place of business solely for any combination of the activities mentioned in subparagraphs a) through e).

5.   Notwithstanding the provisions of paragraphs 1 and 2, where a person—other than an agent of an independent status to whom paragraph 6 applies—is acting on behalf of an enterprise and has and habitually exercises in a Contracting State an authority to conclude contracts that are binding on the enterprise, that enterprise shall be deemed to have a permanent establishment in that State in respect of any activities that the person undertakes for the enterprise, unless the activities of such person are limited to those mentioned in paragraph 4 that, if exercised through a fixed place of business, would not make this fixed place of business a permanent establishment under the provisions of that paragraph.

6. An enterprise shall not be deemed to have a permanent establishment in a Contracting State merely because it carries on business in that State through a broker, general commission agent, or any other agent of an independent status, provided that such persons are acting in the ordinary course of their business as independent agents.

7. The fact that a company that is a resident of a Contracting State controls or is controlled by a company that is a resident of the other Contracting State, or that carries on business in that other State (whether through a permanent establishment or otherwise), shall not constitute either company a permanent establishment of the other.

Article 6
INCOME FROM REAL PROPERTY (IMMOVABLE PROPERTY)

1. Income derived by a resident of a Contracting State from real property (immovable property), including income from agriculture or forestry, situated in the other Contracting State may be taxed in that other State.

2. The term "real property (immovable property)" shall have the meaning which it has under the law of the Contracting State in which the property in question is situated.

3. The provisions of paragraph 1 shall apply to income derived from the direct use, letting, or use in any other form of real property.

4. The provisions of paragraphs 1 and 3 shall also apply to the income from real property of an enterprise and to income from real property used for the performance of independent personal services.

5. A resident of a Contracting State who is liable to tax in the other Contracting State on income from real property situated in the other Contracting State may elect for any taxable year to compute the tax on such income on a net basis as if such income were business profits attributable to a permanent establishment in such other State. Any such election shall be binding for the taxable year of the election and all subsequent taxable years unless the competent authority of the Contracting State in which the property is situated agrees to terminate the election.

Article 7
BUSINESS PROFITS

1. The business profits of an enterprise of a Contracting State shall be taxable only in that State unless the enterprise carries on business in the other Contracting State through a permanent establishment situated therein. If the enterprise carries on business as aforesaid, the business profits of the enterprise may be taxed in the other State but only so much of them as are attributable to that permanent establishment.

2. Subject to the provisions of paragraph 3, where an enterprise of a Contracting State carries on business in the other Contracting State through a permanent establishment situated therein, there shall in each Contracting State be attributed to that permanent establishment the business profits that it might be expected to make if it were a distinct and independent enterprise engaged in the same or similar activities under the same or similar conditions. For this purpose, the business profits to be attributed to the permanent establishment shall include only the profits derived from the assets or activities of the permanent establishment.

3. In determining the business profits of a permanent establishment, there shall be allowed as deductions expenses that are incurred for the purposes of the permanent establishment, including a reasonable allocation of executive and general administrative expenses, research and development expenses, interest, and other expenses incurred for the purposes of the enterprise as a whole (or the part thereof which includes the permanent establishment), whether incurred in the State in which the permanent establishment is situated or elsewhere.

4. No business profits shall be attributed to a permanent establishment by reason of the mere purchase by that permanent establishment of goods or merchandise for the enterprise.

5. For the purposes of the preceding paragraphs, the profits to be attributed to the permanent establishment shall be determined by the same method of accounting year by year unless there is good and sufficient reason to the contrary.

6. Where business profits include items of income that are dealt with separately in other Articles of the Convention, then the provisions of

139

those Articles shall not be affected by the provisions of this Article.

7. For the purposes of the Convention, the term "business profits" means income from any trade or business, including income derived by an enterprise from the performance of personal services, and from the rental of tangible personal property.

8. In applying paragraphs 1 and 2 of Article 7 (Business Profits), paragraph 6 of Article 10 (Dividends), paragraph 3 of Article 11 (Interest), paragraph 3 of Article 12 (Royalties), paragraph 3 of Article 13 (Gains), Article 14 (Independent Personal Services) and paragraph 2 of Article 21 (Other Income), any income or gain attributable to a permanent establishment or fixed base during its existence is taxable in the Contracting State where such permanent establishment or fixed base is situated even if the payments are deferred until such permanent establishment or fixed base has ceased to exist.

Article 8
SHIPPING AND AIR TRANSPORT

1. Profits of an enterprise of a Contracting State from the operation of ships or aircraft in international traffic shall be taxable only in that State.

2. For the purposes of this Article, profits from the operation of ships or aircraft include profits derived from the rental of ships or aircraft on a full (time or voyage) basis. They also include profits from the rental of ships or aircraft on a bareboat basis if such ships or aircraft are operated in international traffic by the lessee, or if the rental income is incidental to profits from the operation of ships or aircraft in international traffic. Profits derived by an enterprise from the inland transport of property or passengers within either Contracting State, shall be treated as profits from the operation of ships or aircraft in international traffic if such transport is undertaken as part of international traffic.

3. Profits of an enterprise of a Contracting State from the use, maintenance, or rental of containers (including trailers, barges, and related equipment for the transport of containers) used in international traffic shall be taxable only in that State.

4. The provisions of paragraphs 1 and 3 shall also apply to profits from participation in a pool, a joint business, or an international operating agency.

Article 9
ASSOCIATED ENTERPRISES

1. Where:

a) an enterprise of a Contracting State participates directly or indirectly in the management, control or capital of an enterprise of the other Contracting State; or

b) the same persons participate directly or indirectly in the management, control, or capital of an enterprise of a Contracting State and an enterprise of the other Contracting State,

and in either case conditions are made or imposed between the two enterprises in their commercial or financial relations that differ from those that would be made between independent enterprises, then, any profits that, but for those conditions, would have accrued to one of the enterprises, but by reason of those conditions have not so accrued, may be included in the profits of that enterprise and taxed accordingly.

2. Where a Contracting State includes in the profits of an enterprise of that State, and taxes accordingly, profits on which an enterprise of the other Contracting State has been charged to tax in that other State, and the other Contracting State agrees that the profits so included are profits that would have accrued to the enterprise of the first-mentioned State if the conditions made between the two enterprises had been those that

would have been made between independent enterprises, then that other State shall make an appropriate adjustment to the amount of the tax charged therein on those profits. In determining such adjustment, due regard shall be paid to the other provisions of this Convention and the competent authorities of the Contracting States shall if necessary consult each other.

Article 10
DIVIDENDS

1. Dividends paid by a resident of a Contracting State to a resident of the other Contracting State may be taxed in that other State.

2. However, such dividends may also be taxed in the Contracting State of which the payor is a resident and according to the laws of that State, but if the dividends are beneficially owned by a resident of the other Contracting State, except as otherwise provided, the tax so charged shall not exceed:

a) 5 percent of the gross amount of the dividends if the beneficial owner is a company that owns directly at least 10 percent of the voting stock of the company paying the dividends;

b) 15 percent of the gross amount of the dividends in all other cases.

This paragraph shall not affect the taxation of the company in respect of the profits out of which the dividends are paid.

3. Subparagraph a) of paragraph 2 shall not apply in the case of dividends paid by a United States person that is a Regulated Investment Company or a Real Estate Investment Trust (REIT). In the case of a United States person that is a REIT, subparagraph b) of paragraph 2 also shall not apply, unless the dividend is beneficially owned by an individual holding a less than 10-percent interest in the REIT.

4. Notwithstanding paragraph 2, dividends may not be taxed in the Contracting State of which the payor is a resident if the beneficial owner of the dividends is a resident of the other Contracting State that is a qualified governmental entity that does not control the payor of the dividend.

5. For purposes of the Convention, the term "dividends" means income from shares or other rights, not being debt-claims, participating in profits, as well as income that is subjected to the same taxation treatment as income from shares under the laws of the State of which the payor is a resident.

6. The provisions of paragraphs 1 and 2 shall not apply if the beneficial owner of the dividends, being a resident of a Contracting State, carries on business in the other Contracting State, of which the payor is a resident, through a permanent establishment situated therein, or performs in that other State independent personal services from a fixed base situated therein, and the dividends are attributable to such permanent establishment or fixed base. In such case the provisions of Article 7 (Business Profits) or Article 14 (Independent Personal Services), as the case may be, shall apply.

7. A Contracting State may not impose any tax on dividends paid by a resident of the other State, except insofar as the dividends are paid to a resident of the first-mentioned State or the dividends are attributable to a permanent establishment or a fixed base situated in that State, nor may it impose tax on a corporation's undistributed profits, except as provided in paragraph 8, even if the dividends paid or the undistributed profits consist wholly or partly of profits or income arising in that State.

8. A corporation that is a resident of one of the States and that has a permanent establishment in the other State or that is subject to tax in the other State on a net basis on its income that may be taxed in the other State under Article 6

(Income from Real Property (Immoveable Property)) or under paragraph 1 of Article 13 (Gains) may be subject in that other State to a tax in addition to the tax allowable under the other provisions of this Convention. Such tax, however, may be imposed on only the portion of the business profits of the corporation attributable to the permanent establishment and the portion of the income referred to in the preceding sentence that is subject to tax under Article 6 (Income from Real Property (Immoveable Property)) or under paragraph 1 of Article 13 (Gains) that, in the case of the United States, represents the dividend equivalent amount of such profits or income and, in the case of _____, is an amount that is analogous to the dividend equivalent amount.

9. The tax referred to in paragraph 8 may not be imposed at a rate in excess of the rate specified in paragraph 2 a).

Article 11
INTEREST

1. Interest arising in a Contracting State and beneficially owned by a resident of the other Contracting State may be taxed only in that other State.

2. The term "interest" as used in this Convention means income from debt-claims of every kind, whether or not secured by mortgage, and whether or not carrying a right to participate in the debtor's profits, and in particular, income from government securities and income from bonds or debentures, including premiums or prizes attaching to such securities, bonds or debentures, and all other income that is subjected to the same taxation treatment as income from money lent by the taxation law of the Contracting State in which the income arises. Income dealt with in Article 10 (Dividends) and penalty charges for late payment shall not be regarded as interest for the purposes of this Convention.

3. The provisions of paragraph 1 shall not apply if the beneficial owner of the interest, being a resident of a Contracting State, carries on business in the other Contracting State, in which the interest arises, through a permanent establishment situated therein, or performs in that other State independent personal services from a fixed base situated therein, and the interest is attributable to such permanent establishment or fixed base. In such case the provisions of Article 7 (Business Profits) or Article 14 (Independent Personal Services), as the case may be, shall apply.

4. Where, by reason of a special relationship between the payer and the beneficial owner or between both of them and some other person, the amount of the interest, having regard to the debt-claim for which it is paid, exceeds the amount which would have been agreed upon by the payer and the beneficial owner in the absence of such relationship, the provisions of this Article shall apply only to the last-mentioned amount. In such case the excess part of the payments shall remain taxable according to the laws of each State, due regard being had to the other provisions of this Convention.

5. Notwithstanding the provisions of paragraph 1:

a) interest paid by a resident of a Contracting State and that is determined with reference to receipts, sales, income, profits or other cash flow of the debtor or a related person, to any change in the value of any property of the debtor or a related person or to any dividend, partnership distribution or similar payment made by the debtor to a related person, and paid to a resident of the other State also may be taxed in the Contracting State in which it arises, and according to the laws of that State, but if the beneficial owner is a resident of the other Contracting State, the gross amount of the interest may be taxed at a rate not exceeding the rate prescribed in subparagraph b) of paragraph 2 of Article 10 (Dividends); and

b) Interest that is an excess inclusion with respect to a residual interest in a real estate mortgage investment conduit may be taxed by each State in accordance with its domestic law.

Article 12
ROYALTIES

1. Royalties arising in a Contracting State and beneficially owned by a resident of the other Contracting State may be taxed only in that other State.

2. The term "royalties" as used in this Convention means:

(a) any consideration for the use of, or the right to use, any copyright of literary, artistic, scientific or other work (including computer software, cinematographic films, audio or video tapes or disks, and other means of image or sound reproduction), any patent, trademark, design or model, plan, secret formula or process, or other like right or property, or for information concerning industrial, commercial, or scientific experience; and

(b) gain derived from the alienation of any property described in subparagraph (a), provided that such gain is contingent on the productivity, use, or disposition of the property.

3. The provisions of paragraph 1 shall not apply if the beneficial owner of the royalties, being a resident of a Contracting State, carries on business in the other Contracting State through a permanent establishment situated therein, or performs in that other State independent personal services from a fixed base situated therein, and the royalties are attributable to such permanent establishment or fixed base. In such case the provisions of Article 7 (Business Profits) or Article 14 (Independent Personal Services), as the case may be, shall apply.

4. Where, by reason of a special relationship between the payer and the beneficial owner or between both of them and some other person, the amount of the royalties, having regard to the use, right, or information for which they are paid, exceeds the amount which would have been agreed upon by the payer and the beneficial owner in the absence of such relationship, the provisions of this Article shall apply only to the last-mentioned amount. In such case the excess part of the payments shall remain taxable according to the laws of each Contracting State, due regard being had to the other provisions of the Convention.

Article 13
GAINS

1. Gains derived by a resident of a Contracting State that are attributable to the alienation of real property situated in the other Contracting State may be taxed in that other State.

2. For the purposes of this Convention the term "real property situated in the other Contracting State" shall include:

a) real property referred to in Article 6 (Income from Real Property (Immovable Property));

b) a United States real property interest; and

c) an equivalent interest in real property situated in _____.

3. Gains from the alienation of personal property that are attributable to a permanent establishment that an enterprise of a Contracting State has in the other Contracting State, or that are attributable to a fixed base that is available to a resident of a Contracting State in the other Contracting State for the purpose of performing independent personal services, and gains from the alienation of such a permanent establishment

143

(alone or with the whole enterprise) or of such a fixed base, may be taxed in that other State.

4. Gains derived by an enterprise of a Contracting State from the alienation of ships, aircraft, or containers operated or used in international traffic or personal property pertaining to the operation or use of such ships, aircraft, or containers shall be taxable only in that State.

5. Gains from the alienation of any property other than property referred to in paragraphs 1 through 4 shall be taxable only in the Contracting State of which the alienator is a resident.

Article 14
INDEPENDENT PERSONAL SERVICES

1. Income derived by an individual who is a resident of a Contracting State in respect of the performance of personal services of an independent character shall be taxable only in that State, unless the individual has a fixed base regularly available to him in the other Contracting State for the purpose of performing his activities. If he has such a fixed base, the income attributable to the fixed base that is derived in respect of services performed in that other State also may be taxed by that other State.

2. For purposes of paragraph 1, the income that is taxable in the other Contracting State shall be determined under the principles of paragraph 3 of Article 7.

Article 15
DEPENDENT PERSONAL SERVICES

1. Subject to the provisions of Articles 16 (Directors' Fees), 18 (Pensions, Social Security, Annuities, Alimony, and Child Support) and 19 (Government Service), salaries, wages, and other remuneration derived by a resident of a Contracting State in respect of an employment shall be taxable only in that State unless the employment is exercised in the other Contracting State. If the employment is so exercised, such

remuneration as is derived therefrom may be taxed in that other State.

2. Notwithstanding the provisions of paragraph 1, remuneration derived by a resident of a Contracting State in respect of an employment exercised in the other Contracting State shall be taxable only in the first-mentioned State if:

a) the recipient is present in the other State for a period or periods not exceeding in the aggregate 183 days in any twelve month period commencing or ending in the taxable year concerned;

b) the remuneration is paid by, or on behalf of, an employer who is not a resident of the other State; and

c) the remuneration is not borne by a permanent establishment or a fixed base which the employer has in the other State.

3. Notwithstanding the preceding provisions of this Article, remuneration described in paragraph 1 that is derived by a resident of a Contracting State in respect of an employment as a member of the regular complement of a ship or aircraft operated in international traffic shall be taxable only in that State.

Article 16
DIRECTORS' FEES

Directors' fees and other compensation derived by a resident of a Contracting State for services rendered in the other Contracting State in his capacity as a member of the board of directors of a company that is a resident of the other Contracting State may be taxed in that other Contracting State.

Article 17
ARTISTES AND SPORTSMEN

1. Income derived by a resident of a Contracting State as an entertainer, such as a theater, motion picture, radio, or television artiste, or a musician, or as a sportsman, from his personal activities as such exercised in the other Contracting State, which income would be exempt from tax in that other Contracting State under the provisions of Articles 14 (Independent Personal Services) and 15 (Dependent Personal Services) may be taxed in that other State, except where the amount of the gross receipts derived by such entertainer or sportsman, including expenses reimbursed to him or borne on his behalf, from such activities does not exceed twenty thousand United States dollars ($20,000) or its equivalent in _____ for the taxable year concerned.

2. Where income in respect of activities exercised by an entertainer or a sportsman in his capacity as such accrues not to the entertainer or sportsman himself but to another person, that income, notwithstanding the provisions of Articles 7 (Business Profits) and 14 (Independent Personal Services), may be taxed in the Contracting State in which the activities of the entertainer or sportsman are exercised, unless it is established that neither the entertainer or sportsman nor persons related thereto participate directly or indirectly in the profits of that other person in any manner, including the receipt of deferred remuneration, bonuses, fees, dividends, partnership distributions, or other distributions.

Article 18
PENSIONS, SOCIAL SECURITY, ANNUITIES, ALIMONY, AND CHILD SUPPORT

1. Subject to the provisions of Article 19 (Government Service), pension distributions and other similar remuneration beneficially owned by a resident of a Contracting State, whether paid periodically or as a single sum, shall be taxable only in that State, but only to the extent not included in taxable income in the other Contracting State prior to the distribution.

2. Notwithstanding the provisions of paragraph 1, payments made by a Contracting State under provisions of the social security or similar legislation of that State to a resident of the other Contracting State or to a citizen of the United States shall be taxable only in the first-mentioned State.

3. Annuities derived and beneficially owned by an individual resident of a Contracting State shall be taxable only in that State. The term "annuities" as used in this paragraph means a stated sum paid periodically at stated times during a specified number of years, under an obligation to make the payments in return for adequate and full consideration (other than services rendered).

4. Alimony paid by a resident of a Contracting State, and deductible therein, to a resident of the other Contracting State shall be taxable only in that other State. The term "alimony" as used in this paragraph means periodic payments made pursuant to a written separation agreement or a decree of divorce, separate maintenance, or compulsory support, which payments are taxable to the recipient under the laws of the State of which he is a resident.

5. Periodic payments, not dealt with in paragraph 4, for the support of a child made pursuant to a written separation agreement or a decree of divorce, separate maintenance, or compulsory support, paid by a resident of a Contracting State to a resident of the other Contracting State, shall be exempt from tax in both Contracting States.

6. For purposes of this Convention, where an individual who is a participant in a pension plan that is established and recognized under the legislation of one of the Contracting States performs personal services in the other Contracting State:

a) Contributions paid by or on behalf of the individual to the plan during the period that he performs such services in the other State shall be deductible (or excludible) in computing his taxable income in that State. Any benefits accrued under the plan or payments made to the plan by or on behalf of his employer during that period shall not be treated as part of the employee's taxable income and shall be allowed as a deduction in computing the profits of his employer in that other State.

b) Income earned but not distributed by the plan shall not be taxable in the other State until such time and to the extent that a distribution is made from the plan.

c) Distributions from the plan to the individual shall not be subject to taxation in the other Contracting State if the individual contributes such amounts to a similar plan established in the other State within a time period and in accordance with any other requirements imposed under the laws of the other State.

d) The provisions of this paragraph shall not apply unless:

(i) contributions by or on behalf of the individual to the plan (or to another similar plan for which this plan was substituted) were made before he arrived in the other State; and

(ii) the competent authority of the other State has agreed that the pension plan generally corresponds to a pension plan recognized for tax purposes by that State.

The benefits granted under this paragraph shall not exceed the benefits that would be allowed by the other State to its residents for contributions to, or benefits otherwise accrued under a pension plan recognized for tax purposes by that State.

Article 19
GOVERNMENT SERVICE

1. Notwithstanding the provisions of Articles 14 (Independent Personal Services), 15 (Dependent Personal Services), 16 (Director's Fees) and 17 (Artistes and Sportsmen):

a) Salaries, wages and other remuneration, other than a pension, paid from the public funds of a Contracting State or a political subdivision or a local authority thereof to an individual in respect of services rendered to that State or subdivision or authority in the discharge of functions of a governmental nature shall, subject to the provisions of subparagraph (b), be taxable only in that State;

b) such remuneration, however, shall be taxable only in the other Contracting State if the services are rendered in that State and the individual is a resident of that State who:

i) is a national of that State; or

ii) did not become a resident of that State solely for the purpose of rendering the services.

2. Notwithstanding the provisions of paragraph 1 of Article 18 (Pensions, Social Security, Annuities, Alimony, and Child Support):

a) any pension paid from the public funds of a Contracting State or a political subdivision or a local authority thereof to an individual in respect of services rendered to that State or subdivision or authority in the discharge of functions of a governmental nature shall, subject to the provisions of subparagraph (b), be taxable only in that State;

b) such pension, however, shall be taxable only in the other Contracting State if the individual is a resident of, and a national of, that State.

Article 20
STUDENTS AND TRAINEES

Payments received by a student, apprentice, or business trainee who is, or was immediately before visiting a Contracting State, a resident of the other Contracting State, and who is present in the first-mentioned State for the purpose of his full-time education at an accredited educational institution, or for his full-time training, shall not be taxed in that State, provided that such payments arise outside that State, and are for the purpose of his maintenance, education or training. The exemption from tax provided by this Article shall apply to an apprentice or business trainee only for a period of time not exceeding one year from the date he first arrives in the first-mentioned Contracting State for the purpose of his training.

Article 21
OTHER INCOME

1. Items of income beneficially owned by a resident of a Contracting State, wherever arising, not dealt with in the foregoing Articles of this Convention shall be taxable only in that State.

2. The provisions of paragraph 1 shall not apply to income, other than income from real property as defined in paragraph 2 of Article 6 (Income from Real Property (Immovable Property)), if the beneficial owner of the income, being a resident of a Contracting State, carries on business in the other Contracting State through a permanent establishment situated therein, or performs in that other State independent personal services from a fixed base situated therein, and the income is attributable to such permanent establishment or fixed base. In such case the provisions of Article 7 (Business Profits) or Article 14 (Independent Personal Services), as the case may be, shall apply.

Article 22
LIMITATION ON BENEFITS

1. A resident of a Contracting State shall be entitled to benefits otherwise accorded to residents of a Contracting State by this Convention only to the extent provided in this Article.

2. A resident of a Contracting State shall be entitled to all the benefits of this Convention if the resident is:

a) an individual;

b) a qualified governmental entity;

c) a company, if

i) all the shares in the class or classes of shares representing more than 50 percent of the voting power and value of the company are regularly traded on a recognized stock exchange, or

ii) at least 50 percent of each class of shares in the company is owned directly or indirectly by companies entitled to benefits under clause i), provided that in the case of indirect ownership, each intermediate owner is a person entitled to benefits of the Convention under this paragraph;

d) described in subparagraph 1(b)(i) of Article 4 (Residence);

e) described in subparagraph 1(b)(ii) of Article 4 (Residence), provided that more than 50 percent of the person's beneficiaries, members or participants are individuals resident in either Contracting State; or

f) a person other than an individual, if:

i) On at least half the days of the taxable year persons described in subparagraphs a), b), c), d) or e) own, directly or indirectly (through a chain of ownership in which each person is entitled to benefits of the Convention under this paragraph), at least 50 percent of each class of shares or other beneficial interests in the person, and

ii) less than 50 percent of the person's gross income for the taxable year is paid or accrued, directly or indirectly, to persons who are not residents of either Contracting State (unless the payment is attributable to a permanent establishment situated in either State), in the form of payments that are deductible for income tax purposes in the person's State of residence.

3. a) A resident of a Contracting State not otherwise entitled to benefits shall be entitled to the benefits of this Convention with respect to an item of income derived from the other State, if:

i) the resident is engaged in the active conduct of a trade or business in the first-mentioned State,

ii) the income is connected with or incidental to the trade or business, and

iii) the trade or business is substantial in relation to the activity in the other State generating the income.

b) For purposes of this paragraph, the business of making or managing investments will not be considered an active trade or business unless the activity is banking, insurance or securities activity conducted by a bank, insurance company or registered securities dealer.

c) Whether a trade or business is substantial for purposes of this paragraph will be determined based on all the facts and circumstances. In any case, however, a trade or business will be deemed substantial if, for the preceding taxable year, or for the average of the three preceding taxable years, the asset value, the gross income, and the payroll expense that are related to the trade or business in the first-mentioned State equal at least 7.5 percent of the resident's (and any related parties') proportionate share of the asset value, gross income and payroll expense, respectively, that are related to the activity that generated the income in the other State, and the average of the three ratios exceeds 10 percent.

d) Income is derived in connection with a trade or business if the activity in the other State generating the income is a line of business that forms a part of or is complementary to the trade or business. Income is incidental to a trade or business if it facilitates the conduct of the trade or business in the other State.

4. A resident of a Contracting State not otherwise entitled to benefits may be granted benefits of the Convention if the competent authority of the State from which benefits are claimed so determines.

5. For purposes of this Article the term "recognized stock exchange" means:

a) the NASDAQ System owned by the National Association of Securities Dealers, Inc. and any stock exchange registered with the U.S. Securities and Exchange Commission as a national securities exchange under the U.S. Securities Exchange Act of 1934; and

b) [stock exchanges of the other Contracting State].

Article 23
RELIEF FROM DOUBLE TAXATION

1. In accordance with the provisions and subject to the limitations of the law of the United States (as it may be amended from time to time without changing the general principle hereof), the United States shall allow to a resident or citizen of the United States as a credit against the United States tax on income

> a) the income tax paid or accrued to _____ by or on behalf of such citizen or resident; and

> b) in the case of a United States company owning at least 10 percent of the voting stock of a company that is a resident of _____ and from which the United States company receives dividends, the income tax paid or accrued to _____ by or on behalf of the payor with respect to the profits out of which the dividends are paid.

For the purposes of this paragraph, the taxes referred to in paragraphs 1(b) and 2 of Article 2 (Taxes Covered) shall be considered income taxes.

2. In accordance with the provisions and subject to the limitations of the law of _____ (as it may be amended from time to time without changing the general principle hereof), _____ shall allow to a resident or citizen of_____ as a credit against the _____ tax on income

> a) the income tax paid or accrued to the United States by or on behalf of such resident of citizen; and

> b) in the case of a _____ company owning at least 10 percent of the voting stock of a company that is a resident of the United States and from which the _____ company receives dividends, the income tax paid or accrued to the United States by or on behalf of the payor with respect to the profits out of which the dividends are paid.

For the purposes of this paragraph, the taxes referred to in paragraphs 1(a) and 2 of Article 2 (Taxes Covered) shall be considered income taxes.

3. Where a United States citizen is a resident of_____:

> a) with respect to items of income that under the provisions of this Convention are exempt from United States tax or that are subject to a reduced rate of United States tax when derived by a resident of _____ who is not a United States citizen, _____ shall allow as a credit against _____ tax, only the tax paid, if any, that the United States may impose under the provisions of this Convention, other than taxes that may be imposed solely by reason of citizenship under the saving clause of paragraph 4 of Article 1 (General Scope);

> b) for purposes of computing United States tax on those items of income referred to in subparagraph (a), the United States shall allow as a credit against United States tax the income tax paid to _____ after the credit referred to in subparagraph (a); the credit so allowed shall not reduce the portion of the United States tax that is creditable against the _____ tax in accordance with subparagraph (a); and

> c) for the exclusive purpose of relieving double taxation in the United States under subparagraph (b), items of income referred to in subparagraph (a) shall be deemed to arise in _____ to the extent necessary to avoid double taxation of such income under subparagraph (b).

Article 24
NON-DISCRIMINATION

1. Nationals of a Contracting State shall not be subjected in the other Contracting State to any taxation or any requirement connected therewith that is more burdensome than the taxation and connected requirements to which nationals of that other State in the same circumstances, particularly with respect to taxation on worldwide income, are or may be subjected. This provision shall also apply to persons who are not residents of one or both of the Contracting States.

2. The taxation on a permanent establishment or fixed base that a resident or enterprise of a Contracting State has in the other Contracting State shall not be less favorably levied in that other State than the taxation levied on enterprises or residents of that other State carrying on the same activities. The provisions of this paragraph shall not be construed as obliging a Contracting State to grant to residents of the other Contracting State any personal allowances, reliefs, and reductions for taxation purposes on account of civil status or family responsibilities that it grants to its own residents.

3. Except where the provisions of paragraph 1 of Article 9 (Associated Enterprises), paragraph 4 of Article 11 (Interest), or paragraph 4 of Article 12 (Royalties) apply, interest, royalties, and other disbursements paid by a resident of a Contracting State to a resident of the other Contracting State shall, for the purpose of determining the taxable profits of the first-mentioned resident, be deductible under the same conditions as if they had been paid to a resident of the first-mentioned State. Similarly, any debts of a resident of a Contracting State to a resident of the other Contracting State shall, for the purpose of determining the taxable capital of the first-mentioned resident, be deductible under the same conditions as if they had been contracted to a resident of the first-mentioned State.

4. Enterprises of a Contracting State, the capital of which is wholly or partly owned or controlled, directly or indirectly, by one or more residents of the other Contracting State, shall not be subjected in the first-mentioned State to any taxation or any requirement connected therewith that is more burdensome than the taxation and connected requirements to which other similar enterprises of the first-mentioned State are or may be subjected.

5. Nothing in this Article shall be construed as preventing either Contracting State from imposing a tax as described in paragraph 8 of Article 10 (Dividends).

6. The provisions of this Article shall, notwithstanding the provisions of Article 2 (Taxes Covered), apply to taxes of every kind and description imposed by a Contracting State or a political subdivision or local authority thereof.

Article 25
MUTUAL AGREEMENT PROCEDURE

1. Where a person considers that the actions of one or both of the Contracting States result or will result for him in taxation not in accordance with the provisions of this Convention, he may, irrespective of the remedies provided by the domestic law of those States, and the time limits prescribed in such laws for presenting claims for refund, present his case to the competent authority of either Contracting State.

2. The competent authority shall endeavor, if the objection appears to it to be justified and if it is not itself able to arrive at a satisfactory solution, to resolve the case by mutual agreement with the competent authority of the other Contracting State, with a view to the avoidance of taxation which is not in accordance with the Convention. Any agreement reached shall be implemented notwithstanding any time limits or other procedural limitations in the domestic law of the Contracting States. Assessment and collection procedures shall be suspended during the pendency of any mutual agreement proceeding.

150

3. The competent authorities of the Contracting States shall endeavor to resolve by mutual agreement any difficulties or doubts arising as to the interpretation or application of the Convention. In particular the competent authorities of the Contracting States may agree:

a) to the same attribution of income, deductions, credits, or allowances of an enterprise of a Contracting State to its permanent establishment situated in the other Contracting State;

b) to the same allocation of income, deductions, credits, or allowances between persons;

c) to the same characterization of particular items of income, including the same characterization of income that is assimilated to income from shares by the taxation law of one of the Contracting States and that is treated as a different class of income in the other State;

d) to the same characterization of persons;

e) to the same application of source rules with respect to particular items of income;

f) to a common meaning of a term;

g) to advance pricing arrangements; and

h) to the application of the provisions of domestic law regarding penalties, fines, and interest in a manner consistent with the purposes of the Convention.

They may also consult together for the elimination of double taxation in cases not provided for in the Convention.

4. The competent authorities also may agree to increases in any specific dollar amounts referred to in the Convention to reflect economic or monetary developments.

5. The competent authorities of the Contracting States may communicate with each other directly for the purpose of reaching an agreement in the sense of the preceding paragraphs.

Article 26
EXCHANGE OF INFORMATION AND
ADMINISTRATIVE ASSISTANCE

1. The competent authorities of the Contracting States shall exchange such information as is relevant for carrying out the provisions of this Convention or of the domestic laws of the Contracting States concerning taxes covered by the Convention insofar as the taxation thereunder is not contrary to the Convention, including information relating to the assessment or collection of, the enforcement or prosecution in respect of, or the determination of appeals in relation to, the taxes covered by the Convention. The exchange of information is not restricted by Article 1 (General Scope). Any information received by a Contracting State shall be treated as secret in the same manner as information obtained under the domestic laws of that State and shall be disclosed only to persons or authorities (including courts and administrative bodies) involved in the assessment, collection, or administration of, the enforcement or prosecution in respect of, or the determination of appeals in relation to, the taxes covered by the Convention or the oversight of the above. Such persons or authorities shall use the information only for such purposes. They may disclose the information in public court proceedings or in judicial decisions.

2. In no case shall the provisions of paragraph 1 be construed so as to impose on a Contracting State the obligation:

a) to carry out administrative measures at variance with the laws and administrative practice of that or of the other Contracting State;

b) to supply information that is not obtainable under the laws or in the normal course of the administration of that or of the other Contracting State;

c) to supply information that would disclose any trade, business, industrial, commercial, or professional secret or trade process, or information the disclosure of which would be contrary to public policy (order public).

3. Notwithstanding paragraph 2, the competent authority of the requested State shall have the authority to obtain and provide information held by financial institutions, nominees or persons acting in an agency or fiduciary capacity, or respecting interests in a person, including bearer shares, regardless of any laws or practices of the requested State that might otherwise preclude the obtaining of such information. If information is requested by a Contracting State in accordance with this Article, the other Contracting State shall obtain that information in the same manner and to the same extent as if the tax of the first-mentioned State were the tax of that other State and were being imposed by that other State, notwithstanding that the other State may not, at that time, need such information for purposes of its own tax. If specifically requested by the competent authority of a Contracting State, the competent authority of the other Contracting State shall provide information under this Article in the form of depositions of witnesses and authenticated copies of unedited original documents (including books, papers, statements, records, accounts, and writings), to the same extent such depositions and documents can be obtained under the laws and administrative practices of that other State with respect to its own taxes.

4. Each of the Contracting States shall endeavor to collect on behalf of the other Contracting State such amounts as may be necessary to ensure that relief granted by the Convention from taxation imposed by that other State does not inure to the benefit of persons not entitled thereto. This paragraph shall not impose upon either of the Contracting States the obligation to carry out administrative measures that would be contrary to its sovereignty, security, or public policy.

5. For the purposes of this Article, the Convention shall apply, notwithstanding the provisions of Article 2 (Taxes Covered), to taxes of every kind imposed by a Contracting State.

6. The competent authority of the requested State shall allow representatives of the applicant State to enter the requested State to interview individuals and examine books and records with the consent of the persons subject to examination.

Article 27
DIPLOMATIC AGENTS AND CONSULAR OFFICERS

Nothing in this Convention shall affect the fiscal privileges of diplomatic agents or consular officers under the general rules of international law or under the provisions of special agreements.

Article 28
ENTRY INTO FORCE

1. This Convention shall be subject to ratification in accordance with the applicable procedures of each Contracting State. Each Contracting State shall notify the other as soon as its procedures have been complied with.

2. The Convention shall enter into force on the date of the receipt of the later of such notifications, and its provisions shall have effect:

a) in respect of taxes withheld at source, for amounts paid or credited on or after the first day of the second month next following the date on which the Convention enters into force;

b) in respect of other taxes, for taxable periods beginning on or after the first day of January next following the date on which the Convention enters into force.

Article 29
TERMINATION

1. This Convention shall remain in force until terminated by a Contracting State. Either Contracting State may terminate the Convention by giving notice of termination to the other Contracting State through diplomatic channels. In such event, the Convention shall cease to have effect:

a) in respect of taxes withheld at source, for amounts paid or credited after the expiration of the 6 month period beginning on the date on which notice of termination was given; and

b) in respect of other taxes, for taxable periods beginning on or after the expiration of the 6 month period beginning on the date on which notice of termination was given.

IN WITNESS WHEREOF, the undersigned, being duly authorized thereto by their respective Governments, have signed this Convention.

DONE at _____ in duplicate, in the English and _____ languages, both texts being equally authentic, this __ day of _(month)_ , 19_.

FOR THE GOVERNMENT OF THE FOR THE GOVERNMENT OF UNITED STATES OF AMERICA: _____:

PART II. OTHER INTERNATIONAL DOCUMENTS

A. UNIDROIT Principles of International Commercial Contracts

Source: UNIDROIT—International Institute for the Unification of Private Law (Rome 1994)

Website information:

http://www.unidroit.org/
This website is the homepage for UNIDROIT. It contains the full text of a number of UNIDROIT documents, including the Principles of International Commercial Contracts, with comments, at http://www.unidroit.org/english/principles/pr-main.htms.

Introduction

The International Institute for the Unification of Private Law (UNIDROIT) developed the Principles of International Commercial Contracts (Principles) in order to help create unification in international commercial law and to provide guidance to national and international legislators. As the Preamble to the Principles articulates, "[t]hey may provide a solution to an issue raised when it proves impossible to establish the relevant rule of the applicable law."

The principles, however, are not law unless parties to a contract choose to be bound by them; they are, perhaps, more like the American Law Institute's Restatements of the Law—persuasive, useful in interpreting private international law (such as the U.N. Sales Convention), but not authoritative. Just as the Restatements look to U.S. law as a guide, UNIDROIT, in developing the Principles, drew from international law (the U.N. Sales Convention), as well as various national legal texts (the American UCC and others, including African and European states).[1] By its own terms, the text invites even parties to purely domestic commercial relationships to employ the Principles.

Two of the Principles' more significant additions to the existing body of rules on international transactions are first, that, unlike the U.N. Sales Convention, they contain extensive comments to the substantive provisions; and, second, the Principles are intended to apply to *any* international commercial contract.

The Principles cover most of the issues encountered in international transactional business: contract formation, validity, interpretation, obligations of the parties (in the chapter on "content"), performance and non-performance. Chapter one sets the tone of the Principles, espousing both the principle of "freedom of contract" and the "binding character of contract."

The Preamble provides that the Principles "may be applied when the parties have agreed that their contract be governed by general principles of law, the lex mercatoria or the like." Because the drafters of the text were legal practitioners rather than members of the international business community, and because the drafters drew piecemeal from existing sets of rules, some *law merchant*, some not, it is probably error to consider the Principles as reflective of the *lex mercatoria*.[2] The hope is that, by their completeness and similarity, if not equivalency to binding law such as the U.N. Sales Convention, the *lex mercatoria* may instead come to reflect the Unidroit Principles. It is too soon to predict the impact of the Principles; since there is no universal recognition of the UNIDROIT

---

[1]*See, e.g.*, Michael Joachim Bonell, *The UNIDROIT Principles of International Commercial Contracts: Why? What? How?*, 69 TUL. L. REV. 1121, 1129-30 (1995).

[2]*See* Dr. Maria del Pilar Perales Viscasillas, *Unidroit Principles of International Commercial Contracts: Sphere of Application and General Provisions*, 13 ARIZ. J. INT'L & COMP. L. 381, 398 (Fall 1996). ("The Principles are not usages. . .").

Principles as an accurate or comprehensive guide to international law, the Principles may not often even be applied.[3]

---

[3]Many of those involved in the preparation of the principles were "'innovators', more open to recent developments, even when these developments belonged to a foreign system and were not yet generally accepted." Bonell, *supra* note 1, at 1131.

UNIDROIT Principles of International Commercial Contracts

157

Principles of International Commercial Contracts, 1994 - Unidroit

Preamble - Purpose of the Principles

These Principles set forth general rules for international commercial contracts.

They shall be applied when the parties have agreed that their contract be governed by them.

They may be applied when the parties have agreed that their contracts be governed by general principles of law, the lex mercatoria or the like.

They may provide a solution to an issue raised when it proves impossible to establish the relevant rule of applicable law.

They may be used to interpret or supplement international uniform law instruments.

They may serve as a model for national and international legislators.

Chapter 1 - General Provisions

Article 1.1 - Freedom of Contract

The parties are free to enter into a contract and determine its content.

Article 1.2 - No Form Required

Nothing in these Principles requires a contract to be concluded in or evidenced by writing. It may be proved by any means, including witnesses.

Article 1.3 - Binding Character of Contract

A contract validly entered into is binding upon the parties. It can only be modified or terminated in accordance with its terms or by agreement or as otherwise provided in these Principles.

Article 1.4 - Mandatory Rules

Nothing in these Principles shall restrict the application of mandatory rules, whether of national, international or supranational origin, which are applicable in accordance with the relevant rules of private international law.

Article 1.5 - Exclusion or Modification by the Parties

The parties may exclude the application of these Principles or derogate from or vary the effect of any of their provisions, except as otherwise provided in the Principles.

Article 1.6 - Interpretation and supplementation of the Principles

(1) In the interpretation of these Principles, regard is to be had to their international character and to their purposes including the need to promote uniformity in their application.

(2) Issues within the scope of these Principles but not expressly settled by them are as far as possible to be settled in accordance with their underlying general principles.

Article 1.7 - Good Faith and Fair Dealing

(1) Each party must act in accordance with good faith and fair dealing in international trade.

(2) The parties may not exclude or limit this duty.

Article 1.8 - Usages and Practices

(1) The parties are bound by any usage to which they have agreed and by any practices which they have established between themselves.

(2) The parties are bound by a usage that is widely known to and regularly observed in international trade by parties in the particular trade concerned except where the application of such usage would be unreasonable.

Article 1.9 - Notice

(1) Where notice is required it may be given by any means appropriate to the circumstances.

(2) A notice is effective when it reaches the person to whom it is given.

(3) For the purpose of paragraph (2) a notice "reaches" a person when given to that person orally or delivered at that person's place of business or mailing address.

(4) For the purpose of this article "notice" includes a declaration, demand, request or any other communication of intention.

Article 1.10 - Definitions

In these Principles

- "court" includes an arbitral tribunal;

- where a party has more than one place of business the relevant "place of business" is that which has the closest relationship to the contract and its performance, having regard to the circumstances known to or contemplated by the parties at any time before or at the conclusion of the contract;

- "obligor" refers to the party who is to perform an obligation and "obligee" refers to the party who is entitled to performance of that obligation.

- "writing" means any mode of communication that preserves a record of the information contained therein and is capable of being reproduced in tangible form.

Chapter 2 - Formation

Article 2.1 - Manner of Formation

A contract may be concluded either by the acceptance of an offer or by conduct of the parties that is sufficient to show agreement.

Article 2.2 - Definition of Offer

A proposal for concluding a contract constitutes an offer if it is sufficiently definite and indicates the intention of the offeror to be bound in case of acceptance.

Article 2.3 - Withdrawal of Offer

(1) An offer becomes effective when it reaches the offeree.

(2) An offer, even if it is irrevocable, may be withdrawn if the withdrawal reaches the offeree before or at the same time as the offer.

Article 2.4 - Revocation of Offer

(1) Until a contract is concluded an offer may be revoked if the revocation reaches the offeree before it has dispatched an acceptance.

(2) However, an offer cannot be revoked

> (a) if it indicates, whether by stating a fixed time for acceptance or otherwise, that it is irrevocable; or

> (b) if it was reasonable for the offeree to rely on the offer as being irrevocable and the offeree has acted in reliance of the offer.

Article 2.5 - Rejection of Offer

An offer is terminated when a rejection reaches the offeror.

Article 2.6 - Mode of Acceptance

(1) A statement made by or other conduct of the offeree indicating assent to an offer is an acceptance. Silence or inactivity does not in itself amount to acceptance.

(2) An acceptance of an offer becomes effective when the indication of assent reaches the offeror.

(3) However, if, by virtue of the offer or as a result of practices which the parties have established between themselves or of usage, the offeree may indicate assent by performing an act without notice to the offeror, the acceptance is effective when the act is performed.

Article 2.7 - Time of Acceptance

An offer must be accepted within the time the offeror has fixed or, if no time is fixed, within a reasonable time having regard to the circumstances, including the rapidity of the means of communication employed by the offeror. An oral offer must be accepted immediately unless the circumstances indicate otherwise.

Article 2.8 - Acceptance Within a Fixed Period of Time

(1) A period of time for acceptance fixed by the offeror in a telegram or a letter begins to run from the moment the telegram is handed in for dispatch or from the date shown on the letter or, if no such date is shown, from the date shown on the envelope. A period of time for acceptance fixed by the offeror by means of instantaneous communication begins to run from the moment that offer reaches the offeree.

(2) Official holidays or non-business days occurring during the period for acceptance are included in calculating the period. However, if a notice of acceptance cannot be delivered at the address of the offeror on the last day of the period because that day falls on an official holiday or a non-business day at the place of business of the offeror, the period is extended until the first business day which follows.

Article 2.9 - Late Acceptance. Delay in Transmission

(1) A late acceptance is nevertheless effective as an acceptance if without undue delay the offeror so informs the offeree or gives notice to that effect.

(2) If a letter or other writing containing a late acceptance shows that it has been sent in such circumstances that if its transmission had been normal it would have reached the offeror in due time, the late acceptance is effective as an acceptance, unless without undue delay, the offeror informs the offeree that it considers the offer as having lapsed.

Article 2.10 - Withdrawal of Acceptance

An acceptance may be withdrawn if the withdrawal reaches the offeror before or at the same time as the acceptance would have become effective.

Article 2.11 - Modified Acceptance

(1) A reply to an offer which purports to be an acceptance but contains additions, limitations or other modifications is a rejection of the offer and constitutes a counter-offer.

(2) However, a reply to an offer which purports to be an acceptance but contains additional or different terms which do not materially alter the terms of the offer constitutes an acceptance, unless the offeror without undue delay, objects to the discrepancy. If the offeror does not object, the terms of the contract are the terms of the offer with the modifications contained in the acceptance.

Article 2.12 - Writings in Confirmation

If a writing which is sent within a reasonable time after the conclusion of the contract and which purports to be a confirmation of the contract contains additional or different terms, such terms become part of the contract, unless they materially alter the contract or the recipient, without undue delay, objects to the discrepancy.

Article 2.13 - Conclusion of Contract Dependent on Agreement on Specific Matters or in a Specific Form

Where in the course of negotiations one of the parties insists that the contract is not concluded until there is agreement on specific matters or in a specific form, no contract is concluded before agreement is reached on those matters or in that form

Article 2.14 - Contract with Terms Deliberately Left Open

(1) If the parties intend to conclude a contract, the fact that they intentionally leave a term to be agreed upon in further negotiations or to be

determined by a third person does not prevent a contract from coming into existence.

(2) The existence of the contract is not affected by the fact that subsequently

(a) the parties reach no agreement on the terms; or

(b) the third person does not determine the term, provided that there is an alternative means of rendering the term definite that is reasonable in the circumstances, having regard to the intention of the parties.

Article 2.15 - Negotiations in Bad Faith

(1) A party is free to negotiate and is not liable for failure to reach an agreement.

(2) However, a party who negotiates or breaks off negotiations in bad faith is liable for the losses caused to the other party.

(3) It is bad faith, in particular, for a party to enter into or continue negotiations when intending not to reach an agreement with the other party.

Article 2.16 - Duty of Confidentiality

Where information is given as confidential by one party in the course of negotiations, the other party is under a duty not to disclose that information or to use it improperly for its own purposes, whether or not a contract is subsequently concluded. Where appropriate, the remedy for breach of that duty may include compensation based on the benefit received by the other party.

Article 2.17 - Merger Clause

A contract in writing which contains a clause indicating that the writing completely embodies the terms on which the parties have agreed cannot be contradicted or supplemented by evidence of prior statements or agreements. However, such statements or agreements may be used to interpret the writing.

Article 2.18 - Written Modification Clauses

A contract in writing which contains a clause requiring any modification or termination by agreement to be in writing may not be otherwise modified or terminated. However, a party may be precluded by its conduct from asserting such a clause to the extent that the other party has acted in reliance on that conduct.

Article 2.19 - Contracting Under Standard Terms

(1) Where one party or both parties use standard terms in concluding a contract, the general rules of formation apply, subject to Articles 2.20 - 2.22.

(2) Standard terms are provisions which are prepared in advance for general and repeated use by one party and which are actually used without negotiation with the other party.

Article 2.20 - Surprising Terms

(1) No term contained in standard terms which is of such a character that the other party could not reasonably have expected it, is effective unless it has been expressly accepted by that party.

(2) In determining whether a term is of such a character regard is to be had to its content, language and presentation.

Article 2.21 - Conflict Between Standard Terms and Non-Standard Terms

In case of conflict between a standard term which is not a standard term the latter prevails.

Article 2.22 - Battle of Forms

Where both parties use standard terms and reach agreement except on those terms, a contract is concluded on the basis of the agreed terms and of any standard terms which are common in substance unless one party clearly indicates in advance, or later and without undue delay informs the other party, that it does not intend to be bound by such a contract.

Chapter 3 - Validity

Article 3.1 - Matters Not Covered

These Principles do not deal with invalidity arising from

(a) lack of capacity;

(b) lack of authority;

(c) immorality or illegality.

Article 3.2 - Validity of Mere Agreement

A contract is concluded, modified or terminated by the mere agreement of the parties, without any further requirements.

Article 3.3 - Initial Impossibility

(1) The mere fact that at the time of the conclusion of the contract the performance of the obligation assumed was impossible does not affect the validity of the contract.

(2) The mere fact that at the time of the conclusion of the contract a party was not entitled to dispose of the assets to which the contract relates does not affect the validity of the contract.

Article 3.4 - Definition of Mistake

Mistake is an erroneous assumption relating to facts or to law existing when the contract was concluded.

Article 3.5 - Relevant Mistake

(1) A party may only avoid the contract for mistake if, when the contract was concluded, the mistake was of such importance that a reasonable person in the same situation as the party would not have concluded it at all if the true state of affairs had been known, and

(a) the other party made the same mistake, or caused the mistake, or knew or ought to have known of the mistake and it was contrary to reasonable commercial standards of fair dealing to leave the mistaken party in error; or

(b) the other party had not at the time of avoidance acted in reliance on the contract

(2) However, a party may not avoid the contract if

(a) it was grossly negligent in committing the mistake; or

(b) the mistake relates to a matter in regard to which the risk of mistake was assumed or, having regard to the circumstances, should be borne by the mistaken party.

Article 3.6 - Error in Expression or Transmission

An error occurring in the expression or transmission of a declaration is considered to be a mistake of the person from whom the declaration emanated.

Article 3.7 - Remedies for Non-Performance

A party is not entitled to avoid the contract on the ground of mistake if the circumstances on which that party relies afford, or could have afforded, a remedy for non-performance.

Article 3.8 - Fraud

A party may avoid the contract when it has been led to conclude the contract by the other party's fraudulent representation, including language or practices, or fraudulent non-disclosure of circumstances which, according to reasonable commercial standards of fair dealing, the latter party should have disclosed.

Article 3.9 - Threat

A party may avoid the contract when it has been led to conclude the contract by the other party's unjustified threat which, having regard to the circumstances, is so imminent and serious as to leave the first party no reasonable alternative. In particular, a threat is unjustified if the act or omission with which a party has been threatened is wrongful in itself, or is wrong to use it as a means to obtain the conclusion of the contract.

Article 3.10 - Gross Disparity

(1) A party may avoid the contract or an individual term of it if, at the time of the conclusion of the contract, the contract term unjustifiably gave the other party an excessive

advantage. Regard is to be had, among other factors, to

(a) the fact that the other party has taken unfair advantage of the first party's dependence, economic distress or urgent needs, or of its improvidence, ignorance, inexperience or lack of bargaining skill; and

(b) the nature and purpose of the contract.

(2) Upon the request of the party entitled to avoidance, a court may adapt the contract or term in order to make it accord with reasonable commercial standards of fair dealing.

(3) A court may also adapt the contract or term upon the request of the party receiving notice of avoidance, provided that that party informs the other party of its request promptly after receiving such notice and before the other party has acted in reliance on it. The provisions of Article 3.13(2) apply accordingly.

Article 3.11 - Third Persons

(1) Where fraud, threat, gross disparity or a party's mistake is imputable to, or is known or ought to be known by, a third person for whose acts the other party is responsible, the contract may be avoided under the same conditions as if the behaviour or knowledge had been that of the party itself.

(2) Where fraud, threat or gross disparity is imputable to a third person for whose acts the other party is not responsible, the contract may be avoided if that party knew or ought to have known of the fraud, threat or disparity, or has not at the time of avoidance acted in reliance on the contract.

Article 3.12 - Confirmation

If the party entitled to avoid the contract expressly or impliedly confirms the contract after the period of time for giving notice of avoidance has begun to run, avoidance of contract is excluded.

Article 3.13 - Loss of Right to Avoid

(1) If a party is entitled to avoid the contract for mistake but the other party declares itself willing to perform or performs the contract as it was understood by the party entitled to avoidance, the contract is considered to have been concluded as the latter party understood it. The other party must make such a declaration or render such performance promptly after having been informed of the manner in which the party entitled to avoidance had understood the contract and before that party has acted in reliance on a notice of avoidance.

(2) After such a declaration or performance the right to avoidance is lost and any earlier notice of avoidance is ineffective.

Article 3.14 - Notice of Avoidance

The right of a party to avoid the contract is exercised by notice to the other party.

Article 3.15 - Time Limits

(1) Notice of avoidance shall be given within a reasonable time, having regard to the circumstances, after the avoiding party knew or could not have been unaware of the relevant facts or became capable of acting freely.

(2) Where an individual term of the contract may be avoided by a party under Article 3.10, the period of time for giving notice of avoidance begins to run when that term is asserted by the other party.

Article 3.16 - Partial Avoidance

Where a ground of avoidance affects only individual terms of the contract, the effect of avoidance is limited to those terms unless, having regard to the circumstances, it is unreasonable to uphold the remaining contract.

Article 3.17 - Retroactive Effect of Avoidance

(1) Avoidance takes effect retroactively.

(2) On avoidance either party may claim restitution of whatever is supplied under the contract or the part of it avoided, provided that it concurrently makes restitution of whatever it has received under the contract or the part of it avoided or, if it cannot make restitution in kind, it makes an allowance for what it has received.

165

Article 3.18 - Damages

Irrespective of whether or not the contract has been avoided, the party who knew or ought to have known of the ground for avoidance is liable for damages so as to put the other party in the same position in which it would have been if it had not concluded the contract.

Article 3.19 - Mandatory Character of the Provisions

The provisions of this Chapter are mandatory, except insofar as they relate to the binding force of mere agreement, initial impossibility or mistake.

Article 3.20 - Unilateral Declarations

The provisions of this Chapter apply with appropriate adaptations to any communication of intention addressed by one party to the other.

Chapter 4 - Interpretation

Article 4.1 - Intention of the Parties

(1) A contract shall be interpreted according to the common intention of the parties.

(2) If such an intention cannot be established, the contract shall be interpreted according to the meaning that reasonable persons of the same kind as the parties would give to it in the same circumstances.

Article 4.2 - Interpretation of Statements and Other Conduct

(1) The statements and other conduct of a party shall be interpreted according to that party's intention if the other party knew or could not have been unaware of that intention.

(2) If the preceding paragraph is not applicable, such statements and other conduct shall be interpreted according to the meaning that a reasonable person of the same kind as the other party would give to it in the same circumstances.

Article 4.3 - Relevant Circumstances

In applying Articles 4.1 and 4.2, regard shall be had to all the circumstances, including

(a) preliminary negotiations between the parties;

(b) practices which the parties have established between themselves;

(c) the conduct of the parties subsequent to the conclusion of the contract;

(d) the nature and purpose of the contract;

(e) the meaning commonly given to terms and expressions in the trade concerned;

(f) usages.

Article 4.4 - Reference to Contract or Statement as a Whole

Terms and expressions shall be interpreted in the light of the whole contract or statement in which they appear.

Article 4.5 - All Terms to be Given Effect

Contract terms shall be interpreted so as to give effect to all the terms rather than to deprive some of them of effect.

Article 4.6 - Contra Proferentem Rule

If contract terms supplied by one party are unclear, an interpretation against that party is preferred.

Article 4.7 - Linguistic Discrepancies

Where a contract is drawn up in two or more language versions which are equally authoritative there is, in case of discrepancy between the versions, a preference for the interpretation according to a version in which the contract was originally drawn up.

Article 4.8 - Supplying an Omitted Term

(1) Where the parties to a contract have not agreed with respect to a term which is important for a determination of their rights and duties, a term which is appropriate in the circumstances shall be supplied.

(2) In determining what is an appropriate term regard shall be had, among other factors to

(a) the intention of the parties;

(b) the nature and purpose of the contract;

(c) good faith and fair dealing;

(d) reasonableness.

Chapter 5 - Content

Article 5.1 - Express and Implied Obligations

The contractual obligations of the parties may be express or implied.

Article 5.2 -Implied Obligations

Implied obligations stem from

(a) the nature and purpose of the contract;

(b) practices established between the parties and usages;

(c) good faith and fair dealing;

(d) reasonableness.

Article 5.3 - Co-operation between the Parties

Each party shall co-operate with the other party when such co-operation may reasonably be expected for the performance of that party's obligations.

Article 5.4 - Duty to Achieve a Specific Result. Duty of Best Efforts

(1) To the extent that an obligation of a party involves a duty to achieve a specific result, that party is bound to achieve that result.

(2) To the extent that an obligation of a party involves a duty of best efforts in the performance of an activity, that party is bound to make such efforts as would be made by a reasonable person of the same kind in the same circumstances.

Article 5.5 - Determination of Kind of Duty Involved

In determining the extent to which an obligation of a party involves a duty of best efforts in the performance of an activity or duty to achieve a specific result, regard shall be had, among other factors, to

(a) the way in which the obligation is expressed in the contract;

(b) the contractual price and other terms of the contract;

(c) the degree of risk normally involved in achieving the expected result;

(d) the ability of the other party to influence the performance of the obligation.

Article 5.6 - Determination of Quality of Performance

Where the quality of performance is neither fixed by, nor determinable from, the contract a party is bound to render a performance of a quality that is reasonable and not less than average in the circumstances.

Article 5.7 - Price Determination

(1) Where a contract does not fix or make provision for determining the price, the parties are considered, in the absence of any indication to the contrary, to have made reference to the price generally charged at the time of the conclusion of the contract for such performance in comparable circumstances in the trade concerned or, if no such price is available, to a reasonable price.

(2) Where the price is to be determined by one party and that determination is manifestly unreasonable, a reasonable price shall be substituted notwithstanding any contract term to the contrary.

(3) Where the price is to be fixed by a third person, and that person cannot or will not do so, the price shall be a reasonable price.

(4) Where the price is to be fixed by reference to factors which do not exist or have ceased to exist or to be accessible, the nearest equivalent factor shall be treated as a substitute.

Article 5.8 - Contract for an Indefinite Period

A contract for an indefinite period may be ended by either party by giving notice a reasonable time in advance.

Chapter 6 - Performance

Section 1 - Performance in General

Article 6.1.1 - Time of Performance

A party must perform its obligations:

(a) if a time is fixed by or determinable from the contract, at that time;

(b) if a period of time is fixed by or determinable from the contract, at any time within that period unless circumstances indicate that the other party is to choose a time;

(c) in any other case, within a reasonable time after the conclusion of the contract.

Article 6.1.2 - Performance at one Time or in Instalments

In cases under Article 6.1(b) or (c), a party must perform its obligations at one time if that performance can be rendered at one time ad the circumstances do not indicate otherwise.

Article 6.1.3 - Partial Performance

(1) The obligee may reject an offer to perform in part at the time performance is due, whether or not such offer is coupled with an assurance as to the balance of the performance, unless the obligee has no legitimate interest in so doing.

(2) Additional expenses caused to the obligee by partial performance are to be borne by the obligor without prejudice to any other remedy.

Article 6.1.4 - Order of Performance

(1) To the extent that the performances of the parties can be rendered simultaneously, the parties are bound to render them simultaneously unless the circumstances indicate otherwise.

(2) To the extent that the performance of only one party requires a period of time, that party is bound to render its performance first, unless the circumstances indicate otherwise.

Article 6.1.5 - Earlier Performance

(1) The obligee may reject an earlier performance unless it has no legitimate interest in so doing.

(2) Acceptability by a party of an earlier performance does not affect the time for the performance of its own obligations if that time has been fixed irrespective of the performance of the other party's obligations.

(3) Additional expenses caused to the obligee by earlier performance are to be borne by the obligor, without prejudice to any other remedy.

Article 6.1.6 - Place of Performance

(1) If the place of performance is neither fixed by, nor determinable from the contract, a party is to perform:

(a) a monetary obligation, at the obligee's place of business;

(b) any other obligation, at its own place of business.

(2) A party must bear any increase in the expenses incidental to performance which is caused by a change in its place of business subsequent to the conclusion of the contract.

Article 6.1.7 - Payment by Cheque or other Instrument

(1) Payment may be made in any form used in the ordinary course of business at the place for payment.

(2) However, an obligee who accepts, either by virtue of paragraph (1) or voluntarily, a cheque, any other order to pay or a promise to pay, is

presumed to do so only on condition that it will be honoured.

Article 6.1.8 - Payment by Funds Transfer

(1) Unless the obligee has indicated a particular account, payment may be made by a transfer to any of the financial institutions in which the obligee has made it known that it has an account.

(2) In case of payment by a transfer of the obligation of the obligor is discharged when the transfer to the obligee's financial institution becomes effective.

Article 6.1.9 - Currency of Payment

(1) If a monetary obligation is expressed in a currency other than that of the place of payment, it may be paid by the obligor in the currency of the place for payment unless

(a) the currency is freely convertible; or

(b) the parties have agreed that payment should be made only in the currency in which the monetary obligation is expressed.

(2) If it is impossible for the obligor to make payment in the currency in which the monetary obligation is expressed, the obligee may require payment in the currency of the place for payment, even in the case referred to in paragraph (1)(b).

(3) Payment in the currency of the place for payment is to be made according to the applicable rate of exchange prevailing there when payment is due.

(4) However, if the obligor has not paid at the time when payment is due, the obligee may require payment according to the applicable rate of exchange prevailing either when payment is due or at the time of actual payment.

Article 6.1.10 - Currency Not Expressed

Where a monetary obligation is not expressed in a particular currency, payment must be made in the currency of the place where payment is to be made.

Article 6.1.11 - Costs of Performance

Each party shall bear the costs of performance of its obligations.

Article 6.1.12 - Imputation of Payments

(1) An obligor owing several monetary obligations to the same obligee may specify at the time of payment the debt to which it intends the payment to be applied. However, the payment discharges first any expenses, then interest due and finally the principal.

(2) If the obligor makes no such specification, the obligee may, within a reasonable time after payment, declare to the obligor the obligation to which it imputes the payment, provided that the obligation is due and undisputed.

(3) In the absence of imputation under paragraphs (1) or (2), payment is imputed to that obligation which satisfies one of the following criteria and in the order indicated:

(a) an obligation which is due or which is the first to fall due;

(b) the obligation for which the obligee has least security;

(c) the obligation which is the most burdensome for the obligor;

(d) the obligation which has arisen first.

If none of the preceding criteria applies, payment is imputed to all the obligations proportionally.

Article 6.1.13 - Imputation of Non-Monetary Obligations

Article 6.1.12 applies with appropriate adaptations to the imputation of performance of non-monetary obligations.

Article 6.1.14 - Application for Public Permission

Where the law of a State requires a public permission affecting the validity of the contract or its performance and neither that law nor the circumstances indicate otherwise

(a) if only one party has its place of business in that State, that party shall take the measures necessary to obtain the permission;

(b) in any other case the party whose performance requires permission shall take the necessary measures.

Article 6.1.15 - Procedure in Applying for Permission

(1) The party required to take the measures necessary to obtain the permission shall do so without undue delay and shall bear any expenses incurred.

(2) That party shall whenever appropriate give the other party notice of the grant or refusal of such permission without undue delay.

Article 6.1.16 - Permission Neither Granted Nor Refused

(1) If, notwithstanding the fact that the party responsible has taken all measures required, permission is neither granted nor refused within an agreed period or, where no period has been agreed, within a reasonable time from the conclusion of the contract, either party is entitled to terminate the contract.

(2) Where the permission affects some terms only, paragraph (1) does not apply if, having regard to the circumstances, it is reasonable to uphold the remaining contract even if the permission is refused.

Article 6.1.17 - Permission Refused

(1) The refusal of a permission affecting the validity of the contract renders the contract void. If the refusal affects the validity of some terms only, only such terms are void if, having regard to the circumstances, it is reasonable to uphold the remaining contract.

(2) Where the refusal of a permission renders the performance of the contract impossible in whole or in part, the rules on non-performance apply.

Section 2 - Hardship

Article 6.2.1 - Contract to be Observed

Where the performance of a contract becomes more onerous for one of the parties, that party is nevertheless bound to perform its obligations subject to the following provisions on hardship.

Article 6.2.2 - Definition of Hardship

There is hardship where the occurrence of events fundamentally alters the equilibrium of the contract either because the cost of a party's performance has increased or because the value of the performance a party receives has diminished, and

(a) the events occur or become known to the disadvantaged party after the conclusion of the contract;

(b) the events could not reasonably have been taken into account by the disadvantaged party at the time of the conclusion of the contract;

(c) the events are beyond the control of the disadvantaged party; and

(d) the risk of the events was not assumed by the disadvantaged party.

Article 6.2.3 - Effects of Hardship

(1) In case of hardship the disadvantaged party is entitled to request renegotiations. The request shall be made without undue delay and shall indicate the grounds on which it is based.

(2) The request for renegotiation does not itself entitle the disadvantaged party to withhold performance.

(3) Upon failure to reach agreement within a reasonable time either party may resort to the court.

(4) If the court finds hardship it may, if reasonable,

(a) terminate the contract at a date and on terms to be fixed; or

(b) adapt the contract with a view to restoring its equilibrium.

Chapter 7 - Non-Performance

Section 1 - Non-Performance in General

Article 7.1.1 - Non-Performance Defined

Non-performance is failure by a party to perform any of its obligations under the contract, including defective performance or late performance.

Article 7.1.2 - Interference by the Other Party

A party may not rely on the non-performance of the other party to the extent that such non-performance was caused by the first party's act or omission or by another event as to which the first party bears the risk.

Article 7.1.3 - Withholding Performance

(1) Where the parties are to perform simultaneously, either party may withhold performance until the other party tenders performance.

(2) Where the parties are to perform consecutively, the party that is to perform later may withhold its performance until the first party has performed.

Article 7.1.4 - Cure by Non-Performing Party

(1) The non-performing party may, at its own expense, cure any non-performance, provided that

(a) without undue delay, it gives notice indicating the proposed manner and timing of the cure;

(b) cure is appropriate in the circumstances;

(c) the aggrieved party has no legitimate interest in refusing cure; and

(d) cure is effected promptly.

(2) The right to cure is not precluded by notice of termination.

(3) Upon effective notice of cure, rights of the aggrieved party that are inconsistent with the nonperforming party's performances are suspended until the time for cure has expired.

(4) The aggrieved party may withhold performance pending cure.

(5) Notwithstanding cure, the aggrieved party retains the right to claim damages for delay as well as for any harm caused or not prevented by the cure.

Article 7.1.5 - Additional Period for Performance

(1) In a case of non-performance the aggrieved party may by notice to the other party allow an additional period of time for performance.

(2) During the additional period the aggrieved party may withhold performance of its own reciprocal obligations and may claim damages but may not resort to any other remedy. If it receives notice from the other party that the latter will not perform within that period, or if upon expiry of that period due performance has not been made, the aggrieved party may resort to any of the remedies that may be available under this Chapter.

(3) Where in a case of delay in performance which is not fundamental the aggrieved party has given notice allowing an additional period of time of reasonable length, it may terminate the contract at the end of that period. If the additional period allowed is not of reasonable length it shall be extended to a reasonable length. The aggrieved party may in its notice provide that if the other party fails to perform within the period allowed by the notice the contract shall automatically terminate.

(4) Paragraph (3) does not apply where the obligation which has not been performed is only a minor part of the contractual obligation of the non-performing party.

Article 7.1.6 - Exemption Clauses

A clause which limits or excludes one party's liability for non-performance or which permits one party to tender performance substantially different from what the other party reasonably expected may not be invoked if it would be grossly unfair to do so, having regard to the purpose of the contract.

Article 7.1.7 - Force Majeure

(1) Non-performance by a party is excused if that party proves that the non-performance was due to an impediment beyond its control and that it could not reasonably be expected to have taken the impediment into account at the time of the conclusion of the contract or to have avoided or overcome it or its consequences.

(2) When the impediment is only temporary, the excuse shall have effect for such period as is reasonable having regard to the effect of the impediment on performance of the contract.

(3) The party who fails to perform must give notice to the other party of the impediment and its effect on its ability to perform. If the notice is not received by the other party within a reasonable time after the party who fails to perform knew or ought to have known of the impediment, it is liable for damages resulting from such non-receipt.

(4) Nothing in this article prevents a party from exercising a right to terminate the contract or to withhold performance or request interest on money due..

Section 2 - Right to Performance

Article 7.2.1 - Performance of monetary Obligation

Where a party who is obliged to pay money does not do so, the other may require payment.

Article 7.2.2 - Performance of Non-Monetary Obligation

Where a party who owes an obligation other than one to pay money does not perform, the other party may require performance, unless

(a) performance is impossible in law or fact;

(b) performance or, where relevant, enforcement is unreasonably burdensome or expensive;

(c) the party entitled to performance may reasonably obtain performance from another source;

(d) performance is of an exclusively personal character; or

(e) the party entitled to performance does not require performance within a reasonable time after it has, or ought to have, become aware of the non-performance.

Article 7.2.3 - Repair and Replacement of Defective Performance

The right to performance includes in appropriate cases the right to require repair, replacement, or other cure of defective performance. The provisions of Articles 7.2.1 and 7.2.2 apply accordingly.

Article 7.2.4 - Judicial Penalty

(1) Where the court orders a party to perform, it may also direct that this party pay a penalty if it does not comply with the order.

(2) The penalty shall be paid to the aggrieved party unless mandatory provisions of the law of the forum provide otherwise. Payment of the penalty to the aggrieved party does not exclude any claim for damages.

Article 7.2.5 - Change of Remedy

(1) An aggrieved party who has required performance of a non-monetary obligation and who has not received performance within a period fixed or otherwise within a reasonable period of time may invoke any other remedy.

(2) Where the decision of a court for performance of a non-monetary obligation cannot be enforced, the aggrieved party may invoke any other remedy.

Section 3 - Termination

Article 7.3.1 - Right to Terminate the Contract

(1) A party may terminate the contract where the failure of the other party to perform an obligation under the contract amounts to a fundamental performance.

172

(2) In determining whether a failure to perform an obligation amounts to a fundamental nonperformance regard shall be had, in particular, to whether

(a) the non-performance substantially deprives the aggrieved party of what it was entitled to expect under the contract unless the other party did not foresee and could not reasonably have foreseen such result;

(b) strict compliance with the obligation which has not been performed is of essence under the contract;

(c) the non-performance is intentional or reckless;

(d) the non-performance gives the aggrieved party reason to believe that it cannot rely on the other party's future performance;

(e) the non-performing party will suffer disproportionate loss as a result of the preparation or performance if the contract is terminated.

(3) In the case of delay the aggrieved party may also terminate the contract if the other party fails to perform before the time allowed under Article 7.1.5 has expired.

Article 7.3.2 - Notice of Termination

(1) The right of a party to terminate the contract is exercised by notice to the other party.

(2) If performance has been offered late or otherwise does not conform to the contract the aggrieved party will lose its right to terminate the contract unless it gives notice to the other party within a reasonable time after it has or ought to have become aware of the non-conforming performance.

Article 7.3.3 - Anticipatory Non-Performance

Where prior to the date for performance by one of the parties it is clear that there will be a fundamental non-performance by that party, the other party may terminate the contract.

Article 7.3.4 - Adequate Assurance of Due Performance

A party who reasonably believes that there will be a fundamental non-performance by the other party may demand adequate assurance of due performance and may meanwhile withhold its own performance. Where this assurance is not provided within a reasonable time the party demanding it may terminate the contract.

Article 7.3.5 - Effects of Termination in General

(1) Termination of the contract releases both parties from their obligation to effect and to receive future performance.

(2) Termination does not preclude a claim for damages for non-performance.

(3) Termination does not affect any provision in the contract for the settlement of disputes or any other term of the contract which is to operate even after termination.

Article 7.3.6 - Restitution

(1) On termination of contract either party may claim restitution of whatever it has supplied, provided that such party concurrently makes restitution of whatever it has received. If restitution in kind is not possible or appropriate allowance should be made in money whenever reasonable.

(2) However, if performance of the contract has extended over a period of time and the contract is divisible, such restitution can only be claimed for the period after termination has taken effect.

Section 4 - Damages

Article 7.4.1 - Right to Damages

Any non-performance gives the aggrieved party a right to damages either exclusively or in conjunction with any other remedies except where the non-performance is excused under these Principles.

Article 7.4.2 - Full Compensation

(1) The aggrieved party is entitled to full compensation for harm sustained as a result of the nonperformance. Such harm includes both any loss which it suffered and any gain of which it was deprived, taking into account any gain to the aggrieved party resulting from its avoidance of cost or harm.

(2) Such harm may be non-pecuniary and includes, for instance, physical suffering or emotional distress.

Article 7.4.3 - Certainty of Harm

(1) Compensation is due only for harm, including future harm, that is established with a reasonable degree of certainty.

(2) Compensation may be due for the loss of a chance in proportion to the stability of its occurrence.

(3) Where the amount of damages cannot be established with a sufficient degree of certainty, the assessment is at the discretion of the court.

Article 7.4.4 - Foreseeability of Harm

The non-performing party is liable only for harm which it foresaw or could reasonably have foreseen at the time of the conclusion of the contract as being likely to result from its non-performance.

Article 7.4.5 - Proof of Harm in case of Replacement Transaction

Where the aggrieved party has terminated the contract and has made a replacement transaction within a reasonable time and in a reasonable manner it may recover the difference between the contract price and the price of the replacement transaction as well as damages for any further harm.

Article 7.4.6 - Proof of Harm by Current Price

(1) Where the aggrieved party has terminated the contract and has not made a replacement transaction but there is a current price for the performance contracted for, it may recover the difference between the contract price and the price

current at the time the contract is terminated as well as damages for any further harm.

(2) Current price is the price generally charged for goods delivered or services rendered in comparable circumstances at the place where the contract should have been performed or, if the re is no current price at that place, the current price at such other place that appears reasonable to take as a reference.

Article 7.4.7 - Harm Due in Part to Aggrieved Party

Where the harm is due in part to an act or omission of the aggrieved party or to another event as to which that party bears the risk, the amount of damages shall be reduced to the extent that these factors have contributed to the harm, having regard to the conduct of the parties.

Article 7.4.8 - Mitigation of Harm

(1) The non-performing party is not liable for harm suffered by the aggrieved party to the extent that the harm could have been reduced by the latter party's taking reasonable steps.

(2) The aggrieved party is entitled to recover any expenses reasonably incurred in attempting to reduce the harm.

Article 7.4.9 - Interest for Failure to Pay Money

(1) I a party does not pay a sum of money when it falls due the aggrieved party is entitled to interest upon that sum from the time when payment is due to the time of payment whether or not the nonpayment is excused.

(2) The rate of interest shall be the average bank short-term lending rate to prime borrowers prevailing for the currency of payment at the place for payment, or where no such rate exists at that place, then the same rate in the State of the currency of payment. In the absence of such a rate at either place the rate of interest shall l be the appropriate rate fixed by the law of the State of the currency of payment.

(3) The aggrieved party is entitled to additional damages if the non-payment caused it a greater harm.

Article 7.4.10 - Interest on Damages

Unless otherwise agreed, interest on damages for non-performance of non-monetary obligations accrues as from the time of non-performance.

Article 7.4.11 - Manner of Monetary Redress

(1) Damages are to be paid in a lump sum. However, they may be payable in instalments where the nature of the harm makes this appropriate.

(2) Damages to be paid in instalments may be indexed.

Article 7.4.12 - Currency in which to Access Damages

Damages are to be assessed either in the currency in which the monetary obligation was expressed or in the currency in which the harm was suffered, whichever is more appropriate.

Article 7.4.13 - Agreed Payment for Non-Performance

(1) Where the contract provides that a party who does not perform is to pay a specified sum to the aggrieved party for such non-performance, the aggrieved party is entitled to that sum irrespective of its actual harm.

(2) However, notwithstanding any agreement to the contrary the specified sum may be reduced to a reasonable amount where it is grossly excessive in relation to the harm resulting from the nonperformance and to the other circumstances.

B. CCBE Code of Conduct for Lawyers in the European Community

Source: Council of the Bars and Law Societies of the European Community (CCBE), adopted at Strasbourg, October 28, 1988.

Website information:

http://www.ccbe.org/
This is the website of the Council of Bars and Law Societies of the European Union. It contains information on the CCBE and its member institutions.

Introduction

The Code of Conduct for Lawyers in the European Community is the product of the Council of the Bars and Law Societies of the European Community (CCBE), which was established in 1960 by the legal profession in response to the 1957 Treaty of Rome and the creation of the European Community (EC). Because the substantive law of the EC did not specifically address the issue of legal ethics in cross-border practice, the CCBE drafted an ethics code to be applied when lawyers cross borders within the Community, thereby subjecting themselves to conflicting ethical responsibilities. The work on the Code began in May 1982, and the CCBE adopted the first completed version in October 1988. This was updated by the 1998 adoption of the Current Code of Conduct by delegations representing the bars of 18 states of the European Union and the European Economic Area.

Although the CCBE Code has not completely coordinated the legal ethics rules from the states involved, it has provided clear rules delineating the conflicts of law choices facing a lawyer, stating in which situations a lawyer's home state ethics rule governs and in which situations a lawyer's host state ethics rule will govern.

Because the CCBE acts only as a representative of the interests of the lawyers in the Member States, and not as a formal decision-making institution within the EU, the Code, as a legal matter and without more, has no real binding effect. However, section 0.2.2 of the Code explicitly proposes that "the rules codified in the following articles . . . be adopted as enforceable rules as soon as possible in accordance with national or EAA procedures in relation to the cross border activities of the lawyer in the European Union and European Economic Area." National organizations with the power to regulate the legal profession have adopted the Code.

CCBE CODE OF CONDUCT FOR LAWYERS IN THE EUROPEAN COMMUNITY

1. *PREAMBLE*

1.1. *The Function of the Lawyer in Society*

In a society founded on respect for the rule of law the lawyer fulfils a special role. His duties do not begin and end with the faithful performance of what he is instructed to do so far as the law permits. A lawyer must serve the interests of justice as well as those whose rights and liberties he is trusted to assert and defend and it is his duty not only to plead his client's cause but to be his adviser.

A lawyer's function therefore lays on him a variety of legal and moral obligations (sometimes appearing to be in conflict with each other) towards:

—the client;

—the courts and other authorities before whom the lawyer pleads his client's cause or acts on his behalf;

—the legal profession in general and each fellow member of it in particular; and

—the public for whom the existence of a free and independent profession, bound together by respect for rules made by the profession itself, is an essential means of safeguarding human rights in face of the power of the state and other interests in society.

1.2. *The Nature of Rules of Professional Conduct*

1.1.1. Rules of professional conduct are designed through their willing acceptance by those to whom they apply to ensure the proper performance by the lawyer of a function which is recognised as essential in all civilized societies. The failure of the lawyer to observe these rules must in the last resort result in a disciplinary sanction.

1.1.2. The particular rules of each Bar or Law Society arise from its own traditions. They are adapted to the organisation and sphere of activity of the profession in the Member State concerned and to its judicial and administrative procedures and to its national legislation. It is neither possible nor desirable that they should be taken out of their context nor that an attempt should be made to give general application to rules which are inherently incapable of such application.

The particular rules of each Bar and Law Society nevertheless are based on the same values and in most cases demonstrate a common foundation.

1.3. *The Purpose of the Code*

1.3.1. The continued integration of the European Union and European Economic Area and the increasing frequency of the cross-border activities of lawyers within the European Economic Area have made necessary in the public interest the statement of common rules which apply to all lawyers from the European Economic Area whatever Bar or Law Society they belong to in relation to their cross-border practice. A particular purpose of the statement of those rules is to mitigate the difficulties which result from the application of "double deontology" as set out in Article 4 of the E.C. Directive 77/249 of 22nd March 1977.

1.3.2. The organisations representing the legal profession through the CCBE propose that the rules codified in the following articles:

—be recognised at the present time as the expression of a consensus of all the Bars and Law Societies of the European Union and European Economic Area;

—be adopted as enforceable rules as soon as possible in accordance with national or EEA procedures in relation to the cross-border activities of the lawyer in the European Union and European Economic Area;

—be taken into account in all revisions of national rules of deontology or professional practice with a view to their progressive harmonisation.

They further express the wish that the national rules of deontology or professional practice be interpreted and applied whenever possible in a way consistent with the rules in this Code.

After the rules in this Code have been adopted as enforceable rules in relation to his cross-border activities the lawyer will remain bound to observe the rules of the Bar or Law Society to which he belongs to the extent that they are consistent with the rules in this Code.

1.4. *Field of Application Ratione Personae*

The following rules shall apply to lawyers of the European Union and the European Economic Area as they are defined by the Directive 77/249 of 22nd March 1977.

1.5. *Field of Application Ratione Materiae*

Without prejudice to the pursuit of a progressive harmonisation of rules of deontology or professional practice which apply only internally within a Member State, the following rules shall apply to the cross-border activities of the lawyer within the European Union and the European Economic Area. Cross-border activities shall mean:

(a) all professional contacts with lawyers of Member States other than his own; and

(b) the professional activities of the lawyer in a Member State other than his own, whether or not the lawyer is physically present in that Member State.

1.6. *Definitions*

In these rules:

"Home Member State" means the Member State of the Bar or Law Society to which the lawyer belongs.

"Host Member State" means any other Member State where the lawyer carries on cross-border activities.

"Competent authority" means the professional organisation(s) or authority(ies) of the Member State concerned responsible for the laying down of rules of professional conduct and the administration of discipline of lawyers.

2. *GENERAL PRINCIPLES*

2.1. *Independence*

2.1.1. The many duties to which a lawyer is subject require his absolute independence, free from all other influence, especially such as may arise from his personal interests or external pressure. Such independence is as necessary to trust in the process of justice as the impartiality of the judge. A lawyer must therefore avoid any impairment of his independence and be careful not to compromise his professional standards in order to please his client, the court or third parties.

2.1.2. This independence is necessary in non-contentious matters as well as in litigation. Advice given by a lawyer to his client has no value if it is given only to ingratiate himself, to serve his personal interests or in response to outside pressure.

2.2. *Trust and Personal Integrity*

Relationship of trust can only exist if a lawyer's personal honour, honesty and integrity are beyond doubt. For the lawyer these traditional virtues are professional obligations.

2.3. *Confidentiality*

2.3.1 It is of the essence of a lawyer's function that he should be told by his client things which the client would not tell to others, and that he should be the recipient of other information on a basis of confidence. Without the certainty of confidentiality there cannot be trust. Confidentiality is therefore a primary and fundamental right and duty of the lawyer.

The lawyer's obligation of confidentiality serves the interest of the administration of justice as well as the interest of the client. It is therefore entitled to special protection by the State.

2.3.2. A lawyer shall respect the confidentiality of all information that becomes known to him in the course of his professional activity.

2.3.3. The obligation of confidentiality is not limited in time.

2.3.4. A lawyer shall require his associates and staff and anyone engaged by him in the course of providing professional services to observe the same obligation of confidentiality.

2.4. *Respect for the Rules of Other Bars and Law Societies*

Under the laws of the European Union and the European Economic Area a lawyer from another Member State may be bound to comply with the rules of the Bar or Law Society of the Host Member State. Lawyers have a duty to inform themselves as to the rules which will affect them in the performance of any particular activity.

Member organisations of CCBE are obliged to deposit their codes of conduct at the Secretariat of CCBE so that any lawyer can get hold of the copy of the current code from the Secretariat.

2.5. *Incompatible Occupations*

2.5.1. In order to perform his functions with due independence and in a manner which is consistent with his duty to participate in the administration of justice a lawyer is excluded from some occupations.

2.5.2. A lawyer who acts in the representation or the defence of a client in legal proceedings or before any public authorities in a Host Member State shall there observe the rules regarding incompatible occupations as they are applied to lawyers of the Host Member State.

2.5.3. A lawyer established in a Host Member State in which he wished to participate directly in commercial or other activities not connected with the practice of the law shall respect the rules regarding forbidden or incompatible occupations as they are applied to lawyers of that Member State.

2.6. *Personal Publicity*

2.6.2. A lawyer should not advertise or seek personal publicity where this is not permitted.

In other cases a lawyer should only advertise or seek personal publicity to the extent and in the manner permitted by the rules to which he is subject.

2.6.2. Advertising and personal publicity shall be regarded as taking place where it is permitted, if the lawyer concerned shows that it was placed for the purpose of reaching clients or potential clients located where such advertising or personal publicity is permitted and its communication elsewhere is incidental.

2.7. *The Client's Interest*

Subject to due observance of all rules of law and professional conduct, a lawyer must always act in the best interests of his client and must put those interests before his own interests or those of fellow members of the legal profession.

2.8. *Limitation of Lawyer's Liability towards his Client*

To the extent permitted by the law of the Home Member State and the Host Member State, the lawyer may limit his liabilities towards his client in accordance with rules of the Code of Conduct to which he is subject.

3. *RELATIONS WITH CLIENTS*

3.1 *Acceptance and Termination of Instructions*

3.1.1. A lawyer shall not handle a case for a party except on his instructions. He may, however, act in a case in which he has been instructed by another lawyer who himself acts for the party or where the case has been assigned to him by a competent body.

The lawyer should make reasonable efforts to ascertain the identity, competence and authority of the person or body who instructs him when the specific circumstances show that the identity, competence and authority are uncertain.

3.1.2. A lawyer shall advise and represent his client promptly, conscientiously and diligently. He shall undertake personal responsibility for the discharge of the instructions given to him. He shall keep his client informed as to the progress of the matter entrusted to him.

3.1.3. A lawyer shall not handle a matter which he knows or ought to know he is not competent to handle, without co-operating with a lawyer who is competent to handle it.

A lawyer shall not accept instructions unless he can discharge those instructions promptly having regard to the pressure of other work.

3.1.4. A lawyer shall not be entitled to exercise his right to withdraw from a case in such a way or in such circumstances that the client may be unable to find other legal assistance in time to prevent prejudice being suffered by the client.

3.2. *Conflict of Interest*

3.2.1. A lawyer may not advise, represent or act on behalf of two or more clients in the same matter if there is a conflict, or a significant risk of a conflict, between the interests of those clients.

3.2.2. A lawyer must cease to act for both client when a conflict of interests arises between those clients and also whenever there is a risk of a breach of confidence or where his independence may be impaired.

3.2.3. A lawyer must also refrain from acting for a new client if there is a risk of a breach of confidence entrusted to the lawyer by a former client or if the knowledge which the lawyer possesses of the affairs of the former client would give an undue advantage to the new client.

3.2.4. Where lawyers are practising in association, paragraphs 3.2.1 to 3.2.3 above shall apply to the association and all its members.

3.3. *Pactum de Quota Litis*

3.3.1. A lawyer shall not be entitled to make a pactum de quota litis.

3.3.2. By "pactum de quota litis" is meant an agreement between a lawyer and his client entered into prior to final conclusion of a matter to which the client is a party, by virtue of which the client undertakes to pay the lawyer a share of the result regardless of whether this is represented by a sum of money or by any other benefit achieved by the client upon the conclusion of the matter.

3.3.2. The pactum de quota litis does not include an agreement that fees be charged in proportion to the value of a matter handled by the lawyer if this is in accordance with an officially approved fee scale or under the control of competent authority having jurisdiction over the lawyer.

3.4 *Regulation of Fees*

3.4.1. A fee charged by a lawyer shall be fully disclosed to his client and shall be fair and reasonable.

3.4.2. Subject to any proper agreement to the contrary between a lawyer and his client fees charged by a lawyer shall be subject to regulation in accordance with the rules applied to members of the Bar or Law Society to which he belongs. If he belongs to more than one Bar or Law Society the rules applied shall be those with the closest connection to the contract between the lawyer and his client.

3.5 *Payment on Account*

If a lawyer requires a payment on account of his fees and/or disbursements such payment should not exceed a reasonable estimate of the fees and probable disbursements involved.

Failing such payment, a lawyer may withdraw from the case or refuse to handle it, but subject always to paragraph 3.1.4 above.

3.6 *Fee Sharing with Non-Lawyers*

3.6.1. Subject as after-mentioned a lawyer may not share his fees with a person who is not a lawyer except where an association between the lawyer and the other person is permitted by the laws of the Member State to which the lawyer belongs.

3.6.2. The provisions of 3.6.1 above shall not preclude a lawyer from paying a fee, commission or other compensation to a deceased lawyer's heirs or to a retired lawyer in respect of taking over the deceased or retired lawyer's practice.

3.7 *Cost Effective Resolution and Availability of Legal Aid*

3.7.1. The lawyer should at all times strive to achieve the most cost effective resolution of the client's dispute and should advise the client at appropriate stages as to the desirability of attempting a settlement and/or a reference to alternative dispute resolution.

3.7.2. A lawyer shall inform his client of the availability of legal aid where applicable.

3.8 *Clients funds*

3.8.1. When lawyers at any time in the course of their practice come into possession of funds on behalf of their clients or third parties (hereinafter called "client's funds") it shall be obligatory:

3.8.1.1. That client's funds shall always be held in an account of a bank or similar institution subject to supervision of Public Authority and that all clients' funds received by a lawyer should be paid into such an account unless the client explicitly or by implication agrees that the funds should be dealt with otherwise.

3.8.1.2. That any account in which the client's funds are held in the name of the lawyer should indicate in the title or designation that the funds are held on behalf of the client or clients of the lawyer.

3.8.1.3. That any account or accounts in which client's funds are held in the name of the lawyer should at all times contain a sum which is not less than the total of the client's funds held by the lawyer.

3.8.1.4. That all funds shall be paid to clients immediately or upon such conditions as the client may authorise.

3.8.1.5. That payments made from client's funds on behalf of a client to any other person including:

a) payments made to or for one client from funds held for another client and

b) payment of the lawyer's fees, be prohibited except to the extent that they are permitted by law or are ordered by the court and have the express or implied authority of the client for whom the payment is being made.

3.8.1.6. That the lawyer shall maintain full and accurate records, available to each client on request, showing all his dealings with his client's funds and distinguishing client's funds from other funds held by him.

3.8.1.7. That the competent authorities in all Member States should have powers to allow them to examine and investigate on a confidential basis the financial records of lawyer's client's funds to ascertain whether or not the rules which they make are being complied with and to impose sanctions upon lawyers who fail to comply with those rules.

3.8.2. Subject as aftermentioned, and without prejudice to the rules set out in 3.8.1 above, a lawyer who holds client's funds in the course of carrying on practice in any Member State must comply with the rules relating to holding and accounting for client's funds which are applied by the competent authorities of the Home Member State.

3.8.3. A lawyer who carries on practice or provides services in a Host Member State may with the agreement of the competent authorities of the Home and Host Member State concerned comply with the requirements of the Host Member State to the exclusion of the requirements of the Home Member State. In that event he shall take reasonable steps to inform his clients that he complies with the requirements in force in the Host Member State.

3.9 *Professional Indemnity Insurance*

3.9.1. Lawyers shall be insured at all times against claims based on professional negligence of an extent which is reasonable having regard to the nature and extent of the risks which each lawyer may incur in his practice.

3.9.2. When a lawyer provides services or carries out practice in a Host Member State, the following shall apply:

3.9.2.2. The lawyer must comply with any Rules relating to his obligation to insure against his professional liability as a lawyer which are in force in his Home Member State.

3.9.2.3. A lawyer who is obliged so to insure in his Home Member State and who provides services or carries out practice in any Host Member State shall use his best endeavours to obtain insurance cover on the basis required in his Home Member State extended to services which he provides or practice which he carries out in a Host Member State.

3.9.9.4. A lawyer who fails to obtain the extended insurance cover referred to in paragraph 3.9.2.2 above or who is not obliged so to insure in his Home Member State and who provides services or carries out practice in a Host Member

State shall in so far as possible obtain insurance cover against his professional liability as a lawyer whilst acting for clients in that Host Member State on at least a basis equivalent to that required of lawyers in the Host Member State.

3.9.9.5. To the extent that a lawyer is unable to obtain the insurance cover required by the foregoing rules, he shall inform such of his clients as might be effected.

3.9.9.6. A lawyer who carries out practice or provides services in a Host Member State may with the agreement of the competent authorities of the Home and Host Member States concerned comply with such insurance requirements as are in force in the Host Member State to the exclusion of the insurance requirements of the Home Member State. In this event he shall take reasonable steps to inform his clients that he is insured according to the requirements in force in the Host Member State.

4. *RELATIONS WITH THE COURTS*

4.1 *Applicable Rules of Conduct in Court*

A lawyer who appears, or takes part in a case before a court or tribunal in a Member State, must comply with the rules of conduct applied before that court or tribunal.

4.2 *Fair Conduct of Proceedings*

A lawyer must always have due regard for the fair conduct of proceedings. He must not, for example, make contact with the judge without first informing the lawyer acting for the opposing party or submit exhibits, notes or documents to the judge without communicating them in good time to the lawyer on the other side unless such steps are permitted under the relevant rules of procedure. To the extent not prohibited by law a lawyer must not divulge or submit to the court any proposals for settlement of the case made by the other party or its lawyer without the express consent by the other party's lawyer.

4.3 *Demeanour in Court*

A lawyer shall while maintaining due respect and courtesy towards the court defend the interests of his client honourably and fearlessly without regard to his own interests or to any consequences to himself or to any other person.

4.4 *False or Misleading Information*

A lawyer shall never knowingly give false or misleading information to the court.

4.5 *Extension to Arbitrators Etc.*

The rules governing a lawyer's relations with the courts apply also to his relations with arbitrators and any other persons exercising judicial or quasi-judicial functions, even on an occasional basis.

5. *RELATIONS BETWEEN LAWYERS*

5.1 *Corporate Spirit of the Profession*

5.1.1. The corporate spirit of the profession requires a relationship of trust and co-operation between lawyers for the benefit of their clients and in order to avoid unnecessary litigation and other behaviour harmful to the reputation of the profession. It can, however, never justify setting the interests of the profession against those of the client.

5.1.2. A lawyer should recognise all other lawyers of Member States as professional colleagues and act fairly and courteously towards them.

5.2. *Co-operation Among Lawyers of Different Member States*

5.9.1. It is the duty of a lawyer who is approached by a colleague from another Member State not to accept instructions in a matter which he is not competent to undertake. He should in such case be prepared to help his colleague to obtain the information necessary to enable him to instruct a lawyer who is capable of providing the service asked for.

5.9.2. Where a lawyer of a Member State co-operates with a lawyer from another Member State, both have a general duty to take into account the differences which may exist between their respective legal systems and the professional organisations, competences and obligations of lawyers in the Member States concerned.

5.3 *Correspondence Between Lawyers*

5.3.1. If a lawyer sending a communication to a lawyer in another Member State wishes it remain confidential or without prejudice he should clearly express this intention when communicating the document.

5.3.2. If the recipient of the communication is unable to ensure its status as confidential or without prejudice he should return it to the sender without revealing the contents to others.

5.4. *Referral Fees*

5.4.1. A lawyer may not demand or accept from another lawyer or any other person a fee, commission or any other compensation for referring or recommending the lawyer to a client.

5.4.2. A lawyer may not pay anyone a fee, commission or any other compensation as a consideration for referring a client to himself.

5.5. *Communication with Opposing Parties*

A lawyer shall not communicate about a particular case or matter directly with any person whom he knows to be represented or advised in the case or matter by another lawyer, without the consent of that other lawyer (and shall keep the other lawyer informed of any such communications).

5.6. *Change of Lawyers*

5.6.1. A lawyer who is instructed to represent a client in substitution for another lawyer in relation to a particular matter should inform that other lawyer and, subject to 5.6.2 below, should not begin to act until he has ascertained that arrangements have been made for the settlement of the other lawyer's fees and disbursements. This duty does not, however, make the new lawyer personally responsible for the former lawyer's fees and disbursements.

5.6.2. If urgent steps have to be taken in the interests of the client before the conditions in 5.6.1 above can be complied with, the lawyer may take such steps provided he informs the other lawyer immediately.

5.7. *Responsibility for Fees*

In professional relations between members of Bars of different Member States, where a lawyer does not confine himself to recommending another lawyer or introducing him to the client but himself entrusts a correspondent with a particular matter or seeks his advice, he is personally bound, even if the client is insolvent, to pay the fees, costs and outlays which are due to the foreign correspondent. The lawyers concerned may, however, at the outset of the relationship between them make special arrangements on this matter.

Further, the instructing lawyer may at any time limit his personal responsibility to the amount of the fees, costs and outlays incurred before intimation to the foreign lawyer of his disclaimer of responsibility for the future.

5.8. *Training Young Lawyers*

In order to improve trust and co-operation amongst lawyers of different Member States for the clients' benefit there is a need to encourage a better knowledge of the laws and procedures in different Member States. Therefore, when considering the need for the profession to give good training to young lawyers, lawyers should take into account the need to give training to young lawyers from other Member States.

5.9. *Disputes amongst Lawyers in Different Member States*

5.9.1. If a lawyer considers that a colleague in another Member State has acted in breach of a rule of professional conduct he shall draw the matter to the attention of his colleague.

5.9.2. If any personal dispute of a professional nature arises amongst lawyers in different Member States they should if possible first try to settle it in a friendly way.

5.9.3. A lawyer shall not commence any form of proceedings against a colleague in another Member State on matters referred to in 5.9.1 or 5.9.2 above without first informing the Bars or Law Societies to which they both belong for the purpose of allowing both Bars or Law Societies concerned an opportunity to assist in reaching a settlement.

ANNEX
Policy Statement Concerning Professional Secrecy of Lawyers and Legislation on Money Laundering

CCBE aims to work for a harmonized attitude amongst its member organisations. It therefore recommends that national lawyer's organization of the CCBE Member States to include, if not already included, in their codes of conduct the following obligations:

1. In whichever case submitted to a lawyer, he or she should check the identity of the client or the intermediary of the client for which the lawyer is acting;

2. To prohibit, when lawyers are asked to handle funds, for any lawyer to receive or handle any fund that do not strictly correspond to a file known by name.

3. For lawyers participating in a legal transaction to withdraw if they seriously suspect that the planned operation will result in money laundering and the client is not prepared to abstain from this operation.

CCBE also aims at including these provisions in its own Code of Conduct for transnational legal business.

PART III. UNITED STATES FEDERAL LAWS, REGULATIONS AND OTHER DOCUMENTS

A. Selected Provisions of the Export Administration Act

Source: 50 App. U.S.C. § 2401 *et seq.*

Website information:

http://www.bxa.doc.gov/
The Bureau of Export Administration (BXA) administers the Export Administration Act by developing export control policies, issuing export licenses, and prosecuting violators. Additionally, BXA enforces the EAA's anti-boycott provisions. This website provides a comprehensive look at the policies, programs and activities of the BXA, as well as practical application of the EAA.

Introduction

The U.S. Export Administration Act (EAA), along with the Export Administration Regulations issued by the U.S. Department of Commerce Bureau of Export Affairs (BXA), regulate nearly all United States commodity and data exports. The EAA evolved out of the Export Control Act of 1949, which first gave the U.S. Department of Commerce responsibility for administering and enforcing export controls on dual-use items that could be used for both civil and military purposes. Such controls were justified by national security, foreign policy, and domestic short supply economic interests. The Export Administration Act (EAA) of 1969 replaced the Export Control Act, and took effect on January 1, 1970. It was reestablished again in 1979. The EAA lapsed on August 20, 1994, and the Department of Commerce was forced to operate under the authority conferred by Executive Order No. 12924 of August 19, 1994 to continue in effect the provisions of the Act, under the authority of the International Emergency Economic Powers Act (IEEPA). Legislation to revive the Export Administration Act has been introduced in each subsequent Congress.

The justifications initially set forth in the 1949 predecessor to the EAA continue to represent the primary policy objectives of the Act. These objectives are 1) "to restrict the export of goods and technology which would make a significant contribution to the military potential of any other country or combination of countries which would prove detrimental to the *national security* of the United States," 2) "to restrict the export of goods and technology where necessary to further significantly the *foreign policy* of the United States or to fulfill its declared international obligations," and 3) "to restrict the export of goods where necessary to protect the domestic economy from the excessive *drain of scarce materials* and to reduce the serious inflationary impact of foreign demand." (emphasis added).

50 App. U.S.C. § 2401

Section 2. Congressional findings

The Congress makes the following findings:

(1) The ability of United States citizens to engage in international commerce is a fundamental concern of United States policy.

(2) Exports contribute significantly to the economic well-being of the United States and the stability of the world economy by increasing employment and production in the United States, and by earning foreign exchange, thereby contributing favorably to the trade balance. The restriction of exports from the United States can have serious adverse effects on the balance of payments and on domestic employment, particularly when restrictions applied by the United States are more extensive than those imposed by other countries.

(3) It is important for the national interest of the United States that both the private sector and the Federal Government place a high priority on exports, consistent with the economic, security, and foreign policy objectives of the United States.

(4) The availability of certain materials at home and abroad varies so that the quantity and composition of United States exports and their distribution among importing countries may affect the welfare of the domestic economy and may have an important bearing upon fulfillment of the foreign policy of the United States.

(5) Exports of goods or technology without regard to whether they make a significant contribution to the military potential of individual countries or combinations of countries may adversely affect the national security of the United States.

(6) Uncertainty of export control policy can inhibit the efforts of United States business and work to the detriment of the overall attempt to improve the trade balance of the United States.

(7) Unreasonable restrictions on access to world supplies can cause worldwide political and economic instability, interfere with free international trade, and retard the growth and development of nations.

(8) It is important that the administration of export controls imposed for national security purposes give special emphasis to the need to control exports of technology (and goods which contribute significantly to the transfer of such technology) which could make a significant contribution to the military potential of any country or combination of countries which would be detrimental to the national security of the United States.

(9) Minimization of restrictions on exports of agricultural commodities and products is of critical importance to the maintenance of a sound agricultural sector, to a positive contribution to the balance of payments, to reducing the level of Federal expenditures for agricultural support programs, and to United States cooperation in efforts to eliminate malnutrition and world hunger.

(10) It is important that the administration of export controls imposed for foreign policy purposes give special emphasis to the need to control exports of goods and substances hazardous to the public health and the environment which are banned or severely restricted for use in the United States, and which, if exported, could affect the international reputation of the United States as a responsible trading partner.

(11) Availability to controlled countries of goods and technology from foreign sources is a fundamental concern of the United States and should be eliminated through negotiations and other appropriate means whenever possible.

(12) Excessive dependence of the United States, its allies, or countries sharing common strategic objectives with the United States, on energy and other critical resources from potential adversaries can be harmful to the mutual and individual security of all those countries.

HISTORY: (Sept. 29, 1979, P.L. 96-72, § 2, 93 Stat. 503; July 12, 1985, P.L. 99-64, Title I, § 102, 99 Stat. 120; Dec. 17, 1993, P.L. 103-199, Title II, § 201(a), 107 Stat. 2320.)

50 App. U.S.C. § 2402

Section 3. Congressional declaration of policy

The Congress makes the following declarations:

(1) It is the policy of the United States to minimize uncertainties in export control policy and to encourage trade with all countries with which the United States has diplomatic or trading relations, except those countries with which such trade has been determined by the President to be against the national interest.

(2) It is the policy of the United States to use export controls only after full consideration of the impact on the economy of the United States and only to the extent necessary—

(A) to restrict the export of goods and technology which would make a significant contribution to the military potential of any other country or combination of countries which would prove detrimental to the national security of the United States;

(B) to restrict the export of goods and technology where necessary to further significantly the foreign policy of the United States or to fulfill its declared international obligations; and

(C) to restrict the export of goods where necessary to protect the domestic economy from the excessive drain of scarce materials and to reduce the serious inflationary impact of foreign demand.

(3) It is the policy of the United States (A) to apply any necessary controls to the maximum extent possible in cooperation with all nations, and (B) to encourage observance of a uniform export control by all nations with which the United States has defense treaty commitments or common strategic directives.

(4) It is the policy of the United States to use its economic resources and trade potential to further the sound growth and stability of its economy as well as to further its national security and foreign policy objectives.

(5) It is the policy of the United States—

(A) to oppose restrictive trade practices or boycotts fostered or imposed by foreign countries against other countries friendly to the United States or against any United States person;

(B) to encourage and, in specified cases, require United States persons engaged in the export of goods or technology or other information to refuse to take actions, including furnishing information or entering into or implementing agreements, which have the effect of furthering or supporting the restrictive trade practices or boycotts fostered or imposed by any foreign country against a country friendly to the United States or against any United States person; and

(C) to foster international cooperation and the development of international rules and institutions to assure reasonable access to world supplies.

(6) It is the policy of the United States that the desirability of subjecting, or continuing to subject, particular goods or technology or other information to United States export controls should be subjected to review by and consultation with representatives of appropriate United States Government agencies and private industry.

(7) It is the policy of the United States to use export controls, including license fees, to secure the removal by foreign countries of restrictions on access to supplies where such restrictions have or may have a serious domestic inflationary impact, have caused or may cause a serious domestic shortage, or have been imposed for purposes of influencing the foreign policy of the United States. In effecting this policy, the President shall make reasonable and prompt efforts to secure the removal or reduction of such restrictions, policies, or actions through international cooperation and agreement before imposing export controls. No action taken in fulfillment of the policy set forth in this paragraph shall apply to the export of medicine or medical supplies.

(8) It is the policy of the United States to use export controls to encourage other countries to take immediate steps to prevent the use of their territories or resources to aid, encourage, or give sanctuary to those persons involved in directing, supporting, or participating in acts of international terrorism. To achieve this objective, the President shall make reasonable and prompt efforts to secure the removal or reduction of such assistance to international terrorists through international cooperation and agreement before imposing export controls.

(9) It is the policy of the United States to cooperate with other countries with which the United States has defense treaty commitments or common strategic objectives in restricting the export of goods and technology which would make a significant contribution to the military potential of any country or combination of countries which would prove detrimental to the security of the United States and of those countries with which the United States has defense treaty commitments or common strategic objectives, and to encourage other friendly countries to cooperate in restricting the sale of goods and technology that can harm the security of the United States.

(10) It is the policy of the United States that export trade by United States citizens be given a high priority and not be controlled except when such controls (A) are necessary to further fundamental national security, foreign policy, or short supply objectives, (B) will clearly further such objectives, and (C) are administered consistent with basic standards of due process.

(11) It is the policy of the United States to minimize restrictions on the export of agricultural commodities and products.

(12) It is the policy of the United States to sustain vigorous scientific enterprise. To do so involves sustaining the ability of scientists and other scholars freely to communicate research findings, in accordance with applicable provisions of law, by means of publication, teaching, conferences, and other forms of scholarly exchange.

(13) It is the policy of the United States to control the export of goods and substances banned or severely restricted for use in the United States in order to foster public health and safety and to prevent injury to the foreign policy of the United States as well as to the credibility of the United States as a responsible trading partner.

(14) It is the policy of the United States to cooperate with countries which are allies of the United States and countries which share common strategic objectives with the United States in minimizing dependence on imports of energy and other critical resources from potential adversaries and in developing alternative supplies of such resources in order to minimize strategic threats posed by excessive hard currency earnings derived from such resource exports by countries with policies adverse to the security interests of the United States.

HISTORY: (Sept. 29, 1979, P.L. 96-72, § 3, 93 Stat. 504; July 12, 1985, P.L. 99-64, Title I, § 103, 99 Stat. 121; Dec. 17, 1993, P.L. 103-199, Title II, § 201(b)(2), 107 Stat. 2321.)

50 App. U.S.C. § 2403

Section 4. General provisions

. . . . .

(c) **Foreign availability.** In accordance with the provisions of this Act, the President shall not impose export controls for foreign policy or national security purposes on the export from the United States of goods or technology which he determines are available without restriction from sources outside the United States in sufficient quantities and comparable in quality to those produced in the United States so as to render the controls ineffective in achieving their purposes, unless the President determines that adequate evidence has been presented to him demonstrating that the absence of such controls would prove detrimental to the foreign policy or national security of the United States. In complying with the provisions of this subsection, the President shall give strong emphasis to bilateral or multilateral negotiations to eliminate foreign availability. The Secretary and the Secretary of Defense shall cooperate in gathering information relating to foreign availability, including the establishment and maintenance of a jointly operated computer system.

. . . . .

HISTORY: (Sept. 29, 1979, P.L. 96-72, § 5, 93 Stat. 506; July 12, 1985, P.L. 99-64, Title I, § 105(a)-(c)(1), (d)-(j), 106, 107, 99 Stat. 123-125, 128, 129; Aug. 23, 1988, P.L. 100-418, Title II, Subtitle D, Part I, §§ 2413-2417, 2418(a), (b), 2419, 2420(a), 2421-2423, 2424(a), Part II, § 2446, 102 Stat. 1347-1358, 1369.)

50 App. U.S.C. § 2405

Section 6. Foreign policy controls

(a) **Authority.**

(1) In order to carry out the policy set forth in paragraph (2)(B), (7), (8), or (13) of section 3 of this Act [50 USC Appx. § 2402(2)(B), (7), (8), or (13)], the President may prohibit or curtail the exportation of any goods, technology, or other information subject to the jurisdiction of the United States or exported by any person subject to the jurisdiction of the United States, to the extent necessary to further significantly the foreign policy of the United States or to fulfill its declared international obligations. The authority granted by this subjection shall be exercised by the Secretary, in consultation with the Secretary of State, the Secretary of Defense, the Secretary of Agriculture, the Secretary of the Treasury, the United States Trade Representative, and such other departments and agencies as the Secretary considers appropriate, and shall be implemented by means of export licenses issued by the Secretary.

(2) Any export control imposed under this section shall apply to any transaction or activity undertaken with the intent to evade that export control, even if that export control would not otherwise apply to that transaction or activity.

(3) Export controls maintained for foreign policy purposes shall expire on December 31, 1979, or one year after imposition, whichever is later, unless extended by the President in accordance with subsections (b) and (f). Any such extension and any subsequent extension shall not be for a period of more than one year.

(4) Whenever the Secretary denies any export license under this subsection, the Secretary shall specify in the notice to the applicant of the denial of such license that the license was denied under the authority contained in this subsection, and the reasons for such denial, with reference to the criteria set forth in subsection (b) of this section. The Secretary shall also include in such notice what, if any, modifications in or restrictions on the goods or technology for which the license was sought would allow such export to be compatible with controls implemented under this section, or the Secretary shall indicate in such notice which officers and employees of the Department of Commerce who are familiar with the application will be made reasonably available to the applicant for consultation with regard to such modifications or restrictions, if appropriate.

(5) In accordance with the provisions of section 10 of this Act [50 USC Appx. § 2409], the Secretary of State shall have the right to review any export license application under this section which the Secretary of State requests to review.

(6) Before imposing, expanding, or extending export controls under this section on exports to a country which can use goods, technology, or information available from foreign sources and so incur little or no economic costs as a result of the controls, the President should, through diplomatic means, employ alternatives to export controls which offer opportunities of distinguishing the United States from, and expressing the displeasure of the United States with, the specific actions of that country in response to which the controls are proposed. Such alternatives include private discussions with foreign leaders, public statements in situations where private diplomacy is unavailable or not effective, withdrawal of ambassadors, and reduction of the size of the diplomatic staff that the country involved is permitted to have in the United States.

(b) Criteria.

(1) Subject to paragraph (2) of this subsection, the President may impose, extend, or expand export controls under this section only if the President determines that—

(A) such controls are likely to achieve the intended foreign policy purpose, in light of other factors, including the availability from other countries of the goods or technology

191

proposed for such controls, and that foreign policy purpose cannot be achieved through negotiations or other alternative means;

(B) the proposed controls are compatible with the foreign policy objectives of the United States and with overall United States policy toward the country to which exports are to be subject to the proposed controls;

(C) the reaction of other countries to the imposition, extension, or expansion of such export controls by the United States is not likely to render the controls ineffective in achieving the intended foreign policy purpose or to be counterproductive to United States foreign policy interests;

(D) the effect of the proposed controls on the export performance of the United States, the competitive position of the United States in the international economy, the international reputation of the United States as a supplier of goods and technology, or on the economic well-being of individual United States companies and their employees and communities does not exceed the benefit to United States foreign policy objectives; and

(E) the United States has the ability to enforce the proposed controls effectively.

(2) With respect to those export controls in effect under this section on the date of the enactment of the Export Administration Amendments Act of 1985 [enacted July 12, 1985], the President, in determining whether to extend those controls, as required by subsection (a)(3) of this section, shall consider the criteria set forth in paragraph (1) of this subsection and shall consider the foreign policy consequences of modifying the export controls.

(c) Consultation with industry. The Secretary in every possible instance shall consult with and seek advice from affected United States industries and appropriate advisory committees established under section 135 of the Trade Act of 1974 [19 USC § 2155] before imposing any export control under this section. Such consultation and advice shall be with respect to the criteria set forth in subsection (b)(1) and such other matters as the Secretary considers appropriate.

(d) Consultation with other countries. When imposing export controls under this section, the President shall, at the earliest appropriate opportunity, consult with the countries with which the United States maintains export controls cooperatively, and with such other countries as the President considers appropriate, with respect to the criteria set forth in subsection (b)(1) and such other matters as the President considers appropriate.

(e) Alternative means. Before resorting to the imposition of export controls under this section, the President shall determine that reasonable efforts have been made to achieve the purposes of the controls through negotiations or other alternative means.

(f) Consultation with the Congress.

(1) The President may impose or expand export controls under this section, or extend such controls as required by subsection (a)(3) of this section, only after consultation with the Congress, including the Committee on Foreign Affairs of the House of Representatives and the Committee on Banking, Housing, and Urban Affairs of the Senate.

(2) The President may not impose, expand, or extend export controls under this section until the President has submitted to the Congress a report—

(A) specifying the purpose of the controls;

(B) specifying the determinations of the President (or, in the case of those export controls described in subsection (b)(2), the considerations of the President) with respect to each of the criteria set forth in subsection (b)(1), the bases for such determinations (or considerations), and any possible adverse foreign policy consequences of the controls;

(C) describing the nature, the subjects, and the results of, or the plans for, the consultation with industry pursuant to subsection (c) and with other countries pursuant to subsection (d);

(D) specifying the nature and results of any alternative means attempted under subsection (e), or the reasons for imposing, expanding, or extending the controls without attempting any such alternative means; and

(E) describing the availability from other countries of goods or technology comparable to the goods or technology subject to the proposed export controls, and describing the nature and results of the efforts made pursuant to subsection (h) to secure the cooperation of foreign governments in controlling the foreign availability of such comparable goods or technology.

Such report shall also indicate how such controls will further significantly the foreign policy of the United States or will further its declared international obligations.

. . . . .

(h) Foreign availability.

(1) In applying export controls under this section, the President shall take all feasible steps to initiate and conclude negotiations with appropriate foreign governments for the purpose of securing the cooperation of such foreign governments in controlling the export to countries and consignees to which the United States export controls apply of any goods or technology comparable to goods or technology controlled under this section.

(2) Before extending any export control pursuant to subsection (a)(3) of this section, the President shall evaluate the results of his actions under paragraph (1) of this subsection and shall include the results of that evaluation in his report to the Congress pursuant to subsection (f) of this section.

(3) If, within 6 months after the date on which export controls under this section are imposed or expanded, or within 6 months after the date of the enactment of the Export Administration Amendments Act of 1985 [enacted July 12, 1985] in the case of export controls in effect on such date of enactment [enacted July 12, 1985], the President's efforts under paragraph (1) are not successful in securing the cooperation of foreign governments described in paragraph (1) with respect to those export controls, the Secretary shall thereafter take into account the foreign availability of the goods or technology subject to the export controls. If the Secretary affirmatively determines that a good or technology subject to the export controls is available in sufficient quantity and comparable quality from sources outside the United States to countries subject to the export controls so that denial of an export license would be ineffective in achieving the purposes of the controls, then the Secretary shall, during the period of such foreign availability, approve any license application which is required for the export of the good or technology and which meets all requirements for such a license. The Secretary shall remove the good or technology from the list established pursuant to subsection (l) of this section if the Secretary determines that such action is appropriate.

(4) In making a determination of foreign availability under paragraph (3) of this subsection, the Secretary shall follow the procedures set forth in section 5(f)(3) of this Act [50 USC Appx. § 2404(f)(3)].

(i) **International obligations**. The provisions of subsections (b), (c), (d), (e), (g), and (h) shall not apply in any case in which the President exercises the authority contained in this section to impose export controls, or to approve or deny export license applications, in order to fulfill obligations of the United States pursuant to treaties to which the United States is a party or pursuant to other international agreements.

(j) Countries supporting international terrorism.

(1) A validated license shall be required for the export of goods or technology to a country if the Secretary of State has made the following determinations:

(A) The government of such country has repeatedly provided support for acts of international terrorism.

(B) The export of such goods or technology could make a significant contribution to the military potential of such country, including its military logistics capability, or could enhance the ability of such country to support acts of international terrorism.

(2) The Secretary and the Secretary of State shall notify the Committee on Foreign Affairs of the House of Representatives and the Committee on Banking, Housing, and Urban Affairs and the Committee on Foreign Relations of the Senate at least 30 days before issuing any validated license required by paragraph (1).

(3) Each determination of the Secretary of State under paragraph (1)(A), including each determination in effect on the date of the enactment of the Antiterrorism and Arms Export Amendments Act of 1989 [enacted Dec. 12, 1989], shall be published in the Federal Register.

(4) A determination made by the Secretary of State under paragraph (1)(A) may not be rescinded unless the President submits to the Speaker of the House of Representatives and the chairman of the Committee on Banking, Housing, and Urban Affairs and the chairman of the Committee on Foreign Relations of the Senate—

(A) before the proposed rescission would take effect, a report certifying that—

(i) there has been a fundamental change in the leadership and policies of the government of the country concerned;

(ii) that government is not supporting acts of international terrorism; and

(iii) that government has provided assurances that it will not support acts of international terrorism in the future; or

. . . . .

(p) **Effect on existing contracts and licenses**. The President may not, under this section, prohibit or curtail the export or reexport of goods, technology, or other information—

(1) in performance of a contract or agreement entered into before the date on which the President reports to the Congress, pursuant to subsection (f) of this section, his intention to impose controls on the export or reexport of such goods, technology, or other information, or

(2) under a validated license or other authorization issued under this Act, unless and until the President determines and certifies to the Congress that—

(A) a breach of the peace poses a serious and direct threat to the strategic interest of the United States,

(B) the prohibition or curtailment of such contracts, agreements, licenses, or authorizations will be instrumental in remedying the situation posing the direct threat, and

(C) the export controls will continue only so long as the direct threat persists.

. . . . .

(r) Expanded authority to impose controls.

(1) In any case in which the President determines that it is necessary to impose controls under this section without any limitation contained in subsection (c), (d), (e), (g), (h), or (m) of this section, the President may impose those controls only if the President submits that determination to the Congress, together with a report pursuant to subsection (f) of this section with respect to the proposed controls, and only if a law is enacted authorizing the imposition of those controls. . . . .

. . . . .

HISTORY: (Sept. 29, 1979, P.L. 96-72, § 6, 93 Stat. 513; Dec. 16, 1980, P.L. 96-533, Title I, § 111, 94 Stat. 3138; Dec. 29, 1981, P.L. 97-145, § 6, 95 Stat. 1728; July 12, 1985, P.L. 99-64, Title I, § 108(a)-(g)(1), (h)-(j)(1), (k), (l)(1), 99 Stat. 131-136; Aug. 27, 1986, P.L. 99-399, Title V, § 509(b), 100 Stat. 874; Aug. 23, 1988, P.L. 100-418, Title II, Subtitle D, Part I, § 2423, 102 Stat. 1358; Dec. 12, 1989, P.L. 101-222, § 4, 103 Stat. 1897; Nov. 5, 1990, P.L. 101-510, Div A, Title XVII, § 1702(a), 104 Stat. 1739; Oct. 28, 1991, P.L. 102-138, Title V, § 504(b), 105 Stat. 724; Dec. 4, 1991, P.L. 102-182, Title III, § 304(b), 105 Stat. 1246; April 30, 1994, P.L. 103-236, Title VII, Part B, § 736, 108 Stat. 506.) (As amended Oct. 19, 1996, P.L. 104-316, Title I, § 128(c), 110 Stat. 3841.)

50 App. U.S.C. § 2406

Section 7. Short supply controls

(a) Authority.

(1) In order to carry out the policy set forth in section 3(2)(C) of this Act [50 USC Appx. § 2402(2)(C)], the President may prohibit or curtail the export of any goods subject to the jurisdiction of the United States or exported by any person subject to the jurisdiction of the United States. In curtailing exports to carry out the policy set forth in section 3(2)(C) of this Act [50 USC Appx. § 2402(2)(C)], the President shall allocate a portion of export licenses on the basis of factors other than a prior history of exportation. Such factors shall include the extent to which a country engages in equitable trade practices with respect to United States goods and treats the United States equitably in times of short supply.

(2) Upon imposing quantitative restrictions on exports of any goods to carry out the policy set forth in section 3(2)(C) of this Act [50 USC Appx. § 2402(2)(C)], the Secretary shall include in a notice published in the Federal Register with respect to such restrictions an invitation to all interested parties to submit written comments within 15 days from the date of

publication on the impact of such restrictions and the method of licensing used to implement them.

(3) In imposing export controls under this section, the President's authority shall include, but not be limited to, the imposition of export license fees.

. . . . .

(g) Agricultural commodities.

. . . . .

(3) (A) If the President imposes export controls on any agricultural commodity in order to carry out the policy set forth in paragraph (2)(B), (2)(C), (7), or (8) of section 3 of this Act [50 USC Appx. § 2402(2)(B), (C), (7), (8)], the President shall immediately transmit a report on such action to the Congress, setting forth the reasons for the controls in detail and specifying the period of time, which may not exceed 1 year, that the controls are proposed to be in effect. In the Congress, within 60 days after the date of its receipt of the report, adopts a joint resolution pursuant to paragraph (4) approving the imposition of the export controls, then such controls shall remain in effect for the period specified in the report, or until terminated by the President, whichever occurs first. If the Congress, within 60 days after the date of its receipt of such report, fails to adopt a joint resolution approving such controls, then such controls shall cease to be effective upon the expiration of that 60-day period.

(B) The provisions of subparagraph (A) and paragraph (4) shall not apply to export controls—

(i) which are extended under this Act if the controls, when imposed, were approved by the Congress under subparagraph (A) and paragraph (4); or

(ii) which are imposed with respect to a country as part of the prohibition or curtailment of all exports to that country,

HISTORY: (Sept. 29, 1979, P.L. 96-72, § 7, 93 Stat. 515; July 12, 1985, P.L. 99-64, Title I, §§ 109, 110, 99 Stat. 137, 139; Dec. 4, 1987, P.L. 100-180, Div A, Title XII, Part E, § 1246, 101 Stat. 1165; Aug. 23, 1988, P.L. 100-418, Title II, Subtitle D, Part I, § 2424(a), 102 Stat. 1359; Sept. 28, 1988, P.L. 100-449, Title III, § 305(a), 102 Stat. 1876.)

Section 16. Definitions

As used in this Act—

(1) the term "person" includes the singular and the plural and any individual, partnership, corporation, or other form of association, including any government or agency thereof;

(2) the term "United States person" means any United States resident or national (other than an individual resident outside the United States and employed by other than a United States person), any domestic concern (including any permanent domestic establishment of any foreign concern) and any foreign subsidiary or affiliate (including any permanent foreign establishment) of any domestic concern which is controlled in fact by such domestic concern, as determined under regulations of the President;

(3) the term "good" means any article, natural or manmade substance, material, supply or manufactured product, including inspection and test equipment, and excluding technical data;

(4) the term "technology" means the information and know-how (whether in tangible form, such as models, prototypes, drawings, sketches, diagrams, blueprints, or manuals, or in intangible form, such as training or technical services) that can be used to design, produce, manufacture, utilize, or reconstruct goods, including computer software and technical data, but not the goods themselves;

(5) the term "export" means—

(A) an actual shipment, transfer, or transmission of goods or technology out of the United States;

(B) a transfer of goods or technology in the United States to an embassy or affiliate of a controlled country; or

(C) a transfer to any person of goods or technology either within the United States or outside of the United States with the knowledge or intent that the goods or technology will be shipped, transferred, or transmitted to an unauthorized recipient;

(6) the term "controlled country" means a controlled country under section 5(b)(1) of this Act [50 USC Appx. § 2404(b)(1)];

(7) the term "United States" means the States of the United States, the District of Columbia, and any commonwealth, territory, dependency, or possession of the United States, and includes the outer Continental Shelf, as defined in section 2(a) of the Outer Continental Shelf Lands Act (43 U.S.C. § 1331(a) [43 USC § 1331(a)]);

(8) the term "Secretary" means the Secretary of Commerce.

HISTORY: (Sept. 29, 1979, P.L. 96-72, § 16, 93 Stat. 533; July 12, 1985, P.L. 99-64, Title I, § 117, 99 Stat. 153.)

B. Selected Provisions of the Federal Arbitration Act

Source: 9 U.S.C. § 1 *et seq.*

Website information:

http://www.adr.org/
The "ADR Law" section of the website of the American Arbitration Association includes links to various U.S. laws dealing with arbitration.

Introduction

The United States Federal Arbitration Act of 1925 represented a major change from years of judicial objection to honoring predispute agreements to arbitrate, and established a body of federal law requiring the enforcement of arbitration agreements and arbitration awards. As a federal statute, it requires the enforcement of arbitration agreements and awards even in the face of contrary state law. Under § 2 of the Act, an agreement to arbitrate "shall be valid, irrevocable, and enforceable, save upon such grounds as exist at law or in equity for the revocation of any contract." The Act applies broadly to all "maritime transactions" and other transactions "involving commerce." (§§ 1 and 2).

The notion of enforceability of arbitration agreements is implemented by §§ 3 and 4. Section 3 requires a federal court to stay any litigation pending arbitration, while 4 confers the remedy of specific performance to arbitrate, so long as the federal court has jurisdiction over the matter and it decides that the matter falls within the categories delineated in § 1.

Sections 5 through 7 establish preliminary procedural rules that govern the application of arbitration proceedings. Section 5 allows for the designation of arbitrators, either in accordance with the intent of the original agreement between the parties, the methods proscribed by the American Arbitration Association (AAA), or the statutorily prescribed method. Section 7 confers powers upon designated arbitrators, providing them with the ability to summon witnesses, enforce arbitrator subpoenas, and request judicial aid from a proper district court.

The confirmation, vacation and modification of arbitration awards by a court is governed by §§ 9, 10, and 11, respectively. The application for confirmation of an arbitration award may be made by either party to the court specified in the agreement, and in the absence of such designation, "the United States court in and for the district within which such an award was made" shall have the power to confirm. (§ 9) Likewise, actions for modification and vacation of an arbitration award may be initiated by either party to the dispute; but unlike an action for confirmation, can only be ordered by the proper United States District Court. Sections 12 and 13 govern the procedures for confirmation, vacation and modification of an arbitration award, while § 16 allows for any appeals of court orders pursuant to the Act.

TITLE 9 - ARBITRATION
(FEDERAL ARBITRATION ACT OF 1925)

CHAPTER 1. GENERAL PROVISIONS

§ 1. "Maritime transactions and "commerce" defined; exceptions to operation of title

"Maritime transactions", as herein defined, means charter parties, bills of lading of water carriers, agreements relating to wharfage, supplies furnished vessels or repairs to vessels, collisions, or any other matters in foreign commerce which, if the subject of controversy, would be embraced within admiralty jurisdiction; "commerce", as herein defined, means commerce among the several States or with foreign nations, or in any Territory of the United States or in the District of Columbia, or between any such Territory and another, or between any such Territory and any State or foreign nation, or between the District of Columbia and any State or Territory or foreign nation, but nothing herein contained shall apply to contracts of employment of seamen, railroad employees, or any other class of workers engaged in foreign or interstate commerce.

HISTORY: (July 30, 1947, ch 392, § 1, 61 Stat. 670.)

§ 2. Validity, irrevocability, and enforcement of agreements to arbitrate

A written provision in any maritime transaction or a contract evidencing a transaction involving commerce to settle by arbitration a controversy thereafter arising out of such contract or transaction, or the refusal to perform the whole or any part thereof, or an agreement in writing to submit to arbitration an existing controversy arising out of such a contract, transaction, or refusal, shall be valid, irrevocable, and enforceable, save upon such grounds as exist at law or in equity for the revocation of any contract.

HISTORY: (July 30, 1947, ch 392, § 1, 61 Stat. 670.)

§ 3. Stay of proceedings where issue therein referable to arbitration

If any suit or proceeding be brought in any of the courts of the United States upon any issue referable to arbitration under an agreement in writing for such arbitration, the court in which such suit is pending, upon being satisfied that the issue involved in such suit or proceeding is referable to arbitration under such an agreement, shall on application of one of the parties stay the trial of the action until such arbitration has been had in accordance with the terms of the agreement, providing the applicant for the stay is not in default in proceeding with such arbitration.

HISTORY: (July 30, 1947, ch 392, § 1, 61 Stat. 670.)

§ 4. Failure to arbitrate under agreement; petition to United States court having jurisdiction for order to compel arbitration; notice and service thereof; hearing and determination

A party aggrieved by the alleged failure, neglect, or refusal of another to arbitrate under a written agreement for arbitration may petition any United States district court which, save for such agreement, would have jurisdiction under Title 28 [28 USC §§ 1 et seq.], in a civil action or in admiralty of the subject matter of a suit arising out of the controversy between the parties, for an order directing that such arbitration proceed in the manner provided for in such agreement. Five days' notice in writing of such application shall be served upon the party in default. Service thereof shall be made in the manner provided by the Federal Rules of Civil Procedure [USC Rules of Civil Procedure]. The court shall hear the parties, and upon being satisfied that the making of the agreement for arbitration or the failure to comply therewith is not in issue, the court shall make an order directing the parties to proceed to arbitration in accordance with the terms of the agreement. The hearing and proceedings, under such agreement, shall be within the district in which the petition for an order directing such arbitration is filed. If the making of the arbitration agreement or the failure, neglect, or refusal to perform the same be in issue, the court shall proceed summarily to the trial thereof. If no jury trial be demanded by the party alleged to be in default, or if the matter in dispute is within admiralty jurisdiction, the court shall hear and determine such issue. Where such an issue is raised, the party alleged to be in default may, except in cases of admiralty, on or before the return day of the notice of application, demand a jury trial of such issue, and upon such demand the court shall make an order referring the issue or issues to a jury in the manner provided by the Federal Rules of Civil Procedure [USC Rules of Civil Procedure], or may specially call a jury for that purpose. If the jury find that no agreement in writing for arbitration was made or that there is no default in proceeding thereunder, the proceeding shall be dismissed. If the jury find that an agreement for arbitration was made in writing and that there is a default in proceeding thereunder, the court shall make an order summarily directing the parties to proceed with the arbitration in accordance with the terms thereof.

HISTORY: (July 30, 1947, ch 392, § 1, 61 Stat. 671; Sept. 3, 1954, ch 1263, § 19, 68 Stat. 1233.)

§ 5. Appointment of arbitrators or umpire

If in the agreement provision be made for a method of naming or appointing an arbitrator or arbitrators or an umpire, such method shall be followed; but if no method be provided therein, or if a method be provided and any party thereto shall fail to avail himself of such method, or if for any other reason there shall be a lapse in the naming of an arbitrator or arbitrators or umpire, or in filling a vacancy, then upon the application of either party to the controversy the court shall designate and appoint an arbitrator or arbitrators or umpire, as the case may require, who shall act under the said agreement with the same force and effect as if he or they had been specifically named therein; and unless otherwise provided in the agreement the arbitration shall be by a single arbitrator.

HISTORY: (July 30, 1947, ch 392, § 1, 61 Stat. 671.)

§ 6. Application heard as motion

Any application to the court hereunder shall be made and heard in the manner provided by law for the making and hearing of motions, except as otherwise herein expressly provided.

HISTORY: (July 30, 1947, ch 392, § 1, 61 Stat. 671.)

§ 7. Witnesses before arbitrators; fees; compelling attendance

The arbitrators selected either as prescribed in this title [9 USC §§ 1 et seq.] or otherwise, or a majority of them, may summon in writing any person to attend before them or any of them as a witness and in a proper case to bring with him or them any book, record, document, or paper which may be deemed material as evidence in the case. The fees for such attendance shall be the same as the fees of witnesses before masters of the United States courts. Said summons shall issue in the name of the arbitrator or arbitrators, or a majority of them, and shall be signed by the arbitrators, or a majority of them, and shall be directed to the said person and shall be served in the same manner as subpoenas to appear and testify before the court; if any person or persons so summoned to testify shall refuse or neglect to obey said summons, upon petition the United States district court for the district in which such arbitrators, or a majority of them, are sitting may compel the attendance of such person or persons before said arbitrator or arbitrators, or punish said person or persons for contempt in the same manner provided by law for securing the attendance of witnesses or their punishment for neglect or refusal to attend in the courts of the United States.

HISTORY: (July 30, 1947, ch 392, § 1, 61 Stat. 672: Oct. 31, 1951, ch 655, § 14, 65 Stat. 715.)

§ 8. Proceedings begun by libel in admiralty and seizure of vessel or property

If the basis of jurisdiction be a cause of action otherwise justiciable in admiralty, then, notwithstanding anything herein to the contrary, the party claiming to be aggrieved may begin his proceeding hereunder by libel and seizure of the vessel or other property of the other party according to the usual course of admiralty proceedings, and the court shall then have jurisdiction to direct the parties to proceed with the arbitration and shall retain jurisdiction to enter its decree upon the award.

HISTORY: (July 30, 1947, ch 392, § 1, 61 Stat. 672.)

§ 9. Award of arbitrators; confirmation; jurisdiction; procedure

If the parties in their agreement have agreed that a judgment of the court shall be entered upon the award made pursuant to the arbitration, and shall specify the court, then at any time within one year after the award is made any party to the arbitration may apply to the court so specified for an order confirming the award, and thereupon the court must grant such an order unless the award is vacated, modified, or corrected as prescribed in sections 10 and 11 of this title [9 USC §§ 10, 11]. If no court is specified in the agreement of the parties, then such application may be made to the United States court in and for the district within which such award was made. Notice of the application shall be served upon the adverse party, and thereupon the court shall have jurisdiction of such party as though he had appeared generally in the proceeding. If the adverse party is a resident of the district within which the award was made, such service shall be made upon the adverse party or his attorney as prescribed by law for service of notice of motion in an action in the same court. If the adverse party shall be a nonresident, then the notice of the application shall be served by the marshal of any district within which the adverse party may be found in like manner as other process of the court.

HISTORY: (July 30, 1947, ch 392, § 1, 61 Stat. 672.)

§ 10. Same; vacation; grounds; rehearing

(a) In any of the following cases the United States court in and for the district wherein the award was made may make an order vacating the award upon the application of any party to the arbitration—

(1) Where the award was procured by corruption, fraud, or undue means.

(2) Where there was evident partiality or corruption in the arbitrators, or either of them.

(3) Where the arbitrators were guilty of misconduct in refusing to postpone the hearing, upon sufficient cause shown, or in refusing to hear evidence pertinent and material to the controversy; or of any other misbehavior by which the rights of any party have been prejudiced.

(4) Where the arbitrators exceeded their powers, or so imperfectly executed them that a mutual, final, and definite award upon the subject matter submitted was not made.

(5) Where an award is vacated and the time within which the agreement required the award to be made has not expired the court may, in its discretion, direct a rehearing by the arbitrators.

(b) The United States district court for the district wherein an award was made that was issued pursuant to section 580 of title 5 may make an order vacating the award upon the application of a person, other than a party to the arbitration, who is adversely affected or aggrieved by the award, if

204

the use of arbitration or the award is clearly inconsistent with the factors set forth in section 572 of title 5.

HISTORY: (July 30, 1947, ch 392, § 1, 61 Stat. 672; as amended Nov. 15, 1990, P.L. 101-552, § 5, 104 Stat. 2745; Aug. 26, 1992, Pub. L. 102-354, § 5(b)(4), 106 Stat. 946.)

§ 11. Same; modification or correction; grounds; order

In either of the following cases the United States court in and for the district wherein the award was made may make an order modifying or correcting the award upon the application of any party to the arbitration—

(a) Where there was an evident material miscalculation of figures or an evident material mistake in the description of any person, thing, or property referred to in the award.

(b) Where the arbitrators have awarded upon a matter not submitted to them, unless it is a matter not affecting the merits of the decision upon the matter submitted.

(c) Where the award is imperfect in matter of form not affecting the merits of the controversy.

The order may modify and correct the award, so as to effect the intent thereof and promote justice between the parties.

HISTORY: (July 30, 1947, ch 392, § 1, 61 Stat. 673.)

§ 12. Notice of motions to vacate or modify; service; stay of proceedings

Notice of a motion to vacate, modify, or correct an award must be served upon the adverse party or his attorney within three months after the award is filed or delivered. If the adverse party is a resident of the district within which the award was made, such service shall be made upon the adverse party or his attorney as prescribed by law for service of notice of motion in an action in the same court. If the adverse party shall be a nonresident then the notice of the application shall be served by the marshal of any district within which the adverse party may be found in like manner as other process of the court. For the purposes of the motion any judge who might make an order to stay the proceedings in an action brought in the same court may make an order, to be served with the notice of motion, staying the proceedings of the adverse party to enforce the award.

HISTORY: (July 30, 1947, ch 392, § 1, 61 Stat. 673.)

§ 13. Papers filed with order on motions; judgment; docketing; force and effect; enforcement

The party moving for an order confirming, modifying, or correcting an award shall, at the time such order is filed with the clerk for the entry of judgment thereon, also file the following papers with the clerk:

(a) The agreement; the selection or appointment, if any, of an additional arbitrator or umpire; and each written extension of the time, if any, within which to make the award.

(b) The award.

(c) Each notice, affidavit, or other paper used upon an application to confirm, modify, or correct the award, and a copy of each order of the court upon such an application.

The judgment shall be docketed as if it was rendered in an action.

The judgment so entered shall have the same force and effect, in all respects, as, and be subject to all the provisions of law relating to, a judgment in an action; and it may be enforced as if it had been rendered in an action in the court in which it is entered.

HISTORY: (July 30, 1947, ch 392, § 1, 61 Stat. 673.)

§ 14. Contracts not affected

This title [9 USC §§ 1 et seq.] shall not apply to contracts made prior to January 1, 1926.

HISTORY: (July 30, 1947, ch 392, § 1, 61 Stat. 674.)

§ 15. Inapplicability of the Act of State doctrine

Enforcement of arbitral agreements, confirmation of arbitral awards, and execution upon judgments based on orders confirming such awards shall not be refused on the basis of the Act of State doctrine.

HISTORY: (Added Nov. 16, 1988, P.L. 100-669, § 1, 102 Stat. 3969.)

§ 16. Appeals

(a) An appeal may be taken from—

(1) an order—

(A) refusing a stay of any action under section 3 of this title,

(B) denying a petition under section 4 of this title to order arbitration to proceed,

(C) denying an application under section 206 of this title to compel arbitration,

(D) confirming or denying confirmation of an award of partial award, or

(E) modifying, correcting, or vacating an award;

(2) an interlocutory order granting, continuing, or modifying an injunction against an arbitration that is subject to this title; or

(3) a final decision with respect to an arbitration that is subject to this title.

(b) Except as otherwise provided in section 1292(b) of title 28, an appeal may not be taken from an interlocutory order—

(1) granting a stay of any action under section 3 of this title;

(2) directing arbitration to proceed under section 4 of this title;

(3) compelling arbitration under section 206 of this title; or

(4) refusing to enjoin an arbitration that is subject to this title.

HISTORY: (Added Nov. 19, 1988, P.L. 100-702, Title X, § 1019(a), 102 Stat. 4671; Dec. 1, 1990, P.L. 101-650, Title III, § 325(a)(1), 104 Stat. 5120.)

CHAPTER 2. CONVENTION ON THE RECOGNITION AND ENFORCEMENT OF FOREIGN ARBITRAL AWARDS

§ 201. Enforcement of Convention

The Convention on the Recognition and Enforcement of Foreign Arbitral Awards of June 10, 1958, shall be enforced in United States courts in accordance with this chapter [9 USC §§ 201 et seq.].

HISTORY: (Added July 31, 1970, P.L. 91-368, § 1, 84 Stat. 692.)

§ 202. Agreement or award falling under the Convention

An arbitration agreement or arbitral award arising out of a legal relationship, whether contractual or not, which is considered as commercial, including a transaction, contract, or agreement described in section 2 of this title [9 USC § 2], falls under the Convention. An agreement or award arising out of such a relationship which is entirely between citizens of the United States shall be deemed not to fall under the Convention unless that relationship involves property located abroad, envisages performance or enforcement abroad, or has some other reasonable relation with one or more foreign states. For the purpose of this section a corporation is a citizen of the United States if it is incorporated or has its principal place of business in the United States.

HISTORY: (Added July 31, 1970, P.L. 91-368, § 1, 84 Stat. 692.)

§ 203. Jurisdiction; amount in controversy

An action or proceeding falling under the Convention shall be deemed to arise under the laws and treaties of the United States. The district courts of the United States (including the courts enumerated in section 460 of title 28 [28 USC § 460]) shall have original jurisdiction over such an action or proceeding, regardless of the amount in controversy.

HISTORY: (Added July 31, 1970, P.L. 91-368, § 1, 84 Stat. 692.)

§ 204. Venue

An action or proceeding over which the district courts have jurisdiction pursuant to section 203 of this title [9 USC § 203] may be brought in any such court in which save for the arbitration agreement an action or proceeding with respect to the controversy between the parties could be brought, or in such court for the district and division which embraces the place designated in the agreement as the place of arbitration if such place is within the United States.

HISTORY: (Added July 31, 1970, P.L. 91-368, § 1, 84 Stat. 692.)

§ 205. Removal of cases from State courts

Where the subject matter of an action or proceeding pending in a State court relates to an arbitration agreement or award falling under the Convention, the defendant or the defendants may, at any time before the trial thereof, remove such action or proceeding to the district court of the United States for the district and division embracing the place where the action or proceeding is pending. The procedure for removal of causes otherwise provided by law shall apply, except that the ground for removal provided in this section need not appear on the face of the complaint but may be shown in the petition for removal. For the purposes of Chapter 1 of this title [9 USC §§ 1 et seq.] any action or proceeding removed under this section shall be deemed to have been brought in the district court to which it is removed.

HISTORY: (Added July 31, 1970, P.L. 91-368, § 1, 84 Stat. 692.)

§ 206. Order to compel arbitration; appointment of arbitrators

A court having jurisdiction under this chapter [9 USC §§ 201 et seq.] may direct that arbitration be held in accordance with the agreement at any place therein provided for, whether that place is within or without the United States. Such court may also appoint arbitrators in accordance with the provisions of the agreement.

HISTORY: (Added July 31, 1970, P.L. 91-368, § 1, 84 Stat. 693.)

§ 207. Award of arbitrators; confirmation; jurisdiction; proceeding

Within three years after an arbitral award falling under the Convention is made, any party to the arbitration may apply to any court having jurisdiction under this chapter [9 USC §§ 201 et seq.] for an order confirming the award as against any other party to the arbitration. The court shall confirm the award unless it finds one of the grounds for refusal or deferral of recognition or enforcement of the award specified in the said Convention.

HISTORY: (Added July 31, 1970, P.L. 91-368, § 1, 84 Stat. 693.)

§ 208. Chapter 1; residual application

Chapter 1 [9 USC §§ 1 et seq.] applies to actions and proceedings brought under this chapter [9 USC §§ 201 et seq.] to the extent that chapter is not in conflict with this chapter [9 USC §§ 201 et seq.] or the Convention as ratified by the United States.

HISTORY: (Added July 31, 1970, P.L. 91-368, § 1, 84 Stat. 693.)

CHAPTER 3. INTER-AMERICAN CONVENTION ON INTERNATIONAL COMMERCIAL ARBITRATION

§ 301. Enforcement of Convention

The Inter-American Convention on International Commercial Arbitration of January 30, 1975, shall be enforced in United States courts in accordance with this chapter [9 USC §§ 301 et seq.].

HISTORY: (Added Aug. 15, 1990, P.L. 101-369, § 1, 104 Stat. 448.)

§ 302. Incorporation by reference

Sections 202, 203, 204, 205, and 207 of this title shall apply to this chapter [9 USC §§ 301 et seq.] as if specifically set forth herein, except that for the purposes of this chapter [9 USC §§ 301 et seq.] "the Convention" shall mean the Inter-American Convention.

HISTORY: (Added Aug. 15, 1990, P.L. 101-369, § 1, 104 Stat. 448.)

§ 303. Order to compel arbitration; appointment of arbitrators; locale

(a) A court having jurisdiction under this chapter [9 USC §§ 301 et seq.] may direct that arbitration be held in accordance with the agreement at any place therein provided for, whether that place is within or without the United States. The court may also appoint arbitrators in accordance with the provisions of the agreement.

(b) In the event the agreement does not make provision for the place of arbitration or the appointment of arbitrators, the court shall direct that the arbitration shall be held and the arbitrators be appointed in accordance with Article 3 of the Inter-American Convention.

HISTORY: (Added Aug. 15, 1990, P.L. 101-369, § 1, 104 Stat. 448.)

§ 304. Recognition and enforcement of foreign arbitral decisions and awards; reciprocity

Arbitral decisions or awards made in the territory of a foreign State shall, on the basis of reciprocity, be recognized and enforced under this chapter [9 USC §§ 301 et seq.] only if that State has ratified or acceded to the Inter-American Convention.

HISTORY: (Added Aug. 15, 1990, P.L. 101-369, § 1, 104 Stat. 449.)

§ 305. Relationship between the Inter-American Convention and the Convention on the Recognition and Enforcement of Foreign Arbitral Awards of June 10, 1958

When the requirements for application of both the Inter-American Convention and the Convention on the Recognition and Enforcement of Foreign Arbitral Awards of June 10, 1958, are met, determination as to which Convention applies shall, unless otherwise expressly agreed, be made as follows:

(1) If a majority of the parties to the arbitration agreement are citizens of a State or States that have ratified or acceded to the Inter-American Convention and are member States of the Organization of American States, the Inter-American Convention shall apply.

(2) In all other cases the Convention on the Recognition and Enforcement of Foreign Arbitral Awards of June 10, 1958, shall apply.

HISTORY: (Added Aug. 15, 1990, P.L. 101-369, § 1, 104 Stat. 449.)

§ 306. Applicable rules of Inter-American Commercial Arbitration Commission

(a) For the purposes of this chapter [9 USC §§ 301 et seq.] the rules of procedure of the Inter-American Commercial Arbitration Commission referred to in Article 3 of the Inter-American Convention shall, subject to subsection (b) of this section, be those rules as promulgated by the Commission on July 1, 1988.

(b) In the event the rules of procedure of the Inter-American Commercial Arbitration Commission are modified or amended in accordance with the procedures for amendment of the rules of that Commission, the Secretary of State, by regulation in accordance with section 553 of title 5, consistent with the aims and purposes of this Convention, may prescribe that such modifications or amendments shall be effective for purposes of this chapter [9 USC §§ 301 et seq.].

HISTORY: (Added Aug. 15, 1990, P.L. 101-369, § 1, 104 Stat. 449.)

§ 307. Chapter 1; residual application

Chapter 1 [9 USC §§ 1 et seq.] applies to actions and proceedings brought under this chapter [9 USC §§ 301 et seq.] to the extent chapter 1 [9 USC §§ 1 et seq.] is not in conflict with this chapter [9 USC §§ 301 et seq.] or the Inter-American Convention as ratified by the United States.

HISTORY: (Added Aug. 15, 1990, P.L. 101-369, § 1, 104 Stat. 449.)

C. Jurisdictional Provisions of Title 28 of the U.S. Code

Source: 28 U.S.C. § 1330 *et seq.*

Website information:

http://wwwsecure.law.cornell.edu/topics/federal_courts.html
This website provides an overview of the U.S. federal court system prepared by the Legal Information Institute, and includes links to some of the most important sections of Title 28 of the U.S. Code. It also allows a textual search of Title 28.

http://travel.state.gov/judicial_assistance.html
This website of the U.S. Department of State provides country-by-country information regarding the availability and source of judicial assistance.

Introduction

Article III of the U.S. Constitution provides that "[t]he judicial Power of the United States, shall be vested in one supreme Court, and in such inferior Courts as the Congress may from time to time establish." Congress has exercised its power to create the system of District Courts at the trial level, and Courts of Appeal at the intermediate appellate level, as well as special courts with exclusive jurisdiction over certain matters. Federal District Courts have limited "subject matter" jurisdiction. Thus, cases brought to them must fall within the Constitution and statutory authorization provided by Congress. The rules of subject matter jurisdiction are found in Title 28 of the United States Code. The most important of these rules are § 1331, providing for "federal question" jurisdiction, and thus allowing actions based on federal law; and § 1332, providing for "diversity jurisdiction," and thus giving the federal courts authority to hear cases involving "citizens" of different states of the United States, as well as cases involving foreign citizens on one side and "citizens" of U.S. states on the other. Title 28 also contains sections providing District Court subject matter jurisdiction over cases suits dealing with admiralty (§ 1333), bankruptcy (§ 1334), antitrust (§ 1337), and intellectual property rights (§ 1338). Special provisions exist for tort claims involving violations of international law (§ 1350), and cases against "consuls or vice consuls of foreign states" and "members of a mission or members of their families." (§ 1351)

Title 28 also has sections dealing with service of process in international litigation (§ 1696), transmittal of letters rogatory to and from foreign courts (§ 1781), and assistance to foreign and international tribunals. (§ 1782).

CHAPTER 85. DISTRICT COURTS; JURISDICTION

§ 1330. Actions against foreign states

(a) The district courts shall have original jurisdiction without regard to amount in controversy of any nonjury civil action against a foreign state as defined in section 1603(a) of this title [28 USC § 1603(a)] as to any claim for relief in personam with respect to which the foreign state is not entitled to immunity either under sections 1605-1607 of this title [28 USC §§ 1605-1607] or under any applicable international agreement.

(b) Personal jurisdiction over a foreign state shall exist as to every claim for relief over which the district courts have jurisdiction under subsection (a) where service has been made under section 1608 of this title [28 USC § 1608].

(c) For purposes of subsection (b), an appearance by a foreign state does not confer personal jurisdiction with respect to any claim for relief not arising out of any transaction or occurrence enumerated in sections 1605-1607 of this title [28 USC §§ 1605-1607].

HISTORY: (Added Oct. 21, 1976, P.L. 94-583, § 2(a), 90 Stat. 2891.)

§ 1331. Federal question

The district courts shall have original jurisdiction of all civil actions arising under the Constitution, laws, or treaties of the United States.

HISTORY: (June 25, 1948, ch 646, § 1, 62 Stat. 930; July 25, 1958, P.L. 85-554, § 1, 72 Stat. 415; Oct. 21, 1976, P.L. 94-574, § 2, 90 Stat. 2721; Dec. 1, 1980, P.L. 96-486, § 2(a), 94 Stat. 2369.)

§ 1332. Diversity of citizenship; amount in controversy; costs

(a) The district courts shall have original jurisdiction of all civil actions where the matter in controversy exceeds the sum or value of $75,000, exclusive of interest and costs, and is between—

(1) citizens of different States;

(2) citizens of a State and citizens or subjects of a foreign state;

(3) citizens of different States and in which citizens or subjects of a foreign state are additional parties; and

214

(4) a foreign state, defined in section 1603(a) of this title [28 USC § 1603(a)], as plaintiff and citizens of a State or of different States.

For the purposes of this section, section 1335, and section 1441, an alien admitted to the United States for permanent residence shall be deemed a citizen of the State in which such alien is domiciled.

(b) Except when express provision therefor is otherwise made in a statute of the United States, where the plaintiff who files the case originally in the Federal courts is finally adjudged to be entitled to recover less than the sum or value of $75,000, computed without regard to any setoff or counterclaim to which the defendant may be adjudged to be entitled, and exclusive of interest and costs, the district court may deny costs to the plaintiff and, in addition, may impose costs on the plaintiff.

(c) For the purposes of this section and section 1441 of this title—

(1) a corporation shall be deemed to be a citizen of any State by which it has been incorporated and of the State where it has its principal place of business, except that in any direct action against the insurer of a policy or contract of liability insurance, whether incorporated or unincorporated, to which action the insured is not joined as a party-defendant, such insurer shall be deemed a citizen of the state of which the insured is a citizen, as well as of any State by which the insurer has been incorporated and of the State where it has its principal place of business; and

(2) the legal representative of the estate of a decedent shall be deemed to be a citizen only of the same State as the decedent, and the legal representative of an infant or incompetent shall be deemed to be a citizen only of the same State as the infant or incompetent.

(d) The word "States", as used in this section, includes the Territories, the District of Columbia, and the Commonwealth of Puerto Rico.

HISTORY: (June 25, 1948, ch 646, § 1, 62 Stat. 930; July 26, 1956, ch 740, 70 Stat. 658; July 25, 1958, P.L. 85-554, § 2, 72 Stat. 415; Aug. 14, 1964, P.L. 88-439, § 1, 78 Stat. 445; Oct. 21, 1976, P.L. 94-583, § 3, 90 Stat. 2891; Nov. 19, 1988, Pub. L. 100-702, Title II, §§ 201(a), 202(a), 203(a), 102 Stat. 4646.) (As amended Oct. 19, 1996, Pub. L. 104-317, Title II, § 205(a), 110 Stat. 3850.)

§ 1333. Admiralty, maritime and prize cases

The district courts shall have original jurisdiction, exclusive of the courts of the States, of:

(1) Any civil case of admiralty or maritime jurisdiction, saving to suitors in all cases all other remedies to which they are otherwise entitled.

(2) Any prize brought into the United States and all proceedings for the condemnation of property taken as prize.

HISTORY: (June 25, 1948, ch 646, § 1, 62 Stat. 931; May 24, 1949, ch 139, § 79, 63 Stat. 101.)

§ 1334. Bankruptcy cases and proceedings

(a) Except as provided in subsection (b) of this section, the district courts shall have original and exclusive jurisdiction of all cases under title 11 [11 USC §§ 101 et seq.].

(b) Notwithstanding any Act of Congress that confers exclusive jurisdiction on a court or courts other than the district courts, the district courts shall have original but not exclusive jurisdiction of all civil proceedings arising under title 11 [11 USC §§ 101 et seq.], or arising in or related to cases under title 11 [11 USC §§ 101 et seq.].

(c) (1) Nothing in this section prevents a district court in the interest of justice, or in the interest of comity with State courts or respect for State law, from abstaining from hearing a particular proceeding arising under title 11 [11 USC §§ 101 et seq.] or arising in or related to a case under title 11 [11 USC §§ 101 et seq.].

(2) Upon timely motion of a party in a proceeding based upon a State law claim or State law cause of action, related to a case under title 11 [11 USC §§ 101 et seq.] but not arising under title 11 [11 USC §§ 101 et seq.], with respect to which an action could not have been commenced in a court of the United States absent jurisdiction under this section, the district court shall abstain from hearing such proceeding if an action is commenced, and can be timely adjudicated, in a State forum of appropriate jurisdiction.

(d) Any decision to abstain or not to abstain made under this subsection (other than a decision not to abstain in a proceeding described in subsection (c)(2)), is not reviewable by appeal or otherwise by the court of appeals under section 158(d), 1291, or 1292 of this title or by the Supreme Court of the United States under section 1254 of this title. This subsection shall not be construed to limit the applicability of the stay provided for by section 362 of title 11, United States Code [11 USC § 362], as such section applies to an action affecting the property of the estate in bankruptcy.

(e) The district court in which a case under title 11 [11 USC §§ 101 et seq.] is commenced or is pending shall have exclusive jurisdiction of all of the property, wherever located, of the debtor as of the commencement of such case, and of property of the estate.

HISTORY: (June 25, 1948, ch 646, § 1, 62 Stat. 931; Nov. 6, 1978, P.L. 95-598, Title II, § 238(a), 92 Stat. 2667; July 10, 1984, P.L. 98-353, Title I, § 101(a), 98 Stat. 333; Oct. 27, 1986, P.L. 99-554, Title I, Subtitle C, § 144(e), 100 Stat. 3096; Dec. 1, 1990, P.L. 101-650, Title III, § 309(b), 104 Stat. 5113; Oct. 22, 1994, P.L. 103-394, Title I, § 104(b), 108 Stat. 4109.)

§ 1337. Commerce and antitrust regulations; amount in controversy, costs

(a) The district courts shall have original jurisdiction of any civil action or proceeding arising under any Act of Congress regulating commerce or protecting trade and commerce against restraints and monopolies: Provided, however, That the district courts shall have original jurisdiction of an action brought under section 11707 or 14706 of title 49 [49 USC § 11707], only if the matter in controversy for each receipt or bill of lading exceeds $10,000, exclusive of interest and costs.

(b) Except when express provision therefor is otherwise made in a statute of the United States, where a plaintiff who files the case under section 11707 or 14706 of title 49 [49 USC § 11707], originally in the Federal courts is finally adjudged to be entitled to recover less than the sum or value of $10,000, computed without regard to any setoff or counterclaim to which the defendant may be adjudged to be entitled, and exclusive of any interest and costs, the district court may deny costs to the plaintiff and, in addition, may impose costs on the plaintiff.

(c) The district courts shall not have jurisdiction under this section of any matter within the exclusive jurisdiction of the Court of International Trade under chapter 95 of this title [28 USC §§ 1581 et seq.].

HISTORY: (June 25, 1948, ch 646, § 1, 62 Stat. 931; Oct. 20, 1978, P.L. 95-486, § 9(a), 92 Stat. 1633; Oct. 10, 1980, P.L. 96-417, Title V, § 505, 94 Stat. 1743; Jan. 12, 1983, P.L. 97-449, § 5(f), 96 Stat. 2442; Dec. 29, 1995, P.L. 104-88, Title III, Subtitle A, § 305(a)(3), 109 Stat. 944.)

§ 1338. Patents, plant variety protection, copyrights, mask works, designs, trade-marks, and unfair competition

(a) The district courts shall have original jurisdiction of any civil action arising under any Act of Congress relating to patents, plant variety protection, copyrights and trade-marks. Such jurisdiction shall be exclusive of the courts of the states in patent, plant variety protection and copyright cases.

(b) The district courts shall have original jurisdiction of any civil action asserting a claim of unfair competition when joined with a substantial and related claim under the copyright, patent, plant variety protection or trade-mark laws.

(c) Subsections (a) and (b) apply to exclusive rights in mask works under chapter 9 of title 17 [17 USC §§ 901 et seq.] and to exclusive rights in designs under chapter 13 of title 17 [19 USC § 1301 et seq.], to the same extent as such subsections apply to copyrights.

HISTORY: (June 25, 1948, ch 646, § 1, 62 Stat. 931; Dec. 24, 1970, P.L. 91-577, Title III, § 143(b), 84 Stat. 1559.) (As amended Nov. 19, 1988, P.L. 100-702, Title X, § 1020(a)(4), 102 Stat. 4671; Oct. 28, 1998, P.L. 105-304, Title V, § 503(b)(1), (2)(A), 112 Stat. 2917.)

§ 1350. Alien's action for tort

The district courts shall have original jurisdiction of any civil action by an alien for a tort only, committed in violation of the law of nations or a treaty of the United States.

HISTORY: (June 25, 1948, ch 646, § 1, 62 Stat. 934.)

§ 1351. Consuls, vice consuls, and members of a diplomatic mission as defendant

The district courts shall have original jurisdiction, exclusive of the courts of the States, of all civil actions and proceedings against—

(1) consuls or vice consuls of foreign states; or

(2) members of a mission or members of their families (as such terms are defined in section 2 of the Diplomatic Relations Act [22 USC § 254a]).

HISTORY: (June 25, 1948, ch 646, § 1, 62 Stat. 934; May 24, 1949, ch 139, § 80(c), 63 Stat. 101; Sept. 30, 1978, P.L. 95-393, § 8(a)(1), 92 Stat. 810.)

CHAPTER 87. DISTRICT COURTS; VENUE

§ 1391. Venue generally

. . . .

(f) A civil action against a foreign state as defined in section 1603(a) of this title may be brought—

(1) in any judicial district in which a substantial part of the events or omissions giving rise to the claim occurred, or a substantial part of property that is the subject of the action is situated;

(2) in any judicial district in which the vessel or cargo of a foreign state is situated, if the claim is asserted under section 1605(b) of this title;

(3) in any judicial district in which the agency or instrumentality is licensed to do business or is doing business, if the action is brought against an agency or instrumentality of a foreign state as defined in section 1603(b) of this title; or

(4) in the United States District Court for the District of Columbia if the action is brought against a foreign state or political subdivision thereof.

HISTORY: (June 25, 1948, ch. 646, § 1, 62 Stat. 935; Oct. 5, 1962, P.L. 87-748, § 2, 76 Stat. 744; Dec. 23, 1963, P.L. 88-234, 77 Stat. 473; Nov. 2, 1966, P.L. 89-714, §§ 1, 2, 80 Stat. 1111; Oct. 21, 1976, P.L. 94-583, §§ 3, 5, 90 Stat. 2721, 2897; Nov. 19, 1988, P.L. 100-702, Title X, § 1013(a), 102 Stat. 4669; Dec. 1, 1990, P.L. 101-650, Title III, § 311, 104 Stat. 5114; Dec. 9, 1991, Pub. L. 102-198, § 3, 105 Stat. 1623; Oct. 29, 1992, Pub. L. 102-572, Title V, § 504, 106 Stat. 4513; Oct. 3, 1995, Pub. L. 104-34, § 1, 109 Stat. 293.)

CHAPTER 89. DISTRICT COURTS; REMOVAL OF CASES FROM STATE COURTS

§ 1441. Actions removable generally

(a) Except as otherwise expressly provided by Act of Congress, any civil action brought in a State court of which the district courts of the United States have original jurisdiction, may be removed by the defendant or the defendants, to the district court of the United States for the district and division embracing the place where such action is pending. For purposes of removal under this chapter [28 USC §§ 1441 et seq.], the citizenship of defendants sued under fictitious names shall be disregarded.

(b) Any civil action of which the district courts have original jurisdiction founded on a claim or right arising under the Constitution, treaties or laws of the United States shall be removable without regard to the citizenship or residence of the parties. Any other such action shall be removable only if none of the parties in interest properly joined and served as defendants is a citizen of the State in which such action is brought.

(c) Whenever a separate and independent claim or cause of action within the jurisdiction conferred by section 1331 of this title is joined with one or more otherwise nonremovable claims or causes of action, the entire case may be removed and the district court may determine all issues therein, or, in its discretion, may remand all matters in which State law predominates.

(d) Any civil action brought in a State court against a foreign state as defined in section 1603(a) of this title may be removed by the foreign state to the district court of the United States for the district and division embracing the place where such action is pending. Upon removal the action shall be tried by the court without jury. Where removal is based upon this subsection, the time limitations of section 1446(b) of this chapter may be enlarged at any time for cause shown.

(e) The court to which such civil action is removed is not precluded from hearing and determining any claim in such civil action because the State court from which such civil action is removed did not have jurisdiction over that claim.

HISTORY: (June 25, 1948, ch 646, § 1, 62 Stat. 937; Oct. 21, 1976, P.L. 94-583, § 6, 90 Stat. 2898; June 19, 1986, P.L. 99-336, § 3(a), 100 Stat. 637; Nov. 19, 1988, P.L. 100-702, Title X, § 1016(a), 102 Stat. 4669; Dec. 1, 1990, P.L. 101-650, Title III, § 312, 104 Stat. 5114; Dec. 9, 1991, Pub. L. 102-198, § 4, 105 Stat. 1623.)

PART V. PROCEDURE

CHAPTER 113. PROCESS

§ 1696. Service in foreign and international litigation

(a) The district court of the district in which a person resides or is found may order service upon him of any document issued in connection with a proceeding in a foreign or international tribunal. The order may be made pursuant to a letter rogatory issued, or request made, by a foreign or international tribunal or upon application of any interested person and shall direct the manner of service. Service pursuant to this subsection does not, of itself, require the recognition or enforcement in the United States of a judgment, decree, or order rendered by a foreign or international tribunal.

(b) This section does not preclude service of such a document without an order of court.

HISTORY: (Added Oct. 3, 1964, P.L. 88-619, § 4(a), 78 Stat. 995.)

CHAPTER 117. EVIDENCE; DEPOSITIONS

§ 1781. Transmittal of letter rogatory or request

(a) The Department of State has power, directly, or through suitable channels—

(1) to receive a letter rogatory issued, or request made, by a foreign or international tribunal, to transmit it to the tribunal, officer, or agency in the United States to whom it is addressed, and to receive and return it after execution; and

(2) to receive a letter rogatory issued, or request made, by a tribunal in the United States, to transmit it to the foreign or international tribunal, officer, or agency to whom it is addressed, and to receive and return it after execution.

(b) This section does not preclude—

(1) the transmittal of a letter rogatory or request directly from a foreign or international tribunal to the tribunal, officer, or agency in the United States to whom it is addressed and its return in the same manner; or

(2) the transmittal of a letter rogatory or request directly from a tribunal in the United States to the foreign or international tribunal, officer, or agency to whom it is addressed and its return in the same manner.

HISTORY: (June 25, 1945, c. 646, § 1, 62 Stat. 949; Oct. 3, 1964, P.L. 88-619, § 8(a), 78 Stat. 996.)

§ 1782. Assistance to foreign and international tribunals and to litigants before such tribunals

(a) The district court of the district in which a person resides or is found may order him to give his testimony or statement or to produce a document or other thing for use in a proceeding in a foreign or international tribunal, including criminal investigations conducted before formal accusation. The order may be made pursuant to a letter rogatory issued, or request made, by a foreign or international tribunal or upon the application of any interested person and may direct that the testimony or statement be given, or the document or other thing be produced, before a person appointed by the court. By virtue of his appointment, the person appointed has power to administer any necessary oath and take the testimony or statement. The order may prescribe the practice and procedure, which may be in whole or part the practice and procedure of the foreign country or the international tribunal, for taking the testimony or statement or producing the document or other thing. To the extent that the order does not prescribe otherwise, the testimony or statement shall be taken, and the document or other thing produced, in accordance with the Federal Rules of Civil Procedure.

A person may not be compelled to give his testimony or statement or to produce a document or other thing in violation of any legally applicable privilege.

(b) This chapter [28 USC §§ 1781 et seq.] does not preclude a person within the United States from voluntarily giving his testimony or statement, or producing a document or other thing, for use in a proceeding in a foreign or international tribunal before any person and in any manner acceptable to him.

HISTORY: (June 25, 1948, c. 646, § 1, 62 Stat. 949; May 24, 1949, c. 139, § 93, 63 Stat. 103; Oct. 3, 1964, P.L. 88-619, § 9(a), 78 Stat. 997; Feb. 10, 1996, P.L. 104-106, Div. A., Title XII, Subtitle E, § 1342(b), 110 Stat. 486.)

§ 1783. Subpoena of person in foreign country

(a) A court of the United States may order the issuance of a subpoena requiring the appearance as a witness before it, or before a person or body designated by it, of a national or resident of the United States who is in a foreign country, or requiring the production of a specified document or other thing by him, if the court finds that particular testimony or the production of the document or other thing by him is necessary in the interest of justice, and, in other than a criminal action or proceeding, if the court finds, in addition, that it is not possible to obtain his testimony in admissible form without his personal appearance or to obtain the production of the document or other thing in any other manner.

(b) The subpoena shall designate the time and place for the appearance or for the production of the document or other thing. Service of the subpoena and any order to show cause, rule, judgment, or decree authorized by this section or by section 1784 of this title [28 USC § 1784] shall be effected in accordance with the provisions of the Federal Rules of Civil Procedure relating to service of process on a person in a foreign country. The person serving the subpoena shall tender to the person to whom the subpoena is addressed his estimated necessary travel and attendance expenses, the amount of which shall be determined by the court and stated in the order directing the issuance of the subpoena.

HISTORY: (June 25, 1948, c. 646, § 1, 62 Stat. 949; Oct. 3, 1964, P.L. 88-619, § 10(a), 78 Stat. 997.)

§ 1784. Contempt

(a) The court of the United States which has issued a subpoena served in a foreign country may order the person who has failed to appear or who has failed to produce a document or other thing as directed therein to show cause before it at a designated time why he should not be punished for contempt.

(b) The court, in the order to show cause, may direct that any of the person's property within the United States be levied upon or seized, in the manner provided by law or court rules governing levy or seizure under execution, and held to satisfy any judgment that may be rendered against him pursuant to subsection (d) of this section if adequate security, in such amount as the court may direct in the order, be given for any damage that he might suffer should he not be found in contempt. Security under this subsection may not be required of the United States.

(c) A copy of the order to show cause shall be served on the person in accordance with section 1783(b) of this title [28 USC § 1783 (b)].

(d) On the return day of the order to show cause or any later day to which the hearing may be continued, proof shall be taken. If the person is found in contempt, the court, notwithstanding any limitation upon its power generally to punish for contempt, may fine him not more than $100,000 and direct that the fine and costs of the proceedings be satisfied by a sale of the property levied upon or seized, conducted upon the notice required and in the manner provided for sales upon execution.

HISTORY: (June 25, 1948, c. 646, § 1, 62 Stat. 949; Oct. 3, 1964, P.L. 88-619, § 11, 78 Stat. 998.)

TITLE 22 - FOREIGN RELATIONS AND INTERCOURSE

CHAPTER 32. FOREIGN ASSISTANCE

§ 2370. Prohibitions against furnishing assistance

. . . .

(e)(2) Notwithstanding any other provision of law, no court in the United States shall decline on the ground of the federal act of state doctrine to make a determination on the merits giving effect to the principles of international law in a case in which a claim of title or other right to property is asserted by any party including a foreign state (or a party claiming through such state) based upon (or traced through) a confiscation or other taking after January 1, 1959, by an act of that state in violation of the principles of international law, including the principles of compensation and the other standards set out in this subsection: Provided, That this subparagraph shall not be applicable (1) in any case in which an act of a foreign state is not contrary to international law or with respect to a claim of title or other right to property acquired pursuant to an irrevocable letter of credit of not more than 180 days duration issued in good faith prior to the time of the confiscation or other taking, or (2) in any case with respect to which the President determines that application of the act of state doctrine is required in that particular case by the foreign policy interests of the United States and a suggestion to this effect is filed on his behalf in that case with the court.

HISTORY: (Pub. L. 87-195, Pt. III, § 620, Sept. 4, 1961, 75 Stat. 444; Pub. L. 87-565, Pt. III, § 301(d), Aug. 1, 1962, 76 Stat. 260; Pub. L. 88-205, Pt. III, § 301(e), Dec. 16, 1963, 77 Stat. 386; Pub. L. 88-633, Pt. III, § 301(d) to (g), Oct. 7, 1964, 78 Stat. 1013; Pub. L. 89-171, Pt. III, § 301(d), Sept. 6, 1965, 79 Stat. 659; Pub. L. 89-583, Pt. III, § 301(h), Sept. 19, 1966, 80 Stat. 805; Pub. L. 90-137, Pt. III, § 301(f), Nov. 14, 1967, 81 Stat. 459; Pub. L. 90-554, Pt. III, § 301(c), Oct. 8, 1968, 82 Stat. 963; Pub. L. 91-175, Pt. III, § 303, Dec. 30, 1969, 83 Stat. 820; Pub. L. 92-226, Pt. III, § 301, Feb. 7, 1972, 86 Stat. 27; Pub. L. 93-189, § 15, Dec. 17, 1973, 87 Stat. 722; Pub. L. 93-559, §§ 22 to 24, 44, Dec. 30, 1974, 88 Stat. 1801, 1802, 1813; Pub. L. 94-104, § 2(c)(1), (2), Oct. 6, 1975, 89 Stat. 509; Pub. L. 94-329, Title IV, § 403, Title VI, § 606, June 30, 1976, 90 Stat. 757, 768; Pub. L. 95-88, Title I, § 123(a), (b), Aug. 3, 1977, 91 Stat. 541; Pub. L. 95-92, § 22(d), Aug. 4, 1977, 91 Stat. 624; Pub. L. 95-384, § 13(a), Sept. 26, 1978, 92 Stat. 737; Pub. L. 95-424, Title I, §§ 102(g)(2)(F), 115(k), Title V, § 502(d)(1), Oct. 6, 1978, 92 Stat. 943, 952, 959; Pub. L. 96-533, Title II, § 203, Dec. 16, 1980, 94 Stat. 3145; Pub. L. 97-113, Title VII, §§ 702, 707, 734(a)(1), (13), (b), Dec. 29, 1981, 95 Stat. 1544, 1546, 1560; Pub. L. 99-83, Title XII, §§ 1202, 1203, Aug. 8,

1985, 99 Stat. 276, 277; Pub. L. 102-511, Title IX, § 901, Oct. 24, 1992, 106 Stat. 3355; Pub. L. 103-199, Title VII, § 705(3), Dec. 17, 1993, 107 Stat. 2328; Pub. L. 103-306, Title V, § 573, Aug. 23, 1994, 108 Stat. 1653; Pub. L. 104-114, Title II, § 204(d)(1), (2), Mar. 12, 1996, 110 Stat. 810; Pub. L. 105-277, Div. G, Title XXVIII, § 2810(a), Oct. 21, 1998, 112 Stat. 2681-850.)

D. Selected Provisions of the Foreign Sovereign Immunities Act of 1976

Source: 28 U.S.C. § 1602 *et seq.*

Website information:

http://travel.state.gov/fsia.html
This website of the U.S. Department of State provides answers to frequently asked questions about the Foreign Sovereign Immunities Act.

Introduction

The Foreign Sovereign Immunities Act of 1976 (FSIA), as amended and codified at 28 U.S.C. § 1603, *et seq.*, specifies the circumstances and procedures by which plaintiffs may sue foreign states, their agents or instrumentalities in United States courts. This act of Congress codifies the modern "restrictive theory" of the principle of sovereign immunity, and supplants the traditional role of the executive branch with that of the judiciary in determining state immunity. Under the restrictive theory of sovereign immunity, a state or state instrumentality remains immune from the jurisdiction of the courts of another state in claims arising out of public matters. However, it is not immune from claims arising out of commercial and non-governmental activities that may be carried on by private persons.

The Act provides specific exceptions to the jurisdictional immunity of a foreign state beyond the limited realm of "commercial activity." Immunity to suit will not exist under § 1605(a) when:
(1) it has been explicitly or implicitly waived by the foreign state;
(2) the suit arises out of commercial activity carried on in the United States that causes a direct effect in the United States;
(3) property has been taken in violation of international law;
(4) property rights in the United States are acquired in immovable property, or by succession or gift;
(5) the claim is for money damages against a foreign state for personal injury or death, damage to or loss of property, occurring in the United States and caused by the tortious act or omission of a foreign state;
(6) the action is brought to enforce an arbitration agreement made by a foreign state with or for the benefit of a private party; or
(7) where the action is for money damages for personal injury or death that was caused by an act of torture, extrajudicial killing, aircraft sabotage, or hostage taking, if the foreign state is designated as a state sponsor of terrorism under § 6(j) of the Export Administration Act of 1979 (50 U.S.C. App 2405(j)) or § 620A of the Foreign Assistance Act of 1961 (22 U.S.C. 2371).

In addition to immunity from suit, the FSIA also contains rules dealing with immunity from attachment and execution of property of a foreign state (§§ 1609-1610), including specific rules on prejudgment attachment (§1610(d)), and rules dealing with immunity from attachment and execution of property of a foreign central bank or monetary authority.

Selected Provisions of the Foreign Sovereign Immunities Act of 1976

28 U.S. Code
CHAPTER 97. JURISDICTIONAL IMMUNITIES OF FOREIGN STATES

§ 1602. Findings and declaration of purpose

The Congress finds that the determination by United States courts of the claims of foreign states to immunity from the jurisdiction of such courts would serve the interests of justice and would protect the rights of both foreign states and litigants in United States courts. Under international law, states are not immune from the jurisdiction of foreign courts insofar as their commercial activities are concerned, and their commercial property may be levied upon for the satisfaction of judgments rendered against them in connection with their commercial activities. Claims of foreign states to immunity should henceforth be decided by courts of the United States and of the States in conformity with the principles set forth in this chapter.

HISTORY: (Added Oct. 21, 1976, P.L. 94-583, § 4(a), 90 Stat. 2892.)

§ 1603. Definitions

For purposes of this chapter—

(a) A "foreign state", except as used in section 1608 of this title [28 USC § 1608], includes a political subdivision of a foreign state or an agency or instrumentality of a foreign state as defined in subsection (b).

(b) An "agency or instrumentality of a foreign state" means any entity—

(1) which is a separate legal person, corporate or otherwise, and

(2) which is an organ of a foreign state or political subdivision thereof, or a majority of whose shares or other ownership interest is owned by a foreign state or political subdivision thereof, and

(3) which is neither a citizen of a State of the United States as defined in section 1332(c) and (d) of this title [28 USC § 1332(c), (d)], nor created under the laws of any third country.

(c) The "United States" includes all territory and waters, continental or insular, subject to the jurisdiction of the United States.

(d) A "commercial activity" means either a regular course of commercial conduct or a particular commercial transaction or act. The commercial character of an activity shall be determined by reference to the nature of the course of conduct or particular transaction or act, rather than by reference to its purpose.

(e) A "commercial activity carried on in the United States by a foreign state" means commercial activity carried on by such state and having substantial contact with the United States.

HISTORY: (Added Oct. 21, 1976, P.L. 94-583, § 4(a), 90 Stat. 2892.)

§ 1604. Immunity of a foreign state from jurisdiction

Subject to existing international agreements to which the United States is a party at the time of enactment of this Act [enacted Oct. 21, 1976] a foreign state shall be immune from the jurisdiction of the courts of the United States and of the States except as provided in sections 1605 to 1607 of this chapter [28 USC §§ 1605-1607].

HISTORY: (Added Oct. 21, 1976, P.L. 94-583, § 4(a), 90 Stat. 2892.)

§ 1605. General exceptions to the jurisdictional immunity of a foreign state

(a) A foreign state shall not be immune from the jurisdiction of courts of the United States or of the States in any case—

(1) in which the foreign state has waived its immunity either explicitly or by implication, notwithstanding any withdrawal of the waiver which the foreign state may purport to effect except in accordance with the terms of the waiver;

(2) in which the action is based upon a commercial activity carried on in the United States by the foreign state; or upon an act performed in the United States in connection with a commercial activity of the foreign state elsewhere; or upon an act outside the territory of the United States in connection with a commercial activity of the foreign state elsewhere and that act causes a direct effect in the United States;

(3) in which rights in property taken in violation of international law are in issue and that property or any property exchanged for such property is present in the United States in connection with a commercial activity carried on in the United States by the foreign state; or that property or any property exchanged for such property is owned or operated by an agency or instrumentality of the foreign state and that agency or instrumentality is engaged in a commercial activity in the United States;

(4) in which rights in property in the United States acquired by succession or gift or rights in immovable property situated in the United States are in issue;

227

(5) not otherwise encompassed in paragraph (2) above, in which money damages are sought against a foreign state for personal injury or death, or damage to or loss of property, occurring in the United States and caused by the tortious act or omission of that foreign state or of any official or employee of that foreign state while acting within the scope of his office or employment; except this paragraph shall not apply to—

(A) any claim based upon the exercise or performance or the failure to exercise or perform a discretionary function regardless of whether the discretion be abused, or

(B) any claim arising out of malicious prosecution, abuse of process, libel, slander, misrepresentation, deceit, or interference with contract rights;

(6) in which the action is brought, either to enforce an agreement made by the foreign state with or for the benefit of a private party to submit to arbitration all or any differences which have arisen or which may arise between the parties with respect to a defined legal relationship, whether contractual or not, concerning a subject matter capable of settlement by arbitration under the laws of the United States, or to confirm an award made pursuant to such an agreement to arbitrate, if (A) the arbitration takes place or is intended to take place in the United States, (B) the agreement or award is or may be governed by a treaty or other international agreement in force for the United States calling for the recognition and enforcement of arbitral awards, (C) the underlying claim, save for the agreement to arbitrate, could have been brought in a United States court under this section or section 1607 [28 USC § 1607], or (D) paragraph (1) of this subsection is otherwise applicable.

(7) not otherwise covered by paragraph (2), in which money damages are sought against a foreign state for personal injury or death that was caused by an act of torture, extrajudicial killing, aircraft sabotage, hostage taking, or the provision of material support or resources (as defined in section 2339A of title 18) for such an act if such act or provision of material support is engaged in by an official, employee, or agent of such foreign state while acting within the scope of his or her office, employment, or agency, except that the court shall decline to hear a claim under this paragraph—

(A) if the foreign state was not designated as a state sponsor of terrorism under section 6(j) of the Export Administration Act of 1979 (50 U.S.C. App. 2405(j)) or section 620A of the Foreign Assistance Act of 1961 (22 U.S.C. 2371) at the time the act occurred, unless later so designated as a result of such act; and

(B) even if the foreign state is or was so designated, if—

(i) the act occurred in the foreign state against which the claim has been brought and the claimant has not afforded the foreign state a reasonable opportunity to arbitrate the claim in accordance with accepted international rules of arbitration; or

Selected Provisions of the Foreign Sovereign Immunities Act of 1976

(ii) neither the claimant nor the victim was a national of the United States (as that term is defined in section 101(a)(22) of the Immigration and Nationality Act [8 USC § 1101(a)(22)]) when the act upon which the claim is based occurred.

(b) A foreign state shall not be immune from the jurisdiction of the courts of the United States in any case in which a suit in admiralty is brought to enforce a maritime lien against a vessel or cargo of the foreign state, which maritime lien is based upon a commercial activity of the foreign state: Provided, That—

(1) notice of the suit is given by delivery of a copy of the summons and of the complaint to the person, or his agent, having possession of the vessel or cargo against which the maritime lien is asserted; and if the vessel or cargo is arrested pursuant to process obtained on behalf of the party bringing the suit, the service of process of arrest shall be deemed to constitute valid delivery of such notice, but the party bringing the suit shall be liable for any damages sustained by the foreign state as a result of the arrest if the party bringing the suit had actual or constructive knowledge that the vessel or cargo of a foreign state was involved; and

(2) notice to the foreign state of the commencement of suit as provided in section 1608 of this title [28 USC § 1608] is initiated within ten days either of the delivery of notice as provided in paragraph (1) of this subsection or, in the case of a party who was unaware that the vessel or cargo of a foreign state was involved, of the date such party determined the existence of the foreign state's interest.

(c) Whenever notice is delivered, under subsection (b)(1), the suit to enforce a maritime lien shall thereafter proceed and shall be heard and determined according to the principles of law and rules of practice of suits in rem whenever it appears that, had the vessel been privately owned and possessed, a suit in rem might have been maintained. A decree against the foreign state may include costs of the suit and, if the decree is for a money judgment, interest as ordered by the court, except that the court may not award judgment against the foreign state in an amount greater than the value of the vessel or cargo upon which the maritime lien arose. Such value shall be determined as of the time notice is served under subsection (b)(1). Decrees shall be subject to appeal and revision as provided in other cases of admiralty and maritime jurisdiction. Nothing shall preclude the plaintiff in any proper case from seeking relief in personam in the same action brought to enforce a maritime lien as provided in this section.

(d) A foreign state shall not be immune from the jurisdiction of the courts of the United States in any action brought to foreclose a preferred mortgage, as defined in the Ship Mortgage Act, 1920 (46 U.S.C. 911 and following). Such action shall be brought, heard, and determined in accordance with the provisions of that Act and in accordance with the principles of law and rules of practice of suits in rem, whenever it appears that had the vessel been privately owned and possessed a suit in rem might have been maintained.

(e) For purposes of paragraph (7) of subsection (a)—

229

(1) the terms "torture" and "extrajudicial killing" have the meaning given those terms in section 3 of the Torture Victim Protection Act of 1991 [28 USC § 1350 note];

(2) the term "hostage taking" has the meaning given that term in Article 1 of the International Convention Against the Taking of Hostages; and

(3) the term "aircraft sabotage" has the meaning given that term in Article 1 of the Convention for the Suppression of Unlawful Acts Against the Safety of Civil Aviation.

(f) No action shall be maintained under subsection (a)(7) unless the action is commenced not later than 10 years after the date on which the cause of action arose. All principles of equitable tolling, including the period during which the foreign state was immune from suit, shall apply in calculating this limitation period.

(g) Limitation on discovery.

(1) In general.

(A) Subject to paragraph (2), if an action is filed that would otherwise be barred by section 1604, but for subsection (a)(7), the court, upon request of the Attorney General, shall stay any request, demand, or order for discovery on the United States that the Attorney General certifies would significantly interfere with a criminal investigation or prosecution, or a national security operation, related to the incident that gave rise to the cause of action, until such time as the Attorney General advises the court that such request, demand, or order will no longer so interfere.

(B) A stay under this paragraph shall be in effect during the 12-month period beginning on the date on which the court issues the order to stay discovery. The court shall renew the order to stay discovery for additional 12-month periods upon motion by the United States if the Attorney General certifies that discovery would significantly interfere with a criminal investigation or prosecution, or a national security operation, related to the incident that gave rise to the cause of action.

(2) Sunset.

(A) Subject to subparagraph (B), no stay shall be granted or continued in effect under paragraph (1) after the date that is 10 years after the date on which the incident that gave rise to the cause of action occurred.

(B) After the period referred to in subparagraph (A), the court, upon request of the Attorney General, may stay any request, demand, or order for discovery on the United States that the court finds a substantial likelihood would—

(i) create a serious threat of death or serious bodily injury to any person;

(ii) adversely affect the ability of the United States to work in cooperation with foreign and international law enforcement agencies in investigating violations of United States law; or

(iii) obstruct the criminal case related to the incident that gave rise to the cause of action or undermine the potential for a conviction in such case.

(3) Evaluation of evidence. The court's evaluation of any request for a stay under this subsection filed by the Attorney General shall be conducted ex parte and in camera.

(4) Bar on motions to dismiss. A stay of discovery under this subsection shall constitute a bar to the granting of a motion to dismiss under rules 12(b)(6) and 56 of the Federal Rules of Civil Procedure.

(5) Construction. Nothing in this subsection shall prevent the United States from seeking protective orders or asserting privileges ordinarily available to the United States.

HISTORY: (Added Oct. 21, 1976, P.L. 94-583, § 4(a), 90 Stat. 2892; Nov. 9, 1988, P.L. 100-640, § 1, 102 Stat. 3333; Nov. 16, 1988, P.L. 100-669, § 2, 102 Stat. 3969.) (As amended Dec. 1, 1990, P.L. 101-650, Title III, § 325(b)(8), 104 Stat. 5121; April 24, 1996, P.L. 104-132, Title II, Subtitle B, § 221(a), 110 Stat. 1241; April 25, 1997, P.L. 105-11, 111 Stat. 22.)

§ 1606. Extent of liability

As to any claim for relief with respect to which a foreign state is not entitled to immunity under section 1605 or 1607 of this chapter [28 USC §§ 1605, 1607], the foreign state shall be liable in the same manner and to the same extent as a private individual under like circumstances; but a foreign state except for an agency or instrumentality thereof shall not be liable for punitive damages, except any action under section 1605(a)(7) or 1610(f); if, however, in any case wherein death was caused, the law of the place where the action or omission occurred provides, or has been construed to provide, for damages only punitive in nature, the foreign state shall be liable for actual or compensatory damages measured by the pecuniary injuries resulting from such death which were incurred by the persons for whose benefit the action was brought.

HISTORY: (Added Oct. 21, 1976, P.L. 94-583, § 4(a), 90 Stat. 2894.) (As amended Oct. 21, 1998, P.L. 105-277, Div A, § 101(h) [Title I, § 117(b)], 112 Stat. 2681-491.)

Selected Provisions of the Foreign Sovereign Immunities Act of 1976

§ 1607. Counterclaims

In any action brought by a foreign state, or in which a foreign state intervenes, in a court of the United States or of a State, the foreign state shall not be accorded immunity with respect to any counterclaim—

(a) for which a foreign state would not be entitled to immunity under section 1605 of this chapter [28 USC § 1605] had such claim been brought in a separate action against the foreign state; or

(b) arising out of the transaction or occurrence that is the subject matter of the claim of the foreign state; or

(c) to the extent that the counterclaim does not seek relief exceeding in amount or differing in kind from that sought by the foreign state.

HISTORY: (Added Oct. 21, 1976, P.L. 94-583, § 4(a), 90 Stat. 2894.)

§ 1608. Service; time to answer; default

(a) Service in the courts of the United States and of the States shall be made upon a foreign state or political subdivision of a foreign state:

(1) by delivery of a copy of the summons and complaint in accordance with any special arrangement for service between the plaintiff and the foreign state or political subdivision; or

(2) if no special arrangement exists, by delivery of a copy of the summons and complaint in accordance with an applicable international convention on service of judicial documents; or

(3) if service cannot be made under paragraphs (1) or (2), by sending a copy of the summons and complaint and a notice of suit, together with a translation of each into the official language of the foreign state, by any form of mail requiring a signed receipt, to be addressed and dispatched by the clerk of the court to the head of the ministry of foreign affairs of the foreign state concerned, or

(4) if service cannot be made within 30 days under paragraph (3), by sending two copies of the summons and complaint and a notice of suit, together with a translation of each into the official language of the foreign state, by any form of mail requiring a signed receipt, to be addressed and dispatched by the clerk of the court to the Secretary of State in Washington, District of Columbia, to the attention of the Director of Special Consular Services—and the Secretary shall transmit one copy of the papers through diplomatic channels to the foreign state

and shall send to the clerk of the court a certified copy of the diplomatic note indicating when the papers were transmitted.

As used in this subsection, a "notice of suit" shall mean a notice addressed to a foreign state and in a form prescribed by the Secretary of State by regulation.

(b) Service in the courts of the United States and of the States shall be made upon an agency or instrumentality of a foreign state:

(1) by delivery of a copy of the summons and complaint in accordance with any special arrangement for service between the plaintiff and the agency or instrumentality; or

(2) if no special arrangement exists, by delivery of a copy of the summons and complaint either to an officer, a managing or general agent, or to any other agent authorized by appointment or by law to receive service of process in the United States; or in accordance with an applicable international convention on service of judicial documents; or

(3) if service cannot be made under paragraphs (1) or (2), and if reasonably calculated to give actual notice, by delivery of a copy of the summons and complaint, together with a translation of each into the official language of the foreign state—

(A) as directed by an authority of the foreign state or political subdivision in response to a letter rogatory or request or

(B) by any form of mail requiring a signed receipt, to be addressed and dispatched by the clerk of the court to the agency or instrumentality to be served, or

(C) as directed by order of the court consistent with the law of the place where service is to be made.

(c) Service shall be deemed to have been made—

(1) in the case of service under subsection (a)(4), as of the date of transmittal indicated in the certified copy of the diplomatic note; and

(2) in any other case under this section, as of the date of receipt indicated in the certification, signed and returned postal receipt, or other proof of service applicable to the method of service employed.

(d) In any action brought in a court of the United States or of a State, a foreign state, a political subdivision thereof, or an agency or instrumentality of a foreign state shall serve an answer or other responsive pleading to the complaint within sixty days after service has been made under this section.

Selected Provisions of the Foreign Sovereign Immunities Act of 1976

(e) No judgment by default shall be entered by a court of the United States or of a State against a foreign state, a political subdivision thereof, or an agency or instrumentality of a foreign state, unless the claimant establishes his claim or right to relief by evidence satisfactory to the court. A copy of any such default judgment shall be sent to the foreign state or political subdivision in the manner prescribed for service in this section.

HISTORY: (Added Oct. 21, 1976, P.L. 94-583, § 4(a), 90 Stat. 2894.)

§ 1609. Immunity from attachment and execution of property of a foreign state

Subject to existing international agreements to which the United States is a party at the time of enactment of this Act [enacted Oct. 21, 1976] the property in the United States of a foreign state shall be immune from attachment arrest and execution except as provided in sections 1610 and 1611 of this chapter [28 USC §§ 1610, 1611].

HISTORY: (Added Oct. 21, 1976, P.L. 94-583, § 4(a), 90 Stat. 2895.)

§ 1610. Exceptions to the immunity from attachment or execution

(a) The property in the United States of a foreign state, as defined in section 1603(a) of this chapter [28 USC § 1603(a)], used for a commercial activity in the United States, shall not be immune from attachment in aid of execution, or from execution, upon a judgment entered by a court of the United States or of a State after the effective date of this Act [see effective date note to 28 USC § 1602], if—

(1) the foreign state has waived its immunity from attachment in aid of execution or from execution either explicitly or by implication, notwithstanding any withdrawal of the waiver the foreign state may purport to effect except in accordance with the terms of the waiver, or

(2) the property is or was used for the commercial activity upon which the claim is based, or

(3) the execution relates to a judgment establishing rights in property which has been taken in violation of international law or which has been exchanged for property taken in violation of international law, or

(4) the execution relates to a judgment establishing rights in property—

(A) which is acquired by succession or gift, or

(B) which is immovable and situated in the United States: Provided, That such property is not used for purposes of maintaining a diplomatic or consular mission or the residence of the Chief of such mission, or

(5) the property consists of any contractual obligation or any proceeds from such a contractual obligation to indemnify or hold harmless the foreign state or its employees under a policy of automobile or other liability or casualty insurance covering the claim which merged into the judgment, or

(6) the judgment is based on an order confirming an arbitral award rendered against the foreign state, provided that attachment in aid of execution, or execution, would not be inconsistent with any provision in the arbitral agreement, or

(7) the judgment relates to a claim for which the foreign state is not immune under section 1605(a)(7), regardless of whether the property is or was involved with the act upon which the claim is based.

(b) In addition to subsection (a), any property in the United States of an agency or instrumentality of a foreign state engaged in commercial activity in the United States shall not be immune from attachment in aid of execution, or from execution, upon a judgment entered by a court of the United States or of a State after the effective date of this Act [see effective date note to 28 USC § 1062], if—

(1) the agency or instrumentality has waived its immunity from attachment in aid of execution or from execution either explicitly or implicitly, notwithstanding any withdrawal of the waiver the agency or instrumentality may purport to effect except in accordance with the terms of the waiver, or

(2) the judgment relates to a claim for which the agency or instrumentality is not immune by virtue of section 1605(a)(2), (3), (5) or (7), or 1605(b) of this chapter [28 USC § 1605 (a)(2), (3), (5), (b)], regardless of whether the property is or was involved in the act upon which the claim is based.

(c) No attachment or execution referred to in subsections (a) and (b) of this section shall be permitted until the court has ordered such attachment and execution after having determined that a reasonable period of time has elapsed following the entry of judgment and the giving of any notice required under section 1608(e) of this chapter [28 USC § 1608(e)].

(d) The property of a foreign state, as defined in section 1603(a) of this chapter [28 USC § 1603(a)], used for a commercial activity in the United States, shall not be immune from attachment prior to the entry of judgment in any action brought in a court of the United States or of a State, or prior to the elapse of the period of time provided in subsection (c) of this section, if—

(1) the foreign state has explicitly waived its immunity from attachment prior to judgment, notwithstanding any withdrawal of the waiver the foreign state may purport to effect except in accordance with the terms of the waiver, and

(2) the purpose of the attachment is to secure satisfaction of a judgment that has been or may ultimately be entered against the foreign state, and not to obtain jurisdiction.

(e) The vessels of a foreign state shall not be immune from arrest in rem, interlocutory sale, and execution in actions brought to foreclose a preferred mortgage as provided in section 1605(d).

(f) (1) (A) Notwithstanding any other provision of law, including but not limited to section 208(f) of the Foreign Missions Act (22 U.S.C. 4308(f)), and except as provided in subparagraph (B), any property with respect to which financial transactions are prohibited or regulated pursuant to section 5(b) of the Trading with the Enemy Act (50 U.S.C. App. 5(b)), section 620(a) of the Foreign Assistance Act of 1961 (22 U.S.C. 2370(a)), sections 202 and 203 of the International Emergency Economic Powers Act (50 U.S.C. 1701-1702), or any other proclamation, order, regulation, or license issued pursuant thereto, shall be subject to execution or attachment in aid of execution of any judgment relating to a claim for which a foreign state (including any agency or instrumentality or such state) claiming such property is not immune under section 1605(a)(7).

(B) Subparagraph (A) shall not apply if, at the time the property is expropriated or seized by the foreign state, the property has been held in title by a natural person or, if held in trust, has been held for the benefit of a natural person or persons.

(2) (A) At the request of any party in whose favor a judgment has been issued with respect to a claim for which the foreign state is not immune under section 1605(a)(7), the Secretary of the Treasury and the Secretary of State shall fully, promptly, and effectively assist any judgment creditor or any court that has issued any such judgment in identifying, locating, and executing against the property of that foreign state or any agency or instrumentality of such state.

(B) In providing such assistance, the Secretaries—

(i) may provide such information to the court under seal; and

(ii) shall provide the information in a manner sufficient to allow the court to direct the United States Marshall's office to promptly and effectively execute against that property.

HISTORY: (Added Oct. 21, 1976, P.L. 94-583, § 4(a), 90 Stat. 2896; Nov. 9, 1988, P.L. 100-640, § 2, 102 Stat. 3333; Nov. 16, 1988, P.L. 100-669, § 3, 102 Stat. 3969.) (As amended Dec. 1, 1990, P.L. 101-650, Title III, § 325(b)(9), 104 Stat. 5121; April 24, 1996, P.L. 104-132, Title II, Subtitle

B, § 221(b), 110 Stat. 1242; Oct. 21, 1998, P.L. 105-277, Div A, § 101(h) [Title I, § 117(a)], 112 Stat. 2681-491.)

§ 1611. Certain types of property immune from execution

(a) Notwithstanding the provisions of section 1610 of this chapter [28 USC § 1610], the property of those organizations designated by the President as being entitled to enjoy the privileges, exemptions, and immunities provided by the International Organizations Immunities Act [22 USC §§ 288 et seq.] shall not be subject to attachment or any other judicial process impeding the disbursement of funds to, or on the order of, a foreign state as the result of an action brought in the courts of the United States or of the States.

(b) Notwithstanding the provisions of section 1610 of this chapter [28 USC § 1610], the property of a foreign state shall be immune from attachment and from execution, if—

(1) the property is that of a foreign central bank or monetary authority held for its own account, unless such bank or authority, or its parent foreign government, has explicitly waived its immunity from attachment in aid of execution, or from execution, notwithstanding any withdrawal of the waiver which the bank, authority or government may purport to effect except in accordance with the terms of the waiver; or

(2) the property is, or is intended to be, used in connection with a military activity and

(A) is of a military character, or

(B) is under the control of a military authority or defense agency.

(c) Notwithstanding the provisions of section 1610 of this chapter, the property of a foreign state shall be immune from attachment and from execution in an action brought under section 302 of the Cuban Liberty and Democratic Solidarity (LIBERTAD) Act of 1996 [22 USC § 6082] to the extent that the property is a facility or installation used by an accredited diplomatic mission for official purposes.

HISTORY: (Added Oct. 21, 1976, P.L. 94-583, § 4(a), 90 Stat. 2897.) (As amended March 12, 1996, P.L. 104-114, Title III, § 302(e), 110 Stat. 818.)

E. The Foreign Corrupt Practices Act

Source: 15 U.S.C. § 78m *et seq.*

Website information:

http://www.usdoj.gov/criminal/fraud/fcpa/
This website of the U.S. Department of Justice contains links to the text of the Foreign Corrupt Practices Act, legislative history, opinion procedures releases, and other information on the Act and related international agreements and developments.

Introduction

The Foreign Corrupt Practices Act, originally enacted in 1977, was amended in 1988 and 1998. It contains both accounting provisions requiring careful record-keeping by public companies regarding disposition of assets, and "anti-bribery" provisions prohibiting payments to foreign officials. Under the anti-bribery provisions, there are six principal elements of a violation, providing that it is unlawful to:

(1) make use of interstate commerce
(2) corruptly
(3) in furtherance of an offer of anything of value
(4) to (a) a foreign official, (b) a foreign political party, party official, or candidate for office or (c) to any person while knowing that all or any portion of such thing of value will be offered or given to a foreign official, political party or candidate
(5) for the purpose of inducing a foreign official to use his influence to affect any act or decision of his government or governmental instrumentality
(6) in order to obtain or retain business, or direct business to any person.[1]

The Act provides an exception to liability for "any facilitating or expediting payment to a foreign official, political party, or party official the purpose of which is to expedite or to secure the

---

[1] 15 U.S.C. § 78dd-1(a) and § 78dd-2(a). Item (5) of this list can further be broken down per the language of the statute, prohibiting a payment to the target individual for purposes of:

(A)(i) influencing any act or decision of such foreign official in his official capacity, (ii) inducing such foreign official to do or omit to do any act in violation of the lawful duty of such official [political party or candidate], to do or omit to do any act in violation of the lawful duty of such official, or (iii) securing any improper advantage; or

(B) inducing such foreign official to use his influence with a foreign government or instrumentality thereof to affect or influence any act or decision of such government or instrumentality . . . .

Id. at § 78dd-1(a)(1). *See also* §§ 78dd-1(a)(2) & (3) and 78dd-2(a)(1), (2) & (3). The "securing any improper advantage" language was added in 1998 to conform to the requirements o the OECD Convention on Combating Bribery of Foreign Public Official in International Business Transactions.

performance of a routine governmental action by a foreign official, political party, or party official."[2] Two affirmative defenses exist to a violation of the Act: (1) where the payment was "lawful under the written laws and regulations of the foreign . . . country," and (2) where the payment "was a reasonable and bonafide expenditure, such as travel and lodging expenses . . . directly related to (A) the promotion, demonstration or explanation of products or services; or (b) the execution or performance of a contract."[3]

The Act also provides for vicarious liability when a person knows that a payment to another person will be offered or given to a foreign official or political party.[4]

The 1998 amendments to the Act, contained in the International Anti-Bribery and Fair Competition Act,[5] implemented changes agreed to in the OECD Convention on Combating Bribery of Foreign Public Officials in International Business Transactions.

---

[2]15 U.S.C. §§ 78dd-1(b) and 78dd-2(b).

[3]15 U.S.C. §§ 78dd-1(c) and 78dd-2(c).

[4]15 U.S.C. §§ 78dd-1(a)(3) and 78dd-2(a)(3).

[5]Pub. L. 105-366; 112 Stat. 3202 (1998).

FOREIGN CORRUPT PRACTICES ACT
(including amendments)

U.S. Code Title 15

§ 78m. Periodical and other reports

(a) Reports by issuer of security; contents. Every issuer of a security registered pursuant to section 12 of this title [15 USC § 78l] shall file with the Commission, in accordance with such rules and regulations as the Commission may prescribe as necessary or appropriate for the proper protection of investors and to insure fair dealing in the security—

(1) such information and documents (and such copies thereof) as the Commission shall require to keep reasonably current the information and documents required to be included in or filed with an application or registration statement filed pursuant to section 12 [15 USC § 78l], except that the Commission may not require the filing of any material contract wholly executed before July 1, 1962.

(2) such annual reports (and such copies thereof), certified if required by the rules and regulations of the Commission by independent public accountants, and such quarterly reports (and such copies thereof), as the Commission may prescribe.

Every issuer of a security registered on a national securities exchange shall also file a duplicate original of such information, documents, and reports with the exchange.

(b) Form of report; books, records, and internal accounting; directives.

(1) The Commission may prescribe, in regard to reports made pursuant to this title, the form or forms in which the required information shall be set forth, the items or details to be shown in the balance sheet and the earning statement, and the methods to be followed in the preparation of reports, in the appraisal or valuation of assets and liabilities, in the determination of depreciation and depletion, in the differentiation of recurring and nonrecurring income, in the differentiation of investment and operating income, and in the preparation, where the Commission deems it necessary or desirable, of separate and/or consolidated balance sheets or income accounts of any person directly or indirectly controlling or controlled by the issuer, or any person under direct or indirect common control with the issuer; but in the case of the reports of any person whose methods of accounting are prescribed under the provisions of any law of the United States, or any rule or regulation thereunder, the rules and regulations of the Commission with respect to reports shall not be inconsistent with the requirements imposed by such law or rule or regulation in respect of the same subject matter (except that such rules and regulations of the Commission may be inconsistent with such requirements to the extent that the Commission determines that the public interest or the protection of investors so requires).

240

(2) Every issuer which has a class of securities registered pursuant to section 12 of this title [15 USC § 78l] and every issuer which is required to file reports pursuant to section 15(d) of this title [15 USC § 78o(d)] shall—

(A) make and keep books, records, and accounts, which, in reasonable detail, accurately and fairly reflect the transactions and dispositions of the assets of the issuer; and

(B) devise and maintain a system of internal accounting controls sufficient to provide reasonable assurances that—

(i) transactions are executed in accordance with management's general or specific authorization;

(ii) transactions are recorded as necessary (I) to permit preparation of financial statements in conformity with generally accepted accounting principles or any other criteria applicable to such statements, and (II) to maintain accountability for assets;

(iii) access to assets is permitted only in accordance with management's general or specific authorization; and

(iv) the recorded accountability for assets is compared with the existing assets at reasonable intervals and appropriate action is taken with respect to any differences.

(3) (A) With respect to matters concerning the national security of the United States, no duty or liability under paragraph (2) of this subsection shall be imposed upon any person acting in cooperation with the head of any Federal department or agency responsible for such matters if such act in cooperation with such head of a department or agency was done upon the specific, written directive of the head of such department or agency pursuant to Presidential authority to issue such directives. Each directive issued under this paragraph shall set forth the specific facts and circumstances with respect to which the provisions of this paragraph are to be invoked. Each such directive shall, unless renewed in writing, expire one year after the date of issuance.

(B) Each head of a Federal department or agency of the United States who issues a directive pursuant to this paragraph shall maintain a complete file of all such directives and shall, on October 1 of each year, transmit a summary of matters covered by such directives in force at any time during the previous year to the Permanent Select Committee on Intelligence of the House of Representatives and the Select Committee on Intelligence of the Senate.

(4) No criminal liability shall be imposed for failing to comply with the requirements of paragraph (2) of this subsection except as provided in paragraph (5) of this subsection.

241

(5) No person shall knowingly circumvent or knowingly fail to implement a system of internal accounting controls or knowingly falsify any book, record, or account described in paragraph (2).

(6) Where an issuer which has a class of securities registered pursuant to section 12 of this title [15 USC § 78l] or an issuer which is required to file reports pursuant to section 15(d) of this title [15 USC § 78o(d)] holds 50 per centum or less of the voting power with respect to a domestic or foreign firm, the provisions of paragraph (2) require only that the issuer proceed in good faith to use its influence, to the extent reasonable under the issuer's circumstances, to cause such domestic or foreign firm to devise and maintain a system of internal accounting controls consistent with paragraph (2). Such circumstances include the relative degree of the issuer's ownership of the domestic or foreign firm and the laws and practices governing the business operations of the country in which such firm is located. An issuer which demonstrates good faith efforts to use such influence shall be conclusively presumed to have complied with the requirements of paragraph (2).

(7) For the purpose of paragraph (2) of this subsection, the terms "reasonable assurances" and "reasonable detail" mean such level of detail and degree of assurance as would satisfy prudent officials in the conduct of their own affairs.

(c) Alternative reports. If in the judgment of the Commission any report required under subsection (a) is inapplicable to any specified class or classes of issuers, the Commission shall require in lieu thereof the submission of such reports of comparable character as it may deem applicable to such class or classes of issuers.

(d) Reports by persons acquiring more than five per centum of certain classes of securities.

(1) Any person who, after acquiring directly or indirectly the beneficial ownership of any equity security of a class which is registered pursuant to section 12 of this title [15 USC § 78l], or any equity security of an insurance company which would have been required to be so registered except for the exemption contained in section 12(g)(2)(G) of this title [15 USC § 78l(g)(2)(G)], or any equity security issued by a closed-end investment company registered under the Investment Company Act of 1940 [15 USC §§ 80a-1 *et seq.*] or any equity security issued by a Native Corporation pursuant to section 37(d)(6) of the Alaska Native Claims Settlement Act [43 USC § 1629c(d)(6)], is directly or indirectly the beneficial owner of more than 5 per centum of such class shall, within ten days after such acquisition, send to the issuer of the security at its principal executive office, by registered or certified mail, send to each exchange where the security is traded, and file with the Commission, a statement containing such of the following information, and such additional information, as the Commission may by rules and regulations, prescribe as necessary or appropriate in the public interest or for the protection of investors—

(A) the background, and identity, residence, and citizenship of, and the nature of such beneficial ownership by, such person and all other persons by whom or on whose behalf the purchases have been or are to be effected;

(B) the source and amount of the funds or other consideration used or to be used in making the purchases, and if any part of the purchase price is represented or is to be represented by funds or other consideration borrowed or otherwise obtained for the purpose of acquiring, holding, or trading such security, a description of the transaction and the names of the parties thereto, except that where a source of funds is a loan made in the ordinary course of business by a bank, as defined in section 3(a)(6) of this title [15 USC § 78c(a)(6)], if the person filing such statement so requests, the name of the bank shall not be made available to the public;

(C) if the purpose of the purchases or prospective purchases is to acquire control of the business of the issuer of the securities, any plans or proposals which such persons may have to liquidate such issuer, to sell its assets to or merge it with any other persons, or to make any other major change in its business or corporate structure;

(D) the number of shares of such security which are beneficially owned, and the number of shares concerning which there is a right to acquire, directly or indirectly, by (i) such person, and (ii) by each associate of such person, giving the background, identity, residence, and citizenship of each such associate; and

(E) information as to any contracts, arrangements, or understandings with any person with respect to any securities of the issuer, including but not limited to transfer of any of the securities, joint ventures, loan or option arrangements, puts or calls, guaranties of loans, guaranties against loss or guaranties of profits, division of losses or profits, or the giving or withholding of proxies, naming the persons with whom such contracts, arrangements, or understandings have been entered into, and giving the details thereof.

(2) If any material change occurs in the facts set forth in the statements to the issuer and the exchange, and in the statement filed with the Commission, an amendment shall be transmitted to the issuer and the exchange and shall be filed with the Commission, in accordance with such rules and regulations as the Commission may prescribe as necessary or appropriate in the public interest or for the protection of investors.

(3) When two or more persons act as a partnership, limited partnership, syndicate, or other group for the purpose of acquiring, holding, or disposing of securities of an issuer, such syndicate or group shall be deemed a "person" for the purposes of this subsection.

(4) In determining, for purposes of this subsection, any percentage of a class of any security, such class shall be deemed to consist of the amount of the outstanding securities of such class,

exclusive of any securities of such class held by or for the account of the issuer or a subsidiary of the issuer.

(5) The Commission, by rule or regulation or by order, may permit any person to file in lieu of the statement required by paragraph (1) of this subsection or the rules and regulations thereunder, a notice stating the name of such person, the number of shares of any equity securities subject to paragraph (1) which are owned by him, the date of their acquisition and such other information as the Commission may specify, if it appears to the Commission that such securities were acquired by such person in the ordinary course of his business and were not acquired for the purpose of and do not have the effect of changing or influencing the control of the issuer nor in connection with or as a participant having such purpose or effect.

(6) The provisions of this subsection shall not apply to—

(A) any acquisition or offer to acquire securities made or proposed to be made by means of a registration statement under the Securities Act of 1933;

(B) any acquisition of the beneficial ownership of a security which, together with all other acquisitions by the same person of securities of the same class during the preceding twelve months, does not exceed 2 per centum of that class;

(C) any acquisition of an equity security by the issuer of such security;

(D) any acquisition or proposed acquisition of a security which the Commission, by rules or regulations or by order, shall exempt from the provisions of this subsection as not entered into for the purpose of, and not having the effect of, changing or influencing the control of the issuer or otherwise as not comprehended within the purposes of this subsection.

(e) Purchase of securities by issuer.

(1) It shall be unlawful for an issuer which has a class of equity securities registered pursuant to section 12 of this title [15 USC § 78l], or which is a closed-end investment company registered under the Investment Company Act of 1940 [15 USC §§ 80a-1 *et seq.*], to purchase any equity security issued by it if such purchase is in contravention of such rules and regulations as the Commission, in the public interest or for the protection of investors, may adopt (A) to define acts and practices which are fraudulent, deceptive, or manipulative, and (B) to prescribe means reasonably designed to prevent such acts and practices. Such rules and regulations may require such issuer to provide holders of equity securities of such class with such information relating to the reasons for such purchase, the source of funds, the number of shares to be purchased, the price to be paid for such securities, the method of purchase, and such additional information, as the Commission deems necessary or appropriate in the public

interest or for the protection of investors, or which the Commission deems to be material to a determination whether such security should be sold.

(2) For the purpose of this subsection, a purchase by or for the issuer or any person controlling, controlled by, or under common control with the issuer, or a purchase subject to control of the issuer or any such person, shall be deemed to be a purchase by the issuer. The Commission shall have power to make rules and regulations implementing this paragraph in the public interest and for the protection of investors, including exemptive rules and regulations covering situations in which the Commission deems it unnecessary or inappropriate that a purchase of the type described in this paragraph shall be deemed to be a purchase by the issuer for purposes of some or all of the provisions of paragraph (1) of this subsection.

(3) At the time of filing such statement as the Commission may require by rule pursuant to paragraph (1) of this subsection, the person making the filing shall pay to the Commission a fee of 1/50 of 1 per centum of the value of securities proposed to be purchased. The fee shall be reduced with respect to securities in an amount equal to any fee paid with respect to any securities issued in connection with the proposed transaction under section 6(b) of the Securities Act of 1933 [15 USC § 77f(b)], or the fee paid under that section [15 USC § 77f(b)] shall be reduced in an amount equal to the fee paid to the Commission in connection with such transaction under this paragraph.

(f) Reports by institutional investment managers.

(1) Every institutional investment manager which uses the mails, or any means or instrumentality of interstate commerce in the course of its business as an institutional investment manager and which exercises investment discretion with respect to accounts holding equity securities of a class described in section 13(d)(1) of this title [subsec. (d)(1) of this section] having an aggregate fair market value on the last trading day in any of the preceding twelve months of at least $100,000,000 or such lesser amount (but in no case less than $10,000,000) as the Commission, by rule, may determine, shall file reports with the Commission in such form, for such periods, and at such times after the end of such periods as the Commission, by rule, may prescribe, but in no event shall such reports be filed for periods longer than one year or shorter than one quarter. Such reports shall include for each such equity security held on the last day of the reporting period by accounts (in aggregate or by type as the Commission, by rule, may prescribe) with respect to which the institutional investment manager exercises investment discretion (other than securities held in amounts which the Commission, by rule, determines to be insignificant for purposes of this subsection), the name of the issuer and the title, class, CUSIP number, number of shares or principal amount, and aggregate fair market value of each such security. Such reports may also include for accounts (in aggregate or by type) with respect to which the institutional investment manager exercises investment discretion such of the following information as the Commission, by rule, prescribes—

(A) the name of the issuer and the title, class, CUSIP number, number of shares or principal amount, and aggregate fair market value or cost or amortized cost of each other security (other than an exempted security) held on the last day of the reporting period by such accounts;

(B) the aggregate fair market value or cost or amortized cost of exempted securities (in aggregate or by class) held on the last day of the reporting period by such accounts;

(C) the number of shares of each equity security of a class described in section 13(d)(1) of this title [subsec. (d)(1) of this section] held on the last day of the reporting period by such accounts with respect to which the institutional investment manager possesses sole or shared authority to exercise the voting rights evidenced by such securities;

(D) the aggregate purchases and aggregate sales during the reporting period of each security (other than an exempted security) effected by or for such accounts; and

(E) with respect to any transaction or series of transactions having a market value of at least $500,000 or such other amount as the Commission, by rule, may determine, effected during the reporting period by or for such accounts in any equity security of a class described in section 13(d)(1) of this title [subsec. (d)(1) of this section]—

(i) the name of the issuer and the title, class, and CUSIP number of the security;

(ii) the number of shares or principal amount of the security involved in the transaction;

(iii) whether the transaction was a purchase or sale;

(iv) the per share price or prices at which the transaction was effected;

(v) the date or dates of the transaction;

(vi) the date or dates of the settlement of the transaction;

(vii) the broker or dealer through whom the transaction was effected;

(viii) the market or markets in which the transaction was effected; and

(ix) such other related information as the Commission, by rule, may prescribe.

(2) The Commission, by rule or order, may exempt, conditionally or unconditionally, any institutional investment manager or security or any class of institutional investment managers or securities from any or all of the provisions of this subsection or the rules thereunder.

(3) The Commission shall make available to the public for a reasonable fee a list of all equity securities of a class described in section 13(d)(1) of this title [subsec. (d)(1) of this section], updated no less frequently than reports are required to be filed pursuant to paragraph (1) of this subsection. The Commission shall tabulate the information contained in any report filed pursuant to this subsection in a manner which will, in the view of the Commission, maximize the usefulness of the information to other Federal and State authorities and the public. Promptly after the filing of any such report, the Commission shall make the information contained therein conveniently available to the public for a reasonable fee in such form as the Commission, by rule, may prescribe, except that the Commission, as it determines to be necessary or appropriate in the public interest or for the protection of investors, may delay or prevent public disclosure of any such information in accordance with section 552 of title 5, United States Code [5 USC § 552]. Notwithstanding the preceding sentence, any such information identifying the securities held by the account of a natural person or an estate or trust (other than a business trust or investment company) shall not be disclosed to the public.

(4) In exercising its authority under this subsection, the Commission shall determine (and so state) that its action is necessary or appropriate in the public interest and for the protection of investors or to maintain fair and orderly markets or, in granting an exemption, that its action is consistent with the protection of investors and the purposes of this subsection. In exercising such authority the Commission shall take such steps as are within its power, including consulting with the Comptroller General of the United States, the Director of the Office of Management and Budget, the appropriate regulatory agencies, Federal and State authorities which, directly or indirectly, require reports from institutional investment managers of information substantially similar to that called for by this subsection, national securities exchanges, and registered securities associations, (A) to achieve uniform, centralized reporting of information concerning the securities holdings of and transactions by or for accounts with respect to which institutional investment managers exercise investment discretion, and (B) consistently with the objective set forth in the preceding subparagraph, to avoid unnecessarily duplicative reporting by, and minimize the compliance burden on, institutional investment managers. Federal authorities which, directly or indirectly, require reports from institutional investment managers of information substantially similar to that called for by this subsection shall cooperate with the Commission in the performance of its responsibilities under the preceding sentence. An institutional investment manager which is a bank, the deposits of which are insured in accordance with the Federal Deposit Insurance Act, shall file with the appropriate regulatory agency a copy of every report filed with the Commission pursuant to this subsection.

(5)   (A) For purposes of this subsection the term "institutional investment manager" includes any person, other than a natural person, investing in or buying and selling securities for its own account, and any person exercising investment discretion with respect to the account of any other person.

247

(B) The Commission shall adopt such rules as it deems necessary or appropriate to prevent duplicative reporting pursuant to this subsection by two or more institutional investment managers exercising investment discretion with respect to the same amount [account].

(g) Statement of equity security ownership.

(1) Any person who is directly or indirectly the beneficial owner of more than 5 per centum of any security of a class described in subsection (d)(1) of this section shall send to the issuer of the security and shall file with the Commission a statement setting forth, in such form and at such time as the Commission may, by rule, prescribe—

(A) such person's identity, residence, and citizenship; and

(B) the number and description of the shares in which such person has an interest and the nature of such interest.

(2) If any material change occurs in the facts set forth in the statement sent to the issuer and filed with the Commission, an amendment shall be transmitted to the issuer and shall be filed with the Commission, in accordance with such rules and regulations as the Commission may prescribe as necessary or appropriate in the public interest or for the protection of investors.

(3) When two or more persons act as a partnership, limited partnership, syndicate, or other group for the purpose of acquiring, holding, or disposing of securities of an issuer, such syndicate or group shall be deemed a "person" for the purposes of this subsection.

(4) In determining, for purposes of this subsection, any percentage of a class of any security, such class shall be deemed to consist of the amount of the outstanding securities of such class, exclusive of any securities of such class held by or for the account of the issuer or a subsidiary of the issuer.

(5) In exercising its authority under this subsection, the Commission shall take such steps as it deems necessary or appropriate in the public interest or for the protection of investors (A) to achieve centralized reporting of information regarding ownership, (B) to avoid unnecessarily duplicative reporting by and minimize the compliance burden on persons required to report, and (C) to tabulate and promptly make available the information contained in any report filed pursuant to this subsection in a manner which will, in the view of the Commission, maximize the usefulness of the information to other Federal and State agencies and the public.

(6) The Commission may, by rule or order, exempt, in whole or in part, any person or class of persons from any or all of the reporting requirements of this subsection as it deems necessary or appropriate in the public interest or for the protection of investors.

(h) Large trader reporting.

(1) Identification requirements for large traders. For the purpose of monitoring the impact on the securities markets of securities transactions involving a substantial volume or a large fair market value or exercise value and for the purpose of otherwise assisting the Commission in the enforcement of this title, each large trader shall—

(A) provide such information to the Commission as the Commission may by rule or regulation prescribe as necessary or appropriate, identifying such large trader and all accounts in or through which such large trader effects such transactions; and

(B) identify, in accordance with such rules or regulations as the Commission may prescribe as necessary or appropriate, to any registered broker or dealer by or through whom such large trader directly or indirectly effects securities transactions, such large trader and all accounts directly or indirectly maintained with such broker or dealer by such large trader in or through which such transactions are effected.

(2) Recordkeeping and reporting requirements for brokers and dealers. Every registered broker or dealer shall make and keep for prescribed periods such records as the Commission by rule or regulation prescribes as necessary or appropriate in the public interest, for the protection of investors, or otherwise in furtherance of the purposes of this title, with respect to securities transactions that equal or exceed the reporting activity level effected directly or indirectly by or through such registered broker or dealer of or for any person that such broker or dealer knows is a large trader, or any person that such broker or dealer has reason to know is a large trader on the basis of transactions in securities effected by or through such broker or dealer. Such records shall be available for reporting to the Commission, or any self-regulatory organization that the Commission shall designate to receive such reports, on the morning of the day following the day the transactions were effected, and shall be reported to the Commission or a self-regulatory organization designated by the Commission immediately upon request by the Commission or such a self-regulatory organization. Such records and reports shall be in a format and transmitted in a manner prescribed by the Commission (including, but not limited to, machine readable form).

(3) Aggregation rules. The Commission may prescribe rules or regulations governing the manner in which transactions and accounts shall be aggregated for the purpose of this subsection, including aggregation on the basis of common ownership or control.

(4) Examination of broker and dealer records. All records required to be made and kept by registered brokers and dealers pursuant to this subsection with respect to transactions effected by large traders are subject at any time, or from time to time, to such reasonable periodic, special, or other examinations by representatives of the Commission as the Commission deems necessary or appropriate in the public interest, for the protection of investors, or otherwise in furtherance of the purposes of this title.

(5) Factors to be considered in Commission actions. In exercising its authority under this subsection, the Commission shall take into account—

(A) existing reporting systems;

(B) the costs associated with maintaining information with respect to transactions effected by large traders and reporting such information to the Commission or self-regulatory organizations; and

(C) the relationship between the United States and international securities markets.

(6) Exemptions. The Commission, by rule, regulation, or order, consistent with the purposes of this title, may exempt any person or class of persons or any transaction or class of transactions, either conditionally or upon specified terms and conditions or for stated periods, from the operation of this subsection, and the rules and regulations thereunder.

(7) Authority of Commission to limit disclosure of information. Notwithstanding any other provision of law, the Commission shall not be compelled to disclose any information required to be kept or reported under this subsection. Nothing in this subsection shall authorize the Commission to withhold information from Congress, or prevent the Commission from complying with a request for information from any other Federal department or agency requesting information for purposes within the scope of its jurisdiction, or complying with an order of a court of the United States in an action brought by the United States or the Commission. For purposes of section 552 of title 5, United States Code, this subsection shall be considered a statute described in subsection (b)(3)(B) of such section 552.

(8) Definitions. For purposes of this subsection—

(A) the term "large trader" means every person who, for his own account or an account for which he exercises investment discretion, effects transactions for the purchase or sale of any publicly traded security or securities by use of any means or instrumentality of interstate commerce or of the mails, or of any facility of a national securities exchange, directly or indirectly by or through a registered broker or dealer in an aggregate amount equal to or in excess of the identifying activity level;

(B) the term "publicly traded security" means any equity security (including an option on individual equity securities, and an option on a group or index of such securities) listed, or admitted to unlisted trading privileges, on a national securities exchange, or quoted in an automated interdealer quotation system;

(C) the term "identifying activity level" means transactions in publicly traded securities at or above a level of volume, fair market value, or exercise value as shall be fixed from time to time by the Commission by rule or regulation, specifying the time interval during which such transactions shall be aggregated;

(D) the term "reporting activity level" means transactions in publicly traded securities at or above a level of volume, fair market value, or exercise value as shall be fixed from time to time by the Commission by rule, regulation, or order, specifying the time interval during which such transactions shall be aggregated; and

(E) the term "person" has the meaning given in section 3(a)(9) of this title [15 USC § 78c(a)(9)] and also includes two or more persons acting as a partnership, limited partnership, syndicate, or other group, but does not include a foreign central bank.

HISTORY: (June 6, 1934, c. 404, Title I, § 13, 48 Stat. 894; Aug. 20, 1964, Pub. L. 88-467, § 4, 78 Stat. 569; July 29, 1968, Pub. L. 90-439, § 2, 82 Stat. 454; Dec. 22, 1970, Pub. L. 91-567, §§ 1, 2, 84 Stat. 1497; June 4, 1975, Pub. L. 94-29, § 10, 89 Stat. 119; Feb. 5, 1976, Pub. L. 94-210, Title III, § 308(b), 90 Stat. 57; Dec. 19, 1977, Pub. L. 95-213, Title I, § 102, Title II, §§ 202, 203, 91 Stat. 1494, 1498, 1499; June 6, 1983, Pub. L. 98-38, § 2(a), 97 Stat. 205; Dec. 4, 1987, Pub. L. 100-181, Title III, §§ 315, 316, 101 Stat. 1256; Feb. 3, 1988, Pub. L. 100-241, § 12(d), 101 Stat. 1810; Aug. 23, 1988, Pub. L. 100-418, Title V, § 5002, 102 Stat. 1415; Oct. 16, 1990, Pub. L. 101-432, § 3, 104 Stat. 964.)

§ 78dd-1. Prohibited foreign trade practices by issuers

(a) Prohibition. It shall be unlawful for any issuer which has a class of securities registered pursuant to section 12 of this title [15 USC § 78 l] or which is required to file reports under section 15(d) of this title [15 USC § 78o(d)], or for any officer, director, employee, or agent of such issuer or any stockholder thereof acting on behalf of such issuer, to make use of the mails or any means or instrumentality of interstate commerce corruptly in furtherance of an offer, payment, promise to pay, or authorization of the payment of any money, or offer, gift, promise to give, or authorization of the giving of anything of value to—

(1) any foreign official for purposes of—

(A) (i) influencing any act or decision of such foreign official in his official capacity,

(ii) inducing such foreign official to do or omit to do any act in violation of the lawful duty of such official, or

(iii) securing any improper advantage; or

251

(B) inducing such foreign official to use his influence with a foreign government or instrumentality thereof to affect or influence any act or decision of such government or instrumentality,

in order to assist such issuer in obtaining or retaining business for or with, or directing business to, any person;

(2) any foreign political party or official thereof or any candidate for foreign political office for purposes of—

(A) (i) influencing any act or decision of such party, official, or candidate in its or his official capacity,

(ii) inducing such party, official, or candidate to do or omit to do an act in violation of the lawful duty of such party, official, or candidate, or

(iii) securing any improper advantage; or

(B) inducing such party, official, or candidate to use its or his influence with a foreign government or instrumentality thereof to affect or influence any act or decision of such government or instrumentality,

in order to assist such issuer in obtaining or retaining business for or with, or directing business to, any person; or

(3) any person, while knowing that all or a portion of such money or thing of value will be offered, given, or promised, directly or indirectly, to any foreign official, to any foreign political party or official thereof, or to any candidate for foreign political office, for purposes of—

(A) (i) influencing any act or decision of such foreign official, political party, party official, or candidate in his or its official capacity,

(ii) inducing such foreign official, political party, party official, or candidate to do or omit to do any act in violation of the lawful duty of such foreign official, political party, party official, or candidate, or

(iii) securing any improper advantage; or

(B) inducing such foreign official, political party, party official, or candidate to use his or its influence with a foreign government or instrumentality thereof to affect or influence any act or decision of such government or instrumentality, in order to assist such issuer in obtaining or retaining business for or with, or directing business to, any person.

(b) Exception for routine governmental action. Subsection (a) and (g) shall not apply to any facilitating or expediting payment to a foreign official, political party, or party official the purpose of which is to expedite or to secure the performance of a routine governmental action by a foreign official, political party, or party official.

(c) Affirmative defenses. It shall be an affirmative defense to actions under subsection (a) that—

(1) the payment, gift, offer, or promise of anything of value that was made, was lawful under the written laws and regulations of the foreign official's, political party's, party official's, or candidate's country; or

(2) the payment, gift, offer, or promise of anything of value that was made, was a reasonable and bona fide expenditure, such as travel and lodging expenses, incurred by or on behalf of a foreign official, party, party official, or candidate and was directly related to—

(A) the promotion, demonstration, or explanation of products or services; or

(B) the execution or performance of a contract with a foreign government or agency thereof.

(d) Guidelines by the Attorney General. Not later than one year after the date of the enactment of the Foreign Corrupt Practices Act Amendments of 1988 [enacted Aug. 23, 1988], the Attorney General, after consultation with the Commission, the Secretary of Commerce, the United States Trade Representative, the Secretary of State, and the Secretary of the Treasury, and after obtaining the views of all interested persons through public notice and comment procedures, shall determine to what extent compliance with this section would be enhanced and the business community would be assisted by further clarification of the preceding provisions of this section and may, based on such determination and to the extent necessary and appropriate, issue—

(1) guidelines describing specific types of conduct, associated with common types of export sales arrangements and business contracts, which for purposes of the Department of Justice's present enforcement policy, the Attorney General determines would be in conformance with the preceding provisions of this section; and

(2) general precautionary procedures which issuers may use on a voluntary basis to conform their conduct to the Department of Justice's present enforcement policy regarding the preceding provisions of this section.

The Attorney General shall issue the guidelines and procedures referred to in the preceding sentence in accordance with the provisions of subchapter II of chapter 5 of title 5, United States Code [5 USC

§§ 551 *et seq.*], and those guidelines and procedures shall be subject to the provisions of chapter 7 of that title [5 USC §§ 701 *et seq.*].

(e) Opinions of the Attorney General.

(1) The Attorney General, after consultation with appropriate departments and agencies of the United States and after obtaining the views of all interested persons through public notice and comment procedures, shall establish a procedure to provide responses to specific inquiries by issuers concerning conformance of their conduct with the Department of Justice's present enforcement policy regarding the preceding provisions of this section. The Attorney General shall, within 30 days after receiving such a request, issue an opinion in response to that request. The opinion shall state whether or not certain specified prospective conduct would, for purposes of the Department of Justice's present enforcement policy, violate the preceding provisions of this section. Additional requests for opinions may be filed with the Attorney General regarding other specified prospective conduct that is beyond the scope of conduct specified in previous requests. In any action brought under the applicable provisions of this section, there shall be a rebuttable presumption that conduct, which is specified in a request by an issuer and for which the Attorney General has issued an opinion that such conduct is in conformity with the Department of Justice's present enforcement policy, is in compliance with the preceding provisions of this section. Such a presumption may be rebutted by a preponderance of the evidence. In considering the presumption for purposes of this paragraph, a court shall weigh all relevant factors, including but not limited to whether the information submitted to the Attorney General was accurate and complete and whether it was within the scope of the conduct specified in any request received by the Attorney General. The Attorney General shall establish the procedure required by this paragraph in accordance with the provisions of subchapter II of chapter 5 of title 5, United States Code [5 USC §§ 551 *et seq.*], and that procedure shall be subject to the provisions of chapter 7 of that title [5 USC §§ 701 *et seq.*].

(2) Any document or other material which is provided to, received by, or prepared in the Department of Justice or any other department or agency of the United States in connection with a request by an issuer under the procedure established under paragraph (1), shall be exempt from disclosure under section 552 of title 5, United States Code, and shall not, except with the consent of the issuer, be made publicly available, regardless of whether the Attorney General responds to such a request or the issuer withdraws such request before receiving a response.

(3) Any issuer who has made a request to the Attorney General under paragraph (1) may withdraw such request prior to the time the Attorney General issues an opinion in response to such request. Any request so withdrawn shall have no force or effect.

(4) The Attorney General shall, to the maximum extent practicable, provide timely guidance concerning the Department of Justice's present enforcement policy with respect to the preceding provisions of this section to potential exporters and small businesses that are unable to obtain specialized counsel on issues pertaining to such provisions. Such guidance shall be

limited to responses to requests under paragraph (1) concerning conformity of specified prospective conduct with the Department of Justice's present enforcement policy regarding the preceding provisions of this section and general explanations of compliance responsibilities and of potential liabilities under the preceding provisions of this section.

(f) Definitions. For purposes of this section:

(1) (A) The term "foreign official" means any officer or employee of a foreign government or any department, agency, or instrumentality thereof, or of a public international organization, or any person acting in an official capacity for or on behalf of any such government or department, agency, or instrumentality, or for or on behalf of any such public international organization.

(B) For purposes of subparagraph (A), the term "public international organization" means—

(i) an organization that is designated by Executive order pursuant to section 1 of the International Organizations Immunities Act (22 U.S.C. 288); or

(ii) any other international organization that is designated by the President by Executive order for the purposes of this section, effective as of the date of publication of such order in the Federal Register.

(2) (A) A person's state of mind is "knowing" with respect to conduct, a circumstance, or a result if—

(i) such person is aware that such person is engaging in such conduct, that such circumstance exists, or that such result is substantially certain to occur; or

(ii) such person has a firm belief that such circumstance exists or that such result is substantially certain to occur.

(B) When knowledge of the existence of a particular circumstance is required for an offense, such knowledge is established if a person is aware of a high probability of the existence of such circumstance, unless the person actually believes that such circumstance does not exist.

(3) (A) The term "routine governmental action" means only an action which is ordinarily and commonly performed by a foreign official in—

(i) obtaining permits, licenses, or other official documents to qualify a person to do business in a foreign country;

(ii) processing governmental papers, such as visas and work orders;

(iii) providing police protection, mail pick-up and delivery, or scheduling inspections associated with contract performance or inspections related to transit of goods across country;

(iv) providing phone service, power and water supply, loading and unloading cargo, or protecting perishable products or commodities from deterioration; or

(v) actions of a similar nature.

(B) The term "routine governmental action" does not include any decision by a foreign official whether, or on what terms, to award new business to or to continue business with a particular party, or any action taken by a foreign official involved in the decisionmaking process to encourage a decision to award new business to or continue business with a particular party.

(g) Alternative jurisdiction.

(1) It shall also be unlawful for any issuer organized under the laws of the United States, or a State, territory, possession, or commonwealth of the United States or a political subdivision thereof and which has a class of securities registered pursuant to section 12 of this title [15 USC § 78l] or which is required to file reports under section 15(d) of this title [15 USC § 78o(d)], or for any United States person that is an officer, director, employee, or agent of such issuer or a stockholder thereof acting on behalf of such issuer, to corruptly do any act outside the United States in furtherance of an offer, payment, promise to pay, or authorization of the payment of any money, or offer, gift, promise to give, or authorization of the giving of anything of value to any of the persons or entities set forth in paragraphs (1), (2), and (3) of subsection (a) of this section for the purposes set forth therein, irrespective of whether such issuer or such officer, director, employee, agent, or stockholder makes use of the mails or any means or instrumentality of interstate commerce in furtherance of such offer, gift, payment, promise, or authorization.

(2) As used in this subsection, the term "United States person" means a national of the United States (as defined in section 101 of the Immigration and Nationality Act (8 U.S.C. 1101)) or any corporation, partnership, association, joint-stock company, business trust, unincorporated organization, or sole proprietorship organized under the laws of the United States or any State, territory, possession, or commonwealth of the United States, or any political subdivision thereof.

HISTORY: (June 6, 1934, ch 404, Title I, § 30A, as added Dec. 19, 1977, P.L. 95-213, Title I, § 103(a), 91 Stat.1495; Aug. 23, 1988, P.L. 100-418, Title V, Subtitle A, Part I, § 5003(a), 102 Stat. 1415.) (As amended Nov. 10, 1998, P.L. 105-366, §§ 2(a)-(c), 112 Stat. 3302.)

§ 78dd-2. Prohibited foreign trade practices by domestic concerns

(a) Prohibition. It shall be unlawful for any domestic concern, other than an issuer which is subject to section 30A of the Securities Exchange Act of 1934 [15 USC § 78dd-1], or for any officer, director, employee, or agent of such domestic concern or any stockholder thereof acting on behalf of such domestic concern, to make use of the mails or any means or instrumentality of interstate commerce corruptly in furtherance of an offer, payment, promise to pay, or authorization of the payment of any money, or offer, gift, promise to give, or authorization of the giving of anything of value to—

(1) any foreign official for purposes of—

(A) (i) influencing any act or decision of such foreign official in his official capacity,

(ii) inducing such foreign official to do or omit to do any act in violation of the lawful duty of such official, or

(iii) securing any improper advantage; or

(B) inducing such foreign official to use his influence with a foreign government or instrumentality thereof to affect or influence any act or decision of such government or instrumentality,

in order to assist such domestic concern in obtaining or retaining business for or with, or directing business to, any person;

(2) any foreign political party or official thereof or any candidate for foreign political office for purposes of—

(A) (i) influencing any act or decision of such party, official, or candidate in its or his official capacity,

(ii) inducing such party, official, or candidate to do or omit to do an act in violation of the lawful duty of such party, official, or candidate, or

(iii) securing any improper advantage; or

(B) inducing such party, official, or candidate to use its or his influence with a foreign government or instrumentality thereof to affect or influence any act or decision of such government or instrumentality,

257

in order to assist such domestic concern in obtaining or retaining business for or with, or directing business to, any person; or

(3) any person, while knowing that all or a portion of such money or thing of value will be offered, given, or promised, directly or indirectly, to any foreign official, to any foreign political party or official thereof, or to any candidate for foreign political office, for purposes of—

(A) (i) influencing any act or decision of such foreign official, political party, party official, or candidate in his or its official capacity,

(ii) inducing such foreign official, political party, party official, or candidate to do or omit to do any act in violation of the lawful duty of such foreign official, political party, party official, or candidate, or

(iii) securing any improper advantage; or

(B) inducing such foreign official, political party, party official, or candidate to use his or its influence with a foreign government or instrumentality thereof to affect or influence any act or decision of such government or instrumentality,

in order to assist such domestic concern in obtaining or retaining business for or with, or directing business to, any person.

(b) Exception for routine governmental action. Subsection (a) and (i) shall not apply to any facilitating or expediting payment to a foreign official, political party, or party official the purpose of which is to expedite or to secure the performance of a routine governmental action by a foreign official, political party, or party official.

(c) Affirmative defenses. It shall be an affirmative defense to actions under subsection (a) that—

(1) the payment, gift, offer, or promise of anything of value that was made, was lawful under the written laws and regulations of the foreign official's, political party's, party official's, or candidate's country; or

(2) the payment, gift, offer, or promise of anything of value that was made, was a reasonable and bona fide expenditure, such as travel and lodging expenses, incurred by or on behalf of a foreign official, party, party official, or candidate and was directly related to—

(A) the promotion, demonstration, or explanation of products or services; or

(B) the execution or performance of a contract with a foreign government or agency thereof.

(d) Injunctive relief.

(1) When it appears to the Attorney General that any domestic concern to which this section applies, or officer, director, employee, agent, or stockholder thereof, is engaged, or about to engage, in any act or practice constituting a violation of subsection (a) of this section, the Attorney General may, in his discretion, bring a civil action in an appropriate district court of the United States to enjoin such act or practice, and upon a proper showing, a permanent injunction or a temporary restraining order shall be granted without bond.

(2) For the purpose of any civil investigation which, in the opinion of the Attorney General, is necessary and proper to enforce this section, the Attorney General or his designee are empowered to administer oaths and affirmations, subpoena witnesses, take evidence, and require the production of any books, papers, or other documents which the Attorney General deems relevant or material to such investigation. The attendance of witnesses and the production of documentary evidence may be required from any place in the United States, or any territory, possession, or commonwealth of the United States, at any designated place of hearing.

(3) In case of contumacy by, or refusal to obey a subpoena issued to, any person, the Attorney General may invoke the aid of any court of the United States within the jurisdiction of which such investigation or proceeding is carried on, or where such person resides or carries on business, in requiring the attendance and testimony of witnesses and the production of books, papers, or other documents. Any such court may issue an order requiring such person to appear before the Attorney General or his designee, there to produce records, if so ordered, or to give testimony touching the matter under investigation. Any failure to obey such order of the court may be punished by such court as a contempt thereof. All process in any such case may be served in the judicial district in which such person resides or may be found. The Attorney General may make such rules relating to civil investigations as may be necessary or appropriate to implement the provisions of this subsection.

(e) Guidelines by the Attorney General. Not later than 6 months after the date of the enactment of the Foreign Corrupt Practices Act Amendments of 1988 [enacted Aug. 23, 1988], the Attorney General, after consultation with the Securities and Exchange Commission, the Secretary of Commerce, the United States Trade Representative, the Secretary of State, and the Secretary of the Treasury, and after obtaining the views of all interested persons through public notice and comment procedures, shall determine to what extent compliance with this section would be enhanced and the business community would be assisted by further clarification of the preceding provisions of this section and may, based on such determination and to the extent necessary and appropriate, issue—

(1) guidelines describing specific types of conduct, associated with common types of export sales arrangements and business contracts, which for purposes of the Department of Justice's present enforcement policy, the Attorney General determines would be in conformance with the preceding provisions of this section; and

259

(2) general precautionary procedures which domestic concerns may use on a voluntary basis to conform their conduct to the Department of Justice's present enforcement policy regarding the preceding provisions of this section.

The Attorney General shall issue the guidelines and procedures referred to in the preceding sentence in accordance with the provisions of subchapter II of chapter 5 of title 5, United States Code [5 USC §§ 551 *et seq.*], and those guidelines and procedures shall be subject to the provisions of chapter 7 of that title [5 USC §§ 701 *et seq.*].

(f) Opinions of the Attorney General.

(1) The Attorney General, after consultation with appropriate departments and agencies of the United States and after obtaining the views of all interested persons through public notice and comment procedures, shall establish a procedure to provide responses to specific inquiries by domestic concerns concerning conformance of their conduct with the Department of Justice's present enforcement policy regarding the preceding provisions of this section. The Attorney General shall, within 30 days after receiving such a request, issue an opinion in response to that request. The opinion shall state whether or not certain specified prospective conduct would, for purposes of the Department of Justice's present enforcement policy, violate the preceding provisions of this section. Additional requests for opinions may be filed with the Attorney General regarding other specified prospective conduct that is beyond the scope of conduct specified in previous requests. In any action brought under the applicable provisions of this section, there shall be a rebuttable presumption that conduct, which is specified in a request by a domestic concern and for which the Attorney General has issued an opinion that such conduct is in conformity with the Department of Justice's present enforcement policy, is in compliance with the preceding provisions of this section. Such a presumption may be rebutted by a preponderance of the evidence. In considering the presumption for purposes of this paragraph, a court shall weigh all relevant factors, including but not limited to whether the information submitted to the Attorney General was accurate and complete and whether it was within the scope of the conduct specified in any request received by the Attorney General. The Attorney General shall establish the procedure required by this paragraph in accordance with the provisions of subchapter II of chapter 5 of title 5, United States Code [5 USC §§ 551 *et seq.*], and that procedure shall be subject to the provisions of chapter 7 of that title [5 USC §§ 701 *et seq.*].

(2) Any document or other material which is provided to, received by, or prepared in the Department of Justice or any other department or agency of the United States in connection with a request by a domestic concern under the procedure established under paragraph (1), shall be exempt from disclosure under section 552 of title 5, United States Code, and shall not, except with the consent of the domestic concern, be made publicly available, regardless of whether the Attorney General responds to such a request or the domestic concern withdraws such request before receiving a response.

(3) Any domestic concern who has made a request to the Attorney General under paragraph (1) may withdraw such request prior to the time the Attorney General issues an opinion in response to such request. Any request so withdrawn shall have no force or effect.

(4) The Attorney General shall, to the maximum extent practicable, provide timely guidance concerning the Department of Justice's present enforcement policy with respect to the preceding provisions of this section to potential exporters and small businesses that are unable to obtain specialized counsel on issues pertaining to such provisions. Such guidance shall be limited to responses to requests under paragraph (1) concerning conformity of specified prospective conduct with the Department of Justice's present enforcement policy regarding the preceding provisions of this section and general explanations of compliance responsibilities and of potential liabilities under the preceding provisions of this section.

(g) Penalties.

    (1) (A) Penalties. Any domestic concern that is not a natural person and that violates subsection (a) or (i) of this section shall be fined not more than $2,000,000.

        (B) Any domestic concern that is not a natural person and that violates subsection (a) or (i) of this section shall be subject to a civil penalty of not more than $10,000 imposed in an action brought by the Attorney General.

    (2) (A) Any natural person that is an officer, director, employee, or agent of a domestic concern, or stockholder acting on behalf of such domestic concern, who willfully violates subsection (a) or (i) of this section shall be fined not more than $100,000 or imprisoned not more than 5 years, or both.

        (B) Any natural person that is an officer, director, employee, or agent of a domestic concern, or stockholder acting on behalf of such domestic concern, who violates subsection (a) or (i) of this section shall be subject to a civil penalty of not more than $10,000 imposed in an action brought by the Attorney General.

(3) Whenever a fine is imposed under paragraph (2) upon any officer, director, employee, agent, or stockholder of a domestic concern, such fine may not be paid, directly or indirectly, by such domestic concern.

(h) Definitions. For purposes of this section:

(1) The term "domestic concern" means—

    (A) any individual who is a citizen, national, or resident of the United States; and

(B) any corporation, partnership, association, joint-stock company, business trust, unincorporated organization, or sole proprietorship which has its principal place of business in the United States, or which is organized under the laws of a State of the United States or a territory, possession, or commonwealth of the United States.

(2) The term "foreign official" means any officer or employee of a foreign government or any department, agency, or instrumentality thereof, or any person acting in an official capacity for or on behalf of any such government or department, agency, or instrumentality.

(3) (A) A person's state of mind is "knowing" with respect to conduct, a circumstance, or a result if—

(i) such person is aware that such person is engaging in such conduct, that such circumstance exists, or that such result is substantially certain to occur; or

(ii) such person has a firm belief that such circumstance exists or that such result is substantially certain to occur.

(B) When knowledge of the existence of a particular circumstance is required for an offense, such knowledge is established if a person is aware of a high probability of the existence of such circumstance, unless the person actually believes that such circumstance does not exist.

(4) (A) For purposes of paragraph (1), the term "routine governmental action" means only an action which is ordinarily and commonly performed by a foreign official in—

(i) obtaining permits, licenses, or other official documents to qualify a person to do business in a foreign country;

(ii) processing governmental papers, such as visas and work orders;

(iii) providing police protection, mail pick-up and delivery, or scheduling inspections associated with contract performance or inspections related to transit of goods across country;

(iv) providing phone service, power and water supply, loading and unloading cargo, or protecting perishable products or commodities from deterioration; or

(v) actions of a similar nature.

(B) The term "routine governmental action" does not include any decision by a foreign official whether, or on what terms, to award new business to or to continue business with a particular party, or any action taken by a foreign official involved in the decision-making

262

process to encourage a decision to award new business to or continue business with a particular party.

(5) The term "interstate commerce" means trade, commerce, transportation, or communication among the several States, or between any foreign country and any State or between any State and any place or ship outside thereof, and such term includes the intrastate use of—

(A) a telephone or other interstate means of communication, or

(B) any other interstate instrumentality.

(i) Alternative jurisdiction

(1) It shall also be unlawful for any United States person to corruptly do any act outside the United States in furtherance of an offer, payment, promise to pay, or authorization of the payment of any money, or offer, gift, promise to give, or authorization of the giving of anything of value to any of the persons or entities set forth in paragraphs (1), (2), and (3) of subsection (a), for the purposes set forth therein, irrespective of whether such United States person makes use of the mails or any means or instrumentality of interstate commerce in furtherance of such offer, gift, payment, promise, or authorization.

(2) As used in this subsection, the term "United States person" means a national of the United States (as defined in section 101 of the Immigration and Nationality Act (8 U.S.C. 1101)) or any corporation, partnership, association, joint-stock company, business trust, unincorporated organization, or sole proprietorship organized under the laws of the United States or any State, territory, possession, or commonwealth of the United States, or any political subdivision thereof."

HISTORY: (Dec. 19, 1977, P.L. 95-213, Title I, § 104, 91 Stat. 1496; Aug. 23, 1988, P.L. 100-418, Title V, Subtitle A, Part I, § 5003(c), 102 Stat. 1419; Sept. 13, 1994, P.L. 103-322, Title XXXIII, § 330005, 108 Stat. 2142.) (As amended Nov. 10, 1998, P.L. 105-366, § 3, 112 Stat. 3304.)

§ 78dd-3. Prohibited foreign trade practices by persons other than issuers or domestic concerns

(a) Prohibition. It shall be unlawful for any person other than an issuer that is subject to section 78dd-1 of this title or a domestic concern (as defined in section 78dd-2 of this title), or for any officer, director, employee, or agent of such person or any stockholder thereof acting on behalf of such person, while in the territory of the United States, corruptly to make use of the mails or any means or instrumentality of interstate commerce or to do any other act in furtherance of an offer, payment, promise to pay, or authorization of the payment of any money, or offer, gift, promise to give, or authorization of the giving of anything of value to—

The Foreign Corrupt Practices Act

(1) any foreign official for purposes of—

    (A) (i) influencing any act or decision of such foreign official in his official capacity,

    (ii) inducing such foreign official to do or omit to do any act in violation of the lawful duty of such official, or

    (iii) securing any improper advantage; or

    (B) inducing such foreign official to use his influence with a foreign government or instrumentality thereof to affect or influence any act or decision of such government or instrumentality,

in order to assist such person in obtaining or retaining business for or with, or directing business to, any person;

(2) any foreign political party or official thereof or any candidate for foreign political office for purposes of—

    (A) (i) influencing any act or decision of such party, official, or candidate in its or his official capacity,

    (ii) inducing such party, official, or candidate to do or omit to do an act in violation of the lawful duty of such party, official, or candidate, or

    (iii) securing any improper advantage; or

    (B) inducing such party, official, or candidate to use its or his influence with a foreign government or instrumentality thereof to affect or influence any act or decision of such government or instrumentality,

in order to assist such person in obtaining or retaining business for or with, or directing business to, any person; or

(3) any person, while knowing that all or a portion of such money or thing of value will be offered, given, or promised, directly or indirectly, to any foreign official, to any foreign political party or official thereof, or to any candidate for foreign political office, for purposes of—

    (A) (i) influencing any act or decision of such foreign official, political party, party official, or candidate in his or its official capacity,

(ii) inducing such foreign official, political party, party official, or candidate to do or omit to do any act in violation of the lawful duty of such foreign official, political party, party official, or candidate, or

(iii) securing any improper advantage; or

(B) inducing such foreign official, political party, party official, or candidate to use his or its influence with a foreign government or instrumentality thereof to affect or influence any act or decision of such government or instrumentality,

in order to assist such person in obtaining or retaining business for or with, or directing business to, any person.

(b) Exception for routine governmental action. Subsection (a) of this section shall not apply to any facilitating or expediting payment to a foreign official, political party, or party official the purpose of which is to expedite or to secure the performance of a routine governmental action by a foreign official, political party, or party official.

(c) Affirmative defenses. It shall be an affirmative defense to actions under subsection (a) of this section that—

(1) the payment, gift, offer, or promise of anything of value that was made, was lawful under the written laws and regulations of the foreign official's, political party's, party official's, or candidate's country; or

(2) the payment, gift, offer, or promise of anything of value that was made, was a reasonable and bona fide expenditure, such as travel and lodging expenses, incurred by or on behalf of a foreign official, party, party official, or candidate and was directly related to—

(A) the promotion, demonstration, or explanation of products or services; or

(B) the execution or performance of a contract with a foreign government or agency thereof.

(d) Injunctive relief.

(1) When it appears to the Attorney General that any person to which this section applies, or officer, director, employee, agent, or stockholder thereof, is engaged, or about to engage, in any act or practice constituting a violation of subsection (a) of this section, the Attorney General may, in his discretion, bring a civil action in an appropriate district court of the United States to enjoin such act or practice, and upon a proper showing, a permanent injunction or a temporary restraining order shall be granted without bond.

(2) For the purpose of any civil investigation which, in the opinion of the Attorney General, is necessary and proper to enforce this section, the Attorney General or his designee are empowered to administer oaths and affirmations, subpoena witnesses, take evidence, and require the production of any books, papers, or other documents which the Attorney General deems relevant or material to such investigation. The attendance of witnesses and the production of documentary evidence may be required from any place in the United States, or any territory, possession, or commonwealth of the United States, at any designated place of hearing.

(3) In case of contumacy by, or refusal to obey a subpoena issued to, any person, the Attorney General may invoke the aid of any court of the United States within the jurisdiction of which such investigation or proceeding is carried on, or where such person resides or carries on business, in requiring the attendance and testimony of witnesses and the production of books, papers, or other documents. Any such court may issue an order requiring such person to appear before the Attorney General or his designee, there to produce records, if so ordered, or to give testimony touching the matter under investigation. Any failure to obey such order of the court may be punished by such court as a contempt thereof.

(4) All process in any such case may be served in the judicial district in which such person resides or may be found. The Attorney General may make such rules relating to civil investigations as may be necessary or appropriate to implement the provisions of this subsection.

(e) Penalties.

    (1) (A) Any juridical person that violates subsection (a) of this section shall be fined not more than $2,000,000.

        (B) Any juridical person that violates subsection (a) of this section shall be subject to a civil penalty of not more than $10,000 imposed in an action brought by the Attorney General.

    (2) (A) Any natural person who willfully violates subsection (a) of this section shall be fined not more than $100,000 or imprisoned not more than 5 years, or both.

        (B) Any natural person who violates subsection (a) of this section shall be subject to a civil penalty of not more than $10,000 imposed in an action brought by the Attorney General.

    (3) Whenever a fine is imposed under paragraph (2) upon any officer, director, employee, agent, or stockholder of a person, such fine may not be paid, directly or indirectly, by such person.

(f) Definitions. For purposes of this section:

(1) The term "person", when referring to an offender, means any natural person other than a national of the United States (as defined in section 101 of the Immigration and Nationality Act [8 U.S.C. § 1101] or any corporation, partnership, association, joint-stock company, business trust, unincorporated organization, or sole proprietorship organized under the law of a foreign nation or a political subdivision thereof.

(2) (A) The term "foreign official" means any officer or employee of a foreign government or any department, agency, or instrumentality thereof, or of a public international organization, or any person acting in an official capacity for or on behalf of any such government or department, agency, or instrumentality, or for or on behalf of any such public international organization.

(B) For purposes of subparagraph (A), the term "public international organization" means—

(i) an organization that is designated by Executive order pursuant to section 1 of the International Organizations Immunities Act [22 U.S.C. § 288]; or

(ii) any other international organization that is designated by the President by Executive order for the purposes of this section, effective as of the date of publication of such order in the Federal Register.

(3) (A) A person's state of mind is knowing, with respect to conduct, a circumstance or a result if—

(i) such person is aware that such person is engaging in such conduct, that such circumstance exists, or that such result is substantially certain to occur; or

(ii) such person has a firm belief that such circumstance exists or that such result is substantially certain to occur.

(B) When knowledge of the existence of a particular circumstance is required for an offense, such knowledge is established if a person is aware of a high probability of the existence of such circumstance, unless the person actually believes that such circumstance does not exist.

(4) (A) The term "routine governmental action" means only an action which is ordinarily and commonly performed by a foreign official in—

(i) obtaining permits, licenses, or other official documents to qualify a person to do business in a foreign country;

(ii) processing governmental papers, such as visas and work orders;

(iii) providing police protection, mail pick-up and delivery, or scheduling inspections associated with contract performance or inspections related to transit of goods across country;

(iv) providing phone service, power and water supply, loading and unloading cargo, or protecting perishable products or commodities from deterioration; or

(v) actions of a similar nature.

(B) The term "routine governmental action" does not include any decision by a foreign official whether, or on what terms, to award new business to or to continue business with a particular party, or any action taken by a foreign official involved in the decision-making process to encourage a decision to award new business to or continue business with a particular party.

(5) The term "interstate commerce" means trade, commerce, transportation, or communication among the several States, or between any foreign country and any State or between any State and any place or ship outside thereof, and such term includes the intrastate use of—

(A) a telephone or other interstate means of communication, or

(B) any other interstate instrumentality.

HISTORY: (Pub. L. 95-213, Title I, S 104A, as added Pub. L. 105-366, S 3, Nov. 10, 1998, 112 Stat. 3306.)

§ 78ff. Penalties

(a) Willful violations; false and misleading statements. Any person who willfully violates any provision of this title (other than section 30A [15 USC § 78dd-1]), or any rule or regulation thereunder the violation of which is made unlawful or the observance of which is required under the terms of this title, or any person who willfully and knowingly makes, or causes to be made, any statement in any application, report, or document required to be filed under this title or any rule or regulation thereunder or any undertaking contained in a registration statement as provided in subsection (d) of section 15 of this title [15 USC § 78 o(d)] or by any self-regulatory organization in connection with an application for membership or participation therein or to become associated with a member thereof[,], which statement was false or misleading with respect to any material fact, shall upon conviction be fined not more than $1,000,000, or imprisoned not more than 10 years, or both, except that when such person is a person other than a natural person, a fine not exceeding

$2,500,000 may be imposed; but no person shall be subject to imprisonment under this section for the violation of any rule or regulation if he proves that he had no knowledge of such rule or regulation.

(b) Failure to file information, documents, or reports. Any issuer which fails to file information, documents, or reports required to be filed under subsection (d) of section 15 of this title [15 USC § 78o(d)] or any rule or regulation thereunder shall forfeit to the United States the sum of $100 for each and every day such failure to file shall continue. Such forfeiture, which shall be in lieu of any criminal penalty for such failure to file which might be deemed to arise under subsection (a) of this section, shall be payable to the Treasury of the United States and shall be recoverable in a civil suit in the name of the United States.

(c) Violations by issuers, officers, directors, stockholders, employees, or agents of issuers.

    (1)   (A) Any issuer that violates subsection (a) or (g) of section 30A [15 USC § 78dd-1] shall be fined not more than $2,000,000.

        (B) Any issuer that violates subsection (a) or (g) of section 30A [15 USC § 78dd-1] shall be subject to a civil penalty of not more than $10,000 imposed in an action brought by the Commission.

    (2)   (A) Any officer, director, employee, or agent of an issuer, or stockholder acting on behalf of such issuer, who willfully violates subsection (a) or (g) of section 30A of this title [15 USC § 78dd-1] shall be fined not more than $100,000, or imprisoned not more than 5 years, or both.

        (B) Any officer, director, employee, or agent of an issuer, or stockholder acting on behalf of such issuer, who violates subsection (a) or (g) of section 30A of this title [15 USC § 78dd-1] shall be subject to a civil penalty of not more than $10,000 imposed in an action brought by the Commission.

    (3) Whenever a fine is imposed under paragraph (2) upon any officer, director, employee, agent, or stockholder of an issuer, such fine may not be paid, directly or indirectly, by such issuer.

HISTORY: (June 6, 1934, ch 404, Title I, § 32, 48 Stat. 904; May 27, 1936, ch 462, § 9, 49 Stat. 1380; June 25, 1938, ch 677, § 4, 52 Stat. 1076; Aug. 20, 1964, P.L. 88-467, § 11, 78 Stat. 580; June 4, 1975, P.L. 94-29, § 23, 27(b), 89 Stat. 162, 163; Dec. 19, 1977, P.L. 95-213, Title I, § 103(b), 91 Stat. 1496; Aug. 10, 1984, P.L. 98-376, § 3, 98 Stat. 1265; Aug. 23, 1988, P.L. 100-418, Title V, Subtitle A, Part I, § 5003(b), 102 Stat. 1419; Nov. 19, 1988, P.L. 100-704, § 4, 102 Stat. 4680.) (As amended Nov. 10, 1998, P.L. 105-366, § 2(d), 112 Stat. 3303.)

F. Statutory Provisions Governing the Overseas Private Investment Corporation (OPIC)

Source: 22 U.S.C. § 2191 *et seq.*

Website information:

http://www.opic.gov/
This website provides a comprehensive description of OPIC's functions, programs and recent publications.

Introduction

The Overseas Private Investment Corporation (OPIC) is chartered by Congress to "mobilize and facilitate the participation of United States private capital and skills in the economic and social development of less developed countries and areas, and countries in transition from nonmarket to market economies." 22 U.S.C. § 2191. By providing insurance, financing and reinsurance for such investments, OPIC complements other foreign assistance programs through inducement of private sector investment in target economies.

OPIC carries out its functions through four types of activities:

1) It provides insurance against the following types of political risks for investments overseas:
   a) inability to convert foreign currencies into U.S. dollars.
   b) loss due to expropriation or confiscation by a foreign government,
   c) loss due to war, revolution, insurrection, or civil strife, and
   d) loss due to business interruption caused by any of the above risks. 22 U.S.C. § 2194(a).
2) It provides loans and loan guaranties for overseas investments. 22 U.S.C. 2194(b).
3) It provides direct investment through equity participation in overseas investments. 22 U.S.C. § 2194(c).
4) It encourages investment by advocating the interests of the American business community overseas. 22 U.S.C. § 2194(d).

OPIC coverage of an investment involves a series of agreements. In the standard OPIC insurance arrangement, there is first an Investment Incentive Agreement between the United States and the host government. This agreement provides that OPIC may offer coverage of investors with projects in the host country, require that such projects be approved by the host government, recognize the U.S. government's right as transferee of the investor's rights should coverage be claimed, and provide for dispute resolution should it be necessary between the two governments.

The second agreement is between the investor and the host government, providing the requisite approval of the investment and acknowledgment that it is in accordance with the government-to-government agreement. This agreement, and the resulting approval of investments, help make certain that any covered investments are not objectionable to the host government. The third agreement is the insurance agreement between OPIC and the investor. This agreement provides in

270

detail the covered investment, the risks covered, and the manner in which coverage will be realized should one of the risks occur.

OPIC has accumulated reserves of more than $3 billion, having recorded a positive net income in every year of its operation. It covers investments in nearly 140 countries worldwide.

§ 2191. Congressional statement of purpose; creation and functions of Corporation

To mobilize and facilitate the participation of United States private capital and skills in the economic and social development of less developed countries and areas, and countries in transition from nonmarket to market economies, thereby complementing the development assistance objectives of the United States, there is hereby created the Overseas Private Investment Corporation (hereinafter called the "Corporation"), which shall be an agency of the United States under the policy guidance of the Secretary of State.

The Corporation, in determining whether to provide insurance, financing, or reinsurance for a project, shall especially—

(1) be guided by the economic and social development impact and benefits of such a project and the ways in which such a project complements, or is compatible with, other development assistance programs or projects of the United States or other donors;

(2) give preferential consideration to investment projects in less developed countries that have per capita incomes of $984 or less in 1986 United States dollars, and restrict its activities with respect to investment projects in less developed countries that have per capita incomes of $4,269 or more in 1986 United States dollars (other than countries designated as beneficiary countries under section 2702 of Title 19, Ireland, and Northern Ireland); and

(3) ensure that the project is consistent with the provisions of section 2151p of this title, section 2151p-1 of this title, and section 2151q of this title relating to the environment and natural resources of, and tropical forests and endangered species in, developing countries, and consistent with the intent of regulations issued pursuant to section 2151p of this title, section 2151p-1 of this title, and section 2151q of this title.

In carrying out its purpose, the Corporation, utilizing broad criteria, shall undertake—

(a) to conduct financing, insurance, and reinsurance operations on a self-sustaining basis, taking into account in its financing operations the economic and financial soundness of projects;

(b) to utilize private credit and investment institutions and the Corporation's guaranty authority as the principal means of mobilizing capital investment funds;

(c) to broaden private participation and revolve its funds through selling its direct investments to private investors whenever it can appropriately do so on satisfactory terms;

(d) to conduct its insurance operations with due regard to principles of risk management including efforts to share its insurance and reinsurance risks;

(e) to the maximum degree possible consistent with its purposes—

(1) to give preferential consideration in its investment insurance, reinsurance, and guaranty activities to investment projects sponsored by or involving United States small business; and

(2) to increase the proportion of projects sponsored by or significantly involving United States small business to at least 30 percent of all projects insured, reinsured, or guaranteed by the Corporation;

(f) to consider in the conduct of its operations the extent to which less developed country governments are receptive to private enterprise, domestic and foreign, and their willingness and ability to maintain conditions which enable private enterprise to make its full contribution to the development process;

(g) to foster private initiative and competition and discourage monopolistic practices;

(h) to further to the greatest degree possible, in a manner consistent with its goals, the balance-of-payments and employment objectives of the United States;

(i) to conduct its activities in consonance with the activities of the agency primarily responsible for administering subchapter I of this chapter and the international trade, investment, and financial policies of the United States Government, and to seek to support those developmental projects having positive trade benefits for the United States;

(j) to advise and assist, within its field of competence, interested agencies of the United States and other organizations, both public and private, national and international, with respect to projects and programs relating to the development of private enterprise in less developed countries and areas;

(k) (1) to decline to issue any contract of insurance or reinsurance, or any guaranty, or to enter into any agreement to provide financing for an eligible investor's proposed investment if the Corporation determines that such investment is likely to cause such investor (or the sponsor of an investment project in which such investor is involved) significantly to reduce the number of his employees in the United States because he is replacing his United States production with production from such investment which involves substantially the same product for substantially the same market as his United States production; and (2) to monitor conformance with the representations of the investor on which the Corporation relied in making the determination required by clause (1);

(l) to decline to issue any contract of insurance or reinsurance, or any guaranty, or to enter into any agreement to provide financing for an eligible investor's proposed investment if the Corporation determines that such investment is likely to cause a significant reduction in the number of employees in the United States;

(m) to refuse to insure, reinsure, or finance any investment subject to performance requirements which would reduce substantially the positive trade benefits likely to accrue to the United States from the investment; and

273

(n) to refuse to insure, reinsure, guarantee, or finance any investment in connection with a project which the Corporation determines will pose an unreasonable or major environmental, health, or safety hazard, or will result in the significant degradation of national parks or similar protected areas.

HISTORY: (Pub. L. 87-195, Pt. I, § 231, as added Pub. L. 91-175, Pt. I, § 105, Dec. 30, 1969, 83 Stat. 809, and amended Pub. L. 93-390, § 2(1), Aug. 27, 1974, 88 Stat. 763; Pub. L. 95-268, § 2, Apr. 24, 1978, 92 Stat. 213; Pub. L. 97-65, § 2, Oct. 16, 1981, 95 Stat. 1021; Pub. L. 99-204, §§ 3, 4(a), Dec. 23, 1985, 99 Stat. 1669; Pub. L. 100-461, Title V, § 555, Oct. 1, 1988, 102 Stat. 2268-36.) (As amended Pub. L. 102-549, Title I, § 101, Oct. 28, 1992, 106 Stat. 3651; Pub. L. 103-392, Title I, § 105, Oct. 22, 1994, 108 Stat. 4099.)

§ 2191a. Additional requirements

(a) Worker rights

(1) Limitation on OPIC activities

The Corporation may insure, reinsure, guarantee, or finance a project only if the country in which the project is to be undertaken is taking steps to adopt and implement laws that extend internationally recognized worker rights, as defined in section 2467(4) of Title 19, to workers in that country (including any designated zone in that country). The Corporation shall also include the following language, in substantially the following form, in all contracts which the Corporation enters into with eligible investors to provide financial support under this subpart:

"The investor agrees not to take actions to prevent employees of the foreign enterprise from lawfully exercising their right of association and their right to organize and bargain collectively. The investor further agrees to observe applicable laws relating to a minimum age for employment of children, acceptable conditions of work with respect to minimum wages, hours of work, and occupational health and safety, and not to use forced labor. The investor is not responsible under this paragraph for the actions of a foreign government."

(2) Use of annual reports on workers rights

The Corporation shall, in making its determinations under paragraph (1), use the reports submitted to the Congress pursuant to section 2464 of Title 19. The restriction set forth in paragraph (1) shall not apply until the first such report is submitted to the Congress.

(3) Waiver

Paragraph (1) shall not prohibit the Corporation from providing any insurance, reinsurance, guaranty, or financing with respect to a country if the President determines that such activities by

274

the Corporation would be in the national economic interests of the United States. Any such determination shall be reported in writing to the Congress, together with the reasons for the determination.

(4) Operations of OPIC in the People's Republic of China

In making a determination under this section for the People's Republic of China, the Corporation shall discuss fully and completely the justification for making such determination with respect to each item set forth in subparagraphs (A) through (E) of section 2467(4) of Title 19.

(b) Environmental Impact.

The Board of Directors of the Corporation shall not vote in favor of any action proposed to be taken by the Corporation that is likely to have significant adverse environmental impacts that are sensitive, diverse, or unprecedented, unless for at least 60 days before the date of the vote

(1) an environmental impact assessment or initial environmental audit, analyzing the environmental impacts of the proposed action and of alternatives to the proposed action has been completed by the project applicant and made available to the Board of Directors; and

(2) such assessment or audit has been made available to the public of the United States, locally affected groups in the host country, and host country nongovernmental organizations.

(c) Public hearings

(1) The Board shall hold at least one public hearing each year in order to afford an opportunity for any person to present views as to whether the Corporation is carrying out its activities in accordance with section 2191 of this title and this section or whether any investment in a particular country should have been or should be extended insurance, reinsurance, guarantees, or financing under this subpart.

(2) In conjunction with each meeting of its Board of Directors, the Corporation shall hold a public hearing in order to afford an opportunity for any person to present views regarding the activities of the Corporation. Such views shall be made part of the record.

HISTORY: (Pub. L. 87-195, Pt. 1, § 231A, as added Pub. L. 99-204, § 5(a), Dec. 23, 1985, 99 Stat. 1670, and amended Pub. L. 100-418, Title II, § 2203(c), Aug. 23, 1988, 102 Stat. 1328.) (As amended Pub. L. 102-549, Title I, § 102, Oct. 28, 1992, 106 Stat. 3651; Pub. L. 104-188, Title I, § 1954(b)(3), Aug. 20, 1996, 110 Stat. 1928.) (As amended PL 106-158, December 9, 1999, 113 Stat. 1745.)

§ 2192. Capital of the Corporation

The President is authorized to pay in as capital of the Corporation, out of dollar receipts made available through the appropriation process from loans made pursuant to subchapter I of this chapter and from loans made under the Mutual Security Act of 1954, as amended, for the fiscal year 1970 not to exceed $20,000,000 and for the fiscal year 1971 not to exceed $20,000,000. Upon the payment of such capital by the President, the Corporation shall issue an equivalent amount of capital stock to the Secretary of the Treasury.

HISTORY: (Pub. L. 87-195, Pt. I, § 232, as added Pub. L. 91-175, Pt. I, § 105, Dec. 30, 1969, 83 Stat. 810.)

§ 2193. Organization and management

(a) Structure

The Corporation shall have a Board of Directors, a President, an Executive Vice President, and such other officers and staff as the Board of Directors may determine.

(b) Board of directors

All powers of the Corporation shall vest in and be exercised by or under the authority of its Board of Directors ("the Board") which shall consist of fifteen Directors, including the Chairman, with eight Directors constituting a quorum for the transaction of business. Eight Directors shall be appointed by the President of the United States, by and with the advice and consent of the Senate, and shall not be officials or employees of the Government of the United States. At least two of the eight Directors appointed under the preceding sentence shall be experienced in small business, one in organized labor, and one in cooperatives. Each such Director shall be appointed for a term of no more than three years. The terms of no more than three such Directors shall expire in any one year. Such Directors shall serve until their successors are appointed and qualified and may be reappointed.

The other Directors shall be officials of the Government of the United States, including the President of the Corporation, the Administrator of the Agency for International Development, the United States Trade Representative, and an official of the Department of Labor, designated by and serving at the pleasure of the President of the United States. The United States Trade Representative may designate a Deputy United States Trade Representative to serve on the Board in place of the United States Trade Representative. There shall be a Chairman and a Vice Chairman of the Board, both of whom shall be designated by the President of the United States from among the Directors of the Board other than those appointed under the second sentence of the first paragraph of this subsection.

All Directors who are not officers of the Corporation or officials of the Government of the United States shall be compensated at a rate equivalent to that of level IV of the Executive Schedule when actually engaged in the business of the Corporation and may be paid per diem in lieu of subsistence at the applicable rate prescribed in the standardized Government travel regulations, as amended from time to time, while away from their homes or usual places of business.

(c) President

The President of the Corporation shall be appointed by the President of the United States, by and with the advice and consent of the Senate, and shall serve at the pleasure of the President. In making such appointment, the President shall take into account private business experience of the appointee. The President of the Corporation shall be its Chief Executive Officer and responsible for the operations and management of the Corporation, subject to bylaws and policies established by the Board.

(d) Officers and staff

The Executive Vice President of the Corporation shall be appointed by the President of the United States, by and with the advice and consent of the Senate, and shall serve at the pleasure of the President. Other officers, attorneys, employees, and agents shall be selected and appointed by the Corporation, and shall be vested with such powers and duties as the Corporation may determine. Of such persons employed by the Corporation, not to exceed twenty may be appointed, compensated, or removed without regard to the civil service laws and regulations: Provided, That under such regulations as the President of the United States may prescribe, officers and employees of the United States Government who are appointed to any of the above positions may be entitled, upon removal from such position, except for cause, to reinstatement to the position occupied at the time of appointment or to a position of comparable grade and salary. Such positions shall be in addition to those otherwise authorized by law, including those authorized by section 5108 of Title 5.

HISTORY: (Pub. L. 87-195, Pt. I, § 233, as added Pub. L. 91-175, Pt. I, § 105, Dec. 30, 1969, 83 Stat. 810, and amended 1979 Reorg. Plan No. 2, § 6(a)(1), eff. Oct. 1, 1979, 44 F.R. 41166, 93 Stat. 1379; Pub. L. 97-65, § 3(a), (b), Oct. 16, 1981, 95 Stat. 1021, 1022.) (As amended PL 106-158, December 9, 1999, 113 Stat. 1745.)

§ 2194. Investment insurance and other programs

The Corporation is hereby authorized to do the following:

(a) Investment insurance

Statutory Provisions Governing the Overseas Private Investment Corporation (OPIC)

(1) To issue insurance, upon such terms and conditions as the Corporation may determine, to eligible investors assuring protection in whole or in part against any or all of the following risks with respect to projects which the Corporation has approved—

(A) inability to convert into United States dollars other currencies, or credits in such currencies, received as earnings or profits from the approved project, as repayment or return of the investment therein, in whole or in part, or as compensation for the sale or disposition of all or any part thereof;

(B) loss of investment, in whole or in part, in the approved project due to expropriation or confiscation by action of a foreign government;

(C) loss due to war, revolution, insurrection, or civil strife; and

(D) loss due to business interruption caused by any of the risks set forth in subparagraphs (A), (B), and (C).

(2) Recognizing that major private investments in less developed friendly countries or areas are often made by enterprises in which there is multinational participation, including significant United States private participation, the Corporation may make arrangements with foreign governments (including agencies, instrumentalities, or political subdivisions thereof) or with multilateral organizations and institutions for sharing liabilities assumed under investment insurance for such investments and may in connection therewith issue insurance to investors not otherwise eligible hereunder, except that liabilities assumed by the Corporation under the authority of this subsection shall be consistent with the purposes of this subpart and that the maximum share of liabilities so assumed shall not exceed the proportionate participation by eligible investors in the project.

(3) Not more than 10 per centum of the maximum contingent liability of investment insurance which the Corporation is permitted to have outstanding under section 2195(a)(1) of this title shall be issued to a single investor.

(4) Before issuing insurance for the first time for loss due to business interruption, and in each subsequent instance in which a significant expansion is proposed in the type of risk to be insured under the definition of "civil strife" or "business interruption", the Corporation shall, at least sixty days before such insurance is issued, submit to the Committee on Foreign Relations of the Senate and the Committee on Foreign Affairs of the House of Representatives a report with respect to such insurance, including a thorough analysis of the risks to be covered, anticipated losses, and proposed rates and reserves and, in the case of insurance for loss due to business interruption, an explanation of the underwriting basis upon which the insurance is to be offered. Any such report with respect to insurance for loss due to business interruption shall be considered in accordance with the procedures applicable to reprogramming notifications pursuant to section 2394-1 of this title.

(b) Investment guaranties

To issue to eligible investors guaranties of loans and other investments made by such investors assuring against loss due to such risks and upon such terms and conditions as the Corporation may determine: Provided, however, That such guaranties on other than loan investments shall not exceed 75 per centum of such investment: Provided further, That except for loan investments for credit unions made by eligible credit unions or credit union associations, the aggregate amount of investment (exclusive of interest and earnings) so guaranteed with respect to any project shall not exceed, at the time of issuance of any such guaranty, 75 per centum of the total investment committed to any such project as determined by the Corporation, which determination shall be conclusive for purposes of the Corporation's authority to issue any such guaranty: Provided further, That not more than 15 per centum of the maximum contingent liability of investment guaranties which the Corporation is permitted to have outstanding under section 2195(a)(2) of this title shall be issued to a single investor.

(c) Direct investment

To make loans in United States dollars repayable in dollars or loans in foreign currencies (including, without regard to section 1306 of Title 31, such foreign currencies which the Secretary of the Treasury may determine to be excess to the normal requirements of the United States and the Director of the Office of Management and Budget may allocate) to firms privately owned or of mixed private and public ownership upon such terms and conditions as the Corporation may determine. Loans may be made under this subsection only for projects that are sponsored by or significantly involve United States small business or cooperatives.

The Corporation may designate up to 25 percent of any loan under this subsection for use in the development or adaptation in the United States of new technologies or new products or services that are to be used in the project for which the loan is made and are likely to contribute to the economic or social development of less developed countries.

No loan may be made under this subsection to finance any operation for the extraction of oil or gas. The aggregate amount of loans under this subsection to finance operations for the mining or other extraction of any deposit of ore or other nonfuel minerals may not in any fiscal year exceed $4,000,000.

(d) Investment encouragement

To initiate and support through financial participation, incentive grant, or otherwise, and on such terms and conditions as the Corporation may determine, the identification, assessment, surveying and promotion of private investment opportunities, utilizing wherever feasible and effective the facilities of private organizations or private investors, except that—

(1) the Corporation shall not finance any survey to ascertain the existence, location, extent, or quality of, or to determine the feasibility of undertaking operations for the extraction of, oil or gas; and

(2) expenditures financed by the Corporation during any fiscal year on surveys to ascertain the existence, location, extent, or quality of, or to determine the feasibility of undertaking operations for the extraction of nonfuel minerals may not exceed $200,000.

In carrying out this authority, the Corporation shall coordinate with such investment promotion activities as are carried out by the Department of Commerce.

(e) Special projects and programs

To administer and manage special projects and programs, including programs of financial and advisory support which provide private technical, professional, or managerial assistance in the development of human resources, skills, technology, capital savings and intermediate financial and investment institutions and cooperatives and including the initiation of incentives, grants, and studies for renewable energy and other small activities. The funds for these projects and programs may, with the Corporation's concurrence, be transferred to it for such purposes under the authority of section 2392(a) of this title or from other sources, public or private. Administrative funds may not be made available for incentives, grants, and studies for renewable energy and other small business activities.

(f) Additional insurance functions

(1) To make and carry out contracts of insurance or reinsurance, or agreements to associate or share risks, with insurance companies, financial institutions, any other persons, or groups thereof, and employing the same, where appropriate, as its agent, or acting as their agent, in the issuance and servicing of insurance, the adjustment of claims, the exercise of subrogation rights, the ceding and accepting of reinsurance, and in any other matter incident to an insurance business; except that such agreements and contracts shall be consistent with the purposes of the Corporation set forth in section 2191 of this title and shall be on equitable terms.

(2) To enter into pooling or other risk-sharing arrangements with multinational insurance or financing agencies or groups of such agencies.

(3) To hold an ownership interest in any association or other entity established for the purposes of sharing risks under investment insurance.

(4) To issue, upon such terms and conditions as it may determine, reinsurance of liabilities assumed by other insurers or groups thereof in respect of risks referred to in subsection (a)(1) of this section.

The amount of reinsurance of liabilities under this subpart which the Corporation may issue shall not in the aggregate exceed at any one time an amount equal to the amount authorized for the maximum contingent liability outstanding at any one time under section 2195(a) (1) of this title. All reinsurance issued by the Corporation under this subsection shall require that the reinsured party retain for his own account specified portions of liability, whether first loss or otherwise.

(g) Pilot equity finance program

(1) Authority for pilot program. In order to study the feasibility and desirability of a program of equity financing, the Corporation is authorized to establish a 4-year pilot program under which it may, on the limited basis prescribed in paragraphs (2) through (5), purchase, invest in, or otherwise acquire equity or quasi-equity securities of any firm or entity, upon such terms and conditions as the Corporation may determine, for the purpose of providing capital for any project which is consistent with the provisions of this subpart, except that—

(A) the aggregate amount of the Corporation's equity investment with respect to any project shall not exceed 30 percent of the aggregate amount of all equity investment made with respect to such project at the time that the Corporation's equity investment is made, except for securities acquired through the enforcement of any lien, pledge, or contractual arrangement as a result of a default by any party under any agreement relating to the terms of the Corporation's investment; and

(B) the Corporation's equity investment under this subsection with respect to any project, when added to any other investments made or guaranteed by the Corporation under subsection (b) or (c) of this section with respect to such project, shall not cause the aggregate amount of all such investment to exceed, at the time any such investment is made or guaranteed by the Corporation, 75 percent of the total investment committed to such project as determined by the Corporation.

The determination of the Corporation under subparagraph (B) shall be conclusive for purposes of the Corporation's authority to make or guarantee any such investment.

(2) Equity authority limited to projects in sub-Saharan Africa and Caribbean basin and marine transportation projects globally. Equity investments may be made under this subsection only in projects in countries eligible for financing under this subpart that are countries in sub-Saharan Africa or countries designated as beneficiary countries under section 2702 of Title 19 and in marine transportation projects in countries and areas eligible for OPIC support worldwide using United States commercial maritime expertise.

(3) Additional criteria. In making investment decisions under this subsection, the Corporation shall give preferential consideration to projects sponsored by or significantly involving United States small business or cooperatives. The Corporation shall also consider the extent to which the Corporation's equity investment will assist in obtaining the financing required for the project.

(4) Disposition of equity interest. Taking into consideration, among other things, the Corporation's financial interests and the desirability of fostering the development of local capital markets in less developed countries, the Corporation shall endeavor to dispose of any equity interest it may acquire under this subsection within a period of 10 years from the date of acquisition of such interest.

(5) Implementation. To the extent provided in advance in appropriations Acts, the Corporation is authorized to create such legal vehicles as may be necessary for implementation of its authorities, which legal vehicles may be deemed non-Federal borrowers for purposes of the Federal Credit Reform Act of 1990. Income and proceeds of investments made pursuant to this subsection may be used to purchase equity or quasi-equity securities in accordance with the provisions of this section: Provided, however, That such purchases shall not be limited to the 4-year period of the pilot program: Provided further, That the limitations contained in paragraph (2) shall not apply to such purchases.

(6) Consultations with Congress. The Corporation shall consult annually with the Committee on Foreign Affairs of the House of Representatives and the Committee on Foreign Relations of the Senate on the implementation of the pilot equity finance program established under this subsection.

HISTORY: (Pub. L. 87-195, Pt. I, § 234, as added Pub. L. 91-175, Pt. I, § 105, Dec. 30, 1969, 83 Stat. 811, and amended 1970 Reorg. Plan No. 2, § 102, eff. July 1, 1970, 35 F.R. 7959, 84 Stat. 2085; Pub. L. 93-390, § 2(2), Aug. 27, 1974, 88 Stat. 764; Pub. L. 95-268, § 3, Apr. 24, 1978, 92 Stat. 214; Pub. L. 97-65, § 4, Oct. 16, 1981, 95 Stat. 1022; Pub. L. 99-204, §§ 6(a), 7, 8, Dec. 23, 1985, 99 Stat. 1671, 1672; Pub. L. 100-461, Title V, § 555, Oct. 1, 1988, 102 Stat. 2268-36; Pub. L. 101-218, § 8(c), Dec. 11, 1989, 103 Stat. 1868.) (As amended Pub. L. 102-549, Title I, § 103, Oct. 28, 1992, 106 Stat. 3651; Pub. L. 106-31, Title VI, § 6001, May 21, 1999, 113 Stat. 112; Pub. L. 106-31, Title VI, § 6001, May 21, 1999, 113 Stat. 112.)

§ 2194a. Contract authority of Corporation; specific authorization in appropriation Acts required

The authority of the Overseas Private Investment Corporation to enter into contracts under section 2194(a) of this title shall be effective for any fiscal year beginning after September 30, 1981, only to such extent or in such amounts as are provided in appropriation Acts.

HISTORY: (Pub. L. 97-65, § 5(b)(2), Oct. 16, 1981, 95 Stat. 1023.)

§ 2194b. Enhancing private political risk insurance industry

(a) Cooperative programs

In order to encourage greater availability of political risk insurance for eligible investors by enhancing the private political risk insurance industry in the United States, and to the extent consistent with this subpart, the Corporation shall undertake programs of cooperation with such industry, and in connection with such programs may engage in the following activities:

(1) Utilizing its statutory authorities, encourage the development of associations, pools, or consortia of United States private political risk insurers.

(2) Share insurance risks (through coinsurance, contingent insurance, or other means) in a manner that is conducive to the growth and development of the private political risk insurance industry in the United States.

(3) Notwithstanding section 2197(e) of this title, upon the expiration of insurance provided by the Corporation for an investment, enter into risk- sharing agreements with United States private political risk insurers to insure any such investment; except that, in cooperating in the offering of insurance under this paragraph, the Corporation shall not assume responsibility for more than 50 percent of the insurance being offered in each separate transaction.

(b) Advisory group

(1) Establishment and membership

The Corporation shall establish a group to advise the Corporation on the development and implementation of the cooperative programs under this section. The group shall be appointed by the Board and shall be composed of up to 12 members, including the following:

(A) Up to seven persons from the private political risk insurance industry, of whom no fewer than two shall represent private political risk insurers, one shall represent private political risk reinsurers, and one shall represent insurance or reinsurance brokerage firms.

(B) Up to four persons, other than persons described in subparagraph (A), who are purchasers of political risk insurance.

(2) Functions

The Corporation shall call upon members of the advisory group, either collectively or individually, to advise it regarding the capability of the private political risk insurance industry to meet the political risk insurance needs of United States investors, and regarding the development of cooperative programs to enhance such capability.

(3) Meetings

The advisory group shall meet not later than September 30, 1989, and at least annually thereafter. The Corporation may from time to time convene meetings of selected members of the advisory group to address particular questions requiring their specialized knowledge.

(4) Federal Advisory Committee Act

The advisory group shall not be subject to the Federal Advisory Committee Act (5 U.S.C. App.).

HISTORY: (Pub. L. 87-195, Pt. I, § 234A, as added Pub. L. 99-204, § 9(a), Dec. 23, 1985, 99 Stat. 1672, and amended Pub. L. 100-461, Title V, § 555, Oct. 1, 1988, 102 Stat. 2268-36.)

§ 2195. Issuing authority, direct investment authority and reserves

(a) Issuing authority

(1) Insurance and financing.—(A) The maximum contingent liability outstanding at any one time pursuant to insurance issued under section 2194(a) of this title, and the amount of financing issued under sections 2194(b) and (c) of this title, shall not exceed in the aggregate $29,000,000,000.

(B) Subject to spending authority provided in appropriations Acts pursuant to section 661c(b) of Title 2, the Corporation is authorized to transfer such sums as are necessary from its noncredit activities to pay for the subsidy cost of the investment guaranties and direct loan programs under subsections (b) and (c) of section 2194 of this title.

(2) Termination of authority

The authority of subsections (a), (b), and (c) of section 2194 of this title shall continue until November 1, 2000.

(b) Repealed. Pub. L. 102-549, Title I, § 104(a)(3), Oct. 28, 1992, 106 Stat. 3652

(c) Insurance Reserve; Guaranty Reserve

There shall be established in the Treasury of the United States an insurance and guaranty fund, which shall have separate accounts to be known as the Insurance Reserve and the Guaranty Reserve, which reserves shall be available for discharge of liabilities, as provided in subsection (d) of this section, until such time as all such liabilities have been discharged or have expired or until all such reserves have been expended in accordance with the provisions of this section. Such fund shall be funded by: (1) the funds heretofore available to discharge liabilities under predecessor guaranty authority (including housing guaranty authorities), less both the amount made available for housing guaranty programs pursuant to section 2183(b) of this title and the amount made available to the Corporation pursuant to subsection (e) of this section of this title; and (2) such sums as shall be appropriated pursuant to subsection (f) of this section for such purpose. The allocation of such funds to each such reserve shall be determined by the Board after consultation with the Secretary of the Treasury. Additional amounts may thereafter be transferred to such reserves pursuant to section 2196 of this title.

(d) Priority of funds used to discharge liabilities

Any payments made to discharge liabilities under investment insurance or reinsurance issued under section 2194 of this title, under similar predecessor guaranty authority, or under section 2194b of this title shall be paid first out of the Insurance Reserve, as long as such reserve remains available, and thereafter out of funds made available pursuant to subsection (f) of this section. Any payments made to discharge liabilities under guaranties issued under section 2194(b) of this title or under similar predecessor guaranty authority shall be paid first out of the Guaranty Reserve as long as such reserve remains available, and thereafter out of funds made available pursuant to subsection (f) of this section.

(e) Reserves from predecessor guaranty authority

There is hereby authorized to be transferred to the Corporation at its call, for the purposes specified in section 2196 of this title, all fees and other revenues collected under predecessor guaranty authority from December 31, 1968, available as of the date of such transfer.

(f) Authorization of appropriations; issuance, etc., of obligations by Corporation for purchase by Secretary of the Treasury

There are authorized to be appropriated to the Corporation, to remain available until expended, such amounts as may be necessary from time to time to replenish or increase the insurance and guaranty fund, to discharge the liabilities under insurance, reinsurance, or guaranties issued by the Corporation or issued under predecessor guaranty authority, or to discharge obligations of the Corporation purchased by the Secretary of the Treasury pursuant to this subsection. However, no appropriations shall be made to augment the Insurance Reserve until the amount of funds in the Insurance Reserve is less than $25,000,000. Any appropriations to augment the Insurance Reserve shall then only be made either pursuant to specific authorization enacted after August 27, 1974, or to satisfy the full faith and credit provision of section 2197(c) of this title. In order to discharge liabilities under investment insurance or reinsurance, the Corporation is authorized to issue from time to time for purchase by the Secretary of the Treasury its notes, debentures, bonds, or other obligations; but the aggregate amount of such obligations outstanding at any one time shall not exceed $100,000,000. Any such obligation shall be repaid to the Treasury within one year after the date of issue of such obligation. Any such obligation shall bear interest at a rate determined by the Secretary of the Treasury, taking into consideration the current average market yield on outstanding marketable obligations of the United States of comparable maturities during the month preceding the issuance of any obligation authorized by this subsection. The Secretary of the Treasury shall purchase any obligation of the Corporation issued under this subsection, and for such purchase he may use as a public debt transaction the proceeds of the sale of any securities issued under chapter 31 of Title 31 after August 27, 1974. The purpose for which securities may be issued under such chapter shall include any such purchase.

HISTORY: (Pub. L. 87-195, Pt. I, § 235, as added Pub. L. 91-175, Pt. I, § 105, Dec. 30, 1969, 83 Stat. 813, and amended Pub. L. 93-189, § 6(1), Dec. 17, 1973, 87 Stat. 717; Pub. L. 93-390, § 2(3), Aug. 27, 1974, 88 Stat. 766; Pub. L. 95-268, § 4, Apr. 24, 1978, 92 Stat. 214; Pub. L. 97-65, § 5(a), (b)(1), (c), Oct. 16, 1981, 95 Stat. 1022, 1023; Pub. L. 99-204, §§ 9(b)(1), 10, 17(b), Dec. 23, 1985, 99 Stat. 1673, 1676; Pub. L. 100-418, Title II, § 2203(b), Aug. 23, 1988, 102 Stat. 1328; Pub. L. 100-461, Title V, § 555, Oct. 1, 1988, 102 Stat. 2268-36.) (As amended Pub. L. 102-549, Title I, § 104, Oct. 28, 1992, 106 Stat. 3652; Pub. L. 103-392, Title I, §§ 101 to 104, Oct. 22, 1994, 108 Stat. 4098; Pub. L. 104-208, Div. A, Title I, § 101(c) [Title I], Sept. 30, 1996, 110 Stat. 3009-123; Pub. L. 105-118, Title V, § 581(a), Nov. 26, 1997, 111 Stat. 2435.) (As amended PL 106-113, November 29, 1999, 113 Stat. 1501.)

§ 2196. Income and revenues

In order to carry out the purposes of the Corporation, all revenues and income transferred to or earned by the Corporation, from whatever source derived, shall be held by the Corporation and shall be available to carry out its purposes, including without limitation—

(a) payment of all expenses of the Corporation, including investment promotion expenses;

(b) transfers and additions to the insurance or guaranty reserves, the Direct Investment Fund established pursuant to section 2195 of this title, and such other funds or reserves as the Corporation may establish, at such time and in such amounts as the Board may determine; and

(c) payment of dividends, on capital stock, which shall consist of and be paid from net earnings of the Corporation after payments, transfers, and additions under subsections (a) and (b) hereof.

HISTORY: (Pub. L. 87-195, Pt. I, § 236, as added Pub. L. 91-175, Pt. I, § 105, Dec. 30, 1969, 83 Stat. 814.)

§ 2197. General provisions relating to insurance, guaranty, financing and reinsurance programs

(a) Scope

Insurance, guaranties, and reinsurance issued under this subpart shall cover investment made in connection with projects in any less developed friendly country or area with the government of which the President of the United States has agreed to institute a program for insurance, guaranties, or reinsurance.

(b) Protection of interest

The Corporation shall determine that suitable arrangements exist for protecting the interest of the Corporation in connection with any insurance, guaranty or reinsurance issued under this subpart, including arrangements concerning ownership, use, and disposition of the currency, credits, assets, or investments on account of which payment under such insurance, guaranty or reinsurance is to be made, and any right, title, claim, or cause of action existing in connection therewith.

(c) Guaranties as obligations backed by full faith and credit of United States

All guaranties issued prior to July 1, 1956, all guaranties issued under sections 1872(b) and 1933(b) of this title, all guaranties heretofore issued pursuant to prior guaranty authorities repealed by the Foreign Assistance Act of 1969, and all insurance, reinsurance and guaranties issued pursuant to this subpart shall constitute obligations, in accordance with the terms of such insurance, reinsurance or guaranties, of the United States of America and the full faith and credit of the United States of America is hereby pledged for the full payment and performance of such obligations.

(d) Fees

(1) In general

Fees may be charged for providing insurance, reinsurance, financing, and other services under this subpart in amounts to be determined by the Corporation. In the event fees charged for insurance, reinsurance, financing, or other services are reduced, fees to be paid under existing contracts for the same type of insurance, reinsurance, financing, or services and for similar guarantees issued under predecessor guarantee authority may be reduced.

(2) Credit transaction costs

Project-specific transaction costs incurred by the Corporation relating to loan obligations or loan guarantee commitments covered by the provisions of the Federal Credit Reform Act of 1990 [2 U.S.C.A. § 661 et seq.], including the costs of project-related travel and expenses for legal representation provided by persons outside the Corporation and other similar expenses which are charged to the borrower, shall be paid out of the appropriate finance account established pursuant to section 505(b) of such Act [2 U.S.C.A. § 661d(b)].

(3) Noncredit transaction costs

Fees paid for the project-specific transaction costs and other direct costs associated with services provided to specific investors or potential investors pursuant to section 2194 of this title (other than those covered in paragraph (2)), including financing, insurance, reinsurance, missions, seminars, conferences, and other preinvestment services, shall be available for obligation for the purposes for which they were collected, notwithstanding any other provision of law.

(e) Maximum term of obligation

No insurance, guaranty, or reinsurance of any equity investment shall extend beyond twenty years from the date of issuance.

(f) Limitations on amounts

Compensation for insurance, reinsurance, or guaranties issued under this subpart shall not exceed the dollar value, as of the date of the investment, of the investment made in the project with the approval of the Corporation plus interest, earnings, or profits actually accrued on such investment to the extent provided by such insurance, reinsurance, or guaranty, except that the Corporation may provide that (1) appropriate adjustments in the insured dollar value be made to reflect the replacement cost of project assets, (2) compensation for a claim of loss under insurance of an equity investment may be computed on the basis of the net book value attributable to such equity investment on the date of loss, and (3) compensation for loss due to business interruption may be computed on a basis to be determined by the Corporation which reflects amounts lost. Notwithstanding the preceding sentence, the Corporation shall limit the amount of direct insurance and reinsurance issued by it under section 2194 or 2194b of this title so that risk of loss as to at least 10 per centum of the total investment of the insured and its affiliates in the project is borne by the insured and such affiliates, except that such limitation shall not apply to direct insurance or reinsurance of loans by banks or other financial institutions to unrelated parties.

(g) Fraud or misrepresentation

No payment may be made under any guaranty, insurance, or reinsurance issued pursuant to this subpart for any loss arising out of fraud or misrepresentation for which the party seeking payment is responsible.

(h) Limits of obligation

Insurance, guaranties, or reinsurance of a loan or equity investment of an eligible investor in a foreign bank, finance company, or other credit institution shall extend only to such loan or equity investment and not to any individual loan or equity investment made by such foreign bank, finance company, or other credit institution.

(i) Claims settlement

Claims arising as a result of insurance, reinsurance, or guaranty operations under this subpart or under predecessor guaranty authority may be settled, and disputes arising as a result thereof may be arbitrated with the consent of the parties, on such terms and conditions as the Corporation may determine. Payment made pursuant to any such settlement, or as a result of an arbitration award, shall be final and conclusive notwithstanding any other provision of law.

(j) Presumption of compliance

Each guaranty contract executed by such officer or officers as may be designated by the Board shall be conclusively presumed to be issued in compliance with the requirements of this chapter.

(k) Balance of payments

In making a determination to issue insurance, guaranties, or reinsurance under this subpart, the Corporation shall consider the possible adverse effect of the dollar investment under such insurance, guaranty, or reinsurance upon the balance of payments of the United States.

(l) Convictions under Foreign Corrupt Practices Act of 1977; prohibition on payments for losses resulting from unlawful activities; suspension from eligibility of receipt of financial support

(1) No payment may be made under any insurance or reinsurance which is issued under this subpart on or after April 24, 1978, for any loss occurring with respect to a project, if the preponderant cause of such loss was an act by the investor seeking payment under this subpart, by a person possessing majority ownership and control of the investor at the time of the act, or by any agent of such investor or controlling person, and a court of the United States has entered a final judgment that such act constituted a violation under the Foreign Corrupt Practices Act of 1977.

(2) Not later than 120 days after April 24, 1978, the Corporation shall adopt regulations setting forth appropriate conditions under which any person convicted under the Foreign Corrupt Practices Act of 1977 for an offense related to a project insured or otherwise supported by the Corporation shall be suspended, for a period of not more than five years, from eligibility to receive any insurance, reinsurance, guaranty, loan, or other financial support authorized by this subpart.

(m) Notification of countries of environmental restrictions on certain activities

(1) Before finally providing insurance, reinsurance, guarantees, or financing under this subpart for any environmentally sensitive investment in connection with a project in a country, the Corporation shall notify appropriate government officials of that country of—

(A) all guidelines and other standards adopted by the International Bank for Reconstruction and Development and any other international organization relating to the public health or safety or the environment which are applicable to the project; and

(B) to the maximum extent practicable, any restriction under any law of the United States relating to public health or safety or the environment that would apply to the project if the project were undertaken in the United States.

The notification under the preceding sentence shall include a summary of the guidelines, standards, and restrictions referred to in subparagraphs (A) and (B), and may include any environmental impact statement, assessment, review, or study prepared with respect to the investment pursuant to section 2199(g) of this title.

(2) Before finally providing insurance, reinsurance, guarantees, or financing for any investment subject to paragraph (1), the Corporation shall take into account any comments it receives on the project involved.

(3) On or before September 30, 1986, the Corporation shall notify appropriate government officials of a country of the guidelines, standards, and legal restrictions described in paragraph (1) that apply to any project in that country—

(A) which the Corporation identifies as potentially posing major hazards to public health and safety or the environment; and

(B) for which the Corporation provided insurance, reinsurance, guarantees, or financing under this subpart before December 23, 1985, and which is in the Corporation's portfolio on that date.

(n) Penalties for fraud

Whoever knowingly makes any false statement or report, or willfully overvalues any land, property, or security, for the purpose of influencing in any way the action of the Corporation with respect to any insurance, reinsurance, guarantee, loan, equity investment, or other activity of the Corporation under section 2194 of this title or any change or extension of any such insurance, reinsurance, guarantee, loan, equity investment, or activity, by renewal, deferment of action or otherwise, or the acceptance, release, or substitution of security therefor, shall be fined not more than $1,000,000 or imprisoned not more than 30 years, or both.

(o) Use of local currencies

Direct loans or investments made in order to preserve the value of funds received in inconvertible foreign currency by the Corporation as a result of activities conducted pursuant to section 2194(a) of this title shall not be considered in determining whether the Corporation has made or has outstanding loans or investments to the extent of any limitation on obligations and equity investment imposed by or pursuant to this subpart. The provisions of section 504(b) of the Federal Credit Reform Act of 1990 [2 U.S.C.A. § 661c(b)] shall not apply to direct loan obligations made with funds described in this subsection.

HISTORY: (Pub. L. 87-195, Pt. I, § 237, as added Pub. L. 91-175, Pt. I, § 105, Dec. 30, 1969, 83 Stat. 814, and amended Pub. L. 93-390, § 2(4), Aug. 27, 1974, 88 Stat. 767; Pub. L. 95-268, §§ 5, 6, Apr. 24, 1978, 92 Stat. 215; Pub. L. 97-65, § 6, Oct. 16, 1981, 95 Stat. 1023; Pub. L. 99-204, §§ 4(b), 6(b), 9(b)(2), Dec. 23, 1985, 99 Stat. 1670, 1671, 1673; Pub. L. 100-461, Title V, § 555, Oct. 1, 1988, 102 Stat. 2268-36.) (As amended Pub. L. 102-549, Title I, § 105, Oct. 28, 1992, 106 Stat. 3652.)

§ 2198. Definitions

As used in this subpart—

(a) the term "investment" includes any contribution or commitment of funds, commodities, services, patents, processes, or techniques, in the form of (1) a loan or loans to an approved project, (2) the purchase of a share of ownership in any such project, (3) participation in royalties, earnings, or profits of any such project, and (4) the furnishing of commodities or services pursuant to a lease or other contract;

(b) the term "expropriation" includes, but is not limited to, any abrogation, repudiation, or impairment by a foreign government of its own contract with an investor with respect to a project, where such abrogation, repudiation, or impairment is not caused by the investor's own fault or misconduct, and materially adversely affects the continued operation of the project;

(c) the term "eligible investor" means: (1) United States citizens; (2) corporations, partnerships, or other associations including nonprofit associations, created under the laws of the United States, any State or territory thereof, or the District of Columbia, and substantially beneficially owned by United States citizens; and (3) foreign corporations, partnerships, of [FN1] other associations wholly owned by one or more such United States citizens, corporations, partnerships, or other associations: Provided, however, That the eligibility of such foreign corporation shall be determined without regard to any shares, in aggregate less than 5 per centum of the total of issued and subscribed share capital, held by other than the United States owners: Provided further, That in the case of any loan investment a final determination of eligibility may be made at the time the insurance or guaranty is issued; in all other cases, the investor must be eligible at the time a claim arises as well as at the time the insurance or guaranty is issued;

(d) the term "noncredit account revolving fund" means the account in which funds under section 2196 of this title and all funds from noncredit activities are held; and

(e) the term "noncredit activities" means all activities of the Corporation other than its loan guarantee program under section 2194(b) of this title and its direct loan program under section 2194(c) of this title;

(f) the term "predecessor guaranty authority" means prior guaranty authorities (other than housing guaranty authorities) repealed by the Foreign Assistance Act of 1969, and sections 1509(b)(3), 1872(b), and 1933(b) of this title (exclusive of authority relating to informational media guaranties).

HISTORY: (Pub. L. 87-195, Pt. I, § 238, as added Pub. L. 91-175, Pt. I, § 105, Dec. 30, 1969, 83 Stat. 815, and amended Pub. L. 92-226, Pt. I, § 104(a), Feb. 7, 1972, 86 Stat. 22; Pub. L. 97-65, § 7, Oct. 16, 1981, 95 Stat. 1024; Pub. L. 99-204, § 17(a), Dec. 23, 1985, 99 Stat. 1676.) (As amended Pub. L. 102-549, Title I, § 106, Oct. 28, 1992, 106 Stat. 3653.)

§ 2199. General provisions and powers

(a) Place of residence

The Corporation shall have its principal office in the District of Columbia and shall be deemed, for purposes of venue in civil actions, to be a resident thereof.

(b) Transfer of prior obligations, etc.; administration prior to transfer

The President shall transfer to the Corporation, at such time as he may determine, all obligations, assets and related rights and responsibilities arising out of, or related to, predecessor programs and authorities similar to those provided for in section 2194(a), (b), and (d) of this title. Until such transfer, the agency heretofore responsible for such predecessor programs shall continue to administer such assets and obligations, and such programs and activities authorized under this subpart as may be determined by the President.

(c) Audits of the Corporation

(1) The Corporation shall be subject to the applicable provisions of chapter 91 of Title 31, except as otherwise provided in this subpart.

(2) An independent certified public accountant shall perform a financial and compliance audit of the financial statements of the Corporation at least once every three years, in accordance with generally accepted Government auditing standards for a financial and compliance audit, as issued by the Comptroller General. The independent certified public accountant shall report the results of such audit to the Board. The financial statements of the Corporation shall be presented in accordance with generally accepted accounting principles. These financial statements and the report of the accountant shall be included in a report which contains, to the extent applicable, the information identified in section 9106 of Title 31 and which the Corporation shall submit to the Congress not later than six and one-half months after the end of the last fiscal year covered by the audit. The General Accounting Office may review the audit conducted by the accountant and the report to the Congress in the manner and at such times as the General Accounting Office considers necessary.

(3) In lieu of the financial and compliance audit required by paragraph (2), the General Accounting Office shall, if the Office considers it necessary or upon the request of the Congress, audit the financial statements of the Corporation in the manner provided in paragraph (2). The Corporation shall reimburse the General Accounting Office for the full cost of any audit conducted under this paragraph.

(4) All books, accounts, financial records, reports, files, workpapers, and property belonging to or in use by the Corporation and the accountant who conducts the audit under paragraph (2), which are necessary for purposes of this subsection, shall be made available to the representatives of the General Accounting Office.

(d) Powers of Corporation

To carry out the purposes of this subpart, the Corporation is authorized to adopt and use a corporate seal, which shall be judicially noticed; to sue and be sued in its corporate name; to adopt, amend, and repeal bylaws governing the conduct of its business and the performance of the powers and duties granted to or imposed upon it by law; to acquire, hold or dispose of, upon such terms and conditions as the Corporation may determine, any property, real, personal, or mixed, tangible or intangible, or any interest therein; to invest funds derived from fees and other revenues in obligations of the United States and to use the proceeds therefrom, including earnings and profits, as it shall deem appropriate; to indemnify directors, officers, employees and agents of the Corporation for liabilities and expenses incurred in connection with their Corporation activities; notwithstanding any other provision of law, to represent itself or to contract for representation in all legal and arbitral proceedings; to enter into limited-term contracts with nationals of the United States for personal services to carry out activities in the United States and abroad under subsections (d) and (e) of section 2194 of this title; to purchase, discount, rediscount, sell, and negotiate, with or without its endorsement or guaranty, and guarantee notes, participation certificates, and other evidence of indebtedness (provided that the Corporation shall not issue its own securities, except participation certificates for the purpose of carrying out section 2191(c) of this title or participation certificates as evidence of indebtedness held by the Corporation in connection with settlement of claims under section 2197(i) of this title); to make and carry out such contracts and agreements as are necessary and advisable in the conduct of its business; to exercise any priority of the Government of the United States in collecting debts from bankrupt, insolvent, or decedents' estates; to determine the character of and the necessity for its obligations and expenditures, and the manner in which they shall be incurred, allowed, and paid, subject to provisions of law specifically applicable to Government corporations; to collect or compromise any obligations assigned to or held by the Corporation, including any legal or equitable rights accruing to the Corporation; and to take such actions as may be necessary or appropriate to carry out the powers herein or hereafter specifically conferred upon it.

(e) Reviews, investigations, and inspections by Inspector General of Agency for International Development

The Inspector General of the Agency for International Development (1) may conduct reviews, investigations, and inspections of all phases of the Corporation's operations and activities and (2) shall conduct all security activities of the Corporation relating to personnel and the control of classified material. With respect to his responsibilities under this subsection, the Inspector General shall report to the Board. The agency primarily responsible for administering subchapter I of this chapter shall be reimbursed by the Corporation for all expenses incurred by the Inspector General in connection with his responsibilities under this subsection.

(f) Programs in Yugoslavia, Poland, Hungary, Romania, the People's Republic of China, or Pakistan; national interest

Except for the provisions of this subpart, no other provision of this chapter or any other law shall be construed to prohibit the operation in Yugoslavia, Poland, Hungary, or any other East European Country, or the People's Republic of China, or Pakistan of the programs authorized by this subpart, if the President determines that the operation of such program in such country is important to the national interest.

(g) Environmental impact assessments

The requirements of section 2151p(c) of this title relating to environmental impact statements and environmental assessments shall apply to any investment which the Corporation insures, reinsures, guarantees, or finances under this subpart in connection with a project in a country.

(h) Preparation, maintenance, and contents of development impact profile for investment projects; development of criteria for evaluating projects

In order to carry out the policy set forth in paragraph (1) of the second undesignated paragraph of section 2191 of this title, the Corporation shall prepare and maintain for each investment project it insures, finances, or reinsures, a development impact profile consisting of data appropriate to measure the projected and actual effects of such project on development. Criteria for evaluating projects shall be developed in consultation with the Director of the United States International Development Cooperation Agency.

(i) Observance of and respect for human rights and fundamental freedoms as considerations for conduct of assistance programs, etc.; provisions applicable for determinations; exceptions

The Corporation shall take into account in the conduct of its programs in a country, in consultation with the Secretary of State, all available information about observance of and respect for human rights and fundamental freedoms in such country and the effect the operation of such programs will have on human rights and fundamental freedoms in such country. The provisions of section 2151n of this title shall apply to any insurance, reinsurance, guaranty, or loan issued by the Corporation for projects in a country, except that in addition to the exception (with respect to benefiting needy people) set forth in subsection (a) of such section, the Corporation may support a project if the national security interest so requires.

(j) Exemption from taxation

The Corporation, including its franchise, capital, reserves, surplus, advances, intangible property, and income, shall be exempt from all taxation at any time imposed by the United States, by any territory, dependency, or possession of the United States, or by any State, the District of Columbia, or any county, municipality, or local taxing authority.

(k) Publication of policy guidelines

The Corporation shall publish, and make available to applicants for insurance, reinsurance, guarantees, financing, or other assistance made available by the Corporation under this subpart, the policy guidelines of the Corporation relating to its programs.

HISTORY: (Pub. L. 87-195, Pt. I, § 239, as added Pub. L. 91-175, Pt. I, § 105, Dec. 30, 1969, 83 Stat. 816, and amended Pub. L. 92-226, Pt. I, § 104(b), Feb. 7, 1972, 86 Stat. 22; Pub. L. 92-310, Title II, § 227(d), June 6, 1972, 86 Stat. 207; Pub. L. 93-390, § 2(5), Aug. 27, 1974, 88 Stat. 768; Pub. L. 95-268, §§ 7, 8, Apr. 24, 1978, 92 Stat. 215, 216; Pub. L. 95-598, Title III, § 318, Nov. 6, 1978, 92 Stat. 2678; 1979 Reorg. Plan No. 2, § 6(a)(1), eff. Oct. 1, 1979, 44 F.R. 41166, 93 Stat. 1379; Pub. L. 96-327, Aug. 8, 1980, 94 Stat. 1026; Pub. L. 97-65, § 8, Oct. 16, 1981, 95 Stat. 1024; Pub. L. 97-113, Title VII, § 705(b)(2), Dec. 29, 1981, 95 Stat. 1545; Pub. L. 99-204, §§ 4(c), 11 to 13, Dec. 23, 1985, 99 Stat. 1670, 1673, 1674; Pub. L. 100-461, Title V, § 555, Oct. 1, 1988, 102 Stat. 2268-36; Pub. L. 101-167, Title V, § 597(a), Nov. 21, 1989, 103 Stat. 1257; Pub. L. 101-179, Title III, § 302(a), Nov. 28, 1989, 103 Stat. 1311.) (As amended Pub. L. 101-513, Title V, § 576(a), Nov. 5, 1990, 104 Stat. 2044; Pub. L. 102-549, Title I, § 107, Oct. 28, 1992, 106 Stat. 3654; Pub. L. 105-118, Title V, § 579(a), Nov. 26, 1997, 111 Stat. 2435.)

§ 2200. Small business development in less developed friendly countries or areas; encouragement by other Federal departments, etc., of broadened participation by United States small business cooperatives and investors; project funding

The Corporation shall undertake, in cooperation with appropriate departments, agencies, and instrumentalities of the United States as well as private entities and others, to broaden the participation of United States small business, cooperatives, and other small United States investors in the development of small private enterprise in less developed friendly countries or areas. The Corporation shall allocate up to 50 per cent of its annual net income, after making suitable provision for transfers and additions to reserves, to assist and facilitate the development of projects consistent with the provisions of this section. Such funds may be expended, notwithstanding the requirements of section 2191(a) of this title, on such terms and conditions as the Corporation may determine, through loans, grants, or other programs authorized by section 2194 and section 2194b of this title.

HISTORY: (Pub. L. 87-195, Pt. I, § 240, as added Pub. L. 95-268, § 9, Apr. 24, 1978, 92 Stat. 216, and amended Pub. L. 99-204, § 9(b)(3), Dec. 23, 1985, 99 Stat. 1673.)

§ 2200a. Report to Congress

(a) Annual report

After the end of each fiscal year, the Corporation shall submit to the Congress a complete and detailed report of its operations during such fiscal year. Such report shall include—

(1) an assessment, based upon the development impact profiles required by section 2199(h) of this title, of the economic and social development impact and benefits of the projects with respect to which such profiles are prepared, and of the extent to which the operations of the Corporation complement or are compatible with the development assistance programs of the United States and other donors; and

(2) a description of any project for which the Corporation—

(A) refused to provide any insurance, reinsurance, guaranty, financing, or other financial support, on account of violations of human rights referred to in section 2199(i) of this title; or

(B) notwithstanding such violations, provided such insurance, reinsurance, guaranty, financing, or financial support, on the basis of a determination (i) that the project will directly benefit the needy people in the country in which the project is located, or (ii) that the national security interest so requires.

(b) Effect of all projects on employment in United States to be included in annual report

(1) Each annual report required by subsection (a) of this section shall contain projections of the effects on employment in the United States of all projects for which, during the preceding fiscal year, the Corporation initially issued any insurance, reinsurance, or guaranty or made any direct loan. Each such report shall include projections of—

(A) the amount of United States exports to be generated by those projects, both during the start-up phase and over a period of years;

(B) the final destination of the products to be produced as a result of those projects; and

(C) the impact such production will have on the production of similar products in the United States with regard to both domestic sales and exports.

(2) The projections required by this subsection shall be based on an analysis of each of the projects described in paragraph (1).

(3) In reporting the projections on employment required by this subsection, the Corporation shall specify, with respect to each project—

(A) any loss of jobs in the United States caused by the project, whether or not the project itself creates other jobs;

(B) any jobs created by the project; and

(C) the country in which the project is located, and the economic sector involved in the project.

No proprietary information may be disclosed under this paragraph.

(c) Repealed. Pub.L. 100-461, Title V, § 555, Oct. 1, 1988, 102 Stat. 2268-36

(d) Maintenance of records

The Corporation shall maintain as part of its records—

(1) all information collected in preparing the report required by subsection (c) of this section (as in effect before October 1, 1988), whether the information was collected by the Corporation itself or by a contractor; and

(2) a copy of the analysis of each project analyzed in preparing the reports required either by subsection (b) of this section, or by subsection (c) of this section (as in effect before October 1, 1988).

(e) Assessment of cooperative political risk insurance program

Each annual report required by subsection (a) of this section shall include an assessment of programs implemented by the Corporation under section 2194b(a) of this title including the following information, to the extent such information is available to the Corporation:

(1) The nature and dollar value of political risk insurance provided by private insurers in conjunction with the Corporation, which the Corporation was not permitted to provide under this subpart.

(2) The nature and dollar value of political risk insurance provided by private insurers in conjunction with the Corporation, which the Corporation was permitted to provide under this subpart.

(3) The manner in which such private insurers and the Corporation cooperated in recovery efforts and claims management.

(f) Information not required to be made available to public excluded from reports

Subsections (b) and (e) of this section do not require the inclusion in any report submitted pursuant to those subsections of any information which would not be required to be made available to the public pursuant to section 552 of Title 5 (relating to freedom of information).

HISTORY: (Pub. L. 87-195, Pt. I, § 240A, as added Pub. L. 91-175, Pt. I, § 105, Dec. 30, 1969, 83 Stat. 818, and amended Pub. L. 93-390, § 2(7), Aug. 27, 1974, 88 Stat. 768; Pub. L. 95-268, § 10, Apr. 24, 1978, 92 Stat. 216; Pub. L. 97-65, § 9, formerly S 9(a), Oct. 16, 1981, 95 Stat. 1024, renumbered § 9, Pub. L. 99-204, § 17(c)(1), Dec. 23, 1985, 99 Stat. 1677; Pub. L. 99-204, § 14(a), Dec. 23, 1985, 99 Stat. 1674; Pub. L. 100-461, Title V, § 555, Oct. 1, 1988, 102 Stat. 2268-36.) (As amended Pub. L. 102-549, Title I, § 108, Oct. 28, 1992, 106 Stat. 3654.)

§ 2200b. Prohibition on noncompetitive awarding of insurance contracts on OPIC supported exports

(a) Requirement for certification

(1) In general

Except as provided in paragraph (3), the investor on whose behalf insurance, reinsurance, guaranties, or other financing is provided under this title with respect to a project shall be required to certify to the Corporation that any contract for the export of goods as part of that project will include a clause requiring that United States insurance companies have a fair and open competitive opportunity to provide insurance against risk of loss of such export.

(2) When certification must be made

The investor shall be required, in every practicable case, to so certify before the insurance, reinsurance, guarantee, or other financing is provided. In any case in which such a certification is not made in advance, the investor shall include in the certification the reasons for the failure to make a certification in advance.

(3) Exception

Paragraph (1) does not apply with respect to an investor who does not, because of the nature of the investment, have a controlling interest in fact in the project in question.

(b) Reports by United States Trade Representative

The United States Trade Representative shall review the actions of the Corporation under subsection (a) of this section and, after consultation with representatives of United States insurance companies, shall report to the Congress in the report required by section 2241(b) of Title 19 with respect to such actions.

(c) Definitions

For purposes of this section—

(1) the term "United States insurance company" includes—

(A) an individual, partnership, corporation, holding company, or other legal entity which is authorized, or in the case of a holding company, subsidiaries of which are authorized, by a State to engage in the business of issuing insurance contracts or reinsuring the risk underwritten by insurance companies; and

(B) foreign operations, branches, agencies, subsidiaries, affiliates, or joint ventures of any entity described in subparagraph (A);

(2) United States insurance companies shall be considered to have had a "fair and open competitive opportunity to provide insurance" if they—

(A) have received notice of the opportunity to provide insurance; and

(B) have been evaluated on a nondiscriminatory basis; and

(3) the term "State" includes the District of Columbia and any commonwealth, territory, or possession of the United States.

HISTORY: (Pub. L. 87-195, Pt. I, § 240B, as added Pub. L. 102-549, Title I, § 109, Oct. 28, 1992, 106 Stat. 3654.)

G. Basic Antitrust Statutes and Regulations

Source: 15 U.S.C. assorted sections; 15 C.F.R.

Website information:

http://www.usdoj.gov/atr/public/international/intdocs.htm
This is the international documents website of the U.S. Department of Justice Antitrust Division.
It includes links to the text of the 1995 Guidelines for International Operations as well as other
current documentation on antitrust law.

Introduction

The following are the primary provisions of U.S. antitrust law applicable to international
transactions. They were enacted as part of the following legislation:

Sherman Act of 1890
Wilson Tariff Act of 1894
Clayton Act of 1914
Federal Trade Commission Act of 1914
Webb-Pomerene Act of 1918
Foreign Trade Antitrust Improvements Act (Title VI of the Export Trading Company Act of
1982

UNITED STATES CODE
TITLE 15. COMMERCE AND TRADE
CHAPTER 1—MONOPOLIES AND COMBINATIONS IN RESTRAINT OF TRADE

§ 1. Trusts, etc., in restraint of trade illegal; penalty (Sherman Act, § 1)

Every contract, combination in the form of trust or otherwise, or conspiracy, in restraint of trade or commerce among the several States, or with foreign nations, is declared to be illegal. Every person who shall make any contract or engage in any combination or conspiracy hereby declared to be illegal shall be deemed guilty of a felony, and, on conviction thereof, shall be punished by fine not exceeding $10,000,000 if a corporation, or, if any other person, $350,000, or by imprisonment not exceeding three years, or by both said punishments, in the discretion of the court.

HISTORY: (July 2, 1890, c. 647, § 1, 26 Stat. 209; Aug. 17, 1937, c. 690, Title VIII, 50 Stat. 693; July 7, 1955, c. 281, 69 Stat. 282; Dec. 21, 1974, Pub. L. 93- 528, § 3, 88 Stat. 1708; Dec. 12, 1975, Pub. L. 94-145, § 2, 89 Stat. 801; Nov. 16, 1990, Pub. L. 101-588, § 4(a), 104 Stat. 2880.)

§ 2. Monopolizing trade a felony; penalty (Sherman Act § 2)

Every person who shall monopolize, or attempt to monopolize, or combine or conspire with any other person or persons, to monopolize any part of the trade or commerce among the several States, or with foreign nations, shall be deemed guilty of a felony, and, on conviction thereof, shall be punished by fine not exceeding $10,000,000 if a corporation, or, if any other person, $350,000, or by imprisonment not exceeding three years, or by both said punishments, in the discretion of the court.

HISTORY: (July 2, 1890, c. 647, S 2, 26 Stat. 209; July 7, 1955, c. 281, 69 Stat. 282; Dec. 21, 1974, Pub. L. 93-528, § 3, 88 Stat. 1708; Nov. 16, 1990, Pub. L. 101- 588, § 4(b), 104 Stat. 2880.)

§ 6a. Conduct involving trade or commerce with foreign nations (Foreign Trade Antitrust Improvements Act § 402)

Sections 1 to 7 of this title shall not apply to conduct involving trade or commerce (other than import trade or import commerce) with foreign nations unless—

(1) such conduct has a direct, substantial, and reasonably foreseeable effect—

(A) on trade or commerce which is not trade or commerce with foreign nations, or on import trade or import commerce with foreign nations; or

302

(B) on export trade or export commerce with foreign nations, of a person engaged in such trade or commerce in the United States; and

(2) such effect gives rise to a claim under the provisions of sections 1 to 7 of this title, other than this section.

If sections 1 to 7 of this title apply to such conduct only because of the operation of paragraph (1) (B), then sections 1 to 7 of this title shall apply to such conduct only for injury to export business in the United States.

HISTORY: (July 2, 1890, c. 647, S 7, as added Oct. 8, 1982, Pub. L. 97-290, Title IV, § 402, 96 Stat. 1246.)

§ 8. Trusts in restraint of import trade illegal; penalty (Wilson Tariff Act § 73)

Every combination, conspiracy, trust, agreement, or contract is declared to be contrary to public policy, illegal, and void when the same is made by or between two or more persons or corporations, either of whom, as agent or principal, is engaged in importing any article from any foreign country into the United States, and when such combination, conspiracy, trust, agreement, or contract is intended to operate in restraint of lawful trade, or free competition in lawful trade or commerce, or to increase the market price in any part of the United States of any article or articles imported or intended to be imported into the United States, or of any manufacture into which such imported article enters or is intended to enter. Every person who shall be engaged in the importation of goods or any commodity from any foreign country in violation of this section, or who shall combine or conspire with another to violate the same, is guilty of a misdemeanor, and on conviction thereof in any court of the United States such person shall be fined in a sum not less than $100 and not exceeding $5,000, and shall be further punished by imprisonment, in the discretion of the court, for a term not less than three months nor exceeding twelve months.

HISTORY: (Aug. 27, 1894, c. 349, § 73, 28 Stat. 570; Feb. 12, 1913, c. 40, 37 Stat. 667.)

§ 15. Suits by persons injured (Clayton Act §15)

(a) Amount of recovery; prejudgment interest

Except as provided in subsection (b) of this section, any person who shall be injured in his business or property by reason of anything forbidden in the antitrust laws may sue therefor in any district court of the United States in the district in which the defendant resides or is found or has an agent, without respect to the amount in controversy, and shall recover threefold the damages by him sustained, and the cost of suit, including a reasonable attorney's fee. The court may award under this section, pursuant to a motion by such person promptly made, simple interest on actual damages for the period beginning on the date of service of such person's pleading setting forth a claim under the antitrust laws and ending on the date of judgment, or for any shorter period therein, if the court finds that the award of such interest for such period is just in the circumstances. In determining whether an award of interest under this section for any period is just in the circumstances, the court shall consider only—

(1) whether such person or the opposing party, or either party's representative, made motions or asserted claims or defenses so lacking in merit as to show that such party or representative acted intentionally for delay, or otherwise acted in bad faith;

(2) whether, in the course of the action involved, such person or the opposing party, or either party's representative, violated any applicable rule, statute, or court order providing for sanctions for dilatory behavior or otherwise providing for expeditious proceedings; and

(3) whether such person or the opposing party, or either party's representative, engaged in conduct primarily for the purpose of delaying the litigation or increasing the cost thereof.

(b) Amount of damages payable to foreign states and instrumentalities of foreign states

(1) Except as provided in paragraph (2), any person who is a foreign state may not recover under subsection (a) of this section an amount in excess of the actual damages sustained by it and the cost of suit, including a reasonable attorney's fee.

(2) Paragraph (1) shall not apply to a foreign state if—

(A) such foreign state would be denied, under section 1605(a) (2) of Title 28, immunity in a case in which the action is based upon a commercial activity, or an act, that is the subject matter of its claim under this section;

(B) such foreign state waives all defenses based upon or arising out of its status as a foreign state, to any claims brought against it in the same action;

(C) such foreign state engages primarily in commercial activities; and

(D) such foreign state does not function, with respect to the commercial activity, or the act, that is the subject matter of its claim under this section as a procurement entity for itself or for another foreign state.

(c) Definitions

For purposes of this section—

(1) the term "commercial activity" shall have the meaning given it in section 1603(d) of Title 28, and

(2) the term "foreign state" shall have the meaning given it in section 1603(a) of Title 28.

HISTORY: (Oct. 15, 1914, c. 323, § 4, 38 Stat. 731; Sept. 12, 1980, Pub. L. 96-349, § 4(a)(1), 94 Stat. 1156; Dec. 29, 1982, Pub. L. 97-393, 96 Stat. 1964.)

§ 18. Acquisition by one corporation of stock of another (Clayton Act § 7)

No person engaged in commerce or in any activity affecting commerce shall acquire, directly or indirectly, the whole or any part of the stock or other share capital and no person subject to the jurisdiction of the Federal Trade Commission shall acquire the whole or any part of the assets of another person engaged also in commerce or in any activity affecting commerce, where in any line of commerce or in any activity affecting commerce in any section of the country, the effect of such acquisition may be substantially to lessen competition, or to tend to create a monopoly.

No person shall acquire, directly or indirectly, the whole or any part of the stock or other share capital and no person subject to the jurisdiction of the Federal Trade Commission shall acquire the whole or any part of the assets of one or more persons engaged in commerce or in any activity affecting commerce, where in any line of commerce or in any activity affecting commerce in any section of the country, the effect of such acquisition, of such stocks or assets, or of the use of such stock by the voting or granting of proxies or otherwise, may be substantially to lessen competition, or to tend to create a monopoly.

This section shall not apply to persons purchasing such stock solely for investment and not using the same by voting or otherwise to bring about, or in attempting to bring about, the substantial lessening of competition. Nor shall anything contained in this section prevent a corporation engaged in commerce or in any activity affecting commerce from causing the formation of subsidiary corporations for the actual carrying on of their immediate lawful business, or the natural and legitimate branches or extensions thereof, or from owning and holding all or a part of the stock of such subsidiary corporations, when the effect of such formation is not to substantially lessen competition.

. . . .

HISTORY: (Oct. 15, 1914, c. 323, § 7, 38 Stat. 731; Dec. 29, 1950, c. 1184, 64 Stat. 1125; Sept. 12, 1980, Pub. L. 96-349, § 6(a), 94 Stat. 1157; Oct. 4, 1984, Pub. L. 98-443, § 9(l), 98 Stat. 1708;

Dec. 29, 1995, Pub. L. 104-88, Title III, § 318(1), 109 Stat. 949; Feb. 8, 1996, Pub. L. 104-104, Title VI, § 601(b)(3), 110 Stat. 143.)

§ 26. Injunctive relief for private parties; exception; costs (Clayton Act § 16)

Any person, firm, corporation, or association shall be entitled to sue for and have injunctive relief, in any court of the United States having jurisdiction over the parties, against threatened loss or damage by a violation of the antitrust laws, including sections 13, 14, 18, and 19 of this title, when and under the same conditions and principles as injunctive relief against threatened conduct that will cause loss or damage is granted by courts of equity, under the rules governing such proceedings, and upon the execution of proper bond against damages for an injunction improvidently granted and a showing that the danger of irreparable loss or damage is immediate, a preliminary injunction may issue: Provided, That nothing herein contained shall be construed to entitle any person, firm, corporation, or association, except the United States, to bring suit for injunctive relief against any common carrier subject to the jurisdiction of the Surface Transportation Board under subtitle IV of Title 49. In any action under this section in which the plaintiff substantially prevails, the court shall award the cost of suit, including a reasonable attorney's fee, to such plaintiff.

HISTORY: (Oct. 15, 1914, c. 323, § 16, 38 Stat. 737; Sept. 30, 1976, Pub. L. 94-435, Title III, § 302(3), 90 Stat. 1396; Dec. 29, 1995, Pub. L. 104-88, Title III, § 318(3), 109 Stat. 949.)

§ 45. Unfair methods of competition unlawful; prevention by Commission (Federal Trade Commission Act § 5)

(a) Declaration of unlawfulness; power to prohibit unfair practices; inapplicability to foreign trade

(1) Unfair methods of competition in or affecting commerce, and unfair or deceptive acts or practices in or affecting commerce, are declared unlawful.

(2) The Commission is empowered and directed to prevent persons, partnerships, or corporations, except banks, savings and loan institutions described in section 57a(f)(3) of this title, Federal credit unions described in section 57a(f)(4) of this title, common carriers subject to the Acts to regulate commerce, air carriers and foreign air carriers subject to the Federal Aviation Act of 1958, and persons, partnerships, or corporations insofar as they are subject to the Packers and Stockyards Act, 1921, as amended [7 U.S.C.A. § 181 et seq.], except as provided in section 406(b) of said Act [7 U.S.C.A. § 227(a)], from using unfair methods of competition in or affecting commerce and unfair or deceptive acts or practices in or affecting commerce.

(3) This subsection shall not apply to unfair methods of competition involving commerce with foreign nations (other than import commerce) unless—

(A) such methods of competition have a direct, substantial, and reasonably foreseeable effect—

(i) on commerce which is not commerce with foreign nations, or on import commerce with foreign nations; or

(ii) on export commerce with foreign nations, of a person engaged in such commerce in the United States; and

(B) such effect gives rise to a claim under the provisions of this subsection, other than this paragraph.

If this subsection applies to such methods of competition only because of the operation of subparagraph (A) (ii), this subsection shall apply to such conduct only for injury to export business in the United States.

. . . .

HISTORY: (Sept. 26, 1914, c. 311, § 5, 38 Stat. 719; Mar. 21, 1938, c. 49, § 3, 52 Stat. 111; June 23, 1938, c. 601, Title XI, § 1107(f), 52 Stat. 1028; June 25, 1948, c. 646, § 32(a), 62 Stat. 991; May 24, 1949, c. 139, § 127, 63 Stat. 107; Mar. 16, 1950, c. 61, § 4(c), 64 Stat. 21; July 14, 1952, c. 745, § 2, 66 Stat. 632; Aug. 23, 1958, Pub. L. 85-726, Title XIV, §§ 1401(b), 1411, 72 Stat. 806, 809; Aug. 28, 1958, Pub. L. 85-791, § 3, 72 Stat. 942; Sept. 2, 1958, Pub. L. 85-909, § 3, 72 Stat. 1750; June 11, 1960, Pub. L. 86-507, § 1(13), 74 Stat. 200; Nov. 16, 1973, Pub. L. 93-153, Title IV, § 408(c), (d), 87 Stat. 591, 592; Jan. 4, 1975, Pub. L. 93-637, Title II, §§ 201(a), 204(b), 205(a), 88 Stat. 2193, 2200; Dec. 12, 1975, Pub. L. 94-145, § 3, 89 Stat. 801; July 23, 1979, Pub. L. 96-37, § 1(a), 93 Stat. 95; May 28, 1980, Pub. L. 96-252, § 2, 94 Stat. 374; Oct. 8, 1982, Pub. L. 97-290, Title IV, § 403, 96 Stat. 1246; Nov. 8, 1984, Pub. L. 98-620, Title IV, §655; Aug. 26, 1994, Pub. L. 103-312, §§ 4, 6, 9, 108 Stat. 1691, 1692, 1695.)

§ 62. Export trade and antitrust legislation (Webb-Pomerene Act § 2)

Nothing contained in sections 1 to 7 of this title shall be construed as declaring to be illegal an association entered into for the sole purpose of engaging in export trade and actually engaged solely in such export trade, or an agreement made or act done in the course of export trade by such association, provided such association, agreement, or act is not in restraint of trade within the United States, and is not in restraint of the export trade of any domestic competitor of such association: Provided, That such association does not, either in the United States or elsewhere, enter into any agreement, understanding, or conspiracy, or do any act which artificially or intentionally enhances or depresses prices within the United States of commodities of the class exported by such association, or which substantially lessens competition within the United States or otherwise restrains trade therein.

HISTORY: (Apr. 10, 1918, c. 50, § 2, 40 Stat. 517.)

CODE OF FEDERAL REGULATIONS
TITLE 28—JUDICIAL ADMINISTRATION
CHAPTER I—DEPARTMENT OF JUSTICE
PART 50—STATEMENTS OF POLICY

§ 50.6 Antitrust Division business review procedure.

Although the Department of Justice is not authorized to give advisory opinions to private parties, for several decades the Antitrust Division has been willing in certain circumstances to review proposed business conduct and state its enforcement intentions. This originated with a "railroad release" procedure under which the Division would forego the initiation of criminal antitrust proceedings. The procedure was subsequently expanded to encompass a "merger clearance" procedure under which the Division would state its present enforcement intention with respect to a merger or acquisition; and the Department issued a written statement entitled "Business Review Procedure." That statement has been revised several times.

1. A request for a business review letter must be submitted in writing to the Assistant Attorney General, Antitrust Division, Department of Justice, Washington, D.C. 20530.

2. The Division will consider only requests with respect to proposed business conduct, which may involve either domestic or foreign commerce.

3. The Division may, in its discretion, refuse to consider a request.

4. A business review letter shall have no application to any party which does not join in the request therefor.

5. The requesting parties are under an affirmative obligation to make full and true disclosure with respect to the business conduct for which review is requested. Each request must be accompanied by all relevant data including background information, complete copies of all operative documents and detailed statements of all collateral oral understandings, if any. All parties requesting the review letter must provide the Division with whatever additional information or documents the Division may thereafter request in order to review the matter. Such additional information, if furnished orally, shall be promptly confirmed in writing. In connection with any request for review the Division will also conduct whatever independent investigation it believes is appropriate.

6. No oral clearance, release or other statement purporting to bind the enforcement discretion of the Division may be given. The requesting party may rely upon only a written business review letter signed by the Assistant Attorney General in charge of the Antitrust Division or his delegate.

7. (a) If the business conduct for which review is requested is subject to approval by a regulatory agency, a review request may be considered before agency approval has been obtained only where it appears that exceptional and unnecessary burdens might otherwise be imposed on the

party or parties requesting review, or where the agency specifically requests that a party or parties request review. However, any business review letter issued in these as in any other circumstances will state only the Department's present enforcement intentions under the antitrust laws. It shall in no way be taken to indicate the Department's views on the legal or factual issues that may be raised before the regulatory agency, or in an appeal from the regulatory agency's decision. In particular, the issuance of such a letter is not to be represented to mean that the Division believes that there are no anticompetitive consequences warranting agency consideration.

(b) The submission of a request for a business review, or its pendency, shall in no way alter any responsibility of any party to comply with the Premerger Notification provisions of the Antitrust Improvements Act of 1976, 15 U.S.C. 18A, and the regulations promulgated thereunder, 16 CFR, Part 801.

8. After review of a request submitted hereunder the Division may: state its present enforcement intention with respect to the proposed business conduct; decline to pass on the request; or take such other position or action as it considers appropriate.

9. A business review letter states only the enforcement intention of the Division as of the date of the letter, and the Division remains completely free to bring whatever action or proceeding it subsequently comes to believe is required by the public interest. As to a stated present intention not to bring an action, however, the Division has never exercised its right to bring a criminal action where there has been full and true disclosure at the time of presenting the request.

10. (a) Simultaneously upon notifying the requesting party of and Division action described in paragraph 8, the business review request, and the Division's letter in response shall be indexed and placed in a file available to the public upon request.

(b) On that date or within thirty days after the date upon which the Division takes any action as described in paragraph 8, the information supplied to support the business review request and any other information supplied by the requesting party in connection with the transaction that is the subject of the business review request, shall be indexed and placed in a file with the request and the Division's letter, available to the public upon request. This file shall remain open for one year, after which time it shall be closed and the documents either returned to the requesting party or otherwise disposed of, at the discretion of the Antitrust Division.

(c) Prior to the time the information described in subparagraphs (a) and (b) is indexed and made publicly available in accordance with the terms of that subparagraph, the requesting party may ask the Division to delay making public some or all of such information. However the requesting party must: (1) Specify precisely the documents or parts thereof that he asks not be made public; (2) state the minimum period of time during which nondisclosure is considered necessary; and (3) justify the request for non-disclosure, both as to content and time, by showing good cause therefor, including a showing that disclosure would have a detrimental effect upon the requesting party's operations or relationships with actual or potential customers, employees, suppliers (including suppliers of credit), stockholders, or competitors. The Department of Justice, in its discretion, shall make the final determination as to whether good cause for non-disclosure has been shown.

(d) Nothing contained in subparagraphs (a), (b) and (c) shall limit the Division's right, in its discretion, to issue a press release describing generally the identity of the requesting party or parties and the nature of action taken by the Division upon the request.

(e) This paragraph reflects a policy determination by the Justice Department and is subject to any limitations on public disclosure arising from statutory restrictions, Executive Order, or the national interest.

11. Any requesting party may withdraw a request for review at any time. The Division remains free, however, to submit such comments to such requesting party as it deems appropriate. Failure to take action after receipt of documents or information whether submitted pursuant to this procedure or otherwise, does not in any way limit or stop the Division from taking such action at such time thereafter as it deems appropriate. The Division reserves the right to retain documents submitted to it under this procedure or otherwise and to use them for all governmental purposes.

[42 FR 11831, Mar. 1, 1977]

CODE OF FEDERAL REGULATIONS
TITLE 16—COMMERCIAL PRACTICES
CHAPTER I—FEDERAL TRADE COMMISSION
SUBCHAPTER A—ORGANIZATION, PROCEDURES AND RULES OF PRACTICE
PART 1—GENERAL PROCEDURES
SUBPART A—INDUSTRY GUIDANCE
ADVISORY OPINIONS

§ 1.1 Policy.

(a) Any person, partnership, or corporation may request advice from the Commission with respect to a course of action which the requesting party proposes to pursue. The Commission will consider such requests for advice and inform the requesting party of the Commission's views, where practicable, under the following circumstances.

(1) The matter involves a substantial or novel question of fact or law and there is no clear Commission or court precedent; or

(2) The subject matter of the request and consequent publication of Commission advice is of significant public interest.

(b) The Commission has authorized its staff to consider all requests for advice and to render advice, where practicable, in those circumstances in which a Commission opinion would not be warranted. Hypothetical questions will not be answered, and a request for advice will ordinarily be considered inappropriate where: (1) The same or substantially the same course of action is under investigation or is or has been the subject of a current proceeding involving the Commission or another governmental agency, or (2) an informed opinion cannot be made or could be made only after extensive investigation, clinical study, testing, or collateral inquiry.

[44 FR 21624, Apr. 11, 1979; 44 FR 23515, Apr. 20, 1979; 54 FR 14072, April 7, 1989]

§ 1.2 Procedure.

(a) Application. The request for advice or interpretation should be submitted in writing (one original and two copies) to the Secretary of the Commission and should: (1) State clearly the question(s) that the applicant wishes resolved; (2) cite the provision of law under which the question arises; and (3) state all facts which the applicant believes to be material. In addition, the identity of the companies and other persons involved should be disclosed. Letters relating to unnamed companies or persons may not be answered. Submittal of additional facts may be requested prior to the rendering of any advice.

(b) Compliance matters. If the request is for advice as to whether the proposed course of action may violate an outstanding order to cease and desist issued by the Commission, such request will be considered as provided for in § 2.41 of this chapter.

[44 FR 21624, Apr. 11, 1979, as amended at 44 FR 40638, July 12, 1979]

§ 1.3 Advice.

(a) On the basis of the materials submitted, as well as any other information available, and if practicable, the Commission or its staff will inform the requesting party of its views.

(b) Any advice given by the Commission is without prejudice to the right of the Commission to reconsider the questions involved and, where the public interest requires, to rescind or revoke the action. Notice of such rescission or revocation will be given to the requesting party so that he may discontinue the course of action taken pursuant to the Commission's advice. The Commission will not proceed against the requesting party with respect to any action taken in good faith reliance upon the Commission's advice under this section, where all the relevant facts were fully, completely, and accurately presented to the Commission and where such action was promptly discontinued upon notification of rescission or revocation of the Commission's approval.

(c) Advice rendered by the staff is without prejudice to the right of the Commission later to rescind the advice and, where appropriate, to commence an enforcement proceeding.

[44 FR 21624, Apr. 11, 1979]

§ 1.4 Public disclosure.

Written advice rendered pursuant to this Section and requests therefor, including names and details, will be placed in the Commission's public record immediately after the requesting party has received the advice, subject to any limitations on public disclosure arising from statutory restrictions, the Commission's rules, and the public interest. A request for confidential treatment of information submitted in connection with the questions should be made separately.

[44 FR 21624, Apr. 11, 1979]

H. The Export Trading Company Act of 1982

Source: 15 U.S.C. § 4001 *et seq.*

§ 4001. Congressional findings and declaration of purpose

(a) The Congress finds that—

(1) United States exports are responsible for creating and maintaining one out of every nine manufacturing jobs in the United States and for generating one out of every seven dollars of total United States goods produced;

(2) the rapidly growing service-related industries are vital to the well-being of the United States economy inasmuch as they create jobs for seven out of every ten Americans, provide 65 per centum of the Nation's gross national product, and offer the greatest potential for significantly increased industrial trade involving finished products;

(3) trade deficits contribute to the decline of the dollar on international currency markets and have an inflationary impact on the United States economy;

(4) tens of thousands of small- and medium-sized United States businesses produce exportable goods or services but do not engage in exporting;

(5) although the United States is the world's leading agricultural exporting nation, many farm products are not marketed as widely and effectively abroad as they could be through export trading companies;

(6) export trade services in the United States are fragmented into a multitude of separate functions, and companies attempting to offer export trade services lack financial leverage to reach a significant number of potential United States exporters;

(7) the United States needs well-developed export trade intermediaries which can achieve economies of scale and acquire expertise enabling them to export goods and services profitably, at low per unit cost to producers;

(8) the development of export trading companies in the United States has been hampered by business attitudes and by Government regulations;

(9) those activities of State and local governmental authorities which initiate, facilitate, or expand exports of goods and services can be an important source for expansion of total United States exports, as well as for experimentation in the development of innovative export programs keyed to local, State, and regional economic needs;

314

(10) if United States trading companies are to be successful in promoting United States exports and in competing with foreign trading companies, they should be able to draw on the resources, expertise, and knowledge of the United States banking system, both in the United States and abroad; and

(11) the Department of Commerce is responsible for the development and promotion of United States exports, and especially for facilitating the export of finished products by United States manufacturers.

(b) It is the purpose of this chapter to increase United States exports of products and services by encouraging more efficient provision of export trade services to United States producers and suppliers, in particular by establishing an office within the Department of Commerce to promote the formation of export trade associations and export trading companies, by permitting bank holding companies, bankers' banks, and Edge Act corporations and agreement corporations that are subsidiaries of bank holding companies to invest in export trading companies, by reducing restrictions on trade financing provided by financial institutions, and by modifying the application of the antitrust laws to certain export trade.

HISTORY: (Pub. L. 97-290, Title I, § 102, Oct. 8, 1982, 96 Stat. 1233.)

§ 4002. Definitions

(a) For purposes of this subchapter—

(1) the term "export trade" means trade or commerce in goods or services produced in the United States which are exported, or in the course of being exported, from the United States to any other country;

(2) the term "services" includes, but is not limited to, accounting, amusement, architectural, automatic data processing, business, communications, construction franchising and licensing, consulting, engineering, financial, insurance, legal, management, repair, tourism, training, and transportation services;

(3) the term "export trade services" includes, but is not limited to, consulting, international market research, advertising, marketing, insurance, product research and design, legal assistance, transportation, including trade documentation and freight forwarding, communication and processing of foreign orders to and for exporters and foreign purchasers, warehousing, foreign exchange, financing, and taking title to goods, when provided in order to facilitate the export of goods or services produced in the United States;

(4) the term "export trading company" means a person, partnership, association, or similar organization, whether operated for profit or as a nonprofit organization, which does business under

315

the laws of the United States or any State and which is organized and operated principally for purposes of—

(A) exporting goods or services produced in the United States; or

(B) facilitating the exportation of goods or services produced in the United States by unaffiliated persons by providing one or more export trade services;

(5) the term "State" means any of the several States of the United States, the District of Columbia, the Commonwealth of Puerto Rico, the Virgin Islands, American Samoa, Guam, the Commonwealth of the Northern Mariana Islands, and the Trust Territory of the Pacific Islands;

(6) the term "United States" means the several States of the United States, the District of Columbia, the Commonwealth of Puerto Rico, the Virgin Islands, American Samoa, Guam, the Commonwealth of the Northern Mariana Islands, and the Trust Territory of the Pacific Islands; and

(7) the term "antitrust laws" means the antitrust laws as defined in section 12(a) of this title, section 45 of this title to the extent that section 45 of this title applies to unfair methods of competition, and any State antitrust or unfair competition law.

(b) The Secretary of Commerce may by regulation further define any term defined in subsection (a) of this section, in order to carry out this subchapter.

HISTORY: (Pub. L. 97-290, Title I, § 103, Oct. 8, 1982, 96 Stat. 1234.)

§ 4003. Office of Export Trade in Department of Commerce

The Secretary of Commerce shall establish within the Department of Commerce an office to promote and encourage to the greatest extent feasible the formation of export trade associations and export trading companies. Such office shall provide information and advice to interested persons and shall provide a referral service to facilitate contact between producers of exportable goods and services and firms offering export trade services. The office shall establish a program to encourage and assist the operation of other export intermediaries, including existing and newly formed export management companies.

HISTORY: (Pub. L. 97-290, Title I, § 104, Oct. 8, 1982, 96 Stat. 1235; Pub. L. 100-418, Title II, § 2310, Aug. 23, 1988, 102 Stat. 1346.)

§ 4011. Export trade promotion; duties of Secretary of Commerce

To promote and encourage export trade, the Secretary may issue certificates of review and advise and assist any person with respect to applying for certificates of review.

HISTORY: (Pub. L. 97-290, Title III, § 301, Oct. 8, 1982, 96 Stat. 1240.)

§ 4012. Application for issuance of certificate of review

(a) Written form; limitation to export trade; compliance with regulations

To apply for a certificate of review, a person shall submit to the Secretary a written application which—

(1) specifies conduct limited to export trade, and

(2) is in a form and contains any information, including information pertaining to the overall market in which the applicant operates, required by rule or regulation promulgated under section 4020 of this title.

(b) Publication of notice of application; transmittal to Attorney General

(1) Within ten days after an application submitted under subsection (a) of this section is received by the Secretary, the Secretary shall publish in the Federal Register a notice that announces that an application for a certificate of review has been submitted, identifies each person submitting the application, and describes the conduct for which the application is submitted.

(2) Not later than seven days after an application submitted under subsection (a) of this section is received by the Secretary, the Secretary shall transmit to the Attorney General—

(A) a copy of the application,

(B) any information submitted to the Secretary in connection with the application, and

(C) any other relevant information (as determined by the Secretary) in the possession of the Secretary, including information regarding the market share of the applicant in the line of commerce to which the conduct specified in the application relates.

HISTORY: (Pub. L. 97-290, Title III, § 302, Oct. 8, 1982, 96 Stat. 1240.)

§ 4013. Issuance of certificate

(a) Requirements

A certificate of review shall be issued to any applicant that establishes that its specified export trade, export trade activities, and methods of operation will—

(1) result in neither a substantial lessening of competition or restraint of trade within the United States nor a substantial restraint of the export trade of any competitor of the applicant,

(2) not unreasonably enhance, stabilize, or depress prices within the United States of the goods, wares, merchandise, or services of the class exported by the applicant,

(3) not constitute unfair methods of competition against competitors engaged in the export of goods, wares, merchandise, or services of the class exported by the applicant, and

(4) not include any act that may reasonably be expected to result in the sale for consumption or resale within the United States of the goods, wares, merchandise, or services exported by the applicant.

(b) Time for determination; specification in certificate

Within ninety days after the Secretary receives an application for a certificate of review, the Secretary shall determine whether the applicant's export trade, export trade activities, and methods of operation meet the standards of subsection (a) of this section. If the Secretary, with the concurrence of the Attorney General, determines that such standards are met, the Secretary shall issue to the applicant a certificate of review. The certificate of review shall specify—

(1) the export trade, export trade activities, and methods of operation to which the certificate applies,

(2) the person to whom the certificate of review is issued, and

(3) any terms and conditions the Secretary or the Attorney General deems necessary to assure compliance with the standards of subsection (a) of this section.

(c) Expedited action

If the applicant indicates a special need for prompt disposition, the Secretary and the Attorney General may expedite action on the application, except that no certificate of review may be issued within thirty days of publication of notice in the Federal Register under section 4012(b)(1) of this title.

(d) Notification of denial; request for reconsideration

(1) If the Secretary denies in whole or in part an application for a certificate, he shall notify the applicant of his determination and the reasons for it.

(2) An applicant may, within thirty days of receipt of notification that the application has been denied in whole or in part, request the Secretary to reconsider the determination. The Secretary, with the concurrence of the Attorney General, shall notify the applicant of the determination upon reconsideration within thirty days of receipt of the request.

(e) Return of documents upon request after denial

If the Secretary denies an application for the issuance of a certificate of review and thereafter receives from the applicant a request for the return of documents submitted by the applicant in connection with the application for the certificate, the Secretary and the Attorney General shall return to the applicant, not later than thirty days after receipt of the request, the documents and all copies of the documents available to the Secretary and the Attorney General, except to the extent that the information contained in a document has been made available to the public.

(f) Fraudulent procurement of certificate

A certificate shall be void ab initio with respect to any export trade, export trade activities, or methods of operation for which a certificate was procured by fraud.

HISTORY: (Pub. L. 97-290, Title III, § 303, Oct. 8, 1982, 96 Stat. 1241.)

§ 4014. Reporting requirement; amendment of certificate; revocation

(a) Report of changes in matters specified; application to amend; treatment as application for issuance

(1) Any applicant who receives a certificate of review—

(A) shall promptly report to the Secretary any change relevant to the matters specified in the certificate, and

(B) may submit to the Secretary an application to amend the certificate to reflect the effect of the change on the conduct specified in the certificate.

(2) An application for an amendment to a certificate of review shall be treated as an application for the issuance of a certificate. The effective date of an amendment shall be the date on which the application for the amendment is submitted to the Secretary.

319

(b) Request for compliance information; failure to provide; notice of noncompliance; revocation or modification; antitrust investigation; no civil investigative demand

(1) If the Secretary or the Attorney General has reason to believe that the export trade, export trade activities, or methods of operation of a person holding a certificate of review no longer comply with the standards of section 4013(a) of this title, the Secretary shall request such information from such person as the Secretary or the Attorney General deems necessary to resolve the matter of compliance. Failure to comply with such request shall be grounds for revocation of the certificate under paragraph (2).

(2) If the Secretary or the Attorney General determines that the export trade, export trade activities, or methods of operation of a person holding a certificate no longer comply with the standards of section 4013(a) of this title, or that such person has failed to comply with a request made under paragraph (1), the Secretary shall give written notice of the determination to such person. The notice shall include a statement of the circumstances underlying, and the reasons in support of, the determination. In the 60-day period beginning 30 days after the notice is given, the Secretary shall revoke the certificate or modify it as the Secretary or the Attorney General deems necessary to cause the certificate to apply only to the export trade, export trade activities, or methods of operation which are in compliance with the standards of section 4013(a) of this title.

(3) For purposes of carrying out this subsection, the Attorney General, and the Assistant Attorney General in charge of the antitrust division of the Department of Justice, may conduct investigations in the same manner as the Attorney General and the Assistant Attorney General conduct investigations under section 1312 of this title, except that no civil investigative demand may be issued to a person to whom a certificate of review is issued if such person is the target of such investigation.

HISTORY: (Pub. L. 97-290, Title III, § 304, Oct. 8, 1982, 96 Stat. 1242.)

§ 4015. Judicial review; admissibility

(a) District court review of grants or denials; erroneous determination

If the Secretary grants or denies, in whole or in part, an application for a certificate of review or for an amendment to a certificate, or revokes or modifies a certificate pursuant to section 4014(b) of this title, any person aggrieved by such determination may, within 30 days of the determination, bring an action in any appropriate district court of the United States to set aside the determination on the ground that such determination is erroneous.

(b) Exclusive provision for review

Except as provided in subsection (a) of this section, no action by the Secretary or the Attorney General pursuant to this subchapter shall be subject to judicial review.

(c) Inadmissibility in antitrust proceedings

If the Secretary denies, in whole or in part, an application for a certificate of review or for an amendment to a certificate, or revokes or amends a certificate, neither the negative determination nor the statement of reasons therefor shall be admissible in evidence, in any administrative or judicial proceeding, in support of any claim under the antitrust laws.

HISTORY: (Pub. L. 97-290, Title III, § 305, Oct. 8, 1982, 96 Stat. 1243.)

§ 4016. Protection conferred by certificate of review

(a) Protection from civil or criminal antitrust actions

Except as provide in subsection (b) of this section, no criminal or civil action may be brought under the antitrust laws against a person to whom a certificate of review is issued which is based on conduct which is specified in, and complies with the terms of, a certificate issued under section 4013 of this title which certificate was in effect when the conduct occurred.

(b) Special restraint of trade civil actions; time limitations; certificate governed conduct presumed in compliance; award of costs to successful defendant; suit by Attorney General

(1) Any person who has been injured as a result of conduct engaged in under a certificate of review may bring a civil action for injunctive relief, actual damages, the loss of interest on actual damages, and the cost of suit (including a reasonable attorney's fee) for the failure to comply with the standards of section 4013(a) of this title. Any action commenced under this subchapter shall proceed as if it were an action commenced under section 15 or section 26 of this title, except that the standards of section 4013(a) of this title and the remedies provided in this paragraph shall be the exclusive standards and remedies applicable to such action.

(2) Any action brought under paragraph (1) shall be filed within two years of the date the plaintiff has notice of the failure to comply with the standards of section 4013(a) of this title but in any event within four years after the cause of action accrues.

(3) In any action brought under paragraph (1), there shall be a presumption that conduct which is specified in and complies with a certificate of review does comply with the standards of section 4013(a) of this title.

(4) In any action brought under paragraph (1), if the court finds that the conduct does comply with the standards of section 4013(a) of this title, the court shall award to the person against whom the claim is brought the cost of suit attributable to defending against the claim (including a reasonable attorney's fee).

(5) The Attorney General may file suit pursuant to section 25 of this title to enjoin conduct threatening clear and irreparable harm to the national interest.

HISTORY: (Pub. L. 97-290, Title III, § 306, Oct. 8, 1982, 96 Stat. 1243.)

§ 4017. Guidelines

(a) Issuance; content

To promote greater certainty regarding the application of the antitrust laws to export trade, the Secretary, with the concurrence of the Attorney General, may issue guidelines—

(1) describing specific types of conduct with respect to which the Secretary, with the concurrence of the Attorney General, has made or would make, determinations under sections 4013 and 4014 of this title, and

(2) summarizing the factual and legal bases in support of the determinations.

(b) Administrative rulemaking requirements not applicable

Section 553 of Title 5 shall not apply to the issuance of guidelines under subsection (a) of this section.

HISTORY: (Pub. L. 97-290, Title III, § 307, Oct. 8, 1982, 96 Stat. 1244.)

§ 4018. Annual reports

Every person to whom a certificate of review is issued shall submit to the Secretary an annual report, in such form and at such time as the Secretary may require, that updates where necessary the information required by section 4012(a) of this title.

HISTORY: (Pub. L. 97-290, Title III, § 308, Oct. 8, 1982, 96 Stat. 1244.)

§ 4019. Disclosure of information

(a) Exemption

Information submitted by any person in connection with the issuance, amendment, or revocation of a certificate of review shall be exempt from disclosure under section 552 of Title 5.

(b) Protection of potentially harmful confidential information; exceptions: Congress; judicial or administrative proceedings; consent; necessity for determination; Federal law; regulations

(1) Except as provided in paragraph (2), no officer or employee of the United States shall disclose commercial or financial information submitted in connection with the issuance, amendment, or revocation of a certificate of review if the information is privileged or confidential and if disclosure of the information would cause harm to the person who submitted the information.

(2) Paragraph (1) shall not apply with respect to information disclosed—

(A) upon a request made by the Congress or any committee of the Congress,

(B) in a judicial or administrative proceeding, subject to appropriate protective orders,

(C) with the consent of the person who submitted the information,

(D) in the course of making a determination with respect to the issuance, amendment, or revocation of a certificate of review, if the Secretary deems disclosure of the information to be necessary in connection with making the determination,

(E) in accordance with any requirement imposed by a statute of the United States, or

(F) in accordance with any rule or regulation promulgated under section 4020 of this title permitting the disclosure of the information to an agency of the United States or of a State on the condition that the agency will disclose the information only under the circumstances specified in subparagraphs (A) through (E).

HISTORY: (Pub. L. 97-290, Title III, § 309, Oct. 8, 1982, 96 Stat. 1244.)

§ 4020. Rules and regulations

The Secretary, with the concurrence of the Attorney General, shall promulgate such rules and regulations as are necessary to carry out the purposes of this chapter.

HISTORY: (Pub. L. 97-290, Title III, § 310, Oct. 8, 1982, 96 Stat. 1245.)

§ 4021. Definitions

As used in this subchapter—

(1) the term "export trade" means trade or commerce in goods, wares, merchandise, or services exported, or in the course of being exported, from the United States or any territory thereof to any foreign nation,

(2) the term "service" means intangible economic output, including, but not limited to—

(A) business, repair, and amusement services,

(B) management, legal, engineering, architectural, and other professional services, and

(C) financial, insurance, transportation, informational and any other data-based services, and communication services,

(3) the term "export trade activities" means activities or agreements in the course of export trade,

(4) the term "methods of operation" means any method by which a person conducts or proposes to conduct export trade,

(5) the term "person" means an individual who is a resident of the United States; a partnership that is created under and exists pursuant to the laws of any State or of the United States; a State or local government entity; a corporation, whether organized as a profit or nonprofit corporation, that is created under and exists pursuant to the laws of any State or of the United States; or any association or combination, by contract or other arrangement, between or among such persons,

(6) the term "antitrust laws" means the antitrust laws, as such term is defined in section 12 of this title, and section 45 of this title (to the extent that section 45 of this title prohibits unfair methods of competition), and any State antitrust or unfair competition law,

(7) the term "Secretary" means the Secretary of Commerce or his designee, and

(8) the term "Attorney General" means the Attorney General of the United States or his designee.

HISTORY: (Pub. L. 97-290, Title III, § 311, Oct. 8, 1982, 96 Stat. 1245.)

§ 4051. Requirement of prior authorization

(a) General rule

Notwithstanding any other provision of law, money appropriated to the Department of Commerce for expenses to carry out any export promotion program may be obligated or expended only if—

(1) the appropriation thereof has been previously authorized by law enacted on or after July 12, 1985; or

(2) the amount of all such obligations and expenditures does not exceed an amount previously prescribed by law enacted on or after such date.

(b) Exception for later legislation authorizing obligations or expenditures

To the extent that legislation enacted after the making of an appropriation to carry out any export promotion program authorizes the obligation or expenditure thereof, the limitation contained in subsection (a) of this section shall have no effect.

(c) Provisions must be specifically superseded

The provisions of this section shall not be superseded except by a provision of law enacted after July 12, 1985, which specifically repeals, modifies, or supersedes the provisions of this section.

(d) "Export promotion program" defined

For purposes of this subchapter, the term "export promotion program" means any activity of the Department of Commerce designed to stimulate or assist United States businesses in marketing their goods and services abroad competitively with businesses from other countries, including, but not limited to—

(1) trade development (except for the trade adjustment assistance program) and dissemination of foreign marketing opportunities and other marketing information to United States producers of goods and services, including the expansion of foreign markets for United States textiles and apparel and any other United States products;

(2) the development of regional and multilateral economic policies which enhance United States trade and investment interests, and the provision of marketing services with respect to foreign countries and regions;

(3) the exhibition of United States goods in other countries;

The Export Trading Company Act of 1982

(4) the operations of the United States and Foreign Commercial Service, or any successor agency; and

(5) the Market Development Cooperator Program established under section 4723 of this title, and assistance for trade shows provided under section 4724 of this title.

(e) Printing outside the United States

(1) Notwithstanding the provisions of section 501 of Title 44, and consistent with other applicable law, the Secretary of Commerce in carrying out any export promotion program, may authorize—

(A) the printing, distribution, and sale of documents outside the contiguous United States, if the Secretary finds that the implementation of such export promotion program would be more efficient, and if such documents will be distributed primarily and sold exclusively outside the United States; and

(B) the acceptance of private notices and advertisements in connection with the printing and distribution of such documents.

(2) Any fees received by the Secretary pursuant to paragraph (1) shall be deposited in a separate account or accounts which may be used to defray directly the costs incurred in conducting activities authorized by paragraph (1) or to repay or make advances to appropriations or other funds available for such activities.

HISTORY: (Pub. L. 99-64, Title II, § 201, July 12, 1985, 99 Stat. 157; Pub. L. 100-418, Title II, §§ 2305(a), 2308(a), Aug. 23, 1988, 102 Stat. 1344, 1346.)

§ 4052. Authorization of appropriations

There are authorized to be appropriated to the Department of Commerce to carry out export promotion programs such sums as are necessary for fiscal years 1995 and 1996.

HISTORY: (Pub. L. 99-64, Title II, § 202, July 12, 1985, 99 Stat. 158; Pub. L. 99-633, § 2, Nov. 7, 1986, 100 Stat. 3522; Pub. L. 100-418, Title II, § 2305(b)(1), Aug. 23, 1988, 102 Stat. 1344; Pub. L. 102-429, Title II, § 208, Oct. 21, 1992, 106 Stat. 2205; Pub. L. 103-392, Title III, § 301, Oct. 22, 1994, 108 Stat. 4099.)

§ 4053. Barter arrangements

(a) Report on status of Federal barter programs

The Secretary of Agriculture and the Secretary of Energy shall, not later than 90 days after July 12, 1985, submit to the Congress a report on the status of Federal programs relating to the barter or exchange of commodities owned by the Commodity Credit Corporation for materials and products produced in foreign countries. Such report shall include details of any changes necessary in existing law to allow the Department of Agriculture and, in the case of petroleum resources, the Department of Energy, to implement fully any barter program.

(b) Authorities of President

The President is authorized—

(1) to barter stocks of agricultural commodities acquired by the Government for petroleum and petroleum products, and for other materials vital to the national interest, which are produced abroad, in situations in which sales would otherwise not occur; and

(2) to purchase petroleum and petroleum products, and other materials vital to the national interest, which are produced abroad and acquired by persons in the United States through barter for agricultural commodities produced in and exported from the United States through normal commercial trade channels.

(c) Other provisions of law not affected

In the case of any petroleum, petroleum products, or other materials vital to the national interest, which are acquired under subsection (b) of this section, nothing in this section shall be construed to render inapplicable the provisions of any law then in effect which apply to the storage, distribution, or use of such petroleum, petroleum products, or other materials vital to the national interest.

(d) Conventional markets not to be displaced by barters

The President shall take steps to ensure that, in making any barter described in subsection (a) or (b)(1) of this section or any purchase authorized by subsection (b)(2) of this section, existing export markets for agricultural commodities operating on conventional business terms are safeguarded from displacement by the barter described in subsection (a), (b)(1), or (b)(2) of this section, as the case may be. In addition, the President shall ensure that any such barter is consistent with the international obligations of the United States, including the General Agreement on Tariffs and Trade.

(e) Report to the Congress

The Secretary of Energy shall report to the Congress on the effect on energy security and on domestic energy supplies of any action taken under this section which results in the acquisition by the Government of petroleum or petroleum products. Such report shall be submitted to the Congress not later than 90 days after such acquisition.

HISTORY: (Pub. L. 99-64, Title II, § 203, July 12, 1985, 99 Stat. 158.)

I. The National Cooperative Research Act of 1984

Source: 15 U.S.C. § 4301 *et seq.*

§ 4301. Definitions

(a) For purposes of this chapter:

(1) The term "antitrust laws" has the meaning given it in subsection (a) of section 12 of this title, except that such term includes section 45 of this title to the extent that such section 45 applies to unfair methods of competition.

(2) The term "Attorney General" means the Attorney General of the United States.

(3) The term "Commission" means the Federal Trade Commission.

(4) The term "person" has the meaning given it in subsection (a) of section 12 of this title.

(5) The term "State" has the meaning given it in section 15g(2) of this title.

(6) The term "joint venture" means any group of activities, including attempting to make, making, or performing a contract, by two or more persons for the purpose of—

(A) theoretical analysis, experimentation, or systematic study of phenomena or observable facts,

(B) the development or testing of basic engineering techniques,

(C) the extension of investigative findings or theory of a scientific or technical nature into practical application for experimental and demonstration purposes, including the experimental production and testing of models, prototypes, equipment, materials, and processes,

(D) the production of a product, process, or service,

(E) the testing in connection with the production of a product, process, or service by such venture,

(F) the collection, exchange, and analysis of research or production information, or

(G) any combination of the purposes specified in subparagraphs (A), (B), (C), (D), (E), and (F),

and may include the establishment and operation of facilities for the conducting of such venture, the conducting of such venture on a protected and proprietary basis, and the prosecuting of applications

329

for patents and the granting of licenses for the results of such venture, but does not include any activity specified in subsection (b) of this section.

(b) The term "joint venture" excludes the following activities involving two or more persons:

(1) exchanging information among competitors relating to costs, sales, profitability, prices, marketing, or distribution of any product, process, or service if such information is not reasonably required to carry out the purpose of such venture,

(2) entering into any agreement or engaging in any other conduct restricting, requiring, or otherwise involving the marketing, distribution, or provision by any person who is a party to such venture of any product, process, or service, other than—

(A) the distribution among the parties to such venture, in accordance with such venture, of a product, process, or service produced by such venture,

(B) the marketing of proprietary information, such as patents and trade secrets, developed through such venture formed under a written agreement entered into before June 10, 1993, or

(C) the licensing, conveying, or transferring of intellectual property, such as patents and trade secrets, developed through such venture formed under a written agreement entered into on or after June 10, 1993,

(3) entering into any agreement or engaging in any other conduct—

(A) to restrict or require the sale, licensing, or sharing of inventions, developments, products, processes, or services not developed through, or produced by, such venture, or

(B) to restrict or require participation by any person who is a party to such venture in other research and development activities,

that is not reasonably required to prevent misappropriation of proprietary information contributed by any person who is a party to such venture or of the results of such venture,

(4) entering into any agreement or engaging in any other conduct allocating a market with a competitor,

(5) exchanging information among competitors relating to production (other than production by such venture) of a product, process, or service if such information is not reasonably required to carry out the purpose of such venture,

330

(6) entering into any agreement or engaging in any other conduct restricting, requiring, or otherwise involving the production (other than the production by such venture) of a product, process, or service,

(7) using existing facilities for the production of a product, process, or service by such venture unless such use involves the production of a new product or technology, and

(8) except as provided in paragraphs (2), (3), and (6), entering into any agreement or engaging in any other conduct to restrict or require participation by any person who is a party to such venture, in any unilateral or joint activity that is not reasonably required to carry out the purpose of such venture.

HISTORY: (Pub. L. 98-462, § 2, Oct. 11, 1984, 98 Stat. 1815; Pub. L. 103-42, § 3(b), (c), June 10, 1993, 107 Stat. 117, 118.)

§ 4302. Rule of reason standard

In any action under the antitrust laws, or under any State law similar to the antitrust laws, the conduct of any person in making or performing a contract to carry out a joint venture shall not be deemed illegal per se; such conduct shall be judged on the basis of its reasonableness, taking into account all relevant factors affecting competition, including, but not limited to, effects on competition in properly defined, relevant research, development, product, process, and service markets. For the purpose of determining a properly defined, relevant market, worldwide capacity shall be considered to the extent that it may be appropriate in the circumstances.

HISTORY: (Pub. L. 98-462, § 3, Oct. 11, 1984, 98 Stat. 1816; Pub. L. 103-42, § 3(d), June 10, 1993, 107 Stat. 119.)

§ 4303. Limitation on recovery

(a) Amount recoverable

Notwithstanding section 15 of this title and in lieu of the relief specified in such section, any person who is entitled to recovery on a claim under such section shall recover the actual damages sustained by such person, interest calculated at the rate specified in section 1961 of Title 28 on such actual damages as specified in subsection (d) of this section, and the cost of suit attributable to such claim, including a reasonable attorney's fee pursuant to section 4304 of this title if such claim—

(1) results from conduct that is within the scope of a notification that has been filed under section 4305(a) of this title for a joint venture, and

(2) is filed after such notification becomes effective pursuant to section 4305(c) of this title.

(b) Recovery by States

Notwithstanding section 15c of this title, and in lieu of the relief specified in such section, any State that is entitled to monetary relief on a claim under such section shall recover the total damage sustained as described in subsection (a)(1) of such section, interest calculated at the rate specified in section 1961 of Title 28 on such total damage as specified in subsection (d) of this section, and the cost of suit attributable to such claim, including a reasonable attorney's fee pursuant to section 15c of this title if such claim—

(1) results from conduct that is within the scope of a notification that has been filed under section 4305(a) of this title for a joint venture, and

(2) is filed after such notification becomes effective pursuant to section 4305(c) of this title.

(c) Conduct similar under State law

Notwithstanding any provision of any State law providing damages for conduct similar to that forbidden by the antitrust laws, any person who is entitled to recovery on a claim under such provision shall not recover in excess of the actual damages sustained by such person, interest calculated at the rate specified in section 1961 of Title 28 on such actual damages as specified in subsection (d) of this section, and the cost of suit attributable to such claim, including a reasonable attorney's fee pursuant to section 4304 of this title if such claim—

(1) results from conduct that is within the scope of a notification that has been filed under section 4305(a) of this title for a joint venture, and

(2) is filed after notification has become effective pursuant to section 4305(c) of this title.

(d) Interest

Interest shall be awarded on the damages involved for the period beginning on the earliest date for which injury can be established and ending on the date of judgment, unless the court finds that the award of all or part of such interest is unjust in the circumstances.

(e) Applicability

This section shall be applicable only if the challenged conduct of a person defending against a claim is not in violation of any decree or order, entered or issued after October 11, 1984, in any case or proceeding under the antitrust laws or any State law similar to the antitrust laws challenging such conduct as part of a joint venture.

332

HISTORY: (Pub. L. 98-462, § 4, Oct. 11, 1984, 98 Stat. 1816; Pub. L. 103-42, § 3(e)(1), June 10, 1993, 107 Stat. 119.)

§ 4304. Award of costs, including attorney's fees, to substantially prevailing party; offset

(a) Notwithstanding sections 15 and 26 of this title, in any claim under the antitrust laws, or any State law similar to the antitrust laws, based on the conducting of a joint venture, the court shall, at the conclusion of the action—

(1) award to a substantially prevailing claimant the cost of suit attributable to such claim, including a reasonable attorney's fee, or

(2) award to a substantially prevailing party defending against any such claim the cost of suit attributable to such claim, including a reasonable attorney's fee, if the claim, or the claimant's conduct during the litigation of the claim, was frivolous, unreasonable, without foundation, or in bad faith.

(b) The award made under subsection (a) of this section may be offset in whole or in part by an award in favor of any other party for any part of the cost of suit, including a reasonable attorney's fee, attributable to conduct during the litigation by any prevailing party that the court finds to be frivolous, unreasonable, without foundation, or in bad faith.

HISTORY: (Pub. L. 98-462, § 5, Oct. 11, 1984, 98 Stat. 1817; Pub. L. 103-42, § 3(e)(2), June 10, 1993, 107 Stat. 119.)

§ 4305. Disclosure of joint venture

(a) Written notifications; filing

Any party to a joint venture, acting on such venture's behalf, may, not later than 90 days after entering into a written agreement to form such venture or not later than 90 days after October 11, 1984, whichever is later, file simultaneously with the Attorney General and the Commission a written notification disclosing—

(1) the identities of the parties to such venture,

(2) the nature and objectives of such venture, and

(3) if a purpose of such venture is the production of a product, process, or service, as referred to in section 4301(a)(6)(D) of this title, the identity and nationality of any person who is a party to

such venture, or who controls any party to such venture whether separately or with one or more other persons acting as a group for the purpose of controlling such party.

Any party to such venture, acting on such venture's behalf, may file additional disclosure notifications pursuant to this section as are appropriate to extend the protections of section 4303 of this title. In order to maintain the protections of section 4303 of this title, such venture shall, not later than 90 days after a change in its membership, file simultaneously with the Attorney General and the Commission a written notification disclosing such change.

(b) Publication; Federal Register; notice

Except as provided in subsection (e) of this section, not later than 30 days after receiving a notification filed under subsection (a) of this section, the Attorney General or the Commission shall publish in the Federal Register a notice with respect to such venture that identifies the parties to such venture and that describes in general terms the area of planned activity of such venture. Prior to its publication, the contents of such notice shall be made available to the parties to such venture.

(c) Effect of notice

If with respect to a notification filed under subsection (a) of this section, notice is published in the Federal Register, then such notification shall operate to convey the protections of section 4303 of this title as of the earlier of—

(1) the date of publication of notice under subsection (b) of this section, or

(2) if such notice is not so published within the time required by subsection (b) of this section, after the expiration of the 30-day period beginning on the date the Attorney General or the Commission receives the applicable information described in subsection (a) of this section.

(d) Exemption; disclosure; information

Except with respect to the information published pursuant to subsection (b) of this section—

(1) all information and documentary material submitted as part of a notification filed pursuant to this section, and

(2) all other information obtained by the Attorney General or the Commission in the course of any investigation, administrative proceeding, or case, with respect to a potential violation of the antitrust laws by the joint venture with respect to which such notification was filed.

shall be exempt from disclosure under section 552 of Title 5 and shall not be made publicly available by any agency of the United States to which such section applies except in a judicial or administrative proceeding in which such information and material is subject to any protective order.

(e) Withdrawal of notification

Any person who files a notification pursuant to this section may withdraw such notification before notice of the joint venture involved is published under subsection (b) of this section. Any notification so withdrawn shall not be subject to subsection (b) of this section and shall not confer the protections of section 4303 of this title on any person with respect to whom such notification was filed.

(f) Judicial review; inapplicable with respect to notifications

Any action taken or not taken by the Attorney General or the Commission with respect to notifications filed pursuant to this section shall not be subject to judicial review.

(g) Admissibility into evidence; disclosure of conduct; publication of notice; supporting or answering claims under antitrust laws

(1) Except as provided in paragraph (2), for the sole purpose of establishing that a person is entitled to the protections of section 4303 of this title, the fact of disclosure of conduct under subsection (a) of this section and the fact of publication of a notice under subsection (b) of this section shall be admissible into evidence in any judicial or administrative proceeding.

(2) No action by the Attorney General or the Commission taken pursuant to this section shall be admissible into evidence in any such proceeding for the purpose of supporting or answering any claim under the antitrust laws or under any State law similar to the antitrust laws.

HISTORY: (Pub. L. 98-462, § 6, Oct. 11, 1984, 98 Stat. 1818; Pub. L. 103-42, § 3(f), June 10, 1993, 107 Stat. 119.)

§ 4306. Application of section 4303 protections to production of products, processes, and services

Notwithstanding sections 4303 and 4305 of this title, the protections of section 4303 of this title shall not apply with respect to a joint venture's production of a product, process, or service, as referred to in section 4301(a)(6)(D) of this title, unless—

(1) the principal facilities for such production are located in the United States or its territories, and

(2) each person who controls any party to such venture (including such party itself) is a United States person, or a foreign person from a country whose law accords antitrust treatment no less favorable to United States persons than to such country's domestic persons with respect to participation in joint ventures for production.

335

The National Cooperative Research Act of 1984

HISTORY: (Pub. L. 98-462, § 7, as added Pub. L. 103-42, § 3(g), June 10, 1993, 107 Stat. 119.)

J. 1995 Department of Justice Antitrust Enforcement Guidelines for International Operations

Source: U.S. Department of Justice Antitrust Division

Website information:

http://www.usdoj.gov/atr/public/international/intdocs.htm
This is the international documents website of the U.S. Department of Justice Antitrust Division. It includes links to the text of the 1995 Guidelines for International Operations as well as other current documentation on antitrust law.

Introduction

The 1995 Department of Justice Antitrust Enforcement Guidelines for International Operations provide the Department's analysis of important issues of international antitrust enforcement, including a review of the basic statutory provisions, some coverage of related trade regulation laws, detailed coverage of jurisdictional issues, and discussion of issues of comity and sovereign immunity in the application of the antitrust laws. The Guidelines are useful both as a partial review of the law in this area, and as an introduction to Justice Department enforcement policy.

The first Antitrust Guide for International Operations was issued by the Department of Justice in 1977. These were replaced by a second set in 1988. The 1995 Guidelines expressly provide that the 1988 Guidelines are not only "revised and updated," but "hereby withdrawn." While the earlier Guidelines are thus not a part of official current policy, they do provide useful historical information. The 1977 Guide provides a review of the historical development of case law applying U.S. antitrust laws to international transactions. The 1988 Guidelines provide a very different approach, with discussion of case law replaced largely by discussion of economic issues in the application of the antitrust laws. The 1995 Guidelines move back to greater discussion of case law, but with a focus limited primarily to the area of legislative (subject matter) jurisdiction. Taken together, the three documents (only the last of which is set forth here) provide a useful historical introduction to the application of U.S. antitrust laws to international transactions, as well as a tour of enforcement attitudes in the later quarter of the twentieth century.

ANTITRUST ENFORCEMENT GUIDELINES
FOR INTERNATIONAL OPERATIONS

ISSUED BY THE U.S. DEPARTMENT OF JUSTICE
AND THE FEDERAL TRADE COMMISSION

APRIL 1995

TABLE OF CONTENTS

TABLE OF CONTENTS (CONT'D)

U.S. DEPARTMENT OF JUSTICE

ANTITRUST ENFORCEMENT
GUIDELINES FOR INTERNATIONAL
OPERATIONS

April 1995

1. INTRODUCTION

For more than a century, the U.S. antitrust laws have stood as the ultimate protector of the competitive process that underlies our free market economy. Through this process, which enhances consumer choice and promotes competitive prices, society as a whole benefits from the best possible allocation of resources.

Although the federal antitrust laws have always applied to foreign commerce, that application is particularly important today. Throughout the world, the importance of antitrust law as a means to ensure open and free markets, protect consumers, and prevent conduct that impedes competition is becoming more apparent. The Department of Justice ("the Department") and the Federal Trade Commission ("the Commission" or "FTC") (when referred to collectively, "the Agencies"), as the federal agencies charged with the responsibility of enforcing the antitrust laws, thus have made it a high priority to enforce the antitrust laws with respect to international operations and to cooperate wherever appropriate with foreign authorities regarding such enforcement. In furtherance of this priority, the Agencies have revised and updated the Department's 1988 Antitrust Enforcement Guidelines for International Operations, which are hereby withdrawn.[6]

The 1995 Antitrust Enforcement Guidelines for International Operations (hereinafter "Guidelines") are intended to provide antitrust guidance to businesses engaged in international operations on questions that relate specifically to the Agencies' international enforcement policy.[7] They do not, therefore, provide a complete statement of the Agencies' general enforcement policies. The topics covered include the Agencies' subject matter jurisdiction over conduct and entities outside the United States and the considerations, issues, policies, and processes that govern their decision to exercise that jurisdiction; comity; mutual assistance in international antitrust enforcement; and the effects of foreign governmental involvement on the antitrust liability of private

---

[6]The U.S. Department of Justice and Federal Trade Commission Antitrust Guidelines for the Licensing of Intellectual Property (1995), the U.S. Department of Justice and Federal Trade Commission Horizontal Merger Guidelines (1992), and the Statements of Antitrust Enforcement Policy and Analytical Principles Relating to Health Care and Antitrust, Jointly Issued by the U.S. Department of Justice and Federal Trade Commission (1994), are not qualified, modified, or otherwise amended by the issuance of these Guidelines.

[7]Readers should separately evaluate the risk of private litigation by competitors, consumers and suppliers, as well as the risk of enforcement by state prosecutors under state and federal antitrust laws.

entities. In addition, the Guidelines discuss the relationship between antitrust and international trade initiatives. Finally, to illustrate how these principles may operate in certain contexts, the Guidelines include a number of examples.

As is the case with all guidelines, users should rely on qualified counsel to assist them in evaluating the antitrust risk associated with any contemplated transaction or activity. No set of guidelines can possibly indicate how the Agencies will assess the particular facts of every case. Persons seeking more specific advance statements of enforcement intentions with respect to the matters treated in these Guidelines should use the Department's Business Review procedure,[8] the Commission's Advisory Opinion procedure,[9] or one of the more specific procedures described below for particular types of transactions.

2. ANTITRUST LAWS ENFORCED BY THE AGENCIES

Foreign commerce cases can involve almost any provision of the antitrust laws. The Agencies do not discriminate in the enforcement of the antitrust laws on the basis of the nationality of the parties. Nor do the Agencies employ their statutory authority to further non-antitrust goals. Once jurisdictional requirements, comity, and doctrines of foreign governmental involvement have been considered and satisfied, the same substantive rules apply to all cases.

The following is a brief summary of the laws enforced by the Agencies that are likely to have the greatest significance for international transactions.

2.1 Sherman Act

Section 1 of the Sherman Act, 15 U.S.C. 1, sets forth the basic antitrust prohibition against contracts, combinations, and conspiracies "in restraint of trade or commerce among the several States or with foreign nations." Section 2 of the Act, 15 U.S.C. 2, prohibits monopolization, attempts to monopolize, and conspiracies to monopolize "any part of trade or commerce among the several States or with foreign nations." Section 6a of the Sherman Act, 15 U.S.C. 6a, defines the jurisdictional reach of the Act with respect to non-import foreign commerce.

Violations of the Sherman Act may be prosecuted as civil or criminal offenses. Conduct that the Department prosecutes criminally is limited to traditional per se offenses of the law, which typically involve price-fixing, customer allocation, bid-rigging or other cartel activities that would also be violations of the law in many countries. Criminal violations of the Act are punishable by fines and imprisonment. The Sherman Act provides that corporate defendants may be fined up to $10 million, other defendants may be fined up to $350,000, and individuals may be sentenced to up

---

[8]28 C.F.R. 50.6 (1994).

[9]16 C.F.R. 1.1-1.4 (1994).

to 3 years imprisonment.[10] The Department has sole responsibility for the criminal enforcement of the Sherman Act. In a civil proceeding, the Department may obtain injunctive relief against prohibited practices. It may also obtain treble damages if the U.S. government is the purchaser of affected goods or services.[11] Private plaintiffs may also obtain injunctive and treble damage relief for violations of the Sherman Act.[12] Before the Commission, conduct that violates the Sherman Act may be challenged pursuant to the Commission's power under Section 5 of the Federal Trade Commission Act, described below.

2.2 Clayton Act

The Clayton Act, 15 U.S.C. 12 et seq., expands on the general prohibitions of the Sherman Act and addresses anticompetitive problems in their incipiency.[13] Section 7 of the Clayton Act, 15 U.S.C. 18, prohibits any merger or acquisition of stock or assets "where in any line of commerce or in any activity affecting commerce in any section of the country, the effect of such acquisition may be substantially to lessen competition, or to tend to create a monopoly."[14] Section 15 of the Clayton Act empowers the Attorney General, and Section 13(b) of the FTC Act empowers the Commission, to seek a court order enjoining consummation of a merger that would violate Section 7. In addition, the Commission may seek a cease and desist order in an administrative proceeding against a merger under Section 11 of the Clayton Act, Section 5 of the FTC Act, or both. Private parties may also seek injunctive relief under 15 U.S.C. 26.

Section 3 of the Clayton Act prohibits any person engaged in commerce from conditioning the lease or sale of goods or commodities upon the purchaser's agreement not to use the products of a competitor, if the effect may be "to substantially lessen competition or to tend to create a monopoly in any line of commerce."[15] In evaluating transactions, the trend of recent authority is to use the

---

[10]Defendants may be fined up to twice the gross pecuniary gain or loss caused by their offense in lieu of the Sherman Act fines, pursuant to 18 U.S.C. 3571(d) (1988 & Supp. 1993). In addition, the U.S. Sentencing Commission Guidelines provide further information about possible criminal sanctions for individual antitrust defendants in 2R1.1 and for organizational defendants in Chapter 8.

[11]See 15 U.S.C. 4 (1988) (injunctive relief); 15 U.S.C. 15(a) (1988 & Supp. 1993) (damages).

[12]See 15 U.S.C. 16, 26 (1988).

[13]Under the Clayton Act, "commerce" includes "trade or commerce among the several States and with foreign nations." "Persons" include corporations or associations existing under or authorized either by the laws of the United States or any of its states or territories, or by the laws of any foreign country. 15 U.S.C. 12 (1988 & Supp. 1993).

[14]15 U.S.C. 18 (1988). The asset acquisition clause applies to "person[s] subject to the jurisdiction of the Federal Trade Commission" under the Clayton Act.

[15]15 U.S.C. 14 (1988).

same analysis employed in the evaluation of tying under Section 1 of the Sherman Act to assess a defendant's liability under Section 3 of the Clayton Act.[16] Section 2 of the Clayton Act, known as the Robinson-Patman Act,[17] prohibits price discrimination in certain circumstances. In practice, the Commission has exercised primary enforcement responsibility for this provision.

2.3 Federal Trade Commission Act

Section 5 of the Federal Trade Commission Act ("FTC Act") declares unlawful "unfair methods of competition in or affecting commerce, and unfair or deceptive acts or practices in or affecting commerce."[18] Pursuant to its authority over unfair methods of competition, the Commission may take administrative action against conduct that violates the Sherman Act and the Clayton Act, as well as anticompetitive practices that do not fall within the scope of the Sherman or Clayton Acts. The Commission may also seek injunctive relief in federal court against any such conduct under Section 13(b) of the FTC Act. Although enforcement at the Commission relating to international deceptive practices has become increasingly important over time, these Guidelines are limited to the Commission's antitrust authority under the unfair methods of competition language of Section 5.

2.4 Hart-Scott-Rodino Antitrust Improvements Act of 1976

Title II of the Hart-Scott-Rodino Antitrust Improvements Act of 1976 ("HSR Act"), 15 U.S.C. 18a, provides the Department and the Commission with several procedural devices to facilitate enforcement of the antitrust laws with respect to anticompetitive mergers and acquisitions.[19] The

---

[16]See, e.g., Mozart Co. v. Mercedes-Benz of N. Am., Inc., 833 F.2d 1342, 1352 (9th Cir. 1987), cert. denied, 488 U.S. 870 (1988).

[17]15 U.S.C. 13-13b, 21a (1988). The Robinson-Patman Act applies only to purchases involving commodities "for use, consumption, or resale within the United States." Id. at 13. It has been construed not to apply to sales for export. See, e.g., General Chem., Inc. v. Exxon Chem. Co., 625 F.2d 1231, 1234 (5th Cir. 1980). Intervening domestic sales, however, would be subject to the Act. See Raul Int'l Corp. v. Sealed Power Corp., 586 F. Supp. 349, 351-55 (D.N.J. 1984).

[18]15 U.S.C. 45 (1988 & Supp. 1993).

[19]The scope of the Agencies' jurisdiction under Clayton 7 exceeds the scope of those transactions subject to the premerger notification requirements of the HSR Act. Whether or not the HSR Act premerger notification thresholds are satisfied, either Agency may request the parties to a merger affecting U.S. commerce to provide information voluntarily concerning the transaction. In addition, the Department may issue Civil Investigative Demands ("CIDs") pursuant to the Antitrust Civil Process Act, 15 U.S.C. 1311-1314 (1988), and the Commission may issue administrative CIDs pursuant to the Act of Aug. 26, 1994, Pub. L. No. 103-312, 7; 108 Stat. 1691 (1994). The Commission may also issue administrative subpoenas and orders to file special reports under Sections 9 and 6(b) of the FTC Act, respectively. 15 U.S.C. 49, 46(b) (1988). Authority in particular cases is allocated to either the Department or the Commission pursuant to a voluntary clearance protocol. See Antitrust & Trade Reg. Daily (BNA), Dec. 6, 1993, and U.S. Department of Justice

HSR Act requires persons engaged in commerce or in any activity affecting commerce to notify the Agencies of proposed mergers or acquisitions that would exceed statutory size-of-party and size-of-transaction thresholds,[20] to provide certain information relating to reportable transactions, and to wait for a prescribed period-15 days for cash tender offers and 30 days for most other transactions-before consummating the transaction.[21] The Agency may, before the end of the waiting period, request additional information concerning a transaction (make a "Second Request") and thereby extend the waiting period beyond the initial one prescribed, to a specified number of days after the receipt of the material required by the Second Request—10 days for cash tender offers and 20 days for most other transactions.[22]

The HSR Act and the FTC rules implementing the HSR Act[23] exempt from the premerger notification requirements certain international transactions (typically those having little nexus to U.S. commerce) that otherwise meet the statutory thresholds.[24] Failure to comply with the HSR Act is punishable by court-imposed civil penalties of up to $10,000 for each day a violation continues. The court may also order injunctive relief to remedy a failure substantially to comply with the HSR Act.

---

and Federal Trade Commission, Hart-Scott-Rodino Premerger Program Improvements (March 23, 1995).

[20]Unless exempted pursuant to the HSR Act, the parties must provide premerger notification to the Agencies if (1) the acquiring person, or the person whose voting securities or assets are being acquired, is engaged in commerce or any activity affecting commerce; and (2)(a) any voting securities or assets of a person engaged in manufacturing which has annual net sales or total assets of $10 million or more are being acquired by any person which has total assets or annual net sales of $100 million or more, or (b) any voting securities or assets of a person not engaged in manufacturing which has total assets of $10 million or more are being acquired by any person which has total assets or annual sales of $100 million or more; or (c) any voting securities or assets of a person with annual net sales or total assets of $100 million or more are being acquired by any person with total assets or annual net sales of $10 million or more; and (3) as a result of such acquisition, the acquiring person would hold (a) 15 percent or more of the voting securities or assets of the acquired person, or (b) an aggregate total amount of the voting securities and assets of the acquired person of $15 million. 15 U.S.C. 18a(a) (1988). The size of the transaction test set forth in (3) must be read in conjunction with 16 C.F.R. 802.20 (1994). This Section exempts asset acquisitions valued at $15 million or less. It also exempts voting securities acquisitions of $15 million or less unless, if as a result of the acquisition, the acquiring person would hold 50 percent or more of the voting securities of an issuer that has annual net sales or total assets of $25 million or more. The HSR rules are necessarily technical, contain other exemptions, and should be consulted, rather than relying on this summary.

[21]15 U.S.C. 18a(b) (1988 & Supp. 1993); 16 C.F.R. 803.1 (1994); see also 11 U.S.C. 363 (b)(2).

[22]15 U.S.C. 18a(e) (1988).

[23]16 C.F.R. 801-803 (1994).

[24]16 C.F.R. 801.1(e), (k), 802.50-52 (1994). See infra at Section 4.22.

Businesses may seek an interpretation of their obligations under the HSR Act from the Commission.[25]

2.5 National Cooperative Research and Production Act

The National Cooperative Research and Production Act ("NCRPA"), 15 U.S.C. 4301-06, clarifies the substantive application of the U.S. antitrust laws to joint research and development ("R&D") activities and joint production activities. Originally drafted to encourage research and development by providing a special antitrust regime for research and development joint ventures, the NCRPA requires U.S. courts to judge the competitive effects of a challenged joint R&D or joint production venture, or a combination of the two, in properly defined relevant markets and under a rule-of-reason standard. The statute specifies that the conduct "shall be judged on the basis of its reasonableness, taking into account all relevant factors affecting competition, including, but not limited to, effects on competition in properly defined, relevant research, development, product, process, and service markets."[26] This approach is consistent with the Agencies' general analysis of joint ventures.[27]

The NCRPA also establishes a voluntary procedure pursuant to which the Attorney General and the FTC may be notified of a joint R&D or production venture. The statute limits the monetary relief that may be obtained in private civil suits against the participants in a notified venture to actual rather than treble damages, if the challenged conduct is within the scope of the notification. With respect to joint production ventures, the National Cooperative Production Amendments of 1993[28] provide that the benefits of the limitation on recoverable damages for claims resulting from conduct within the scope of a notification are not available unless (1) the principal facilities for the production are located within the United States or its territories, and (2) "each person who controls any party to such venture (including such party itself) is a United States person, or a foreign person

---

[25]See 16 C.F.R. 803.30 (1994).

[26]15 U.S.C. 4302 (1988 & Supp. 1993).

[27]See, e.g., U.S. Department of Justice and Federal Trade Commission Antitrust Guidelines for the Licensing of Intellectual Property, 4 (1995); Statements of Antitrust Enforcement Policy and Analytical Principles Relating to Health Care and Antitrust, Jointly Issued by the U.S. Department of Justice and the Federal Trade Commission (1994), Statement 2 (outlining a four-step approach for joint venture analysis). See generally National Collegiate Athletic Ass'n v. Board of Regents of Univ. of Okla., 468 U.S. 85 (1984); Federal Trade Comm'n v. Indiana Fed'n of Dentists, 476 U.S. 447 (1986). See also Massachusetts Board of Registration in Optometry, 110 F.T.C. 549 (1988).

[28]Pub. L. No. 103-42, 107 Stat. 117, 119 (1993).

from a country whose law accords antitrust treatment no less favorable to United States persons than to such country's domestic persons with respect to participation in joint ventures for production."[29]

2.6 Webb-Pomerene Act

The Webb-Pomerene Act, 15 U.S.C. 61-65, provides a limited antitrust exemption for the formation and operation of associations of otherwise competing businesses to engage in collective export sales. The exemption applies only to the export of "goods, wares, or merchandise."[30] It does not apply to conduct that has an anticompetitive effect in the United States or that injures domestic competitors of the members of an export association. Nor does it provide any immunity from prosecution under foreign antitrust laws.[31] Associations seeking an exemption under the Webb-Pomerene Act must file their articles of agreement and annual reports with the Commission, but pre-formation approval from the Commission is not required.

2.7 Export Trading Company Act of 1982

The Export Trading Company Act of 1982 (the "ETC Act"), Pub. L. No. 97-290, 96 Stat. 1234, is designed to increase U.S. exports of goods and services. It addresses that goal in several ways. First, in Title II, it encourages more efficient provision of export trade services to U.S. producers and suppliers by reducing restrictions on trade financing provided by financial institutions.[32] Second, in Title III, it reduces uncertainty concerning the application of the U.S. antitrust laws to export trade through the creation of a procedure by which persons engaged in U.S. export trade may obtain an export trade certificate of review ("ETCR").[33] Third, in Title IV, it clarifies the jurisdictional rules applicable to non-import cases brought under the Sherman Act and the FTC Act.[34] The Title III certificates are discussed briefly here; the jurisdictional rules are treated below in Section 3.1.

Export trade certificates of review are issued by the Secretary of Commerce with the concurrence of the Attorney General. Persons named in the ETCR obtain limited immunity from suit under both state and federal antitrust laws for activities that are specified in the certificate and

---

[29]15 U.S.C. 4306(2) (Supp. 1993).

[30]15 U.S.C. 61 (1988).

[31]See, e.g., Cases 89/85, etc., A. Ahlstrom Osakeyhtio v. Commission ("Wood Pulp"), 1988 E.C.R. 5193, [1987-1988 Transfer Binder] Common Mkt. Rep. (CCH) 14,491 (1988).

[32]See 12 U.S.C. 372, 635 a-4, 1841, 1843 (1988 & Supp. 1993) (Because Title II does not implicate the antitrust laws, it is not discussed further in these Guidelines.)

[33]15 U.S.C. 4011-21 (1988 & Supp. 1993).

[34]15 U.S.C. 6a (1988); 15 U.S.C. 45(a)(3) (1988).

that comply with the terms of the certificate. To obtain an ETCR, an applicant must show that proposed export conduct will:

(1) result in neither a substantial lessening of competition or restraint of trade within the United States nor a substantial restraint of the export trade of any competitor of the applicant;

(2) not unreasonably enhance, stabilize, or depress prices in the United States of the class of goods or services covered by the application;

(3) not constitute unfair methods of competition against competitors engaged in the export of the class of goods or services exported by the applicant; and

(4) not include any act that may reasonably be expected to result in the sale for consumption or resale in the United States of such goods or services.[35]

Congress intended that these standards "encompass the full range of the antitrust laws," as defined in the ETC Act.[36] Although an ETCR provides significant protection under the antitrust laws, it has certain limitations. First, conduct that falls outside the scope of a certificate remains fully subject to private and governmental enforcement actions. Second, an ETCR that is obtained by fraud is void from the outset and thus offers no protection under the antitrust laws. Third, any person that has been injured by certified conduct may recover actual (though not treble) damages if that conduct is found to violate any of the statutory criteria described above. In any such action, certified conduct enjoys a presumption of legality, and the prevailing party is entitled to recover costs and attorneys' fees.[37] Fourth, an ETCR does not constitute, explicitly or implicitly, an endorsement or opinion by the Secretary of Commerce or by the Attorney General concerning the legality of such business plans under the laws of any foreign country.

The Secretary of Commerce may revoke or modify an ETCR if the Secretary or the Attorney General determines that the applicant's export activities have ceased to comply with the statutory criteria for obtaining a certificate. The Attorney General may also bring suit under Section 15 of the Clayton Act to enjoin conduct that threatens "a clear and irreparable harm to the national interest,"[38] even if the conduct has been pre-approved as part of an ETCR.

---

[35] 15 U.S.C. 4013(a) (1988).

[36] H.R. Rep. No. 924, 97th Cong., 2d Sess. 26 (1982). See 15 U.S.C. 4021(6).

[37] See 15 U.S.C. 4016(b)(1) (1988) (injured party) and 4016(b)(4) (1988) (party against whom claim is brought).

[38] 15 U.S.C. 4016(b)(5) (1988); see 15 U.S.C. 25 (1988).

The Commerce Department, in consultation with the Department, has issued guidelines setting forth the standards used in reviewing ETCR applications.[39] The ETC Guidelines contain several examples illustrating application of the certification standards to specific export trade conduct, including the use of vertical and horizontal restraints and technology licensing arrangements. In addition, the Commerce Department's Export Trading Company Guidebook[40] provides information on the functions and advantages of establishing or using an export trading company, including factors to consider in applying for an ETCR. The Commerce Department's Office of Export Trading Company Affairs provides advice and information on the formation of export trading companies and facilitates contacts between producers of exportable goods and services and firms offering export trade services.

2.8 Other Pertinent Legislation

2.81 Wilson Tariff Act

The Wilson Tariff Act, 15 U.S.C. 8-11, prohibits "every combination, conspiracy, trust, agreement, or contract" made by or between two or more persons or corporations, either of whom is engaged in importing any article from a foreign country into the United States, where the agreement is intended to restrain trade or increase the market price in any part of the United States of the imported articles, or of "any manufacture into which such imported article enters or is intended to enter." Violation of the Act is a misdemeanor, punishable by a maximum fine of $5,000 or one year in prison. The Act also provides for seizure of the imported articles.[41]

2.82 Antidumping Act of 1916

The Revenue Act of 1916, better known as the Antidumping Act, 15 U.S.C. 71-74, is not an antitrust statute, but its subject matter is closely related to the antitrust rules regarding predation. It is a trade statute that creates a private claim against importers who sell goods into the United States at prices substantially below the prices charged for the same goods in their home market. In order to state a claim, a plaintiff must show both that such lower prices were commonly and systematically charged, and that the importer had the specific intent to injure or destroy an industry in the United States, or to prevent the establishment of an industry. Dumping cases are more commonly brought using the administrative procedures of the Tariff Act of 1930, discussed below.

---

[39]See Department of Commerce, International Trade Administration, Guidelines for the Issuance of Export Trade Certificates of Review (2d ed.), 50 Fed. Reg. 1786 (1985) (hereinafter "ETC Guidelines").

[40]U.S. Department of Commerce, International Trade Administration, The Export Trading Company Guidebook (1984).

[41]15 U.S.C. 11 (1988).

2.83 Tariff Act of 1930

A comprehensive discussion of the trade remedies available under the Tariff Act is beyond the scope of these Guidelines. However, because antitrust questions sometimes arise in the context of trade actions, it is appropriate to describe these laws briefly.

2.831 Countervailing Duties

Pursuant to Title VII.A of the Tariff Act,[42] U.S. manufacturers, producers, wholesalers, unions, and trade associations may petition for the imposition of offsetting duties on subsidized foreign imports.[43] The Department of Commerce's International Trade Administration ("ITA") must make a determination that the foreign government in question is subsidizing the imports, and in almost all cases the International Trade Commission ("ITC") must determine that a domestic industry is materially injured or threatened with material injury by reason of these imports.

2.832 Antidumping Duties

Pursuant to Title VII.B of the Tariff Act,[44] parties designated in the statute (the same parties as in the countervailing duties provision) may petition for antidumping duties, which must be imposed on foreign merchandise that is being, or is likely to be, sold in the United States at "less than fair value" ("LTFV"), if the U.S. industry is materially injured or threatened with material injury by imports of the foreign merchandise. The ITA makes the LTFV determination, and the ITC is responsible for the injury decision.

2.833 Section 337

Section 337 of the Tariff Act, 19 U.S.C. 1337, prohibits "unfair methods of competition and unfair acts in the importation of articles into the United States," if the effect is to destroy or substantially injure a U.S. industry, or where the acts relate to importation of articles infringing U.S. patents, copyrights, trademarks, or registered mask works.[45] Complaints are filed with the ITC. The

---

[42]See 19 U.S.C. 1671 et seq. (1988 & Supp. 1993), amended by Uruguay Round Agreements Act, Pub. L. No. 103-465, 108 Stat. 4809 (1994).

[43]Some alternative procedures exist under Tariff Act 701(c) for countries that have not subscribed to the World Trade Organization ("WTO") Agreement on Subsidies and Countervailing Measures or measures equivalent to it. 19 U.S.C. 1671(c) (1988 & Supp. 1993), amended by the Uruguay Round Agreements Act, Pub. L. No. 103-465, 108 Stat. 4809 (1994).

[44]See 19 U.S.C. 1673 et seq. (1988).

[45]19 U.S.C. 1337 (1988), amended by the Uruguay Round Agreements Act, Pub. L. No. 103-465, 108 Stat. 4809 (1994).

principal remedies under Section 337 are an exclusion order directing that any offending goods be excluded from entry into the United States, and a cease and desist order directed toward any offending U.S. firms and individuals.[46] The ITC is required to give the Agencies an opportunity to comment before making a final determination.[47] In addition, the Department participates in the interagency group that prepares recommendations for the President to approve, disapprove, or allow to take effect the import relief proposed by the ITC.

2.84 Trade Act of 1974

2.841 Section 201

Section 201 of the Trade Act of 1974, 19 U.S.C. 2251 et seq., provides that American businesses claiming serious injury due to significant increases in imports may petition the ITC for relief or modification under the so-called "escape clause." If the ITC makes a determination that "an article is being imported into the United States in such increased quantities as to be a substantial cause of serious injury, or the threat thereof, to the domestic industry producing an article like or directly competitive with the imported article," and formulates its recommendation for appropriate relief, the Department participates in the interagency committee that conducts the investigations and advises the President whether to adopt, modify, or reject the import relief recommended by the ITC.

2.842 Section 301

Section 301 of the Trade Act of 1974, 19 U.S.C. 2411, provides that the U.S. Trade Representative ("USTR"), subject to the specific direction, if any, of the President, may take action, including restricting imports, to enforce rights of the United States under any trade agreement, to address acts inconsistent with the international legal rights of the United States, or to respond to unjustifiable, unreasonable or discriminatory practices of foreign governments that burden or restrict U.S. commerce. Interested parties may initiate such actions through petitions to the USTR, or the USTR may itself initiate proceedings.[48] Of particular interest to antitrust enforcement is Section 301(d)(3)(B)(i)(IV), which includes among the "unreasonable" practices of foreign governments that might justify a proceeding the "toleration by a foreign government of systematic anticompetitive activities by enterprises or among enterprises in the foreign country that have the effect of restricting

---

[46]19 U.S.C. 1337(d), (f) (1988).

[47]19 U.S.C. 1337(b)(2) (1988).

[48]19 U.S.C. 2412(a), (b) (1988), amended by the Uruguay Round Agreements Act, Pub. L. No. 103-465, 108 Stat. 4809 (1994); see also Identification of Trade Expansion Priorities, Exec. Order No. 12,901, 59 Fed. Reg. 10,727 (1994).

... access of United States goods or services to a foreign market."[49] The Department participates in the interagency committee that makes recommendations to the President on what actions, if any, should be taken.

2.9 Relevant International Agreements

To further the twin goals of promoting enforcement cooperation between the United States and foreign governments and of reducing any tensions that may arise in particular proceedings, the Agencies have developed close relationships with antitrust and competition policy officials of many different countries. In some instances, understandings have been reached with respect to notifications, consultations, and cooperation in antitrust matters.[50] In other instances, more general rules endorsed by multilateral organizations such as the Organization for Economic Cooperation and Development ("OECD") provide the basis for the Agencies' cooperative policies. Finally, even in the absence of specific or general international understandings or recommendations, the Agencies often seek cooperation with foreign authorities.

2.91 Bilateral Cooperation Agreements

Formal written bilateral arrangements exist between the United States and the Federal Republic of Germany, Australia, and Canada.[51] International antitrust cooperation can also occur through

---

[49]19 U.S.C. 2411(d)(3)(B)(i)(IV) (1988), amended by the Uruguay Round Agreements Act, Pub. L. No. 103-465, 108 Stat. 4809 (1994), 314(c).

[50]Chapter 15 of the North American Free Trade Agreement ("NAFTA") addresses competition policy matters and commits the Parties to cooperate on antitrust matters. North American Free Trade Agreement Between the Government of the United States of America, the Government of Canada and the Government of the United Mexican States, 32 I.L.M. 605, 663 (1993), reprinted in H.R. Doc. No. 159, 103d Cong., 1st Sess. 712, 1170-1174 (1993).

[51]See Agreement Relating to Mutual Cooperation Regarding Restrictive Business Practices, June 23, 1976, U.S.-Federal Republic of Germany, 27 U.S.T. 1956, T.I.S. No. 8291, reprinted in 4 Trade Reg. Rep. (CCH) 13,501; Agreement Between the Government of the United States of America and the Government of Australia Relating to Cooperation on Antitrust Matters, June 29, 1982, U.S.-Australia, T.I.A.S. No. 10365, reprinted in 4 Trade Reg. Rep. (CCH) 13,502; and Memorandum of Understanding as to Notification, Consultation, and Cooperation with Respect to the Application of National Antitrust Laws, March 9, 1984, U.S.-Canada, reprinted in 4 Trade Reg. Rep. (CCH) 13,503. The Agencies also signed a similar agreement with the Commission of the European Communities in 1991. See Agreement Between the Government of the United States of America and the Commission of the European Communities Regarding the Application of Their Competition Laws, Sept. 23, 1991, 30 I.L.M. 1491 (Nov. 1991), reprinted in 4 Trade Reg. Rep. (CCH) 13,504. However, on August 9, 1994, the European Court of Justice ruled that the conclusion of the Agreement did not comply with institutional requirements of the law of the European Union ("EU"). Under the Court's decision, action by the EU Council of Ministers is necessary for this type of agreement. See French Republic v. Commission of European Communities (No. C-327/91) (Aug. 9, 1994).

mutual legal assistance treaties ("MLATs"), which are treaties of general application pursuant to which the United States and a foreign country agree to assist one another in criminal law enforcement matters. MLATs currently are in force with over one dozen countries, and many more are in the process of ratification or negotiation. However, only the MLAT with Canada has been used to date to obtain assistance in antitrust investigations.[52] The Agencies also hold regular consultations with the antitrust officials of Canada, the European Commission, and Japan, and have close, informal ties with the antitrust authorities of many other countries. Since 1990, the Agencies have cooperated closely with countries in the process of establishing competition agencies, assisted by funding provided by the Agency for International Development.

On November 2, 1994, President Clinton signed into law the International Antitrust Enforcement Assistance Act of 1994,[53] which authorizes the Agencies to enter into antitrust mutual assistance agreements in accordance with the legislation.

2.92 International Guidelines and Recommendations

The Agencies have agreed with respect to member countries of the OECD to consider the legitimate interests of other nations in accordance with relevant OECD recommendations.[54] Under the terms of a 1986 recommendation, the United States agency with responsibility for a particular case notifies a member country whenever an antitrust enforcement action may affect important interests of that country or its nationals.[55] Examples of potentially notifiable actions include requests for documents located outside the United States, attempts to obtain information from potential witnesses located outside the United States, and cases or investigations with significant foreign conduct or involvement of foreign persons.

---

[52]Treaty with Canada on Mutual Legal Assistance in Criminal Matters, S. Treaty Doc. No. 28, 100th Cong., 2d Sess. (1988).

[53]Pub. L. No. 103-438, 108 Stat. 4597 (1994).

[54]See Revised Recommendation of the OECD Council Concerning Cooperation Between Member Countries on Restrictive Business Practices Affecting International Trade, OECD Doc. No. C(86)44 (Final) (May 21, 1986). The Recommendation also calls for countries to consult with each other in appropriate situations, with the aim of promoting enforcement cooperation and minimizing differences that may arise.

[55]The OECD has 25 member countries and the European Commission takes part in its work. The OECD's membership includes many of the most advanced market economies in the world. The OECD also has several observer nations, which have made rapid progress toward open market economies. The Agencies follow recommended OECD practices with respect to all member countries.

3. THRESHOLD INTERNATIONAL ENFORCEMENT ISSUES

3.1 Jurisdiction

Just as the acts of U.S. citizens in a foreign nation ordinarily are subject to the law of the country in which they occur, the acts of foreign citizens in the United States ordinarily are subject to U.S. law. The reach of the U.S. antitrust laws is not limited, however, to conduct and transactions that occur within the boundaries of the United States. Anticompetitive conduct that affects U.S. domestic or foreign commerce may violate the U.S. antitrust laws regardless of where such conduct occurs or the nationality of the parties involved.

Under the Sherman Act and the FTC Act, there are two principal tests for subject matter jurisdiction in foreign commerce cases. With respect to foreign import commerce, the Supreme Court has recently stated in Hartford Fire Insurance Co. v. California that "the Sherman Act applies to foreign conduct that was meant to produce and did in fact produce some substantial effect in the United States."[56] There has been no such authoritative ruling on the scope of the FTC Act, but both Acts apply to commerce "with foreign nations" and the Commission has held that terms used by both Acts should be construed together.[57] Second, with respect to foreign commerce other than imports, the Foreign Trade Antitrust Improvements Act of 1982 ("FTAIA") applies to foreign conduct that has a direct, substantial, and reasonably foreseeable effect on U.S. commerce.[58]

3.11 Jurisdiction Over Conduct Involving Import Commerce

Imports into the United States by definition affect the U.S. domestic market directly, and will, therefore, almost invariably satisfy the intent part of the Hartford Fire test. Whether they in fact produce the requisite substantial effects will depend on the facts of each case.

---

[56]113 S. Ct. 2891, 2909 (1993). In a world in which economic transactions observe no boundaries, international recognition of the "effects doctrine" of jurisdiction has become more widespread. In the context of import trade, the "implementation" test adopted in the European Court of Justice usually produces the same outcome as the "effects" test employed in the United States. See Cases 89/85, etc., Ahlstrom v. Commission, supra at note 26. The merger laws of the European Union, Canada, Germany, France, Australia, and the Czech and Slovak Republics, among others, take a similar approach.

[57]In re Massachusetts Bd. of Registration in Optometry, 110 F.T.C. 598, 609 (1988).

[58]15 U.S.C. 6a (1988) (Sherman Act) and 45(a)(3) (1988) (FTC Act).

****

ILLUSTRATIVE EXAMPLE A[59]

Situation: A, B, C, and D are foreign companies that produce a product in various foreign countries. None has any U.S. production, nor any U.S. subsidiaries. They organize a cartel for the purpose of raising the price for the product in question. Collectively, the cartel members make substantial sales into the United States, both in absolute terms and relative to total U.S. consumption.

Discussion: These facts present the straightforward case of cartel participants selling products directly into the United States. In this situation, the transaction is unambiguously an import into the U.S. market, and the sale is not complete until the goods reach the United States. Thus, U.S. subject matter jurisdiction is clear under the general principles of antitrust law expressed most recently in Hartford Fire. The facts presented here demonstrate actual and intended participation in U.S. commerce.[60] The separate question of personal jurisdiction under the facts presented here would be analyzed using the principles discussed infra in Section 4.1.

****

3.12 Jurisdiction Over Conduct Involving Other Foreign Commerce

With respect to foreign commerce other than imports, the jurisdictional limits of the Sherman Act and the FTC Act are delineated in the FTAIA. The FTAIA amended the Sherman Act to provide that it:

shall not apply to conduct involving trade or commerce (other than import trade or commerce) with foreign nations unless

(1) such conduct has a direct, substantial, and reasonably foreseeable effect: (A) on trade or commerce which is not trade or commerce with foreign nations, or on import trade or import commerce with foreign nations; or (B) on export trade or export commerce with foreign nations, of a person engaged in such trade or commerce in the

---

[59]The examples incorporated into the text are intended solely to illustrate how the Agencies would apply the principles articulated in the Guidelines in differing fact situations. In each case, of course, the ultimate outcome of the analysis, i.e. whether or not a violation of the antitrust laws has occurred, would depend on the specific facts and circumstances of the case. These examples, therefore, do not address many of the factual and economic questions the Agencies would ask in analyzing particular conduct or transactions under the antitrust laws. Therefore, certain hypothetical situations presented here may, when fully analyzed, not violate any provision of the antitrust laws.

[60]See infra at Section 3.12.

United States;[61] (2) such effect gives rise to a claim under the provisions of [the Sherman Act], other than this section.

The FTAIA uses slightly different statutory language for the FTC Act,[62] but produces the same jurisdictional outcomes.

3.121 Jurisdiction in Cases Under Subsection 1(A) of the FTAIA

To the extent that conduct in foreign countries does not "involve" import commerce but does have an "effect" on either import transactions or commerce within the United States, the Agencies apply the "direct, substantial, and reasonably foreseeable" standard of the FTAIA. That standard is applied, for example, in cases in which a cartel of foreign enterprises, or a foreign monopolist, reaches the U.S. market through any mechanism that goes beyond direct sales, such as the use of an unrelated intermediary, as well as in cases in which foreign vertical restrictions or intellectual property licensing arrangements have an anticompetitive effect on U.S. commerce.

****

ILLUSTRATIVE EXAMPLE B

Situation: As in Illustrative Example A, the foreign cartel produces a product in several foreign countries. None of its members has any U.S. production, nor do any of them have U.S. subsidiaries. They organize a cartel for the purpose of raising the price for the product in question. Rather than selling directly into the United States, however, the cartel sells to an intermediary outside the United States, which they know will resell the product in the United States. The intermediary is not part of the cartel.

Discussion: The jurisdictional analysis would change slightly from the one presented in Example A, because not only is the conduct being challenged entered into by cartelists in a foreign country, but it is also initially implemented through a sale made in a foreign country. Despite the different test, however, the outcome on these facts would in all likelihood remain the same. The fact that the illegal conduct occurs prior to the import would trigger the application of the FTAIA. The Agencies would have to determine whether the challenged conduct had "direct, substantial and reasonably foreseeable effects" on U.S. domestic or import commerce. Furthermore, since "the essence of any violation of Section 1 [of the Sherman Act] is the illegal agreement itself—rather than the overt acts performed in furtherance of it,"[63] the Agencies would focus on the potential harm that

---

[61] If the Sherman Act applies to such conduct only because of the operation of paragraph (1)(B), then that Act shall apply to such conduct only for injury to export business in the United States. 15 U.S.C. 6a (1988).

[62] See 15 U.S.C. 45(a)(3) (1988).

[63] Summit Health, Ltd. v. Pinhas, 500 U.S. 322, 330-31 (1991).

would ensue if the conspiracy were successful, not on whether the actual conduct in furtherance of the conspiracy had in fact the prohibited effect upon interstate or foreign commerce.

****

ILLUSTRATIVE EXAMPLE C

Situation: Variant (1): Widgets are manufactured in both the United States and various other countries around the world. The non-U.S. manufacturers meet privately outside the United States and agree among themselves to raise prices to specified levels. Their agreement clearly indicates that sales in or into the United States are not within the scope of the agreement, and thus that each participant is free independently to set its prices for the U.S. market. Over time, the cartel members begin to sell excess production into the United States. These sales have the effect of stabilizing the cartel for the foreign markets. In the U.S. market, these "excess" sales are priced at levels below those that would have prevailed in the U.S. market but for the cartel, but there is no evidence that the prices are predatory. As a result of these events, several U.S. widget manufacturers curtail their production, overall domestic output falls, and remaining manufacturers fail to invest in new or improved capacity.

Variant (2): Assume now that the cartel agreement specifically provides that cartel members will set agreed prices for the U.S. market at levels designed to soak up excess quantities that arise as a result of price increases in foreign markets. The U.S. price level is set at periodic meetings where each participant indicates how much it must off-load in this way. Thus, the cartel members sell goods in the U.S. market at fixed prices that undercut prevailing U.S. price levels, with consequences similar to those in Variant 1. Discussion: Variant (1): The jurisdictional issue is whether the predictable economic consequences of the original cartel agreement and the independent sales into the United States are sufficient to support jurisdiction. The mere fact that the existence of U.S. sales or the level of U.S. prices may ultimately be affected by the cartel agreement is not enough for either Hartford Fire jurisdiction or the FTAIA.[64] Furthermore, in the absence of an agreement with respect to the U.S. market, sales into the U.S. market at non-predatory levels do not raise antitrust concerns.[65]

Variant (2): The critical element of a foreign price-fixing agreement with direct, intended effects in the United States is now present. The fact that the cartel believes its U.S. prices are "reasonable," or that it may be exerting downward pressure on U.S. price levels, does not exonerate

---

[64]If the Agencies lack jurisdiction under the FTAIA to challenge the cartel, the facts of this example would nonetheless lend themselves well to cooperative enforcement action among antitrust agencies. Virtually every country with an antitrust law prohibits horizontal cartels and the Agencies would willingly cooperate with foreign authorities taking direct action against the cartel in the countries where the agreement has raised the price of widgets to the extent such cooperation is allowed under U.S. law and any agreement executed pursuant to U.S. law with foreign agencies or governments.

[65]Cf. Matsushita Elec. Indus. Co. v. Zenith Radio Corp., 475 U.S. 574 (1986).

it.[66] Variant 2 presents a case where the Agencies would need clear evidence of the prohibited agreement before they would consider moving forward. They would be particularly cautious if the apparent effects in the U.S. market appeared to be beneficial to consumers.

****

3.122 Jurisdiction in Cases Under Subsection 1(B) of the FTAIA

Two categories of "export cases" fall within the FTAIA's jurisdictional test. First, the Agencies may, in appropriate cases, take enforcement action against anticompetitive conduct, wherever occurring, that restrains U.S. exports, if (1) the conduct has a direct, substantial, and reasonably foreseeable effect on exports of goods or services from the United States, and (2) the U.S. courts can obtain jurisdiction over persons or corporations engaged in such conduct.[67] As Section 3.2 below explains more fully, if the conduct is unlawful under the importing country's antitrust laws as well, the Agencies are also prepared to work with that country's authorities if they are better situated to remedy the conduct, and if they are prepared to take action that will address the U.S. concerns, pursuant to their antitrust laws. Second, the Agencies may in appropriate cases take enforcement action against conduct by U.S. exporters that has a direct, substantial, and reasonably foreseeable effect on trade or commerce within the United States, or on import trade or commerce. This can arise in two principal ways. First, if U.S. supply and demand were not particularly elastic, an agreement among U.S. firms accounting for a substantial share of the relevant market, regarding the level of their exports, could reduce supply and raise prices in the United States.[68] Second, conduct ostensibly export-related could affect the price of products sold or resold in the United States. This kind of effect could occur if, for example, U.S. firms fixed the price of an input used to manufacture a product overseas for ultimate resale in the United States.

****

ILLUSTRATIVE EXAMPLE D

Situation: Companies E and F are the only producers of product Q in country Epsilon, one of the biggest markets for sales of Q in the world. E and F together account for 99 percent of the sales

---

[66]Cf. Arizona v. Maricopa County Medical Soc'y, 457 U.S. 332 (1982); United States v. Socony-Vacuum Oil Co., 310 U.S. 150 (1940); United States v. Trenton Potteries Co., 273 U.S. 392 (1927).

[67]See U.S. Department of Justice Press Release dated April 3, 1992 (announcing enforcement policy that would permit the Department to challenge foreign business conduct that harms U.S. exports when the conduct would have violated U.S. antitrust laws if it occurred in the United States).

[68]One would need to show more than indirect price effects resulting from legitimate export efforts to support an antitrust challenge. See ETC Guidelines, supra at note 34, 50 Fed. Reg. at 1791.

of product Q in Epsilon.[69] In order to prevent a competing U.S. producer from entering the market in Epsilon, E and F agree that neither one of them will purchase or distribute the U.S. product, and that they will take "all feasible" measures to keep the U.S. company out of their market. Without specifically discussing what other measures they will take to carry out this plan, E and F meet with their distributors and, through a variety of threats and inducements, obtain agreement of all of the distributors not to carry the U.S. product. There are no commercially feasible substitute distribution channels available to the U.S. producer. Because of the actions of E and F, the U.S. producer cannot find any distributors to carry its product and is unable to make any sales in Epsilon.

Discussion: The agreement between E and F not to purchase or distribute the U.S. product would clearly have a direct and reasonably foreseeable effect on U.S. export commerce, since it is aimed at a U.S. exporter. The substantiality of the effects on U.S. exports would depend on the significance of E and F as purchasers and distributors of Q, although on these facts the virtually total foreclosure from Epsilon would almost certainly qualify as a substantial effect for jurisdictional purposes. However, if the Agencies believe that they may encounter difficulties in establishing personal jurisdiction or in obtaining effective relief, the case may be one in which the Agencies would seek to resolve their concerns by working with other authorities who are examining the transaction.

****

ILLUSTRATIVE EXAMPLE E

Situation: Companies P, Q, R, and S, organized under the laws of country Alpha, all manufacture and distribute construction equipment. Much of that equipment is protected by patents in the various countries where it is sold, including Alpha. The companies all belong to a private trade association, which develops industry standards that are often (although not always) adopted by Alpha's regulatory authorities. Feeling threatened by competition from the United States, the companies agree at a trade association meeting (1) to refuse to adopt any U.S. company technology as an industry standard, and (2) to boycott the distribution of U.S. construction equipment. The U.S. companies have taken all necessary steps to protect their intellectual property under the law of Alpha. Discussion: In this example, the collective activity impedes U.S. companies in two ways: their technology is boycotted (even if U.S. companies are willing to license their intellectual property) and they are foreclosed from access to distribution channels. The jurisdictional question is whether these actions create a direct, substantial, and reasonably foreseeable effect on the exports of U.S. companies. The mere fact that only the market of Alpha appears to be foreclosed is not enough to defeat such an effect. Only if exclusion from Alpha as a quantitative measure were so de minimis in terms of actual volume of trade that there would not be a substantial effect on U.S. export

---

[69]That E and F together have an overwhelmingly dominant share in Epsilon may or may not, depending on the market conditions for Q, satisfy the requirement of "substantial effect on U.S. exports" as required by the FTAIA. Foreclosure of exports to a single country, such as Epsilon, may satisfy the statutory threshold if that country's market accounts for a significant part of the export opportunities for U.S. firms.

commerce would jurisdiction be lacking. Given that this example involves construction equipment, a generally highly priced capital good, the exclusion from Alpha would probably satisfy the substantiality requirement for FTAIA jurisdiction. This arrangement appears to have been created with particular reference to competition from the United States, which indicates that the effects on U.S. exports are both direct and foreseeable.

****

3.13 Jurisdiction When U.S. Government Finances or Purchases

The Agencies may, in appropriate cases, take enforcement action when the U.S. Government is a purchaser, or substantially funds the purchase, of goods or services for consumption or use abroad. Cases in which the effect of anticompetitive conduct with respect to the sale of these goods or services falls primarily on U.S. taxpayers may qualify for redress under the federal antitrust laws.[70] As a general matter, the Agencies consider there to be a sufficient effect on U.S. commerce to support the assertion of jurisdiction if, as a result of its payment or financing, the U.S. Government bears more than half the cost of the transaction. For purposes of this determination, the Agencies apply the standards used in certifying export conduct under the ETC Act of 1982, 15 U.S.C. 4011-21(1982).[71]

---

[70]Cf. United States v. Concentrated Phosphate Export Ass'n, 393 U.S. 199, 208 (1968) ("[A]lthough the fertilizer shipments were consigned to Korea and although in most cases Korea formally let the contracts, American participation was the overwhelmingly dominant feature. The burden of noncompetitive pricing fell, not on any foreign purchaser, but on the American taxpayer. The United States was, in essence, furnishing fertilizer to Korea. . . . The foreign elements in the transaction were, by comparison, insignificant."); United States v. Standard Tallow Corp., 1988-1 Trade Cas. (CCH) 67,913 (S.D.N.Y. 1988) (consent decree) (barring suppliers from fixing prices or rigging bids for the sale of tallow financed in whole or in part through grants or loans by the U.S. Government); United States v. Anthracite Export Ass'n, 1970 Trade Cas. (CCH) 73,348 (M.D. Pa. 1970) (consent decree) (barring price-fixing, bid-rigging, and market allocation in Army foreign aid program).

[71]See ETC Guidelines, supra at note 34, 50 Fed. Reg. at 1799-1800. The requisite U.S. Government involvement could include the actual purchase of goods by the U.S. Government for shipment abroad, a U.S. Government grant to a foreign government that is specifically earmarked for the transaction, or a U.S. Government loan specifically earmarked for the transaction that is made on such generous terms that it amounts to a grant. U.S. Government interests would not be considered to be sufficiently implicated with respect to a transaction that is funded by an international agency, or a transaction in which the foreign government received non-earmarked funds from the United States as part of a general government-to-government aid program.

****

ILLUSTRATIVE EXAMPLE F

Situation: A combination of U.S. firms and local firms in country Beta create a U.S.-based joint venture for the purpose of building a major pollution control facility for Beta's Environmental Control Agency ("BECA"). The venture has received preferential funding from the U.S. Government, which has the effect of making the present value of expected future repayment of the principal and interest on the loan less than half its face value. Once the venture has begun work, it appears that its members secretly have agreed to inflate the price quoted to BECA, in order to secure more funding. Discussion: The fact that the U.S. Government bears more than half the financial risk of the transaction is sufficient for jurisdiction. With jurisdiction established, the Agencies would proceed to investigate whether the apparent bid-rigging actually occurred.[72]

****

ILLUSTRATIVE EXAMPLE G

Situation: The United States has many military bases and other facilities located in other countries. These facilities procure substantial goods and services from suppliers in the host country. In country X, it comes to the attention of the local U.S. military base commander that bids to supply certain construction services have been rigged.

Discussion: Sales made by a foreign party to the U.S. Government, including to a U.S. facility located in a foreign country, are within U.S. antitrust jurisdiction when they fall within the rule of Section 3.13. Bid-rigging of sales to the U.S. Government represents the kind of conduct that can lead to an antitrust action. Indeed, in the United States this type of behavior is normally prosecuted by the Department as a criminal offense. In practice, the Department has whenever possible worked closely with the host country antitrust authorities to explore remedies under local law. This has been successful in a number of instances.[73]

****

---

[72]Such conduct might also violate the False Claims Act, 31 U.S.C. 3729-3733 (1988 & Supp. 1993).

[73]If, however, local law does not provide adequate remedies, or the local authorities are not prepared to take action, the Department will weigh the comity factors, discussed infra at Section 3.2, and take such action as is appropriate.

3.14 Jurisdiction Under Section 7 of the Clayton Act

Section 7 of the Clayton Act applies to mergers and acquisitions between firms that are engaged in commerce or in any activity affecting commerce. The Agencies would apply the same principles regarding their foreign commerce jurisdiction to Clayton Section 7 cases as they would apply in Sherman Act cases.

****

ILLUSTRATIVE EXAMPLE H

Situation: Two foreign firms, one in Europe and the other in Canada, account together for a substantial percentage of U.S. sales of a particular product through direct imports. Both firms have sales offices and are subject to personal jurisdiction in the United States, although neither has productive assets in the United States. They enter into an agreement to merge.

Discussion: The express language of Section 7 of the Clayton Act reaches the stock and asset acquisitions of persons engaged in trade and commerce "with foreign nations."[74] Thus, in assessing jurisdiction for this merger outside the United States the Agencies could establish U.S. subject matter jurisdiction based on its effect on U.S. imports. If the facts stated above were modified to show that the proposed merger would have effects on U.S. export commerce, as opposed to import trade, then in assessing jurisdiction under the Clayton Act the Agencies would analyze the question of effects on commerce in a manner consistent with the FTAIA: that is, they would look to see whether the effects on U.S. domestic or import commerce are direct, substantial, and reasonably foreseeable.[75] It is appropriate to do so because the FTAIA sheds light on the type of effects Congress considered necessary for foreign commerce cases, even though the FTAIA did not amend the Clayton Act.

In both these situations, the Agencies would conclude that Section 7 jurisdiction technically exists. However, if effective relief is difficult to obtain, the case may be one in which the Agencies would seek to coordinate their efforts with other authorities who are examining the transaction.[76]

****

---

[74]Clayton Act 1, 15 U.S.C. 12 (1988).

[75]See supra at Section 3.121.

[76]Through concepts such as "positive comity," one country's authorities may ask another country to take measures that address possible harm to competition in the requesting country's market.

3.2 Comity

In enforcing the antitrust laws, the Agencies consider international comity. Comity itself reflects the broad concept of respect among co-equal sovereign nations and plays a role in determining "the recognition which one nation allows within its territory to the legislative, executive or judicial acts of another nation."[77] Thus, in determining whether to assert jurisdiction to investigate or bring an action, or to seek particular remedies in a given case, each Agency takes into account whether significant interests of any foreign sovereign would be affected.[78]

In performing a comity analysis, the Agencies take into account all relevant factors. Among others, these may include (1) the relative significance to the alleged violation of conduct within the United States, as compared to conduct abroad; (2) the nationality of the persons involved in or affected by the conduct; (3) the presence or absence of a purpose to affect U.S. consumers, markets, or exporters; (4) the relative significance and foreseeability of the effects of the conduct on the United States as compared to the effects abroad; (5) the existence of reasonable expectations that would be furthered or defeated by the action; (6) the degree of conflict with foreign law or articulated foreign economic policies; (7) the extent to which the enforcement activities of another country with respect to the same persons, including remedies resulting from those activities, may be affected; and (8) the effectiveness of foreign enforcement as compared to U.S. enforcement action.[79]

The relative weight that each factor should be given depends on the facts and circumstances of each case. With respect to the factor concerning conflict with foreign law, the Supreme Court made clear in Hartford Fire[80] that no conflict exists for purposes of an international comity analysis in the courts if the person subject to regulation by two states can comply with the laws of both. Bearing this in mind, the Agencies first ask what laws or policies of the arguably interested foreign jurisdictions are implicated by the conduct in question. There may be no actual conflict between the antitrust enforcement interests of the United States and the laws or policies of a foreign sovereign. This is increasingly true as more countries adopt antitrust or competition laws that are compatible with those of the United States. In these cases, the anticompetitive conduct in question may also be prohibited under the pertinent foreign laws, and thus the possible conflict would relate to

---

[77]Hilton v. Guyot, 159 U.S. 113, 164 (1895).

[78]The Agencies have agreed to consider the legitimate interests of other nations in accordance with the recommendations of the OECD and various bilateral agreements, see supra at Section 2.9.

[79]The first six of these factors are based on previous Department Guidelines. The seventh and eighth factors are derived from considerations in the U.S.-EC Antitrust Cooperation Agreement. See supra at note 46.

[80]113 S. Ct. 2891, 2910.

enforcement practices or remedy. If the laws or policies of a foreign nation are neutral, it is again possible for the parties in question to comply with the U.S. prohibition without violating foreign law.

The Agencies also take full account of comity factors beyond whether there is a conflict with foreign law. In deciding whether or not to challenge an alleged antitrust violation, the Agencies would, as part of a comity analysis, consider whether one country encourages a certain course of conduct, leaves parties free to choose among different strategies, or prohibits some of those strategies. In addition, the Agencies take into account the effect of their enforcement activities on related enforcement activities of a foreign antitrust authority. For example, the Agencies would consider whether their activities would interfere with or reinforce the objectives of the foreign proceeding, including any remedies contemplated or obtained by the foreign antitrust authority. The Agencies also will consider whether the objectives sought to be obtained by the assertion of U.S. law would be achieved in a particular instance by foreign enforcement. In lieu of bringing an enforcement action, the Agencies may consult with interested foreign sovereigns through appropriate diplomatic channels to attempt to eliminate anticompetitive effects in the United States. In cases where the United States decides to prosecute an antitrust action, such a decision represents a determination by the Executive Branch that the importance of antitrust enforcement outweighs any relevant foreign policy concerns.[81] The Department does not believe that it is the role of the courts to "second-guess the executive branch's judgment as to the proper role of comity concerns under these circumstances."[82] To date, no Commission cases have presented the issue of the degree of deference that courts should give to the Commission's comity decisions.[83] It is important also to note that in disputes between private parties, many courts are willing to undertake a comity analysis.[84]

****

ILLUSTRATIVE EXAMPLE I

Situation: A group of buyers in one foreign country decide that they will agree on the price that they will offer to U.S. suppliers of a particular product. The agreement results in substantial loss of sales and capacity reductions in the United States.

---

[81]Foreign policy concerns may also lead the United States not to prosecute a case. See, e.g., U.S. Department of Justice Press Release dated Nov. 19, 1984 (announcing the termination, based on foreign policy concerns, of a grand jury investigation into passenger air travel between the United States and the United Kingdom).

[82]United States v. Baker Hughes, Inc., 731 F. Supp. 3, 6 n.5 (D.D.C. 1990), aff'd, 908 F.2d 981 (D.C. Cir. 1990).

[83]Like the Department, the Commission considers comity issues and consults with foreign antitrust authorities, but the Commission is not part of the Executive Branch.

[84]See, e.g., Timberlane Lumber Co. v. Bank of America, 549 F.2d 597 (9th Cir. 1976).

Discussion: From a jurisdictional point of view, the FTAIA standard appears to be satisfied because the effects on U.S. exporters presented here are direct and the percentage of supply accounted for by the buyers' cartel is substantial given the fact that the U.S. suppliers are "major." The Agencies, however, would also take into consideration the comity aspects presented before deciding whether or not to proceed.

Consistent with their consideration of comity and its obligations under various international agreements, the Agencies would ordinarily notify the antitrust authority in the cartel's home country. If that authority were in a better position to address the competitive problem, and were prepared to take effective action to address the adverse effects on U.S. commerce, the Agencies would consider working cooperatively with the foreign authority or staying their own remedy pending enforcement efforts by the foreign country. In deciding whether to proceed, the Agencies would weigh the factors relating to comity set forth above. Factors weighing in favor of bringing such an action include the substantial and purposeful harm caused by the cartel to the United States.

****

ILLUSTRATIVE EXAMPLE J

Situation: A and B manufacture a consumer product for which there are no readily available substitutes in ten different countries around the world, including the United States, Canada, Mexico, Spain, Australia, and others. When they decide to merge, it becomes necessary for them to file premerger notifications in many of these countries, and to subject themselves to the merger law of all ten.[85] Discussion: Under the 1986 OECD Recommendation, OECD countries notify one another when a proceeding such as a merger review is underway that might affect the interests of other countries. Within the strict limits of national confidentiality laws, agencies attempt to cooperate with one another in processing these reviews. This might extend to exchanges of publicly available information, agreements to let the other agencies know when a decision to institute a proceeding is taken, and to consult for purposes of international comity with respect to proposed remedial measures and investigatory methods. The parties can facilitate faster resolution of these cases if they are willing voluntarily to waive confidentiality protections and to cooperate with a joint investigation. At present, confidentiality provisions in U.S. and foreign laws do not usually permit effective coordination of a single international investigation in the absence of such waivers.

****

---

[85]Not every country has compulsory premerger notification, and the events triggering duties to notify vary from country to country.

3.3 Effects of Foreign Government Involvement

Foreign governments may be involved in a variety of ways in conduct that may have antitrust consequences. To address the implications of such foreign governmental involvement, Congress and the courts have developed four special doctrines: the doctrine of foreign sovereign immunity; the doctrine of foreign sovereign compulsion; the act of state doctrine; and the application of the Noerr-Pennington doctrine to immunize the lobbying of foreign governments. Although these doctrines are interrelated, for purposes of discussion the Guidelines discuss each one individually.

3.31 Foreign Sovereign Immunity

The scope of immunity of a foreign government or its agencies and instrumentalities (hereinafter foreign government)[86] from the jurisdiction of the U.S. courts for all causes of action, including antitrust, is governed by the Foreign Sovereign Immunities Act of 1976 ("FSIA").[87] Subject to the treaties in place at the time of FSIA's enactment, a foreign government is immune from suit except where designated in the FSIA.[88] Under the FSIA, a U.S. court has jurisdiction if the foreign government has:

(a) waived its immunity explicitly or by implication,
(b) engaged in commercial activity as described in the statute,
(c)expropriated property in violation of international law,
(d) acquired rights to U.S. property,
(e) committed certain torts within the United States, or agreed to arbitration of a dispute.[89]

The commercial activities exception is a frequently invoked exception to sovereign immunity under the FSIA. Under the FSIA, a foreign government is not immune in any case:

in which the action is based upon a commercial activity carried on in the United States by the foreign state; or upon an act performed in the United States in connection with a

---

[86]Section 1603(b) of the Foreign Sovereign Immunities Act of 1976 defines an "agency or instrumentality of a foreign state" to be any entity "(1) which is a separate legal person, corporate or otherwise; and (2) which is an organ of a foreign state or political subdivision thereof, or a majority of whose shares or other ownership interest is owned by a foreign state or political subdivision thereof; and (3) which is neither a citizen of a State of the United States as defined in Section 1332(c) and (d) of [Title 28, U.S. Code], nor created under the laws of any third country." 28 U.S.C. 1603(b) (1988). It is not uncommon in antitrust cases to see state-owned enterprises meeting this definition.

[87]28 U.S.C. 1602, et seq. (1988).

[88]28 U.S.C. 1604 (1988 & Supp. 1993).

[89]28 U.S.C. 1605(a)(1-6) (1988).

commercial activity of the foreign state elsewhere; or upon an act outside the territory of the United States in connection with a commercial activity of the foreign state elsewhere and that act causes a direct effect in the United States.[90]

"Commercial activity of the foreign state" is not defined in the FSIA, but is to be determined by the "nature of the course of conduct or particular transaction or act, rather than by reference to its purpose."[91] In attempting to differentiate commercial from sovereign activity, courts have considered whether the conduct being challenged is customarily performed for profit[92] and whether the conduct is of a type that only a sovereign government can perform.[93] As a practical matter, most activities of foreign government-owned corporations operating in the commercial marketplace will be subject to U.S. antitrust laws to the same extent as the activities of foreign privately-owned firms.

The commercial activity also must have a substantial nexus with the United States before a foreign government is subject to suit. The FSIA sets out three different standards for meeting this requirement. First, the challenged conduct by the foreign government may occur in the United States.[94] Alternatively, the challenged commercial activity may entail an act performed in the United States in connection with a commercial activity of the foreign government elsewhere.[95] Or, finally, the challenged commercial activity of a foreign government outside of the United States may

---

[90]28 U.S.C. 1605(a)(2) (1988).

[91]28 U.S.C. 1603(d) (1988).

[92]See, e.g., Republic of Argentina v. Weltover, Inc., 112 S. Ct. 2160 (1992); Schoenberg v. Exportadora de Sal, S.A. de C.V., 930 F.2d 777 (9th Cir. 1991); Rush-Presbyterian-St. Luke's Medical Ctr. v. Hellenic Republic, 877 F.2d 574, 578 n.4 (7th Cir.), cert. denied, 493 U.S. 937 (1989).

[93]See, e.g., Saudi Arabia v. Nelson, 113 S. Ct. 1471 (1993); de Sanchez v. Banco Central de Nicaragua, 770 F.2d 1385 (5th Cir. 1985); Letelier v. Republic of Chile, 748 F.2d 790, 797-98 (2d Cir. 1984), cert. denied, 471 U.S. 1125 (1985); International Ass'n of Machinists & Aerospace Workers v. Organization of Petroleum Exporting Countries, 477 F. Supp. 553 (C.D. Cal. 1979), aff'd on other grounds, 649 F.2d 1354 (9th Cir. 1981), cert. denied, 454 U.S. 1163 (1982).

[94]28 U.S.C. 1603(e) (1988).

[95]See H.R. Rep. No. 1487, 94th Cong., 2d Sess. 18-19 (1976), reprinted in 1976 U.S.C.C.A.N. 6604, 6617-18 (providing as an example the wrongful termination in the United States of an employee of a foreign state employed in connection with commercial activity in a third country.) But see Filus v. LOT Polish Airlines, 907 F.2d 1328, 1333 (2d Cir. 1990) (holding as too attenuated the failure to warn of a defective product sold outside of the United States in connection with an accident outside the United States.)

produce a direct effect within the United States, i.e., an effect which follows "as an immediate consequence of the defendant's . . . activity."[96]

3.32 Foreign Sovereign Compulsion

Although U.S. antitrust jurisdiction extends to conduct and parties in foreign countries whose actions have the required effects on U.S. commerce, as discussed above, those parties may find themselves subject to conflicting requirements from the other country (or countries) where they are located.[97] Under Hartford Fire, if it is possible for the party to comply both with the foreign law and the U.S. antitrust laws, the existence of the foreign law does not provide any legal excuse for actions that do not comply with U.S. law. However, a direct conflict may arise when the facts demonstrate that the foreign sovereign has compelled the very conduct that the U.S. antitrust law prohibits.

In these circumstances, at least one court has recognized a defense under the U.S. antitrust laws, and the Agencies will also recognize it.[98] There are two rationales underlying the defense of foreign sovereign compulsion. First, Congress enacted the U.S. antitrust laws against the background of well recognized principles of international law and comity among nations, pursuant to which U.S. authorities give due deference to the official acts of foreign governments. A defense for actions taken under the circumstances spelled out below serves to accommodate two equal sovereigns. Second, important considerations of fairness to the defendant require some mechanism that provides a predictable rule of decision for those seeking to conform their behavior to all pertinent laws.

---

[96]Republic of Argentina, 112 S. Ct. at 2168. This test is similar to proximate cause formulations adopted by other courts. See Martin v. Republic of South Africa, 836 F.2d 91, 95 (2d Cir. 1987) (a direct effect is one with no intervening element which flows in a straight line without deviation or interruption), quoting Upton v. Empire of Iran, 459 F. Supp. 264, 266 (D.D.C. 1978), aff'd mem., 607 F.2d 494 (D.C. Cir. 1979).

[97]Conduct by private entities not required by law is entirely outside of the protections afforded by this defense. See Continental Ore Co. v. Union Carbide & Carbon Corp., 370 U.S. 690, 706 (1962); United States v. Watchmakers of Switzerland Info. Ctr., Inc., 1963 Trade Cas. (CCH) 70,600 at 77,456-57 (S.D.N.Y. 1962) ("[T]he fact that the Swiss Government may, as a practical matter, approve the effects of this private activity cannot convert what is essentially a vulnerable private conspiracy into an unassailable system resulting from a foreign government mandate.") See supra at Section 3.2.

[98]Interamerican Refining Corp. v. Texaco Maracaibo, Inc., 307 F. Supp. 1291 (D. Del. 1970) (defendant, having been ordered by the government of Venezuela not to sell oil to a particular refiner out of favor with the current political regime, held not subject to antitrust liability under the Sherman Act for an illegal group boycott). The defense of foreign sovereign compulsion is distinguished from the federalism-based state action doctrine. The state action doctrine applies not just to the actions of states and their subdivisions, but also to private anticompetitive conduct that is both undertaken pursuant to clearly articulated state policies, and is actively supervised by the state. See Federal Trade Comm'n v. Ticor Title Insurance Co., 112 S. Ct. 2169 (1992); California Retail Liquor Dealers Ass'n v. Midcal Aluminum, Inc., 445 U.S. 97, 105 (1980); Parker v. Brown, 317 U.S. 341 (1943).

Because of the limited scope of the defense, the Agencies will refrain from enforcement actions on the ground of foreign sovereign compulsion only when certain criteria are satisfied. First, the foreign government must have compelled the anticompetitive conduct under circumstances in which a refusal to comply with the foreign government's command would give rise to the imposition of penal or other severe sanctions. As a general matter, the Agencies regard the foreign government's formal representation that refusal to comply with its command would have such a result as being sufficient to establish that the conduct in question has been compelled, as long as that representation contains sufficient detail to enable the Agencies to see precisely how the compulsion would be accomplished under local law.[99] Foreign government measures short of compulsion do not suffice for this defense, although they can be relevant in a comity analysis.

Second, although there can be no strict territorial test for this defense, the defense normally applies only when the foreign government compels conduct which can be accomplished entirely within its own territory. If the compelled conduct occurs in the United States, the Agencies will not recognize the defense.[100] For example, no defense arises when a foreign government requires the U.S. subsidiaries of several firms to organize a cartel in the United States to fix the price at which products would be sold in the United States, or when it requires its firms to fix mandatory resale prices for their U.S. distributors to use in the United States.

Third, with reference to the discussion of foreign sovereign immunity in Section 3.31 above, the order must come from the foreign government acting in its governmental capacity. The defense does not arise from conduct that would fall within the FSIA commercial activity exception.

****

ILLUSTRATIVE EXAMPLE K

Situation: Greatly increased quantities of commodity X have flooded into the world market over the last two or three years, including substantial amounts indirectly coming into the United States. Because they are unsure whether they would prevail in an antidumping and countervailing duty case, U.S. industry participants have refrained from filing trade law petitions. The officials of three foreign countries meet with their respective domestic firms and urge them to "rationalize" production by cooperatively cutting back. Going one step further, one of the interested governments orders cutbacks from its firms, subject to substantial penalties for non-compliance. Producers from the other two countries agree among themselves to institute comparable cutbacks, but their governments do not require them to do so.

---

[99]For example, the Agencies may not regard as dispositive a statement that is ambiguous or that on its face appears to be internally inconsistent. The Agencies may inquire into the circumstances underlying the statement and they may also request further information if the source of the power to compel is unclear.

[100]See Linseman v. World Hockey Ass'n, 439 F. Supp. 1315, 1325 (D. Conn. 1977).

Discussion: Assume for the purpose of this example that the overseas production cutbacks have the necessary effects on U.S. commerce to support jurisdiction. As for the participants from the two countries that did not impose any penalty for a failure to reduce production, the Agencies would not find that sovereign compulsion precluded prosecution of this agreement.[101] As for participants from the country that did compel production cut-backs through the imposition of severe penalties, the Agencies would acknowledge a defense of sovereign compulsion.

****

3.33 Acts of State

The act of state doctrine is a judge-made rule of federal common law.[102] It is a doctrine of judicial abstention based on considerations of international comity and separation of powers, and applies only if the specific conduct complained of is a public act of the foreign sovereign within its territorial jurisdiction on matters pertaining to its governmental sovereignty. The act of state doctrine arises when the validity of the acts of a foreign government is an unavoidable issue in a case.[103]

Courts have refused to adjudicate claims or issues that would require the court to judge the legality (as a matter of U.S. law or international law) of the sovereign act of a foreign state.[104] Although in some cases the sovereign act in question may compel private behavior, such compulsion is not required by the doctrine.[105] While the act of state doctrine does not compel dismissal as a matter of course, judicial abstention is appropriate in a case where the court must "declare invalid, and thus ineffective as a rule of decision in the U.S. courts, . . . the official act of a foreign sovereign."[106]

When a restraint on competition arises directly from the act of a foreign sovereign, such as the grant of a license, award of a contract, expropriation of property, or the like, the Agencies may

---

[101]As in all such cases, the Agencies would consider comity factors as part of their analysis. See supra at Section 3.2.

[102]Banco Nacional de Cuba v. Sabbatino, 376 U.S. 398, 421-22 n.21 (1964) (noting that other countries do not adhere in any formulaic way to an act of state doctrine).

[103]See W.S. Kirkpatrick & Co. v. Environmental Tectonics Corp., 493 U.S. 400 (1990).

[104]International Ass'n of Machinists and Aerospace Workers v. Organization of Petroleum Exporting Countries, 649 F.2d 1354, 1358 (9th Cir. 1981), cert. denied, 454 U.S. 1163 (1982).

[105]See Timberlane, supra at note 79, 549 F.2d at 606-08.

[106]Kirkpatrick, 493 U.S. at 405, quoting Ricaud v. American Metal Co., 246 U.S. 304, 310 (1918).

refrain from bringing an enforcement action based on the act of state doctrine. For example, the Agencies will not challenge foreign acts of state if the facts and circumstances indicate that: (1) the specific conduct complained of is a public act of the sovereign, (2) the act was taken within the territorial jurisdiction of the sovereign, and (3) the matter is governmental, rather than commercial.

3.34 Petitioning of Sovereigns

Under the Noerr-Pennington doctrine, a genuine effort to obtain or influence action by governmental entities in the United States is immune from application of the Sherman Act, even if the intent or effect of that effort is to restrain or monopolize trade.[107] Whatever the basis asserted for Noerr-Pennington immunity (either as an application of the First Amendment or as a limit on the statutory reach of the Sherman Act, or both), the Agencies will apply it in the same manner to the petitioning of foreign governments and the U.S. Government.

****

ILLUSTRATIVE EXAMPLE L

Situation: In the course of preparing an antidumping case, which requires the U.S. industry to demonstrate that it has been injured through the effects of the dumped imports, producers representing 75 percent of U.S. output exchange the information required for the adjudication. All the information is exchanged indirectly through third parties and in an aggregated form that makes the identity of any particular producer's information impossible to discern.

Discussion: Information exchanged by competitors within the context of an antidumping proceeding implicates the Noerr-Pennington petitioning immunity. To the extent that these exchanges are reasonably necessary in order for them to prepare their joint petition, which is permitted under the trade laws, Noerr is available to protect against antitrust liability that would otherwise arise. On these facts the parties are likely to be immunized by Noerr if they have taken the necessary measures to ensure that the provision of sensitive information called for by the Commerce Department and the ITC cannot be used for anticompetitive purposes. In such a situation, the information exchange is incidental to genuine petitioning and is not subject to the antitrust laws. Conversely, were the parties directly to exchange extensive information relating to their costs, the prices each has charged for the product, pricing trends, and profitability, including information about

---

[107]See Eastern R.R. Presidents Conference v. Noerr Motor Freight, Inc., 365 U.S. 127 (1961); United Mine Workers of Am. v. Pennington, 381 U.S. 657 (1965); California Motor Transp. Co. v. Trucking Unlimited, 404 U.S. 508 (1972) (extending protection to petitioning before "all departments of Government," including the courts); Professional Real Estate Investors, Inc. v. Columbia Pictures Indus., 113 S. Ct. 1920 (1993). However, this immunity has never applied to "sham" activities, in which petitioning "ostensibly directed toward influencing governmental action, is a mere sham to cover . . . an attempt to interfere directly with the business relationships of a competitor." Professional Real Estate Investors, 113 S. Ct. at 1926, quoting Noerr, 365 U.S. at 144. See also USS-Posco Indus. v. Contra Costa Cty. Bldg. Constr. Council, AFL-CIO, 31 F.3d 800 (9th Cir. 1994).

specific transactions that went beyond the scope of those facts required for the adjudication, such conduct would go beyond the contemplated protection of Noerr immunity.

****

3.4 Antitrust Enforcement and International Trade Regulation

There has always been a close relationship between the international application of the antitrust laws and the policies and rules governing the international trade of the United States. Restrictions such as tariffs or quotas on the free flow of goods affect market definition, consumer choice, and supply options for U.S. producers. In certain instances, the U.S. trade laws set forth specific procedures for settling disputes under those laws, which can involve price and quantity agreements by the foreign firms involved. When those procedures are followed, an implied antitrust immunity results.[108] However, agreements among competitors that do not comply with the law, or go beyond the measures authorized by the law, do not enjoy antitrust immunity. In the absence of legal authority, the fact, without more, that U.S. or foreign government officials were involved in or encouraged measures that would otherwise violate the antitrust laws does not immunize such arrangements.[109]

If a particular voluntary export restraint does not qualify for express or implied immunity from the antitrust laws, then the legality of the arrangement would depend upon the existence of the ordinary elements of an antitrust offense, such as whether or not a prohibited agreement exists or whether defenses such as foreign sovereign compulsion can be invoked.

---

[108]See, e.g., Letter from Charles F. Rule, Acting Assistant Attorney General, Antitrust Division, Department of Justice, to Mr. Makoto Kuroda, Vice-Minister for International Affairs, Japanese Ministry of International Trade and Industry, July 30, 1986 (concluding that a suspension agreement did not violate U.S. antitrust laws on the basis of factual representations that the agreement applied only to products under investigation, that it did not require pricing above levels needed to eliminate sales below foreign market value, and that assigning weighted-average foreign market values to exporters who were not respondents in the investigation was necessary to achieve the purpose of the antidumping law).

[109]Cf. United States v. Socony-Vacuum Oil Co., 310 U.S. 150, 226 (1940) ("Though employees of the government may have known of those programs and winked at them or tacitly approved them, no immunity would have thereby been obtained. For Congress had specified the precise manner and method of securing immunity [in the National Industrial Recovery Act]. None other would suffice . . . ."); see also Otter Tail Power Co. v. United States, 410 U.S. 366, 378-79 (1973).

****

ILLUSTRATIVE EXAMPLE M

Situation: Six U.S. producers of product Q have initiated an antidumping action alleging that imports of Q from country Sigma at less than fair value are causing material injury to the U.S. Q industry. The ITC has made a preliminary decision that there is a reasonable indication that the U.S. industry is suffering material injury from Q imported from Sigma. The Department of Commerce has preliminarily concluded that the foreign market value of Q imported into the United States by Sigma's Q producers exceeds the price at which they are selling Q in this country by margins of 10 to 40 percent. Sigma's Q producers jointly initiate discussions with the Department of Commerce that lead to suspension of the investigation in accordance with Section 734 of the Tariff Act of 1930, 19 U.S.C. 1673c. The suspension agreement provides that each of Sigma's Q producers will sell product Q in the United States at no less than its individual foreign market value, as determined periodically by the Department of Commerce in accordance with the Tariff Act. Before determining to suspend the investigation, the Department of Commerce provides copies of the proposed agreement to the U.S. Q producers, who jointly advise the Department that they do not object to the suspension of the investigation on the terms proposed. The Department also determines that suspension of the investigation would be in the public interest. As a result of the suspension agreement, prices in the United States of Q imported from Sigma rise by an average of 25 percent from the prices that prevailed before the antidumping action was initiated.

Discussion: While an unsupervised agreement among foreign firms to raise their U.S. sales prices ordinarily would violate the Sherman Act, the suspension agreement outlined above qualifies for an implied immunity from the antitrust laws. As demonstrated here, the parties have engaged only in conduct contemplated by the Tariff Act and none of the participants have engaged in conduct beyond what is necessary to implement that statutory scheme.

****

ILLUSTRATIVE EXAMPLE N

Situation: The Export Association is a Webb-Pomerene association that has filed the appropriate certificates and reports with the Commission. The Association exports a commodity to markets around the world, and fixes the price at which all of its members sell the commodity in the foreign markets. Nearly 80 percent of all U.S. producers of the commodity belong to the Association, and on a world-wide level, the Association's members account for approximately 40 percent of annual sales.

Discussion: The Webb-Pomerene Act addresses only the question of antitrust liability under U.S. law. Although the U.S. antitrust laws confer an immunity on such associations, the Act does not purport to confer immunity under the law of any foreign country, nor does the Act compel the members of a Webb-Pomerene association to act in any particular way. Thus, a foreign government retains the ability to initiate proceedings if such an association allegedly violates that country's competition law.

****

4. PERSONAL JURISDICTION AND PROCEDURAL RULES

4.1 Personal Jurisdiction and Venue

The Agencies will bring suit only if they conclude that personal jurisdiction exists under the due process clause of the U.S. Constitution.[110] The Constitution requires that the defendant have affiliating or minimum contacts with the United States, such that the proceeding comports with "fair play and substantial justice."[111]

Section 12 of the Clayton Act, 15 U.S.C. 22, provides that any suit under the antitrust laws against a corporation may be brought in the judicial district where it is an inhabitant, where it may be found, or where it transacts business. The concept of transacting business is interpreted pragmatically by the Agencies. Thus, a company may transact business in a particular district directly through an agent, or through a related corporation that is actually the "alter ego" of the foreign party.[112]

4.2 Investigatory Practice Relating to Foreign Nations

In conducting investigations that require documents that are located outside the United States, or contacts with persons located outside the United States, the Agencies first consider requests for voluntary cooperation when practical and consistent with enforcement objectives. When compulsory measures are needed, they seek whenever possible to work with the foreign government involved. U.S. law also provides authority in some circumstances for the use of compulsory measures directed

---

[110]See also International Shoe Co. v. Washington, 326 U.S. 310 (1945); Asahi Metal Industry Co. Ltd. v. Superior Court, 480 U.S. 102 (1987).

[111]Go-Video, Inc. v. Akai Elec. Co., Ltd., 885 F.2d 1406, 1414 (9th Cir. 1989); Wells Fargo & Co. v. Wells Fargo Express Co., 556 F.2d 406, 418 (9th Cir. 1977). To establish jurisdiction, parties must also be served in accordance with the Federal Rules of Civil Procedure or other relevant authority. Fed. R. Civ. P. 4(k); 15 U.S.C. 22, 44.

[112]See, e.g., Letter from Donald S. Clark, Secretary of the Federal Trade Commission, to Caswell O. Hobbs, Esq., Morgan, Lewis & Bockius, Jan. 17, 1990 (Re: Petition to Quash Subpoena Nippon Sheet Glass, et al., File No. 891-0088, at page 3) ("The Commission . . . may exercise jurisdiction over and serve process on, a foreign entity that has a related company in the United States acting as its agent or alter ego."); see also Fed. R. Civ. P. 4; Volkswagenwerk AG v. Schlunk, 486 U.S. 694, 707-708 (1988); United States v. Scophony Corp., 333 U.S. 795, 810-818 (1948).

to parties over whom the courts have personal jurisdiction, which the Agencies may use when other efforts to obtain information have been exhausted or would be unavailing.[113]

Conflicts can arise, however, where foreign statutes purport to prevent persons from disclosing documents or information for use in U.S. proceedings. However, the mere existence of such statutes does not excuse noncompliance with a request for information from one of the Agencies.[114] To enable the Agencies to obtain evidence located abroad more effectively, as noted in Section 2.91 above, Congress recently has enacted legislation authorizing the Agencies to negotiate bilateral agreements with foreign governments or antitrust enforcement agencies to facilitate the exchange of documents and evidence in civil and criminal investigations.[115]

4.22 Hart-Scott-Rodino: Special Foreign Commerce Rules

As noted above in Section 2.4, qualifying mergers and acquisitions, defined both in terms of size of party and size of transaction, must be reported to the Agencies, along with certain information about the parties and the transaction, prior to their consummation, pursuant to the HSR Amendments to the Clayton Act, 15 U.S.C. 18a.

In some instances, the HSR implementing regulations exempt otherwise reportable foreign transactions.[116] First, some acquisitions by U.S. persons are exempt. Acquisitions of foreign assets by a U.S. person are exempt when (i) no sales in or into the United States are attributable to those assets, or (ii) some sales in or into the United States are attributable to those assets, but the acquiring person would not hold assets of the acquired person to which $25 million or more of such sales in the acquired person's most recent fiscal year were attributable.[117] Acquisitions by a U.S. person of voting securities of a foreign issuer are exempt unless the issuer holds assets in the United States having an aggregate book value of $15 million or more, or made aggregate sales in or into the United States of $25 million or more in its most recent fiscal year.[118]

---

[113]For example, 28 U.S.C. 1783(a) (1988) authorizes a U.S. court to order the issuance of a subpoena "requiring the appearance as a witness before it, or before a person or body designated by it, of a national or resident of the United States who is in a foreign country, or requiring the production of a specified document or other thing by him," under circumstances spelled out in the statute.

[114]See Societe Internationale pour Participations Industrielles et Commerciales, S.A. v. Rogers, 357 U.S. 197 (1958).

[115]International Antitrust Enforcement Assistance Act of 1994, Pub. L. No. 103-438, 108 Stat. 4597 (1994).

[116]See 16 C.F.R. 802.50-52 (1994).

[117]See 16 C.F.R. 802.50(a) (1994).

[118]See 16 C.F.R. 802.50(b) (1994).

Second, some acquisitions by foreign persons are exempt. An exemption exists for acquisitions by foreign persons if (i) the acquisition is of voting securities of a foreign issuer and would not confer control of a U.S. issuer having annual net sales or total assets of $25 million or more, or of any issuer with assets located in the United States having a book value of $15 million or more; or (ii) the acquired person is also a foreign person and the aggregate annual net sales of the merging firms in or into the United States is less than $110 million and their aggregate total assets in the United States are less than $110 million.[119] In addition, an acquisition by a foreign person of assets located outside the United States is exempt. Acquisitions by foreign persons of U.S. issuers or assets are not exempt.

Finally, acquisitions are exempt if the ultimate parent entity of either the acquiring or the acquired person is controlled by a foreign state, and the acquisition is of assets located within that foreign state, or of voting securities of an issuer organized under its laws.[120] The HSR rules are necessarily technical, and should be consulted rather than relying on the summary description herein.

United States Department of Justice and Federal Trade Commission

ANTITRUST ENFORCEMENT GUIDELINES FOR INTERNATIONAL OPERATIONS

April 1995

---

[119]See 16 C.F.R. 802.51 (1994).

[120]See 16 C.F.R. 802.52 (1994).

K. Selected Provisions of the Internal Revenue Code

Source: 26 U.S.C. § 1 *et seq.*

Website information:

http://www.irs.gov
This is the website of the International Revenue Service and includes links to the sections of the Internal Revenue Code, Regulations and other useful documents.

SELECTED PROVISIONS OF THE
INTERNAL REVENUE CODE

§ 1. Tax imposed.

(a) Married individuals filing joint returns and surviving spouses.

There is hereby imposed on the taxable income of --

(1) every married individual (as defined in section 7703) who makes a single return jointly with his spouse under section 6013, and

If taxable income is:	The tax is:
Not over $36,900...............	15% of taxable income.
Over $36,900 but not over $89,150	$5,535, plus 28% of the excess over $36,900.
Over $89,150 but not over $140,000	$20,165, plus 31% of the excess over $89,150.
Over $140,000 but not over $250,000	$35,928.50, plus 36% of the excess over $140,000.
Over $250,000....................	$75,528.50, plus 39.6% of the excess over $250,000.

(b) Heads of households.

There is hereby imposed on the taxable income of every head of a household (as defined in section 2(b)) a tax determined in accordance with the following table:

If taxable income is:	The tax is:
Not over $29,600.................	15% of taxable income.
Over $29,600 but not over $76,400	$4,440, plus 28% of the excess over $29,600.
Over $76,400 but not over $127,500	$17,544, plus 31% of the excess over $76,400.
Over $127,500 but not over $250,000	$33,385, plus 36% of the excess over $127,500.
Over $250,000....................	$77,485, plus 39.6% of the excess over $250,000.

(c) Unmarried individuals (other than surviving spouses and heads of households).

There is hereby imposed on the taxable income of every individual (other than a surviving spouse as defined in section 2(a) or the head of a household as defined in section 2(b)) who is not a married individual (as defined in section 7703) a tax determined in accordance with the following table:

If taxable income is:	The tax is:
Not over $22,100................	15% of taxable income.
Over $22,100 but not over $53,500	$3,315, plus 28% of the excess over $22,100.
Over $53,500 but not over $115,000	$12,107, plus 31% of the excess over $53,500.
Over $115,000 but not over $250,000	$31,172, plus 36% of the excess over $115,000.
Over $250,000....................	$79,772, plus 39.6% of the excess over $250,000.

(d) Married individuals filing separate returns.

There is hereby imposed on the taxable income of every married individual (as defined in section 7703) who does not make a single return jointly with his spouse under section 6013, a tax determined in accordance with the following table:

If taxable income is:	The tax is:
Not over $18,450..............	15% of taxable income.
Over $18,450 but not over $44,575	$2,767.50, plus 28% of the excess over $18,450.
Over $44,575 but not over $70,000	$10,082.50, plus 31% of the excess over $44,575.
Over $70,000 but not over $125,000	$17,964.25, plus 36% of the excess over $70,000.
Over $125,000..................	$37,764.25, plus 39.6% of the excess over $125,000.

(e) Estates and trusts.

There is hereby imposed on the taxable income of --

(1) every estate, and

(2) every trust, taxable under this subsection a tax determined in accordance with the following table:

If taxable income is:	The tax is:
Not over $1,500.................	15% of taxable income.
Over $1,500 but not over $3,500	$225, plus 28% of the excess over $1,500.
Over $3,500 but not over $5,500	$785, plus 31% of the excess over $3,500.
Over $5,500 but not over $7,500	$1,405, plus 36% of the excess over $5,500.
Over $7,500....................	$2,125, plus 39.6% of the excess over $7,500.

(f) Adjustments in tax tables so that inflation will not result in tax increases.

(1) In general. Not later than December 15 of 1993, and each subsequent calendar year, the Secretary shall prescribe tables which shall apply in lieu of the tables contained in subsections (a), (b), (c), (d), and (e) with respect to taxable years beginning in the succeeding calendar year.

* * * *

(h) Maximum capital gains rate.
(1) In general. If a taxpayer has a net capital gain for any taxable year, the tax imposed by this section for such taxable year shall not exceed the sum of--
(A) a tax computed at the rates and in the same manner as if this subsection had not been enacted on the greater of--
(i) taxable income reduced by the net capital gain, or
(ii) the lesser of--
(I) the amount of taxable income taxed at a rate below 28 percent, or
(II) taxable income reduced by the adjusted net capital gain, plus
(B) 10 percent of so much of the adjusted net capital gain (or, if less, taxable income) as does not exceed the excess (if any) of --
(i) the amount of taxable income which would (without regard to this paragraph) be taxed at a rate below 28 percent, over
(ii) the taxable income reduced by the adjusted net capital gain;
(C) 20 percent of the adjusted net capital gain (or, if less, taxable income) in excess of the amount on which a tax is determined under subparagraph (B);
(D) 25 percent of the excess (if any) of --
(i) the unrecaptured section 1250 gain (or, if less, the net capital gain), over
(ii) the excess (if any) of --
(I) the sum of the amount on which tax is determined under subparagraph (A) plus the net capital gain, over
(II) taxable income; and

378

(E) 28 percent of the amount of taxable income in excess of the sum of the amounts on which tax is determined under the preceding subparagraphs of this paragraph.

(2) Reduced capital gain rates for qualified 5-year gain.--

(A) Reduction in 10-percent rate.--In the case of any taxable year beginning after December 31, 2000, the rate under paragraph (1)(B) shall be 8 percent with respect to so much of the amount to which the 10-percent rate would otherwise apply as does not exceed qualified 5-year gain, and 10 percent with respect to the remainder of such amount.

(B) Reduction in 20-percent rate.--The rate under paragraph (1)(C) shall be 18 percent with respect to so much of the amount to which the 20-percent rate would otherwise apply as does not exceed the lesser of --

(i) the excess of qualified 5-year gain over the amount of such gain taken into account under subparagraph (A) of this paragraph; or

(ii) the amount of qualified 5-year gain (determined by taking into account only property the holding period for which begins after December 31, 2000), and 20 percent with respect to the remainder of such amount. For purposes of determining under the preceding sentence whether the holding period of property begins after December 31, 2000, the holding period of property acquired pursuant to the exercise of an option (or other right or obligation to acquire property) shall include the period such option (or other right or obligation) was held.

* * * *

(9) **Qualified 5-year gain.** For purposes of this subsection, the term qualified 5-year gain' means the amount of long-term capital gain which would be computed for the taxable year if only gains from the sale or exchange of property held by the taxpayer for more than 5 years were taken into account. The determination under the preceding sentence shall be made without regard to collectibles gain, unrecaptured section 1250 gain (determined without regard to subparagraph (B) of paragraph (6)), section 1202 gain, or mid-term gain.

§ 11. Tax imposed.

(a) Corporations in general.

A tax is hereby imposed for each taxable year on the taxable income of every corporation.

(b) Amount of tax.

(1) In general. The amount of the tax imposed by subsection (a) shall be the sum of --

(A) 15 percent of so much of the taxable income as does not exceed $50,000,

(B) 25 percent of so much of the taxable income as exceeds $50,000 but does not exceed $75,000,

(C) 34 percent of so much of the taxable income as exceeds $75,000 but does not exceed $10,000,000, and

(D) 35 percent of so much of the taxable income as exceeds $10,000,000.

In the case of a corporation which has taxable income in excess of $100,000 for any taxable year, the amount of tax determined under the preceding sentence for such taxable year shall be increased by the lesser of (i) 5 percent of such excess, or (ii) $11,750. In the case of a corporation which has taxable income in excess of $15,000,000, the amount of the tax determined under the foregoing provisions of this paragraph shall be increased by an additional amount equal to the lesser of (i) 3 percent of such excess, or (ii) $100,000.

(2) Certain personal service corporations not eligible for graduated rates. Notwithstanding paragraph (1), the amount of the tax imposed by subsection (a) on the taxable income of a qualified personal service corporation (as defined in section 448(d)(2)) shall be equal to 35 percent of the taxable income.

(c) Exceptions.

Subsection (a) shall not apply to a corporation subject to a tax imposed by --

(1) section 594 (relating to mutual savings banks conducting life insurance business),

(2) subchapter L (sec. 801 and following, relating to insurance companies), or

(3) subchapter M (sec. 851 and following, relating to regulated investment companies and real estate investment trusts).

(d) Foreign corporations.

In the case of a foreign corporation, the taxes imposed by subsection (a) and section 55 shall apply only as provided by section 882.

§ 61. Gross income defined.

(a) General definition.

Except as otherwise provided in this subtitle, gross income means all income from whatever source derived, including (but not limited to) the following items:

(1) Compensation for services, including fees, commissions, fringe benefits, and similar items;

(2) Gross income derived from business;

(3) Gains derived from dealings in property;

(4) Interest;

(5) Rents;

(6) Royalties;

(7) Dividends;

(8) Alimony and separate maintenance payments;

(9) Annuities;

(10) Income from life insurance and endowment contracts;

(11) Pensions;

(12) Income from discharge of indebtedness;

(13) Distributive share of partnership gross income;

(14) Income in respect of a decedent; and

(15) Income from an interest in an estate or trust.

(b) Cross references.

For items specifically included in gross income, see part II (sec. 71 and following). For items specifically excluded from gross income, see part III 101 and following).

§ 63. Taxable income defined.

(a) In general.

Except as provided in subsection (b), for purposes of this subtitle, the term "taxable income" means gross income minus the deductions allowed by this chapter (other than the standard deduction).

§ 78. Dividends received from certain foreign corporations by domestic corporations choosing foreign tax credit.

If a domestic corporation chooses to have the benefits of subpart A of part III of subchapter N (relating to foreign tax credit) for any taxable year, an amount equal to the taxes deemed to be paid by such corporation under section 902(a) (relating to credit for corporate stockholder in foreign corporation) or under section 960(a)(1) (relating to taxes paid by foreign corporation) for such taxable year shall be treated for purposes of this title (other than section 245) as a dividend received by such domestic corporation from the foreign corporation.

§ 164. Taxes.

(a) General rule.

Except as otherwise provided in this section, the following taxes shall be allowed as a deduction for the taxable year within which paid or accrued:

(1) State and local, and foreign, real property taxes.

(2) State and local personal property taxes.

(3) State and local, and foreign, income, war profits, and excess profits taxes.

(4) The GST tax imposed on income distributions.

(5) The environmental tax imposed by section 59A.

In addition, there shall be allowed as a deduction State and local, and foreign, taxes not described in the preceding sentence which are paid or accrued within the taxable year in carrying on a trade or business or an activity described in section 212 (relating to expenses for production of income).

Notwithstanding the preceding sentence, any tax (not described in the first sentence of this subsection) which is paid or accrued by the taxpayer in connection with an acquisition or disposition of property shall be treated as part of the cost of the acquired property or, in the case of a disposition, as a reduction in the amount realized on the disposition.

§ 275. Certain taxes.

(a) General rule.

No deduction shall be allowed for the following taxes:

(4) Income, war profits, and excess profits taxes imposed by the authority of any foreign country or possession of the United States if --

(A) the taxpayer chooses to take to any extent the benefits of section 901, or

(B) such taxes are paid or accrued with respect to foreign trade income (within the meaning of section 923(b)) of a FSC.

§ 301. Distributions of property.

(a) In general. Except as otherwise provided in this chapter, a distribution of property (as defined in section 317(a)) made by a corporation to a shareholder with respect to its stock shall be treated in the manner provided in subsection (c).

(b) Amount distributed.

(1) General rule. For purposes of this section, the amount of any distribution shall be the amount of money received, plus the fair market value of the other property received.

(2) Reduction for liabilities. The amount of any distribution determined under paragraph (1) shall be reduced (but not below zero) by --

(A) the amount of any liability of the corporation assumed by the shareholder in connection with the distribution, and

(B) the amount of any liability to which the property received by the shareholder is subject immediately before, and immediately after, the distribution.

(3) Determination of fair market value. For purposes of this section, fair market value shall be determined as of the date of the distribution.

(c) Amount taxable. In the case of a distribution to which subsection (a) applies --

(1) Amount constituting dividend. That portion of the distribution which is a dividend (as defined in section 316) shall be included in gross income.

(2) Amount applied against basis. That portion of the distribution which is not a dividend shall be applied against and reduce the adjusted basis of the stock.

(3) Amount in excess of basis.

(A) In general. Except as provided in subparagraph (B), that portion of the distribution which is not a dividend, to the extent that it exceeds the adjusted basis of the stock, shall be treated as gain from the sale or exchange of property.

(B) Distributions out of increase in value accrued before March 1, 1913. That portion of the distribution which is not a dividend, to the extent that it exceeds the adjusted basis of the stock and to the extent that it is out of increase in value accrued before March 1, 1913, shall be exempt from tax.

§ 316. Dividend defined.

(a) General rule. For purposes of this subtitle, the term "dividend" means any distribution of property made by a corporation to its shareholders --

(1) out of its earnings and profits accumulated after February 28, 1913, or

(2) out of its earnings and profits of the taxable year (computed as of the close of the taxable year without diminution by reason of any distributions made during the taxable year), without regard to the amount of the earnings and profits at the time the distribution was made.

Except as otherwise provided in this subtitle, every distribution is made out of earnings and profits to the extent thereof, and from the most recently accumulated earnings and profits. To the extent that any distribution is, under any provision of this subchapter, treated as a distribution of property to which section 301 applies, such distribution shall be treated as a distribution of property for purposes of this subsection.

(b) Special rules.

(1) Certain insurance company dividends. The definition in subsection (a) shall not apply to the term "dividend" as used in subchapter L in any case where the reference is to dividends of insurance companies paid to policyholders as such.

(2) Distributions by personal holding companies.

(A) In the case of a corporation which --

(i) under the law applicable to the taxable year in which the distribution is made, is a personal holding company (as defined in section 542), or

(ii) for the taxable year in respect of which the distribution is made under section 563(b) (relating to dividends paid after the close of the taxable year), or section 547 (relating to deficiency dividends), or the corresponding provisions of prior law, is a personal holding company under the law applicable to such taxable year, the term "dividend" also means any distribution of property (whether or not a dividend as defined in subsection (a) made by the corporation to its shareholders, to the extent of its undistributed personal holding company income (determined under section 545 without regard to distributions under this paragraph) for such year.

(B) For purposes of subparagraph (A), the term "distribution of property" includes a distribution in complete liquidation occurring within 24 months after the adoption of a plan of liquidation, but --

(i) only to the extent of the amounts distributed to distributees other than corporate shareholders, and

(ii) only to the extent that the corporation designates such amounts as a dividend distribution and duly notifies such distributees of such designation, under regulations prescribed by the Secretary, but

(iii) not in excess of the sum of such distributees' allocable share of the undistributed personal holding company income for such year, computed without regard to this subparagraph or section 562(b).

(3) Deficiency dividend distributions by a regulated investment company or real estate investment trust. The term "dividend" also means any distribution of property (whether or not a dividend as defined in subsection (a)) which constitutes a "deficiency dividend" as defined in section 860(f).

§ 332. Complete liquidations of subsidiaries

(a) General rule.

No gain or loss shall be recognized on the receipt by a corporation of property distributed in complete liquidation of another corporation.

§ 351. Transfer to corporation controlled by transferor.

(a) General rule.

No gain or loss shall be recognized if property is transferred to a corporation by one or more persons solely in exchange for stock in such corporation and immediately after the exchange such person or persons are in control (as defined in section 368(c)) of the corporation.

(b) Receipt of property.

If subsection (a) would apply to an exchange but for the fact that there is received, in addition to the stock permitted to be received under subsection (a), other property or money, then --

(1) gain (if any) to such recipient shall be recognized, but not in excess of --

(A) the amount of money received, plus

(B) the fair market value of such other property received; and

(2) no loss to such recipient shall be recognized.

(c) Special rules where distribution to shareholders.

(1) In general. In determining control for purposes of this section, the fact that any corporate transferor distributes part or all of the stock in the corporation which it receives in the exchange to its shareholders shall not be taken into account.

(2) Special rule for section 355. If the requirements of section 355 (or so much of section 356 as relates to section 355) are met with respect to a distribution described in paragraph (1), then, solely for purposes of determining the tax treatment of the transfers of property to the controlled corporation by the distributing corporation, the fact that the shareholders of the distributing corporation dispose of part or all of the distributed stock, or the fact that the corporation whose stock was distributed issues additional stock, shall not be taken into account in determining control for purposes of this section.

(d) Services, certain indebtedness, and accrued interest not treated as property.

For purposes of this section, stock issued for --

(1) services,

(2) indebtedness of the transferee corporation which is not evidenced by a security, or

(3) interest on indebtedness of the transferee corporation which accrued on or after the beginning of the transferor's holding period for the debt, shall not be considered as issued in return for property.

§ 367. Foreign corporations.

(a) Transfers of property from the United States.

(1) General rule. If, in connection with any exchange described in section 332, 351, 354, 356, or 361, a United States person transfers property to a foreign corporation, such foreign corporation shall not, for purposes of determining the extent to which gain shall be recognized on such transfer, be considered to be a corporation.

(2) Exception for certain stock or securities. Except to the extent provided in regulations, paragraph (1) shall not apply to the transfer of stock or securities of a foreign corporation which is a party to the exchange or a party to the reorganization.

(3) Exception for transfers of certain property used in the active conduct of a trade or business.

(A) In general. Except as provided in regulations prescribed by the Secretary, paragraph (1) shall not apply to any property transferred to a foreign corporation for use by such foreign corporation in the active conduct of a trade or business outside of the United States.

(B) Paragraph not to apply to certain property. Except as provided in regulations prescribed by the Secretary, subparagraph (A) shall not apply to any --

(i) property described in paragraph (1) or (3) of section 1221 (relating to inventory and copyrights, etc.),

(ii) installment obligations, accounts receivable, or similar property,

(iii) foreign currency or other property denominated in foreign currency,

(iv) intangible property (within the meaning of section 936(h)(3)(B)), or

(v) property with respect to which the transferor is a lessor at the time of the transfer, except that this clause shall not apply if the transferee was the lessee.

(C) Transfer of foreign branch with previously deducted losses. Except as provided in regulations prescribed by the Secretary, subparagraph (A) shall not apply to gain realized on the transfer of the assets of a foreign branch of a United States person to a foreign corporation in an exchange described in paragraph (1) to the extent that --

(i) the sum of losses --

(I) which were incurred by the foreign branch before the transfer, and

(II) with respect to which a deduction was allowed to the taxpayer, exceeds

(ii) the sum of --

(I) any taxable income of such branch for a taxable year after the taxable year in which the loss was incurred and through the close of the taxable year of the transfer, and

(II) the amount which is recognized under section 904(f)(3) on account of the transfer.

Any gain recognized by reason of the preceding sentence shall be treated for purposes of this chapter as income from sources outside the United States having the same character as such losses had.

(4) Special rule for transfer of partnership interests. Except as provided in regulations prescribed by the Secretary, a transfer by a United States person of an interest in a partnership to a foreign corporation in an exchange described in paragraph (1) shall, for purposes of this subsection, be treated as a transfer to such corporation of such person's pro rata share of the assets of the partnership.

(5) Paragraphs (2) and (3) not to apply to certain section 361 transactions. Paragraphs (2) and (3) shall not apply in the case of an exchange described in subsection (a) or (b) of section 361. Subject to such basis adjustments and such other conditions as shall be provided in regulations, the preceding sentence shall not apply if the transferor corporation is controlled (within the meaning of section 368(c)), by 5 or fewer domestic corporations. For purposes of the preceding sentence, all members of the same affiliated group (within the meaning of section 1504) shall be treated as 1 corporation.

(6) Secretary may exempt certain transactions from application of this subsection. Paragraph (1) shall not apply to the transfer of any property which the Secretary, in order to carry out the purposes of this subsection, designates by regulation.

(b) Other transfers.

(1) Effect of section to be determined under regulations. In the case of any exchange described in section 332, 351, 354, 355, 356, or 361 in connection with which there is no transfer of property described in subsection (a)(1), a foreign corporation shall be considered to be a corporation except to the extent provided in regulations prescribed by the Secretary which are necessary or appropriate to prevent the avoidance of Federal income taxes.

(2) Regulations relating to sale or exchange of stock in foreign corporations. The regulations prescribed pursuant to paragraph (1) shall include (but shall not be limited to) regulations dealing with the sale or exchange of stock or securities in a foreign corporation by a United States person, including regulations providing --

(A) the circumstances under which --

(i) gain shall be recognized currently, or amounts included in gross income currently as a dividend, or both, or

(ii) gain or other amounts may be deferred for inclusion in the gross income of a shareholder (or his successor in interest) at a later date, and

(B) the extent to which adjustments shall be made to earnings and profits, basis of stock or securities, and basis of assets.

(c) Transactions to be treated as exchanges.

(1) Section 355 distribution. For purposes of this section, any distribution described in section 355 (or so much of section 356 as relates to section 355) shall be treated as an exchange whether or not it is an exchange.

(2) Contribution of capital to controlled corporations. For purposes of this chapter, any transfer of property to a foreign corporation as a contribution to the capital of such corporation by one or more persons who, immediately after the transfer, own (within the meaning of section 318) stock possessing at least 80 percent of the total combined voting power of all classes of stock of such corporation entitled to vote shall be treated as an exchange of such property for stock of the foreign corporation equal in value to the fair market value of the property transferred.

(d) Special rules relating to transfers of intangibles.

(1) In general. Except as provided in regulations prescribed by the Secretary, if a United States person transfers any intangible property (within the meaning of section 936(h)(3)(B)) to a foreign corporation in an exchange described in section 351 or 361 --

(A) subsection (a) shall not apply to the transfer of such property, and

(B) the provisions of this subsection shall apply to such transfer.

(2) Transfer of intangibles treated as transfer pursuant to sale of contingent payments.

(A) In general. If paragraph (1) applies to any transfer, the United States person transferring such property shall be treated as --

(i) having sold such property in exchange for payments which are contingent upon the productivity, use, or disposition of such property, and

(ii) receiving amounts which reasonably reflect the amounts which would have been received --

(I) annually in the form of such payments over the useful life of such property, or

(II) in the case of a disposition following such transfer (whether direct or indirect), at the time of the disposition.

The amounts taken into account under clause (ii) shall be commensurate with the income attributable to the intangible.

(B) **Effect on earnings and profits.** For purposes of this chapter, the earnings and profits of a foreign corporation to which the intangible property was transferred shall be reduced by the amount required to be included in the income of the transferor of the intangible property under subparagraph (A)(ii).

(C) Amounts received treated as ordinary income. For purposes of this chapter, any amount included in gross income by reason of this subsection shall be treated as ordinary income.

(3) Regulations relating to transfers of intangibles to partnerships. The Secretary may provide by regulations that the rules of paragraph (2) also apply to the transfer of intangible property by a United States person to a partnership in circumstances consistent with the purposes of this subsection.

(e) Treatment of distributions described in section 355 or liquidations under section 332.

(1) Distributions described in section 355. In the case of any distribution described in section 355 (or so much of section 356 as relates to section 355) by a domestic corporation to a person who is not a United States person, to the extent provided in regulations, gain shall be recognized under principles similar to the principles of this section.

(2) Liquidations under section 332. In the case of any liquidation to which section 332 applies, except as provided in regulations, subsections (a) and (b)(1) of section 337 shall not apply where the 80-percent distributee (as defined in section 337(c)) is a foreign corporation.

§ 482. Allocation of income and deductions among taxpayers.

In any case of two or more organizations, trades, or businesses (whether or not incorporated, whether or not organized in the United States, and whether or not affiliated) owned or controlled directly or indirectly by the same interests, the Secretary may distribute, apportion, or allocate gross income, deductions, credits, or allowances between or among such organizations, trades, or businesses, if he determines that such distribution, apportionment, or allocation is necessary in order to prevent evasion of taxes or clearly to reflect the income of any of such organizations, trades, or businesses. In the case of any transfer (or license) of intangible property (within the meaning of section 936(h)(3)(B)), the income with respect to such transfer or license shall be commensurate with the income attributable to the intangible.

§ 861. Income from sources within the United States.

(a) Gross income from sources within United States.

The following items of gross income shall be treated as income from sources within the United States:

(1) Interest. Interest from the United States, or the District of Columbia, and interest on bonds, notes, or other interest-bearing obligations of noncorporate residents or domestic corporations not including --

(A) interest from a resident alien individual or domestic corporation, if such individual or corporation meets the 80-percent foreign business requirements of subsection (c)(1), and

(B) interest --

(i) on deposits with a foreign branch of a domestic corporation or a domestic partnership if such branch is engaged in the commercial banking business, and

(ii) on amounts satisfying the requirements of subparagraph (B) of section 871(i)(3) which are paid by a foreign branch of a domestic corporation or a domestic partnership.

(2) Dividends. The amount received as dividends --

(A) from a domestic corporation other than a corporation which has an election in effect under section 936, or

(B) from a foreign corporation unless less than 25 percent of the gross income from all sources of such foreign corporation for the 3-year period ending with the close of its taxable year preceding the declaration of such dividends (or for such part of such period as the corporation has been in existence) was effectively connected (or treated as effectively connected other than income described in section 884(d)(2)) with the conduct of a trade or business within the United States; but only in an amount which bears the same ratio to such dividends as the gross income of the corporation for such period which was effectively connected (or treated as effectively connected other than income described in section 884(d)(2)) with the conduct of a trade or business within the United States bears to its gross income from all sources; but dividends (other than dividends for which a deduction is allowable under section 245(b)) from a foreign corporation shall, for purposes of subpart A of part III (relating to foreign tax credit), be treated as income from sources without the United States to the extent (and only to the extent) exceeding the amount which is 100/70th of the amount of the deduction allowable under section 245 in respect of such dividends, or

(C) from a foreign corporation to the extent that such amount is required by section 243(e) (relating to certain dividends from foreign corporations) to be treated as dividends from a domestic corporation which is subject to taxation under this chapter, and to such extent subparagraph (B) shall not apply to such amount, or

(D) from a DISC or former DISC (as defined in section 992(a)) except to the extent attributable (as determined under regulations prescribed by the Secretary) to qualified export receipts described in section 993(a)(1) (other than interest and gains described in section 995(b)(1)).

In the case of any dividend from a 20-percent owned corporation (as defined in section 243(c)(2)), subparagraph (B) shall be applied by substituting "100/80th" for "100/70th".

(3) Personal services. Compensation for labor or personal services performed in the United States; except that compensation for labor or services performed in the United States shall not be deemed to be income from sources within the United States if --

(A) the labor or services are performed by a nonresident alien individual temporarily present in the United States for a period or periods not exceeding a total of 90 days during the taxable year,

(B) such compensation does not exceed $3,000 in the aggregate, and

(C) the compensation is for labor or services performed as an employee of or under a contract with --

(i) a nonresident alien, foreign partnership, or foreign corporation, not engaged in trade or business within the United States, or

(ii) an individual who is a citizen or resident of the United States, a domestic partnership, or a domestic corporation, if such labor or services are performed for an office or place of business maintained in a foreign country or in a possession of the United States by such individual, partnership, or corporation.

(4) Rentals and royalties. Rentals or royalties from property located in the United States or from any interest in such property, including rentals or royalties for the use of or for the privilege of using in the United States patents, copyrights, secret processes and formulas, good will, trade-marks, trade brands, franchises, and other like property.

(5) Disposition of United States real property interest. Gains, profits, and income from the disposition of a United States real property interest (as defined in section 897(c)).

(6) Sale or exchange of inventory property. Gains, profits, and income derived from the purchase of inventory property (within the meaning of section 865(i)(1)) without the United States (other than within a possession of the United States) and its sale or exchange within the United States.

(7) Amounts received as underwriting income (as defined in section 832(b)(3)) derived from the issuing (or reinsuring) of any insurance or annuity contract --

(8) Social security benefits. Any social security benefit (as defined in section 86(d)).

(b) Taxable income from sources within United States.

From the items of gross income specified in subsection (a) as being income from sources within the United States there shall be deducted the expenses, losses, and other deductions properly apportioned or allocated thereto and a ratable part of any expenses, losses, or other deductions which cannot definitely be allocated to some item or class of gross income. The remainder, if any, shall be included in full as taxable income from sources within the United States. In the case of an individual who does not itemize deductions, an amount equal to the standard deduction shall be considered a deduction which cannot definitely be allocated to some item or class of gross income.

(c) Foreign business requirements.

(1) Foreign business requirements.

(A) In general. An individual or corporation meets the 80-percent foreign business requirements of this paragraph if it is shown to the satisfaction of the Secretary that at least 80 percent of the gross income from all sources of such individual or corporation for the testing period is active foreign business income.

(B) Active foreign business income. For purposes of subparagraph (A), the term "active foreign business income" means gross income which --

(i) is derived from sources outside the United States (as determined under this subchapter) or, in the case of a corporation, is attributable to income so derived by a subsidiary of such corporation, and

(ii) is attributable to the active conduct of a trade or business in a foreign country or possession of the United States by the individual or corporation (or by a subsidiary).

For purposes of this subparagraph, the term "subsidiary" means any corporation in which the corporation referred to in this subparagraph owns (directly or indirectly) stock meeting the requirements of section 1504(a)(2) (determined by substituting "50 percent" for "80 percent" each place it appears).

(C) Testing period. For purposes of this subsection, the term "testing period" means the 3-year period ending with the close of the taxable year of the individual or corporation preceding the payment (or such part of such period as may be applicable). If the individual or corporation has no gross income for such 3-year period (or part thereof), the testing period shall be the taxable year in which the payment is made.

(2) Look-thru where related person receives interest.

(A) In general. In the case of interest received by a related person from a resident alien individual or domestic corporation meeting the 80-percent foreign business requirements of paragraph (1), subsection (a)(1)(A) shall apply only to a percentage of such interest equal to the percentage which --

(i) the gross income of such individual or corporation for the testing period from sources outside the United States (as determined under this subchapter), is of

(ii) the total gross income of such individual or corporation for the testing period.

(B) Related person. For purposes of this paragraph, the term "related person" has the meaning given such term by section 954(d)(3), except that --

(i) such section shall be applied by substituting "the individual or corporation making the payment" for "controlled foreign corporation" each place it appears, and

(ii) such section shall be applied by substituting "10 percent or more" for "more than 50 percent" each place it appears.

(d) Special rule for application of subsection (a)(2)(B).

For purposes of subsection (a)(2)(B), if the foreign corporation has no gross income from any source for the 3-year period (or part thereof) specified, the requirements of such subsection shall be applied with respect to the taxable year of such corporation in which the payment of the dividend is made.

(e) Income from certain railroad rolling stock treated as income from sources within the United States.

(1) General rule. For purposes of subsection (a) and section 862(a), if --

(A) a taxpayer leases railroad rolling stock which is section 1245 property (as defined in section 1245(a)(3)) to a domestic common carrier by railroad or a corporation which is controlled, directly or indirectly, by one or more such common carriers, and

(B) the use under such lease is expected to be use[d] within the United States, all amounts includible in gross income by the taxpayer with respect to such railroad rolling stock (including gain from sale or other disposition of such railroad rolling stock) shall be treated as income from sources within the United States. The requirements of subparagraph (B) of the preceding sentence shall be treated as satisfied if the only expected use outside the United States is use by a person (whether or not a United States person) in Canada or Mexico on a temporary basis which is not expected to exceed a total of 90 days in any taxable year.

(2) Paragraph (1) not to apply where lessor is a member of controlled group which includes a railroad. Paragraph (1) shall not apply to a lease between two members of the same controlled group of corporations (as defined in section 1563) if any member of such group is a domestic common carrier by railroad or a switching or terminal company all of whose stock is owned by one or more domestic common carriers by railroad.

(3) Denial of foreign tax credit. No credit shall be allowed under section 901 for any payments to foreign countries with respect to any amount received by the taxpayer with respect to railroad rolling stock which is subject to paragraph (1).

§ 862. Income from sources without the United States.

(a) Gross income from sources without United States.

The following items of gross income shall be treated as income from sources without the United States:

(1) interest other than that derived from sources within the United States as provided in section 861(a)(1);

(2) dividends other than those derived from sources within the United States as provided in section 861(a)(2);

(3) compensation for labor or personal services performed without the United States;

(4) rentals or royalties from property located without the United States or from any interest in such property, including rentals or royalties for the use of or for the privilege of using without the United States patents, copyrights, secret processes and formulas, good will, trade-marks, trade brands, franchises, and other like properties;

(5) gains, profits, and income from the sale or exchange of real property located without the United States;

(6) gains, profits, and income derived from the purchase of inventory property (within the meaning of section 865(i)(1)) within the United States and its sale or exchange without the United States;

(7) underwriting income other than that derived from sources within the United States as provided in section 861(a)(7); and

(8) gains, profits, and income from the disposition of a United States real property interest (as defined in section 897(c)) when the real property is located in the Virgin Islands.

(b) Taxable income from sources without United States.

From the items of gross income specified in subsection (a) there shall be deducted the expenses, losses, and other deductions properly apportioned or allocated thereto, and a ratable part of any expenses, losses, or other deductions which cannot definitely be allocated to some item or class of gross income. The remainder, if any, shall be treated in full as taxable income from sources without the United States. In the case of an individual who does not itemize deductions, an amount equal to the standard deduction shall be considered a deduction which cannot definitely be allocated to some item or class of gross income.

§ 863. Special rules for determining source.

(a) Allocation under regulations.

Items of gross income, expenses, losses, and deductions, other than those specified in sections 861(a) and 862(a), shall be allocated or apportioned to sources within or without the United States, under regulations prescribed by the Secretary. Where items of gross income are separately allocated to sources within the United States, there shall be deducted (for the purpose of computing the taxable income therefrom) the expenses, losses, and other deductions properly apportioned or allocated thereto and a ratable part of other expenses, losses, or other deductions which cannot definitely be allocated to some item or class of gross income. The remainder, if any, shall be included in full as taxable income from sources within the United States.

(b) Income partly from within and partly from without the United States.

In the case of gross income derived from sources partly within and partly without the United States, the taxable income may first be computed by deducting the expenses, losses, or other deductions apportioned or allocated thereto and a ratable part of any expenses, losses, or other deductions which cannot definitely be allocated to some item or class of gross income; and the portion of such taxable income attributable to sources within the United States may be determined by processes or formulas of general apportionment prescribed by the Secretary. Gains, profits, and income --

(1) from services rendered partly within and partly without the United States,

(2) from the sale or exchange of inventory property (within the meaning of section 865(i)(1)) produced (in whole or in part) by the taxpayer within and sold or exchanged without the United States, or produced (in whole or in part) by the taxpayer without and sold or exchanged within the United States, or

(3) derived from the purchase of inventory property (within the meaning of section 865(i)(1)) within a possession of the United States and its sale or exchange within the United States, shall be treated as derived partly from sources within and partly from sources without the United States.

(c) Source rule for certain transportation income.

(1) Transportation beginning and ending in the United States. All transportation income attributable to transportation which begins and ends in the United States shall be treated as derived from sources within the United States.

(2) Other transportation having United States connection.

(A) In general. 50 percent of all transportation income attributable to transportation which --

(i) is not described in paragraph (1), and

(ii) begins or ends in the United States, shall be treated as from sources in the United States.

(B) Special rule for personal service income. Subparagraph (A) shall not apply to any transportation income which is income derived from personal services performed by the taxpayer, unless such income is attributable to transportation which --

(i) begins in the United States and ends in a possession of the United States, or

(ii) begins in a possession of the United States and ends in the United States.

In the case of transportation income derived from, or in connection with, a vessel, this subparagraph shall only apply if the taxpayer is a citizen or resident alien.

(3) Transportation income. For purposes of this subsection, the term "transportation income" means any income derived from, or in connection with --

(A) the use (or hiring or leasing for use) of a vessel or aircraft, or

(B) the performance of services directly related to the use of a vessel or aircraft.

For purposes of the preceding sentence, the term "vessel or aircraft" includes any container used in connection with a vessel or aircraft.

(d) Source rules for space and certain ocean activities.

(1) In general. Except as provided in regulations, any income derived from a space or ocean activity --

(A) if derived by a United States person, shall be sourced in the United States, and

(B) if derived by a person other than a United States person, shall be sourced outside the United States.

(2) Space or ocean activity. For purposes of paragraph (1) --

393

(A) In general. The term "space or ocean activity" means --

(i) any activity conducted in space, and

(ii) any activity conducted on or under water not within the jurisdiction (as recognized by the United States) of a foreign country, possession of the United States, or the United States.

Such term includes any activity conducted in Antarctica.

(B) Exception for certain activities. The term "space or ocean activity" shall not include --

(i) any activity giving rise to transportation income (as defined in section 863(c)),

(ii) any activity giving rise to international communications income (as defined in subsection (e)(2)), and

(iii) any activity with respect to mines, oil and gas wells, or other natural deposits to the extent within the United States or any foreign country or possession of the United States (as defined in section 638).

For purposes of applying section 638, the jurisdiction of any foreign country shall not include any jurisdiction not recognized by the United States.

(e) International communications income.

(1) Source rules.

(A) United States persons. In the case of any United States person, 50 percent of any international communications income shall be sourced in the United States and 50 percent of such income shall be sourced outside the United States.

(B) Foreign persons.

(i) In general. Except as provided in regulations or clause (ii), in the case of any person other than a United States person, any international communications income shall be sourced outside the United States.

(ii) Special rule for income attributable to office or fixed place of business in the United States. In the case of any person (other than a United States person) who maintains an office or other fixed place of business in the United States, any international communications income attributable to such office or other fixed place of business shall be sourced in the United States.

(2) Definition. For purposes of this section, the term "international communications income" includes all income derived from the transmission of communications or data from the United States to any foreign country (or possession of the United States) or from any foreign country (or possession of the United States) to the United States.

§ 864. Definitions and special rules.

(a) Produced.

For purposes of this part, the term "produced" includes created, fabricated, manufactured, extracted, processed, cured, or aged.

(b) Trade or business within the United States.

For purposes of this part, part II, and chapter 3, the term "trade or business within the United States" includes the performance of personal services within the United States at any time within the taxable year, but does not include --

(1) Performance of personal services for foreign employer. The performance of personal services --

(A) for a nonresident alien individual, foreign partnership, or foreign corporation, not engaged in trade or business within the United States, or

(B) for an office or place of business maintained in a foreign country or in a possession of the United States by an individual who is a citizen or resident of the United States or by a domestic partnership or a domestic corporation, by a nonresident alien individual temporarily present in the United States for a period or periods not exceeding a total of 90 days during the taxable year and whose compensation for such services does not exceed in the aggregate $3,000.

(2) Trading in securities or commodities.

(A) Stocks and securities.

(i) In general. Trading in stocks or securities through a resident broker, commission agent, custodian, or other independent agent.

(ii) Trading for taxpayer's own account. Trading in stocks or securities for the taxpayer's own account, whether by the taxpayer or his employees or through a resident broker, commission agent, custodian, or other agent, and whether or not any such employee or agent has discretionary authority to make decisions in effecting the transactions. This clause shall not apply in the case of a dealer in stocks or securities.

(B) Commodities.

(i) In general. Trading in commodities through a resident broker, commission agent, custodian, or other independent agent.

(ii) Trading for taxpayer's own account. Trading in commodities for the taxpayer's own account, whether by the taxpayer or his employees or through a resident broker, commission agent, custodian, or other agent, and whether or not any such employee or agent has discretionary authority to make decisions in effecting the transactions. This clause shall not apply in the case of a dealer in commodities.

(iii) Limitation. Clauses (i) and (ii) shall apply only if the commodities are of a kind customarily dealt in on an organized commodity exchange and if the transaction is of a kind customarily consummated at such place.

(C) Limitation. Subparagraphs (A)(i) and (B)(i) shall apply only if, at no time during the taxable year, the taxpayer has an office or other fixed place of business in the United States through which or by the direction of which the transactions in stocks or securities, or in commodities, as the case may be, are effected.

(c) Effectively connected income, etc.

(1) General rule. For purposes of this title --

(A) In the case of a nonresident alien individual or a foreign corporation engaged in trade or business within the United States during the taxable year, the rules set forth in paragraphs (2), (3), (4), (6), and (7) shall apply in determining the income, gain, or loss which shall be treated as effectively connected with the conduct of a trade or business within the United States.

(B) Except as provided in paragraph (6) or (7) or in section 871(d) or sections 882(d) and (e), in the case of a nonresident alien individual or a foreign corporation not engaged in trade or business within the United States during the taxable year, no income, gain, or loss shall be treated as effectively connected with the conduct of a trade or business within the United States.

(2) Periodical, etc., income from sources within United States -- factors. In determining whether income from sources within the United States of the types described in section 871(a)(1), section 871(h), section 881(a), or section 881(c), or whether gain or loss from sources within the United States from the sale or exchange of capital assets, is effectively connected with the conduct of a trade or business within the United States, the factors taken into account shall include whether --

(A) the income, gain, or loss is derived from assets used in or held for use in the conduct of such trade or business, or

(B) the activities of such trade or business were a material factor in the realization of the income, gain, or loss.

In determining whether an asset is used in or held for use in the conduct of such trade or business or whether the activities of such trade or business were a material factor in realizing an item of income, gain, or loss, due regard shall be given to whether or not such asset or such income, gain, or loss was accounted for through such trade or business.

(3) Other income from sources within United States. All income, gain, or loss from sources within the United States (other than income, gain, or loss to which paragraph (2) applies) shall be treated as effectively connected with the conduct of a trade or business within the United States.

(4) Income from sources without United States.

(A) Except as provided in subparagraphs (B) and (C), no income, gain, or loss from sources without the United States shall be treated as effectively connected with the conduct of a trade or business within the United States.

(B) Income, gain, or loss from sources without the United States shall be treated as effectively connected with the conduct of a trade or business within the United States by a nonresident alien individual or a foreign corporation if such person has an office or other fixed place of business within the United States to which such income, gain, or loss is attributable and such income, gain, or loss --

(i) consists of rents or royalties for the use of or for the privilege of using intangible property described in section 862(a)(4) derived in the active conduct of such trade or business;

(ii) consists of dividends or interest, and either is derived in the active conduct of a banking, financing, or similar business within the United States or is received by a corporation the principal business of which is trading in stocks or securities for its own account; or

(iii) is derived from the sale or exchange (outside the United States) through such office or other fixed place of business of personal property described in section 1221(1), except that this clause shall not apply if the property is sold or exchanged for use, consumption, or disposition outside the United States and an office or other fixed place of business of the taxpayer in a foreign country participated materially in such sale.

(C) In the case of a foreign corporation taxable under part I or part II of subchapter L, any income from sources without the United States which is attributable to its United States business shall be treated as effectively connected with the conduct of a trade or business within the United States.

(D) No income from sources without the United States shall be treated as effectively connected with the conduct of a trade or business within the United States if it either --

(i) consists of dividends, interest, or royalties paid by a foreign corporation in which the taxpayer owns (within the meaning of section 958(a)), or is considered as owning (by applying the ownership rules of section 958(b)), more than 50 percent of the total combined voting power of all classes of stock entitled to vote, or

(ii) is subpart F income within the meaning of section 952(a).

(5) Rules for application of paragraph (4)(B). For purposes of subparagraph (B) of paragraph (4) --

(A) in determining whether a nonresident alien individual or a foreign corporation has an office or other fixed place of business, an office or other fixed place of business of an agent shall be disregarded unless such agent (i) has the authority to negotiate and conclude contracts in the name of the nonresident alien individual or foreign corporation and regularly exercises that authority or has a stock of merchandise from which he regularly fills orders on behalf of such individual or foreign corporation, and (ii) is not a general commission agent, broker, or other agent of independent status acting in the ordinary course of his business,

(B) income, gain, or loss shall not be considered as attributable to an office or other fixed place of business within the United States unless such office or fixed place of business is a material factor in the production of such income, gain, or loss and such office or fixed place of business regularly carries on activities of the type from which such income, gain, or loss is derived, and

(C) the income, gain, or loss which shall be attributable to an office or other fixed place of business within the United States shall be the income, gain, or loss property allocable thereto, but, in the case of a sale or exchange described in clause (iii) of such subparagraph, the income which shall be treated as attributable to an office or other fixed place of business within the United States shall not exceed the income which would be derived from sources within the United States if the sale or exchange were made in the United States.

(6) Treatment of certain deferred payments, etc. For purposes of this title, in the case of any income or gain of a nonresident alien individual or a foreign corporation which --

(A) is taken into account for any taxable year, but

(B) is attributable to a sale or exchange of property or the performance of services (or any other transaction) in any other taxable year, the determination of whether such income or gain is taxable under section 871(b) or 882 (as the case may be) shall be made as if such income or gain were taken into account in such other taxable year and without regard to the requirement that the taxpayer be engaged in a trade or business within the United States during the taxable year referred to in subparagraph (A).

(7) Treatment of certain property transactions. For purposes of this title, if --

(A) any property ceases to be used or held for use in connection with the conduct of a trade or business within the United States, and

(B) such property is disposed of within 10 years after such cessation, the determination of whether any income or gain attributable to such disposition is taxable under section 871(b) or 882 (as the case may be) shall be made as if such sale or exchange occurred immediately before such cessation and without regard to the requirement that the taxpayer be engaged in a trade or business within the United States during the taxable year for which such income or gain is taken into account.

(d) Treatment of related person factoring income.

(1) In general. -- For purposes of the provisions set forth in paragraph (2), if any person acquires (directly or indirectly) a trade or service receivable from a related person, any income of such person from the trade or service receivable so acquired shall be treated as if it were interest on a loan to the obligor under the receivable.

(2) Provisions to which paragraph (1) applies. The provisions set forth in this paragraph are as follows:

(A) Part III of subchapter G of this chapter (relating to foreign personal holding companies).

(B) Section 904 (relating to limitation on foreign tax credit).

(C) Subpart F of part III of this subchapter (relating to controlled foreign corporations).

(3) Trade or service receivable. For purposes of this subsection, the term "trade or service receivable" means any account receivable or evidence of indebtedness arising out of --

(A) the disposition by a related person of property described in section 1221(1), or

(B) the performance of services by a related person.

(4) Related person. -- For purposes of this subsection, the term "related person" means --

(A) any person who is a related person (within the meaning of section 267(b)), and

(B) any United States shareholder (as defined in section 951(b)) and any person who is a related person (within the meaning of section 267(b)) to such a shareholder.

(5) Certain provisions not to apply.

(A) Certain exceptions. The following provisions shall not apply to any amount treated as interest under paragraph (1) or (6):

(i) Subparagraphs (A)(iii)(II), (B)(ii), and (C)(iii)(III) of section 904(d)(2) (relating to exceptions for export financing interest).

(ii) Subparagraph (A) of section 954(b)(3) (relating to exception where foreign base company income is less than 5 percent or $1,000,000).

(iii) Subparagraph (B) of section 954(c)(2) (relating to certain export financing).

(iv) Clause (i) of section 954(c)(3)(A) (relating to certain income received from related persons).

(B) Special rules for possessions. An amount treated as interest under paragraph (1) shall not be treated as income described in subparagraph (A) or (B) of section 936(a)(1) unless such amount is from sources within a possession of the United States (determined after the application of paragraph (1)).

(6) Special rule for certain income from loans of a controlled foreign corporation. Any income of a controlled foreign corporation (within the meaning of section 957(a)) from a loan to a person for the purpose of financing --

(A) the purchase of property described in section 1221(1) of a related person, or

(B) the payment for the performance of services by a related person, shall be treated as interest described in paragraph (1).

(7) **Exception for certain related persons doing business in same foreign country.** Paragraph (1) shall not apply to any trade or service receivable acquired by any person from a related person if --

(A) the person acquiring such receivable and such related person are created or organized under the laws of the same foreign country and such related person has a substantial part of its assets used in its trade or business located in such same foreign country, and

(B) such related person would not have derived any foreign base company income (as defined in section 954(a), determined without regard to section 954(b)(3)(A)), or any income effectively connected with the conduct of a trade or business within the United States, from such receivable if it had been collected by such related person.

(8) **Regulations.** The Secretary shall prescribe such regulations as may be necessary to prevent the avoidance of the provisions of this subsection or section 956(b)(3).

(e) Rules for allocating interest, etc.

For purposes of this subchapter --

(1) **Treatment of affiliated groups.** The taxable income of each member of an affiliated group shall be determined by allocating and apportioning interest expense of each member as if all members of such group were a single corporation.

(2) **Gross income method may not be used for interest.** All allocations and apportionments of interest expense shall be made on the basis of assets rather than gross income.

(3) **Tax-exempt assets not taken into account.** For purposes of allocating and apportioning any deductible expense, any tax-exempt asset (and any income from such an asset) shall not be taken into account. A similar rule shall apply in the case of the portion of any dividend (other than a qualifying dividend as defined in section 243(b)) equal to the deduction allowable under section 243 or 245(a) with respect to such dividend and in the case of a like portion of any stock the dividends on which would be so deductible and would not be qualifying dividends (as so defined).

(4) **Basis of stock in nonaffiliated 10-percent owned corporations adjusted for earnings and profits changes.**

(A) **In general.** For purposes of allocating and apportioning expenses on the basis of assets, the adjusted basis of any stock in a nonaffiliated 10-percent owned corporation shall be --

(i) increased by the amount of the earnings and profits of such corporation attributable to such stock and accumulated during the period the taxpayer held such stock, or

(ii) reduced (but not below zero) by any deficit in earnings and profits of such corporation attributable to such stock for such period.

(B) **Nonaffiliated 10-percent owned corporation.** For purposes of this paragraph, the term "nonaffiliated 10-percent owned corporation" means any corporation if --

(i) such corporation is not included in the taxpayer's affiliated group, and

(ii) members of such affiliated group own 10 percent or more of the total combined voting power of all classes of stock of such corporation entitled to vote.

(C) Earnings and profits of lower tier corporations taken into account.

(i) In general. If, by reason of holding stock in a nonaffiliated 10-percent owned corporation, the taxpayer is treated under clause (iii) as owning stock in another corporation with respect to which the stock ownership requirements of clause (ii) are met, the adjustment under subparagraph (A) shall include an adjustment for the amount of the earnings and profits (or deficit therein) of such other corporation which are attributable to the stock the taxpayer is so treated as owning and to the period during which the taxpayer is treated as owning such stock.

(ii) Stock ownership requirements. The stock ownership requirements of this clause are met with respect to any corporation if members of the taxpayer's affiliated group own (directly or through the application of clause (iii)) 10 percent or more of the total combined voting power of all classes of stock of such corporation entitled to vote.

(iii) Stock owned through entities. For purposes of this subparagraph, stock owned (directly or indirectly) by a corporation, partnership, or trust shall be treated as being owned proportionately by its shareholders, partners, or beneficiaries. Stock considered to be owned by a person by reason of the application of the preceding sentence, shall, for purposes of applying such sentence, be treated as actually owned by such person.

(D) Coordination with subpart F, etc. For purposes of this paragraph, proper adjustment shall be made to the earnings and profits of any corporation to take into account any earnings and profits included in gross income under section 951 or under any other provision of this title and reflected in the adjusted basis of the stock.

(5) Affiliated group. For purposes of this subsection --

(A) In general. Except as provided in subparagraph (B), the term "affiliated group" has the meaning given such term by section 1504 (determined without regard to paragraph (4) of section 1504(b)).

(B) Treatment of certain financial institutions. For purposes of subparagraph (A), any corporation described in subparagraph (C) shall be treated as an includible corporation for purposes of section 1504 only for purposes of applying such section separately to corporations so described. This subparagraph shall not apply for purposes of paragraph (6).

(C) Description. A corporation is described in this subparagraph if --

(i) such corporation is a financial institution described in section 581 or 591,

(ii) the business of such financial institution is predominantly with persons other than related persons (within the meaning of subsection (d)(4)) or their customers, and

(iii) such financial institution is required by State or Federal law to be operated separately from any other entity which is not such an institution.

(D) Treatment of bank holding companies. To the extent provided in regulations --

(i) a bank holding company (within the meaning of section 2(a) of the Bank Holding Company Act of 1956), and

(ii) any subsidiary of a financial institution described in section 581 or 591 or of any bank holding company if such subsidiary is predominantly engaged (directly or indirectly) in the active conduct of a banking, financing, or similar business, shall be treated as a corporation described in subparagraph (C).

(6) Allocation and apportionment of other expenses. Expenses other than interest which are not directly allocable or apportioned to any specific income producing activity shall be allocated and apportioned as if all members of the affiliated group were a single corporation.

(7) Regulations. The secretary shall prescribe such regulations as may be necessary or appropriate to carry out the purposes of this section, including regulations providing --

(A) for the resourcing of income of any member of an affiliated group or modifications to the consolidated return regulations to the extent such resourcing or modification is necessary to carry out the purposes of this section,

(B) for direct allocation of interest expense incurred to carry out an integrated financial transaction to any interest (or interest-type income) derived from such transaction,

(C) for the apportionment of expenses allocated to foreign source income among the members of the affiliated group and various categories of income described in section 904(d)(1),

(D) for direct allocation of interest expense in the case of indebtedness resulting in a disallowance under section 246A,

(E) for appropriate adjustments in the application of paragraph (3) in the case of an insurance company, and

(F) that this subsection shall not apply for purposes of any provision of this subchapter to the extent the Secretary determines that the application of this subsection for such purposes would not be appropriate.

§ 865. Source rules for personal property sales.

(a) General rule.

Except as otherwise provided in this section, income from the sale of personal property --

(1) by a United States resident shall be sourced in the United States, or

(2) by a nonresident shall be sourced outside the United States.

(b) Exception for inventory property.

In the case of income derived from the sale of inventory property --

(1) this section shall not apply, and

(2) such income shall be sourced under the rules of sections 861(a)(6), 862(a)(6), and 863(b).

Notwithstanding the preceding sentence, any income from the sale of any unprocessed timber which is a softwood and was cut from an area in the United States shall be sourced in the United States and the rules of sections 862(a)(6) and 863(b) shall not apply to any such income. For purposes of the preceding sentence, the term "unprocessed timber" means any log, cant, or similar form of timber.

(c) Exception for depreciable personal property.

(1) In general. Gain (not in excess of the depreciation adjustments) from the sale of depreciable personal property shall be allocated between sources in the United States and sources outside the United States --

(A) by treating the same proportion of such gain as sourced in the United States as the United States depreciation adjustments with respect to such property bear to the total depreciation adjustments, and

(B) by treating the remaining portion of such gain as sourced outside the United States.

(2) Gain in excess of depreciation. Gain (in excess of the depreciation adjustments) from the sale of depreciable personal property shall be sourced as if such property were inventory property.

(3) United States depreciation adjustments. For purposes of this subsection --

(A) In general. The term "United States depreciation adjustments" means the portion of the depreciation adjustments to the adjusted basis of the property which are attributable to the depreciation deductions allowable in computing taxable income from sources in the United States.

(B) Special rule for certain property. Except in the case of property of a kind described in section 168(g)(4), if, for any taxable year --

(i) such property is used predominantly in the United States, or

(ii) such property is used predominantly outside the United States, all of the depreciation deductions allowable for such year shall be treated as having been allocated to income from sources in the United States (or, where clause (ii) applies, from sources outside the United States).

(4) Other definitions. For purposes of this subsection --

(A) Depreciable personal property. The term "depreciable personal property" means any personal property if the adjusted basis of such property includes depreciation adjustments.

(B) Depreciation adjustments. The term "depreciation adjustments" means adjustments reflected in the adjusted basis of any property on account of depreciation deductions (whether allowed with respect to such property or other property and whether allowed to the taxpayer or to any other person).

(C) Depreciation deductions. The term "depreciation deductions" means any deductions for depreciation or amortization or any other deduction allowable under any provision of this chapter which treats an otherwise capital expenditure as a deductible expense.

(d) Exception for intangibles.

(1) In general. In the case of any sale of an intangible --

(A) this section shall apply only to the extent the payments in consideration of such sale are not contingent on the productivity, use, or disposition of the intangible, and

(B) to the extent such payments are so contingent, the source of such payments shall be determined under this part in the same manner as if such payments were royalties.

(2) Intangible. For purposes of paragraph (1), the term "intangible" means any patent, copyright, secret process or formula, goodwill, trademark, trade brand, franchise or other like property.

(3) Special rule in the case of goodwill. To the extent this section applies to the sale of goodwill, payments in consideration of such sale shall be treated as from sources in the country in which such goodwill was generated.

(4) Coordination with subsection (c).

(A) Gain not in excess of depreciation adjustments sourced under subsection (c). Notwithstanding paragraph (1), any gain from the sale of an intangible shall be sourced under subsection (c) to the extent such gain does not exceed the depreciation adjustments with respect to such intangible.

(B) Subsection (c)(2) not to apply to intangibles. Paragraph (2) of subsection (c) shall not apply to any gain from the sale of an intangible.

(e) Special rules for sales through offices or fixed places of business.

(1) Sales by residents.

(A) In general. In the case of income not sourced under subsection (b), (c), (d)(1)(B) or (3), or (f), if a United States resident maintains an office or other fixed place of business in a foreign country, income from sales of personal property attributable to such office or other fixed place of business shall be sourced outside the United States.

(B) Tax must be imposed. Subparagraph (A) shall not apply unless an income tax equal to at least 10 percent of the income from the sale is actually paid to a foreign country with respect to such income.

(2) Sales by nonresidents.

(A) In general. Notwithstanding any other provisions of this part, if a nonresident maintains an office or other fixed place of business in the United States, income from any sale of personal property (including inventory property) attributable to such office or other fixed place of business shall be sourced in the United States. The preceding sentence shall not apply for purposes of section 971 (defining export trade corporation).

(B) Exception. -- Subparagraph (A) shall not apply to any sale of inventory property which is sold for use, disposition, or consumption outside the United States if an office or other fixed place of business of the taxpayer in a foreign country materially participated in the sale.

(3) Sales attributable to an office or other fixed place of business. The principles of section 864(c)(5) shall apply in determining whether a taxpayer has an office or other fixed place of business and whether a sale is attributable to such an office or other fixed place of business.

(f) Stock of affiliates.

If --

(1) a United States resident sells stock in an affiliate which is a foreign corporation,

(2) such sale occurs in a foreign country in which such affiliate is engaged in the active conduct of a trade or business, and

(3) more than 50 percent of the gross income of such affiliate for the 3-year period ending with the close of such affiliate's taxable year immediately preceding the year in which the sale occurred was derived from the active conduct of a trade or business in such foreign country, any gain from such sale shall be sourced outside the United States. For purposes of paragraphs (2) and (3), the United States resident may elect to treat an affiliate and all other corporations which are wholly owned (directly or indirectly) by the affiliate as one corporation.

(g) United States resident; nonresident.

For purposes of this section --

(1) In general. Except as otherwise provided in this subsection --

(A) United States resident. The term "United States resident" means --

(i) any individual who --

(I) is a United States citizen or a resident alien and does not have a tax home (as defined in section 911(d)(3)) in a foreign country, or

(II) is a nonresident alien and has a tax home (as so defined) in the United States, and

(ii) any corporation, trust, or estate which is a United States person (as defined in section 7701(a)(30)).

(B) Nonresident. The term "nonresident" means any person other than a United States resident.

(2) Special rules for United States citizens and resident aliens. For purposes of this section, a United States citizen or resident alien shall not be treated as a nonresident with respect to any sale of personal property unless an income tax equal to at least 10 percent of the gain derived from such sale is actually paid to a foreign country with respect to that gain.

(3) Special rule for certain stock sales by residents of Puerto Rico. Paragraph (2) shall not apply to the sale by an individual who was a bona fide resident of Puerto Rico during the entire taxable year of stock in a corporation if

(A) such corporation is engaged in the active conduct of a trade or business in Puerto Rico, and

(B) more than 50 percent of its gross income for the 3 year period ending with the close of such corporation's taxable year immediately preceding the year in which such sale occurred was derived from the active conduct of a trade or business in Puerto Rico.

For purposes of the preceding sentence, the taxpayer may elect to treat a corporation and all other corporations which are wholly owned (directly or indirectly) by such corporation as one corporation.

(h) Treatment of gains from sale of certain stock or intangibles and from certain liquidations.

(1) In general. In the case of gain to which this subsection applies --

(A) such gain shall be sourced outside the United States, but

(B) subsections (a), (b), and (c) of section 904 and sections 902, 907, and 960 shall be applied separately with respect to such gain.

(2) Gain to which subsection applies. This subsection shall apply to --

(A) Gain from sale of certain stock or intangibles. Any gain --

(i) which is from the sale of stock in a foreign corporation or an intangible (as defined in subsection (d)(2)) and which would otherwise be sourced in the United States under this section,

404

(ii) which, under a treaty obligation of the United States (applied without regard to this section), would be sourced outside the United States, and

(iii) with respect to which the taxpayer chooses the benefits of this subsection.

(B) Gain from liquidation in possession. Any gain which is derived from the receipt of any distribution in liquidation of a corporation --

(i) which is organized in a possession of the United States, and

(ii) more than 50 percent of the gross income of which during the 3-taxable year period ending with the close of the taxable year immediately preceding the taxable year in which the distribution is received from the active conduct of a trade or business in such possession.

(i) Other definitions.

For purposes of this section --

(1) Inventory property. The term "inventory property" means personal property described in paragraph (1) of section 1221.

(2) Sale includes exchange. The term "sale" includes an exchange or any other disposition.

(3) Treatment of possessions. Any possession of the United States shall be treated as a foreign country.

(4) Affiliate. The term "affiliate" means a member of the same affiliated group (within the meaning of section 1504(a) without regard to section 1504(b)).

(5) Treatment of partnerships. In the case of a partnership, except as provided in regulations, this section shall be applied at the partner level.

(j) Regulations.

The Secretary shall prescribe such regulations as may be necessary or appropriate to carry out the purpose of this section, including regulations --

(1) relating to the treatment of losses from sales of personal property,

(2) applying the rules of this section to income derived from trading in futures contracts, forward contracts, options contracts, and other instruments, and

(3) providing that, subject to such conditions (which may include provisions comparable to section 877) as may be provided in such regulations, subsections (e)(1)(B) and (g)(2) shall not apply for purposes of sections 931, 933, and 936.

(k) Cross references.

(1) For provisions relating to the characterization as dividends for source purposes of gains from the sale of stock in certain foreign corporations, see section 1248.

(2) For sourcing of income from certain foreign currency transactions, see section 988.

§ 871. Tax on nonresident alien individuals.

(a) Income not connected with United States business -- 30 percent tax.

(1) Income other than capital gains. Except as provided in subsection (h), there is hereby imposed for each taxable year a tax of 30 percent of the amount received from sources within the United States by a nonresident alien individual as --

(A) interest (other than original issue discount as defined in section 1273), dividends, rents, salaries, wages, premiums, annuities, compensations, remunerations, emoluments, and other fixed or determinable annual or periodical gains, profits, and income,

(B) gains described in section 631(b) or (c), and gains on transfers described in section 1235 made on or before October 4, 1966,

(C) in the case of --

(i) a sale or exchange of an original issue discount obligation, the amount of the original issue discount accruing while such obligation was held by the nonresident alien individual (to the extent such discount was not theretofore taken into account under clause (ii)), and

(ii) a payment on an original issue discount obligation, an amount equal to the original issue discount accruing while such obligation was held by the nonresident alien individual (except that such original issue discount shall be taken into account under this clause only to the extent such discount was not theretofore taken into account under this clause and only to the extent that the tax thereon does not exceed the payment less the tax imposed by subparagraph (A) thereon), and

(D) gains from the sale or exchange after October 4, 1966, of patents, copyrights, secret processes and formulas, good will, trademarks, trade brands, franchises, and other like property, or of any interest in any such property, to the extent such gains are from payments which are contingent on the productivity, use, or disposition of the property or interest sold or exchanged, but only to the extent the amount so received is not effectively connected with the conduct of a trade or business within the United States.

(2) Capital gains of aliens present in the United States 183 days or more. In the case of a nonresident alien individual present in the United States for a period or periods aggregating 183 days or more during the taxable year, there is hereby imposed for such year a tax of 30 percent of the amount by which his gains, derived from sources within the United States, from the sale or exchange at an y time during such year of capital assets exceed his losses, allocable to sources within the United States, from the sale or exchange at any time during such year of capital assets. For purposes of this paragraph, gains and losses shall be taken into account only if, and to the extent that, they would be recognized and taken into account if such gains and losses were effectively connected with the conduct of a trade or business within the United States, except that such gains and losses shall be determined without regard to section 1202 and such losses shall be determined without the benefits of the capital loss carryover provided in section 1212. Any gain or loss which is taken into account in determining the tax under paragraph (1) or subsection (b) shall not be taken into account in determining the tax under this paragraph. For purposes of the 183-day requirement of this paragraph, a nonresident alien individual not engaged in trade or business within the United States who has not established a taxable year for any prior period shall be treated as having a taxable year which is the calendar year.

(3) Taxation of social security benefits. For purposes of this section and section 1441 --

(A) one-half of any social security benefit (as defined in section 86(d)) shall be included in gross income (notwithstanding section 207 of the Social Security Act), and

(B) section 86 shall not apply.

For treatment of certain citizens of possessions of the United States, see section 932(c).

(b) Income connected with United States business -- graduated rate of tax.

(1) Imposition of tax. A nonresident alien individual engaged in trade or business within the United States during the taxable year shall be taxable as provided in section 1, 55, on his taxable income which is effectively connected with the conduct of a trade or business within the United States.

(2) Determination of taxable income. In determining taxable income for purposes of paragraph (1), gross income includes only gross income which is effectively connected with the conduct of a trade or business within the United States.

(c) Participants in certain exchange or training programs.

For purposes of this section, a nonresident alien individual who (without regard to this subsection) is not engaged in trade or business within the United States and who is temporarily present in the United States as a nonimmigrant under subparagraph (F), (J), (M), or (Q) of section 101(a)(15) of the Immigration and Nationality Act, as amended (8 U.S.C. 1101(a)(15)(F), (J), (M), or (Q), shall be treated as a nonresident alien individual engaged in trade or business within the United States, and any income described in the second sentence of section 1441(b) which is received by such individual shall, to the extent derived from sources within the United States, be treated as effectively connected with the conduct of a trade or business within the United States.

(d) Election to treat real property income as income connected with United States business.

(1) In general. A nonresident alien individual who during the taxable year derives any income --

(A) from real property held for the production of income and located in the United States, or from any interest in such real property, including (i) gains from the sale or exchange of such real property or an interest therein, (ii) rents or royalties from mines, wells, or other natural deposits, and (iii) gains described in section 631(b) or (c), and

(B) which, but for this subsection, would not be treated as income which is effectively connected with the conduct of a trade or business within the United States, may elect for such taxable year to treat all such income as income which is effectively connected with the conduct of a trade or business within the United States. In such case, such income shall be taxable as provided in subsection (b)(1) whether or not such individual is engaged in trade or business within the United States during the taxable year. An election under this paragraph for any taxable year shall remain in effect for all subsequent taxable years, except that it may be revoked with the consent of the Secretary with respect to any taxable year.

(2) Election after revocation. If an election has been made under paragraph (1) and such election has been revoked, a new election may not be made under such paragraph for any taxable year before the 5th taxable year which begins after the first taxable year for which such revocation is effective, unless the Secretary consents to such new election.

(3) Form and time of election and revocation. An election under paragraph (1), and any revocation of such an election, may be made only in such manner and at such time as the Secretary may by regulations prescribe.

(e) Repealed.

(f) Certain annuities received under qualified plans.

(1) In general. For purposes of this section, gross income does not include any amount received as an annuity under a qualified annuity plan described in section 403(a)(1), or from a qualified trust described in section 401(a) which is exempt from tax under section 501(a), if --

(A) all of the personal services by reason of which the annuity is payable were either --

(i) personal services performed outside the United States by an individual who, at the time of performance of such personal services, was a nonresident alien, or

(ii) personal services described in section 864(b)(1) performed within the United States by such individual, and

(B) at the time the first amount is paid as an annuity under the annuity plan or by the trust, 90 percent or more of the employees for whom contributions or benefits are provided under such annuity plan, or under the plan or plans of which the trust is a part, are citizens or residents of the United States.

(2) Exclusion. Income received during the taxable year which would be excluded from gross income under this subsection but for the requirement of paragraph (1)(B) shall not be included in gross income if --

(A) the recipient's country of residence grants a substantially equivalent exclusion to residents and citizens of the United States; or

(B) the recipient's country of residence is a beneficiary developing country within the meaning of section 502 of the Trade Act of 1974 (19 U.S.C. 2461).

(g) Special rules for original issue discount.

For purposes of this section and section 881 --

(1) Original issue discount obligation.

(A) In general. Except as provided in subparagraph (B), the term "original issue discount obligation" means any bond or other evidence of indebtedness having original issue discount (within the meaning of section 1273).

(B) Exceptions. The term "original issue discount obligation" shall not include --

(i) Certain short-term obligations. Any obligation payable 183 days or less from the dat e of original issue (without regard to the period held by the taxpayer).

(ii) Tax-exempt obligations. Any obligation the interest on which is exempt from tax under section 103 or under any other provision of law without regard to the identity of the holder.

(2) Determination of portion of original issue discount accruing during any period. The determination of the amount of the original issue discount which accrues during any period shall be made under the rules of section 1272 (or the corresponding provisions of prior law) without regard to any exception for short-term obligations.

(3) Source of original issue discount. Except to the extent provided in regulations prescribed by the Secretary, the determination of whether any amount described in subsection (a)(1)(C) is from sources within the United States shall be made at the time of the payment (or sale or exchange) as if such payment (or sale or exchange) involved the payment of interest.

(4) Stripped bonds. The provisions of section 1286 (relating to the treatment of stripped bonds and stripped coupons as obligations with original issue discount) shall apply for purposes of this section.

(h) Repeal of tax on interest of nonresident alien individuals received from certain portfolio debt investments.

(1) In general. In the case of any portfolio interest received by a nonresident individual from sources within the United States, no tax shall be imposed under paragraph (1)(A) or (1)(C) of subsection (a).

(2) Portfolio interest. For purposes of this subsection, the term "portfolio interest" means any interest (including original issue discount) which would be subject to tax under subsection (a) but for this subsection and which is described in any of the following subparagraphs:

(A) Certain obligations which are not registered. Interest which is paid on any obligation which --

(i) is not in registered form, and

(ii) is described in section 163(f)(2)(B).

(B) Certain registered obligations. Interest which is paid on an obligation --

(i) which is in registered form, and

(ii) with respect to which the United States person who would otherwise be required to deduct and withhold tax from such interest under section 1441(a) receives a statement (which meets the requirements of paragraph (5)) that the beneficial owner of the obligation is not a United States person.

(3) Portfolio interest not to include interest received by 10-percent shareholders. For purposes of this subsection --

(A) In general. The term "portfolio interest" shall not include any interest described in subparagraph (A) or (B) of paragraph (2) which is received by a 10-percent shareholder.

(B) 10-Percent shareholder. The term "10-percent shareholder" means --

(i) in the case of an obligation issued by a corporation, any person who owns 10 percent or more of the total combined voting power of all classes of stock of such corporation entitled to vote, or

(ii) in the case of an obligation issued by a partnership, any person who owns 10 percent or more of the capital or profits interest in such partnership.

(C) Attribution rules. For purposes of determining ownership of stock under subparagraph (B)(i) the rules of section 318(a) shall apply, except that --

(i) section 318(a)(2)(C) shall be applied without regard to the 50-percent limitation therein,

(ii) section 318(a)(3)(C) shall be applied[md ash]

(I) without regard to the 50-percent limitation therein; and

(II) in any case where such section would not apply but for subclause (I), by considering a corporation as owning the stock (other than stock in such corporation) which is owned by or for any shareholder of such corporation in that proportion which the value of the stock which such shareholder owns in such corporation bears to the value of all stock in such corporation, and

(iii) any stock which a person is treated as owning after application of section 318(a)(4) shall not, for purposes of applying paragraphs (2) and (3) of section 318(a), be treated as actually owned by such person.

Under regulations prescribed by the Secretary, rules similar to the rules of the preceding sentence shall be applied in determining the ownership of the capital or profits interest in a partnership for purposes of subparagraph (B)(ii).

(4) Portfolio interest not to include certain contingent interest. For purposes of this subsection --

(A) In general. Except as otherwise provided in this paragraph, the term "portfolio interest" shall not include --

(i) any interest if the amount of such interest is determined by reference to --

(I) any receipts, sales or other cash flow of the debtor or a related person,

(II) any income or profits of the debtor or a related person,

(III) any change in value of any property of the debtor or a related person, or

(IV) any dividend, partnership distributions, or similar payments made by the debtor or a related person, or

(ii) any other type of contingent interest that is identified by the Secretary by regulation, where a denial of the portfolio interest exemption is necessary or appropriate to prevent avoidance of Federal income tax.

(B) Related person. The term "related person" means any person who is related to the debtor within the meaning of section 267(b) or 707(b)(1), or who is a party to any arrangement undertaken for a purpose of avoiding the application of this paragraph.

(C) Exceptions. Subparagraph (A)(i) shall not apply to --

(i) any amount of interest solely by reason of the fact that the timing of any interest or principal payment is subject to a contingency,

(ii) any amount of interest solely by reason of the fact that the interest is paid with respect to nonrecourse or limited recourse indebtedness,

(iii) any amount of interest all or substantially all of which is determined by reference to any other amount of interest not described in subparagraph (A) (or by reference to the principal amount of indebtedness on which such other interest is paid),

(iv) any amount of interest solely by reason of the fact that the debtor or a related person enters into a hedging transaction to reduce the risk of interest rate or currency fluctuations with respect to such interest,

(v) any amount of interest determined by reference to --

(I) changes in the value of property (including stock) that is actively traded (within the meaning of section 1092(d)) other than property described in section 897(c)(1) or (g),

410

(II) the yield on property described in subclause (I), other than a debt instrument that pays interest described in subparagraph (A), or stock or other property that represents a beneficial interest in the debtor or a related person, or

(III) changes in any index of the value of property described in subclause (I) or of the yield on property described in subclause (II), and

(vi) any other type of interest identified by the Secretary by regulation.

(D) Exception for certain existing indebtedness. Subparagraph (A) shall not apply to any interest paid or accrued with respect to any indebtedness with a fixed term --

(i) which was issued on or before April 7, 1993, or

(ii) which was issued after such date pursuant to a written binding contract in effect on such date and at all times thereafter before such indebtedness was issued.

(5) Certain statements. A statement with respect to any obligation meets the requirements of this paragraph if such statement is made by --

(A) the beneficial owner of such obligation, or

(B) a securities clearing organization, a bank, or other financial institution that holds customers' securities in the ordinary course of its trade or business.

The preceding sentence shall not apply to any statement with respect to payment of interest on any obligation by any person if, at least one month before such payment, the Secretary has published a determination that any statement from such person (or any class including such person) does not meet the requirements of this paragraph.

(6) Secretary may provide subsection not to apply in cases of inadequate information exchange.

(A) In general. If the Secretary determines that the exchange of information between the United States and a foreign country is inadequate to prevent evasion of the United States income tax by United States persons, the Secretary may provide in writing (and publish a statement) that the provisions of this subsection shall not apply to payments of interest to any person within such foreign country (or payments addressed to, or for the account of, persons within such foreign country) during the period --

(i) beginning on the date specified by the Secretary, and

(ii) ending on the date that the Secretary determines that the exchange of information between the United States and the foreign country is adequate to prevent the evasion of United States income tax by United States persons.

(B) Exception for certain obligations. Subparagraph (A) shall not apply to the payment of interest on any obligation which is issued on or before the date of the publication of the Secretary's determination under such subparagraph.

(7) Registered form. For purposes of this subsection, the term "registered form" has the same meaning given such term by section 163(f).

(i) Tax not to apply to certain interest and dividends.

(1) **In general.** No tax shall be imposed under paragraph (1)(A) or (1)(C) of subsection (a) on any amount described in paragraph (2).

(2) **Amounts to which paragraph (1) applies.** The amounts described in this paragraph are as follows:

(A) Interest on deposits, if such interest is not effectively connected with the conduct of a trade or business within the United States.

(B) A percentage of any dividend paid by a domestic corporation meeting the 80-percent foreign business requirements of section 861(c)(1) equal to the percentage determined for purposes of section 861(c)(2)(A).

(C) Income derived by a foreign central bank of issue from bankers' acceptances.

(3) **Deposits.** For purposes of paragraph (2), the term "deposits" means amounts which are --

(A) deposits with persons carrying on the banking business,

(B) deposits or withdrawable accounts with savings institutions chartered and supervised as savings and loan or similar associations under Federal or State law, but only to the extent that amounts paid or credited on such deposits or accounts are deductible under section 591 (determined without regard to sections 265 and 291) in computing the taxable income of such institutions, and

(C) amounts held by an insurance company under an agreement to pay interest thereon.

(j) Exemption for certain gambling winnings.

No tax shall be imposed under paragraph (1)(A) of subsection (a) on the proceeds from a wager placed in any of the following games: blackjack, baccarat, craps, roulette, or big-6 wheel. The preceding sentence shall not apply in any case where the Secretary determines by regulation that the collection of the tax is administratively feasible.

(k) Cross references.

(1) For tax treatment of certain amounts distributed by the United States to nonresident alien individuals, see section 402(e)(2).

(2) For taxation of nonresident alien individuals who are expatriate United States citizens, see section 877.

(3) For doubling of tax on citizens of certain foreign countries, see section 891.

(4) For adjustment of tax in case of nationals or residents of certain foreign countries, see section 896.

(5) For withholding of tax at source on nonresident alien individuals, see section 1441.

(6) For election to treat married nonresident alien individual as resident of United States in certain cases, see subsections (g) and (h) of section 6013.

(7) For special tax treatment of gain or loss from the disposition by a nonresident alien individual of a United States real property interest, see section 897.

§ 872. Gross income.

(a) General rule.

In the case of a nonresident alien individual, except where the context clearly indicates otherwise gross income includes only --

(1) gross income which is derived from sources within the United States and which is not effectively connected with the conduct of a trade or business within the United States, and

(2) gross income which is effectively connected with the conduct of a trade or business within the United States.

(b) Exclusions.

The following items shall not be included in gross income of a nonresident alien individual, and shall be exempt from taxation under this subtitle:

(1) **Ships operated by certain nonresidents.** Gross income derived by an individual resident of a foreign country from the international operation of a ship or ships if such foreign country grants an equivalent exemption to individual residents of the United States.

(2) **Aircraft operated by certain nonresidents.** Gross income derived by an individual resident of a foreign country from the international operation of aircraft if such foreign country grants an equivalent exemption to individual residents of the United States.

(3) **Compensation of participants in certain exchange or training programs.** Compensation paid by a foreign employer to a nonresident alien individual for the period he is temporarily present in the United States as a non-immigrant under subparagraph (F), (J), or (Q) of section 101(a)(15) of the Immigration and Nationality Act, as amended. For purposes of this paragraph, the term "foreign employer" means --

(A) a nonresident alien individual, foreign partnership, or foreign corporation, or

(B) an office or place of business maintained in a foreign country or in a possession of the United States by a domestic corporation, a domestic partnership, or an individual who is a citizen or resident of the United States.

(4) Certain bond income of residents of the Ryukyu Islands or the Trust Territory of the Pacific Islands. Income derived by a nonresident alien individual from a series E or series H United States savings bond, if such individual acquired such bond while a resident of the Ryukyu Islands or the Trust Territory of the Pacific Islands.

(5) Certain rental income. Income to which paragraphs (1) and (2) apply shall include income which is derived from the rental on a full or bareboat basis of a ship or ships or aircraft, as the case may be.

(6) **Application to different types of transportation.** The Secretary may provide that this subsection be applied separately with respect to income from different types of transportation.

(7) **Treatment of possessions.** To the extent provided in regulations, a possession of the United States shall be treated as a foreign country for purposes of this subsection.

§ 877. Expatriation to avoid tax.

(a) Treatment of expatriates.

(1) In general. Every nonresident alien individual who at any time after March 8, 1965, and within the 10-year period immediately preceding the close of the taxable year lost United States citizenship, unless such loss did not have for one of its principal purposes the avoidance of taxes under this subtitle or subtitle B, shall be taxable for such taxable year in the manner provided in subsection (b) if the tax imposed pursuant to such subsection exceeds the tax which, without regard to this section, is imposed pursuant to section 871.

(2) Certain individuals treated as having tax avoidance purpose. For purposes of paragraph (1), an individual shall be treated as having a principal purpose to avoid such taxes if --

(A) the average annual net income tax (as defined in section 38(c)(1)) of such individual for the period of 5 taxable years ending before the date of the loss of United States citizenship is greater than $100,000, or

(B) the net worth of the individual as of such date is $500,000 or more.

In the case of the loss of United States citizenship in any calendar year after 1996, such $100,000 and $500,000 amounts shall be increased by an amount equal to such dollar amount multiplied by the cost-of-living adjustment determined under section 1(f)(3) for such calendar year by substituting '1994' for '1992' in subparagraph (B) thereof. Any increase under the preceding sentence shall be rounded to the nearest multiple of $1,000.

(b) Alternative tax [Caution: For provisions applicable to taxable years beginning on or before 12/31/99, see note below relating to amendment made by Sec. 1401 of P.L. 104-188.]. A nonresident alien individual described in subsection (a) shall be taxable for the taxable year as provided in section 1 or 55, except that --

(1) the gross income shall include only the gross income described in section 872(a) (as modified by subsection (c) of this section), and

(2) the deductions shall be allowed if and to the extent that they are connected with the gross income included under this section, except that the capital loss carryover provided by section 1212(b) shall not be allowed; and the proper allocation and apportionment of the deductions for this purpose shall be determined as provided under regulations prescribed by the Secretary.

For purposes of paragraph (2), the deductions allowed by section 873(b) shall be allowed; and the deduction (for losses not connected with the trade or business if incurred in transactions entered into for profit) allowed by section 165(c)(2) shall be allowed, but only if the profit, if such transaction had resulted in a profit, would be included in gross income under this section. The tax imposed solely by reason of this section shall be reduced (but not below zero) by the amount of any income, war profits, and excess profits taxes (within the meaning of section 903) paid to any foreign country or possession of the United States on any income of the taxpayer on which tax is imposed solely by reason of this section.

(c) Tax avoidance not presumed in certain cases.

(1) In general. Subsection (a)(2) shall not apply to an individual if --

(A) such individual is described in a subparagraph of paragraph (2) of this subsection, and

(B) within the 1-year period beginning on the date of the loss of United States citizenship, such individual submits a ruling request for the Secretary's determination as to whether such loss has for one of its principal purposes the avoidance of taxes under this subtitle or subtitle B.

(2) Individuals described.

(A) Dual citizenship, etc. An individual is described in this subparagraph if --

(i) the individual became at birth a citizen of the United States and a citizen of another country and continues to be a citizen of such other country, or

(ii) the individual becomes (not later than the close of a reasonable period after loss of United States citizenship) a citizen of the country in which --

(I) such individual was born,

(II) if such individual is married, such individual's spouse was born, or

(III) either of such individual's parents were born.

(B) Long-term foreign residents. An individual is described in this subparagraph if, for each year in the 10-year period ending on the date of loss of United States citizenship, the individual was present in the United States for 30 days or less. The rule of section 7701(b)(3)(D)(ii) shall apply for purposes of this subparagraph.

(C) Renunciation upon reaching age of majority. An individual is described in this subparagraph if the individual's loss of United States citizenship occurs before such individual attains age 18 1/2.

(D) Individuals specified in regulations. An individual is described in this subparagraph if the individual is described in a category of individuals prescribed by regulation by the Secretary.

§ 881. Tax on income of foreign corporations not connected with United States business.

(a) Imposition of tax. Except as provided in subsection (c), there is hereby imposed for each taxable year a tax of 30 percent of the amount received from sources within the United States by a foreign corporation as --

(1) interest (other than original issue discount as defined in section 1273), dividends, rents, salaries, wages, premiums, annuities, compensations, remunerations, emoluments, and other fixed or determinable annual or periodical gains, profits, and income,

(2) gains described in section 631(b) or (c),

(3) in the case of --

(A) a sale or exchange of an original issue discount obligation, the amount of the original issue discount accruing while such obligation was held by the foreign corporation (to the extent such discount was not theretofore taken into account under subparagraph (B)), and

(B) a payment on an original issue discount obligation, an amount equal to the original issue discount accruing while such obligation was held by the foreign corporation (except that such original issue discount shall be taken into account under this subparagraph only to the extent such discount was not theretofore taken into account under this subparagraph and only to the extent that the tax thereon does not exceed the payment less the tax imposed by paragraph (1) thereon), and

(4) gains from the sale or exchange after October 4, 1966, of patents, copyrights, secret processes and formulas, good will, trademarks, trade brands, franchises, and other like property, or of any interest in any such property, to the extent such gains are from payments which are contingent on the productivity, use, or disposition of the property or interest sold or exchanged,

but only to the extent the amount so received is not effectively connected with the conduct of a trade or business within the United States.

(b) Exception for certain Guam and Virgin Islands corporations.

(1) In general. For purposes of this section and section 884, a corporation created or organized in Guam, American Samoa, the Northern Mariana Islands, or the Virgin Islands or under the law of any such possession shall not be treated as a foreign corporation for any taxable year if --

(A) at all times during such taxable year less than 25 percent in value of the stock of such corporation is beneficially owned (directly or indirectly) by foreign persons,

(B) at least 65 percent of the gross income of such corporation is shown to the satisfaction of the Secretary to be effectively connected with the conduct of a trade or business in such a possession or the United States for the 3-year period ending with the close of the taxable year of such corporation (or for such part of such period as the corporation or any predecessor has been in existence), and

(C) no substantial part of the income of such corporation is used (directly or indirectly) to satisfy obligations to persons who are not bona fide residents of such a possession or the United States.

(2) Definitions.

(A) Foreign person. For purposes of paragraph (1), the term "foreign person" means any person other than --

(i) a United States person, or

(ii) a person who would be a United States person if references to the United States in section 7701 included references to a possession of the United States.

(B) Indirect ownership rules. For purposes of paragraph (1), the rules of section 318(a)(2) shall apply except that "5 percent" shall be substituted for "50 percent" in subparagraph (C) thereof.

(c) Repeal of tax on interest of foreign corporations received from certain portfolio debt investments.

(1) In general. In the case of any portfolio interest received by a foreign corporation from sources within the United States, no tax shall be imposed under paragraph (1) or (3) of subsection (a).

(2) Portfolio interest. For purposes of this subsection, the term "portfolio interest" means any interest (including original issue discount) which would be subject to tax under subsection (a) but for this subsection and which is described in any of the following subparagraphs:

(A) Certain obligations which are not registered. Interest which is paid on any obligation which is described in section 871(h)(2)(A).

(B) Certain registered obligations. Interest which is paid on an obligation --

(i) which is in registered form, and

(ii) with respect to which the person who would otherwise be required to deduct and withhold tax from such interest under section 1442(a) receives a statement which meets the requirements of section 871(h)(5) that the beneficial owner of the obligation is not a United States person.

(3) Portfolio interest shall not include interest received by certain persons. For purposes of this subsection, the term "portfolio interest" shall not include any portfolio interest which --

(A) except in the case of interest paid on an obligation of the United States, is received by a bank on an extension of credit made pursuant to a loan agreement entered into in the ordinary course of its trade or business,

(B) is received by a 10-percent shareholder (within the meaning of section 871(h)(3)(B)), or

(C) is received by a controlled foreign corporation from a related person (within the meaning of section 864(d)(4)).

(4) Portfolio interest not to include certain contingent interest. For purposes of this subsection, the term "portfolio interest" shall not include any interest which is treated as not being portfolio interest under the rules of section 871(h)(4).

(5) Special rules for controlled foreign corporations.

(A) In general. In the case of any portfolio interest received by a controlled foreign corporation, the following provisions shall not apply:

(i) Subparagraph (A) of section 954(b)(3) (relating to exception where foreign base company income is less than 5 percent or $1,000,000).

(ii) Paragraph (4) of section 954(b) (relating to exception for certain income subject to high foreign taxes).

(iii) Clause (i) of section 954(c)(3)(A) (relating to certain income received from related persons).

(B) Controlled foreign corporation. For purposes of this subsection, the term "controlled foreign corporation" has the meaning given to such term by section 957(a).

(6) Secretary may cease application of this subsection. Under rules similar to the rules of section 871(h)(5), the Secretary may provide that this subsection shall not apply to payments of interest described in section 871(h)(6).

(7) Registered form. For purposes of this subsection, the term "registered form" has the meaning given such term by section 163(f).

(d) Tax not to apply to certain interest and dividends.

No tax shall be imposed under paragraph (1) or (3) of subsection (a) on any amount described in section 871(i)(2).

(e) Cross Reference.

For doubling of tax on corporations of certain foreign countries, see section 891. For special rules for original issue discount, see section 871(g).

§ 882. Tax on income of foreign corporations connected with United States business.

(a) Imposition of tax.

(1) In general. A foreign corporation engaged in trade or business within the United States during the taxable year shall be taxable as provided in section 11, 55, 59A, or 1201(a) on its taxable income which is effectively connected with the conduct of a trade or business within the United States.

(2) Determination of taxable income. In determining taxable income for purposes of paragraph (1), gross income includes only gross income which is effectively connected with the conduct of a trade or business within the United States.

(3) For special tax treatment of gain or loss from the disposition by a foreign corporation of a United States real property interest, see section 897.

(b) Gross income.

In the case of a foreign corporation, except where the context clearly indicates otherwise, gross income includes only --

(1) gross income which is derived from sources within the United States and which is not effectively connected with the conduct of a trade or business within the United States, and

(2) gross income which is effectively connected with the conduct of a trade or business within the United States.

(c) Allowance of deductions and credits.

(1) Allocation of deductions.

(A) General rule. In the case of a foreign corporation, the deductions shall be allowed only for purposes of subsection (a) and (except as provided by subparagraph (B)) only if and to the extent that they are connected with income which is effectively connected with the conduct of a trade or business within the United States; and the proper apportionment and allocation of the deductions for this purpose shall be determined as provided in regulations prescribed by the Secretary.

(B) Charitable contributions. The deduction for charitable contributions and gifts provided by section 170 shall be allowed whether or not connected with income which is effectively connected with the conduct of a trade or business within the United States.

(2) Deductions and credits allowed only if return filed. A foreign corporation shall receive the benefit of the deductions and credits allowed to it in this subtitle only by filing or causing to be filed with the Secretary a true and accurate return, in the manner prescribed in subtitle F, including therein all the information which the Secretary may deem necessary for the calculation of such deductions and credits. The preceding sentence shall not apply for purposes of the tax imposed by section 541 (relating to personal holding company tax), and shall not be construed to deny the credit provided by section 33 for tax withheld at source or the credit provided by section 34 for certain uses of gasoline.

(3) Foreign tax credit. Except as provided by section 906, foreign corporations shall not be allowed the credit against the tax for taxes of foreign countries and possessions of the United States allowed by section 901.

(4) Cross reference. For rule that certain foreign taxes are not to be taken into account in determining deduction or credit, see section 906(b)(1).

(d) Election to treat real property income as income connected with United States business.

(1) In general. A foreign corporation which during the taxable year derives any income --

(A) from real property located in the United States, or from any interest in such real property, including (i) gains from the sale or exchange of real property or an interest therein, (ii) rents or royalties from mines, wells or other natural deposits, and (iii) gains described in section 631(b) or (c), and

(B) which, but for this subsection, would not be treated as income effectively connected with the conduct of a trade or business within the United States, may elect for such taxable year to treat all such income as income which is effectively connected with the conduct of a trade or business within the United States. In such case, such income shall be taxable as provided in subsection (a)(1) whether or not such corporation is engaged in trade or business within the United States during the taxable year. An election under this paragraph for any taxable year shall remain in effect for all subsequent taxable years, except that it may be revoked with the consent of the Secretary with respect to any taxable year.

(2) Election after revocation, etc. Paragraphs (2) and (3) of section 871(d) shall apply in respect of elections under this subsection in the same manner and to the same extent as they apply in respect of elections under section 871(d).

(e) Interest on United States obligations received by banks organized in possessions.

In the case of a corporation created or organized in, or under the law of, a possession of the United States which is carrying on the banking business in a possession of the United States, interest on obligations of the United States which is not portfolio interest (as defined in section 881(c)(2)) shall --

(1) for purposes of this subpart, be treated as income which is effectively connected with the conduct of a trade or business within the United States, and

(2) shall be taxable as provided in subsection (a)(1) whether or not such corporation is engaged in trade or business within the United States during the taxable year.

(f) Returns of tax by agent.

If any foreign corporation has no office or place of business in the United States but has an agent in the United States, the return required under section 6012 shall be made by the agent.

419

§ 883. Exclusions from gross income.

(a) Income of foreign corporations from ships and aircraft.

The following items shall not be included in gross income of a foreign corporation, and shall be exempt from taxation under this subtitle:

(1) Ships operated by certain foreign corporations. Gross income derived by a corporation organized in a foreign country from the international operation of a ship or ships if such foreign country grants an equivalent exemption to corporations organized in the United States.

(2) Aircraft operated by certain foreign corporations. Gross income derived by a corporation organized in a foreign country from the international operation of aircraft if such foreign country grants an equivalent exemption to corporations organized in the United States.

(3) Railroad rolling stock of foreign corporations. Earnings derived from payments by a common carrier for the use on a temporary basis (not expected to exceed a total of 90 days in any taxable year) of railroad rolling stock owned by a corporation of a foreign country which grants an equivalent exemption to corporations organized in the United States.

(4) Special rules. The rules of paragraphs (5), (6), and (7) of section 872(b) shall apply for purposes of this subsection.

(5) Special rule for countries which tax on residence basis. For purposes of this subsection, there shall not be taken into account any failure of a foreign country to grant an exemption to a corporation organized in the United States if such corporation is subject to tax by such foreign country on a residence basis pursuant to provisions of foreign law which meets such standards (if any) as the Secretary may prescribe.

(b) Earnings derived from communications satellite system.

The earnings derived from the ownership or operation of a communications satellite system by a foreign entity designated by a foreign government to participate in such ownership or operation shall be exempt from taxation under this subtitle, if the United States, through its designated entity, participates in such system pursuant to the Communications Satellite Act of 1962 (47 U.S.C. 701 and following).

(c) Treatment of certain foreign corporations.

(1) In general. Paragraph (1) or (2) of subsection (a) (as the case may be) shall not apply to any foreign corporation if 50 percent or more of the value of the stock of such corporation is owned by individuals who are not residents of such foreign country or another foreign country meeting the requirements of such paragraph.

(2) Treatment of controlled foreign corporations. Paragraph (1) shall not apply to any foreign corporation which is a controlled foreign corporation (as defined in section 957(a)).

(3) Special rules for publicly traded corporations.

(A) Exception. Paragraph (1) shall not apply to any corporation which is organized in a foreign country meeting the requirements of paragraph (1) or (2) of subsection (a) (as the case may be) and the stock of which is primarily and regularly traded on an established securities market in such foreign country, another foreign country meeting the requirements of such paragraph, or the United States.

(B) Treatment of stock owned by publicly traded corporation. Any stock in another corporation which is owned (directly or indirectly) by a corporation meeting the requirements of subparagraph (A) shall be treated as owned by individuals who are residents of the foreign country in which the corporation meeting the requirements of subparagraph (A) is organized.

(4) Stock ownership through entities. For purposes of paragraph (1), stock owned (directly or indirectly) by or for a corporation, partnership, trust, or estate shall be treated as being owned proportionately by its shareholders, partners, or beneficiaries. Stock considered to be owned by a person by reason of the application of the preceding sentence shall, for purposes of applying such sentence, be treated as actually owned by such person.

§ 884. Branch profits tax.

(a) Imposition of tax.

In addition to the tax imposed by section 882 for any taxable year, there is hereby imposed on any foreign corporation a tax equal to 30 percent of the dividend equivalent amount for the taxable year.

(b) Dividend equivalent amount.

For purposes of subsection (a), the term "dividend equivalent amount" means the foreign corporation's effectively connected earnings and profits for the taxable year adjusted as provided in this subsection:

(1) Reduction for increase in U.S. net equity. If --

(A) the U.S. net equity of the foreign corporation as of the close of the taxable year, exceeds

(B) the U.S. net equity of the foreign corporation as of the close of the preceding taxable year,

the effectively connected earnings and profits for the taxable year shall be reduced (but not below zero) by the amount of such excess.

(2) Increase for decrease in net equity.

(A) In general. If --

(i) the U.S. net equity of the foreign corporation as of the close of the preceding taxable year, exceeds

(ii) the U.S. net equity of the foreign corporation as of the close of the taxable year,

the effectively connected earnings and profits for the taxable year shall be increased by the amount of such excess.

(B) Limitation.

(i) In general. The increase under subparagraph (A) for any taxable year shall not exceed the accumulated effectively connected earnings and profits as of the close of the preceding taxable year.

(ii) Accumulated effectively connected earnings and profits. For purposes of clause (i), the term "accumulated effectively connected earnings and profits" means the excess of --

(I) the aggregate effectively connected earnings and profits for preceding taxable years beginning after December 31, 1986, over

(II) the aggregate dividend equivalent amounts determined for such preceding taxable years.

(c) U.S. net equity.

For purposes of this section --

(1) In general. The term "U.S. net equity" means --

(A) U.S. assets, reduced (including below zero) by

(B) U.S. liabilities.

(2) U.S. assets and U.S. liabilities. For purposes of paragraph (1) --

(A) U.S. assets. The term "U.S. assets" means the money and aggregate adjusted bases of property of the foreign corporation treated as connected with the conduct of a trade or business in the United States under regulations prescribed by the Secretary. For purposes of the preceding sentence, the adjusted basis of any property shall be its adjusted basis for purposes of computing earnings and profits.

(B) U.S. liabilities. The term "U.S. liabilities" means the liabilities of the foreign corporation treated as connected with the conduct of a trade or business in the United States under regulations prescribed by the Secretary.

(C) Regulations to be consistent with allocation of deductions. The regulations prescribed under subparagraphs (A) and (B) shall be consistent with the allocation of deductions under section 882(c)(1).

(d) Effectively connected earnings and profits.

For purposes of this section --

(1) In general. The term "effectively connected earnings and profits" means earnings and profits (without diminution by reason of any distributions made during the taxable year) which are attributable to income which is effectively connected (or treated as effectively connected) with the conduct of a trade or business within the United States.

(2) Exception for certain income. The term "effectively connected earnings and profits" shall not include any earnings and profits attributable to --

(A) income not includible in gross income under paragraph (1) or (2) of section 883(a),

(B) income treated as effectively connected with the conduct of a trade or business within the United States under section 921(d) or 926(b),

(C) gain on the disposition of a United States real property interest described in section 897(c)(1)(A)(ii),

(D) income treated as effectively connected with the conduct of a trade or business within the United States under section 953(c)(3)(C), or

(E) income treated as effectively connected with the conduct of a trade or business within the United States under section 882(e).

Property and liabilities of the foreign corporation treated as connected with such income under regulations prescribed by the Secretary shall not be taken into account in determining the U.S. assets or U.S. liabilities of the foreign corporation.

(e) Coordination with income tax treaties; etc.

(1) Limitation on treaty exemption. No treaty between the United States and a foreign country shall exempt any foreign corporation from the tax imposed by subsection (a) (or reduce the amount thereof) unless --

(A) such treaty is an income tax treaty, and

(B) such foreign corporation is a qualified resident of such foreign country.

(2) Treaty modifications. If a foreign corporation is a qualified resident of a foreign country with which the United States has an income tax treaty --

(A) the rate of tax under subsection (a) shall be the rate of tax specified in such treaty --

(i) on branch profits if so specified, or

(ii) if not so specified, on dividends paid by a domestic corporation to a corporation resident in such country which wholly owns such domestic corporation, and

(B) any other limitations under such treaty on the tax imposed by subsection (a) shall apply.

(3) Coordination with withholding tax.

(A) In general. If a foreign corporation is subject to the tax imposed by subsection (a) for any taxable year (determined after the application of any treaty), no tax shall be imposed by section 871(a), 881(a), 1441, or 1442 on any dividends paid by such corporation out of its earnings and profits for such taxable year.

(B) Limitation on certain treaty benefits. If --

(i) any dividend described in section 861(a)(2)(B) is received by a foreign corporation, and

(ii) subparagraph (A) does not apply to such dividend, rules similar to the rules of subparagraphs (A) and (B) of subsection (f)(3) shall apply to such dividend.

(4) Qualified resident. For purposes of this subsection --

(A) In general. Except as otherwise provided in this paragraph, the term "qualified resident" means, with respect to any foreign country, any foreign corporation which is a resident of such foreign country unless --

(i) 50 percent or more (by value) of the stock of such foreign corporation is owned (within the meaning of section 883(c)(4)) by individuals who are not residents of such foreign country and who are not United States citizens or resident aliens, or

(ii) 50 percent or more of its income is used (directly or indirectly) to meet liabilities to persons who are not residents of such foreign country or citizens or residents of the United States.

(B) Special rule for publicly traded corporations. A foreign corporation which is a resident of a foreign country shall be treated as a qualified resident of such foreign country if --

(i) the stock of such corporation is primarily and regularly traded on an established securities market in such foreign country, or

(ii) such corporation is wholly owned (either directly or indirectly) by another foreign corporation which is organized in such foreign country and the stock of which is so traded.

(C) Corporations owned by publicly traded domestic corporations. A foreign corporation which is a resident of a foreign country shall be treated as a qualified resident of such foreign country if --

(i) such corporation is wholly owned (directly or indirectly) by a domestic corporation, and

(ii) the stock of such domestic corporation is primarily and regularly traded on an established securities market in the United States.

(D) Secretarial authority. The Secretary may, in his sole discretion, treat a foreign corporation as being a qualified resident of a foreign country if such corporation establishes to the satisfaction of the Secretary that such corporation meets such requirements as the Secretary may establish to ensure that individuals who are not residents of such foreign country do not use the treaty between such foreign country and the United States in a manner inconsistent with the purposes of this subsection.

(5) Exception for international organizations. This section shall not apply to an international organization (as defined in section 7701(a)(18)).

(f) Treatment of interest allocable to effectively connected income.

(1) In general. In the case of a foreign corporation engaged in a trade or business in the United States (or having gross income treated as effectively connected with the conduct of a trade or business in the United States), for purposes of this subtitle --

(A) any interest paid by such trade or business in the United States shall be treated as if it were paid by a domestic corporation, and

(B) to the extent the amount of interest allowable as a deduction under section 882 in computing the effectively connected taxable income of such foreign corporation exceeds the interest described in subparagraph (A), such foreign corporation shall be liable for tax under section 881(a) in the same manner as if such excess were interest paid to such foreign corporation by a wholly owned domestic corporation on the last day of such foreign corporation's taxable year.

To the extent provided in regulations, subparagraph (A) shall not apply to interest in excess of the amounts reasonably expected to be deductible under section 882 in computing the effectively connected taxable income of such foreign corporation.

(2) Allocable interest. For purposes of this subsection, the term "allocable interest" means any interest which is allocable to income which is effectively connected (or treated as effectively connected) with the conduct of a trade or business in the United States.

(3) Coordination with treaties.

(A) Payor must be qualified resident. In the case of any interest described in paragraph (1) which is paid or accrued by a foreign corporation, no benefit under any treaty between the United States and the foreign country of which such corporation is a resident shall apply unless --

(i) such treaty is an income tax treaty, and

424

(ii) such foreign corporation is a qualified resident of such foreign country.

(B) Recipient must be qualified resident. In the case of any interest described in paragraph (1) which is received or accrued by any corporation, no benefit under any treaty between the United States and the foreign country of which such corporation is a resident shall apply unless --

(i) such treaty is an income tax treaty, and

(ii) such foreign corporation is a qualified resident of such foreign country.

(g) Regulations.

The Secretary shall prescribe such regulations as may be necessary or appropriate to carry out the purposes of this section, including regulations providing for appropriate adjustments in the determination of the dividend equivalent amount in connection with the distribution to shareholders or transfer to a controlled corporation of the taxpayer's U.S. assets and other adjustments in such determination as are necessary or appropriate to carry out the purposes of this section.

§ 901. Taxes of foreign countries and of possessions of United States.

(a) Allowance of credit.

If the taxpayer chooses to have the benefits of this subpart, the tax imposed by this chapter shall, subject to the limitation of section 904, be credited with the amounts provided in the applicable paragraph of subsection (b) plus, in the case of a corporation, the taxes deemed to have been paid under sections 902 and 960. Such choice for any taxable year may be made or changed at any time before the expiration of the period prescribed for making a claim for credit or refund of the tax imposed by this chapter for such taxable year. The credit shall not be allowed against any tax treated as a tax not imposed by this chapter under section 26(b).

(b) Amount allowed.

Subject to the limitation of section 904, the following amounts shall be allowed as the credit under subsection (a):

(1) Citizens and domestic corporations. In the case of a citizen of the United States and of a domestic corporation, the amount of any income, war profits, and excess profits taxes paid or accrued during the taxable year to any foreign country or to any possession of the United States; and

(2) Resident of the United States or Puerto Rico. In the case of a resident of the United States and in the case of an individual who is a bona fide resident of Puerto Rico during the entire taxable year, the amount of any such taxes paid or accrued during the taxable year to any possession of the United States; and

(3) Alien resident of the United States or Puerto Rico. In the case of an alien resident of the United States and in the case of an alien individual who is a bona fide resident of Puerto Rico during the entire taxable year, the amount of any such taxes paid or accrued during the taxable year to any foreign country; and

(4) Nonresident alien individuals and foreign corporations. In the case of any nonresident alien individual not described in section 876 and in the case of any foreign corporation, the amount determined pursuant to section 906; and

(5) Partnerships and estates. In the case of any individual described in paragraph (1), (2), or (3), or (4), who is a member of a partnership or a beneficiary of an estate or trust, the amount of his proportionate share of the taxes (described in such paragraph) of the partnership or the estate or trust paid or accrued during the taxable year to a foreign country or to any possession of the United States, as the case may be. Under rules or regulations prescribed by the Secretary, in the case of any foreign trust of which the settlor or another person would be treated as owner of any portion of the trust under subpart E but for section 672(f), the allocable amount of any income, war profits, and excess profits taxes imposed by any foreign country or possession of the United States on the settlor or such other person in respect of trust income.

(c) Similar credit required for certain alien residents.

Whenever the President finds that --

(1) a foreign country, in imposing income, war profits, and excess profits taxes, does not allow to citizens of the United States residing in such foreign country a credit for any such taxes paid or accrued to the United States or any foreign country, as the case may be, similar to the credit allowed under subsection (b)(3),

(2) such foreign country, when requested by the United States to do so, has not acted to provide such a similar credit to citizens of the United States residing in such foreign country, and

(3) it is in the public interest to allow the credit under subsection (b)(3) to citizens or subjects of such foreign country only if it allows such a similar credit to citizens of the United States residing in such foreign country, the President shall proclaim that, for taxable years beginning while the proclamation remains in effect, the credit under subsection (b)(3) shall be allowed to citizens or subjects of such foreign country only if such foreign country, in imposing income, war profits, and excess profits taxes, allows to citizens of the United States residing in such foreign country such a similar credit.

(d) Treatment of dividends from a DISC or former DISC.

For purposes of this subpart, dividends from a DISC or former DISC (as defined in section 992(a)) shall be treated as dividends from a foreign corporation to the extent such dividends are treated under part I as income from sources without the United States.

(e) Foreign taxes on mineral income.

(1) Reduction in amount allowed. Notwithstanding subsection (b), the amount of any income, war profits, and excess profits taxes paid or accrued during the taxable year to any foreign country or possession of the United States with respect to foreign mineral income from sources within such country or possession which would (but for this paragraph) be allowed under such subsection shall be reduced by the amount (if any) by which --

(A) the amount of such taxes (or, if smaller, the amount of the tax which would be computed under this chapter with respect to such income determined without the deduction allowed under section 613), exceeds

(B) the amount of the tax computed under this chapter with respect to such income.

(2) Foreign mineral income defined. For purposes of paragraph (1), the term "foreign mineral income" means income derived from the extraction of minerals from mines, wells, or other natural deposits, the processing of such minerals into their primary products, and the transportation, distribution, or sale of such minerals or primary products. Such term includes, but is not limited to --

(A) dividends received from a foreign corporation in respect of which taxes are deemed paid by the taxpayer under section 902, to the extent such dividends are attributable to foreign mineral income, and

(B) that portion of the taxpayer's distributive share of the income of partnerships attributable to foreign mineral income.

(f) Certain payments for oil or gas not considered as taxes.

Notwithstanding subsection (b) and sections 902 and 960, the amount of any income, or profits, and excess profits taxes paid or accrued during the taxable year to any foreign country in connection with the purchase and sale of oil or gas extracted in such country is not to be considered as tax for purposes of section 275(a) and this section if --

(1) the taxpayer has no economic interest in the oil or gas to which section 611(a) applies, and

(2) either such purchase or sale is at a price which differs from the fair market value for such oil or gas at the time of such purchase or sale.

(g) Certain taxes paid with respect to distributions from possessions corporations.

(1) In general. For purposes of this chapter, any tax of a foreign country or possession of the United States which is paid or accrued with respect to any distribution from a corporation --

(A) to the extent that such distribution is attributable to periods during which such corporation is a possessions corporation, and

(B)(i) if a dividends received deduction is allowable with respect to such distribution under part VIII of subchapter B, or

(ii) to the extent that such distribution is received in connection with a liquidation or other transaction with respect to which gain or loss is not recognized, shall not be treated as income, war profits, or excess profits taxes paid or accrued to a foreign country or possession of the United States, and no deduction shall be allowed under this title with respect to any amount so paid or accrued.

(2) Possessions corporation. For purposes of paragraph (1), a corporation shall be treated as a possessions corporation for any period during which an election under section 936 applied to such corporation, or during which section 931 (as in effect on the day before the date of the enactment of the Tax Reform Act of 1976) applied to such corporation, or during which section 957(c) (as in effect on the day before the date of the enactment of the Tax Reform Act of 1986) applied to such corporation.

(h) Taxes paid with respect to foreign trade income.

No credit shall be allowed under this section for any income, war profits, and excess profits taxes paid or accrued with respect to the foreign trade income (within the meaning of section 923(b)) of a FSC, other than section 923(a)(2) non-exempt income (within the meaning of section 927(d)(6)).

(i) Taxes used to provide subsidies.

Any income, war profits, or excess profits tax shall not be treated as a tax for purposes of this title to the extent --

(1) the amount of such tax is used (directly or indirectly) by the country imposing such tax to provide a subsidy by any means to the taxpayer, a related person (within the meaning of section 482), or any party to the transaction or to a related transaction, and

(2) such subsidy is determined (directly or indirectly) by reference to the amount of such tax, or the base used to compute the amount of such tax.

(j) Denial of foreign tax credit, etc., with respect to certain foreign countries.

(1) In general. Notwithstanding any other provision of this part --

(A) no credit shall be allowed under subsection (a) for any income, war profits, or excess profits taxes paid or accrued (or deemed paid under section 902 or 960) to any country if such taxes are with respect to income attributable to a period during which this subsection applies to such country, and

(B) subsections (a), (b), and (c) of section 904 and sections 902 and 960 shall be applied separately with respect to income attributable to such a period from sources within such country

(2) Countries to which subsection applies.

(A) In general. This subsection shall apply to any foreign country --

(i) the government of which the United States does not recognize, unless such government is otherwise eligible to purchase defense articles or services under the Arms Export Control Act,

(ii) with respect to which the United States has severed diplomatic relations,

(iii) with respect to which the United States has not severed diplomatic relations but does not conduct such relations, or

(iv) which the Secretary of State has, pursuant to section 6(j) of the Export Administration Act of 1979, as amended, designated as a foreign country which repeatedly provides support for acts of international terrorisms.

(B) Period for which subsection applies. This subsection shall apply to any foreign country described in subparagraph (A) during the period --

(i) beginning on the later of --

(I) January 1, 1987, or

(II) 6 months after such country becomes a country described in subparagraph (A), and

(ii) ending on the date the Secretary of State certifies to the Secretary of the Treasury that such country is no longer described in subparagraph (A).

(C) Repealed.

(3) Taxes allowed as a deduction, etc. Sections 275 and 78 shall not apply to any tax which is not allowable as a credit under subsection (a) by reason of this subsection.

(4) Regulations. The Secretary shall prescribe such regulations as may be necessary or appropriate to carry out the purposes of this subsection, including regulations which treat income paid through 1 or more entities as derived from a foreign country to which this subsection applies if such income was, without regard to such entities, derived from such country.

(k) Minimum holding period for certain taxes.

(1) Withholding Taxes.

(A) In General -- In no event shall a credit be allowed under subsection (a) for any withholding tax on a dividend with respect to stock in a corporation if --

(i) such stock is held by the recipient of the dividend for 15 days or less during the 30-day period beginning on the date which is 15 days before the date on which such share becomes ex-dividend with respect to such dividend, or

(ii) to the extent that the recipient of the dividend is under an obligation (whether pursuant to a short sale or otherwise) to make related payments with respect to positions in substantially similar or related property.

(B) Withholding Tax. For purposes of this paragraph, the term "withholding tax" includes any tax determined on a gross basis; but does not include any tax which is in the nature of a prepayment of a tax imposed on a net basis.

(2) Deemed Paid Taxes -- In the case of income, war profits, or excess profits taxes deemed paid under section 853, 902, or 960 through a chain of ownership of stock in 1 or more corporations, no credit shall be allowed under subsection (a) if --

(A) any stock of any corporation in such chain (the ownership of which is required to obtain credit under subsection (a) for such taxes) is held for less than the period described in paragraph (1)(A)(i), or

(B) the corporation holding the stock in under the obligation referred to in paragraph (1)(A)(ii).

(3) 45-day Rule in the Case of Certain Preference Dividends -- In the case of stock having preference in dividends and dividends with respect to such stock which are attributable to a period or periods aggregating in excess of 366 days, paragraph (1)(A)(I) shall be applied --

(A) by substituting "45 days" for "15 days" each place it appears, and

(B) by substituting "90 day period" for "30 day period".

(4) Exception for Certain Taxes Paid by Securities Dealers.

(A) In General. Paragraphs (1) and (2) shall not apply to any qualified tax with respect to any security held in the active conduct in a foreign country of a business as a securities dealer of any person

(i) who is registered as a securities broker or dealer under section 15(a) of the Securities Exchange Act of 1934,

(ii) who is registered as a Government securities broker or dealer under section 15C(a) of such Act, or

(iii) who is licensed or authorized in such foreign country to conduct securities activities in such country and is subject to bona fide regulation by a securities regulating authority of such country.

(B) Qualified Tax. For purposes of subparagraph (A), the term "qualified tax" means a tax paid to a foreign country (other than the foreign country referred to in subparagraph (A)) if --

(i) the dividend to which such tax is attributable is subject to taxation on a net basis by the country referred to in subparagraph (A), and

(ii) such country allows a credit against its net basis tax for the full amount of the tax paid to such other foreign country.

(5) Certain Rules to Apply. For purposes of this section, the rules of paragraphs (2) and (3) of section 246(c) shall apply.

(6) Treatment of Bona Fide Sales. If a person's holding period is reduced by reason of the application of the rules of section 246(c)(4) to any contract for the bona fide sale of stock, the determination of whether such person's holding period meets the requirements of paragraph (2) with respect to taxes deemed paid under section 902 or 960 shall be   made as of the date such contract is entered into.

(7) Taxes Allowed as Deduction, etc. Section 275 and 78 shall not apply to any tax which is not allowable as a credit under subsection (a) by reason of this subsection.

(l) Cross reference.

(1) For deductions of income, war profits, and excess profits taxes paid to a foreign country or a possession of the United States, see sections 164 and 175.

(2) For right of each partner to make election under this section, see section 703(b).

(3) For right of estate or trust to the credit for taxes imposed by foreign countries and possessions of the United States under this section, see section 642(a).

(4) For reduction of credit for failure of a United States person to furnish certain information with respect to a foreign corporation controlled by him, see section 6038.

§ 902. Deemed paid credit where domestic corporation owns 10 percent or more of voting stock of foreign corporation.

(a) Taxes paid by foreign corporation treated as paid by domestic corporation.

For purposes of this subpart, a domestic corporation which owns 10 percent or more of the voting stock of a foreign corporation from which it receives dividends in any taxable year shall be deemed to have paid the same proportion of such foreign corporation's post-1986 foreign income taxes as --

(1) the amount of such dividends (determined without regard to section 78), bears to

(2) such foreign corporation's post-1986 undistributed earnings.

(b) Deemed Taxes Increased in Case of Certain Lower Tier Corporations.

(1) In General. If

(A) any foreign corporation is a member of a qualified group, and

(B) such foreign corporation owns 10 percent or more of the voting stock of another member of such group from which it receives dividends in any taxable year, such foreign corporation shall be deemed to have paid the same proportion of such other member's post-1986 foreign income taxes as would be determined under subsection (a) if such foreign corporation were a domestic corporation.

(2) **Qualified** Group. For the purpose of paragraph (1), the term "qualified group" means

(A) the foreign corporation describe in subsection (a), and

(B) any other foreign corporation if

(i) the domestic corporation owns at least 5 percent of the voting stock of such other foreign corporation indirectly through a chain of foreign corporations connected through stock ownership of at least 10 percent of their voting stock,

(ii) the foreign corporation described in subsection (a) is the first tier corporation in such chain, and

(iii) such other corporation is not below the sixth tier in such chain.

The term "qualified group" shall not include any foreign corporation below the third tier in the chain referred to in clause (i) unless such foreign corporation is a controlled foreign corporation (as defined in section 957) and the domestic corporation is a United States shareholder (as defined in section 951(b)) in such foreign corporation. Paragraph (1) shall apply only to those taxes paid by a member of the qualified group below the third tier only with respect to periods during which it was a controlled foreign corporation.

(b) Deemed taxes increased in case of certain 2nd and 3rd tier foreign corporations.

(1) 2nd tier. If the foreign corporation described in subsection (a) (hereinafter in this section referred to as the "1st tier corporation") owns 10 percent or more of the voting stock of a 2nd foreign corporation from which it receives dividends in any taxable year, the 1st tier corporation shall be deemed to have paid the same proportion of such 2nd foreign corporation's post-1986 foreign income taxes as would be determined under subsection (a) if such 1st tier corporation were a domestic corporation.

(2) 3rd tier. If such 1st tier corporation owns 10 percent or more of the voting stock of a 2nd foreign corporation which, in turn, owns 10 percent or more of the voting stock of a 3rd foreign corporation from which the 2nd corporation receives dividends in any taxable year, such 2nd foreign corporation shall be deemed to have paid the same proportion of such 3rd foreign corporation's post-1986 foreign income taxes as would be determined under subsection (a) if such 2nd foreign corporation were a domestic corporation.

(3) 5 percent stock requirement. For purposes of this subpart --

(A) **For 2nd tier.** Paragraph (1) shall not apply unless the percentage of voting stock owned by the domestic corporation in the 1st tier corporation and the percentage of voting stock owned by the 1st tier corporation in the 2nd foreign corporation when multiplied together equal at least 5 percent.

(B) **For 3rd tier.** Paragraph (2) shall not apply unless the percentage arrived at for purposes of applying paragraph (1) when multiplied by the percentage of voting stock owned by the 2nd foreign corporation in the 3rd foreign corporation is equal to at least 5 percent.

(c) Definitions and special rules.

For purposes of this section --

(1) Post-1986 undistributed earnings. The term "post-1986 undistributed earnings" means the amount of the earnings and profits of the foreign corporation (computed in accordance with sections 964(a) and 986) accumulated in taxable years beginning after December 31, 1986 --

(A) as of the close of the taxable year of the foreign corporation in which the dividend is distributed, and

(B) without diminution by reason of dividends distributed during such taxable year.

(2) Post-1986 foreign income taxes. The term "post-1986 foreign income taxes" means the sum of --

(A) the foreign income taxes with respect to the taxable year of the foreign corporation in which the dividend is distributed, and

(B) the foreign income taxes with respect to prior taxable years beginning after December 31, 1986, to the extent such foreign taxes were not deemed paid with respect to dividends distributed by the foreign corporation in prior taxable years.

(3) Special rule where domestic corporation acquires 10 percent of foreign corporation after December 31, 1986.

(A) In general. If the 1st day on which the ownership requirements of subparagraph (B) are met with respect to any foreign corporation is in a taxable year of such corporation beginning after December 31, 1986, the post-1986 undistributed earnings and the post-1986 foreign income taxes of such foreign corporation shall be determined by taking into account only periods beginning on and after the 1st day of the 1st taxable year in which such ownership requirements are met.

(B) Ownership requirements. The ownership requirements of this subparagraph are met with respect to any foreign corporation if --

(i) 10 percent or more of the voting stock of such foreign corporation is owned by a domestic corporation,

(ii) the requirements of subsection (b)(3)(A) are met with respect to such foreign corporation and 10 percent or more of the voting stock of such foreign corporation is owned by another foreign corporation described in clause (i), or

(iii) the requirements of subsection (b)(3)(B) are met with respect to such foreign corporation and 10 percent or more of the voting stock of such foreign corporation is owned by another foreign corporation described in clause (ii).

(4) Foreign income taxes.

(A) In general. The term "foreign income taxes" means any income, war profits, or excess profits taxes paid by the foreign corporation to any foreign country or possession of the United States.

(B) Treatment of deemed taxes. Except for purposes of determining the amount of the post-1986 foreign income taxes of a 3rd foreign corporation referred to in subsection (b)(2), the term "foreign income taxes" includes any such taxes deemed to be paid by the foreign corporation under this section.

(5) Accounting periods. In the case of a foreign corporation the income, war profits, and excess profits taxes of which are determined on the basis of an accounting period of less than 1 year, the word "year" as used in this subsection shall be construed to mean such accounting period.

(6) Treatment of distributions from earnings before 1987.

(A) In general. In the case of any dividend paid by a foreign corporation out of accumulated profits (as defined in this section as in effect on the day before the date of the enactment of the Tax Reform Act of 1986) for taxable years beginning before the 1st taxable year taken into account in determining the post-1986 undistributed earnings of such corporation --

(i) this section (as amended by the Tax Reform Act of 1986) shall not apply, but

(ii) this section (as in effect on the day before the date of the enactment of such Act) shall apply.

(B) Dividends paid first out of post-1986 earnings. Any dividend in a taxable year beginning after December 31, 1986, shall be treated as made out of post-1986 undistributed earnings to the extent thereof.

(7) Regulations. The Secretary shall provide such regulations as may be necessary or appropriate to carry out the provisions of this section and section 960, including provisions which provide for the separate application of this section and section 960 to reflect the separate application of section 904 to separate types of income and loss.

(d) Cross references.

(1) For inclusion in gross income of an amount equal to taxes deemed paid under subsection (a), see section 78.

(2) For application of subsections (a) and (b) with respect to taxes deemed paid in a prior taxable year by a United States shareholder with respect to a controlled foreign corporation, see section 960.

(3) For reduction of credit with respect to dividends paid out of post-1986 undistributed earnings for years for which certain information is not furnished, see section 6038.

§ 903. Credit for taxes in lieu of income, etc., taxes

For purposes of this part and of sections 164(a) and 275(a), the term "income, war profits, and excess profits taxes" shall include a tax paid in lieu of a tax on income, war profits, or excess profits otherwise generally imposed by any foreign country or by any possession of the United States.

§ 904. Limitation on credit.

(a) Limitation.

The total amount of the credit taken under section 901(a) shall not exceed the same proportion of the tax against which such credit is taken which the taxpayer's taxable income from sources without the United States (but not in excess of the taxpayer's entire taxable income) bears to his entire taxable income for the same taxable year.

(b) Taxable income for purpose of computing limitation.

(1) **Personal exemptions.** For purposes of subsection (a), the taxable income in the case of an individual, estate, or trust shall be computed without any deduction for personal exemptions under section 151 or 642(b).

(2) **Capital gains.** For purposes of this section --

(A) **In general.** Taxable income from sources outside the United States shall include gain from the sale or exchange of capital assets only to the extent of foreign source capital gain net income.

(B) **Special rules where capital gain rate differential.** In the case of any taxable year for which there is a capital gain rate differential --

(i) in lieu of applying subparagraph (A), the taxable income from sources outside the United States shall include gain from the sale or exchange of capital assets only in an amount equal to foreign source capital gain net income reduced by the rate differential portion of foreign source net capital gain,

(ii) the entire taxable income shall include gain from the sale or exchange of capital assets only in an amount equal to capital gain net income reduced by the rate differential portion of net capital gain, and

(iii) for purposes of determining taxable income from sources outside the United States, any net capital loss (and any amount which is a short-term capital loss under section 1212(a)) from sources outside the United States to the extent taken into account in determining capital gain net income for the taxable year shall be reduced by an amount equal to the rate differential portion of the excess of net capital gain from sources within the United States over net capital gain.

(C) **Coordination With the Capital gains Rate.** The Secretary may by regulations modify the application of this paragraph and paragraph (3) to the extent necessary to properly reflect any capital gain rate differential under section 1(h) or 120(a) and the computation of net capital gain.

(3) **Definitions.** For purposes of this subsection --

(A) **Foreign source capital gain net income.** The term "foreign source capital gain net income" means the lesser of --

(i) capital gain net income from sources without the United States, or

(ii) capital gain net income.

(B) **Foreign source net capital gain.** The term "foreign source net capital gain" means the lesser of --

(i) net capital gain from sources without the United States, or

(ii) net capital gain.

(C) **Section 1231 gains.** The term "gain from the sale or exchange of capital assets" includes any gain so treated under section 1231.

(D) **Capital gain rate differential.** There is a capital gain rate differential for any taxable year if --

(i) in the case of a taxpayer other than a corporation, subsection (h) of section 1 applies to such taxable year, or

(ii) in the case of a corporation, any rate of tax imposed by section 11, 511, or 831(a) or (b) (whichever applies) exceeds the alternative rate of tax under section 1201(a) (determined without regard to the last sentence of section 11(b)(1)).

(E) Rate differential portion.

(i) In general. The rate differential portion of foreign source net capital gain, net capital gain, or the excess of net capital gain from sources within the United States over net capital gain, as the case may be, is the same proportion of such amount as --

(I) the excess of the highest applicable tax rate over the alternative tax rate, bears to

(II) the highest applicable tax rate.

(ii) Highest applicable tax rate. For purposes of clause (i), the term "highest applicable tax rate" means --

(I) in the case of a taxpayer other than a corporation, the highest rate of tax set forth in subsection (a), (b), (c), (d), or (e) of section 1 (whichever applies), or

(II) in the case of a corporation, the highest rate of tax specified in section 11(b).

(iii) Alternative tax rate. For purposes of clause (i), the term "alternative tax rate" means --

(I) in the case of a taxpayer other than a corporation, the alternative rate of tax determined under section 1(h), or

(II) in the case of a corporation, the alternative rate of tax under section 1201(a).

(4) Coordination with section 936 - effective for tax. yrs. begin. before 1/1/94. For purposes of subsection (a), in the case of a corporation, the taxable income shall not include any portion thereof taken into account for purposes of the credit (if any) allowed by section 936.

(4) Coordination with section 936 - effective for tax. yrs. begin. after 12/31/93. For purposes of subsection (a), in the case of a corporation, the taxable income shall not include any portion thereof taken into account for purposes of the credit (if any) allowed by section 936 (without regard to subsections (a)(4) and (i) thereof).

(c) Carryback and carryover of excess tax paid.

Any amount by which all taxes paid or accrued to foreign countries or possessions of the United States for any taxable year for which the taxpayer chooses to have the benefits of this subpart exceed the limitation under subsection (a) shall be deemed taxes paid or accrued to foreign countries or possessions of the United States in the second preceding taxable year, in the first preceding taxable year, and in the first, second, third, fourth, or fifth succeeding taxable years, in that order and to the extent not deemed taxes paid or accrued in a prior taxable year, in the amount by which the limitation under subsection (a) for such preceding or succeeding taxable year exceeds the sum of the taxes paid or accrued to foreign countries or possessions of the United States for such preceding or succeeding taxable year and the amount of the taxes for any taxable year earlier than the current taxable year which shall be deemed to have been paid or accrued in such preceding or subsequent taxable year (whether or not the taxpayer chooses to have the benefits of this subpart with respect to such earlier taxable year). Such amount deemed paid or accrued in any year may be availed of only as a tax credit and not as a deduction and only if the taxpayer for such year chooses to have the benefits of this subpart as to taxes paid or accrued for that year to foreign countries or possessions of the United States.

(d) Separate application of section with respect to certain categories of income.

   (1) In general. The provisions of subsections (a), (b), and (c) and sections 902, 907, and 960 shall be applied separately with respect to each of the following items of income:

   (A) passive income,

   (B) high withholding tax interest,

   (C) financial services income,

   (D) shipping income,

   (E) in the case of a corporation, dividends from noncontrolled section 902 corporations, out of earnings and profits accumulated in taxable years beginning before January 1, 2003.

   (F) dividends from a DISC or former DISC (as defined in section 992(a)) to the extent such dividends are treated as income from sources without the United States,

   (G) taxable income attributable to foreign trade income (within the meaning of section 923(b)),

   (H) distributions from a FSC (or a former FSC) out of earnings and profits attributable to foreign trade income (within the meaning of section 923(b)) or interest or carrying charges (as defined in section 927(d)(1)) derived from a transaction which results in foreign trade income (as defined in section 923(b)), and

   (I) income other than income described in any of the preceding subparagraphs.

   (2) Definitions and special rules. For purposes of this subsection --

   (A) Passive income.

   (i) In general. Except as otherwise provided in this subparagraph, the term "passive income" means any income received or accrued by any person which is of a kind which would be foreign personal holding company income (as defined in section 954(c)).

   (ii) Certain amounts included. Except as provided in clause (iii), the term "passive income" includes any amount includible in gross income under section 551 or, except as provided in subparagraph (E)(iii) or paragraph (3)(I), section 1293 (relating to certain passive foreign investment companies).

   (iii) Exceptions. The term "passive income" shall not include --

   (I) any income described in a subparagraph of paragraph (1) other than subparagraph (A),

   (II) any export financing interest, and

   (III) any high-taxed income.

   (iv) Clarification of application of section 864(d)(6). In determining whether any income is of a kind which would be foreign personal holding company income, the rules of section 864(d)(6) shall apply only in the case of income of a controlled foreign corporation.

(B) High withholding tax interest.

(i) In general. Except as otherwise provided in this subparagraph, the term "high withholding tax interest" means any interest if --

(I) such interest is subject to a withholding tax of a foreign country or possession of the United States (or other tax determined on a gross basis), and

(II) the rate of such tax applicable to such interest is at least 5 percent.

(ii) Exception for export financing. The term "high withholding tax interest" shall not include any export financing interest.

(iii) Regulations. The Secretary may by regulations provide that --

(I) amounts (not otherwise high withholding tax interest) shall be treated as high withholding tax interest where necessary to prevent avoidance of the purposes of this subparagraph, and

(II) a tax shall not be treated as a withholding tax or other tax imposed on a gross basis if such tax is in the nature of a prepayment of a tax imposed on a net basis.

(C) Financial services income.

(i) In general. Except as otherwise provided in this subparagraph, the term "financial services income" means any income which is received or accrued by any person predominantly engaged in the active conduct of a banking, insurance, financing, or similar business, and which is --

(I) described in clause (ii),

(II) passive income (determined without regard to subclauses (I) and (III) of subparagraph (A)(iii)), or

(III) export financing interest which (but for subparagraph (B)(ii)) would be high withholding tax interest.

(ii) General description of financial services income. Income is described in this clause if such income is --

(I) derived in the active conduct of a banking, financing, or similar business,

(II) derived from the investment by an insurance company of its unearned premiums or reserves ordinary and necessary for the proper conduct of its insurance business, or

(III) of a kind which would be insurance income as defined in section 953(a) determined without regard to those provisions of paragraph (1)(A) of such section which limit insurance income to income from countries other than the country in which the corporation was created or organized.

(iii) Exceptions. The term "financial services income" does not include --

(I) any high withholding tax interest,

(II) any dividend from a noncontrolled section 902 corporation, out of earnings and profits accumulated in taxable years beginning before January 1, 2003, and

(III) any export financing interest not described in clause (i)(III).

437

(D) Shipping income. The term "shipping income" means any income received or accrued by any person which is of a kind which would be foreign base company shipping income (as defined in section 954(f)). Such term does not include any dividend from a noncontrolled section 902 corporation and does not include any financial services income.

(E) Noncontrolled section 902 corporation.

(i) In general. The term "noncontrolled section 902 corporation" means any foreign corporation with respect to which the taxpayer meets the stock ownership requirements of section 902(a) (or, for purposes of applying paragraph (3), the requirements of section 902(b)). A controlled foreign corporation shall not be treated as a noncontrolled section 902 corporation with respect to any distribution out of its earnings and profits for periods during which it was a controlled foreign corporation.

(ii) Special rule for taxes on high-withholding tax interest. If a foreign corporation is a noncontrolled section 902 corporation with respect to the taxpayer, taxes on high withholding tax interest (to the extent imposed at a rate in excess of 5 percent) shall not be treated as foreign taxes for purposes of determining the amount of foreign taxes deemed paid by the taxpayer under section 902.

(iii) Treatment of inclusions under section 1293. If any foreign corporation is a non-controlled section 902 corporation with respect to the taxpayer, any inclusion under section 1293 with respect to such corporation shall be treated as a dividend from such corporation.

(iv) All non-PFICs treated as one.--All noncontrolled section 902 corporations which are not passive foreign investment companies (as defined in section 1297) shall be treated as one noncontrolled section 902 corporation for purposes of paragraph (1).

(F) High-taxed income. The term "high-taxed income" means any income which (but for this subparagraph) would be passive income if the sum of --

(i) the foreign income taxes paid or accrued by the taxpayer with respect to such income, and

(ii) the foreign income taxes deemed paid by the taxpayer with respect to such income under section 902 or 960, exceeds the highest rate of tax specified in section 1 or 11 (whichever applies) multiplied by the amount of such income (determined with regard to section 78). For purposes of the preceding sentence, the term "foreign income taxes" means any income, war profits, or excess profits tax imposed by any foreign country or possession of the United States.

(G) Export financing interest. For purposes of this paragraph, the term "export financing interest" means any interest derived from financing the sale (or other disposition) for use or consumption outside the United States of any property --

(i) which is manufactured, produced, grown, or extracted in the United States by the taxpayer or a related person, and

(ii) not more than 50 percent of the fair market value of which is attributable to products imported into the United States.

For purposes of clause (ii), the fair market value of any property imported into the United States shall be its appraised value, as determined by the Secretary under section 402 of the Tariff Act of 1930 (19 U.S.C. 1401a) in connection with its importation.

(H) Related person. For purposes of this paragraph, the term "related person" has the meaning given such term by section 954(d)(3), except that such section shall be applied by substituting "the person with respect to whom the determination is being made" for "controlled foreign corporation" each place it appears.

(I) Transitional rule. For purposes of paragraph (1) --

(i) taxes paid or accrued in a taxable year beginning before January 1, 1987, with respect to income which was described in subparagraph (A) of paragraph (1) (as in effect on the day before the date of the enactment of the Tax Reform Act of 1986) shall be treated as taxes paid or accrued with respect to income described in subparagraph (A) of paragraph (1) (as in effect after such date),

(ii) taxes paid or accrued in a taxable year beginning before January 1, 1987, with respect to income which was described in subparagraph (E) of paragraph (1) (as in effect on the day before the date of the enactment of the Tax Reform Act of 1986) shall be treated as taxes paid or accrued with respect to income described in subparagraph (I) of paragraph (1) (as in effect after such date) except that --

(I) such taxes shall be treated as paid or accrued with respect to shipping income to the extent the taxpayer establishes to the satisfaction of the Secretary that such taxes were paid or accrued with respect to such income,

(II) in the case of a person described in subparagraph (C)(i), such taxes shall be treated as paid or accrued with respect to financial services income to the extent the taxpayer establishes to the satisfaction of the Secretary that such taxes were paid or accrued with respect to such income, and

(III) such taxes shall be treated as paid or accrued with respect to high withholding tax interest to the extent the taxpayer establishes to the satisfaction of the Secretary that such taxes were paid or accrued with respect to such income, and

(iii) taxes paid or accrued in a taxable year beginning before January 1, 1987, with respect to income described in any other subparagraph of paragraph (1) (as so in effect before such date) shall be treated as taxes paid or accrued with respect to income described in the corresponding subparagraph of paragraph (1) (as so in effect after such date).

(3) Look-thru in case of controlled foreign corporations.

(A) In general. Except as otherwise provided in this paragraph, dividends, interest, rents, and royalties received or accrued by the taxpayer from a controlled foreign corporation in which the taxpayer is a United States shareholder shall not be treated as income in a separate category.

(B) Subpart F inclusions. Any amount included in gross income under section 951(a)(1)(A) shall be treated as income in a separate category to the extent the amount so included is attributable to income in such category.

(C) Interest, rents, and royalties. Any interest, rent, or royalty which is received or accrued from a controlled foreign corporation in which the taxpayer is a United States shareholder shall be treated as income in a separate category to the extent it is properly allocable (under regulations prescribed by the Secretary) to income of the controlled foreign corporation in such category.

(D) Dividends. Any dividend paid out of the earnings and profits of any controlled foreign corporation in which the taxpayer is a United States shareholder shall be treated as income in a separate category in proportion to the ratio of --

(i) the portion of the earnings and profits attributable to income in such category, to

(ii) the total amount of earnings and profits.

(E) Look-thru applies only where subpart F applies. If a controlled foreign corporation meets the requirements of section 954(b)(3)(A) (relating to de minimis rule) for any taxable year, for purposes of this paragraph, none of its foreign base company income (as defined in section 954(a) without regard to section 954(b)(5)) and none of its gross insurance income (as defined in section 954(b)(3)(C)) for such taxable year shall be treated as income in a separate category, except that this sentence shall not apply to any income which (without regard to this sentence) would be treated as financial services income. Solely for purposes of applying subparagraph (D), passive income of a controlled foreign corporation shall not be treated as income in a separate category if the requirements of section 954(b)(4) are met with respect to such income.

(F) Separate category. For purposes of this paragraph --

(i) In general. Except as provided in clause (ii), the term "separate category" means any category of income described in subparagraph (A), (B), (C), (D), or (E) of paragraph (1).

(ii) Coordination with high-taxed income provisions.

(I) In determining whether any income of a controlled foreign corporation is in a separate category, subclause (III) of paragraph (2)(A)(iii) shall not apply.

(II) Any income of the taxpayer which is treated as income in a separate category under this paragraph shall be so treated notwithstanding any provision of paragraph (2); except that the determination of whether any amount is high-taxed income shall be made after the application of this paragraph.

(G) Dividend. For purposes of this paragraph, the term "dividend" includes any amount included in gross income in section 951(a)(1)(B). Any amount included in gross income under section 78 to the extent attributable to amounts included in gross income in section 951(a)(1)(A) shall not be treated as a dividend but shall be treated as included in gross income under section 951(a)(1)(A).

(H) Exception for certain high withholding tax interest. This paragraph shall not apply to any amount which --

(i) without regard to this paragraph, is high withholding tax interest (including any amount treated as high withholding tax interest under paragraph (2)(B)(iii)), and

(ii) would (but for this subparagraph) be treated as financial services income under this paragraph.

The amount to which this paragraph does not apply by reason of the preceding sentence shall not exceed the interest or equivalent income of the controlled foreign corporation taken into account in determining financial services income without regard to this subparagraph.

(I) Look-thru applies to passive foreign investment company inclusion if --

(i) a passive foreign investment company is a controlled foreign corporation, and

(ii) the taxpayer is a United States shareholder in such controlled foreign corporation, any amount included in gross income under section 1293 shall be treated as income in a separate category to the extent such amount is attributable to income in such category.

(4) Look-Thru Applies to Dividends From Noncontrolled Section 902 Corporations.

(A) In General. For purposes of this subsection, any applicable dividend shall be treated as income in a separate category in proportion to the ratio of

(i) the portion of the earnings and profits described in subparagraph (B)(ii) attributable to income in such category,
to

(ii) the total amount of such earnings and profits.

(B) Applicable Dividend. For purposes of subparagraph (A), the term "applicable dividend" means any dividend

(i) from a noncontrolled section 902 corporation with respect to the taxpayer, and

(ii) paid out of earnings and profits accumulated in taxable years beginning after December 31, 2002.

(C) Special Rules.

(i) In General. Rules similar to the rules of paragraph (3)(F) shall apply for purposes of this paragraph.

(ii) Earnings and Profits. For purposes of this paragraph and paragraph (1)(E)

(I) In general. The rules of section 316 shall apply.

(II) Regulations. The Secretary may prescribe regulations regarding the treatment of distributions out of earnings and profits for periods prior to the taxpayer's acquisition of such stock.

(5) Controlled foreign corporation; United States shareholder. For purposes of this subsection --

(A) Controlled foreign corporation. The term "controlled foreign corporation" has the meaning given such term by section 957 (taking into account section 953(c)).

(B) United States shareholder. The term "United States shareholder" has the meaning given such term by section 951(b) (taking into account section 953(c)).

(6) Regulations. The Secretary shall prescribe such regulations as may be necessary or appropriate for the purposes of this subsection, including regulations --

(A) for the application of paragraph (3) and subsection (f)(5) in the case of income paid (or loans made) through 1 or more entities or between 2 or more chains of entities,

(B) preventing the manipulation of the character of income the effect of which is to avoid the purposes of this subsection, and

(C) providing that rules similar to the rules of paragraph (3)(C) shall apply to interest, rents, and royalties received or accrued from entities which would be controlled foreign corporations if they were foreign corporations.

(e) Repealed.

(f) Recapture of overall foreign loss.

(1) General rule. For purposes of this subpart and section 936, in the case of any taxpayer who sustains an overall foreign loss for any taxable year, that portion of the taxpayer's taxable income from sources without the United States for each succeeding taxable year which is equal to the lesser of --

(A) the amount of such loss (to the extent not used under this paragraph in prior taxable years), or

(B) 50 percent (or such larger percent as the taxpayer may choose) of the taxpayer's taxable income from sources without the United States for such succeeding taxable year, shall be treated as income from sources within the United States (and not as income from sources without the United States).

(2) Overall foreign loss defined. For purposes of this subsection, the term "overall foreign loss" means the amount by which the gross income for the taxable year from sources without the United States (whether or not the taxpayer chooses the benefits of this subpart for such taxable year) for such year is exceeded by the sum of the deductions properly apportioned or allocated thereto, except that there shall not be taken into account --

(A) any net operating loss deduction allowable for such year under section 172(a), and

(B) any --

(i) foreign expropriation loss for such year, as defined in section 172(h), or

(ii) loss for such year which arises from fire, storm, shipwreck, or other casualty, or from theft, to the extent such loss is not compensated for by insurance or otherwise.

(3) Dispositions.

(A) In general. For purposes of this chapter, if property which has been used predominantly without the United States in a trade or business is disposed of during any taxable year --

(i) the taxpayer, notwithstanding any other provision of this chapter (other than paragraph (1)), shall be deemed to have received and recognized taxable income from sources without the United States in the taxable year of the disposition, by reason of such disposition, in an amount equal to the lesser of the excess of the fair market value of such property over the taxpayer's adjusted basis in such property or the remaining amount of the overall foreign losses which were not used under paragraph (1) for such taxable year or any prior taxable year, and

(ii) paragraph (1) shall be applied with respect to such income by substituting "100 percent" for "50 percent".

In determining for purposes of this subparagraph whether the predominant use of any property has been without the United States, there shall be taken into account use during the 3-year period ending on the date of the disposition (or, if shorter, the period during which the property has been used in the trade or business).

(B) Disposition defined and special rules.

(i) For purposes of this subsection, the term "disposition" includes a sale, exchange, distribution, or gift of property whether or not gain or loss is recognized on the transfer.

(ii) Any taxable income recognized solely by reason of subparagraph (A) shall have the same characterization it would have had if the taxpayer had sold or exchanged the property.

(iii) The Secretary shall prescribe such regulations as he may deem necessary to provide for adjustments to the basis of property to reflect taxable income recognized solely by reason of subparagraph (A).

(C) Exceptions. Notwithstanding subparagraph (B), the term "disposition" does not include --

(i) a disposition of property which is not a material factor in the realization of income by the taxpayer, or

(ii) a disposition of property to a domestic corporation in a distribution or transfer described in section 381(a).

(4) Accumulation distributions of foreign trust. For purposes of this chapter, in the case of amounts of income from sources without the United States which are treated under section 666 (without regard to subsections (b) and (c) thereof if the taxpayer chose to take a deduction with respect to the amounts described in such subsections under section 667(d)(1)(B)) as having been distributed by a foreign trust in a preceding taxable year, that portion of such amounts equal to the amount of any overall foreign loss sustained by the beneficiary in a year prior to the taxable year of the beneficiary in which such distribution is received from the trust shall be treated as income from sources within the United States (and not income from sources without the United States) to the extent that such loss was not used under this subsection in prior taxable years, or in the current taxable year, against other income of the beneficiary.

(5) Treatment of separate limitation losses.

(A) In general. The amount of the separate limitation losses for any taxable year shall reduce income from sources within the United States for such taxable year only to the extent the aggregate amount of such losses exceeds the aggregate amount of the separate limitation incomes for such taxable year.

(B) Allocation of losses. The separate limitation losses for any taxable year (to the extent such losses do not exceed the separate limitation incomes for such year) shall be allocated among (and operate to reduce) such incomes on a proportionate basis.

(C) Recharacterization of subsequent income. If --

(i) a separate limitation loss from any income category (hereinafter in this subparagraph referred to as "the loss category") was allocated to income from any other category under subparagraph (B), and

(ii) the loss category has income for a subsequent taxable year,

such income (to the extent it does not exceed the aggregate separate limitation losses from the loss category not previously recharacterized under this subparagraph) shall be recharacterized as income from such other category in proportion to the prior reductions under subparagraph (B) in such other category not previously taken into account under this subparagraph. Nothing in the preceding sentence shall be construed as recharacterizing any tax.

(D) Special rules for losses from sources in the United States. Any loss from sources in the United States for any taxable year (to the extent such loss does not exceed the separate limitation incomes from such year) shall be allocated among (and operate to reduce) such incomes on a proportionate basis. This subparagraph shall be applied after subparagraph (B).

(E) Definitions. For purposes of this paragraph --

(i) Income category. The term "income category" means each separate category of income described in subsection (d)(1).

(ii) Separate limitation income. The term "separate limitation income" means, with respect to any income category, the taxable income from sources outside the United States, separately computed for such category.

(iii) Separate limitation loss. The term "separate limitation loss" means, with respect to any income category, the loss from such category determined under the principles of section 907(c)(4)(B).

(F) Dispositions. If any separate limitation loss for any taxable year is allocated against any separate limitation income for such taxable year, except to the extent provided in regulations, rules similar to the rules of paragraph (3) shall apply to any disposition of property if gain from such disposition would be in the income category with respect to which there was such separate limitation loss.

(g) Source rules in case of United States-owned foreign corporations.

(1) In general. The following amounts which are derived from a United States-owned foreign corporation and which would be treated as derived from sources outside the United States without regard to this subsection shall, for purposes of this section, be treated as derived from sources within the United States to the extent provided in this subsection:

(A) Any amount included in gross income under --

(i) section 951(a) (relating to amounts included in gross income of United States shareholders),

(ii) section 551 (relating to foreign personal holding company income taxed to United States shareholders), or

(iii) section 1293 (relating to current taxation of income from qualified funds).

(B) Interest.

(C) Dividends.

(2) Subpart F and foreign personal holding or passive foreign investment company inclusions. Any amount described in subparagraph (A) of paragraph (1) shall be treated as derived from sources within the United States to the extent such amount is attributable to income of the United States-owned foreign corporation from sources within the United States.

(3) Certain interest allocable to United States source income. Any interest which --

(A) is paid or accrued by a United States-owned foreign corporation during any taxable year,

(B) is paid or accrued to a United States shareholder (as defined in section 951(b)) or a related person (within the meaning of section 267(b)) to such a shareholder, and

(C) is properly allocable (under regulations prescribed by the Secretary) to income of such foreign corporation for the taxable year from sources within the United States,

shall be treated as derived from sources within the United States.

(4) Dividends.

(A) In general. The United States source ratio of any dividend paid or accrued by a United States-owned foreign corporation shall be treated as derived from sources within the United States.

(B) United States source ratio. For purposes of subparagraph (A), the term "United States source ratio" means, with respect to any dividend paid out of the earnings and profits for any taxable year, a fraction --

(i) the numerator of which is the portion of the earnings and profits for such taxable year from sources within the United States, and

(ii) the denominator of which is the total amount of earnings and profits for such taxable year.

(5) Exception where United States-owned foreign corporation has small amount of United States source income. Paragraph (3) shall not apply to interest paid or accrued during any taxable year (and paragraph (4) shall not apply to any dividends paid out of the earnings and profits for such taxable year) if --

(A) the United States-owned foreign corporation has earnings and profits for such taxable year, and

(B) less than 10 percent of such earnings and profits is attributable to sources within the United States.

For purposes of the preceding sentence, earnings and profits shall be determined without any reduction for interest described in paragraph (3) (determined without regard to subparagraph (C) thereof).

(6) United States-owned foreign corporation. For purposes of this subsection, the term "United States-owned foreign corporation" means any foreign corporation if 50 percent or more of --

(A) the total combined voting power of all classes of stock of such corporation entitled to vote, or

(B) the total value of the stock of such corporation,

is held directly (or indirectly through applying paragraphs (2) and (3) of section 958(a) and paragraph (4) of section 318(a)) by United States persons (as defined in section 7701(a)(30)).

(7) Dividend. For purposes of this subsection, the term "dividend" includes any gain treated as ordinary income under section 1246 or as a dividend under section 1248.

(8) Coordination with subsection (f). This subsection shall be applied before subsection (f).

(9) Treatment of certain domestic corporations. For purposes of this subsection --

(A) in the case of interest treated as not from sources within the United States under section 861(a)(1)(A), the corporation paying such interest shall be treated as a United States-owned foreign corporation, and

(B) in the case of any dividend treated as not from sources within the United States under section 861(a)(2)(A), the corporation paying such dividend shall be treated as a United States-owned foreign corporation.

(10) Coordination with treaties.

(A) In general. If --

(i) any amount derived from a United States-owned foreign corporation would be treated as derived from sources within the United States under this subsection by reason of an item of income of such United States-owned foreign corporation,

(ii) under a treaty obligation of the United States (applied without regard to this subsection and by treating any amount included in gross income under section 951(a)(1) as a dividend), such amount would be treated as arising from sources outside the United States, and

(iii) the taxpayer chooses the benefits of this paragraph,

this subsection shall not apply to such amount to the extent attributable to such item of income (but subsections (a), (b) and (c) of this section and sections 902, 907, and 960 shall be applied separately with respect to such amount to the extent so attributable).

(B) Special rule. Amounts included in gross income under section 951(a)(1) shall be treated as a dividend under subparagraph (A)(ii) only if dividends paid by each corporation (the stock in which is taken into account in determining whether the shareholder is a United States shareholder in the United States-owned foreign corporation), if paid to the

445

United States shareholder, would be treated under a treaty obligation of the United States as arising from sources outside the United States (applied without regard to this subsection).

(11) Regulations. The Secretary shall prescribe such regulations as may be necessary or appropriate for purposes of this subsection, including --

(A) regulations for the application of this subsection in the case of interest or dividend payments through 1 or more entities, and

(B) regulations providing that this subsection shall apply to interest paid or accrued to any person (whether or not a United States shareholder).

(h) Coordination with nonrefundable personal credits.

In the case of an individual, for purposes of subsection (a), the tax against which the credit is taken is such tax reduced by the sum of the credits allowable under subpart A of part IV of subchapter A of this chapter.

This subsection shall not apply to taxable years beginning during 2000 or 2001.

(i) Limitation on use of deconsolidation to avoid foreign tax credit limitations.

If 2 or more domestic corporations would be members of the same affiliated group if --

(1) section 1504(b) were applied without regard to the exceptions contained therein, and

(2) the constructive ownership rules of section 1563(e) applied for purposes of section 1504(a),

the Secretary may by regulations provide for resourcing the income of any of such corporations or for modifications to the consolidated return regulations to the extent that such resourcing or modifications are necessary to prevent the avoidance of the provisions of this subpart.

(j) Certain Individuals Exempt.

(1) In General. In the case of an individual to whom this subsection applies for any taxable year

(A) the limitation of subsection (a) shall not apply,

(B) no taxes paid or accrued by the individual during such taxable year may be deemed paid or accrued under subsection (c) in any other taxable year, and

(C) no taxes paid or accrued by the individual during any other taxable year may be deemed paid or accrued under subsection (c) in such taxable year.

(2) Individuals to Whom Subsection Applies. This subsection shall apply to an individual for any taxable year if

(A) the entire amount of such individual's gross income for the taxable year from sources without the United States consists of qualified passive   income,

(B) the amount of the creditable foreign taxes paid or accrued by the individual during the taxable year does not exceed $300 ($600 in the case of a joint return), and

(C) such individual elects to have this subsection apply for the taxable year.

(3) **Definitions**. For purposes of this subsection

(A) Qualified Passive Income. The term "qualified passive income" means any item of gross income if

(i) such item of income is passive income (as defined in subsection (d)(2)(A) without regard to clause (iii) thereof), and

(ii) such item of income is shown on a payee statement furnished to the individual.

(B) **Creditable Foreign Taxes**. The term "creditable foreign taxes" means any taxes for which a credit is allowable under section 901; except that such term shall not include any tax unless such tax is shown on a payee statement furnished to such individual.

(C) **Payee Statement**. The term "payee statement" has the meaning given to such term by section 6724(d)(2).

(D) **Estates and Trusts not Eligible**. This subsection shall not apply to any estate or trust.

(k) Cross references.

(1) For increase of limitation under subsection (a) for taxes paid with respect to amounts received which were included in the gross income of the taxpayer for a prior taxable year as a United States shareholder with respect to a controlled foreign corporation, see section 960(b).

(2) For modification of limitation under subsection (a) for purposes of determining the amount of credit which can be taken against the alternative minimum tax, see section 59(a).

§ 905. Applicable rules.

(a) Year in which credit taken.

The credits provided in this subpart may, at the option of the taxpayer and irrespective of the method of accounting employed in keeping his books, be taken in the year in which the taxes of the foreign country or the possession of the United States accrued, subject, however, to the conditions prescribed in subsection (c). If the taxpayer elects to take such credits in the year in which the taxes of the foreign country or the possession of the United States accrued, the credits for all subsequent years shall be taken on the same basis, and no portion of any such taxes shall be allowed as a deduction in the same or any succeeding year.

(b) Proof of credits.

The credits provided in this subpart shall be allowed only if the taxpayer establishes to the satisfaction of the Secretary --

(1) the total amount of income derived from sources without the United States, determined as provided in part I,

(2) the amount of income derived from each country, the tax paid or accrued to which is claimed as a credit under this subpart, such amount to be determined under regulations prescribed by the Secretary, and

(3) all other information necessary for the verification and computation of such credits.

(c) Adjustments to accrued taxes.

(1) in General. If

(A) accrued taxes when paid differ from the amounts claimed as credits by the taxpayer,

(B) accrued taxes are not paid before the date 2 years after the close of the taxable year to which such taxes relate, or

(C) any tax paid is refunded in whole or in part,

the taxpayer shall notify the Secretary, who shall redetermine the amount of the tax for the year or years affected. The Secretary may prescribe adjustments to the pools of post-1986 foreign income taxes and the pools of post-1986 undistributed earnings under sections 902 and 960 in lieu of the redetermination under the preceding sentence.

(2) Special Rule for Taxes Not Paid Within 2 Years.

(A) In General. Except as provided in subparagraph (B), in making the redetermination under paragraph (1), no credit shall be allowed for accrued taxes not paid before the date referred to in subparagraph (B) of paragraph (1).

(B) Taxes Subsequently Paid. Any taxes if subsequently paid

(i) shall be taken into account

(I) in the case of taxes deemed paid under section 902 or section 960, for the taxable year in which paid (and no redetermination shall be made under this section by reason of such payment), and

(II) in any other case, for the taxable year to which the taxes relate, and

(ii) shall be translated as provided in section 986(a)(2)(A).

(3) Adjustments. The amount of tax (if any) due on any redetermination under paragraph (1) shall be paid by the taxpayer on notice and demand by the Secretary, and the amount of tax overpaid (if any) shall be credited or refunded to the taxpayer in accordance withe subchapter B of chapter 66 (section 6511 et seq.)

(4) Bond Requirements. In the case of any tax accrued but not paid, the Secretary, as a condition precedent to the allowance of the credit provided in this subpart, may require the taxpayer to give a bond, with securities satisfactory to and approved by the Secretary, in such sum as the Secretary may require,   conditioned on the payment by the taxpayer of any amount of tax found due on any such redetermination. Any such bond shall contain such further conditions as the Secretary may require.

(5) Other Special Rules. In any redetermination under paragraph (1) by the Secretary of the amount of tax due from the taxpayer for the year or years affected by a refund, the amount of the taxes refunded for which credit has been allowed under this section shall be reduced by the amount of any tax described in section 901 imposed by the foreign country or possession of the United states with respect to such refund; but no credit under this subpart, or deduction under section 164, shall be allowed for any taxable year with respect to any such tax imposed on the refund. No interest shall be assessed or collected on any amount of the tax due on any redetermination by the Secretary, resulting from a refund to the taxpayer, for any period before the receipt of such refund, except to the extent interest was paid by the foreign country or possession of the United States on such refund for such period.

§ 906. Nonresident alien individuals and foreign corporations.

(a) Allowance of credit.

A nonresident alien individual or a foreign corporation engaged in trade or business within the United States during the taxable year shall be allowed a credit under section 901 for the amount of any income, war profits, and excess profits taxes paid or accrued during the taxable year (or deemed, under section 902, paid or accrued during the taxable year) to any foreign country or possession of the United States with respect to income effectively connected with the conduct of a trade or business within the United States.

(b) Special rules.

(1) For purposes of subsection (a) and for purposes of determining the deductions allowable under sections 873(a) and 882(c), in determining the amount of any tax paid or accrued to any foreign country or possession there shall not be taken into account any amount of tax to the extent the tax so paid or accrued is imposed with respect to income from sources within the United States which would not be taxed by such foreign country or possession but for the fact that --

(A) in the case of a nonresident alien individual, such individual is a citizen or resident of such foreign country or possession, or

(B) in the case of a foreign corporation, such corporation was created or organized under the law of such foreign country or possession or is domiciled for tax purposes in such country or possession.

(2) For purposes of subsection (a), in applying section 904 the taxpayer's taxable income shall be treated as consisting only of the taxable income effectively connected with the taxpayer's conduct of a trade or business within the United States.

(3) The credit allowed pursuant to subsection (a) shall not be allowed against any tax imposed by section 871(a) (relating to income of nonresident alien individual not connected with United States business) or 881 (relating to income of foreign corporations not connected with United States business).

(4) For purposes of sections 902(a) and 78, a foreign corporation choosing the benefits of this subpart which receives dividends shall, with respect to such dividends, be treated as a domestic corporation.

(5) No credit shall be allowed under this section for any income, war profits, and excess profits taxes paid or accrued with respect to the foreign trade income (within the meaning of section 923(b)) of a FSC.

(6) For purposes of section 902, any income, war profits, and excess profits taxes paid or accrued (or deemed paid or accrued) to any foreign country or possession of the United States with respect to income effectively connected with the conduct of a trade or business within the United States shall not be taken into account, and any accumulated profits attributable to such income shall not be taken into account.

(7) No credit shall be allowed under this section against the tax imposed by section 884.

§ 907. Special rules in case of foreign oil and gas income.

. . . . .

§ 908. Reduction of credit for participation in or cooperation with an international boycott.

(a) In general.

If a person, or a member of a controlled group (within the meaning of section 993(a)(3)) which includes such person, participates in or cooperates with an international boycott during the taxable year (within the meaning of section 999(b)), the amount of the credit allowable under section 901 to such person, or under section 902 or 960 to United States shareholders of such person, for foreign taxes paid during the taxable year shall be reduced by an amount equal to the product of --

(1) the amount of the credit which, but for this section, would be allowed under section 901 for the taxable year, multiplied by

(2) the international boycott factor (determined under section 999).

(b) Application with sections 275(a)(4) and 78.

Section 275(a)(4) and section 78 shall not apply to any amount of taxes denied credit under subsection (a).

§ 911. Citizens or residents of the United States living abroad.

(a) Exclusion from gross income.

At the election of a qualified individual (made separately with respect to paragraphs (1) and (2)), there shall be excluded from the gross income of such individual, and exempt from taxation under this subtitle, for any taxable year --

(1) the foreign earned income of such individual, and

(2) the housing cost amount of such individual.

(b) Foreign earned income.

(1) Definition. For purposes of this section --

(A) In general. The term "foreign earned income" with respect to any individual means the amount received by such individual from sources within a foreign country or countries which constitute earned income attributable to services performed by such individual during the period described in subparagraph (A) or (B) of subsection (d)(1), whichever is applicable.

(B) Certain amounts not included in foreign earned income. The foreign earned income for an individual shall not include amounts --

(i) received as a pension or annuity,

(ii) paid by the United States or an agency thereof to an employee of the United States or an agency thereof,

(iii) included in gross income by reason of section 402(b) (relating to taxability of beneficiary of nonexempt trust) or section 403(c) (relating to taxability of beneficiary under a nonqualified annuity), or

(iv) received after the close of the taxable year following the taxable year in which the services to which the amounts are attributable are performed.

(2) Limitation on foreign earned income.

(A) In general. The foreign earned income of an individual which may be excluded under subsection (a)(1) for any taxable year shall not exceed the amount of foreign earned income computed on a daily basis at an annual rate equal to the exclusion amount for the calendar year in which such taxable year begins.

(B) Attribution to year in which services are performed. For purposes of applying subparagraph (A), amounts received shall be considered received in the taxable year in which the services to which the amounts are attributable are performed.

(C) Treatment of community income. In applying subparagraph (A) with respect to amounts received from services performed by a husband or wife which are community income under community property laws applicable to such income, the aggregate amount which may be excludable from the gross income of such husband and wife under subsection (a)(1) for any taxable year shall equal the amount which would be so excludable if such amounts did not constitute community income.

(D) Exclusion Amount.

(i) In General. The exclusion amount for any calendar year is the exclusion amount determined in accordance with the following table (as adjusted by clause (ii)):

For calendar year:	The exclusion amount is:
1998	$ 72,000
1999	74,000
2000	76,000
2001	78,000
2002 and thereafter	80,000

(ii) Inflation Adjustment. In the case of any taxable year beginning in a calendar year after 2007, the $80,000 amount in clause (i) shall be increased by an amount equal to the product of

(I) such dollar amount, and

(II) the cost-of-living adjustment under section 1(f)(3) for the calendar year in which the taxable year begins, determined by substituting "2006"   for "1992" in subparagraph (B) thereof.

If any increase determined under the preceding sentence is not a multiple of $100, such increase shall be rounded to the next lowest multiple of $100.

(c) Housing cost amount.

For purposes of this section --

(1) In general. The term "housing cost amount" means an amount equal to the excess of --

(A) the housing expenses of an individual for the taxable year, over

(B) an amount equal to the product of --

(i) 16 percent of the salary (computed on a daily basis) of an employee of the United States who is compensated at a rate equal to the annual rate paid for step 1 of grade GS-14, multiplied by

(ii) the number of days of such taxable year within the applicable period described in subparagraph (A) or (B) of subsection (d)(1).

(2) Housing expenses.

(A) In general. The term "housing expenses" means the reasonable expenses paid or incurred during the taxable year by or on behalf of an individual for housing for the individual (and, if they reside with him, for his spouse and dependents) in a foreign country. The term --

(i) includes expenses attributable to the housing (such as utilities and insurance), but

(ii) does not include interest and taxes of the kind deductible under section 163 or 164 or any amount allowable as a deduction under section 216(a).

Housing expenses shall not be treated as reasonable to the extent such expenses are lavish or extravagant under the circumstances.

(B) Second foreign household.

(i) In general. Except as provided in clause (ii), only housing expenses incurred with respect to that abode which bears the closest relationship to the tax home of the individual shall be taken into account under paragraph (1).

(ii) Separate household for spouse and dependents. If an individual maintains a separate abode outside the United States for his spouse and dependents and they do not reside with him because of living conditions which are dangerous, unhealthful, or otherwise adverse, then --

(I) the words "if they reside with him" in subparagraph (A) shall be disregarded, and

(II) the housing expenses incurred with respect to such abode shall be taken into account under paragraph (1).

(3) Special rules where housing expenses not provided by employer.

(A) In general. To the extent the housing cost amount of any individual for any taxable year is not attributable to employer provided amounts, such amount shall be treated as a deduction allowable in computing adjusted gross income to the extent of the limitation of subparagraph (B).

(B) Limitation. For purposes of subparagraph (A), the limitation of this subparagraph is the excess of --

(i) the foreign earned income of the individual for the taxable year, over

(ii) the amount of such income excluded from gross income under subsection (a) for the taxable year.

(C) 1-year carryover of housing amounts not allowed by reason of subparagraph (B).

(i) In general. The amount not allowable as a deduction for any taxable year under subparagraph (A) by reason of the limitation of subparagraph (B) shall be treated as a deduction allowable in computing adjusted gross income for the succeeding taxable year (and only for the succeeding taxable year) to the extent of the limitation of clause (ii) for such succeeding taxable year.

(ii) Limitation. For purposes of clause (i), the limitation of this clause for any taxable year is the excess of --

(I) the limitation of subparagraph (B) for such taxable year, over

(II) amounts treated as a deduction under subparagraph (A) for such taxable year.

(D) Employer provided amounts. For purposes of this paragraph, the term "employer provided amounts" means any amount paid or incurred on behalf of the individual by the individual's employer which is foreign earned income included in the individual's gross income for the taxable year (without regard to this section).

(E) Foreign earned income. For purposes of this paragraph, an individual's foreign earned income for any taxable year shall be determined without regard to the limitation of subparagraph (A) of subsection (b)(2).

(d) Definitions and special rules.

For purposes of this section --

(1) Qualified individual. The term "qualified individual" means an individual whose tax home is in a foreign country and who is --

(A) a citizen of the United States and establishes to the satisfaction of the Secretary that he has been a bona fide resident of a foreign country or countries for an uninterrupted period which includes an entire taxable year, or

(B) a citizen or resident of the United States and who, during any period of 12 consecutive months, is present in a foreign country or countries during at least 330 full days in such period.

(2) Earned income.

(A) In general. The term "earned income" means wages, salaries, or professional fees, and other amounts received as compensation for personal services actually rendered, but does not include that part of the compensation derived by the taxpayer for personal services rendered by him to a corporation which represents a distribution of earnings or profits rather than a reasonable allowance as compensation for the personal services actually rendered.

(B) Taxpayer engaged in trade or business. In the case of a taxpayer engaged in a trade or business in which both personal services and capital are material income-producing factors, under regulations prescribed by the Secretary, a reasonable allowance as compensation for the personal services rendered by the taxpayer, not in excess of 30 percent of his share of the net profits of such trade or business, shall be considered as earned income.

(3) Tax home. The term "tax home" means, with respect to any individual, such individual's home for purposes of section 162(a)(2) (relating to traveling expenses while away from home). An individual shall not be treated as having a tax home in a foreign country for any period for which his abode is within the United States.

(4) Waiver of period of stay in foreign country. Notwithstanding paragraph (1), an individual who --

(A) is a bona fide resident of, or is present in, a foreign country for any period,

(B) leaves such foreign country after August 31, 1978 --

(i) during any period during which the Secretary determines, after consultation with the Secretary of State or his delegate, that individuals were required to leave such foreign country because of war, civil unrest, or similar adverse conditions in such foreign country which precluded the normal conduct of business by such individuals, and

(ii) before meeting the requirements of such paragraph (1), and

(C) establishes to the satisfaction of the Secretary that such individual could reasonably have been expected to have met such requirements but for the conditions referred to in clause (i) of subparagraph (B),

shall be treated as a qualified individual with respect to the period described in subparagraph (A) during which he was a bona fide resident of, or was present in, the foreign country, and in applying subsections (b)(2)(A) and (c)(1)(B)(ii) with respect to such individual, only the days within such period shall be taken into account.

(5) Test of bona fide residence. If --

(A) an individual who has earned income from sources within a foreign country submits a statement to the authorities of that country that he is not a resident of that country, and

(B) such individual is held not subject as a resident of that country to the income tax of that country by its authorities with respect to such earnings,

then such individual shall not be considered a bona fide resident of that country for purposes of paragraph (1)(A).

(6) Denial of double benefits. No deduction or exclusion from gross income under this subtitle or credit against the tax imposed by this chapter (including any credit or deduction for the amount of taxes paid or accrued to a foreign country or possession of the United States) shall be allowed to the extent such deduction, exclusion, or credit is properly allocable to or chargeable against amounts excluded from gross income under subsection (a).

(7) Aggregate benefit cannot exceed foreign earned income. The sum of the amount excluded under subsection (a) and the amount deducted under subsection (c)(3)(A) for the taxable year shall not exceed the individual's foreign earned income for such year.

(8) Limitation on income earned in restricted country.

(A) In general. If travel (or any transaction in connection with such travel) with respect to any foreign country is subject to the regulations described in subparagraph (B) during any period --

(i) the term "foreign earned income" shall not include any income from sources within such country attributable to services performed during such period,

(ii) the term "housing expenses" shall not include any expenses allocable to such period for housing in such country or for housing of the spouse or dependents of the taxpayer in another country while the taxpayer is present in such country, and

(iii) an individual shall not be treated as a bona fide resident of, or as present in, a foreign country for any day during which such individual was present in such country during such period.

(B) Regulations. For purposes of this paragraph, regulations are described in this subparagraph if such regulations --

(i) have been adopted pursuant to the Trading With the Enemy Act (50 U.S.C. App. 1 et seq.), or the International Emergency Economic Powers Act (50 U.S.C. 1701 et seq.), and

(ii) include provisions generally prohibiting citizens and residents of the United States from engaging in transactions related to travel to, from, or within a foreign country.

(C) Exception. Subparagraph (A) shall not apply to any individual during any period in which such individual's activities are not in violation of the regulations described in subparagraph (B).

(9) Regulations. The Secretary shall prescribe such regulations as may be necessary or appropriate to carry out the purposes of this section, including regulations providing rules --

(A) for cases where a husband and wife each have earned income from sources outside the United States, and

(B) for married individuals filing separate returns.

(e) Election.

(1) In general. An election under subsection (a) shall apply to the taxable year for which made and to all subsequent taxable years unless revoked under paragraph (2).

(2) Revocation. A taxpayer may revoke an election made under paragraph (1) for any taxable year after the taxable year for which such election was made. Except with the consent of the Secretary, any taxpayer who makes such a revocation for any taxable year may not make another election under this section for any subsequent taxable year before the 6th taxable year after the taxable year for which such revocation was made.

(f) Cross references.

For administrative and penal provisions relating to the exclusions provided for in this section, see sections 6001, 6011, 6012(c), and the other provisions of subtitle F.

§ 921. Exempt foreign trade income excluded from gross income.

(a) Exclusion.

Exempt foreign trade income of a FSC shall be treated as foreign source income which is not effectively connected with the conduct of a trade or business within the United States.

(b) Proportionate allocation of deductions to exempt foreign trade income.

Any deductions of the FSC properly apportioned and allocated to the foreign trade income derived by a FSC from any transaction shall be allocated between --

(1) the exempt foreign trade income derived from such transaction, and

(2) the foreign trade income (other than exempt foreign trade income) derived from such transaction, on a proportionate basis.

(c) Denial of credits.

Notwithstanding any other provision of this chapter, no credit (other than a credit allowable under section 27(a), 33, or 34) shall be allowed under this chapter to any FSC.

(d) Foreign trade income, investment income, and carrying charges treated as effectively connected with United States business.

For purposes of this chapter --

(1) all foreign trade income of a FSC other than --

(A) exempt foreign trade income, and

(B) section 923(a)(2) non-exempt income,

(2) all interest, dividends, royalties, and other investment income received or accrued by a FSC, and

(3) all carrying charges received or accrued by a FSC, shall be treated as income effectively connected with a trade or business conducted through a permanent establishment of such corporation within the United States. Income described in paragraph (1) shall be treated as derived from sources within the United States.

§ 922. FSC defined.

(a) FSC defined.

For purposes of this title, the term "FSC" means any corporation --

(1) which --

(A) was created or organized --

(i) under the laws of any foreign country which meets the requirements of section 927(e)(3), or

(ii) under the laws applicable to any possession of the United States,

(B) has no more than 25 shareholders at any time during the taxable year,

(C) does not have any preferred stock outstanding at any time during the taxable year,

(D) during the taxable year --

(i) maintains an office located outside the United States in a foreign country which meets the requirements of section 927(e)(3) or in any possession of the United States,

(ii) maintains a set of the permanent books of account (including invoices) of such corporation at such office, and

(iii) maintains at a location within the United States the records which such corporation is required to keep under section 6001,

(E) at all times during the taxable year, has a board of directors which includes at least one individual who is not a resident of the United States, and

(F) is not a member, at any time during the taxable year, of any controlled group of corporations of which a DISC is a member, and

(2) which has made an election (at the time and in the manner provided in section 927(f)(1)) which is in effect for the taxable year to be treated as a FSC.

(b) Small FSC defined.

For purposes of this title, a FSC is a small FSC with respect to any taxable year if --

(1) such corporation has made an election (at the time and in the manner provided in section 927(f)(1)) which is in effect for the taxable year to be treated as a small FSC, and

(2) such corporation is not a member, at any time during the taxable year, of a controlled group of corporations which includes a FSC unless such other FSC has also made an election under paragraph (1) which is in effect for such year.

§ 951. Amounts included in gross income of United States shareholders.

(a) Amounts included.

(1) In general. If a foreign corporation is a controlled foreign corporation for an uninterrupted period of 30 days or more during any taxable year, every person who is a United States shareholder (as defined in subsection (b)) of such corporation and who owns (within the meaning of section 958(a)) stock in such corporation on the last day, in such year, on which such corporation is a controlled foreign corporation shall include in his gross income, for his taxable year in which or with which such taxable year of the corporation ends --

(A) the sum of --

(i) his pro rata share (determined under paragraph (2)) of the corporation's subpart F income for such year,

(ii) his pro rata share (determined under section 955(a)(3) as in effect before the enactment of the Tax Reduction Act of 1975) of the corporation's previously excluded subpart F income withdrawn from investment in less developed countries for such year, and

(iii) his pro rata share (determined under section 955(a)(3)) of the corporation's previously excluded subpart F income withdrawn from foreign base company shipping operations for such year; and

(B) the amount determined under section 956 with respect to such shareholder for such year (but only to the extent not excluded from gross income under section 959(a)(2)).

(2) Pro rata share of subpart F income. The pro rata share referred to in paragraph (1)(A)(i) in the case of any United States shareholder is the amount --

(A) which would have been distributed with respect to the stock which such shareholder owns (within the meaning of section 958(a)) in such corporation if on the last day, in its taxable year, on which the corporation is a controlled foreign corporation it had distributed pro rata to its shareholders an amount (i) which bears the same ratio to its subpart F income for the taxable year, as (ii) the part of such year during which the corporation is a controlled foreign corporation bears to the entire year, reduced by

(B) the amount of distributions received by any other person during such year as a dividend with respect to such stock, but only to the extent of the dividend which would have been received if the distribution by the corporation had been the amount (i) which bears the same ratio to the subpart F income of such corporation for the taxable year, as (ii) the part of such year during which such shareholder did not own (within the meaning of section 958(a)) such stock bears to the entire year. For purposes of subparagraph (B), any gain included in the gross income of any person as a dividend under section 1248 shall be treated as a distribution received by such person with respect to the stock involved.

(3) Limitation on pro rata share of previously excluded subpart F income withdrawn from investment. For purposes of paragraph (1)(A)(iii), the pro rata share of any United States shareholder of the previously excluded subpart F income of a controlled foreign corporation with-drawn from investment in foreign base company shipping operations shall not exceed an amount --

(A) which bears the same ratio to his pro rata share of such income withdrawn (as determined under section 955(a)(3)) for the taxable year, as

(B) the part of such year during which the corporation is a controlled foreign corporation bears to the entire year.

(b) United States shareholder defined.

For purposes of this subpart, the term "United States shareholder" means, with respect to any foreign corporation, a United States person (as defined in section 957(c)) who owns (within the meaning of section 958(a)), or is considered as owning by applying the rules of ownership of section 958(b), 10 percent or more of the total combined voting power of all classes of stock entitled to vote of such foreign corporation.

(c) Coordination with election of a foreign investment company to distribute income.

A United States shareholder who, for his taxable year, is a qualified shareholder (within the meaning of section 1247(c)) of a foreign investment company with respect to which an election under section 1247 is in effect shall not be required to include in gross income, for such taxable year, any amount under subsection (a) with respect to such company.

(d) Coordination with foreign personal holding company provisions.

If, but for this subsection, an amount would be included in the gross income of a United States shareholder for any taxable year both under subsection (a)(1)(A)(i) and under section 551(b) (relating to foreign personal holding company income included in gross income of United States shareholder), such amount shall be included in the gross income of such shareholder only under subsection (a)(1)(A).

(e) Foreign trade income not taken into account.

(1) In general. The foreign trade income of a FSC and any deductions which are apportioned or allocated to such income shall not be taken into account under this subpart.

(2) Foreign trade income. For purposes of this subsection, the term "foreign trade income" has the meaning given such term by section 923(b), but does not include section 923(a)(2) non-exempt income (within the meaning of section 927(d)(6)).

(f) Coordination with passive foreign investment company provisions.

If, but for this subsection, an amount would be included in the gross income of a United States shareholder for any taxable year both under subsection (a)(1)(A)(i) and under section 1293 (relating to current taxation of income from certain passive foreign investment companies), such amount shall be included in the gross income of such shareholder only under subsection (a)(1)(A).

§ 952. Subpart F income defined.

(a) In general.

For purposes of this subpart, the term "subpart F income" means, in the case of any controlled foreign corporation, the sum of --

(1) insurance income (as defined under section 953),

(2) the foreign base company income (as determined under section 954),

(3) an amount equal to the product of --

(A) the income of such corporation other than income which --

(i) is attributable to earnings and profits of the foreign corporation included in the gross income of a United States person under section 951 (other than by reason of this paragraph), or

(ii) is described in subsection (b),

multiplied by

(B) the international boycott factor (as determined under section 999),

(4) the sum of the amounts of any illegal bribes, kickbacks, or other payments (within the meaning of section 162(c)) paid by or on behalf of the corporation during the taxable year of the corporation directly or indirectly to an official, employee, or agent in fact of a government, and

(5) the income of such corporation derived from any foreign country during any period during which section 901(j) applies to such foreign country.

The payments referred to in paragraph (4) are payments which would be unlawful under the Foreign Corrupt Practices Act of 1977 if the payor were a United States person. For purposes of paragraph (5), the income described therein shall be reduced, under regulations prescribed by the Secretary, so as to take into account deductions (including taxes) properly allocable to such income.

(b) Exclusion of United States income.

In the case of a controlled foreign corporation, subpart F income does not include any item of income from sources within the United States which is effectively connected with the conduct by such corporation of a trade or business within the United States unless such item is exempt from taxation (or is subject to a reduced rate of tax) pursuant to a treaty obligation of the United States. For purposes of the preceding sentence, income described in paragraph (2) or (3) of section 921(d) shall be treated as derived from sources within the United States. For purposes of this subsection, any exemption (or reduction) with respect to the tax imposed by section 884 shall not be take into account.

459

(c) Limitation.

(1) In general.

(A) Subpart F income limited to current earnings and profits. For purposes of subsection (a), the subpart F income of any controlled foreign corporation for any taxable year shall not exceed the earnings and profits of such corporation for such taxable year.

(B) Certain prior year deficits may be taken into account.

(i) In general. The amount included in the gross income of any United States shareholder under section 951(a)(1)(A)(i) for any taxable year and attributable to a qualified activity shall be reduced by the amount of such shareholder's pro rata share of any qualified deficit.

(ii) Qualified deficit. The term "qualified deficit" means any deficit in earnings and profits of the controlled foreign corporation for any prior taxable year which began after December 31, 1986, and for which the controlled foreign corporation was a controlled foreign corporation; but only to the extent such deficit --

(I) is attributable to the same qualified activity as the activity giving rise to the income being offset, and

(II) has not previously been taken into account under this subparagraph.

In determining the deficit attributable to qualified activities described in clause (iii)(III) or (IV), deficits in earnings and profits (to the extent not previously taken into account under this section) for taxable years beginning after 1962 and before 1987 also shall be taken into account. In the case of the qualified activity described in clause (iii)(II), the rule of the preceding sentence shall apply, except that "1982" shall be substituted for "1962".

(iii) Qualified activity. For purposes of this paragraph, the term "qualified activity" means any activity giving rise to --

(I) foreign base company shipping income,

(II) foreign base company oil related income,

(III) foreign base company sales income,

(IV) foreign base company services income,

(V) in the case of a qualified insurance company, insurance income or foreign personal holding company income, or

(VI) in the case of a qualified financial institution, foreign personal holding company income.

(iv) Pro rata share. For purposes of this paragraph, the shareholder's pro rata share of any deficit for any prior taxable year shall be determined under rules similar to rules under section 951(a)(2) for whichever of the following yields the smaller share:

(I) the close of the taxable year, or

(II) the close of the taxable year in which the deficit arose.

(v) Qualified insurance company. For purposes of this subparagraph, the term "qualified insurance company" means any controlled foreign corporation predominantly engaged in the active conduct of an insurance business in the taxable year and in the prior taxable years in which the deficit arose.

(vi) Qualified financial institution. For purposes of this paragraph, the term "qualified financial institution" means any controlled foreign corporation predominantly engaged in the active conduct of a banking, financing, or similar business in the taxable year and in the prior taxable year in which the deficit arose.

(vii) Special rules for insurance income.

(I) In general. An election may be made under this clause to have section 953(a) applied for purposes of this title without regard to the same country exception under paragraph (1)(A) thereof. Such election, once made, may be revoked only with the consent of the Secretary.

(II) Special rules for affiliated groups. In the case of an affiliated group of corporations (within the meaning of section 1504 but without regard to section 1504(b)(3) and by substituting "more than 50 percent" for "at least 80 percent" each place it appears), no election may be made under subclause (I) for any controlled foreign corporation unless such election is made for all other controlled foreign corporations who are members of such group and who were created or organized under the laws of the same country as such controlled foreign corporation. For purposes of clause (v), in determining whether any controlled corporation described in the preceding sentence is a qualified insurance company, all such corporations shall be treated as 1 corporation.

(C) Certain deficits of member of the same chain of corporations may be taken into account.

(i) In general. A controlled foreign corporation may elect to reduce the amount of its subpart F income for any taxable year which is attributable to any qualified activity by the amount of any deficit in earnings and profits of a qualified chain member for a taxable year ending with (or within) the taxable year of such controlled foreign corporation to the extent such deficit is attributable to such activity. To the extent any deficit reduces subpart F income under the preceding sentence, such deficit shall not be taken into account under subparagraph (B).

(ii) Qualified chain member. For purposes of this subparagraph, the term "qualified chain member" means, with respect to any controlled foreign corporation, any other corporation which is created or organized under the laws of the same foreign country as the controlled foreign corporation but only if --

(I) all the stock of such other corporation (other than directors' qualifying shares) is owned at all times during the taxable year in which the deficit arose (directly or through 1 or more corporations other than the common parent) by such controlled foreign corporation, or

(II) all the stock of such controlled foreign corporation (other than directors' qualifying shares) is owned at all times during the taxable year in which the deficit arose (directly or through 1 or more corporations other than the common parent) by such other corporation.

(iii) Coordination. This subparagraph shall be applied after subparagraphs (A) and (B).

(2) Recharacterization in subsequent taxable years. If the subpart F income of any controlled foreign corporation for any taxable year was reduced by reason of paragraph (1)(A), any excess of the earnings and profits of such corporation for any subsequent taxable year over the subpart F income of such foreign corporation for such taxable year shall be recharacterized as subpart F income under rules similar to the rules applicable under section 904(f)(5).

(3) Special rule for determining earnings and profits. For purposes of this subsection, earnings and profits of any controlled foreign corporation shall be determined without regard to paragraphs (4), (5), and (6) of section 312(n).

461

Under regulations, the preceding sentence shall not apply to the extent it would increase earnings and profits by an amount which was previously distributed by the controlled foreign corporation.

(d) Income derived from foreign country.

The Secretary shall prescribe such regulations as may be necessary or appropriate to carry out the purposes of subsection (a)(5), including regulations which treat income paid through 1 or more entities as derived from a foreign country to which section 901(j) applies if such income was, without regard to such entities, derived from such country.

§ 953. Insurance income.

. . . . .

§ 954. Foreign base company income.

(a) Foreign base company income.

For purposes of section 952(a)(2), the term "foreign base company income" means for any taxable year the sum of --

(1) the foreign personal holding company income for the taxable year (determined under subsection (c) and reduced as provided in subsection (b)(5)),

(2) the foreign base company sales income for the taxable year (determined under subsection (d) and reduced as provided in subsection (b)(5)),

(3) the foreign base company services income for the taxable year (determined under subsection (e) and reduced as provided in subsection (b)(5)),

(4) the foreign base company shipping income for the taxable year (determined under subsection (f) and reduced as provided in subsection (b)(5)), and

(5) the foreign base company oil related income for the taxable year (determined under subsection (g) and reduced as provided in subsection (b)(5)).

(b) Exclusions and special rules.

(1) Repealed.

(2) Repealed.

(3) De minimis, etc., rules. For purposes of subsection (a) and section 953 --

(A) De minimis rule. If the sum of foreign base company income (determined without regard to paragraph (5)) and the gross insurance income for the taxable year is less than the lesser of --

(i) 5 percent of gross income, or

(ii) $1,000,000,

no part of the gross income for the taxable year shall be treated as foreign base company income or insurance income.

(B) Foreign base company income and insurance income in excess of 70 percent of gross income. If the sum of the foreign base company income (determined without regard to paragraph (5)) and the gross insurance income for the taxable year exceeds 70 percent of gross income, the entire gross income for the taxable year shall, subject to the provisions of paragraphs (4) and (5), be treated as foreign base company income or insurance income (whichever is appropriate).

(C) Gross insurance income. For purposes of subparagraphs (A) and (B), the term "gross insurance income" means any item of gross income taken into account in determining insurance income under section 953.

(4) Exception for certain income subject to high foreign taxes. For purposes of subsection (a) and section 953, foreign base company income and insurance income shall not include any item of income received by a controlled foreign corporation if the taxpayer establishes to the satisfaction of the Secretary that such income was subject to an effective rate of income tax imposed by a foreign country greater than 90 percent of the maximum rate of tax specified in section 11. The preceding sentence shall not apply to foreign base company oil-related income described in subsection (a)(5).

(5) Deductions to be taken into account. For purposes of subsection (a), the foreign personal holding company income, the foreign base company sales income, the foreign base company services income, the foreign base company shipping income, and the foreign base company oil related income shall be reduced, under regulations prescribed by the Secretary, so as to take into account deductions (including taxes) properly allocable to such income. Except to the extent provided in regulations prescribed by the Secretary, any interest which is paid or accrued by the controlled foreign corporation to any United States shareholder in such corporation (or any controlled foreign corporation related to such a shareholder) shall be allocated first to foreign personal holding company income which is passive income (within the meaning of section 904(d)(2)) of such corporation to the extent thereof. The Secretary may, by regulations, provide that the preceding sentence shall apply also to interest paid or accrued to other persons.

(6) Special rules for foreign base company shipping income. Income of a corporation which is foreign base company shipping income under paragraph (4) of subsection (a) --

(A) shall not be considered foreign base company income of such corporation under any other paragraph of subsection (a) and

(B) if distributed through a chain of ownership described under section 958(a), shall not be included in foreign base company income of another controlled foreign corporation in such chain.

(7) Special exclusion for foreign base company shipping income. Income of a corporation which is foreign base company shipping income under paragraph (4) of subsection (a) shall be excluded from foreign base company income if derived by a controlled foreign corporation from, or in connection with, the use (or hiring or leasing for use) of an aircraft or vessel in foreign commerce between two points within the foreign country in which such corporation is created or organized and such aircraft or vessel is registered.

(8) Foreign base company oil related income not treated as another kind of base company income. Income of a corporation which is foreign base company oil related income shall not be considered foreign base company income of such corporation under paragraph (2), or (3) of subsection (a).

(c) Foreign personal holding company income.

(1) In general. For purposes of subsection (a)(1), the term "foreign personal holding company income" means the portion of the gross income which consists of:

(A) Dividends, etc. Dividends, interest, royalties, rents, and annuities.

(B) Certain property transactions. The excess of gains over losses from the sale or exchange of property --

(i) which gives rise to income described in subparagraph (A) (after application of paragraph (2)(A) other than property which gives rise to income not treated as foreign personal holding company income by reason of subsection (h) or (i) for the taxable year.

(ii) which is an interest in a trust, partnership, or REMIC, or

(iii) which does not give rise to any income.

In the case of any regular dealer in property, gains and losses from the sale or exchange of any such property or arising out of bona fide hedging transactions reasonably necessary to the conduct of the business of being a dealer in such property shall not be taken into account under this subparagraph. Gains and losses from the sale or exchange of any property which, in the hands of the controlled foreign corporation, is property described in section 1221(1) also shall not be taken into account under this subparagraph.

(C) Commodities transactions. The excess of gains over losses from transactions (including futures, forward, and similar transactions) in any commodities. This subparagraph shall not apply to gains or losses which --

(i) arise out of bona fide hedging transactions reasonably necessary to the conduct of any business by a producer, processor, merchant, or handler of a commodity in the manner in which such business is customarily and usually conducted by others,

(ii) are active business gains or losses from the sale of commodities, but only if substantially all of the controlled foreign corporation's business is as an active producer, processor, merchant, or handler of commodities, or

(iii) are foreign currency gains or losses (as defined in section 988(b)) attributable to any section 988 transactions.

(D) Foreign currency gains. The excess of foreign currency gains over foreign currency losses (as defined in section 988(b)) attributable to any section 988 transactions. This subparagraph shall not apply in the case of any transaction directly related to the business needs of the controlled foreign corporation.

(E) Income equivalent to interest. Any income equivalent to interest, including income from commitment fees (or similar amounts) for loans actually made.

(F) Income from notional principle contracts. Net income from notional principal contracts. Any item of income, gain, deduction, or loss from a notional principal contract entered into for the purposes of hedging any item described in any preceding subparagraph shall not be taken into account for purposes of this subparagraph but shall be taken into account under such other subparagraph.

(G) Payments in Lieu of Dividends. Payments in lieu of dividends which are made pursuant to an arrangement to which section 1058 applies.

(2) Exception for certain amounts.

(A) Rents and royalties derived in active business. Foreign personal holding company income shall not include rents and royalties which are derived in the active conduct of a trade or business and which are received from a person other than a related person (within the meaning of subsection (d)(3)).

(B) Certain export financing. Foreign personal holding company income shall not include any interest which is derived in the conduct of a banking business and which is export financing interest (as defined in section 904(d)(2)(G)).

(C) Exception for dealers. Except as provided by regulations, in the case of a regular dealer in property which is property described in paragraph (1)(B), forward contracts, option contracts, or similar financial instruments (including notional principal contracts and all instruments referenced to commodities), there shall not be taken into account in computing foreign personal holding company income

(i) any item of income, gain, deduction, or loss (other than any item described in subparagraph (A), (E), or (G) of paragraph (1)) from any transaction (including hedging transactions) entered into in the ordinary course of such dealer's trade or business as such a dealer, and

(ii) if such dealer is a dealer in securities (within the meaning of section 475), any interest or dividend or equivalent amount described in subparagraph (E) or (G) of paragraph (1) from any transaction (including any hedging transaction or transaction described in section 956(c)(2)(J)) entered into in the ordinary course of such dealer's trade or business as such a dealer in securities, but only if the income from the transaction is attributable to activities of the dealer in the country under the laws of which the dealer is created or organized (or in the case of a qualified business unit described in section 989(a), is attributable to activities of the unit in the country in which the unit both maintains its principal office and conducts substantial business activity).

(3) Certain income received from related persons.

(A) In general. Except as provided in subparagraph (B), the term "foreign personal holding company income" does not include --

(i) dividends and interest received from a related person which (I) is a corporation created or organized under the laws of the same foreign country under the laws of which the controlled foreign corporation is created or organized, and (II) has a substantial part of its assets used in its trade or business located in such same foreign country, and

(ii) rents and royalties received from a corporation which is a related person for the use of, or the privilege of using, property within the country under the laws of which the controlled foreign corporation is created or organized.

To the extent provided in regulations, payments made by a partnership with 1 or more corporate partners shall be treated as made by such corporate partners in proportion to their respective interests in the partnership.

(B) Exception not to apply to items which reduce subpart F income. Subparagraph (A) shall not apply in the case of any interest, rent, or royalty to the extent such interest, rent, or royalty reduces the payor's subpart F income or creates (or increases) a deficit which under section 952(c) may reduce the subpart F income of the payor or another controlled foreign corporation.

(C) Exception for certain dividends. Subparagraph (A)(i) shall not apply to any dividend with respect to any stock which is attributable to earnings and profits of the distributing corporation accumulated during any period during which the person receiving such dividend did not hold such stock either directly, or indirectly through a chain of one or more subsidiaries each of which meets the requirements of subparagraph (A)(i).

(d) Foreign base company sales income.

(1) In general. For purposes of subsection (a)(2), the term "foreign base company sales income" means income (whether in the form of profits, commissions, fees, or otherwise) derived in connection with the purchase of personal property from a related person and its sale to any person, the sale of personal property to any person on behalf of a related person, the purchase of personal property from any person and its sale to a related person, or the purchase of personal property from any person on behalf of a related person where --

(A) the property which is purchased (or in the case of property sold on behalf of a related person, the property which is sold) is manufactured, produced, grown, or extracted outside the country under the laws of which the controlled foreign corporation is created or organized, and

(B) the property is sold for use, consumption, or disposition outside such foreign country, or, in the case of property purchased on behalf of a related person, is purchased for use, consumption, or disposition outside such foreign country.

For purposes of this subsection, personal property does not include agricultural commodities which are not grown in the United States in commercially marketable quantities.

(2) Certain branch income. For purposes of determining foreign base company sales income in situations in which the carrying on of activities by a controlled foreign corporation through a branch or similar establishment outside the country of incorporation of the controlled foreign corporation has substantially the same effect as if such branch or similar establishment were a wholly owned subsidiary corporation deriving such income, under regulations prescribed by the Secretary, the income attributable to the carrying on of such activities of such branch or similar establishment shall be treated as income derived by a wholly owned subsidiary of the controlled foreign corporation and shall constitute foreign base company sales income of the controlled foreign corporation.

(3) Related person defined. For purposes of this section, a person is a related person with respect to a controlled foreign corporation, if --

(A) such person is an individual, corporation, partnership, trust, or estate which controls, or is controlled by, the controlled foreign corporation, or

(B) such person is a corporation, partnership, trust, or estate which is controlled by the same person or persons which control the controlled foreign corporation.

For purposes of the preceding sentence, control means, with respect to a corporation, the ownership, directly or indirectly, of stock possessing more than 50 percent of the total voting power of all classes of stock entitled to vote or of the total value of stock of such corporation. In the case of a partnership, trust, or estate, control means the ownership, directly or indirectly, of more than 50 percent (by value) of the beneficial interests in such partnership, trust, or estate. For purposes of this paragraph, rules similar to the rules of section 958 shall apply.

(4) Special rule for certain timber products. For purposes of subsection (a)(2), the term "foreign base company sales income" includes any income (whether in the form of profits, commissions, fees, or otherwise) derived in connection with --

(A) the sale of any unprocessed timber referred to in section 865(b), or

(B) the milling of any such timber outside the United States.

Subpart G shall not apply to any amount treated as subpart F income by reason of this paragraph.

(e) Foreign base company services income.

(1) In general. For purposes of subsection (a)(3), the term "foreign base company services income" means income (whether in the form of compensation, commissions, fees, or otherwise) derived in connection with the performance of technical, managerial, engineering, architectural, scientific, skilled, industrial, commercial, or like services which --

(A) are performed for or on behalf of any related person (within the meaning of subsection (d)(3), and

(B) are performed outside the country under the laws of which the controlled foreign corporation is created or organized.

(2) Exception. Paragraph (1) shall not apply to income derived in connection with the performance of services which are directly related to --

(A) the sale or exchange by the controlled foreign corporation of property manufactured, produced, grown, or extracted by it and which are performed before the time of the sale or exchange, or

(B) an offer or effort to sell or exchange such property.

(3) Paragraph (1) shall also not apply to income which is exempt insurance income (as defined in section 953(e)) or which is not treated as foreign personal holding income by reason of subsection (c)(2)(C)(ii), (h), or (i).

(f) Foreign base company shipping income.

For purposes of subsection (a)(4), the term "foreign base company shipping income" means income derived from, or in connection with, the use (or hiring or leasing for use) of any aircraft or vessel in foreign commerce, or from, or in connection with, the performance of services directly related to the use of any such aircraft, or vessel, or from the sale, exchange, or other disposition of any such aircraft or vessel. Such term includes, but is not limited to --

(1) dividends and interest received from a foreign corporation in respect of which taxes are deemed paid under section 902, and gain from the sale, exchange, or other disposition of stock or obligations of such a foreign corporation to the extent that such dividends, interest, and gains are attributable to foreign base company shipping income, and

(2) that portion of the distributive share of the income of a partnership attributable to foreign base company shipping income.

Such term includes any income derived from a space or ocean activity (as defined in section 863(d)(2)). Except as provided in paragraph (1), such term shall not include any dividend or interest income which is foreign personal holding company income (as defined in subsection (c)).

(g) Foreign base company oil related income.

For purposes of this section --

(1) In general. Except as otherwise provided in this subsection, the term "foreign base company oil related income" means foreign oil related income (within the meaning of paragraphs (2) and (3) of section 907(c)) other than income derived from a source within a foreign country in connection with --

(A) oil or gas which was extracted from an oil or gas well located in such foreign country, or

(B) oil, gas, or a primary product of oil or gas which is sold by the foreign corporation or a related person for use or consumption within such country or is loaded in such country on a vessel or aircraft as fuel for such vessel or aircraft.

Such term shall not include any foreign personal holding company income (as defined in subsection (c)).

(2) Paragraph (1) applies only where corporation has produced 1,000 barrels per day or more.

(A) In general. The term "foreign base company oil related income" shall not include any income of a foreign corporation if such corporation is not a large oil producer for the taxable year.

(B) Large oil producer. For purposes of subparagraph (A), the term "large oil producer" means any corporation if, for the taxable year or for the preceding taxable year, the average daily production of foreign crude oil and natural gas of the related group which includes such corporation equaled or exceeded 1,000 barrels.

(C) Related group. The term "related group" means a group consisting of the foreign corporation and any other person who is a related person with respect to such corporation.

(D) Average daily production of foreign crude oil and natural gas. For purposes of this paragraph, the average daily production of foreign crude oil or natural gas of any related group for any taxable year (and the conversion of cubic feet of natural gas into barrels) shall be determined under rules similar to the rules of section 613A except that only crude oil or natural gas from a well located outside the United States shall be taken into account.

. . . . .

§ 955. Withdrawal of previously excluded subpart F income from qualified investment.

. . . . .

§ 956. Investment of earnings in United States property.

(a) General rule.

In the case of any controlled foreign corporation, the amount determined under this section with respect to any United States shareholder for any taxable year is the lesser of --

(1) the excess (if any) of --

(A) such shareholder's pro rata share of the average of the amounts of United States property held (directly or indirectly) by the controlled foreign corporation as of the close of each quarter of such taxable year, over

(B) the amount of earnings and profits described in section 959(c)(1)(A) with respect to such shareholder, or

(2) such shareholder's pro rata share of the applicable earnings of such controlled foreign corporation.

The amount taken into account under paragraph (1) with respect to any property shall be its adjusted basis as determined for purposes of computing earnings and profits, reduced by any liability to which the property is subject.

(b) Special rules.

(1) Applicable earnings. For purposes of this section, the term "applicable earnings" means, with respect to any controlled foreign corporation, the sum of --

(A) the amount (not including a deficit) referred to in section 316(a)(1) to the extent such amount was accumulated in prior taxable years, and

(B) the amount referred to in section 316(a)(2),

(2) Special rule for U.S. property acquired before corporation is a controlled foreign corporation. In applying subsection (a) to any taxable year, there shall be disregarded any item of United States property which was acquired by the controlled foreign corporation before the first day on which such corporation was treated as a controlled foreign corporation. The aggregate amount of property disregarded under the preceding sentence shall not exceed the portion of the applicable earnings of such controlled foreign corporation which were accumulated during periods before such first day.

(3) Special rule where corporation ceases to be controlled foreign corporation. If any foreign corporation ceases to be a controlled foreign corporation during any taxable year --

(A) the determination of any United States shareholder's pro rata share shall be made on the basis of stock owned (within the meaning of section 958(a)) by such shareholder on the last day during the taxable year on which the foreign corporation is a controlled foreign corporation,

(B) the average referred to in subsection (a)(1)(A) for such taxable year shall be determined by only taking into account quarters ending on or before such last day, and

(C) in determining applicable earnings, the amount taken into account by reason of being described in paragraph (2) of section 316(a) shall be the portion of the amount so described which is allocable (on a pro rata basis) to the part of such year during which the corporation is a controlled foreign corporation.

(c) United States property defined.

(1) In general. For purposes of subsection (a), the term "United States property" means any property acquired after December 31, 1962, which is --

(A) tangible property located in the United States;

(B) stock of a domestic corporation;

(C) an obligation of a United States person; or

(D) any right to the use in the United States of --

(i) a patent or copyright,

(ii) an invention, model, or design (whether or not patented),

(iii) a secret formula or process, or

(iv) any other similar property right,

469

which is acquired or developed by the controlled foreign corporation for use in the United States.

(2) Exceptions. For purposes of subsection (a), the term "United States property" does not include --

(A) obligations of the United States, money, or deposits with persons carrying on the banking business;

(B) property located in the United States which is purchased in the United States for export to, or use in, foreign countries;

(C) any obligation of a United States person arising in connection with the sale or processing of property if the amount of such obligation outstanding at no time during the taxable year exceeds the amount which would be ordinary and necessary to carry on the trade or business of both the other party to the sale or processing transaction and the United States person had the sale or processing transaction been made between unrelated persons;

(D) any aircraft, railroad rolling stock, vessel, motor vehicle, or container used in the transportation of persons or property in foreign commerce and used predominantly outside the United States;

(E) an amount of assets of an insurance company equivalent to the unearned premiums or reserves ordinary and necessary for the proper conduct of its insurance business attributable to contracts which are not contracts described in section 953(a)(1);

(F) the stock or obligations of a domestic corporation which is neither a United States shareholder (as defined in section 951(b)) of the controlled foreign corporation, nor a domestic corporation, 25 percent or more of the total combined voting power of which, immediately after the acquisition of any stock in such domestic corporation by the controlled foreign corporation, is owned, or is considered as being owned, by such United States shareholders in the aggregate;

(G) any movable property (other than a vessel or aircraft) which is used for the purpose of exploring for, developing, removing, or transporting resources from ocean waters or under such waters when used on the Continental Shelf of the United States;

(H) an amount of assets of the controlled foreign corporation equal to the earnings and profits accumulated after December 31, 1962, and excluded from subpart F income under section 952(b); and

(I) to the extent provided in regulations prescribed by the Secretary, property which is otherwise United States property which is held by a FSC and which is related to the export activities of such FSC.

(J) deposits of cash or securities made or received an commercial terms in the ordinary course of a United States or foreign person's business as a dealer in securities or in commodities, but only to the extent such deposits are made or received as collateral or margin for (I) a securities load, notional principal contract, options contract, forward contract, or futures contract, or (ii) any other financial transaction in which the   Secretary determines that it is customary to post collateral or margin; and

(K) an obligation of a United States person to the extent the principal amount of the obligation does not exceed the fair market value of readily marketable securities sold or purchased pursuant to a sale and repurchase agreement or otherwise posted or received as collateral for the obligation in the ordinary course of its business by a United States or foreign person which is a dealer in securities of commodities.

For purposes of subparagraphs (J) and (K), the term "dealer in securities" has the meaning given such term by section 475(c)(1), and the term "dealer in commodities" has the meaning given such term by section 475(e), except that such term shall include a futures commission merchant.

(3) Certain trade or service receivables acquired from related United States persons.

(A) In general. Notwithstanding paragraph (2) (other than subparagraph (H) thereof), the term "United States property" includes any trade or service receivable if --

(i) such trade or service receivable is acquired (directly or indirectly) from a related person who is a United States person, and

(ii) the obligor under such receivable is a United States person.

(B) Definitions. For purposes of this paragraph, the term "trade or service receivable" and "related person" have the respective meanings given to such terms by section 864(d).

(d) Pledges and guarantees.

For purposes of subsection (a), a controlled foreign corporation shall, under regulations prescribed by the Secretary, be considered as holding an obligation of a United States person if such controlled foreign corporation is a pledgor or guarantor of such obligation.

(e) Regulations.

The Secretary shall prescribe such regulations as may be necessary to carry out the purposes of this section, including regulations to prevent the avoidance of the provisions of this section through reorganizations or otherwise.

§ 957. Controlled foreign corporations; United States persons.

(a) General rule.

For purposes of this subpart, the term "controlled foreign corporation" means any foreign corporation if more than 50 percent of --

(1) the total combined voting power of all classes of stock of such corporation entitled to vote, or

(2) the total value of the stock of such corporation,

is owned (within the meaning of section 958(a)), or is considered as owned by applying the rules of ownership of section 958(b), by United States shareholders on any day during the taxable year of such foreign corporation.
(b) Special rule for insurance.

For purposes only of taking into account income described in section 953(a) (relating to insurance income), the term "controlled foreign corporation" includes not only a foreign corporation as defined by subsection (a) but also one of which more than 25 percent of the total combined voting power of all classes of stock (or more than 25 percent of the total value of stock) is owned (within the meaning of section 958(a)), or is considered as owned by applying the rules of ownership of section 958(b), by United States shareholders on any day during the taxable year of such corporation, if the gross amount of premiums or other consideration in respect of the reinsurance or the issuing of insurance or annuity contracts described in section 953(a)(1) exceeds 75 percent of the gross amount of all premiums or other consideration in respect of all risks.

(c) United States person.

For purposes of this subpart, the term "United States person" has the meaning assigned to it by section 7701(a)(30) except that --

(1) with respect to a corporation organized under the laws of the Commonwealth of Puerto Rico, such term does not include an individual who is a bona fide resident of Puerto Rico, if a dividend received by such individual during the taxable year from such corporation would, for purposes of section 933(1), be treated as income derived from sources within Puerto Rico, and

(2) with respect to a corporation organized under the laws of Guam, American Samoa, or the Northern Mariana Islands --

(A) 80 percent or more of the gross income of which for the 3-year period ending at the close of the taxable year (or for such part of such period as such corporation or any predecessor has been in existence) was derived from sources within such a possession or was effectively connected with the conduct of a trade or business in such a possession, and

(B) 50 percent or more of the gross income of which for such period (or part) was derived from the conduct of an active trade or business within such a possession,

such term does not include an individual who is a bona fide resident of Guam, American Samoa, or the Northern Mariana Islands.

For purposes of subparagraphs (A) and (B) of paragraph (2), the determination as to whether income was derived from sources within a possession, was effectively connected with the conduct of a trade or business within a possession, or derived from the active conduct of a trade or business within a possession shall be made under regulations prescribed by the Secretary.

§ 958. Rules for determining stock ownership.

(a) Direct and indirect ownership.

(1) General rule. For purposes of this subpart (other than section 960(a)(1)), stock owned means --

(A) stock owned directly, and

(B) stock owned with the application of paragraph (2).

(2) Stock ownership through foreign entities. For purposes of subparagraph (B) of paragraph (1), stock owned, directly or indirectly, by or for a foreign corporation, foreign partnership, or foreign trust or foreign estate (within the meaning of section 7701(a)(31)) shall be considered as being owned proportionately by its shareholders, partners, or beneficiaries. Stock considered to be owned by a person by reason of the application of the preceding sentence shall, for purposes of applying such sentence, be treated as actually owned by such person.

(3) Special rule for mutual insurance companies. For purposes of applying paragraph (1) in the case of a foreign mutual insurance company, the term "stock" shall include any certificate entitling the holder to voting power in the corporation.

(b) Constructive ownership.

For purposes of sections 951(b), 954(d)(3), 956(b)(2), and 957, section 318(a) (relating to constructive ownership of stock) shall apply to the extent that the effect is to treat any United States person as a United States shareholder within the meaning of section 951(b), to treat a person as a related person within the meaning of section 954(d)(3), to treat the stock of a domestic corporation as owned by a United States shareholder of the controlled foreign corporation for purposes of section 956(b)(2), or to treat a foreign corporation as a controlled foreign corporation under section 957, except that --

(1) In applying paragraph (1)(A) of section 318(a), stock owned by a nonresident alien individual (other than a foreign trust or foreign estate) shall not be considered as owned by a citizen or by a resident alien individual.

(2) In applying subparagraphs (A), (B), and (C) of section 318(a)(2), if a partnership, estate, trust, or corporation owns, directly or indirectly, more than 50 percent of the total combined voting power of all classes of stock entitled to vote of a corporation, it shall be considered as owning all the stock entitled to vote.

(3) In applying subparagraph (C) of section 318(a)(2), the phrase "10 percent" shall be substituted for the phrase "50 percent" used in subparagraph (C).

(4) Subparagraphs (A), (B), and (C) of section 318(a)(3) shall not be applied so as to consider a United States person as owning stock which is owned by a person who is not a United States person.

Paragraphs (1) and (4) shall not apply for purposes of section 956(b)(2) to treat stock of a domestic corporation as not owned by a United States shareholder.

§ 959. Exclusion from gross income of previously taxed earnings and profits.

(a) Exclusion from gross income of United States persons.

For purposes of this chapter, the earnings and profits of a foreign corporation attributable to amounts which are, or have been, included in the gross income of a United States shareholder under section 951(a) shall not, when --

(1) such amounts are distributed to, or

(2) such amounts would, but for this subsection, be included under section 951(a)(1)(B) in the gross income of

such shareholder (or any other United States person who acquires from any person any portion of the interest of such United States shareholder in such foreign corporation, but only to the extent of such portion, and subject to such proof of the identity of such interest as the Secretary may by regulations prescribe) directly or indirectly through a chain of ownership described under section 958(a), be again included in the gross income of such United States shareholder (or of such other United States person). The rules of subsection (c) shall apply for purposes of paragraph (1) of this subsection and the rules of subsection (f) shall apply for purposes of paragraphs (2) of this subsection.

(b) Exclusion from gross income of certain foreign subsidiaries.

For purposes of section 951(a), the earnings and profits of a controlled foreign corporation attributable to amounts which are, or have been, included in the gross income of a United States shareholder under section 951(a), shall not, when distributed through a chain of ownership described under section 958(a), be also included in the gross income of another controlled foreign corporation in such chain for purposes of the application of section 951(a) to such other controlled foreign corporation with respect to such United States shareholder (or to any other United States shareholder who acquires from any person any portion of the interest of such United States shareholder in the controlled foreign corporation, but only to the extent of such portion, and subject to such proof of identity of such interest as the Secretary may prescribe by regulations).

(c) Allocation of distributions.

For purposes of subsections (a) and (b), section 316(a) shall be applied by applying paragraph (2) thereof, and then paragraph (1) thereof --

(1) first to the aggregate of --

(A) earnings and profits attributable to amounts included in gross income under section 951(a)(1)(B) (or which would have been included except for subsection (a)(2) of this section), and

(B) earnings and profits attributable to amounts included in gross income under section 951(a)(1)(C) (or which would have been included except for subsection (a)(3) of this section),

with any distribution being allocated between earnings and profits described in subparagraph (A) and earnings and profits described in subparagraph (B) proportionately on the basis of the respective amounts of such earnings and profits,

(2) then to earnings and profits attributable to amounts included in gross income under section 951(a)(1)(A) (but reduced by amounts not included under subparagraph (B) or (C) of section 951(a)(1) because of the exclusions in paragraphs (2) and (3) of subsection (a) of this section), and

(3) then to other earnings and profits.

(d) Distributions excluded from gross income not to be treated as dividends.

Except as provided in section 960(a)(3), any distribution excluded from gross income under subsection (a) shall be treated, for purposes of this chapter, as a distribution which is not a dividend; except that such distributions shall immediately reduce earnings and profits.

(e) Coordination with amounts previously taxed under section 1248.

For purposes of this section and section 960(b), any amount included in the gross income of any person as a dividend by reason of subsection (a) or (f) of section 1248 shall be treated as an amount included in the gross income of such person (or, in any case to which section 1248(e) applies, of the domestic corporation referred to in section 1248(e)(2)) under section 951(a)(1)(A).

(f) Allocation rules for certain inclusions.

(1) In general. For purposes of this section --

(A) amounts that would be included under subparagraph (B) of section 951(a)(1) (determined without regard to this section) shall be treated as attributable first to earnings described in subsection (c)(2), and then to earnings described in subsection (c)(3), and

(B) amounts that would be included under subparagraph (C) of section 951(a)(1) (determined without regard to this section) shall be treated as attributable first to earnings described in subsection (c)(2) to the extent the earnings so described were accumulated in taxable years beginning after September 30, 1993, and then to earnings described in subsection (c)(3).

(2) Treatment of distributions. In applying this section, actual distributions shall be taken into account before amounts that would be included under subparagraphs (B) and (C) of section 951(a)(1) (determined without regard to this section).

§ 960. Special rules for foreign tax credit.

(a) Taxes paid by a foreign corporation.

(1) Deemed Paid Credit. For purposes of subpart A of this part, if there is included under section 951(a) in the gross income of a domestic corporation any amount attributable to earnings and profits of a foreign corporation which is a member of a qualified group (as defined in section 902(b)) with respect to the domestic corporation, then, to the extent provided in regulations, section 902 shall be applied as if the amount so included were a dividend paid by such foreign corporation (determined by applying section 902(c) in accordance with section 904(d)(3)(B)).

(2) Taxes previously deemed paid by domestic corporation. If a domestic corporation receives a distribution from a foreign corporation, any portion of which is excluded from gross income under section 959, the income, war profits, and excess profits taxes paid or deemed paid by such foreign corporation to any foreign country or to any possession of the United States in connection with the earnings and profits of such foreign corporation from which such distribution is made shall not be taken into account for purposes of section 902, to the extent such taxes were deemed paid by a domestic corporation under paragraph (1) for any prior taxable year.

(3) Taxes paid by foreign corporation and not previously deemed paid by domestic corporation. Any portion of a distribution from a foreign corporation received by a domestic corporation which is excluded from gross income under section 959(a) shall be treated by the domestic corporation as a dividend, solely for purposes of taking into account under section 902 any income, war profits, or excess profits taxes paid to any foreign country or to any possession of the United States, on or with respect to the accumulated profits of such foreign corporation from which such distribution is made, which were not deemed paid by the domestic corporation under paragraph (1) for any prior taxable year.

(b) Special rules for foreign tax credit in year of receipt of previously taxed earnings and profits.

(1) Increase in section 904 limitation. In the case of any taxpayer who --

(A) either (i) chose to have the benefits of subpart A of this part for a taxable year beginning after September 30, 1993, in which he was required under section 951(a) to include any amount in his gross income, or (ii) did not pay or accrue for such taxable year any income, war profits, or excess profits taxes to any foreign country or to any possession of the United States,

(B) chooses to have the benefits of subpart A of this part for any taxable year in which he receives 1 or more distributions or amounts which are excludable from gross income under section 959(a) and which are attributable to amounts included in his gross income for taxable years referred to in subparagraph (A), and

(C) for the taxable year in which such distributions or amounts are received, pays, or is deemed to have paid, or accrues income, war profits, or excess profits taxes to a foreign country or to any possession of the United States with respect to such distributions or amounts,

the limitation under section 904 for the taxable year in which such distributions or amounts are received shall be increased by the lesser of the amount of such taxes paid, or deemed paid, or accrued with respect to such distributions or amounts or the amount in the excess limitation account as of the beginning of such taxable year.

(2) Excess limitation account.

(A) Establishment of account. Each taxpayer meeting the requirements of paragraph (1)(A) shall establish an excess limitation account. The opening balance of such account shall be zero.

(B) Increases in account. For each taxable year beginning after September 30, 1993, the taxpayer shall increase the amount in the excess limitation account by the excess (if any) of --

(i) the amount by which the limitation under section 904(a) for such taxable year was increased by reason of the total amount of the inclusions in gross income under section 951(a) for such taxable year, over

(ii) the amount of any income, war profits, and excess profits taxes paid, or deemed paid, or accrued to any foreign country or possession of the United States which were allowable as a credit under section 901 for such taxable year and which would not have been allowable but for the inclusions in gross income described in clause (i).

Proper reductions in the amount added to the account under the preceding sentence for any taxable year shall be made for any increase in the credit allowable under section 901 for such taxable year by reason of a carryback if such increase would not have been allowable but for the inclusions in gross income described in clause (i).

(C) Decreases in account. For each taxable year beginning after September 30, 1993, for which the limitation under section 904 was increased under paragraph (1), the taxpayer shall reduce the amount in the excess limitation account by the amount of such increase.

(3) Distributions of income previously taxed in years beginning before October 1, 1993. If the taxpayer receives a distribution or amount in a taxable year beginning after September 30, 1993, which is excluded from gross income under section 959(a) and is attributable to any amount included in gross income under section 951(a) for a taxable year beginning before October 1, 1993, the limitation under section 904 for the taxable year in which such amount or distribution is received shall be increased by the amount determined under this subsection as in effect on the day before the date of the enactment of the Revenue Reconciliation Act of 1993.

(4) Cases in which taxes not to be allowed as deduction. In the case of any taxpayer who --

(A) chose to have the benefits of subpart A of this part for a taxable year in which he was required under section 951(a) to include in his gross income an amount in respect of a controlled foreign corporation, and

(B) does not choose to have the benefits of subpart A of this part for the taxable year in which he receives a distribution or amount which is excluded from gross income under section 959(a) and which is attributable to earnings and profits of the controlled foreign corporation which was included in his gross income for the taxable year referred to in subparagraph (A),

no deduction shall be allowed under section 164 for the taxable year in which such distribution or amount is received for any income, war profits, or excess profits taxes paid or accrued to any foreign country or to any possession of the United States on or with respect to such distribution or amount.

(5) Insufficient taxable income. If an increase in the limitation under this subsection exceeds the tax imposed by this chapter for such year, the amount of such excess shall be deemed an overpayment of tax for such year.

§ 961. Adjustments to basis of stock in controlled foreign corporations and of other property.

(a) Increase in basis.

Under regulations prescribed by the Secretary, the basis of a United States shareholder's stock in a controlled foreign corporation, and the basis of property of a United States shareholder by reason of which he is considered under section 958(a)(2) as owning stock of a controlled foreign corporation, shall be increased by the amount required to be included in his gross income under section 951(a) with respect to such stock or with respect to such property, as the case may be, but only to the extent to which such amount was included in the gross income of such United States shareholder. In the case of a United States shareholder who has made an election under section 962 for the taxable year, the increase in basis provided by this subsection shall not exceed an amount equal to the amount of tax paid under this chapter with respect to the amounts required to be included in his gross income under section 951(a).

(b) Reduction in basis.

(1) In general. Under regulations prescribed by the Secretary, the adjusted basis of stock or other property with respect to which a United States shareholder or a United States person receives an amount which is excluded from gross income under section 959(a) shall be reduced by the amount so excluded. In the case of a United States shareholder who has made an election under section 962 for any prior taxable year, the reduction in basis provided by this paragraph shall not exceed an amount equal to the amount received which is excluded from gross income under section 959(a) after the application of section 962(d).

(2) Amount in excess of basis. To the extent that an amount excluded from gross income under section 959(a) exceeds the adjusted basis of the stock or other property with respect to which it is received, the amount shall be treated as gain from the sale or exchange of property.

(c) Basis Adjustment in Stock Held in Foreign Corporation. Under regulations prescribed by the Secretary, if a United States shareholder is treated under section 958(a)(2) as owing any stock in a controlled foreign corporation which is actually owned by another controlled foreign corporation, adjustments similar to the adjustments provided by subsections (a) and (b) shall be made to the basis of such stock in the hands of such other controlled foreign corporation, but only for the purposes of determining the amount included under section 951 in the gross income of such United States shareholder (or any other United States shareholder who acquires from any person any portion of the interest of such United States shareholder by reason of which such shareholder was treated as owning such stock, but only to the extent of such portion, and subject to such proof of identity of such interest as the Secretary may prescribe by regulations).

§ 962. Election by individuals to be subject to tax at corporate rates.

. . . . .

§ 964. Miscellaneous provisions.

(a) Earnings and profits.

Except as provided in section 312(k)(4), for purposes of this subpart the earnings and profits of any foreign corporation, and the deficit in earnings and profits of any foreign corporation, for any taxable year shall be determined according to rules substantially similar to those applicable to domestic corporations, under regulations prescribed by the Secretary. In determining such earnings and profits, or the deficit in such earnings and profits, the amount of any illegal bribe, kickback, or other payment (within the meaning of section 162(c)) shall not be taken into account to decrease such earnings and profits or to increase such deficit. The payments referred to in the preceding sentence are payments which would be unlawful under the Foreign Corrupt Practices Act of 1977 if the payor were a United States person.

(b) Blocked foreign income.

Under regulations prescribed by the Secretary, no part of the earnings and profits of a controlled foreign corporation for any taxable year shall be included in earnings and profits for purposes of sections 952, 955, and 956, if it is established to the satisfaction of the Secretary that such part could not have been distributed by the controlled foreign corporation to United States shareholders who own (within the meaning of section 958(a)) stock of such controlled foreign corporation because of currency or other restrictions or limitations imposed under the laws of any foreign country.

(c) Records and accounts of United States shareholders.

(1) Records and accounts to be maintained. The Secretary may by regulations require each person who is, or has been, a United States shareholder of a controlled foreign corporation to maintain such records and accounts as may be prescribed by such regulations as necessary to carry out the provisions of this subpart and subpart G.

(2) Two or more persons required to maintain or furnish the same records and accounts with respect to the same foreign corporation. Where, but for this paragraph, two or more United States persons would be required to maintain or furnish the same records and accounts as may by regulations be required under paragraph (1) with respect to the same controlled foreign corporation for the same period, the Secretary may by regulations provide that the maintenance or furnishing of such records and accounts by only one such person shall satisfy the requirements of paragraph (1) for such other persons.

(d) Treatment of certain branches.

(1) In general. For purposes of this chapter, section 6038, section 6046, and such other provisions as may be specified in regulations --

(A) a qualified insurance branch of a controlled foreign corporation shall be treated as a separate foreign corporation created under the laws of the foreign country with respect to which such branch qualifies under paragraph (2), and

(B) except as provided in regulations, any amount directly or indirectly transferred or credited from such branch to one or more other accounts of such controlled foreign corporation shall be treated as a dividend paid to such controlled foreign corporation.

(2) Qualified insurance branch. For purposes of paragraph (1), the term "qualified insurance branch" means any branch of a controlled foreign corporation which is licensed and predominantly engaged on a permanent basis in the active conduct of an insurance business in a foreign country if --

(A) separate books and accounts are maintained for such branch,

(B) the principal place of business of such branch is. in such foreign country,

(C) such branch would be taxable under subchapter L if it were a separate domestic corporation, and

(D) an election under this paragraph applies to such branch.

An election under this paragraph shall apply to the taxable year for which made and all subsequent taxable years unless revoked with the consent of the Secretary.

(3) Regulations. The Secretary shall prescribe such regulations as may be necessary or appropriate to carry out the purposes of this subsection.

(E) Gain on certain stock sales by controlled foreign corporations treated as dividends.

(1) In general. If a controlled foreign corporation sells or exchanges stock in any other foreign corporation, gain recognized on such sale or exchange shall be included in the gross income of such controlled foreign corporation as a dividend to the same extent that it would have been so included under section 1248(a) if such controlled foreign corporation were a United States person. For purposes of determining the amount which would have been so includible, the determination of whether such other foreign corporation was a controlled foreign corporation shall be made without regard to the preceding sentence.

(2) Same country exception not applicable.--Clause (i) of section 954(c)(3)(A) shall not apply to any amount treated as a dividend by reason of paragraph (1).

(3) Clarification of deemed sales.--For purposes of this subsection, a controlled foreign corporation shall be treated as having sold or exchanged any stock if, under any provision of this subtitle, such controlled foreign corporation is treated as having gain from the sale or exchange of such stock.

§ 1221. Capital asset defined.

(a) In general. For purposes of this subtitle, the term "capital asset" means property held by the taxpayer (whether or not connected with his trade or business), but does not include --

(1) stock in trade of the taxpayer or other property of a kind which would properly be included in the inventory of the taxpayer if on hand at the close of the taxable year, or property held by the taxpayer primarily for sale to customers in the ordinary course of his trade or business;

(2) property, used in his trade or business, of a character which is subject to the allowance for depreciation provided in section 167, or real property used in his trade or business;

(3) a copyright, a literary, musical, or artistic composition, a letter or memorandum, or similar property, held by --

(A) a taxpayer whose personal efforts created such property,

(B) in the case of a letter, memorandum, or similar property, a taxpayer for whom such property was prepared or produced, or

(C) a taxpayer in whose hands the basis of such property is determined, for purposes of determining gain from a sale or exchange, in whole or part by reference to the basis of such property in the hands of a taxpayer described in subparagraph (A) or (B);

(4) accounts or notes receivable acquired in the ordinary course of trade or business for services rendered or from the sale of property described in paragraph (1);

(5) a publication of the United States Government (including the Congressional Record) which is received from the United States Government or any agency thereof, other than by purchase at the price at which it is offered for sale to the public, and which is held by --

(A) a taxpayer who so received such publication, or

(B) a taxpayer in whose hands the basis of such publication is determined, for purposes of determining gain from a sale or exchange, in whole or in part by reference to the basis of such publication in the hands of a taxpayer described in subparagraph (A).

(6) any commodities derivative financial instrument held by a commodities derivatives dealer, unless

(A) it is established to the satisfaction of the Secretary that such instrument has no connection to the activities of such dealer as a dealer, and

(B) such instrument is clearly identified in such dealer's records as being described in subparagraph (A) before the close of the day on which it was acquired, originated, or entered into (or such other time as the Secretary may by regulations prescribe);

(7) any hedging transaction which is clearly identified as such before the close of the day on which it was acquired, originated, or entered into (or such other time as the Secretary may by regulations prescribe); or

(8) supplies of a type regularly used or consumed by the taxpayer in the ordinary course of a trade or business of the taxpayer.

. . . . .

§ 1231. Property used in the trade or business and involuntary conversions.

(a) General rule.

(1) Gains exceed losses. If --

(A) the section 1231 gains for any taxable year, exceed

(B) the section 1231 losses for such taxable year,

such gains and losses shall be treated as long-term capital gains or long-term capital losses, as the case may be.

(2) Gains do not exceed losses. If --

(A) the section 1231 gains for any taxable year, do not exceed

(B) the section 1231 losses for such taxable year,

such gains and losses shall not be treated as gains and losses from sales or exchanges of capital assets.

(3) Section 1231 gains and losses. For purposes of this subsection --

(A) Section 1231 gain. The term "section 1231 gain" means --

(i) any recognized gain on the sale or exchange of property used in the trade or business, and

(ii) any recognized gain from the compulsory or involuntary conversion (as a result of destruction in whole or in part, theft or seizure, or an exercise of the power of requisition or condemnation or the threat or imminence thereof) into other property or money of --

(I) property used in the trade or business, or

(II) any capital asset which is held for more than 1 year and is held in connection with a trade or business or a transaction entered into for profit.

(B) Section 1231 loss. The term "section 1231 loss" means any recognized loss from a sale or exchange or conversion described in subparagraph (A).

(4) Special rules. For purposes of this subsection --

(A) In determining under this subsection whether gains exceed losses --

(i) the section 1231 gains shall be included only if and to the extent taken into account in computing gross income, and

(ii) the section 1231 losses shall be included only if and to the extent taken into account in computing taxable income, except that section 1211 shall not apply.

(B) Losses (including losses not compensated for by insurance or otherwise) on the destruction, in whole or in part, theft or seizure, or requisition or condemnation of --

(i) property used in the trade or business, or

(ii) capital assets which are held for more than 1 year and are held in connection with a trade or business or a transaction entered into for profit,
shall be treated as losses from a compulsory or involuntary conversion.

(C) In the case of any involuntary conversion (subject to the provisions of this subsection but for this sentence) arising from fire, storm, shipwreck, or other casualty, or from theft, of any --

(i) property used in the trade or business, or

(ii) any capital asset which is held for more than 1 year and is held in connection with a trade or business or a transaction entered into for profit,

this subsection shall not apply to such conversion (whether resulting in gain or loss) if during the taxable year the recognized losses from such conversions exceed the recognized gains from such conversions.

(b) Definition of property used in the trade or business.

For purposes of this section --

(1) General rule. The term "property used in the trade or business" means property used in the trade or business, of a character which is subject to the allowance for depreciation provided in section 167, held for more than 1 year, and real property used in the trade or business, held for more than 1 year, which is not --

(A) property of a kind which would properly be includible in the inventory of the taxpayer if on hand at the close of the taxable year,

(B) property held by the taxpayer primarily for sale to customers in the ordinary course of his trade or business,

(C) a copyright, a literary, musical, or artistic composition, a letter or memorandum, or similar property, held by a taxpayer described in paragraph (3) of section 1221, or

(D) a publication of the United States Government (including the Congressional Record) which is received from the United States Government, or any agency thereof, other than by purchase at the price at which it is offered for sale to the public, and which is held by a taxpayer described in paragraph (5) of section 1221.

(2) Timber, coal, or domestic iron ore. Such term includes timber, coal, and iron ore with respect to which section 631 applies.

(3) Livestock. Such term includes --

(A) cattle and horses, regardless of age, held by the taxpayer for draft, breeding, dairy, or sporting purposes, and held by him for 24 months or more from the date of acquisition, and

(B) other livestock, regardless of age, held by the taxpayer for draft, breeding, dairy, or sporting purposes, and held by him for 12 months or more from the date of acquisition.

Such term does not include poultry.

(4) Unharvested crop. In the case of an unharvested crop on land used in the trade or business and held for more than 1 year, if the crop and the land are sold or exchanged (or compulsorily or involuntarily converted) at the same time and to the same person, the crop shall be considered as "property used in the trade or business."

(c) Recapture of net ordinary losses.

(1) In general. The net section 1231 gain for any taxable year shall be treated as ordinary income to the extent such gain does not exceed the non-recaptured net section 1231 losses.

(2) Non-recaptured net section 1231 losses. For purposes of this subsection, the term "non-recaptured net section 1231 losses" means the excess of --

(A) the aggregate amount of the net section 1231 losses for the 5 most recent preceding taxable years beginning after December 31, 1981, over

(B) the portion of such losses taken into account under paragraph (1) for such preceding taxable years.

(3) Net section 1231 gain. For purposes of this subsection, the term "net section 1231 gain" means the excess of --

(A) the section 1231 gains, over

(B) the section 1231 losses.

(4) Net section 1231 loss. For purposes of this subsection, the term "net section 1231 loss" means the excess of --

(A) the section 1231 losses, over

(B) the section 1231 gains.

(5) Special rules. For purposes of determining the amount of the net section 1231 gain or loss for any taxable year, the rules of paragraph (4) of subsection (a) shall apply.

§ 1235. Sale or exchange of patents.

(a) General.

A transfer (other than by gift, inheritance, or devise) of property consisting of all substantial rights to a patent, or an undivided interest therein which includes a part of all such rights, by any holder shall be considered the sale or exchange of a capital asset held for more than 1 year, regardless of whether or not payments in consideration of such transfer are --

(1) payable periodically over a period generally coterminous with the transferee's use of the patent, or

(2) contingent on the productivity, use, or disposition of the property transferred.

(b) "Holder" defined.

For purposes of this section, the term "holder" means --

(1) any individual whose efforts created such property, or

(2) any other individual who has acquired his interest in such property in exchange for consideration in money or money's worth paid to such creator prior to actual reduction to practice of the invention covered by the patent, if such individual is neither --

(A) the employer of such creator, nor

(B) related to such creator (within the meaning of subsection (d)).
(c) Effective date.

This section shall be applicable with regard to any amounts received, or payments made, pursuant to a transfer described in subsection (a) in any taxable year to which this subtitle applies, regardless of the taxable year in which such transfer occurred.

(d) Related persons.

Subsection (a) shall not apply to any transfer, directly or indirectly, between persons specified within any one of the paragraphs of section 267(b) or persons described in section 707(b); except that, in applying section 267(b) and (c) and section 707(b) for purposes of this section --

(1) the phrase "25 percent or more" shall be substituted for the phrase "more than 50 percent" each place it appears in section 267(b) or 707(b), and

(2) paragraph (4) of section 267(c) shall be treated as providing that the family of an individual shall include only his spouse, ancestors, and lineal descendants.

(e) Cross reference.

For special rule relating to nonresident aliens, see section 871(a).

§ 1248. Gain from certain sales or exchanges of stock in certain foreign corporations.

(a) General rule.

If --

(1) a United States person sells or exchanges stock in a foreign corporation, and

(2) such person owns, within the meaning of section 958(a), or is considered as owning by applying the rules of ownership of section 958(b), 10 percent or more of the total combined voting power of all classes of stock entitled to vote of such foreign corporation at any time during the 5-year period ending on the date of the sale or exchange when such foreign corporation was a controlled foreign corporation (as defined in section 957),

then the gain recognized on the sale or exchange of such stock shall be included in the gross income of such person as a dividend, to the extent of the earnings and profits of the foreign corporation attributable (under regulations prescribed by the Secretary) to such stock which were accumulated in taxable years of such foreign corporation beginning after December 31, 1962, and during the period or periods the stock sold or exchanged was held by such person while such foreign corporation was a controlled foreign corporation. For purposes of this section, a United States person shall be treated as having sold or exchanged any stock if, under any provision of this subtitle, such person is treated as realizing gain from the sale or exchange of such stock.

(b) Limitation on tax applicable to individuals.

In the case of an individual, if the stock sold or exchanged is a capital asset (within the meaning of section 1221) and has been held for more than 1 year, the tax attributable to an amount included in gross income as a dividend under subsection (a) shall not be greater than a tax equal to the sum of --

(1) a pro rata share of the excess of --

(A) the taxes that would have been paid by the foreign corporation with respect to its income had it been taxed under this chapter as a domestic corporation (but without allowance for deduction of, or credit for, taxes described in subparagraph (B)), for the period or periods the stock sold or exchanged was held by the United States person in taxable years beginning after December 31, 1962, while the foreign corporation was a controlled foreign corporation, adjusted for distributions and amounts previously included in gross income of a United States shareholder under section 951, over

(B) the income, war profits, or excess profits taxes paid by the foreign corporation with respect to such income; and

(2) an amount equal to the tax that would result by including in gross income, as gain from the sale or exchange of a capital asset held for more than 1 year, an amount equal to the excess of (A) the amount included in gross income as a dividend under subsection (a), over (B) the amount determined under paragraph (1).

(c) Determination of earnings and profits.

(1) In general. Except as provided in section 312(k)(4), for purposes of this section the earnings and profits of any foreign corporation for any taxable year shall be determined according to rules substantially similar to those applicable to domestic corporations, under regulations prescribed by the Secretary.

(2) Earnings and profits of subsidiaries of foreign corporations. If --

(A) subsection (a) or (f) applies to a sale, exchange, or distribution by a United States person of stock of a foreign corporation and, by reason of the ownership of the stock sold or exchanged, such person owned within the meaning of section 958(a)(2) stock of any other foreign corporation; and

(B) such person owned, within the meaning of section 958(a), or was considered as owning by applying the rules of ownership of section 958(b), 10 percent or more of the total combined voting power of all classes of stock entitled to vote of such other foreign corporation at any time during the 5-year period ending on the date of the sale or exchange when such other foreign corporation was a controlled foreign corporation (as defined in section 957),

then, for purposes of this section, the earnings and profits of the foreign corporation the stock of which is sold or exchanged which are attributable to the stock sold or exchanged shall be deemed to include the earnings and profits of such other foreign corporation which --

(C) are attributable (under regulations prescribed by the Secretary) to the stock of such other foreign corporation which such person owned within the meaning of section 958(a)(2) (by reason of his ownership within the meaning of section 958(a)(1)(A) of the stock sold or exchanged) on the date of such sale or exchange (or on the date of any sale or exchange of the stock of such other foreign corporation occurring during the 5-year period ending on the date of the sale or exchange of the stock of such foreign corporation, to the extent not otherwise taken into account under this section but not in excess of the fair market value of the stock of such other foreign corporation sold or exchanged over the basis of such stock (for determining gain) in the hands of the transferor); and

(D) were accumulated in taxable years of such other corporation beginning after December 31, 1962, and during the period or periods --

(i) such other corporation was a controlled foreign corporation, and

(ii) such person owned within the meaning of section 958(a) the stock of such other foreign corporation.

(d) Exclusions from earnings and profits.

For purposes of this section, the following amounts shall be excluded, with respect to any United States person, from the earnings and profits of a foreign corporation:

(1) Amounts included in gross income under section 951. Earnings and profits of the foreign corporation attributable to any amount previously included in the gross income of such person under section 951, with respect to the stock sold or exchanged, but only to the extent the inclusion of such amount did not result in an exclusion of an amount from gross income under section 959.

(2) Repealed.

(3) Less developed country corporations under prior law. Earnings and profits of a foreign corporation which were accumulated during any taxable year beginning before January 1, 1976, while such corporation was a less developed country corporation under section 902(d) as in effect before the enactment of the Tax Reduction Act of 1975.

(4) United States income. Any item includible in gross income of the foreign corporation under this chapter --

(A) for any taxable year beginning before January 1, 1967, as income derived from sources within the United States of a foreign corporation engaged in trade or business within the United States, or

(B) for any taxable year beginning after December 31, 1966, as income effectively connected with the conduct by such corporation of a trade or business within the United States.

This paragraph shall not apply with respect to any item which is exempt from taxation (or is subject to a reduced rate of tax) pursuant to a treaty obligation of the United States.

(5) Amounts included in gross income under section 1247. If the United States person whose stock is sold or exchanged was a qualified shareholder (as defined in section 1247(c)) of a foreign corporation which was a foreign investment company (as described in section 1246(b)(1)), the earnings and profits of the foreign corporation for taxable years in which such person was a qualified shareholder.

(6) Foreign trade income. Earnings and profits of the foreign corporation attributable to foreign trade income of a FSC other than foreign trade income which --

(A) is section 923(a)(2) non-exempt income (within the meaning of section 927(d)(6)), or

(B) would not (but for section 923(a)(4)) be treated as exempt foreign trade income.

For purposes of the preceding sentence, the terms "foreign trade income" and "exempt foreign trade income" have the respective meanings given such terms by section 923.

(7) Amounts included in gross income under section 1293. Earnings and profits of the foreign corporation attributable to any amount previously included in the gross income of such person under section 1293 with respect to the stock sold or exchanged, but only to the extent the inclusion of such amount did not result in an exclusion of an amount under section 1293(c).

(e) Sales or exchanges of stock in certain domestic corporations.

Except as provided in regulations prescribed by the Secretary, if --

(1) a United States person sells or exchanges stock of a domestic corporation, and

(2) such domestic corporation was formed or availed of principally for the holding, directly or indirectly, of stock of one or more foreign corporations,

such sale or exchange shall, for purposes of this section, be treated as a sale or exchange of the stock of the foreign corporation or corporations held by the domestic corporation.

(f) Certain nonrecognition transactions.

Except as provided in regulations prescribed by the Secretary --

(1) In general. If --

(A) a domestic corporation satisfies the stock ownership requirements of subsection (a)(2) with respect to a foreign corporation, and

(B) such domestic corporation distributes stock of such foreign corporation in a distribution to which section 311(a), 337, or 361(c)(1) applies,

then, notwithstanding any other provision of this subtitle, an amount equal to the excess of the fair market value of such stock over its adjusted basis in the hands of the domestic corporation shall be included in the gross income of the domestic corporation as a dividend to the extent of the earnings and profits of the foreign corporation attributable (under regulations prescribed by the Secretary) to such stock which were accumulated in taxable years of such foreign corporation beginning after December 31, 1962, and during the period or periods the stock was held by such domestic corporation while such foreign corporation was a controlled foreign corporation. For purposes of subsections (c)(2), (d), and (h), a distribution of stock to which this subsection applies shall be treated as a sale of stock to which subsection (a) applies.

(2) Exception for certain distributions. In the case of any distribution of stock of a foreign corporation, paragraph (1) shall not apply if such distribution is to a domestic corporation --

(A) which is treated under this section as holding such stock for the period for which the stock was held by the distributing corporation, and

(B) which, immediately after the distribution, satisfies the stock ownership requirements of subsection (a)(2) with respect to such foreign corporation.

(3) Application to cases described in subsection (e). To the extent that earnings and profits are taken into account under this subsection, they shall be excluded and not taken into account for purposes of subsection (e).

(g) Exceptions.

This section shall not apply to --

(1) distributions to which section 303 (relating to distributions in redemption of stock to pay death taxes) applies; or

(2) any amount to the extent that such amount is, under any other provision of this title, treated as --

(A) a dividend (other than an amount treated as a dividend under subsection (f)),

(B) ordinary income, or

(C) gain from the sale of an asset held for not more than 1 year.

(h) Taxpayer to establish earnings and profits.

Unless the taxpayer establishes the amount of the earnings and profits of the foreign corporation to be taken into account under subsection (a) or (f), all gain from the sale or exchange shall be considered a dividend under subsection (a) or (f), and unless the taxpayer establishes the amount of foreign taxes to be taken into account under subsection (b), the limitation of such subsection shall not apply.

(i) Treatment of certain indirect transfers.

(1) In general. If any shareholder of a 10-percent corporate shareholder of a foreign corporation exchanges stock of the 10-percent corporate shareholder for stock of the foreign corporation, for purposes of this section, the stock of the foreign corporation received in such exchange shall be treated as if it had been --

(A) issued to the 10-percent corporate shareholder, and

(B) then distributed by the 10-percent corporate shareholder to such shareholder in redemption or liquidation (whichever is appropriate).

The amount of gain recognized by such 10-percent corporate shareholder under the preceding sentence shall not exceed the amount treated as a dividend under this section.

(2) 10-percent corporate shareholder defined. For purposes of this subsection, the term "10-percent corporate shareholder" means any domestic corporation which, as of the day before the exchange referred to in paragraph (1), satisfies the stock ownership requirements of subsection (a)(2) with respect to the foreign corporation.

(j) Cross reference.

For provision excluding amounts previously taxed under this section from gross income when subsequently distributed, see section 959(e).

§ 1249. Gain from certain sales or exchanges of patents, etc., to foreign corporations.

(a) General rule.

Gain from the sale or exchange after December 31, 1962, of a patent, an invention, model, or design (whether or not patented), a copyright, a secret formula or process, or any other similar property right to any foreign corporation by any United States person (as defined in section 7701(a)(30)) which controls such foreign corporation shall, if such gain would (but for the provisions of this subsection) be gain from the sale or exchange of a capital asset or of property described in section 1231, be considered as ordinary income.

(b) Control.

For purposes of subsection (a), control means, with respect to any foreign corporation, the ownership, directly or indirectly, of stock possessing more than 50 percent of the total combined voting power of all classes of stock entitled to vote. For purposes of this subsection, the rules for determining ownership of stock prescribed by section 958 shall apply.

§ 1441. Withholding of tax on nonresident aliens.

(a) General rule.

Except as otherwise provided in subsection (c), all persons, in whatever capacity acting (including lessees or mortgagors of real or personal property, fiduciaries, employers, and all officers and employees of the United States) having the control, receipt, custody, disposal, or payment of any of the items of income specified in subsection (b) (to the extent that any of such items constitutes gross income from sources within the United States), of any nonresident alien individual, or of any foreign partnership shall (except as otherwise provided in regulations prescribed by the Secretary under section 874) deduct and withhold from such items a tax equal to 30 percent thereof, except that in the case of an y item of income specified in the second sentence of subsection (b), the tax shall be equal to 14 percent of such item.

(b) Income items.

The items of income referred to in subsection (a) are interest (other than original issue discount as defined in section 1273), dividends, rent, salaries, wages, premiums, annuities, compensations, remunerations, emoluments, or other fixed or determinable annual or periodical gains, profits, and income, gains described in section 631(b) or (c), amounts subject to tax under section 871(a)(1)(C), gains subject to tax under section 871(a)(1)(D), and gains on transfers described in section 1235 made on or before October 4, 1966. The items of income referred to in subsection (a) from which tax shall be deducted and withheld at the rate of 14 percent are amounts which are received by a nonresident alien individual who is temporarily present in the United States as a nonimmigrant under subparagraph (F), (J), (M), or (Q) of section 101(a)(15) of the Immigration and Nationality Act and which are --

(1) incident to a qualified scholarship to which section 117(a) applies, but only to the extent includible in gross income; or

(2) in the case of an individual who is not a candidate for a degree at an educational organization described in section 170(b)(1)(A)(ii), granted by --

(A) an organization described in section 501(c)(3) which is exempt from tax under section 501(a),

(B) a foreign government,

(C) an international organization, or a binational or multinational educational and cultural foundation or commission created or continued pursuant to the Mutual Educational and Cultural Exchange Act of 1961, or

(D) the United States, or an instrumentality or agency thereof, or a State, or a possession of the United States, or any political subdivision thereof, or the District of Columbia, as a scholarship or fellowship for study, training, or research in the United States. In the case of a nonresident alien individual who is a member of a domestic partnership, the items of income referred to in subsection (a) shall be treated as referring to items specified in this subsection included in his distributive share of the income of such partnership.

(c) Exceptions.

(1) **Income connected with United States business.** No deduction or withholding under subsection (a) shall be required in the case of any item of income (other than compensation for personal services) which is effectively connected with the conduct of a trade or business within the United States and which is included in the gross income of the recipient under section 871(b)(2) for the taxable year.

(2) **Owner unknown.** The Secretary may authorize the tax under subsection (a) to be deducted and withheld from the interest upon any securities the owners of which are not known to the withholding agent.

(3) **Bonds with extended maturity dates.** The deduction and withholding in the case of interest on bonds, mortgages, or deeds of trust or other similar obligations of a corporation, within subsections (a), (b), and (c) of section 1451 (as in effect before its repeal by the Tax Reform Act of 1984) were it not for the fact that the maturity date of such obligations has been extended on or after January 1, 1934, and the liability assumed by the debtor exceeds 27 1/2 percent of the interest, shall not exceed the rate of 27 1/2 percent per annum.

(4) **Compensation of certain aliens.** Under regulations prescribed by the Secretary, compensation for personal services may be exempted from deduction and withholding under subsection (a).

(5) **Special items.** In the case of gains described in section 631(b) or (c), gains subject to tax under section 871(a)(1)(D), and gains on transfers described in section 1235 made on or before October 4, 1966, the amount required to be deducted and withheld shall, if the amount of such gain is not known to the withholding agent, be such amount,

not exceeding 30 percent of the amount payable, as may be necessary to assure that the tax deducted and withheld shall not be less than 30 percent of such gain.

(6) Per diem of certain aliens. No deduction or withholding under subsection (a) shall be required in the case of amounts of per diem for subsistence paid by the United States Government (directly or by contract) to any nonresident alien individual who is engaged in any program of training in the United States under the Mutual Security Act of 1954, as amended.

(7) Certain annuities received under qualified plans. No deduction or withholding under subsection (a) shall be required in the case of any amount received as an annuity if such amount is, under section 871(f), exempt from the tax imposed by section 871(a).

(8) Original issue discount. The Secretary may prescribe such regulations as may be necessary for the deduction and withholding of the tax on original issue discount subject to tax under section 871(a)(1)(C) including rules for the deduction and withholding of the tax on original issue discount from payments of interest.

(9) Interest income from certain portfolio debt investments. In the case of portfolio interest (within the meaning of 871(h)), no tax shall be required to be deducted and withheld from such interest unless the person required to deduct and withhold tax from such interest knows, or has reason to know, that such interest is not portfolio interest by reason of section 871(h)(3) or (4).

(10) Exception for certain interest and dividends. No tax shall be required to be deducted and withheld under subsection (a) from any amount described in section 871(i)(2).

(11) Certain gambling winnings. No tax shall be required to be deducted and withheld under subsection (a) from any amount exempt from the tax imposed by section 871(a)(1)(A) by reason of section 871(j).

(d) Exemption of certain foreign partnerships.

Subject to such terms and conditions as may be provided by regulations prescribed by the Secretary, subsection (a) shall not apply in the case of a foreign partnership engaged in trade or business within the United States if the Secretary determines that the requirements of subsection (a) impose an undue administrative burden and that the collection of the tax imposed by section 871(a) on the members of such partnership who are nonresident alien individuals will not be jeopardized by the exemption.

(e) Alien resident of Puerto Rico.

For purposes of this section, the term "nonresident alien individual" includes an alien resident of Puerto Rico.

(f) Continental shelf areas.

For sources of income derived from, or for services performed with respect to, the exploration or exploitation of natural resources on submarine areas adjacent to the territorial waters of the United States, see section 638.

(g) Cross reference.

For provision treating 85 percent of social security benefits as subject to withholding under this section, see section 871(a)(3).

§ 1442. Withholding of tax on foreign corporations.

(a) General rule.

In the case of foreign corporations subject to taxation under this subtitle, there shall be deducted and withheld at the source in the same manner and on the same items of income as is provided in section 1441 a tax equal to 30 percent thereof. For purposes of the preceding sentence, the references in section 1441(b) to sections 871(a)(1)(C) and (D) shall be treated as referring to sections 881(a)(3) and (4), the reference in section 1441(c)(1) to section 871(b)(2) shall be treated as referring to section 842 or section 882(a)(2), as the case may be, the reference in section 1441(c)(5) to section 871(a)(1)(D) shall be treated as referring to section 881(a)(4), the reference in section 1441(c)(8) to section 871(a)(1)(C) shall be treated as referring to section 881(a)(3), the references in section 1441(c)(9) to sections 871(h) and 871(h)(3) or (4) shall be treated as referring to sections 881(c) and 881(c)(3) or (4), and the reference in section 1441(c)(10) to section 871(i)(2) shall be treated as referring to section 881(d).

(b) Exemption.

Subject to such terms and conditions as may be provided by regulations prescribed by the Secretary, subsection (a) shall not apply in the case of a foreign corporation engaged in trade or business within the United States if the Secretary determines that the requirements of subsection (a) impose an undue administrative burden and that the collection of the tax imposed by section 881 on such corporation will not be jeopardized by the exemption.

(c) Exception for certain possessions corporations.

For purposes of this section, the term "foreign corporation" does not include a corporation created or organized in Guam, American Samoa, the Northern Mariana Islands, or the Virgin Islands or under the law of any such possession if the requirements of subparagraphs (A), (B), and (C) of section 881(b)(1) are met with respect to such corporation.

§ 1443. Foreign tax-exempt organizations.

(a) Income subject to section 511.

In the case of income of a foreign organization subject to the tax imposed by section 511, this chapter shall apply to income includible under section 512 in computing its unrelated business taxable income, but only to the extent and subject to such conditions as may be provided under regulations prescribed by the Secretary.

(b) Income subject to section 4948.

In the case of income of a foreign organization subject to the tax imposed by section 4948(a), this chapter shall apply, except that the deduction and withholding shall be at the rate of 4 percent and shall be subject to such conditions as may be provided under regulations prescribed by the Secretary.

§ 1444. Withholding on Virgin Islands source income.

For purposes of determining the withholding tax liability incurred in the Virgin Islands pursuant to this title (as made applicable to the Virgin Islands) with respect to amounts received from sources within the Virgin Islands by citizens and resident alien individuals of the United States, and corporations organized in the United States, the rate of withholding tax under sections 1441 and 1442 on income subject to tax under section 871(a)(1) or 881 shall not exceed the rate of tax on such income under section 871(a)(1) or 881, as the case may be.

§ 1445. Withholding of tax on dispositions of United States real property interests.

(a) General rule.

Except as otherwise provided in this section, in the case of any disposition of a United States real property interest (as defined in section 897(c)) by a foreign person, the transferee shall be required to deduct and withhold a tax equal to 10 percent of the amount realized on the disposition.

(b) Exemptions.

(1) In general. No person shall be required to deduct and withhold any amount under subsection (a) with respect to a disposition if paragraph (2), (3), (4), (5), or (6) applies to the transaction.

(2) Transferor furnishes nonforeign affidavit. Except as provided in paragraph (7), this paragraph applies to the disposition if the transferor furnishes to the transferee an affidavit by the transferor stating, under penalty of perjury, the transferor's United States taxpayer identification number and that the transferor is not a foreign person.

(3) Nonpublicly traded domestic corporation furnishes affidavit that interests in corporation not United States real property interests. Except as provided in paragraph (7), this paragraph applies in the case of a disposition of any interest in any domestic corporation if the domestic corporation furnishes to the transferee an affidavit by the domestic corporation stating, under penalty of perjury, that --

(A) the domestic corporation is not and has not been a United States real property holding corporation (as defined in section 897(c)(2)) during the applicable period specified in section 897(c)(1)(A)(ii), or

(B) as of the date of the disposition, interests in such corporation are not United States real property interests by reason of section 897(c)(1)(B).

(4) Transferee receives qualifying statement.

(A) In general. This paragraph applies to the disposition if the transferee receives a qualifying statement at such time, in such manner, and subject to such terms and conditions as the Secretary may by regulations prescribe.

(B) Qualifying statement. For purposes of subparagraph (A), the term "qualifying statement" means a statement by the Secretary that --

(i) the transferor either --

(I) has reached agreement with the Secretary (or such agreement has been reached by the transferee) for the payment of any tax imposed by section 871(b)(1) or 882(a)(1) on any gain recognized by the transferor on the disposition of the United States real property interest, or

(II) is exempt from any tax imposed by section 871(b)(1) or 882(a)(1) on any gain recognized by the transferor on the disposition of the United States real property interest, and

(ii) the transferor or transferee has satisfied any transferor's unsatisfied withholding liability or has provided adequate security to cover such liability.

(5) Residence where amount realized does not exceed $300,000. This paragraph applies to the disposition if --

(A) the property is acquired by the transferee for use by him as a residence, and

(B) the amount realized for the property does not exceed $300,000.

(6) Stock regularly traded on established securities market. This paragraph applies if the disposition is of a share of a class of stock that is regularly traded on an established securities market.

(7) Special rules for paragraphs (2) and (3). Paragraph (2) or (3) (as the case may be) shall not apply to any disposition --

(A) if --

(i) the transferee has actual knowledge that the affidavit referred to in such paragraph is false, or

(ii) the transferee receives a notice (as described in subsection (d)) from a transferor's agent or a transferee's agent that such affidavit is false, or

(B) if the Secretary by regulations requires the transferee to furnish a copy of such affidavit to the Secretary and the transferee fails to furnish a copy of such affidavit to the Secretary at such time and in such manner as required by such regulations.

(c) Limitations on amount required to be withheld.

(1) Cannot exceed transferor's maximum tax liability.

(A) In general. The amount required to be withheld under this section with respect to any disposition shall not exceed the amount (if any) determined under subparagraph (B) as the transferor's maximum tax liability.

(B) Request. At the request of the transferor or transferee, the Secretary shall determine, with respect to any disposition, the transferor's maximum tax liability.

(C) Refund of excess amounts withheld. Subject to such terms and conditions as the Secretary may by regulations prescribe, a transferor may seek and obtain a refund of any amounts withheld under this section in excess of the transferor's maximum tax liability.

(2) Authority of secretary to prescribe reduced amount. At the request of the transferor or transferee, the Secretary may prescribe a reduced amount to be withheld under this section if the Secretary determines that to substitute such reduced amount will not jeopardize the collection of the tax imposed by section 871(b)(1) or 882(a)(1).

(3) Procedural rules.

(A) Regulations. Requests for --

(i) qualifying statements under subsection (b)(4),

(ii) determinations of transferor's maximum tax liability under paragraph (1), and

(iii) reductions under paragraph (2) in the amount required to be withheld,

shall be made at the time and manner, and shall include such information, as the Secretary shall prescribe by regulations.

(B) Requests to be handled within 90 days. The Secretary shall take action with respect to any request described in subparagraph (A) within 90 days after the Secretary receives the request.

(d) Liability of transferor's agents or transferee's agents.

(1) Notice of false affidavit; foreign corporations. If --

(A) the transferor furnishes the transferee an affidavit described in paragraph (2) of subsection (b) or a domestic corporation furnishes the transferee an affidavit described in paragraph (3) of subsection (b), and

(B) in the case of --

(i) any transferor's agent --

(I) such agent has actual knowledge that such affidavit is false, or

(II) in the case of an affidavit described in subsection (b)(2) furnished by a corporation, such corporation is a foreign corporation, or

(ii) any transferee's agent, such agent has actual knowledge that such affidavit is false, such agent shall so notify the transferee at such time and in such manner as the Secretary shall require by regulations.

(2) Failure to furnish notice.

(A) In general. If any transferor's agent or transferee's agent is required by paragraph (1) to furnish notice, but fails to furnish such notice at such time or times and in such manner as may be required by regulations, such agent shall have the same duty to deduct and withhold that the transferee would have had if such agent had complied with paragraph (1).

(B) Liability limited to amount of compensation. An agent's liability under subparagraph (A) shall be limited to the amount of compensation the agent derives from the transaction.

(3) Transferor's agent. For purposes of this subsection, the term "transferor's agent" means any person who represents the transferor --

(A) in any negotiation with the transferee or any transferee's agent related to the transaction, or

(B) in settling the transaction.

(4) Transferee's agent. For purposes of this subsection, the term "transferee's agent" means any person who represents the transferee --

(A) in any negotiation with the transferor or any transferor's agent related to the transaction, or

(B) in settling the transaction.

(5) Settlement officer not treated as transferor's agent. For purposes of this subsection, a person shall not be treated as a transferor's agent or transferee's agent with respect to any transaction merely because such person performs 1 or more of the following acts:

(A) The receipt and the disbursement of any portion of the consideration for the transaction.

(B) The recording of any document in connection with the transaction.

(e) Special rules relating to distributions, etc., by corporations, partnerships, trusts, or estates.

(1) Certain domestic partnerships, trusts, and estates. In the case of any disposition of a United States real property interest as defined in section 897(c) (other than a disposition described in paragraph (4) or 5)) by a domestic partnership, domestic trust, or domestic estate, such partnership, the trustee of such trust, or the executor of such estate (as the case may be) shall be required to deduct and withhold under subsection (a) a tax equal to 35 percent (or, to the extent provided in regulations, 20 percent) of the gain realized to the extent such gain --

(A) is allocable to a foreign person who is a partner or beneficiary of such partnership, trust, or estate, or

(B) is allocable to a portion of the trust treated as owned by a foreign person under subpart E of part I of subchapter J.

(2) Certain distributions by foreign corporations. In the case of any distribution by a foreign corporation on which gain is recognized under subsection (d) or (e) of section 897, the foreign corporation shall deduct and withhold under subsection (a) a tax equal to 35 percent of the amount of gain recognized on such distribution under such subsection.

(3) Distributions by certain domestic corporations to foreign shareholders. If a domestic corporation which is or has been a United States real property holding corporation (as defined in section 897(c)(2)) during the applicable period specified in section 897(c)(1)(A)(ii) distributes property to a foreign person in a transaction to which section 302 or part II of subchapter C applies, such corporation shall deduct and withhold under subsection (a) a tax equal to 10 percent of the amount realized by the foreign shareholder. The preceding sentence shall not apply if, as of the date of the distribution, interests in such corporation are not United States real property interests by reason of section 897(c)(1)(B). Rules similar to the rules of the preceding provisions of this paragraph shall apply in the case of any distribution to which section 301 applies and which is not made out of the earnings and profits of such a domestic corporation.

(4) Taxable distributions by domestic or foreign partnerships, trusts, or estates. A domestic or foreign partnership, the trustee of a domestic or foreign trust, or the executor of a domestic or foreign estate shall be required to deduct and withhold under subsection (a) a tax equal to 10 percent of the fair market value (as of the time of the taxable distribution) of any United States real property interest distributed to a partner of the partnership or a beneficiary of the trust or estate, as the case may be, who is a foreign person in a transaction which would constitute a taxable distribution under the regulations promulgated by the Secretary pursuant to section 897.

(5) Rules relating to dispositions of interest in partnerships, trusts, or estates. To the extent provided in regulations, the transferee of a partnership interest or of a beneficial interest in a trust or estate shall be required to deduct and withhold under subsection (a) a tax equal to 10 percent of the amount realized on the disposition.

(6) Regulations. The Secretary shall prescribe such regulations as may be necessary to carry out the purposes of this subsection, including regulations providing for exceptions from provisions of this subsection and regulations for the application of this subsection in the case of payments through 1 or more entities.

(f) Definitions.

For purposes of this section --

(1) Transferor. The term "transferor" means the person disposing of the United States real property interest.

(2) Transferee. The term "transferee" means the person acquiring the United States real property interest.

(3) Foreign person. The term "foreign person" means any person other than a United States person.

(4) Transferor's maximum tax liability. The term "transferor's maximum tax liability" means, with respect to the disposition of any interest, the sum of --

(A) the maximum amount which the Secretary determines could be imposed as tax under section 871(b)(1) or 882(a)(1) by reason of the disposition, plus

(B) the amount the Secretary determines to be the transferor's unsatisfied withholding liability with respect to such interest.

(5) Transferor's unsatisfied withholding liability. The term "transferor's unsatisfied withholding liability" means the withholding obligation imposed by this section on the transferor's acquisition of the United States real property interest or on the acquisition of a predecessor interest, to the extent such obligation has not been satisfied.

§ 1446. Withholding of tax on foreign partners' share of effectively connected income.

(a) General rule.

If --

(1) a partnership has effectively connected taxable income for any taxable year, and

(2) any portion of such income is allocable under section 704 to a foreign partner, such partnership shall pay a withholding tax under this section at such time and in such manner as the Secretary shall by regulations prescribe.

(b) Amount of withholding tax.

(1) In general. The amount of the withholding tax payable by any partnership under subsection (a) shall be equal to the applicable percentage of the effectively connected taxable income of the partnership which is allocable under section 704 to foreign partners.

(2) Applicable percentage. For purposes of paragraph (1), the term "applicable percentage" means --

(A) the highest rate of tax specified in section 1 in the case of the portion of the effectively connected taxable income which is allocable under section 704 to foreign partners who are not corporations, and

(B) the highest rate of tax specified in section 11(b)(1) in the case of the portion of the effectively connected taxable income which is allocable under section 704 to foreign partners which are corporations.

(c) Effectively connected taxable income.

For purposes of this section, the term "effectively connected taxable income" means the taxable income of the partnership which is effectively connected (or treated as effectively connected) with the conduct of a trade or business in the United States computed with the following adjustments:

(1) Paragraph (1) of section 703(a) shall not apply.

(2) The partnership shall be allowed a deduction for depletion with respect to oil and gas wells but the amount of such deduction shall be determined without regard to sections 613 and 613A.

(3) There shall not be taken into account any item of income, gain, loss, or deduction to the extent allocable under section 704 to any partner who is not a foreign partner.

(d) Treatment of foreign partners.

(1) Allowance of credit. Each foreign partner of a partnership shall be allowed a credit under section 33 for such partner's share of the withholding tax paid by the partnership under this section. Such credit shall be allowed for the partner's taxable year in which (or with which) the partnership taxable year (for which such tax was paid) ends.

(2) Credit treated as distributed to partner. Except as provided in regulations, a foreign partner's share of any withholding tax paid by the partnership under this section shall be treated as distributed to such partner by such partnership on the earlier of --

(A) the day on which such tax was paid by the partnership, or

(B) the last day of the partnership's taxable year for which such tax was paid.

(e) Foreign partner.

For purposes of this section, the term "foreign partner" means any partner who is not a United States person.

(f) Regulations.

The Secretary shall prescribe such regulations as may be necessary to carry out the purposes of this section, including --

(1) regulations providing for the application of this section in the case of publicly traded partnerships, and

(2) regulations providing --

(A) that, for purposes of section 6655, the withholding tax imposed under this section shall be treated as a tax imposed by section 11 and any partnership required to pay such tax shall be treated as a corporation, and

(B) appropriate adjustments in applying section 6655 with respect to such withholding tax.

§ 6038B. Notice of certain transfers to foreign persons.

(a) In general. Each United States person who --

(1) transfers property to --

(A) a foreign corporation in an exchange described in section 332, 351, 354, 355, 356, or 361, or

(B) a foreign partnership in a contribution described in section 721 or in any other contribution described in regulations prescribed by the Secretary,

(2) makes a distribution described in section 336 to a person who is not a United States person,

497

shall furnish to the Secretary, at such time and in such manner as the Secretary shall by regulations prescribe, such iInformation with respect to such exchange or distribution as the Secretary may require in such regulations.

(b) Exceptions for certain transfers to foreign partnerships; special rule.

(1) Exceptions. Subsection (a)(1)(B) shall apply to a transfer by a United States person to a foreign partnership only if

(A) the United States person holds (immediately after the transfer) directly or indirectly at least a 10-percent interest (as defined in section 6046A(d)) in the partnership, or

(B) the value of the property transferred (when added to the value of the property transferred by such person or any related person to such partnership or a related partnership during the 12-month period ending on the date of the transfer) exceeds $100,000.

For purposes of the preceding sentence, the value of any transferred property is its fair market value at the time of its transfer.

(2) Special rule. If by reason of an adjustment under section 482 or otherwise, a contribution described in subsection (a)(1) is deemed to have been made, such contribution shall be treated for purposes of this section as having been made not earlier than the date specified by the Secretary.

(c) Penalty for failure to furnish information.

(1) In general. If any United States person fails to furnish the information described in subsection (a) at the time and in the manner required by regulations, such person shall pay a penalty equal to 10 percent of the fair market value of the property at the time of the exchange (and, in the case of a contribution described in subsection (a)(1)(B), such person shall recognize gain as if the contributed property had been sold for such value at the time of such contribution).

(2) Reasonable cause exception. Paragraph (1) shall not apply to any failure if the United States person shows such failure is due to reasonable cause and not to willful neglect.

(3) Limit on penalty. The penalty under paragraph (1) with respect to any exchange shall not exceed $100,000 unless the failure with respect to such exchange was due to intentional disregard.

§ 7701. Definitions.

(a) When used in this title, where not otherwise distinctly expressed or manifestly incompatible with the intent thereof --

(4) Domestic. The term "domestic" when applied to a corporation or partnership means created or organized in the United States or under the law of the United States or of any State unless, in the case of partnership, the Secretary provides otherwise by regulations.

(5) Foreign. The term "foreign" when applied to a corporation or partnership means a corporation or partnership which is not domestic.

(30) United States person. The term "United States person" means --

(A) a citizen or resident of the United States,

(B) a domestic partnership,

(C) a domestic corporation,

(D) any estate (other than a foreign estate, within the meaning of paragraph 31)), and

(E) any trust if–

PART IV. UNIFORM LAWS AND MODEL RULES

A. Selected Provisions of the Uniform Commercial Code (UCC)

Source: National Conference of Commissioners on Uniform State Laws
211 E. Ontario Street
Suite 1300
Chicago, IL 60611
tel: (312) 915-0195
fax: (312) 915-0187

Website information:

http://www.law.cornell.edu/uniform/ucc.html
This website, entitled "Uniform Commercial Code Locator," provides links to the text of the U.C.C. and its provisions in all states.

Introduction

Article 2 of the Uniform Commercial Code (UCC) was the subject of substantial revisions considered but not adopted at the annual meeting of the National Conference of Commissioners on Uniform State Laws (NCCUSL) July 23-30, 1999. Those revisions can have a significant impact on international trade when the UCC applies to a transaction. For example, definitions of price-delivery terms found in the 1995 Official Text (§§ 2-109 through 2-324) have all been eliminated in the 1999 draft, and replaced with a simple statement in § 2-309 that "[t]he effect of a party's use of shipment terms such as 'FOB', 'CIF', or the like, must be interpreted in light of any applicable usage of trade or course of performance or course of dealing between the parties."

Article 5 of the UCC was revised in 1995. While some states have not yet adopted the 1995 revisions to Article 5, the majority have. For this reason, the 1995 text of Article 5 is used in this volume.

SELECTED PROVISIONS OF THE UNIFORM COMMERCIAL CODE

§ 1-201 General Definitions.

Subject to additional definitions contained in the subsequent Articles of this Act which are applicable to specific Articles or Parts thereof, and unless the context otherwise requires, in this Act:

(15) "Document of title" includes bill of lading, dock warrant, dock receipt, warehouse receipt or order for the delivery of goods, and also any other document which in the regular course of business or financing is treated as adequately evidencing that the person in possession of it is entitled to receive, hold and dispose of the document and the goods it covers. To be a document of title a document must purport to be issued by or addressed to a bailee and purport to cover goods in the bailee's possession which are either identified or are fungible portions of an identified mass.

OFFICIAL COMMENT

15. "Document of title". From Section 76, Uniform Sales Act, but rephrased to eliminate certain ambiguities. Thus, by making it explicit that the obligation or designation of a third party as "bailee" is essential to a document of title, this definition clearly rejects any such result as obtained in *Hixson v. Ward*, 254 Ill App 505 (1929), which treated a conditional sales contract as a document of title. Also the definition is left open so that new types of documents may be included. It is unforeseeable what documents may one day serve the essential purpose now filled by warehouse receipts and bills of lading. Truck transport has already opened up problems which do not fit the patterns of practice resting upon the assumption that a draft can move through banking channels faster than the goods themselves can reach their destination. There lie ahead air transport and such probabilities as teletype transmission of what may some day be regarded commercially as "Documents of Title". The definition is stated in terms of the function of the documents with the intention that any document which gains commercial recognition as accomplishing the desired result shall be included within its scope. Fungible goods are adequately identified within the language of the definition by identification of the mass of which they are a part.

Dock warrants were within the Sales Act definition of document of title apparently for the purpose of recognizing a valid tender by means of such paper. In current commercial practice a dock warrant or receipt is a kind of interim certificate issued by steamship companies upon delivery of the goods at the dock, entitling a designated person to have issued to him at the company's office a bill of lading. The receipt itself is invariably nonnegotiable in form although it may indicate that a negotiable bill is to be forthcoming. Such a document is not within the general compass of the definition, although trade usage may in some cases entitle such paper to be treated as a document of title. If the dock receipt actually represents a storage obligation undertaken by the shipping company, then it is a warehouse receipt within this Section regardless of the name given to the instrument.

The goods must be "described", but the description may be by marks or labels and may be qualified in such a way as to disclaim personal knowledge of the issuer regarding contents or condition. However, baggage and parcel checks and similar "tokens" of storage which identify stored goods only as those received in exchange for the token are not covered by this Article.

The definition is broad enough to include an airway bill.

§ 1-205 Course of Dealing and Usage of Trade.

(1) A course of dealing is a sequence of previous conduct between the parties to a particular transaction which is fairly to be regarded as establishing a common basis of understanding for interpreting their expressions and other conduct.

(2) A usage of trade is any practice or method of dealing having such regularity of observance in a place, vocation or trade as to justify an expectation that it will be observed with respect to the transaction in question. The existence and scope of such a usage are to be proved as facts. If it is established that such a usage is embodied in a written trade code or similar writing the interpretation of the writing is for the court.

(3) A course of dealing between parties and any usage of trade in the vocation or trade in which they are engaged or of which they are or should be aware give particular meaning to and supplement or qualify terms of an agreement.

(4) The express terms of an agreement and an applicable course of dealing or usage of trade shall be construed wherever reasonable as consistent with each other; but when such construction is unreasonable express terms control both course of dealing and usage of trade and course of dealing controls usage of trade.

(5) An applicable usage of trade in the place where any part of performance is to occur shall be used in interpreting the agreement as to that part of the performance.

(6) Evidence of a relevant usage of trade offered by one party is not admissible unless and until he has given the other party such notice as the court finds sufficient to prevent unfair surprise to the latter.

§ 2-105 Definitions: Transferability; "Goods"; "Future" Goods; "Lot"; "Commercial Unit".

(1) "Goods" means all things (including specially manufactured goods) which are movable at the time of identification to the contract for sale other than the money in which the price is to be paid, investment securities (Article 8) and things in action. "Goods" also includes the unborn young of animals and growing crops and other identified things attached to realty as described in the section on goods to be severed from realty (Section 2-107).

(2) Goods must be both existing and identified before any interest in them can pass. Goods which are not both existing and identified are "future" goods. A purported present sale of future goods or of any interest therein operates as a contract to sell.

(3) There may be a sale of a part interest in existing identified goods.

(4) An undivided share in an identified bulk of fungible goods is sufficiently identified to be sold although the quantity of the bulk is not determined. Any agreed proportion of such a bulk or any quantity thereof agreed upon by number, weight or other measure may to the extent of the seller's interest in the bulk be sold to the buyer who then becomes an owner in common.

(5) "Lot" means a parcel or a single article which is the subject matter of a separate sale or delivery, whether or not it is sufficient to perform the contract.

(6) "Commercial unit" means such a unit of goods as by commercial usage is a single whole for purposes of sale and division of which materially impairs its character or value on the market or in use. A commercial unit may be a single article (as a machine) or a set of articles (as a suite of furniture or an assortment of sizes) or a quantity (as a bale, gross, or carload) or any other unit treated in use or in the relevant market as a single whole.

§ 2-319 F.O.B. and F.A.S. Terms.

(1) Unless otherwise agreed the term F.O.B. (which means "free on board") at a named place, even though used only in connection with the stated price, is a delivery term under which

(a) when the term is F.O.B. the place of shipment, the seller must at that place ship the goods in the manner provided in this Article (Section 2-504) and bear the expense and risk of putting them into the possession of the carrier; or

(b) when the term is F.O.B. the place of destination, the seller must at his own expense and risk transport the goods to that place and there tender delivery of them in the manner provided in this Article (Section 2-503);

(c) when under either (a) or (b) the term is also F.O.B. vessel, car or other vehicle, the seller must in addition at his own expense and risk load the goods on board. If the term is F.O.B. vessel the buyer must name the vessel and in an appropriate case the seller must comply with the provisions of this Article on the form of bill of lading (Section 2-323).

(2) Unless otherwise agreed the term F.A.S. vessel (which means "free alongside") at a named port, even though used only in connection with the stated price, is a delivery term under which the seller must

504

(a) at his own expense and risk deliver the goods alongside the vessel in the manner usual in that port or on a dock designated and provided by the buyer; and

(b) obtain and tender a receipt for the goods in exchange for which the carrier is under a duty to issue a bill of lading.

(3) Unless otherwise agreed in any case falling within subsection (1)(a) or (c) or subsection (2) the buyer must seasonably give any needed instructions for making delivery, including when the term is F.A.S. or F.O.B. the loading berth of the vessel and in an appropriate case its name and sailing date. The seller may treat the failure of needed instructions as a failure of cooperation under this Article (Section 2-311). He may also at his option move the goods in any reasonable manner preparatory to delivery or shipment.

(4) Under the term F.O.B. vessel or F.A.S. unless otherwise agreed the buyer must make payment against tender of the required documents and the seller may not tender nor the buyer demand delivery of the goods in substitution for the documents.

OFFICIAL COMMENT

Purposes:

1. This section is intended to negate the uncommercial line of decision which treats an "F.O.B." term as "merely a price term." The distinctions taken in subsection (1) handle most of the issues which have on occasion led to the unfortunate judicial language just referred to. Other matters which have led to sound results being based on unhappy language in regard to F.O.B. clauses are dealt with in this Act by Section 2-311(2) (seller's option re arrangements relating to shipment) and Sections 2-614 and 615 (substituted performance and seller's excuse).

2. Subsection (1)(c) not only specifies the duties of a seller who engages to deliver "F.O.B. vessel," or the like, but ought to make clear that no agreement is soundly drawn when it looks to reshipment from San Francisco or New York, but speaks merely of "F.O.B." the place.

3. The buyer's obligations stated in subsection (1)(c) and subsection (3) are, as shown in the text, obligations of cooperation. The last sentence of subsection (3) expressly, though perhaps unnecessarily, authorizes the seller, pending instructions, to go ahead with such preparatory moves as shipment from the interior to the named point of delivery. The sentence presupposes the usual case in which instructions "fail"; a prior repudiation by the buyer, giving notice that breach was intended, would remove the reason for the sentence, and would normally bring into play, instead, the second sentence of Section 2-704, which duly calls for lessening damages.

4. The treatment of "F.O.B. vessel" in conjunction with F.A.S. fits, in regard to the need for payment against documents, with standard practice and case law; but "F.O.B. vessel" is a term which by its very language makes express the need for an "on board" document. In this respect, that term is stricter than the ordinary overseas "shipment" contract (C.I.F., etc., Section 2-320).

§ 2-320 C.I.F. and C. & F. Terms.

(1) The term C.I.F. means that the price includes in a lump sum the cost of the goods and the insurance and freight to the named destination. The term C. & F. or C.F. means that the price so includes cost and freight to the named destination.

(2) Unless otherwise agreed and even though used only in connection with the stated price and destination, the term C.I.F. destination or its equivalent requires the seller at his own expense and risk to

(a) put the goods into the possession of a carrier at the port for shipment and obtain a negotiable bill or bills of lading covering the entire transportation to the named destination; and

(b) load the goods and obtain a receipt from the carrier (which may be contained in the bill of lading) showing that the freight has been paid or provided for; and

(c) obtain a policy or certificate of insurance, including any war risk insurance, of a kind and on terms then current at the port of shipment in the usual amount, in the currency of the contract, shown to cover the same goods covered by the bill of lading and providing for payment of loss to the order of the buyer or for the account of whom it may concern; but the seller may add to the price the amount of the premium for any such war risk insurance; and

(d) prepare an invoice of the goods and procure any other documents required to effect shipment or to comply with the contract; and

(e) forward and tender with commercial promptness all the documents in due form and with any indorsement necessary to perfect the buyer's rights.

(3) Unless otherwise agreed the term C. & F. or its equivalent has the same effect and imposes upon the seller the same obligations and risks as a C.I.F. term except the obligation as to insurance.

(4) Under the term C.I.F. or C. & F. unless otherwise agreed the buyer must make payment against tender of the required documents and the seller may not tender nor the buyer demand delivery of the goods in substitution for the documents.

OFFICIAL COMMENT

Purposes: To make it clear that:

1. The C.I.F. contract is not a destination but a shipment contract with risk of subsequent loss or damage to the goods passing to the buyer upon shipment if the seller has properly performed all his obligations with respect to the goods. Delivery to the carrier is delivery to the buyer for purposes of risk and "title". Delivery of possession of the goods is accomplished by delivery of the bill of lading, and upon tender of the required documents the buyer must pay the agreed price without awaiting the arrival of the goods and if they have been lost or damaged after proper shipment he must seek his remedy against the carrier or insurer. The buyer has no right of inspection prior to payment or acceptance of the documents.

2. The seller's obligations remain the same even though the C.I.F. term is "used only in connection with the stated price and destination".

3. The insurance stipulated by the C.I.F. term is for the buyer's benefit, to protect him against the risk of loss or damage to the goods in transit. A clause in a C.I.F. contract "insurance—for the account of sellers" should be viewed in its ordinary mercantile meaning that the sellers must pay for the insurance and not that it is intended to run to the seller's benefit.

4. A bill of lading covering the entire transportation from the port of shipment is explicitly required but the provision on this point must be read in the light of its reason to assure the buyer of as full protection as the conditions of shipment reasonably permit, remembering always that this type of contract is designed to move the goods in the channels commercially available. To enable the buyer to deal with the goods while they are afloat the bill of lading must be one that covers only the quantity of goods called for by the contract. The buyer is not required to accept his part of the goods without a bill of lading because the latter covers a larger quantity, nor is he required to accept a bill of lading for the whole quantity under a stipulation to hold the excess for the owner. Although the buyer is not compelled to accept either goods or documents under such circumstances he may of course claim his rights in any goods which have been identified to his contract.

5. The seller is given the option of paying or providing for the payment of freight. He has no option to ship "freight collect" unless the agreement so provides. The rule of the common law that the buyer need not pay the freight if the goods do not arrive is preserved.

Unless the shipment has been sent "freight collect" the buyer is entitled to receive documentary evidence that he is not obligated to pay the freight; the seller is therefore required to obtain a receipt "showing that the freight has been paid or provided for." The usual notation in the appropriate space on the bill of lading that the freight has been prepaid is a sufficient receipt, as at common law. The phrase "provided for" is intended to cover the frequent situation in which the carrier extends credit to a shipper for the freight on successive shipments and receives periodical payments of the accrued freight charges from him.

6. The requirement that unless otherwise agreed the seller must procure insurance "of a kind and on terms then current at the port for shipment in the usual amount, in the currency of the contract, sufficiently shown to cover the same goods covered by the bill of lading", applies to both marine and war risk insurance. As applied to marine insurance, it means such insurance as is usual or customary at the port for shipment with reference to the particular kind of goods involved, the character and equipment of the vessel, the route of the voyage, the port of destination and any other considerations that affect the risk. It is the substantial equivalent of the ordinary

insurance in the particular trade and on the particular voyage and is subject to agreed specifications of type or extent of coverage. The language does not mean that the insurance must be adequate to cover all risks to which the goods may be subject in transit. There are some types of loss or damage that are not covered by the usual marine insurance and are excepted in bills of lading or in applicable statutes from the causes of loss or damage for which the carrier or the vessel is liable. Such risks must be borne by the buyer under this Article.

Insurance secured in compliance with a C.I.F. term must cover the entire transportation of the goods to the named destination.

7. An additional obligation is imposed upon the seller in requiring him to procure customary war risk insurance at the buyer's expense. This changes the common law on the point. The seller is not required to assume the risk of including in the C.I.F. price the cost of such insurance, since it often fluctuates rapidly, but is required to treat it simply as a necessary for the buyer's account. What war risk insurance is "current" or usual turns on the standard forms of policy or rider in common use.

8. The C.I.F. contract calls for insurance covering the value of the goods at the time and place of shipment and does not include any increase in market value during transit or any anticipated profit to the buyer on a sale by him.

The contract contemplates that before the goods arrive at their destination they may be sold again and again on C.I.F. terms and that the original policy of insurance and bill of lading will run with the interest in the goods by being transferred to each successive buyer. A buyer who becomes the seller in such an intermediate contract for sale does not thereby, if his sub-buyer knows the circumstances, undertake to insure the goods again at an increased price fixed in the new contract or to cover the increase in price by additional insurance, and his buyer may not reject the documents on the ground that the original policy does not cover such higher price. If such a sub-buyer desires additional insurance he must procure it for himself.

Where the seller exercises an option to ship "freight collect" and to credit the buyer with the freight against the C.I.F. price, the insurance need not cover the freight since the freight is not at the buyer's risk. On the other hand, where the seller prepays the freight upon shipping under a bill of lading requiring prepayment and providing that the freight shall be deemed earned and shall be retained by the carrier "ship and/or cargo lost or not lost," or using words of similar import, he must procure insurance that will cover the freight, because notwithstanding that the goods are lost in transit the buyer is bound to pay the freight as part of the C.I.F. price and will be unable to recover it back from the carrier.

9. Insurance "for the account of whom it may concern" is usual and sufficient. However, for a valid tender the policy of insurance must be one which can be disposed of together with the bill of lading and so must be "sufficiently shown to cover the same goods covered by the bill of lading." It must cover separately the quantity of goods called for by the buyer's contract and not merely insure his goods as part of a larger quantity in which others are interested, a case provided for in American mercantile practice by the use of negotiable certificates of insurance which are expressly authorized by this section. By usage these certificates are treated as the equivalent of separate policies and are good tender under C.I.F. contracts. The term "certificate of insurance", however, does not of itself include certificates or "cover notes" issued by the insurance broker and stating that the goods are covered by a policy. Their sufficiency as substitutes for policies will depend upon proof of an established usage or course of dealing. The present section rejects the English rule that not only brokers' certificates and "cover notes" but also certain forms of American insurance

508

certificates are not the equivalent of policies and are not good tender under a C.I.F. contract.

The seller's failure to tender a proper insurance document is waived if the buyer refuses to make payment on other and untenable grounds at a time when proper insurance could have been obtained and tendered by the seller if timely objection had been made. Even a failure to insure on shipment may be cured by seasonable tender of a policy retroactive in effect; e.g., one insuring the goods "lost or not lost." The provisions of this Article on cure of improper tender and on waiver of buyer's objections by silence are applicable to insurance tenders under a C.I.F. term. Where there is no waiver by the buyer as described above, however, the fact that the goods arrive safely does not cure the seller's breach of his obligations to insure them and tender to the buyer a proper insurance document.

10. The seller's invoice of the goods shipped under a C.I.F. contract is regarded as a usual and necessary document upon which reliance may properly be placed. It is the document which evidences points of description, quality and the like which do not readily appear in other documents. This Article rejects those statements to the effect that the invoice is a usual but not a necessary document under a C.I.F. term.

11. The buyer needs all of the documents required under a C.I.F. contract, in due form and with necessary endorsements, so that before the goods arrive he may deal with them by negotiating the documents or may obtain prompt possession of the goods after their arrival. If the goods are lost or damaged in transit the documents are necessary to enable him promptly to assert his remedy against the carrier or insurer. The seller is therefore obligated to do what is mercantilely reasonable in the circumstances and should make every reasonable exertion to send forward the documents as soon as possible after the shipment. The requirement that the documents be forwarded with "commercial promptness" expresses a more urgent need for action than that suggested by the phrase "reasonable time".

12. Under a C.I.F. contract the buyer, as under the common law, must pay the price upon tender of the required documents without first inspecting the goods, but his payment in these circumstances does not constitute an acceptance of the goods nor does it impair his right of subsequent inspection or his options and remedies in the case of improper delivery. All remedies and rights for the seller's breach are reserved to him. The buyer must pay before inspection and assert his remedy against the seller afterward unless the nonconformity of the goods amounts to a real failure of consideration, since the purpose of choosing this form of contract is to give the seller protection against the buyer's unjustifiable rejection of the goods at a distant port of destination which would necessitate taking possession of the goods and suing the buyer there.

13. A valid C.I.F. contract may be made which requires part of the transportation to be made on land and part on the sea, as where the goods are to be brought by rail from an inland point to a seaport and thence transported by vessel to the named destination under a "through" or combination bill of lading issued by the railroad company. In such a case shipment by rail from the inland point within the contract period is a timely shipment notwithstanding that the loading of the goods on the vessel is delayed by causes beyond the seller's control.

14. Although subsection (2) stating the legal effects of the C.I.F. term is an "unless otherwise agreed" provision, the express language used in an agreement is frequently a precautionary, fuller statement of the normal C.I.F. terms and hence not intended as a departure or variation from them. Moreover, the dominant outlines of the C.I.F. term are so well understood commercially that any variation should, whenever reasonably possible, be read as falling within those dominant outlines rather than as destroying the whole meaning of a term which essentially indicates a

contract for proper shipment rather than one for delivery at destination. Particularly careful consideration is necessary before a printed form or clause is construed to mean agreement otherwise and where a C.I.F. contract is prepared on a printed form designed for some other type of contract, the C.I.F. terms must prevail over printed clauses repugnant to them.

15. Under subsection (4) the fact that the seller knows at the time of the tender of the documents that the goods have been lost in transit does not affect his rights if he has performed his contractual obligations. Similarly, the seller cannot perform under a C.I.F. term by purchasing and tendering landed goods.

16. Under the C. & F. term, as under the C.I.F. term, title and risk of loss are intended to pass to the buyer on shipment. A stipulation in a C. & F. contract that the seller shall effect insurance on the goods and charge the buyer with the premium (in effect that he shall act as the buyer's agent for that purpose) is entirely in keeping with the pattern. On the other hand, it often happens that the buyer is in a more advantageous position than the seller to effect insurance on the goods or that he has in force an "open" or "floating" policy covering all shipments made by him or to him, in either of which events the C. & F. term is adequate without mention of insurance.

17. It is to be remembered that in a French contract the term "C.A.F." does not mean "Cost and Freight" but has exactly the same meaning as the term "C.I.F." since it is merely the French equivalent of that term. The "A" does not stand for "and" but for "assurance" which means insurance.

§ 2-321 C.I.F. or C. & F.: "Net Landed Weights"; "Payment on Arrival"; Warranty of Condition on Arrival.

Under a contract containing a term C.I.F. or C. & F.

(1) Where the price is based on or is to be adjusted according to "net landed weights", "delivered weights", "out turn" quantity or quality or the like, unless otherwise agreed the seller must reasonably estimate the price. The payment due on tender of the documents called for by the contract is the amount so estimated, but after final adjustment of the price a settlement must be made with commercial promptness.

(2) An agreement described in subsection (1) or any warranty of quality or condition of the goods on arrival places upon the seller the risk of ordinary deterioration, shrinkage and the like in transportation but has no effect on the place or time of identification to the contract for sale or delivery or on the passing of the risk of loss.

(3) Unless otherwise agreed where the contract provides for payment on or after arrival of the goods the seller must before payment allow such preliminary inspection as is feasible; but if the goods are lost delivery of the documents and payment are due when the goods should have arrived.

OFFICIAL COMMENT

Purposes:

This section deals with two variations of the C.I.F. contract which have evolved in mercantile practice but are entirely consistent with the basic C.I.F. pattern. Subsections (1) and (2), which provide for a shift to the seller of the risk of quality and weight deterioration during shipment, are designed to conform the law to the best mercantile practice and usage without changing the legal consequences of the C.I.F. or C. & F. term as to the passing of marine risks to the buyer at the point of shipment. Subsection (3) provides that where under the contract documents are to be presented for payment after arrival of the goods, this amounts merely to a postponement of the payment under the C.I.F. contract and is not to be confused with the "no arrival, no sale" contract. If the goods are lost, delivery of the documents and payment against them are due when the goods should have arrived. The clause for payment on or after arrival is not to be construed as such a condition precedent to payment that if the goods are lost in transit the buyer need never pay and the seller must bear the loss.

§ 2-322 Delivery "Ex-Ship".

(1) Unless otherwise agreed a term for delivery of goods "ex-ship" (which means from the carrying vessel) or in equivalent language is not restricted to a particular ship and requires delivery from a ship which has reached a place at the named port of destination where goods of the kind are usually discharged.

(2) Under such a term unless otherwise agreed

(a) the seller must discharge all liens arising out of the carriage and furnish the buyer with a direction which puts the carrier under a duty to deliver the goods; and

(b) the risk of loss does not pass to the buyer until the goods leave the ship's tackle or are otherwise properly unloaded.

OFFICIAL COMMENT

Purposes:

1. The delivery term, "ex ship", as between seller and buyer, is the reverse of the f.a.s. term covered.

2. Delivery need not be made from any particular vessel under a clause calling for delivery "ex ship", even though a vessel on which shipment is to be made originally is named in the contract, unless the agreement by appropriate language, restricts the clause to delivery from a named vessel.

3. The appropriate place and manner of unloading at the port of destination depend upon the nature of the goods and the facilities and usages of the port.

4. A contract fixing a price "ex ship" with payment "cash against documents" calls only for such documents as are appropriate to the contract. Tender of a delivery order and of a receipt for the freight after the arrival of the carrying vessel is adequate. The seller is not required to tender a bill of lading as a document of title nor is he required to insure the goods for the buyer's benefit, as the goods are not at the buyer's risk during the voyage.

§ 2-323 Form of Bill of Lading Required in Overseas Shipment; "Overseas".

(1) Where the contract contemplates overseas shipment and contains a term C.I.F. or C. & F. or F.O.B. vessel, the seller unless otherwise agreed must obtain a negotiable bill of lading stating that the goods have been loaded on board or, in the case of a term C.I.F. or C. & F., received for shipment.

(2) Where in a case within subsection (1) a bill of lading has been issued in a set of parts, unless otherwise agreed if the documents are not to be sent from abroad the buyer may demand tender of the full set; otherwise only one part of the bill of lading need be tendered. Even if the agreement expressly requires a full set

(a) due tender of a single part is acceptable within the provisions of this Article on cure of improper delivery (subsection (1) of Section 2-508); and

(b) even though the full set is demanded, if the documents are sent from abroad the person tendering an incomplete set may nevertheless require payment upon furnishing an indemnity which the buyer in good faith deems adequate.

(3) A shipment by water or by air or a contract contemplating such shipment is "overseas" insofar as by usage of trade or agreement it is subject to the commercial, financing or shipping practices characteristic of international deep water commerce.

OFFICIAL COMMENT

Purposes:

1. Subsection (1) follows the "American" rule that a regular bill of lading indicating delivery of the goods at the dock for shipment is sufficient, except under a term "F.O.B. vessel." See Section 2-319 and comment thereto.

2. Subsection (2) deals with the problem of bills of lading covering deep water shipments, issued not as a single bill of lading but in a set of parts, each part referring to the other parts and the entire set constituting in commercial practice and at law a single bill of lading. Commercial practice in international commerce is to accept and pay against presentation of the first part of a set if the part is sent from overseas even though the contract of the buyer requires presentation of a full set of bills of lading provided adequate indemnity for the missing parts is forthcoming.

This subsection codifies that practice as between buyer and seller. Article 5 (Section 5-113) authorizes banks presenting drafts under letters of credit to give indemnities against the missing parts, and this subsection means that the buyer must accept and act on such indemnities if he in good faith deems them adequate. But neither this subsection nor Article 5 decides whether a bank which has issued a letter of credit is similarly bound. The issuing bank's obligation under a letter of credit is independent and depends on its own terms. See Article 5.

§ 2-324 "No Arrival, No Sale" Term.

(1) Under a term "no arrival, no sale" or terms of like meaning, unless otherwise agreed,

(a) the seller must properly ship conforming goods and if they arrive by any means he must tender them on arrival but he assumes no obligation that the goods will arrive unless he has caused the non-arrival; and

(b) where without fault of the seller the goods are in part lost or have so deteriorated as no longer to conform to the contract or arrive after the contract time, the buyer may proceed as if there had been casualty to identified goods (Section 2-613).

OFFICIAL COMMENT

Purposes:

1. The "no arrival, no sale" term in a "destination" overseas contract leaves risk of loss on the seller but gives him an exemption from liability for nondelivery. Both the nature of the case and the duty of good faith require that the seller must not interfere with the arrival of the goods in any way. If the circumstances impose upon him the responsibility for making or arranging the shipment, he must have a shipment made despite the exemption clause. Further, the shipment made must be a conforming one, for the exemption under a "no arrival, no sale" term applies only to the hazards of transportation and the goods must be proper in all other respects.

The reason of this section is that where the seller is reselling goods bought by him as shipped by another and this fact is known to the buyer, so that the seller is not under any obligation to make the shipment himself, the seller is entitled under the "no arrival, no sale" clause to exemption from payment of damages for non-delivery if the goods do not arrive or if the goods which actually arrive are non-conforming. This does not extend to sellers who arrange shipment by their own agents, in which case the clause is limited to casualty due to marine hazards. But sellers who make known that they are contracting only with respect to what will be delivered to them by parties over whom they assume no control are entitled to the full quantum of the exemption.

2. The provisions of this Article on identification must be read together with the present section in order to bring the exemption into application. Until there is some designation of the goods in a particular shipment or on a particular ship as being those to which the contract refers there can be no application of an exemption for their non-arrival.

3. The seller's duty to tender the agreed or declared goods if they do arrive is not impaired because of their delay in arrival or by their arrival after transshipment.

4. The phrase "to arrive" is often employed in the same sense as "no arrival, no sale" and may then be given the same effect. But a "to arrive" term, added to a C.I.F. or C. & F. contract, does not have the full meaning given by this section to "no arrival, no sale". Such a "to arrive" term is usually intended to operate only to the extent that the risks are not covered by the agreed insurance and the loss or casualty is due to such uncovered hazards. In some instances the "to arrive" term may be regarded as a time of payment term, or, in the case of the reselling seller discussed in point

1 above, as negating responsibility for conformity of the goods, if they arrive, to any description which was based on his good faith belief of the quality. Whether this is the intention of the parties is a question of fact based on all the circumstances surrounding the resale and in case of ambiguity the rules of Sections 2-316 and 2-317 apply to preclude dishonor.

5. Paragraph (b) applies where goods arrive impaired by damage or partial loss during transportation and makes the policy of this Article on casualty to identified goods applicable to such a situation. For the term cannot be regarded as intending to give the seller an unforeseen profit through casualty; it is intended only to protect him from loss due to causes beyond his control.

§ 2-401 Passing of Title; Reservation for Security; Limited Application of This Section.

Each provision of this Article with regard to the rights, obligations and remedies of the seller, the buyer, purchasers or other third parties applies irrespective of title to the goods except where the provision refers to such title. Insofar as situations are not covered by the other provisions of this Article and matters concerning title become material the following rules apply:

(1) Title to goods cannot pass under a contract for sale prior to their identification to the contract (Section 2-501), and unless otherwise explicitly agreed the buyer acquires by their identification a special property as limited by this Act. Any retention or reservation by the seller of the title (property) in goods shipped or delivered to the buyer is limited in effect to a reservation of a security interest. Subject to these provisions and to the provisions of the Article on Secured Transactions (Article 9), title to goods passes from the seller to the buyer in any manner and on any conditions explicitly agreed on by the parties.

(2) Unless otherwise explicitly agreed title passes to the buyer at the time and place at which the seller completes his performance with reference to the physical delivery of the goods, despite any reservation of a security interest and even though a document of title is to be delivered at a different time or place; and in particular and despite any reservation of a security interest by the bill of lading

(a) if the contract requires or authorizes the seller to send the goods to the buyer but does not require him to deliver them at destination, title passes to the buyer at the time and place of shipment; but

(b) if the contract requires delivery at destination, title passes on tender there.

(3) Unless otherwise explicitly agreed where delivery is to be made without moving the goods,

(a) if the seller is to deliver a document of title, title passes at the time when and the place where he delivers such documents; or

(b) if the goods are at the time of contracting already identified and no documents are to be delivered, title passes at the time and place of contracting.

(4) A rejection or other refusal by the buyer to receive or retain the goods, whether or not justified, or a justified revocation of acceptance revests title to the goods in the seller. Such revesting occurs by operation of law and is not a "sale".

OFFICIAL COMMENT

1. This Article deals with the issues between seller and buyer in terms of step by step performance or non-performance under the contract for sale and not in terms of whether or not "title" to the goods has passed. That the rules of this section in no way alter the rights of either the buyer, seller or third parties declared elsewhere in the Article is made clear by the preamble of this section. This section, however, in no way intends to indicate which line of interpretation should be followed in cases where the applicability of "public" regulation depends upon a "sale" or upon location of "title" without further definition. The basic policy of this Article that known purpose and reason should govern interpretation cannot extend beyond the scope of its own provisions. It is therefore necessary to state what a "sale" is and when title passes under this Article in case the courts deem any public regulation to incorporate the defined term of the "private" law.

2. "Future" goods cannot be the subject of a present sale. Before title can pass the goods must be identified in the manner set forth in Section 2-501. The parties, however, have full liberty to arrange by specific terms for the passing of title to goods which are existing.

3. The "special property" of the buyer in goods identified to the contract is excluded from the definition of "security interest"; its incidents are defined in provisions of this Article such as those on the rights of the seller's creditors, on good faith purchase, on the buyer's right to goods on the seller's insolvency, and on the buyer's right to specific performance or replevin.

4. The factual situations in subsections (2) and (3) upon which passage of title turn actually base the test upon the time when the seller has finally committed himself in regard to specific goods. Thus in a "shipment" contract he commits himself by the act of making the shipment. If shipment is not contemplated subsection (3) turns on the seller's final commitment, i.e. the delivery of documents or the making of the contract.

§ 2-501 Insurable Interest in Goods; Manner of Identification of Goods.

(1) The buyer obtains a special property and an insurable interest in goods by identification of existing goods as goods to which the contract refers even though the goods so identified are non-conforming and he has an option to return or reject them. Such identification can be made at any time and in any manner explicitly agreed to by the parties. In the absence of explicit agreement identification occurs

(a) when the contract is made if it is for the sale of goods already existing and identified;

(b) if the contract is for the sale of future goods other than those described in paragraph (c), when goods are shipped, marked or otherwise designated by the seller as goods to which the contract refers;

(c) when the crops are planted or otherwise become growing crops or the young are conceived if the contract is for the sale of unborn young to be born within twelve months after contracting or for the sale of crops to be harvested within twelve months or the next normal harvest season after contracting whichever is longer.

(2) The seller retains an insurable interest in goods so long as title to or any security interest in the goods remains in him and where the identification is by the seller alone he may until default or insolvency or notification to the buyer that the identification is final substitute other goods for those identified.

(3) Nothing in this section impairs any insurable interest recognized under any other statute or rule of law.

OFFICIAL COMMENT

1. The present section deals with the manner of identifying goods to the contract so that an insurable interest in the buyer and the rights set forth in the next section will accrue. Generally speaking, identification may be made in any manner "explicitly agreed to" by the parties. The rules of paragraphs (a), (b) and (c) apply only in the absence of such "explicit agreement".

2. In the ordinary case identification of particular existing goods as goods to which the contract refers is unambiguous and may occur in one of many ways. It is possible, however, for the identification to be tentative or contingent. In

view of the limited effect given to identification by this Article, the general policy is to resolve all doubts in favor of identification.

3. The provision of this section as to "explicit agreement" clarifies the present confusion in the law of sales which has arisen from the fact that under prior uniform legislation all rules of presumption with reference to the passing of title or to appropriation (which in turn depended upon identification) were regarded as subject to the contrary intention of the parties or of the party appropriating. Such uncertainty is reduced to a minimum under this section by

requiring "explicit agreement" of the parties before the rules of paragraphs (a), (b) and (c) are displaced—as they would be by a term giving the buyer power to select the goods. An "explicit" agreement, however, need not necessarily be found in the terms used in the particular transaction. Thus, where a usage of the trade has previously been made explicit by reduction to a standard set of "rules and regulations" currently incorporated by reference into the contracts of the parties, a relevant provision of those "rules and regulations" is "explicit" within the meaning of this section.

4. In view of the limited function of identification there is no requirement in this section that the goods be in deliverable state or that all of the seller's duties with respect to the processing of the goods be completed in order that identification occur. For example, despite identification the risk of loss remains on the seller under the risk of loss provisions until completion of his duties as to the goods and all of his remedies remain dependent upon his not defaulting under the contract.

5. Undivided shares in an identified fungible bulk, such as grain in an elevator or oil in a storage tank, can be sold. The mere making of the contract with reference to an undivided share in an identified fungible bulk is enough under subsection (a) to effect an identification if there is no explicit agreement otherwise. The seller's duty, however, to segregate and deliver according to the contract is not affected by such an identification but is controlled by other provisions of this Article.

6. Identification of crops under paragraph (c) is made upon planting only if they are to be harvested within the year or within the next normal harvest season. The phrase "next normal harvest season" fairly includes nursery stock raised for normally quick "harvest," but plainly excludes a "timber" crop to which the concept of a harvest "season" is inapplicable.

Paragraph (c) is also applicable to a crop of wool or the young of animals to be born within twelve months after contracting. The product of a lumbering, mining or fishing operation, though seasonal, is not within the concept of "growing". Identification under a contract for all or part of the output of such an operation can be effected early in the operation.

518

§ 2-503 Manner of Seller's Tender of Delivery.

(1) Tender of delivery requires that the seller put and hold conforming goods at the buyer's disposition and give the buyer any notification reasonably necessary to enable him to take delivery. The manner, time and place for tender are determined by the agreement and this Article, and in particular

(a) tender must be at a reasonable hour, and if it is of goods they must be kept available for the period reasonably necessary to enable the buyer to take possession; but

(b) unless otherwise agreed the buyer must furnish facilities reasonably suited to the receipt of the goods.

(2) Where the case is within the next section respecting shipment tender requires that the seller comply with its provisions.

(3) Where the seller is required to deliver at a particular destination tender requires that he comply with subsection (1) and also in any appropriate case tender documents as described in subsections (4) and (5) of this section.

(4) Where goods are in the possession of a bailee and are to be delivered without being moved

(a) tender requires that the seller either tender a negotiable document of title covering such goods or procure acknowledgment by the bailee of the buyer's right to possession of the goods; but

(b) tender to the buyer of a non-negotiable document of title or of a written direction to the bailee to deliver is sufficient tender unless the buyer seasonably objects, and receipt by the bailee of notification of the buyer's rights fixes those rights as against the bailee and all third persons; but risk of loss of the goods and of any failure by the bailee to honor the non-negotiable document of title or to obey the direction remains on the seller until the buyer has had a reasonable time to present the document or direction, and a refusal by the bailee to honor the document or to obey the direction defeats the tender.

(5) Where the contract requires the seller to deliver documents

(a) he must tender all such documents in correct form, except as provided in this Article with respect to bills of lading in a set (subsection (2) of Section 2-323); and

(b) tender through customary banking channels is sufficient and dishonor of a draft accompanying the documents constitutes non-acceptance or rejection.

OFFICIAL COMMENT

Changes: The general policy of the above sections is continued and supplemented but subsection (3) changes the rule of prior section 19(5) as to what constitutes a "destination" contract and subsection (4) incorporates a minor correction as to tender of delivery of goods in the possession of a bailee.

Purposes of Changes:

1. The major general rules governing the manner of proper or due tender of delivery are gathered in this section. The term "tender" is used in this Article in two different senses. In one sense it refers to "due tender" which contemplates an offer coupled with a present ability to fulfill all the conditions resting on the tendering party and must be followed by actual performance if the other party shows himself ready to proceed. Unless the context unmistakably indicates otherwise this is the meaning of "tender" in this Article and the occasional addition of the word "due" is only for clarity and emphasis. At other times it is used to refer to an offer of goods or documents under a contract as if in fulfillment of its conditions even though there is a defect when measured against the contract obligation. Used in either sense, however, "tender" connotes such performance by the tendering party as puts the other party in default if he fails to proceed in some manner.

2. The seller's general duty to tender and deliver is laid down in Section 2-301 and more particularly in Section 2-507. The seller's right to a receipt if he demands one and receipts are customary is governed by Section 2-205. Subsection (1) of the present section proceeds to set forth two primary requirements of tender: first, that the seller "put and hold conforming goods at the buyer's disposition" and, second, that he "give the buyer any notice reasonably necessary to enable him to take delivery."

In case in which payment is due and demanded upon delivery the "buyer's disposition" is qualified by the seller's right to retain control of the goods until payment by the provision of this Article on delivery on condition. However, where the seller is demanding payment on delivery he must first allow the buyer to inspect the goods in order to avoid impairing his tender unless the contract for sale is on C.I.F., C.O.D., cash against documents or similar terms negating the privilege of inspection before payment.

In the case of contracts involving documents the seller can "put and hold conforming goods at the buyer's disposition" under subsection (1) by tendering documents which give the buyer complete control of the goods under the provisions of Article 7 on due negotiation.

3. Under paragraph (a) of subsection (1) usage of the trade and the circumstances of the particular case determine what is a reasonable hour for tender and what constitutes a reasonable period of holding the goods available.

4. The buyer must furnish reasonable facilities for the receipt of the goods tendered by the seller under subsection (1), paragraph (b). This obligation of the buyer is no part of the seller's tender.

5. For the purposes of subsections (2) and (3) there is omitted from this Article the rule under prior uniform legislation that a term requiring the seller to pay the freight or cost of transportation to the buyer is equivalent to an agreement by the seller to deliver to the buyer or at an agreed destination. This omission is with the specific intention of negating the rule, for under this Article the "shipment" contract is regarded as the normal one and the "destination" contract as the variant type. The seller is not obligated to deliver at a named destination and bear the concurrent risk of loss until arrival, unless he has specifically agreed so to deliver or

520

the commercial understanding of the terms used by the parties contemplates such delivery.

6. Paragraph (a) of subsection (4) continues the rule of the prior uniform legislation as to acknowledgment by the bailee. Paragraph (b) of subsection (4) adopts the rule that between the buyer and the seller the risk of loss remains on the seller during a period reasonable for securing acknowledgment of the transfer from the bailee, while as against all other parties the buyer's rights are fixed as of the time the bailee receives notice of the transfer.

7. Under subsection (5) documents are never "required" except where there is an express contract term or it is plainly implicit in the peculiar circumstances of the case or in a usage of trade. Documents may, of course, be "authorized" although not required, but such cases are not within the scope of this subsection. When documents are required, there are three main requirements of this subsection: (1) "All": each required document is essential to a proper tender; (2) "Such": the documents must be the ones actually required by the contract in terms of source and substance; (3) "Correct form": All documents must be in correct form.

When a prescribed document cannot be procured, a question of fact arises under the provision of this Article on substituted performance as to whether the agreed manner of delivery is actually commercially impracticable and whether the substitute is commercially reasonable.

§ 2-504 Shipment by Seller.

Where the seller is required or authorized to send the goods to the buyer and the contract does not require him to deliver them at a particular destination, then unless otherwise agreed he must

(a) put the goods in the possession of such a carrier and make such a contract for their transportation as may be reasonable having regard to the nature of the goods and other circumstances of the case; and

(b) obtain and promptly deliver or tender in due form any document necessary to enable the buyer to obtain possession of the goods or otherwise required by the agreement or by usage of trade; and

(c) promptly notify the buyer of the shipment.

Failure to notify the buyer under paragraph (c) or to make a proper contract under paragraph (a) is a ground for rejection only if material delay or loss ensues.

OFFICIAL COMMENT

Changes: Rewritten.

Purposes of Changes: To continue the general policy of the prior uniform statutory provision while incorporating certain modifications with respect to the requirement that the contract with the carrier be made expressly on behalf of the buyer and as to the necessity of giving notice of the shipment to the buyer, so that:

1. The section is limited to "shipment" contracts as contrasted with "destination" contracts or contracts for delivery at the place where the goods are located. The general principles embodied in this section cover the special cases of F.O.B. point of shipment contracts and C.I.F. and C. & F. contracts. Under the preceding section on manner of tender of delivery, due tender by the seller requires that he comply with the requirements of this section in appropriate cases.

2. The contract to be made with the carrier under paragraph (a) must conform to all express terms of the agreement, subject to any substitution necessary because of failure of agreed facilities as provided in the later provision on substituted performance. However, under the policies of this Article on good faith and commercial standards and on buyer's rights on improper delivery, the requirements of explicit provisions must be read in terms of their commercial and not their literal meaning. This policy is made express with respect to bills of lading in a set in the provision of this Article on form of bills of lading required in overseas shipment.

3. In the absence of agreement, the provision of this Article on options and cooperation respecting performance gives the seller the choice of any reasonable carrier, routing and other arrangements. Whether or not the shipment is at the buyer's expense the seller must see to any arrangements, reasonable in the circumstances, such as refrigeration, watering of live stock, protection against cold, the sending along of any necessary help, selection of specialized cars and the like for paragraph (a) is intended to cover all necessary arrangements whether made by contract with the carrier or otherwise. There is, however, a proper relaxation of such requirements if the buyer is himself in a position to make the appropriate arrangements and the seller gives him reasonable notice

of the need to do so. It is an improper contract under paragraph (a) for the seller to agree with the carrier to a limited valuation below the true value and thus cut off the buyer's opportunity to recover from the carrier in the event of loss, when the risk of shipment is placed on the buyer by his contract with the seller.

4. Both the language of paragraph (b) and the nature of the situation it concerns indicate that the requirement that the seller must obtain and deliver promptly to the buyer in due form any document necessary to enable him to obtain possession of the goods is intended to cumulate with the other duties of the seller such as those covered in paragraph (a).

In this connection, in the case of pool car shipments a delivery order furnished by the seller on the pool car consignee, or on the carrier for delivery out of a larger quantity, satisfies the requirements of paragraph (b) unless the contract requires some other form of document.

5. This Article, unlike the prior uniform statutory provision, makes it the seller's duty to notify the buyer of shipment in all cases. The consequences of his failure to do so, however, are limited in that the buyer may reject on this ground only where material delay or loss ensues.

A standard and acceptable manner of notification in open credit shipments is the sending of an invoice and in the case of documentary contracts is the prompt forwarding of the documents as under paragraph (b) of this section. It is also usual to send on a straight bill of lading but this is not necessary to the required notification. However, should such a document prove necessary or convenient to the buyer, as in the case of loss and claim against the carrier, good faith would require the seller to send it on request.

Frequently the agreement expressly requires prompt notification as by wire or cable. Such a term may be of the essence and the final clause of paragraph (c) does not prevent the parties from making this a particular ground for rejection. To have this vital and irreparable effect upon the seller's duties, such a term should be part of the "dickered" terms written in any "form," or should otherwise be called seasonably and sharply to the seller's attention.

6. Generally, under the final sentence of the section, rejection by the buyer is justified only when the seller's dereliction as to any of the requirements of this section in fact is followed by material delay or damage. It rests on the seller, so far as concerns matters not within the peculiar knowledge of the buyer, to establish that his error has not been followed by events which justify rejection.

§ 2-513 Buyer's Right to Inspection of Goods.

(1) Unless otherwise agreed and subject to subsection (3), where goods are tendered or delivered or identified to the contract for sale, the buyer has a right before payment or acceptance to inspect them at any reasonable place and time and in any reasonable manner. When the seller is required or authorized to send the goods to the buyer, the inspection may be after their arrival.

(2) Expenses of inspection must be borne by the buyer but may be recovered from the seller if the goods do not conform and are rejected.

(3) Unless otherwise agreed and subject to the provisions of this Article on C.I.F. contracts (subsection (3) of Section 2-321), the buyer is not entitled to inspect the goods before payment of the price when the contract provides

(a) for delivery "C.O.D." or on other like terms; or

(b) for payment against documents of title, except where such payment is due only after the goods are to become available for inspection.

(4) A place or method of inspection fixed by the parties is presumed to be exclusive but unless otherwise expressly agreed it does not postpone identification or shift the place for delivery or for passing the risk of loss. If compliance becomes impossible, inspection shall be as provided in this section unless the place or method fixed was clearly intended as an indispensable condition failure of which avoids the contract.

OFFICIAL COMMENT

Purposes of Changes and New Matter: To correspond in substance with the prior uniform statutory provision and to incorporate in addition some of the results of the better case law so that:

1. The buyer is entitled to inspect goods as provided in subsection (1) unless it has been otherwise agreed by the parties. The phrase "unless otherwise agreed" is intended principally to cover such situations as those outlined in subsections (3) and (4) and those in which the agreement of the parties negates inspection before tender of delivery. However, no agreement by the parties can displace the entire right of inspection except where the contract is simply for the sale of "this thing." Even in a sale of boxed goods "as is" inspection is a right of the buyer, since if the boxes prove to contain some other merchandise altogether the price can be recovered back; nor do the limitations of the provision on effect of acceptance apply in such a case.

2. The buyer's right of inspection is available to him upon tender, delivery or appropriation of the goods with notice to him. Since inspection is available to him on tender, where payment is due against delivery he may, unless otherwise agreed, make his inspection before payment of the price. It is also available to him after receipt of the goods and so may be postponed after receipt for a reasonable time. Failure to inspect before payment does not impair

the right to inspect after receipt of the goods unless the case falls within subsection (4) on agreed and exclusive inspection provisions. The right to inspect goods which have been appropriated with notice to the buyer holds whether or not the sale was by sample.

3. The buyer may exercise his right of inspection at any reasonable time or place and in any reasonable manner. It is not necessary that he select the most appropriate time, place or manner to inspect or that his selection be the customary one in the trade or locality. Any reasonable time, place or manner is available to him and the reasonableness will be determined by trade usages, past practices between the parties and the other circumstances of the case.

The last sentence of subsection (1) makes it clear that the place of arrival of shipped goods is a reasonable place for their inspection.

4. Expenses of an inspection made to satisfy the buyer of the seller's performance must be assumed by the buyer in the first instance. Since the rule provides merely for an allocation of expense there is no policy to prevent the parties from providing otherwise in the agreement. Where the buyer would normally bear the expenses of the inspection but the goods are rightly rejected because of what the inspection reveals, demonstrable and reasonable costs of the inspection are part of his incidental damage caused by the seller's breach.

5. In the case of payment against documents, subsection (3) requires payment before inspection, since shipping documents against which payment is to be made will commonly arrive and be tendered while the goods are still in transit. This Article recognizes no exception in any peculiar case in which the goods happen to arrive before the documents. However, where by the agreement payment is to await the arrival of the goods, inspection before payment becomes proper since the goods are then "available for inspection."

Where by the agreement the documents are to be held until arrival the buyer is entitled to inspect before payment since the goods are then "available for inspection". Proof of usage is not necessary to establish this right, but if inspection before payment is disputed the contrary must be established by usage or by an explicit contract term to that effect.

For the same reason, that the goods are available for inspection, a term calling for payment against storage documents or a delivery order does not normally bar the buyer's right to inspection before payment under subsection (3)(b). This result is reinforced by the buyer's right under subsection (1) to inspect goods which have been appropriated with notice to him.

6. Under subsection (4) an agreed place or method of inspection is generally held to be intended as exclusive. However, where compliance with such an agreed inspection term becomes impossible, the question is basically one of intention. If the parties clearly intend that the method of inspection named is to be a necessary condition without which the entire deal is to fail, the contract is at an end if that method becomes impossible. On the other hand, if the parties merely seek to indicate a convenient and reliable method but do not intend to give up the deal in the event of its failure, any reasonable method of inspection may be substituted under this Article.

Since the purpose of an agreed place of inspection is only to make sure at that point whether or not the goods will be thrown back, the "exclusive" feature of the named place is satisfied under this Article if the buyer's failure to inspect there is held to be an acceptance with the knowledge of such defects as inspection would have revealed within the section on waiver of buyer's objections by failure to particularize. Revocation of the acceptance is limited to the situations stated in the section pertaining to that subject. The reasonable time within which to give notice of defects within the section on notice of

525

breach begins to run from the point of the "acceptance."

7. Clauses on time of inspection are commonly clauses which limit the time in which the buyer must inspect and give notice of defects. Such clauses are therefore governed by the section of this Article which requires that such a time limitation must be reasonable.

8. Inspection under this Article is not to be regarded as a "condition precedent to the passing of title" so that risk until inspection remains on

the seller. Under subsection (4) such an approach cannot be sustained. Issues between the buyer and seller are settled in this Article almost wholly by special provisions and not by the technical determination of the locus of the title. Thus "inspection as a condition to the passing of title" becomes a concept almost without meaning. However, in peculiar circumstances inspection may still have some of the consequences hitherto sought and obtained under that concept.

9. "Inspection" under this section has to do with the buyer's check-up on whether the seller's performance is in accordance with a contract previously made and is not to be confused with the "examination" of the goods or of a sample or model of them at the time of contracting which may affect the warranties involved in the contract.

§ 2-613 Casualty to Identified Goods.

Where the contract requires for its performance goods identified when the contract is made, and the goods suffer casualty without fault of either party before the risk of loss passes to the buyer, or in a proper case under a "no arrival, no sale" term (Section 2-324) then

(a) if the loss is total the contract is avoided; and

(b) if the loss is partial or the goods have so deteriorated as no longer to conform to the contract the buyer may nevertheless demand inspection and at his option either treat the contract as avoided or accept the goods with due allowance from the contract price for the deterioration or the deficiency in quantity but without further right against the seller.

OFFICIAL COMMENT

Purposes of Changes:

1. Where goods whose continued existence is presupposed by the agreement are destroyed without fault of either party, the buyer is relieved from his obligation but may at his option take the surviving goods at a fair adjustment. "Fault" is intended to include negligence and not merely wilful wrong. The buyer is expressly given the right to inspect the goods in order to determine whether he wishes to avoid the contract entirely or to take the goods with a price adjustment.

2. The section applies whether the goods were already destroyed at the time of contracting without the knowledge of either party or whether they are destroyed subsequently but before the risk of loss passes to the buyer. Where under the agreement, including of course usage of trade, the risk has passed to the buyer before the casualty, the section has no application. Beyond this, the essential question in determining whether the rules of this section are to be applied is whether the seller has or has not undertaken the responsibility for the continued existence of the goods in proper condition through the time of agreed or expected delivery.

3. The section on the term "no arrival, no sale" makes clear that delay in arrival, quite as much as physical change in the goods, gives the buyer the options set forth in this section.

§ 2-615 Excuse by Failure of Presupposed Conditions.

Except so far as a seller may have assumed a greater obligation and subject to the preceding section on substituted performance:

(a) Delay in delivery or non-delivery in whole or in part by a seller who complies with paragraphs (b) and (c) is not a breach of his duty under a contract for sale if performance as agreed has been made impracticable by the occurrence of a contingency the non-occurrence of which was a basic assumption on which the contract was made or by compliance in good faith with any applicable foreign or domestic governmental regulation or order whether or not it later proves to be invalid.

(b) Where the causes mentioned in paragraph (a) affect only a part of the seller's capacity to perform, he must allocate production and deliveries among his customers but may at his option include regular customers not then under contract as well as his own requirements for further manufacture. He may so allocate in any manner which is fair and reasonable.

(c) The seller must notify the buyer seasonably that there will be delay or non-delivery and, when allocation is required under paragraph (b), of the estimated quota thus made available for the buyer.

OFFICIAL COMMENT

Purposes:

1. This section excuses a seller from timely delivery of goods contracted for, where his performance has become commercially impracticable because of unforeseen supervening circumstances not within the contemplation of the parties at the time of contracting. The destruction of specific goods and the problem of the use of substituted performance on points other than delay or quantity, treated elsewhere in this Article, must be distinguished from the matter covered by this section.

2. The present section deliberately refrains from any effort at an exhaustive expression of contingencies and is to be interpreted in all cases sought to be brought within its scope in terms of its underlying reason and purpose.

3. The first test for excuse under this Article in terms of basic assumption is a familiar one. The additional test of commercial impracticability (as contrasted with "impossibility," "frustration of performance" or "frustration of the venture") has been adopted in order to call attention to the commercial character of the criterion chosen by this Article.

4. Increased cost alone does not excuse performance unless the rise in cost is due to some unforeseen contingency which alters the essential nature of the performance. Neither is a rise or a collapse in the market in itself a justification, for that is exactly the type of business risk which business contracts made at fixed prices are intended to cover. But a severe shortage of raw materials or of supplies due to a contingency such as war, embargo, local crop failure, unforeseen shutdown of major sources of supply or the like, which either causes a marked increase in cost or altogether prevents the seller from securing supplies necessary to his performance, is within the contemplation of this section. (See *Ford & Sons, Ltd., v. Henry Leetham & Sons, Ltd.*, 21 Com Cas 55 (1915, KBD)).

5. Where a particular source of supply is exclusive under the agreement and fails through casualty, the present section applies rather than the provision on destruction or deterioration of specific goods. The same holds true where a particular source of supply is shown by the circumstances to have been contemplated or assumed by the parties at the time of contracting. (See *Davis Co. v. Hoffman-La Roche Chemical Works*, 178 App Div 855, 166 NYS 179 (1917)

528

and *International Paper Co. v. Rockefeller*, 161 App Div 180, 146 NYS 371 (1914)). There is no excuse under this section, however, unless the seller has employed all due measures to assure himself that his source will not fail. (See *Canadian Industrial Alcohol Co., Ltd. v. Dunbar Molasses Co.*, 258 NY 194, 179 NE 383, 80 ALR 1173 (1932) and *Washington Mfg. Co. v. Midland Lumber Co.*, 113 Wash 593, 194 P 777 (1921)).

In the case of failure of production by an agreed source for causes beyond the seller's control, the seller should, if possible, be excused since production by an agreed source is without more a basic assumption of the contract. Such excuse should not result in relieving the defaulting supplier from liability nor in dropping into the seller's lap an unearned bonus of damages over. The flexible adjustment machinery of this Article provides the solution under the provision on the obligation of good faith. A condition to his making good the claim of excuse is the turning over to the buyer of his rights against the defaulting source of supply to the extent of the buyer's contract in relation to which excuse is being claimed.

6. In situations in which neither sense nor justice is served by either answer when the issue is posed in flat terms of "excuse" or "no excuse," adjustment under the various provisions of this Article is necessary, especially the sections on good faith, on insecurity and assurance and on the reading of all provisions in the light of their purposes, and the general policy of this Act to use equitable principles in furtherance of commercial standards and good faith.

7. The failure of conditions which go to convenience or collateral values rather than to the commercial practicability of the main performance does not amount to a complete excuse. However, good faith and the reason of the present section and of the preceding one may properly be held to justify and even to require any needed delay involved in a good faith inquiry seeking a readjustment of the contract terms to meet the new conditions.

8. The provisions of this section are made subject to assumption of greater liability by agreement and such agreement is to be found not only in the expressed terms of the contract but in the circumstances surrounding the contracting, in trade usage and the like. Thus the exemptions of this section do not apply when the contingency in question is sufficiently foreshadowed at the time of contracting to be included among the business risks which are fairly to be regarded as part of the dickered terms, either consciously or as a matter of reasonable, commercial interpretation from the circumstances. (See *Madeirense Do Brasil, S.A. v. Stulman-Emrick Lumber Co.*, 147 F2d 399 (CCA, 2 Cir. 1945).) The exemption otherwise present through usage of trade under the present section may also be expressly negated by the language of the agreement. Generally, express agreements as to exemptions designed to enlarge upon or supplant the provisions of this section are to be read in the light of mercantile sense and reason, for this section itself sets up the commercial standard for normal and reasonable interpretation and provides a minimum beyond which agreement may not go.

Agreement can also be made in regard to the consequences of exemption as laid down in paragraphs (b) and (c) and the next section on procedure on notice claiming excuse.

9. The case of a farmer who has contracted to sell crops to be grown on designated land may be regarded as falling either within the section on casualty to identified goods or this section, and he may be excused, when there is a failure of the specific crop, either on the basis of the destruction of identified goods or because of the failure of a basic assumption of the contract.

Exemption of the buyer in the case of a "requirements" contract is covered by the "Output and Requirements" section both as to assumption and allocation of the relevant risks. But when a contract by a manufacturer to buy fuel or raw material makes no specific reference to a particular venture and no such reference may be drawn from the circumstances, commercial understanding views it as a general deal in the general market and not conditioned on any assumption of the continuing operation of the buyer's plant. Even when notice is given by the buyer that the supplies are needed to fill a specific contract of a normal commercial kind, commercial understanding does not see such a supply contract as conditioned on the continuance of the buyer's further contract for outlet. On the other hand, where the buyer's contract is in reasonable commercial understanding conditioned on a definite and specific venture or assumption as, for instance, a war procurement subcontract known to be based on a prime contract which is subject to termination, or a supply contract for a particular construction venture, the reason of the present section may well apply and entitle the buyer to the exemption.

10. Following its basic policy of using commercial practicability as a test for excuse, this section recognizes as of equal significance either a foreign or domestic regulation and disregards any technical distinctions between "law," "regulation," "order" and the like. Nor does it make the present action of the seller depend upon the eventual judicial determination of the legality of the particular governmental action. The seller's good faith belief in the validity of the regulation is the test under this Article and the best evidence of his good faith is the general commercial acceptance of the regulation. However, governmental interference cannot excuse unless it truly "supervenes" in such a manner as to be beyond the seller's assumption of risk. And any action by the party claiming excuse which causes or colludes in inducing the governmental action preventing his performance would be in breach of good faith and would destroy his exemption.

11. An excused seller must fulfill his contract to the extent which the supervening contingency permits, and if the situation is such that his customers are generally affected he must take account of all in supplying one. Subsections (a) and (b), therefore, explicitly permit in any proration a fair and reasonable attention to the needs of regular customers who are probably relying on spot orders for supplies. Customers at different stages of the manufacturing process may be fairly treated by including the seller's manufacturing requirements. A fortiori, the seller may also take account of contracts later in date than the one in question. The fact that such spot orders may be closed at an advanced price causes no difficulty, since any allocation which exceeds normal past requirements will not be reasonable. However, good faith requires, when prices have advanced, that the seller exercise real care in making his allocations, and in case of doubt his contract customers should be favored and supplies prorated evenly among them regardless of price. Save for the extra care thus required by changes in the market, this section seeks to leave every reasonable business leeway to the seller.

§ 2-616 Procedure on Notice Claiming Excuse.

(1) Where the buyer receives notification of a material or indefinite delay or an allocation justified under the preceding section he may by written notification to the seller as to any delivery concerned, and where the prospective deficiency substantially impairs the value of the whole contract under the provisions of this Article relating to breach of installment contracts (Section 2-612), then also as to the whole,

(a) terminate and thereby discharge any unexecuted portion of the contract; or

(b) modify the contract by agreeing to take his available quota in substitution.

(2) If after receipt of such notification from the seller the buyer fails so to modify the contract within a reasonable time not exceeding thirty days the contract lapses with respect to any deliveries affected.

(3) The provisions of this section may not be negated by agreement except in so far as the seller has assumed a greater obligation under the preceding section.

OFFICIAL COMMENT

Purposes:

This section seeks to establish simple and workable machinery for providing certainty as to when a supervening and excusing contingency "excuses" the delay, "discharges" the contract, or may result in a waiver of the delay by the buyer. When the seller notifies, in accordance with the preceding section, claiming excuse, the buyer may acquiesce, in which case the contract is so modified. No consideration is necessary in a case of this kind to support such a modification. If the buyer does not elect so to modify the contract, he may terminate it and under subsection (2) his silence after receiving the seller's claim of excuse operates as such a termination. Subsection (3) denies effect to any contract clause made in advance of trouble which would require the buyer to stand ready to take delivery whenever the seller is excused from delivery by unforeseen circumstances.

531

§ 2-708 Seller's Damages for Non-acceptance or Repudiation.

(1) Subject to subsection (2) and to the provisions of this Article with respect to proof of market price (Section 2-723), the measure of damages for non-acceptance or repudiation by the buyer is the difference between the market price at the time and place for tender and the unpaid contract price together with any incidental damages provided in this Article (Section 2-710), but less expenses saved in consequence of the buyer's breach.

(2) If the measure of damages provided in subsection (1) is inadequate to put the seller in as good a position as performance would have done then the measure of damages is the profit (including reasonable overhead) which the seller would have made from full performance by the buyer, together with any incidental damages provided in this Article (Section 2-710), due allowance for costs reasonably incurred and due credit for payments or proceeds of resale.

OFFICIAL COMMENT

Purposes of Changes: To make it clear that:

1. The prior uniform statutory provision is followed generally in setting the current market price at the time and place for tender as the standard by which damages for non-acceptance are to be determined. The time and place of tender is determined by reference to the section on manner of tender of delivery, and to the sections on the effect of such terms as FOB, FAS, CIF, C&F, Ex Ship and No Arrival, No Sale.

In the event that there is no evidence available of the current market price at the time and place of tender, proof of a substitute market may be made under the section on determination and proof of market price. Furthermore, the section on the admissibility of market quotations is intended to ease materially the problem of providing competent evidence.

2. The provision of this section permitting recovery of expected profit including reasonable overhead where the standard measure of damages is inadequate, together with the new requirement that price actions may be sustained only where resale is impractical, are designed to eliminate the unfair and economically wasteful results arising under the older law when fixed price articles were involved. This section permits the recovery of lost profits in all appropriate cases, which would include all standard priced goods. The normal measure there would be list price less cost to the dealer or list price less manufacturing cost to the manufacturer. It is not necessary to a recovery of "profit" to show a history of earnings, especially if a new venture is involved.

3. In all cases the seller may recover incidental damages.

§ 2-713 Buyer's Damages for Non-Delivery or Repudiation.

(1) Subject to the provisions of this Article with respect to proof of market price (Section 2-723), the measure of damages for non-delivery or repudiation by the seller is the difference between the market price at the time when the buyer learned of the breach and the contract price together with any incidental and consequential damages provided in this Article (Section 2-715), but less expenses saved in consequence of the seller's breach.

(2) Market price is to be determined as of the place for tender or, in cases of rejection after arrival or revocation of acceptance, as of the place of arrival.

OFFICIAL COMMENT

Purposes of Changes: To clarify the former rule so that:

1. The general baseline adopted in this section uses as a yardstick the market in which the buyer would have obtained cover had he sought that relief. So the place for measuring damages is the place of tender (or the place of arrival if the goods are rejected or their acceptance is revoked after reaching their destination) and the crucial time is the time at which the buyer learns of the breach.

2. The market or current price to be used in comparison with the contract price under this section is the price for goods of the same kind and in the same branch of trade.

3. When the current market price under this section is difficult to prove the section on determination and proof of market price is available to permit a showing of a comparable market price or, where no market price is available, evidence of spot sale prices is proper. Where the unavailability of a market price is caused by a scarcity of goods of the type involved, a good case is normally made for specific performance under this Article. Such scarcity conditions, moreover, indicate that the price has risen and under the section providing for liberal administration of remedies, opinion evidence as to the value of the goods would be admissible in the absence of a market price and a liberal construction of allowable consequential damages should also result.

4. This section carries forward the standard rule that the buyer must deduct from his damages any expenses saved as a result of the breach.

5. The present section provides a remedy which is completely alternative to cover under the preceding section and applies only when and to the extent that the buyer has not covered.

533

§ 2-714 Buyer's Damages for Breach in Regard to Accepted Goods.

(1) Where the buyer has accepted goods and given notification (subsection (3) of Section 2-607) he may recover as damages for any non-conformity of tender the loss resulting in the ordinary course of events from the seller's breach as determined in any manner which is reasonable.

(2) The measure of damages for breach of warranty is the difference at the time and place of acceptance between the value of the goods accepted and the value they would have had if they had been as warranted, unless special circumstances show proximate damages of a different amount.

(3) In a proper case any incidental and consequential damages under the next section may also be recovered.

OFFICIAL COMMENT

Purposes of Changes:

1. This section deals with the remedies available to the buyer after the goods have been accepted and the time for revocation of acceptance has gone by. In general this section adopts the rule of the prior uniform statutory provision for measuring damages where there has been a breach of warranty as to goods accepted, but goes further to lay down an explicit provision as to the time and place for determining the loss.

The section on deduction of damages from price provides an additional remedy for a buyer who still owes part of the purchase price, and frequently the two remedies will be available concurrently. The buyer's failure to notify of his claim under the section on effects of acceptance, however, operates to bar his remedies under either that section or the present section.

2. The "non-conformity" referred to in subsection (1) includes not only breaches of warranties but also any failure of the seller to perform according to his obligations under the contract. In the case of such non-conformity, the buyer is permitted to recover for his loss "in any manner which is reasonable."

3. Subsection (2) describes the usual, standard and reasonable method of ascertaining damages in the case of breach of warranty but it is not intended as an exclusive measure. It departs from the measure of damages for non-delivery in utilizing the place of acceptance rather than the place of tender. In some cases the two may coincide, as where the buyer signifies his acceptance upon the tender. If, however, the non-conformity is such as would justify revocation of acceptance, the time and place of acceptance under this section is determined as of the buyer's decision not to revoke.

4. The incidental and consequential damages referred to in subsection (3), which will usually accompany an action brought under this section, are discussed in detail in the comment on the next section.

§ 2-715 Buyer's Incidental and Consequential Damages.

(1) Incidental damages resulting from the seller's breach include expenses reasonably incurred in inspection, receipt, transportation and care and custody of goods rightfully rejected, any commercially reasonable charges, expenses or commissions in connection with effecting cover and any other reasonable expense incident to the delay or other breach.

(2) Consequential damages resulting from the seller's breach include

(a) any loss resulting from general or particular requirements and needs of which the seller at the time of contracting had reason to know and which could not reasonably be prevented by cover or otherwise; and

(b) injury to person or property proximately resulting from any breach of warranty.

OFFICIAL COMMENT

Purposes of Changes and New Matter:

1. Subsection (1) is intended to provide reimbursement for the buyer who incurs reasonable expenses in connection with the handling of rightfully rejected goods or goods whose acceptance may be justifiably revoked, or in connection with effecting cover where the breach of the contract lies in non-conformity or non-delivery of the goods. The incidental damages listed are not intended to be exhaustive but are merely illustrative of the typical kinds of incidental damage.

2. Subsection (2) operates to allow the buyer, in an appropriate case, any consequential damages which are the result of the seller's breach. The "tacit agreement" test for the recovery of consequential damages is rejected. Although the older rule at common law which made the seller liable for all consequential damages of which he had "reason to know" in advance is followed, the liberality of that rule is modified by refusing to permit recovery unless the buyer could not reasonably have prevented the loss by cover or otherwise. Subparagraph (2) carries forward the provisions of the prior uniform statutory provision as to consequential damages resulting from breach of warranty, but modifies the rule by requiring first that the buyer attempt to minimize his damages in good faith, either by cover or otherwise.

3. In the absence of excuse under the section on merchant's excuse by failure of presupposed conditions, the seller is liable for consequential damages in all cases where he had reason to know of the buyer's general or particular requirements at the time of contracting. It is not necessary that there be a conscious acceptance of an insurer's liability on the seller's part, nor is his obligation for consequential damages limited to cases in which he fails to use due effort in good faith.

Particular needs of the buyer must generally be made known to the seller while general needs must rarely be made known to charge the seller with knowledge.

Any seller who does not wish to take the risk of consequential damages has available the section on contractual limitation on remedy.

4. The burden of proving the extent of loss incurred by way of consequential damage is on the buyer, but the section on liberal administration of remedies rejects any doctrine of certainty which requires almost mathematical precision in the proof of loss. Loss may be determined in any manner which is reasonable under the circumstances.

5. Subsection (2)(b) states the usual rule as to breach of warranty, allowing recovery for injuries "proximately" resulting from the breach. Where the injury involved follows the use of goods without discovery of the defect causing the damage, the question of "proximate" cause turns on whether it was reasonable for the buyer to use the goods without such inspection as would have revealed the defect. If it was not reasonable for him to do so, or if he did in fact discover the defect prior to his use, the injury would not proximately result from the breach of warranty.

6. In the case of sale of wares to one in the business of reselling them, resale is one of the requirements of which the seller has reason to know within the meaning of subsection (2)(a).

2-719 Contractual Modification or Limitation of Remedy.

(1) Subject to the provisions of subsections (2) and (3) of this section and of the preceding section on liquidation and limitation of damages,

(a) the agreement may provide for remedies in addition to or in substitution for those provided in this Article and may limit or alter the measure of damages recoverable under this Article, as by limiting the buyer's remedies to return of the goods and repayment of the price or to repair and replacement of non-conforming goods or parts; and

(b) resort to a remedy as provided is optional unless the remedy is expressly agreed to be exclusive, in which case it is the sole remedy.

(2) Where circumstances cause an exclusive or limited remedy to fail of its essential purpose, remedy may be had as provided in this Act.

(3) Consequential damages may be limited or excluded unless the limitation or exclusion is unconscionable. Limitation of consequential damages for injury to the person in the case of consumer goods is prima facie unconscionable but limitation of damages where the loss is commercial is not.

Purposes:

1. Under this section parties are left free to shape their remedies to their particular requirements and reasonable agreements limiting or modifying remedies are to be given effect.

However, it is of the very essence of a sales contract that at least minimum adequate remedies be available. If the parties intend to conclude a contract for sale within this Article they must accept the legal consequence that there be at least a fair quantum of remedy for breach of the obligations or duties outlined in the contract. Thus any clause purporting to modify or limit the remedial provisions of this Article in an unconscionable manner is subject to deletion and in that event the remedies made available by this Article are applicable as if the stricken clause had never existed. Similarly, under subsection (2), where an apparently fair and reasonable clause because of circumstances fails in its purpose or operates to deprive either party of the substantial value of the bargain, it must give way to the general remedy provisions of this Article.

2. Subsection (1)(b) creates a presumption that clauses prescribing remedies are cumulative rather than exclusive. If the parties intend the term to describe the sole remedy under the contract, this must be clearly expressed.

3. Subsection (3) recognizes the validity of clauses limiting or excluding consequential damages but makes it clear that they may not operate in an unconscionable manner. Actually such terms are merely an allocation of unknown or undeterminable risks. The seller in all cases is free to disclaim warranties in the manner provided in Section 2-316.

§ 3-301 Rights of a Holder.

The holder of an instrument whether or not he is the owner may transfer or negotiate it and, except as otherwise provided in Section 3-603 on payment or satisfaction, discharge it or enforce payment in his own name.

OFFICIAL COMMENT

Purposes of Changes: The section is revised to state in one provision all the rights of a holder, and to make it clear that every holder has such rights. The only limitations are those found in Section 3-603 on payment or satisfaction. That section provides (with stated exceptions) that payment to a holder discharges the liability of the party paying even though made with knowledge of a claim of another person to the instrument, unless the adverse claimant posts indemnity or procures the issuance of appropriate legal process restraining the payment. Thus payment to a holder in an adverse claim situation would not give discharge if the adverse claimant had followed either of the procedures provided for in the "unless" clause of Section 3-603; nor would a discharge result from payment in two other specific situations described in Section 3-603.

§ 3-302 Holder in Due Course.

(1) A holder in due course is a holder who takes the instrument

(a) for value; and

(b) in good faith; and

(c) without notice that it is overdue or has been dishonored or of any defense against or claim to it on the part of any person.

(2) A payee may be a holder in due course.

(3) A holder does not become a holder in due course of an instrument:

(a) by purchase of it at judicial sale or by taking it under legal process; or

(b) by acquiring it in taking over an estate; or

(c) by purchasing it as part of a bulk transaction not in regular course of business of the transferor.

(4) A purchaser of a limited interest can be a holder in due course only to the extent of the interest purchased.

OFFICIAL COMMENT

Purposes of Changes and New Matter: The changes are intended to remove uncertainties arising under the original section.

1. The language "without notice that it is overdue" is substituted for that of the original subsection (2) in order to make it clear that the purchaser of an instrument which is in fact overdue may be a holder in due course if he takes it without notice that it is overdue. Such notice is covered by the section on notice to purchaser (Section 3-304).

2. Subsection (2) is intended to settle the long continued conflict over the status of the payee as a holder in due course. This conflict has turned very largely upon the word "negotiated" in the original Section 52(4), which is now eliminated. The position here taken is that the payee may become a holder in due course to the same extent and under the same circumstances as any other holder. This is true whether he takes the instrument by purchase from a third person or directly from the obligor. All that is necessary is that the payee meet the requirements of this section. In the following cases, among others, the payee is a holder in due course:

a. A remitter, purchasing goods from P, obtains a bank draft payable to P and forwards it to P, who takes it for value, in good faith and without notice as required by this section.

b. The remitter buys the bank draft payable to P, but it is forwarded by the bank directly to P, who takes it in good faith and without notice in payment of the remitter's obligation to him.

c. A and B sign a note as co-makers. A induces B to sign by fraud, and without authority from B delivers the note to P, who takes it for value, in good faith and without notice.

d. A defrauds the maker into signing an instrument payable to P. P pays A for it in good faith and without notice, and the maker delivers the instrument directly to P.

e. D draws a check payable to P and gives it to his agent to be delivered to P in payment of D's debt. The agent delivers it to P, who takes it in good faith and without notice in payment of the agent's debt to P. But as to this case see Section 3-304(2), which may apply.

f. D draws a check payable to P but blank as to the amount, and gives it to his agent to be delivered to P. The agent fills in the check with an excessive amount, and P takes it for value, in good faith and without notice.

g. D draws a check blank as to the name of the payee, and gives it to his agent to be filled in with the name of A and delivered to A. The agent fills in the name of P, and P takes the check in good faith, for value and without notice.

3. Subsection (3) is intended to state existing case law. It covers a few situations in which the purchaser takes the instrument under unusual circumstances which indicate that he is merely a successor in interest to the prior holder and can acquire no better rights. (If such prior holder was himself a holder in due course, the purchaser succeeds to that status under Section 3-201 on Transfer.) The provision applies to a purchaser at an execution sale, a sale in bankruptcy or a sale by a state bank commissioner of the assets of an insolvent bank. It applies equally to an attaching creditor or any other person who acquires the instrument by legal process, even under an antecedent claim; and equally to a representative, such as an executor, administrator, receiver or assignee for the benefit of creditors, who takes over the instrument as part of an estate, even though he is representing antecedent creditors.

Subsection (3)(c) applies to bulk purchases lying outside of the ordinary course of business of the seller. It applies, for example, when a new partnership takes over for value all of the assets of an old one after a new member has entered the firm, or to a reorganized or consolidated corporation taking over in bulk the assets of a predecessor. It has particular application to the purchase by one bank of a substantial part of the paper held by another bank which is threatened with insolvency and seeking to liquidate its assets.

4. A purchaser of a limited interest—as a pledgee in a security transaction—may become a holder in due course, but he may enforce the instrument over defenses only to the extent of his interest, and defenses good against the pledgor remain available insofar as the pledgor retains an equity in the instrument. This is merely a special application of the general rule (Section 1-201) that a purchaser of a limited interest acquires rights only to the extent of the interest purchased. Section 27 of the original Act contained a similar provision.

540

§ 3-307 Burden of Establishing Signatures, Defenses and Due Course.

(1) Unless specifically denied in the pleadings each signature on an instrument is admitted. When the effectiveness of a signature is put in issue

(a) the burden of establishing it is on the party claiming under the signature; but

(b) the signature is presumed to be genuine or authorized except where the action is to enforce the obligation of a purported signer who has died or become incompetent before proof is required.

(2) When signatures are admitted or established, production of the instrument entitles a holder to recover on it unless the defendant establishes a defense.

(3) After it is shown that a defense exists a person claiming the rights of a holder in due course has the burden of establishing that he or some person under whom he claims is in all respects a holder in due course.

OFFICIAL COMMENT

Purposes of Changes and New Matter:

1. Subsection (1) is new, although similar provisions are found in a number of states. The purpose of the requirement of a specific denial in the pleadings is to give the plaintiff notice that he must meet a claim of forgery or lack of authority as to the particular signature, and to afford him an opportunity to investigate and obtain evidence. Where local rules of pleading permit, the denial may be on information and belief, or it may be a denial of knowledge or information sufficient to form a belief. It need not be under oath unless the local statutes or rules require verification. In the absence of such specific denial the signature stands admitted, and is not in issue. Nothing in this section is intended, however, to prevent amendment of the pleading in a proper case.

The question of the burden of establishing the signature arises only when it has been put in issue by specific denial. "Burden of establishing" is defined in the definitions section of this Act (Section 1-201). The burden is on the party claiming under the signature, but he is aided by the presumption that it is genuine or authorized stated in paragraph (b). "Presumption" is also defined in this Act (Section 1-201). It means that until some evidence is introduced which would support a finding that the signature is forged or unauthorized the plaintiff is not required to prove that it is authentic. The presumption rests upon the fact that in ordinary experience forged or unauthorized signatures are very uncommon, and normally any evidence is within the control of the defendant or more accessible to him. He is therefore required to make some sufficient showing of the grounds for his denial before the plaintiff is put to his proof. His evidence need not be sufficient to require a directed verdict in his favor, but it must be enough to support his denial by permitting a finding in his favor. Until he introduces such evidence the presumption requires a finding for the plaintiff. Once such evidence is introduced the burden of establishing the signature by a preponderance of the total evidence is on the plaintiff.

Under paragraph (b) this presumption does not arise where the action is to enforce the obligation of a purported signer who has died or become incompetent before the evidence is required, and so is disabled from obtaining or introducing it. "Action" of course includes a claim asserted against the estate of a deceased or an incompetent.

2. Subsection (2) is substituted for the first clause of the original Section 59. Once signatures are proved or admitted, a holder makes out his case by mere production of the instrument, and is entitled to recover in the absence of any further evidence. The defendant has the burden of establishing any and all defenses, not only in the first instance but by a preponderance of the total evidence. The provision applies only to a holder, as defined in this Act (Section 1-201). Any other person in possession of an instrument must prove his right to it and account for the absence of any necessary indorsement. If he establishes a transfer which gives him the rights of a holder (Section 3-201), this provision becomes applicable, and he is then entitled to recover unless the defendant establishes a defense.

3. Subsection (3) rephrases the last clause of the first sentence of the original Section 59. Until it is shown that a defense exists the issue as to whether the holder is a holder in due course does not arise. In the absence of a defense any holder is entitled to recover and there is no occasion to say that he is deemed prima facie to be a holder in due course. When it is shown that a defense exists the plaintiff may, if he so elects, seek to cut off the defense by establishing that he is himself a holder in due course, or that he has acquired the rights of a prior holder in due course (Section 3-201). On this issue he has the full burden of proof by a preponderance of the total evidence. "In all respects" means that he must sustain this burden by affirmative proof that the instrument was taken for value, that it was taken in good faith, and that it was taken without notice (Section 3-302).

Nothing in this section is intended to say that the plaintiff must necessarily prove that he is a holder in due course. He may elect to introduce no further evidence, in which case a verdict may be directed for the plaintiff or the defendant, or the issue of the defense may be left to the jury, according to the weight and sufficiency of the defendant's evidence. He may elect to rebut the defense itself by proof to the contrary, in which case again a verdict may be directed for either party or the issue may be for the jury. This subsection means only that if the plaintiff claims the rights of a holder in due course against the defense he has the burden of proof upon that issue.

§ 3-301 Person Entitled To Enforce Instrument.

"Person entitled to enforce" an instrument means (i) the holder of the instrument, (ii) a nonholder in possession of the instrument who has the rights of a holder, or (iii) a person not in possession of the instrument who is entitled to enforce the instrument pursuant to Section 3-309 or 3-418(d). A person may be a person entitled to enforce the instrument even though the person is not the owner of the instrument or is in wrongful possession of the instrument.

OFFICIAL COMMENT

This section replaces former Section 3-301 that stated the rights of a holder. The rights stated in former Section 3-301 to transfer, negotiate, enforce, or discharge an instrument are stated in other sections of Article 3. In revised Article 3, Section 3-301 defines "person entitled to enforce" an instrument. The definition recognizes that enforcement is not limited to holders. The quoted phrase includes a person enforcing a lost or stolen instrument. Section 3-309. It also includes a person in possession of an instrument who is not a holder. A nonholder in possession of an instrument includes a person that acquired rights of a holder by subrogation or under Section 3-203(a). It also includes any other person who under applicable law is a successor to the holder or otherwise acquires the holder's rights.

3-302 Holder in Due Course.

(a) Subject to subsection (c) and Section 3-106(d), "holder in due course" means the holder of an instrument if:

(1) the instrument when issued or negotiated to the holder does not bear such apparent evidence of forgery or alteration or is not otherwise so irregular or incomplete as to call into question its authenticity; and

(2) the holder took the instrument (i) for value, (ii) in good faith, (iii) without notice that the instrument is overdue or has been dishonored or that there is an uncured default with respect to payment of another instrument issued as part of the same series, (iv) without notice that the instrument contains an unauthorized signature or has been altered,

543

(v) without notice of any claim to the instrument described in Section 3-306, and (vi) without notice that any party has a defense or claim in recoupment described in Section 3-305(a).

(b) Notice of discharge of a party, other than discharge in an insolvency proceeding, is not notice of a defense under subsection (a), but discharge is effective against a person who became a holder in due course with notice of the discharge. Public filing or recording of a document does not of itself constitute notice of a defense, claim in recoupment, or claim to the instrument.

(c) Except to the extent a transferor or predecessor in interest has rights as a holder in due course, a person does not acquire rights of a holder in due course of an instrument taken (i) by legal process or by purchase in an execution, bankruptcy, or creditor's sale or similar proceeding, (ii) by purchase as part of a bulk transaction not in ordinary course of business of the transferor, or (iii) as the successor in interest to an estate or other organization.

(d) If, under Section 3-303(a)(1), the promise of performance that is the consideration for an instrument has been partially performed, the holder may assert rights as a holder in due course of the instrument only to the fraction of the amount payable under the instrument equal to the value of the partial performance divided by the value of the promised performance.

(e) If (i) the person entitled to enforce an instrument has only a security interest in the instrument and (ii) the person obliged to pay the instrument has a defense, claim in recoupment, or claim to the instrument that may be asserted against the person who granted the security interest, the person entitled to enforce the instrument may assert rights as a holder in due course only to an amount payable under the instrument which, at the time of enforcement of the instrument, does not exceed the amount of the unpaid obligation secured.

(f) To be effective, notice must be received at a time and in a manner that gives a reasonable opportunity to act on it.

(g) This section is subject to any law limiting status as a holder in due course in particular classes of transactions.

OFFICIAL COMMENT

1. Subsection (a)(1) is a return to the N.I.L. rule that the taker of an irregular or incomplete instrument is not a person the law should protect against defenses of the obligor or claims of prior owners. This reflects a policy choice against extending the holder in due course doctrine to an instrument that is so incomplete or irregular "as to call into question its authenticity." The term "authenticity" is used to make it clear that the irregularity or incompleteness must indicate that the instrument may not be what it purports to be. Persons who purchase or pay such instruments should do so at their own risk. Under subsection (1) of former Section 3-304, irregularity or

incompleteness gave a purchaser notice of a claim or defense. But it was not clear from that provision whether the claim or defense had to be related to the irregularity or incomplete aspect of the instrument. This ambiguity is not present in subsection (a)(1).

2. Subsection (a)(2) restates subsection (1) of former Section 3-302. Section 3-305(a) makes a distinction between defenses to the obligation to pay an instrument and claims in recoupment by the maker or drawer that may be asserted to reduce the amount payable on the instrument. Because of this distinction, which was not made in former Article 3, the reference in subsection (a)(2)(vi) is to both a defense and a claim in recoupment. Notice of forgery or alteration is stated separately because forgery and alteration are not technically defenses under subsection (a) of Section 3-305.

3. Discharge is also separately treated in the first sentence of subsection (b). Except for discharge in an insolvency proceeding, which is specifically stated to be a real defense in Section 3-305(a)(1), discharge is not expressed

in Article 3 as a defense and is not included in Section 3-305(a)(2). Discharge is effective against anybody except a person having rights of a holder in due course who took the instrument without notice of the discharge. Notice of discharge does not disqualify a person from becoming a holder in due course. For example, a check certified after it is negotiated by the payee may subsequently be negotiated to a holder. If the holder had notice that the certification occurred after negotiation by the payee, the holder necessarily had notice of the discharge of the payee as indorser. Section 3-415(d). Notice of that discharge does not prevent the holder from becoming a holder in due course, but the discharge is effective against the holder. Section 3-601(b). Notice of a defense under Section 3-305(a)(1) of a maker, drawer or acceptor based on a bankruptcy discharge is different. There is no reason to give holder in due course status to a

person with notice of that defense. The second sentence of subsection (b) is from former Section 3-304(5).

4. Professor Britton in his treatise Bills and Notes 309 (1961) stated: "A substantial number of decisions before the [N.I.L.] indicates that at common law there was nothing in the position of the payee as such which made it impossible for him to be a holder in due course." The courts were divided, however, about whether the payee of an instrument could be a holder in due course under the N.I.L. Some courts read N.I.L. § 52(4) to mean that a person could be a holder in due course only if the instrument was "negotiated" to that person. N.I.L. § 30 stated that "an instrument is negotiated when it is transferred from one person to another in such manner as to constitute the transferee the holder thereof." Normally, an instrument is "issued" to the payee; it is not transferred to the payee. N.I.L. § 191 defined "issue" as the "first delivery of the instrument . . . to a person who takes it as a holder." Thus, some courts concluded that the payee never could be a holder in due course. Other courts concluded that there was no evidence that the N.I.L. was intended to change the common law rule that the payee could be a holder in due course. Professor Britton states on p.318: "The typical situations which raise the [issue] are those where the defense of a maker is interposed because of fraud by a [maker who is] principal debtor . . . against a surety co-maker, or where the defense of fraud by a purchasing remitter is interposed by the drawer of the instrument against the good faith purchasing payee."

Former Section 3-302(2) stated: "A payee may be a holder in due course." This provision was intended to resolve the split of authority under the N.I.L. It made clear that there was no intent to change the common-law rule that allowed a payee to become a holder in due course. See Comment 2 to former Section 3-302. But there was no need to put subsection (2) in former Section 3-302 because the split in authority under the N.I.L. was caused by the particular wording of

N.I.L. § 52(4). The troublesome language in that section was not repeated in former Article 3 nor is it repeated in revised Article 3. Former Section 3-302(2) has been omitted in revised Article 3 because it is surplusage and may be misleading. The payee of an instrument can be a holder in due course, but use of the holder-in-due-course doctrine by the payee of an instrument is not the normal situation.

The primary importance of the concept of holder in due course is with respect to assertion of defenses or claims in recoupment (Section 3-305) and of claims to the instrument (Section 3-306). The holder-in-due-course doctrine assumes the following case as typical. Obligor issues a note or check to Obligee. Obligor is the maker of the note or drawer of the check. Obligee is the payee. Obligor has some defense to Obligor's obligation to pay the instrument. For example,

Obligor issued the instrument for goods that Obligee promised to deliver. Obligee never delivered the goods. The failure of Obligee to deliver the goods is a defense. Section 3-303(b). Although Obligor has a defense against Obligee, if the instrument is negotiated to Holder and the requirements of subsection (a) are met, Holder may enforce the instrument against Obligor free of the defense. Section 3-305(b). In the typical case the holder in due course is not the payee of the instrument. Rather, the holder in due course is an immediate or remote transferee of the payee. If Obligor in our example is the only obligor on the check or note, the holder-in-due-course doctrine is irrelevant in determining rights between Obligor and Obligee with respect to the instrument.

But in a small percentage of cases it is appropriate to allow the payee of an instrument to assert rights as a holder in due course. The cases are like those referred to in the quotation from Professor Britton referred to above, or other cases in which conduct of some third party is the basis of the defense of the issuer of the instrument. The following are examples:

Case No. 1. Buyer pays for goods bought from Seller by giving to Seller a cashier's check bought from Bank. Bank has a defense to its obligation to pay the check because Buyer bought the check from Bank with a check known to be drawn on an account with insufficient funds to cover the check. If Bank issued the check to Buyer as payee and Buyer indorsed it over to Seller, it is clear that Seller can be a holder in due course taking free of the defense if Seller had no notice of the defense. Seller is a transferee of the check. There is no good reason why Seller's position should be any different if Bank drew the check to the order of Seller as payee. In that case, when Buyer took delivery of the check from Bank, Buyer became the owner of the check even though Buyer was not the holder. Buyer was a remitter. Section 3-103(a)(11). At that point nobody was the holder. When Buyer delivered the check to Seller, ownership of the check was transferred to Seller who also became the holder. This is a negotiation. Section 3-201. The rights of Seller should not be affected by the fact that in one case the negotiation to Seller was by a holder and in the other case the negotiation was by a remitter. Moreover, it should be irrelevant whether Bank delivered the check to Buyer and Buyer delivered it to Seller or whether Bank delivered it directly to Seller. In either case Seller can be a holder in due course that takes free of Bank's defense.

Case No. 2. X fraudulently induces Y to join X in a spurious venture to purchase a business. The purchase is to be financed by a bank loan for part of the price. Bank lends money to X and Y by deposit in a joint account of X and Y who sign a note payable to Bank for the amount of the loan. X then withdraws the money from the joint account and absconds. Bank acted in good faith and without notice of the fraud of X against Y. Bank is payee of the note executed by Y, but its right to enforce the note against Y should not be affected by the fact that Y was induced to execute the note by the fraud of X. Bank can be a holder in due course that takes free of the defense of Y. Case No. 2 is similar to Case No. 1. In each case the payee of the instrument has given value to the person committing the fraud in exchange for the obligation of the person against whom the fraud was committed. In each case the payee was not party to the fraud and had no notice of it.

Suppose in Case No. 2 that the note does not meet the requirements of Section 3-104(a) and thus is not a negotiable instrument covered by Article 3. In that case, Bank cannot be a holder in due course but the result should be the same. Bank's rights are determined by general principles of contract law.

Restatement Second, Contracts § 164(2) governs the case. If Y is induced to enter into a contract with Bank by a fraudulent misrepresentation by X, the contract is voidable by Y unless Bank "in good faith and without reason to know of the misrepresentation either gives value or relies materially on the transaction." Comment e to § 164(2) states:

"This is the same principle that protects an innocent person who purchases goods or commercial paper in good faith, without notice and for value from one who obtained them from the original owner by a misrepresentation. See Uniform Commercial Code §§ 2-403(1), 3-305. In the cases that fall within [§ 164(2)], however, the innocent person deals directly with the recipient of the misrepresentation, which is made by one not a party to the contract."

The same result follows in Case No. 2 if Y had been induced to sign the note as an accommodation party (Section 3-419). If Y signs as co-maker of a note for the benefit of X, Y is a surety with respect to the obligation of X to pay the note but is liable as maker of the note to pay Bank. Section 3-419(b). If Bank is a holder in due course, the fraud of X cannot be asserted against Bank under Section 3-305(b). But the result is the same without resort to holder-in-due-course doctrine. If the note is not a negotiable instrument governed by Article 3, general rules of suretyship apply. Restatement, Security § 119

states that the surety (Y) cannot assert a defense against the creditor (Bank) based on the fraud of the principal (X) if the creditor "without knowledge of the fraud . . . extended credit to the principal on the security of the surety's promise . . . ." The underlying principle of § 119 is the same as that of § 164(2) of Restatement Second, Contracts.

Case No. 3. Corporation draws a check payable to Bank. The check is given to an officer of Corporation who is instructed to deliver it to Bank in payment of a debt owed by Corporation to Bank. Instead, the officer, intending to defraud Corporation, delivers the check to Bank in payment of the officer's personal debt, or the check is delivered to Bank for deposit to the officer's personal account. If Bank obtains payment of the check, Bank has received funds of Corporation which have been used for the personal benefit of the officer. Corporation in this case will assert a claim to the proceeds of the check against Bank. If Bank was a holder in due course of the check it took the check free of Corporation's claim. Section 3-306. The issue in this case is whether Bank had notice of the claim when it took the check. If Bank knew that the officer was a fiduciary with respect to the check, the issue is governed by Section 3-307.

Case No. 4. Employer, who owed money to X, signed a blank check and delivered it to Secretary with instructions to complete the check by typing in X's name and the amount owed to X. Secretary fraudulently completed the check by typing in the name of Y, a creditor to whom Secretary owed money. Secretary then delivered the check to Y in payment of Secretary's debt. Y obtained payment of the check. This case is similar to Case No. 3. Since Secretary was authorized to complete the check, Employer is bound by Secretary's act in making the check payable to Y. The drawee bank properly paid the check. Y received funds of Employer which were used for the personal benefit of Secretary. Employer asserts a claim to these funds against Y. If Y is a holder in due course, Y takes free of the claim. Whether Y is a holder in due course depends upon whether Y had notice of Employer's claim.

5. Subsection (c) is based on former Section 3-302(3). Like former Section 3-302(3), subsection (c) is intended to state existing case law. It covers a few situations in which the purchaser takes an instrument under unusual circumstances. The purchaser is treated as a successor in interest to the prior holder and can acquire no better rights. But if the prior holder was a holder in due course, the purchaser obtains rights of a holder in due course.

Subsection (c) applies to a purchaser in an execution sale or sale in bankruptcy. It applies equally to an attaching creditor or any other person who acquires the instrument by legal process or to a representative, such as an executor, administrator, receiver or assignee for the benefit of creditors, who takes the instrument as part of an estate. Subsection (c) applies to bulk purchases lying outside of the ordinary course of business of the seller. For example, it applies to the purchase by one bank of a substantial part of the paper held by another bank which is threatened with insolvency and seeking to liquidate its assets. Subsection (c) would also apply when a new partnership takes over for value all of the assets of an old one after a new member has entered the firm, or to a reorganized or consolidated corporation taking over the assets of a predecessor.

In the absence of controlling state law to the contrary, subsection (c) applies to a sale by a state bank commissioner of the assets of an insolvent bank. However, subsection (c) may be preempted by federal law if the Federal Deposit Insurance Corporation takes over an insolvent bank. Under the governing federal law, the FDIC and similar financial institution insurers are given holder in due course status and that status is also acquired by their assignees under the shelter doctrine.

6. Subsection (d) and (e) clarify two matters not specifically addressed by former Article 3:

Case No. 5. Payee negotiates a $1,000 note to Holder who agrees to pay $900 for it. After paying $500, Holder learns that Payee defrauded Maker in the transaction giving rise to the note. Under subsection (d) Holder may assert rights as a holder in due course to the extent of $555.55 ($500/$900 = .555 x $1,000 = $555.55). This formula rewards Holder with a ratable portion of the bargained for profit.

Case No. 6. Payee negotiates a note of Maker for $1,000 to Holder as security for payment of Payee's debt to Holder of $600. Maker has a defense which is good against Payee but of which Holder has no notice. Subsection (e) applies. Holder may assert rights as a holder in due course only to the extent of $600. Payee does not get the benefit of the holder-in-due-course status of Holder. With respect to $400 of the note, Maker may assert any rights that Maker has against Payee. A different result follows if the payee of a note negotiated it to a person who took it as a holder in due course and that person pledged the note as security for a debt. Because the defense cannot be asserted against the pledgor, the pledgee can assert rights as a holder in due course for the full amount of the note for the benefit of both the pledgor and the pledgee.

7. There is a large body of state statutory and case law restricting the use of the holder in due course doctrine in consumer transactions as well as some business transactions that raise similar issues. Subsection (g) subordinates Article 3 to that law and any other similar law that may evolve in the future. Section 3-106(d) also relates to statutory or administrative law intended to restrict use of the holder-in-due-course doctrine. See Comment 3 to Section 3-106.

§ 3-307 Notice of Breach of Fiduciary Duty.

(a) In this section:

(1) "Fiduciary" means an agent, trustee, partner, corporate officer or director, or other representative owing a fiduciary duty with respect to an instrument.

(2) "Represented person" means the principal, beneficiary, partnership, corporation, or other person to whom the duty stated in paragraph (1) is owed.

(b) If (i) an instrument is taken from a fiduciary for payment or collection or for value, (ii) the taker has knowledge of the fiduciary status of the fiduciary, and (iii) the represented person makes a claim to the instrument or its proceeds on the basis that the transaction of the fiduciary is a breach of fiduciary duty, the following rules apply:

(1) Notice of breach of fiduciary duty by the fiduciary is notice of the claim of the represented person.

(2) In the case of an instrument payable to the represented person or the fiduciary as such, the taker has notice of the breach of fiduciary duty if the instrument is (i) taken in payment of or as security for a debt known by the taker to be the personal debt of the fiduciary, (ii) taken in a transaction known by the taker to be for the personal benefit of the fiduciary, or (iii) deposited to an account other than an account of the fiduciary, as such, or an account of the represented person.

(3) If an instrument is issued by the represented person or the fiduciary as such, and made payable to the fiduciary personally, the taker does not have notice of the breach of fiduciary duty unless the taker knows of the breach of fiduciary duty.

(4) If an instrument is issued by the represented person or the fiduciary as such, to the taker as payee, the taker has notice of the breach of fiduciary duty if the instrument is (i) taken in payment of or as security for a debt known by the taker to be the personal debt of the fiduciary, (ii) taken in a transaction known by the taker to be for the personal benefit of the fiduciary, or (iii) deposited to an account other than an account of the fiduciary, as such, or an account of the represented person.

OFFICIAL COMMENT

1. This section states rules for determining when a person who has taken an instrument from a fiduciary has notice of a breach of fiduciary duty that occurs as a result of the transaction with the fiduciary. Former Section 3-304(2) and (4)(e) related to this issue, but those provisions were unclear in their meaning. Section 3-307 is intended to clarify the law by stating rules that comprehensively cover the issue of when the taker of an instrument has notice of breach of a fiduciary duty and thus notice of a claim to the instrument or its proceeds.

2. Subsection (a) defines the terms "fiduciary" and "represented person" and the introductory paragraph of subsection (b) describes the transaction to which the section applies. The basic scenario is one in which the fiduciary in effect embezzles money of the represented person by applying the proceeds of an instrument that belongs to the represented person to the personal use of the fiduciary. The person dealing with the fiduciary may be a depositary bank that takes the instrument for collection or a bank or other person that pays value for the instrument. The section also covers a transaction in which an instrument is presented for payment to a payor bank that pays the instrument by giving value to the fiduciary. Subsections (b)(2), (3), and (4) state rules for determining when the person dealing with the fiduciary has notice of breach of fiduciary duty. Subsection (b)(1) states that notice of breach of fiduciary duty is notice of the represented person's claim to the instrument or its proceeds.

Under Section 3-306, a person taking an instrument is subject to a claim to the instrument or its proceeds, unless the taker has rights of a holder in due course. Under Section 3-302(a)(2)(v), the taker cannot be a holder in due course if the instrument was taken with notice of a claim under Section 3-306. Section 3-307 applies to cases in which a represented person is asserting a claim because a breach of fiduciary duty resulted in a misapplication of the proceeds

of an instrument. The claim of the represented person is a claim described in Section 3-306. Section 3-307 states rules for determining when a person taking an instrument has notice of the claim which will prevent assertion of rights as a holder in due course. It also states rules for determining when a payor bank pays an instrument with notice of breach of fiduciary duty.

Section 3-307(b) applies only if the person dealing with the fiduciary "has knowledge of the fiduciary status of the fiduciary." Notice which does not amount to knowledge is not enough to cause Section 3-307 to apply. "Knowledge" is defined in Section 1-201(25). In most cases, the "taker" referred to in Section 3-307 will be a bank or other organization. Knowledge of an organization is determined by the rules stated in Section 1-201(27). In many cases, the individual who receives and processes an instrument on behalf of the organization that is the taker of the instrument "for payment or collection or for value" is a clerk who has no knowledge of any fiduciary status of the person from whom the instrument is received. In such cases, Section 3-307 doesn't apply because, under Section 1-201(27), knowledge of the organization is determined by the knowledge of the "individual conducting that transaction," i.e. the clerk who receives and processes the instrument. Furthermore, paragraphs (2) and (4) each require that the person acting for the organization have knowledge of facts that indicate a breach of fiduciary duty. In the case of an instrument taken for deposit to an account, the knowledge is found in the fact that the deposit is made to an account other than that of the represented person or a fiduciary account for benefit of that person. In other cases the person acting for the organization must know that the instrument is taken in payment or as security for a personal debt of the fiduciary or for the personal benefit of the fiduciary. For example, if the instrument is being used to buy goods or services, the person acting for the organization must know that the goods or services are for the personal benefit of the fiduciary. The requirement that the taker have knowledge rather than notice is meant to limit Section 3-307 to relatively uncommon cases in which the person who deals with the fiduciary knows all the relevant facts: the fiduciary status and that the proceeds of the instrument are being used for the personal debt or benefit of the fiduciary or are being paid to an account that is not an account of the represented person or of the fiduciary, as such. Mere notice of these facts is not enough to put the taker on notice of the breach of fiduciary duty and does not give rise to any duty of investigation by the taker.

3. Subsection (b)(2) applies to instruments payable to the represented person or the fiduciary as such. For example, a check payable to Corporation is indorsed in the name of Corporation by Doe as its President. Doe gives the check to Bank as partial repayment of a personal loan that Bank had made to Doe. The check was indorsed either in blank or to Bank. Bank collects the check and applies the proceeds to reduce the amount owed on Doe's loan. If the person acting for Bank in the transaction knows that Doe is a fiduciary and that the check is being used to pay a personal obligation of Doe, subsection (b)(2) applies. If Corporation has a claim to the proceeds of the check because the use of the check by Doe was a breach of fiduciary duty, Bank has notice of the claim and did not take the check as a holder in due course. The same result follows if Doe had indorsed the check to himself before giving it to Bank. Subsection (b)(2) follows Uniform Fiduciaries Act § 4 in providing that if the instrument is payable to the fiduciary, as such, or to the represented person, the taker has notice of a claim if the instrument is negotiated for the fiduciary's personal debt. If fiduciary funds are deposited to a personal account of the fiduciary or to an account that is not an account of the represented person or of the fiduciary, as such, there is a split of authority concerning whether the bank is on notice of a breach of fiduciary duty. Subsection (b)(2)(iii) states that the bank is given notice of breach of

fiduciary duty because of the deposit. The Uniform Fiduciaries Act § 9 states that the bank is not on notice unless it has knowledge of facts that makes its receipt of the deposit an act of bad faith.

The rationale of subsection (b)(2) is that it is not normal for an instrument payable to the represented person or the fiduciary, as such, to be used for the personal benefit of the fiduciary. It is likely that such use reflects an unlawful use of the proceeds of the instrument. If the fiduciary is entitled to compensation from the represented person for services rendered or for expenses incurred by the fiduciary the normal mode of payment is by a check drawn on the fiduciary account to the order of the fiduciary.

4. Subsection (b)(3) is based on Uniform Fiduciaries Act § 6 and applies when the instrument is drawn by the represented person or the fiduciary as such to the fiduciary personally. The term "personally" is used as it is used in the Uniform Fiduciaries Act to mean that the instrument is payable to the payee as an individual and not as a fiduciary. For example, Doe as President of Corporation writes a check on Corporation's account to the order of Doe personally. The check is then indorsed over to Bank as in Comment 3. In this case there is no notice of breach of fiduciary duty because there is nothing unusual about the transaction. Corporation may have owed Doe money for salary, reimbursement for expenses incurred for the benefit of Corporation, or for any other reason. If Doe is authorized to write checks on behalf of Corporation to pay debts of Corporation, the check is a normal way of paying a debt owed to Doe. Bank may assume that Doe may use the instrument for his personal benefit.

5. Subsection (b)(4) can be illustrated by a hypothetical case. Corporation draws a check payable to an organization. X, an officer or employee of Corporation, delivers the check to a person acting for the organization. The person signing the check on behalf of Corporation is X or another person. If the person acting for the

organization in the transaction knows that X is a fiduciary, the organization is on notice of a claim by Corporation if it takes the instrument under the same circumstances stated in subsection (b)(2). If the organization is a bank and the check is taken in repayment of a personal loan of the bank to X, the case is like the case discussed in Comment 3. It is unusual for Corporation, the represented person, to pay a personal debt of Doe by issuing a check to the bank. It is more likely that the use of the check by Doe reflects an unlawful use of the proceeds of the check. The same analysis applies if the check is made payable to an organization in payment of goods or services. If the person acting for the organization knew of the fiduciary status of X and that the goods or services were for X's personal benefit, the organization is on notice of a claim by Corporation to the proceeds of the check. See the discussion in the last paragraph of Comment 2.

§ 5-101 Short Title.

This article may be cited as Uniform Commercial Code—Letters of Credit.

OFFICIAL COMMENT

The Official Comment to the original Section 5-101 was a remarkably brief inaugural address. Noting that letters of credit had not been the subject of statutory enactment and that the law concerning them had been developed in the cases, the Comment stated that Article 5 was intended "within its limited scope" to set an independent theoretical frame for the further development of letters of credit. That statement addressed accurately conditions as they existed when the statement was made, nearly half a century ago. Since Article 5 was originally drafted, the use of letters of credit has expanded and developed, and the case law concerning these developments is, in some respects, discordant.

Revision of Article 5 therefore has required reappraisal both of the statutory goals and of the extent to which particular statutory provisions further or adversely affect achievement of those goals.

The statutory goal of Article 5 was originally stated to be: (1) to set a substantive theoretical frame that describes the function and legal nature of letters of credit; and (2) to preserve procedural flexibility in order to accommodate further development of the efficient use of letters of credit. A letter of credit is an idiosyncratic form of undertaking that supports performance of an obligation incurred in a separate financial, mercantile, or other transaction or arrangement.

The objectives of the original and revised Article 5 are best achieved (1) by defining the peculiar characteristics of a letter of credit that distinguish it and the legal consequences of its use from other forms of assurance such as secondary guarantees, performance bonds, and insurance policies, and from ordinary contracts, fiduciary engagements, and escrow arrangements; and (2) by preserving flexibility through variation by agreement in order to respond to and accommodate developments in custom and usage that are not inconsistent with the essential definitions and substantive mandates of the statute. No statute can, however, prescribe the manner in which such substantive rights and duties are to be enforced or imposed without risking stultification of wholesome developments in the letter of credit mechanism. Letter of credit law should remain responsive to commercial reality and in particular to the customs and expectations of the international banking and mercantile community. Courts should read the terms of this article in a manner consistent with these customs and expectations.

The subject matter in Article 5, letters of credit, may also be governed by an international convention that is now being drafted by UNCITRAL, the draft Convention on Independent Guarantees and Standby Letters of Credit. The Uniform Customs and Practice is an international body of trade practice that is commonly adopted by international and domestic letters of credit and as such is the "law of the transaction" by agreement of the parties. Article 5 is consistent with and was influenced by the rules in the existing version of the UCP. In addition to the UCP and the international convention, other bodies of law apply to letters of credit. For example, the federal bankruptcy law applies to letters of credit with respect to applicants and beneficiaries that are in bankruptcy; regulations of the Federal Reserve Board and the Comptroller of the Currency lay out requirements for banks that issue letters of credit and describe how letters of credit are to be treated for calculating asset risk and for the purpose of loan limitations. In addition there is an array of anti-boycott and other similar laws that may affect the issuance and performance of letters of credit. All of these laws are beyond the scope of Article 5, but in certain circumstances they will override Article 5.

§ 5-102 Definitions.

(a) In this article:

(1) "Adviser" means a person who, at the request of the issuer, a confirmer, or another adviser, notifies or requests another adviser to notify the beneficiary that a letter of credit has been issued, confirmed, or amended.

(2) "Applicant" means a person at whose request or for whose account a letter of credit is issued. The term includes a person who requests an issuer to issue a letter of credit on behalf of another if the person making the request undertakes an obligation to reimburse the issuer.

(3) "Beneficiary" means a person who under the terms of a letter of credit is entitled to have its complying presentation honored. The term includes a person to whom drawing rights have been transferred under a transferable letter of credit.

(4) "Confirmer" means a nominated person who undertakes, at the request or with the consent of the issuer, to honor a presentation under a letter of credit issued by another.

(5) "Dishonor" of a letter of credit means failure timely to honor or to take an interim action, such as acceptance of a draft, that may be required by the letter of credit.

(6) "Document" means a draft or other demand, document of title, investment security, certificate, invoice, or other record, statement, or representation of fact, law, right, or opinion (i) which is presented in a written or other medium permitted by the letter of credit or, unless prohibited by the letter of credit, by the standard practice referred to in Section 5-108(e) and (ii) which is capable of being examined for compliance with the terms and conditions of the letter of credit. A document may not be oral.

(7) "Good faith" means honesty in fact in the conduct or transaction concerned.

(8) "Honor" of a letter of credit means performance of the issuer's undertaking in the letter of credit to pay or deliver an item of value. Unless the letter of credit otherwise provides, "honor" occurs

(i) upon payment,

(ii) if the letter of credit provides for acceptance, upon acceptance of a draft and, at maturity, its payment, or

(iii) if the letter of credit provides for incurring a deferred obligation, upon incurring the obligation and, at maturity, its performance.

(9) "Issuer" means a bank or other person that issues a letter of credit, but does not include an individual who makes an engagement for personal, family, or household purposes.

(10) "Letter of credit" means a definite undertaking that satisfies the requirements of Section 5-104 by an issuer to a beneficiary at the request or for the account of an applicant or, in the case of a financial institution, to itself or for its own account, to honor a documentary presentation by payment or delivery of an item of value.

(11) "Nominated person" means a person whom the issuer (i) designates or authorizes to pay, accept, negotiate, or otherwise give value under a letter of credit and (ii) undertakes by agreement or custom and practice to reimburse.

(12) "Presentation" means delivery of a document to an issuer or nominated person for honor or giving of value under a letter of credit.

(13) "Presenter" means a person making a presentation as or on behalf of a beneficiary or nominated person.

(14) "Record" means information that is inscribed on a tangible medium, or that is stored in an electronic or other medium and is retrievable in perceivable form.

(15) "Successor of a beneficiary" means a person who succeeds to substantially all of the rights of a beneficiary by operation of law, including a corporation with or into which the beneficiary has been merged or consolidated, an administrator, executor, personal representative, trustee in bankruptcy, debtor in possession, liquidator, and receiver.

(b) Definitions in other Articles applying to this article and the sections in which they appear are:

"Accept" or "Acceptance"	Section 3-409
"Value"	Sections 3-303, 4-211

(c) Article 1 contains certain additional general definitions and principles of construction and interpretation applicable throughout this article.

OFFICIAL COMMENT

1. Since no one can be a confirmer unless that person is a nominated person as defined in Section 5-102(a)(11), those who agree to "confirm" without the designation or authorization of the issuer are not confirmers under Article 5. Nonetheless, the undertakings to the beneficiary of such persons may be enforceable by the beneficiary as letters of credit issued by the "confirmer" for its own account or as guarantees or contracts outside of Article 5.

2. The definition of "document" contemplates and facilitates the growing recognition of electronic and other nonpaper media as "documents," however, for the time being, data in those media constitute documents only in certain circumstances. For example, a facsimile received by an issuer would be a document only if the letter of credit explicitly permitted it, if the standard practice authorized it and the letter did not prohibit it, or the agreement of the issuer and beneficiary permitted it. The fact that data transmitted in a nonpaper (unwritten) medium can be recorded on paper by a recipient's computer printer, facsimile machine, or the like does not under current practice render the data so transmitted a "document." A facsimile or S.W.I.F.T. message received directly by the issuer is in an electronic medium when it crosses the boundary of the issuer's place of business. One wishing to make a presentation by facsimile (an electronic medium) will have to procure the explicit agreement of the issuer (assuming that the standard practice does not authorize it). Where electronic transmissions are authorized neither by the letter of credit nor by the practice, the beneficiary may transmit the data electronically to its agent who may be able to put it in written form and make a conforming presentation.

3. "Good faith" continues in revised Article 5 to be defined as "honesty in fact." "Observance of reasonable standards of fair dealing" has not been added to the definition. The narrower definition of "honesty in fact" reinforces the "independence principle" in the treatment of "fraud," "strict compliance," "preclusion," and other tests affecting the performance of obligations that are unique to letters of credit. This narrower definition—which does not include "fair dealing"—is appropriate to the decision to honor or dishonor a presentation of documents specified in a letter of credit. The narrower definition is also appropriate for other parts of revised Article 5 where greater certainty of obligations is necessary and is consistent with the goals of speed and low cost. It is important that U.S. letters of credit have continuing vitality and competitiveness in international transactions.

For example, it would be inconsistent with the "independence" principle if any of the following occurred: (i) the beneficiary's failure to adhere to the standard of "fair dealing" in the underlying transaction or otherwise in presenting documents were to provide applicants and issuers with an "unfairness" defense to dishonor even when the documents complied with the terms of the letter of credit; (ii) the issuer's obligation to honor in "strict compliance in accordance with standard practice" were changed to "reasonable compliance" by use of the "fair dealing" standard, or (iii) the preclusion against the issuer (Section 5-108(d)) were modified under the "fair dealing" standard to enable the issuer later to raise additional deficiencies in the presentation. The rights and obligations arising from presentation, honor, dishonor and reimbursement, are independent and strict, and thus "honesty in fact" is an appropriate standard.

The contract between the applicant and beneficiary is not governed by Article 5, but by applicable contract law, such as Article 2 or the general law of contracts. "Good faith" in that contract is defined by other law, such as Section 2-103(1)(b) or Restatement of Contracts 2d, § 205, which incorporate the principle of "fair dealing" in most cases, or a State's common law or other statutory provisions that may apply to that contract.

The contract between the applicant and the issuer (sometimes called the "reimbursement" agreement) is governed in part by this article (e.g., Sections 5-108(i), 5-111(b), and 5-103(c)) and partly by other law (e.g., the general law of contracts). The definition of good faith in Section 5-102(a)(7) applies only to the extent that the reimbursement contract is governed by provisions in this article; for other purposes good faith is defined by other law.

4. Payment and acceptance are familiar modes of honor. A third mode of honor, incurring an unconditional obligation, has legal effects similar to an acceptance of a time draft but does not technically constitute an acceptance. The practice of making letters of credit available by "deferred payment undertaking" as now provided in UCP 500 has grown up in other countries and spread to the United States. The definition of "honor" will accommodate that practice.

5. The exclusion of consumers from the definition of "issuer" is to keep creditors from using a letter of credit in consumer transactions in which the consumer might be made the issuer and the creditor would be the beneficiary. If that transaction were recognized under Article 5, the effect would be to leave the consumer without defenses against the creditor. That outcome would violate the policy behind the Federal Trade Commission Rule in 16 CFR Part 433. In a consumer transaction, an individual cannot be an issuer where that person would otherwise be either the principal debtor or a guarantor.

6. The label on a document is not conclusive; certain documents labelled "guarantees" in accordance with European (and occasionally, American) practice are letters of credit. On the other hand, even documents that are labelled "letter of credit" may not constitute letters of credit under the definition in Section 5-102(a). When a document labelled a letter of credit requires the issuer to pay not upon the presentation of documents, but upon the determination of an extrinsic fact such as applicant's failure to perform a construction contract, and where that condition appears on its face to be fundamental and would, if ignored, leave no obligation to the issuer under the document labelled letter of credit, the issuer's undertaking is not a letter of credit. It is probably some form of suretyship or other contractual arrangement and may be enforceable as such. See Sections 5-102(a)(10) and 5-103(d). Therefore, undertakings whose fundamental term requires an issuer to look beyond documents and beyond conventional reference to the clock, calendar, and practices concerning the form of various documents are not governed by Article 5. Although Section 5-108(g) recognizes that certain nondocumentary conditions can be included in a letter of credit without denying the undertaking the status of letter of credit, that section does not apply to cases where the nondocumentary condition is fundamental to the issuer's obligation. The rules in Sections 5-102(a)(10), 5-103(d), and 5-108(g) approve the conclusion in Wichita Eagle & Beacon Publishing Co. v. Pacific Nat. Bank, 493 F.2d 1285 (9th Cir.1974).

The adjective "definite" is taken from the UCP. It approves cases that deny letter of credit status to documents that are unduly vague or incomplete. See, e.g., *Transparent Products Corp. v. Paysaver Credit Union*, 864 F.2d 60 (7th Cir.1988). Note, however, that no particular phrase or label is necessary to establish a letter of credit. It is sufficient if the undertaking of the issuer shows that it is intended to be a letter of credit. In most cases the parties' intention will be indicated by a label on the undertaking itself indicating that it is a "letter of credit," but no such language is necessary.

A financial institution may be both the issuer and the applicant or the issuer and the beneficiary. Such letters are sometimes issued by a bank in support of the bank's own lease obligations or on behalf of one of its divisions as an applicant or to one of its divisions as beneficiary, such as an overseas branch. Because wide use of letters of credit in which the issuer and the applicant or the issuer and the beneficiary are the same would endanger the unique status of letters of credit, only financial institutions are authorized to issue them.

In almost all cases the ultimate performance of the issuer under a letter of credit is the payment of money. In rare cases the issuer's obligation is to deliver stock certificates or the like. The definition of letter of credit in Section 5-102(a)(10) contemplates those cases.

557

7. Under the UCP any bank is a nominated bank where the letter of credit is "freely negotiable." A letter of credit might also nominate by the following: "We hereby engage with the drawer, indorsers, and bona fide holders of drafts drawn under and in compliance with the terms of this credit that the same will be duly honored on due presentation" or "available with any bank by negotiation." A restricted negotiation credit might be "available with x bank by negotiation" or the like.

Several legal consequences may attach to the status of nominated person. First, when the issuer nominates a person, it is authorizing that person to pay or give value and is authorizing the beneficiary to make presentation to that person. Unless the letter of credit provides otherwise, the beneficiary need not present the documents to the issuer before the letter of credit expires; it need only present those documents to the nominated person. Secondly, a nominated person that gives value in good faith has a right to payment from the issuer despite fraud. Section 5-109(a)(1).

8. A "record" must be in or capable of being converted to a perceivable form. For example, an electronic message recorded in a computer memory that could be printed from that memory could constitute a record. Similarly, a tape recording of an oral conversation could be a record.

9. Absent a specific agreement to the contrary, documents of a beneficiary delivered to an issuer or nominated person are considered to be presented under the letter of credit to which they refer, and any payment or value given for them is considered to be made under that letter of credit. As the court held in *Alaska Textile Co. v. Chase Manhattan Bank, N.A.*, 982 F.2d 813, 820 (2d Cir.1992), it takes a "significant showing" to make the presentation of a beneficiary's documents for "collection only" or otherwise outside letter of credit law and practice.

10. Although a successor of a beneficiary is one who succeeds "by operation of law," some of the successions contemplated by Section 5-102(a)(15) will have resulted from voluntary action of the beneficiary such as merger of a corporation. Any merger makes the successor corporation the "successor of a beneficiary" even though the transfer occurs partly by operation of law and partly by the voluntary action of the parties. The definition excludes certain transfers, where no part of the transfer is "by operation of law"—such as the sale of assets by one company to another.

11. "Draft" in Article 5 does not have the same meaning it has in Article 3. For example, a document may be a draft under Article 5 even though it would not be a negotiable instrument, and therefore would not qualify as a draft under Section 3-104(e).

§ 5-103 Scope.

(a) This article applies to letters of credit and to certain rights and obligations arising out of transactions involving letters of credit.

(b) The statement of a rule in this article does not by itself require, imply, or negate application of the same or a different rule to a situation not provided for, or to a person not specified, in this article.

(c) With the exception of this subsection, subsections (a) and (d), Sections 5-102(a)(9) and (10), 5-106(d), and 5-114(d), and except to the extent prohibited in Sections 1-102(3) and 5-117(d), the effect of this article may be varied by agreement or by a provision stated or incorporated by reference in an undertaking. A term in an agreement or undertaking generally excusing liability or generally limiting remedies for failure to perform obligations is not sufficient to vary obligations prescribed by this article.

(d) Rights and obligations of an issuer to a beneficiary or a nominated person under a letter of credit are independent of the existence, performance, or nonperformance of a contract or arrangement out of which the letter of credit arises or which underlies it, including contracts or arrangements between the issuer and the applicant and between the applicant and the beneficiary.

OFFICIAL COMMENT

1. Sections 5-102(a)(10) and 5-103 are the principal limits on the scope of Article 5. Many undertakings in commerce and contract are similar, but not identical to the letter of credit. Principal among those are "secondary," "accessory," or "suretyship" guarantees. Although the word "guarantee" is sometimes used to describe an independent obligation like that of the issuer of a letter of credit (most often in the case of European bank undertakings but occasionally in the case of undertakings of American banks), in the United States the word "guarantee" is more typically used to describe a suretyship transaction in which the "guarantor" is only secondarily liable and has the right to assert the underlying debtor's defenses. This article does not apply to secondary or accessory guarantees and it is important to recognize the distinction between letters of credit and those guarantees. It is often a defense to a secondary or accessory guarantor's liability that the underlying debt has been discharged or that the debtor has other defenses to the underlying liability. In letter of credit law, on the other hand, the independence principle recognized throughout Article 5 states that the issuer's liability is independent of the underlying obligation. That the beneficiary may have breached the underlying contract and thus have given a good defense on that contract to the applicant against the beneficiary is no defense for the issuer's refusal to honor. Only staunch recognition of this principle by the issuers and the courts will give letters of credit the continuing vitality that arises from the certainty and speed of payment under letters of credit. To that end, it is important that the law not carry into letter of credit transactions rules that properly apply only

to secondary guarantees or to other forms of engagement.

2. Like all of the provisions of the Uniform Commercial Code, Article 5 is supplemented by Section 1-103 and, through it, by many rules of statutory and common law. Because this article is quite short and has no rules on many issues that will affect liability with respect to a letter of credit transaction, law beyond Article 5 will often determine rights and liabilities in letter of credit transactions. Even within letter of credit law, the article is far from comprehensive; it deals only with "certain" rights of the parties. Particularly with respect to the standards of performance that are set out in Section 5-108, it is appropriate for the parties and the courts to turn to customs and practice such as the Uniform Customs and Practice for Documentary Credits, currently published by the International Chamber of Commerce as I.C.C. Pub. No. 500 (hereafter UCP). Many letters of credit specifically adopt the UCP as applicable to the particular transaction. Where the UCP are adopted but conflict with Article 5 and except where variation is prohibited, the UCP terms are permissible contractual modifications under Sections 1-102(3) and 5-103(c). See Section 5-116(c). Normally Article 5 should not be considered to conflict with practice except when a rule explicitly stated in the UCP or other practice is different from a rule explicitly stated in Article 5.

Except by choosing the law of a jurisdiction that has not adopted the Uniform Commercial Code, it is not possible entirely to escape the Uniform Commercial Code. Since incorporation of the UCP avoids only "conflicting" Article 5 rules, parties who do not wish to be governed by the nonconflicting provisions of Article 5 must normally either adopt the law of a jurisdiction other than a State of the United States or state explicitly the rule that is to govern. When rules of custom and practice are incorporated by reference, they are considered to be explicit terms of the agreement or undertaking.

Neither the obligation of an issuer under Section 5-108 nor that of an adviser under Section 5-107 is an obligation of the kind that is invariable under Section 1-102(3). Section 5-103(c) and Comment 1 to Section 5-108 make it clear that the applicant and the issuer may agree to almost any provision establishing the obligations of the issuer to the applicant. The last sentence of subsection (c) limits the power of the issuer to achieve that result by a nonnegotiated disclaimer or limitation of remedy.

What the issuer could achieve by an explicit agreement with its applicant or by a term that explicitly defines its duty, it cannot accomplish by a general disclaimer. The restriction on disclaimers in the last sentence of subsection (c) is based more on procedural than on substantive unfairness. Where, for example, the reimbursement agreement provides explicitly that the issuer need not examine any documents, the applicant understands the risk it has undertaken. A term in a reimbursement agreement which states generally that an issuer will not be liable unless it has acted in "bad faith" or committed "gross negligence" is ineffective under Section 5-103(c). On the other hand, less general terms such as terms that permit issuer reliance on an oral or electronic message believed in good faith to have been received from the applicant or terms that entitle an issuer to reimbursement when it honors a "substantially" though not "strictly" complying presentation, are effective. In each case the question is whether the disclaimer or limitation is sufficiently clear and explicit in reallocating a liability or risk that is allocated differently under a variable Article 5 provision.

Of course, no term in a letter of credit, whether incorporated by reference to practice rules or stated specifically, can free an issuer from a conflicting contractual obligation to its applicant. If, for example, an issuer promised its applicant that it would pay only against an inspection certificate of a particular company but failed to require such a certificate in its letter of credit or made the requirement only a nondocumentary condition that had to be disregarded, the issuer might be obliged to pay the beneficiary even though its payment might violate its contract with its applicant.

3. Parties should generally avoid modifying the definitions in Section 5-102. The effect of such an agreement is almost inevitably unclear. To say that something is a "guarantee" in the typical domestic transaction is to say that the parties intend that particular legal rules apply to it. By acknowledging that something is a guarantee, but asserting that it is to be treated as a "letter of credit," the parties leave a court uncertain about where the rules on guarantees stop and those concerning letters of credit begin.

4. Section 5-102(2) and (3) of Article 5 are omitted as unneeded; the omission does not change the law.

§ 5-104 Formal Requirements.

A letter of credit, confirmation, advice, transfer, amendment, or cancellation may be issued in any form that is a record and is authenticated (i) by a signature or (ii) in accordance with the agreement of the parties or the standard practice referred to in Section 5-108(e).

OFFICIAL COMMENT

1. Neither Section 5-104 nor the definition of letter of credit in Section 5-102(a)(10) requires inclusion of all the terms that are normally contained in a letter of credit in order for an undertaking to be recognized as a letter of credit under Article 5. For example, a letter of credit will typically specify the amount available, the expiration date, the place where presentation should be made, and the documents that must be presented to entitle a person to honor. Undertakings that have the formalities required by Section 5-104 and meet the conditions specified in Section 5-102(a)(10) will be recognized as letters of credit even though they omit one or more of the items usually contained in a letter of credit.

2. The authentication specified in this section is authentication only of the identity of the issuer, confirmer, or adviser.

An authentication agreement may be by system rule, by standard practice, or by direct agreement between the parties. The reference to practice is intended to incorporate future developments in the UCP and other practice rules as well as those that may arise spontaneously in commercial practice.

3. Many banking transactions, including the issuance of many letters of credit, are now conducted mostly by electronic means. For example, S.W.I.F.T. is currently used to transmit letters of credit from issuing to advising banks. The letter of credit text so transmitted may be printed at the advising bank, stamped "original" and provided to the beneficiary in that form. The printed document may then be used as a way of controlling and recording payments and of recording and authorizing assignments of proceeds or transfers of rights under the letter of credit. Nothing in this section should be construed to conflict with that practice.

To be a record sufficient to serve as a letter of credit or other undertaking under this section, data must have a durability consistent with that function. Because consideration is not required for a binding letter of credit or similar undertaking (Section 5-105) yet those undertakings are to be strictly construed (Section 5-108), parties to a letter of credit transaction are especially dependent on the continued availability of the terms and conditions of the letter of credit or other undertaking. By declining to specify any particular medium in which the letter of credit must be established or communicated, Section 5-104 leaves room for future developments.

§ 5-105 Consideration.

Consideration is not required to issue, amend, transfer, or cancel a letter of credit, advice, or confirmation.

OFFICIAL COMMENT

It is not to be expected that any issuer will issue its letter of credit without some form of remuneration. But it is not expected that the beneficiary will know what the issuer's remuneration was or whether in fact there was any identifiable remuneration in a given case. And it might be difficult for the beneficiary to prove the issuer's remuneration. This section dispenses with this proof and is consistent with the position of Lord Mansfield in *Pillans v. Van Mierop*, 97 Eng.Rep. 1035 (K.B. 1765) in making consideration irrelevant.

§ 5-106 Issuance, Amendment, Cancellation, and Duration.

(a) A letter of credit is issued and becomes enforceable according to its terms against the issuer when the issuer sends or otherwise transmits it to the person requested to advise or to the beneficiary. A letter of credit is revocable only if it so provides.

(b) After a letter of credit is issued, rights and obligations of a beneficiary, applicant, confirmer, and issuer are not affected by an amendment or cancellation to which that person has not consented except to the extent the letter of credit provides that it is revocable or that the issuer may amend or cancel the letter of credit without that consent.

(c) If there is no stated expiration date or other provision that determines its duration, a letter of credit expires one year after its stated date of issuance or, if none is stated, after the date on which it is issued.

(d) A letter of credit that states that it is perpetual expires five years after its stated date of issuance, or if none is stated, after the date on which it is issued.

OFFICIAL COMMENT

1. This section adopts the position taken by several courts, namely that letters of credit that are silent as to revocability are irrevocable. See, e.g., *Weyerhaeuser Co. v. First Nat. Bank*, 27 UCC Rep.Serv. 777 (S.D. Iowa 1979); *West Va. Hous. Dev. Fund v. Sroka*, 415 F.Supp. 1107 (W.D.Pa.1976). This is the position of the current UCP (500). Given the usual commercial understanding and purpose of letters of credit, revocable letters of credit offer unhappy possibilities for misleading the parties who deal with them.

2. A person can consent to an amendment by implication. For example, a beneficiary that tenders documents for honor that conform to an amended letter of credit but not to the original letter of credit has probably consented to the amendment. By the same token an applicant that has procured the issuance of a transferable letter of credit has consented to its transfer and to performance under the letter of credit by a person to whom the beneficiary's rights are duly transferred. If some, but not all of the persons involved in a letter of credit transaction consent to performance that does not strictly conform to the original letter of credit, those persons assume the risk that other nonconsenting persons may insist on strict compliance with the original letter of credit. Under subsection (b) those not consenting are not bound. For example, an issuer might agree to amend its letter of credit or honor documents presented after the expiration date in the belief that the applicant has consented or will consent to the amendment or will waive presentation after the original expiration date. If that belief is mistaken, the issuer is bound to the beneficiary by the terms of the letter of credit as amended or waived, even though it may be unable to recover from the applicant.

In general, the rights of a recognized transferee beneficiary cannot be altered without the transferee's consent, but the same is not true of the rights of assignees of proceeds from the beneficiary. When the beneficiary makes a complete transfer of its interest that is effective under the terms for transfer established by the issuer, adviser, or other party controlling transfers, the beneficiary no longer has an interest in the letter of credit, and the transferee steps into the shoes of the beneficiary as the one with rights under the letter of credit. Section 5-102(a)(3). When there is a partial transfer, both the original beneficiary and the transferee beneficiary have an interest in performance of the letter of credit and each expects that its rights will not be altered by amendment unless it consents.

The assignee of proceeds under a letter of credit from the beneficiary enjoys no such expectation. Notwithstanding an assignee's notice to the issuer of the assignment of proceeds, the assignee is not a person protected by subsection (b). An assignee of proceeds should understand that its rights can be changed or completely extinguished by amendment or cancellation of the letter of credit. An assignee's claim is precarious, for it depends entirely upon the continued existence of the letter of credit and upon the beneficiary's preparation and presentation of documents that would entitle the beneficiary to honor under Section 5-108.

3. The issuer's right to cancel a revocable letter of credit does not free it from a duty to reimburse a nominated person who has honored, accepted, or undertaken a deferred obligation prior to receiving notice of the amendment or cancellation. Compare UCP Article 8.

4. Although all letters of credit should specify the date on which the issuer's engagement expires, the failure to specify an expiration date does not invalidate the letter of credit, or diminish or relieve the obligation of any party with respect to the letter of credit. A letter of credit that may be revoked or terminated at the discretion of the issuer by notice to the beneficiary is not "perpetual."

§ 5-107 Confirmer, Nominated Person, and Adviser.

(a) A confirmer is directly obligated on a letter of credit and has the rights and obligations of an issuer to the extent of its confirmation. The confirmer also has rights against and obligations to the issuer as if the issuer were an applicant and the confirmer had issued the letter of credit at the request and for the account of the issuer.

(b) A nominated person who is not a confirmer is not obligated to honor or otherwise give value for a presentation.

(c) A person requested to advise may decline to act as an adviser. An adviser that is not a confirmer is not obligated to honor or give value for a presentation. An adviser undertakes to the issuer and to the beneficiary accurately to advise the terms of the letter of credit, confirmation, amendment, or advice received by that person and undertakes to the beneficiary to check the apparent authenticity of the request to advise. Even if the advice is inaccurate, the letter of credit, confirmation, or amendment is enforceable as issued.

(d) A person who notifies a transferee beneficiary of the terms of a letter of credit, confirmation, amendment, or advice has the rights and obligations of an adviser under subsection (c). The terms in the notice to the transferee beneficiary may differ from the terms in any notice to the transferor beneficiary to the extent permitted by the letter of credit, confirmation, amendment, or advice received by the person who so notifies.

OFFICIAL COMMENT

1. A confirmer has the rights and obligations identified in Section 5-108. Accordingly, unless the context otherwise requires, the terms "confirmer" and "confirmation" should be read into this article wherever the terms "issuer" and "letter of credit" appear.

A confirmer that has paid in accordance with the terms and conditions of the letter of credit is entitled to reimbursement by the issuer even if the beneficiary committed fraud (see Section 5-109(a)(1)(ii)) and, in that sense, has greater rights against the issuer than the beneficiary has. To be entitled to reimbursement from the issuer under the typical confirmed letter of credit, the confirmer must submit conforming documents, but the confirmer's presentation to the issuer need not be made before the expiration date of the letter of credit.

A letter of credit confirmation has been analogized to a guarantee of issuer performance, to a parallel letter of credit issued by the confirmer for the account of the issuer or the letter of credit applicant or both, and to a back-to-back letter of credit in which the confirmer is a kind of beneficiary of the original issuer's letter of credit. Like letter of credit undertakings, confirmations are both unique and flexible, so that no one of these analogies is perfect, but unless otherwise indicated in the letter of credit or confirmation, a confirmer should be viewed by the letter of credit issuer and the beneficiary as an issuer of a parallel letter of credit for the account of the original letter of credit issuer. Absent a direct agreement between the applicant and a confirmer, normally the obligations of a confirmer are to the issuer not the applicant, but the applicant might have a right to injunction against a confirmer under Section 5-109 or warranty claim under Section 5-110, and either might have claims against the other under Section 5-117.

2. No one has a duty to advise until that person agrees to be an adviser or undertakes to act in accordance with the instructions of the issuer. Except where there is a prior agreement to serve or where the silence of the adviser would be an acceptance of an offer to contract, a person's failure to respond to a request to advise a letter of credit does not in and of itself create any liability, nor does it establish a relationship of issuer and adviser between the two. Since there is no duty to advise a letter of credit in the absence of a prior agreement, there can be no duty to advise it timely or at any particular time. When the adviser manifests its agreement to advise by actually doing so (as is normally the case), the adviser cannot have violated any duty to advise in a timely way. This analysis is consistent with the result of *Sound of Market Street v. Continental Bank International*, 819 F.2d 384 (3d Cir.1987) which held that there is no such duty. This section takes no position on the reasoning of that case, but does not overrule the result. By advising or agreeing to advise a letter of credit, the adviser assumes a duty to the issuer and to the beneficiary accurately to report what it has received from the issuer, but, beyond determining the apparent authenticity of the letter, an adviser has no duty to investigate the accuracy of the message it has received from the issuer. "Checking" the apparent authenticity of the request to advise means only that the prospective adviser must attempt to authenticate the message (e.g., by "testing" the telex that comes from the purported issuer), and if it is unable to authenticate the message must report that fact to the issuer and, if it chooses to advise the message, to the beneficiary. By proper agreement, an adviser may disclaim its obligation under this section.

3. An issuer may issue a letter of credit which the adviser may advise with different terms. The issuer may then believe that it has undertaken a certain engagement, yet the text in the hands of the beneficiary will contain different terms, and the beneficiary would not be entitled to honor if the documents it submitted did not comply with the terms of the letter of credit as originally issued. On the other hand, if the adviser also confirmed the letter of credit, then as a confirmer it will be independently liable on the letter of credit as advised and confirmed. If in that situation the beneficiary's ultimate presentation entitled it to honor under the terms of the confirmation but not under those in the original letter of credit, the confirmer would have to honor but might not be entitled to reimbursement from the issuer.

4. When the issuer nominates another person to "pay," "negotiate," or otherwise to take up the documents and give value, there can be confusion about the legal status of the nominated person. In rare cases the person might actually be an agent of the issuer and its act might be the act of the issuer itself. In most cases the nominated person is not an agent of the issuer and has no authority to act on the issuer's behalf. Its "nomination" allows the beneficiary to present to it and earns it certain rights to payment under Section 5-109 that others do not enjoy. For example, when an issuer issues a "freely negotiable credit," it contemplates that banks or others might take up documents under that credit and advance value against them, and it is agreeing to pay those persons but only if the presentation to the issuer made by the nominated person complies with the credit. Usually there will be no agreement to pay, negotiate, or to serve in any other capacity by the nominated person, therefore the nominated person will have the right to decline to take the documents. It may return them or agree merely to act as a forwarding agent for the documents but without giving value against them or taking any responsibility for their conformity to the letter of credit.

§ 5-108 Issuer's Rights and Obligations.

(a) Except as otherwise provided in Section 5-109, an issuer shall honor a presentation that, as determined by the standard practice referred to in subsection (e), appears on its face strictly to comply with the terms and conditions of the letter of credit. Except as otherwise provided in Section 5-113 and unless otherwise agreed with the applicant, an issuer shall dishonor a presentation that does not appear so to comply.

(b) An issuer has a reasonable time after presentation, but not beyond the end of the seventh business day of the issuer after the day of its receipt of documents:

(1) to honor,

(2) if the letter of credit provides for honor to be completed more than seven business days after presentation, to accept a draft or incur a deferred obligation, or

(3) to give notice to the presenter of discrepancies in the presentation.

(c) Except as otherwise provided in subsection (d), an issuer is precluded from asserting as a basis for dishonor any discrepancy if timely notice is not given, or any discrepancy not stated in the notice if timely notice is given.

(d) Failure to give the notice specified in subsection (b) or to mention fraud, forgery, or expiration in the notice does not preclude the issuer from asserting as a basis for dishonor fraud or forgery as described in Section 5-109(a) or expiration of the letter of credit before presentation.

(e) An issuer shall observe standard practice of financial institutions that regularly issue letters of credit. Determination of the issuer's observance of the standard practice is a matter of interpretation for the court. The court shall offer the parties a reasonable opportunity to present evidence of the standard practice.

(f) An issuer is not responsible for:

(1) the performance or nonperformance of the underlying contract, arrangement, or transaction,

(2) an act or omission of others, or

(3) observance or knowledge of the usage of a particular trade other than the standard practice referred to in subsection (e).

567

(g) If an undertaking constituting a letter of credit under Section 5-102(a)(10) contains nondocumentary conditions, an issuer shall disregard the nondocumentary conditions and treat them as if they were not stated.

(h) An issuer that has dishonored a presentation shall return the documents or hold them at the disposal of, and send advice to that effect to, the presenter.

(i) An issuer that has honored a presentation as permitted or required by this article:

(1) is entitled to be reimbursed by the applicant in immediately available funds not later than the date of its payment of funds;

(2) takes the documents free of claims of the beneficiary or presenter;

(3) is precluded from asserting a right of recourse on a draft under Sections 3-414 and 3-415;

(4) except as otherwise provided in Sections 5-110 and 5-117, is precluded from restitution of money paid or other value given by mistake to the extent the mistake concerns discrepancies in the documents or tender which are apparent on the face of the presentation; and

(5) is discharged to the extent of its performance under the letter of credit unless the issuer honored a presentation in which a required signature of a beneficiary was forged.

OFFICIAL COMMENT

1. This section combines some of the duties previously included in Sections 5-114 and 5-109. Because a confirmer has the rights and duties of an issuer, this section applies equally to a confirmer and an issuer. See Section 5-107(a).

The standard of strict compliance governs the issuer's obligation to the beneficiary and to the applicant. By requiring that a "presentation" appear strictly to comply, the section requires not only that the documents themselves appear on their face strictly to comply, but also that the other terms of the letter of credit such as those dealing with the time and place of presentation are strictly complied with. Typically, a letter of credit will provide that presentation is timely if made to the issuer, confirmer, or any other nominated person prior to expiration of the letter of credit. Accordingly, a nominated person that has honored a demand or otherwise given value before expiration will have a right to reimbursement from the issuer even though presentation to the issuer is made after the expiration of the letter of credit. Conversely, where the beneficiary negotiates documents to one who is not a nominated person, the beneficiary or that person acting on behalf of the beneficiary must make presentation to a nominated person, confirmer, or issuer prior to the expiration date.

This section does not impose a bifurcated standard under which an issuer's right to reimbursement might be broader than a beneficiary's right to honor. However, the explicit deference to standard practice in Section 5-108(a) and (e) and elsewhere expands issuers' rights of reimbursement where that practice so provides. Also, issuers can and often do contract with their applicants for expanded rights of reimbursement. Where that is done, the beneficiary will have to meet a more stringent standard of compliance as to the issuer than the issuer will have to meet as to the applicant. Similarly, a nominated person may have reimbursement and other rights against the issuer based on this article, the UCP, bank-to-bank reimbursement rules, or other agreement or undertaking of the issuer. These rights may allow the nominated person to recover from the issuer even when the nominated person would have no right to obtain honor under the letter of credit.

The section adopts strict compliance, rather than the standard that commentators have called "substantial compliance," the standard arguably applied in *Banco Espanol de Credito v. State Street Bank and Trust Company*, 385 F.2d 230 (1st Cir.1967) and *Flagship Cruises Ltd. v. New England Merchants Nat. Bank*, 569 F.2d 699 (1st Cir.1978). Strict compliance does not mean slavish conformity to the terms of the letter of credit. For example, standard practice (what issuers do) may recognize certain presentations as complying that an unschooled layman would regard as discrepant. By adopting standard practice as a way of measuring strict compliance, this article indorses the conclusion of the court in *New Braunfels Nat. Bank v. Odiorne*, 780 S.W.2d 313 (Tex.Ct.App. 1989) (beneficiary could collect when draft requested payment on "Letter of Credit No. 86-122-5" and letter of credit specified "Letter of Credit No. 86-122-S" holding strict compliance does not demand oppressive perfectionism). The section also indorses the result in *Tosco Corp. v. Federal Deposit Insurance Corp.*, 723 F.2d 1242 (6th Cir.1983). The letter of credit in that case called for "drafts Drawn under Bank of Clarksville Letter of Credit Number 105." The draft presented stated "drawn

under Bank of Clarksville, Clarksville, Tennessee letter of Credit No. 105." The court correctly found that despite the change of upper case "L" to a lower case "l" and the use of the word "No." instead of "Number," and despite the addition of the words "Clarksville, Tennessee," the presentation conformed. Similarly a document addressed by a foreign person to General Motors as "Jeneral Motors" would strictly conform in the absence of other defects.

Identifying and determining compliance with standard practice are matters of interpretation for the court, not for the jury. As with similar rules in Sections 4A-202(c) and 2-302, it is hoped that there will be more consistency in the outcomes and speedier resolution of disputes if the responsibility for determining the nature and scope of standard practice is granted to the court, not to a jury. Granting the court authority to make these decisions will also encourage the salutary practice of courts' granting summary judgment in circumstances where there are no significant factual disputes. The statute encourages outcomes such as *American Coleman Co. v. Intrawest Bank*, 887 F.2d 1382 (10th Cir.1989), where summary judgment was granted.

In some circumstances standards may be established between the issuer and the applicant by agreement or by custom that would free the issuer from liability that it might otherwise have. For example, an applicant might agree that the issuer would have no duty whatsoever to examine documents on certain presentations (e.g., those below a certain dollar amount). Where the transaction depended upon the issuer's payment in a very short time period (e.g., on the same day or within a few hours of presentation), the issuer and the applicant might agree to reduce the issuer's responsibility for failure to discover discrepancies. By the same token, an agreement between the applicant and the issuer might permit the issuer to examine documents exclusively by electronic or electro-optical means. Neither those agreements nor others like them explicitly made by issuers and applicants violate the terms of Section 5-108(a) or (b) or Section 5-103(c).

2. Section 5-108(a) balances the need of the issuer for time to examine the documents against the possibility that the examiner (at the urging of the applicant or for fear that it will not be reimbursed) will take excessive time to search for defects. What is a "reasonable time" is not extended to accommodate an issuer's procuring a waiver from the applicant. See Article 14c of the UCP.

Under both the UCC and the UCP the issuer has a reasonable time to honor or give notice. The outside limit of that time is measured in business days under the UCC and in banking days under the UCP, a difference that will rarely be significant. Neither business nor banking days are defined in Article 5, but a court may find useful analogies in Regulation CC, 12 CFR 229.2, in state law outside of the Uniform Commercial Code, and in Article 4.

Examiners must note that the seven-day period is not a safe harbor. The time within which the issuer must give notice is the lesser of a reasonable time or seven business days. Where there are few documents (as, for example, with the mine run standby letter of credit), the reasonable time would be less than seven days. If more than a reasonable time is consumed in examination, no timely notice is possible. What is a "reasonable time" is to be determined by examining the behavior of those in the business of examining documents, mostly banks. Absent prior agreement of the issuer, one could not expect a bank issuer to examine documents while the beneficiary waited in the lobby if the normal practice was to give the documents to a person who had the opportunity to examine those together with many others in an orderly process. That the applicant has not yet paid the issuer or that the applicant's account with the issuer is insufficient to cover the amount of the draft is not a basis for extension of the time period.

This section does not preclude the issuer from contacting the applicant during its examination; however, the decision to honor rests with the issuer, and it has no duty to seek a waiver from the applicant or to notify the applicant of receipt of the documents. If the issuer dishonors a conforming presentation, the beneficiary will be entitled to the remedies under Section 5-111, irrespective of the applicant's views.

Even though the person to whom presentation is made cannot conduct a reasonable examination of documents within the time after presentation and before the expiration date, presentation establishes the parties' rights. The beneficiary's right to honor or the issuer's right to dishonor arises upon presentation at the place provided in the letter of credit even though it might take the person to whom presentation has been made several days to determine whether honor or dishonor is the proper course. The issuer's time for honor or giving notice of dishonor may be extended or shortened by a term in the letter of credit. The time for the issuer's performance may be otherwise modified or waived in accordance with Section 5-106.

The issuer's time to inspect runs from the time of its "receipt of documents." Documents are considered to be received only when they are received at the place specified for presentation by the issuer or other party to whom presentation is made.

Failure of the issuer to act within the time permitted by subsection (b) constitutes dishonor. Because of the preclusion in subsection (c) and the liability that the issuer may incur under Section 5-111 for wrongful dishonor, the effect of such a silent dishonor may ultimately be the same as though the issuer had honored, i.e., it may owe damages in the amount drawn but unpaid under the letter of credit.

3. The requirement that the issuer send notice of the discrepancies or be precluded from asserting discrepancies is new to Article 5. It is

taken from the similar provision in the UCP and is intended to promote certainty and finality.

The section thus substitutes a strict preclusion principle for the doctrines of waiver and estoppel that might otherwise apply under Section 1-103. It rejects the reasoning in *Flagship Cruises Ltd. v. New England Merchants' Nat. Bank*, 569 F.2d 699 (1st Cir.1978) and *Wing On Bank Ltd. v. American Nat. Bank & Trust Co.*, 457 F.2d 328 (5th Cir.1972) where the issuer was held to be estopped only if the beneficiary relied on the issuer's failure to give notice.

Assume, for example, that the beneficiary presented documents to the issuer shortly before the letter of credit expired, in circumstances in which the beneficiary could not have cured any discrepancy before expiration. Under the reasoning of *Flagship* and *Wing On*, the beneficiary's inability to cure, even if it had received notice, would absolve the issuer of its failure to give notice. The virtue of the preclusion obligation adopted in this section is that it forecloses litigation about reliance and detriment.

Even though issuers typically give notice of the discrepancy of tardy presentation when presentation is made after the expiration of a credit, they are not required to give that notice and the section permits them to raise late presentation as a defect despite their failure to give that notice.

4. To act within a reasonable time, the issuer must normally give notice without delay after the examining party makes its decision. If the examiner decides to dishonor on the first day, it would be obliged to notify the beneficiary shortly thereafter, perhaps on the same business day. This rule accepts the reasoning in cases such as *Datapoint Corp. v. M & I Bank*, 665 F.Supp. 722 (W.D.Wis.1987) and *Esso Petroleum Canada, Div. of Imperial Oil, Ltd. v. Security Pacific Bank*, 710 F.Supp. 275 (D.Or.1989).

The section deprives the examining party of the right simply to sit on a presentation that is made within seven days of expiration. The section requires the examiner to examine the documents and make a decision and, having made a decision to dishonor, to communicate promptly with the presenter. Nevertheless, a beneficiary who presents documents shortly before the expiration of a letter of credit runs the risk that it will never have the opportunity to cure any discrepancies.

5. Confirmers, other nominated persons, and collecting banks acting for beneficiaries can be presenters and, when so, are entitled to the notice provided in subsection (b). Even nominated persons who have honored or given value against an earlier presentation of the beneficiary and are themselves seeking reimbursement or honor need notice of discrepancies in the hope that they may be able to procure complying documents. The issuer has the obligations imposed by this section whether the issuer's performance is characterized as "reimbursement" of a nominated person or as "honor."

6. In many cases a letter of credit authorizes presentation by the beneficiary to someone other than the issuer. Sometimes that person is identified as a "payor" or "paying bank," or as an "acceptor" or "accepting bank," in other cases as a "negotiating bank," and in other cases there will be no specific designation. The section does not impose any duties on a person other than the issuer or confirmer, however a nominated person or other person may have liability under this article or at common law if it fails to perform an express or implied agreement with the beneficiary.

7. The issuer's obligation to honor runs not only to the beneficiary but also to the applicant. It is possible that an applicant who has made a favorable contract with the beneficiary will be injured by the issuer's wrongful dishonor. Except to the extent that the contract between the issuer and the applicant limits that liability, the issuer will have liability to the applicant for wrongful dishonor under Section 5-111 as a matter of

contract law. A good faith extension of the time in Section 5-108(b) by agreement between the issuer and beneficiary binds the applicant even if the applicant is not consulted or does not consent to the extension.

The issuer's obligation to dishonor when there is no apparent compliance with the letter of credit runs only to the applicant. No other party to the transaction can complain if the applicant waives compliance with terms or conditions of the letter of credit or agrees to a less stringent standard for compliance than that supplied by this article. Except as otherwise agreed with the applicant, an issuer may dishonor a noncomplying presentation despite an applicant's waiver.

Waiver of discrepancies by an issuer or an applicant in one or more presentations does not waive similar discrepancies in a future presentation. Neither the issuer nor the beneficiary can reasonably rely upon honor over past waivers as a basis for concluding that a future defective presentation will justify honor. The reasoning of *Courtaulds of North America Inc. v. North Carolina Nat. Bank*, 528 F.2d 802 (4th Cir.1975) is accepted and that expressed in *Schweibish v. Pontchartrain State Bank*, 389 So.2d 731 (La.App.1980) and *Titanium Metals Corp. v. Space Metals, Inc.*, 529 P.2d 431 (Utah 1974) is rejected.

8. The standard practice referred to in subsection (e) includes (i) international practice set forth in or referenced by the Uniform Customs and Practice, (ii) other practice rules published by associations of financial institutions, and (iii) local and regional practice. It is possible that standard practice will vary from one place to another. Where there are conflicting practices, the parties should indicate which practice governs their rights. A practice may be overridden by agreement or course of dealing. See Section 1-205(4).

9. The responsibility of the issuer under a letter of credit is to examine documents and to make a prompt decision to honor or dishonor based upon that examination. Nondocumentary conditions have no place in this regime and are better accommodated under contract or suretyship law and practice. In requiring that nondocumentary conditions in letters of credit be ignored as surplusage, Article 5 remains aligned with the UCP (see UCP 500 Article 13c), approves cases like *Pringle-Associated Mortgage Corp. v. Southern National Bank*, 571 F.2d 871, 874 (5th Cir.1978), and rejects the reasoning in cases such as *Sherwood & Roberts, Inc. v. First Security Bank*, 682 P.2d 149 (Mont. 1984).

Subsection (g) recognizes that letters of credit sometimes contain nondocumentary terms or conditions. Conditions such as a term prohibiting "shipment on vessels more than 15 years old," are to be disregarded and treated as surplusage. Similarly, a requirement that there be an award by a "duly appointed arbitrator" would not require the issuer to determine whether the arbitrator had been "duly appointed." Likewise a term in a standby letter of credit that provided for differing forms of certification depending upon the particular type of default does not oblige the issuer independently to determine which kind of default has occurred. These conditions must be disregarded by the issuer. Where the nondocumentary conditions are central and fundamental to the issuer's obligation (as for example a condition that would require the issuer to determine in fact whether the beneficiary had performed the underlying contract or whether the applicant had defaulted) their inclusion may remove the undertaking from the scope of Article 5 entirely. See Section 5-102(a)(10) and Comment 6 to Section 5-102.

Subsection (g) would not permit the beneficiary or the issuer to disregard terms in the letter of credit such as place, time, and mode of presentation. The rule in subsection (g) is intended to prevent an issuer from deciding or even investigating extrinsic facts, but not from consulting the clock, the calendar, the relevant law and practice, or its own general knowledge of documentation or transactions of the type underlying a particular letter of credit.

Even though nondocumentary conditions must be disregarded in determining compliance of a presentation (and thus in determining the issuer's duty to the beneficiary), an issuer that has promised its applicant that it will honor only on the occurrence of those nondocumentary conditions may have liability to its applicant for disregarding the conditions.

10. Subsection (f) condones an issuer's ignorance of "any usage of a particular trade"; that trade is the trade of the applicant, beneficiary, or others who may be involved in the underlying transaction. The issuer is expected to know usage that is commonly encountered in the course of document examination. For example, an issuer should know the common usage with respect to documents in the maritime shipping trade but would not be expected to understand synonyms used in a particular trade for product descriptions appearing in a letter of credit or an invoice.

11. Where the issuer's performance is the delivery of an item of value other than money, the applicant's reimbursement obligation would be to make the "item of value" available to the issuer.

12. An issuer is entitled to reimbursement from the applicant after honor of a forged or fraudulent drawing if honor was permitted under Section 5-109(a).

13. The last clause of Section 5-108(i)(5) deals with a special case in which the fraud is not committed by the beneficiary, but is committed by a stranger to the transaction who forges the beneficiary's signature. If the issuer pays against documents on which a required signature of the beneficiary is forged, it remains liable to the true beneficiary.

§ 5-109 Fraud and Forgery.

(a) If a presentation is made that appears on its face strictly to comply with the terms and conditions of the letter of credit, but a required document is forged or materially fraudulent, or honor of the presentation would facilitate a material fraud by the beneficiary on the issuer or applicant:

> (1) the issuer shall honor the presentation, if honor is demanded by (i) a nominated person who has given value in good faith and without notice of forgery or material fraud, (ii) a confirmer who has honored its confirmation in good faith, (iii) a holder in due course of a draft drawn under the letter of credit which was taken after acceptance by the issuer or nominated person, or (iv) an assignee of the issuer's or nominated person's deferred obligation that was taken for value and without notice of forgery or material fraud after the obligation was incurred by the issuer or nominated person; and

> (2) the issuer, acting in good faith, may honor or dishonor the presentation in any other case.

(b) If an applicant claims that a required document is forged or materially fraudulent or that honor of the presentation would facilitate a material fraud by the beneficiary on the issuer or applicant, a court of competent jurisdiction may temporarily or permanently enjoin the issuer from honoring a presentation or grant similar relief against the issuer or other persons only if the court finds that:

> (1) the relief is not prohibited under the law applicable to an accepted draft or deferred obligation incurred by the issuer;

> (2) a beneficiary, issuer, or nominated person who may be adversely affected is adequately protected against loss that it may suffer because the relief is granted;

> (3) all of the conditions to entitle a person to the relief under the law of this State have been met; and

> (4) on the basis of the information submitted to the court, the applicant is more likely than not to succeed under its claim of forgery or material fraud and the person demanding honor does not qualify for protection under subsection (a)(1).

OFFICIAL COMMENT

1. This recodification makes clear that fraud must be found either in the documents or must have been committed by the beneficiary on the issuer or applicant. See *Cromwell v. Commerce & Energy Bank*, 464 So.2d 721 (La.1985).

Secondly, it makes clear that fraud must be "material." Necessarily courts must decide the breadth and width of "materiality." The use of the word requires that the fraudulent aspect of a document be material to a purchaser of that document or that the fraudulent act be significant to the participants in the underlying transaction. Assume, for example, that the beneficiary has a contract to deliver 1,000 barrels of salad oil. Knowing that it has delivered only 998, the beneficiary nevertheless submits an invoice showing 1,000 barrels. If two barrels in a 1,000 barrel shipment would be an insubstantial and immaterial breach of the underlying contract, the beneficiary's act, though possibly fraudulent, is not materially so and would not justify an injunction. Conversely, the knowing submission of those invoices upon delivery of only five barrels would be materially fraudulent. The courts must examine the underlying transaction when there is an allegation of material fraud, for only by examining that transaction can one determine whether a document is fraudulent or the beneficiary has committed fraud and, if so, whether the fraud was material.

Material fraud by the beneficiary occurs only when the beneficiary has no colorable right to expect honor and where there is no basis in fact to support such a right to honor. The section indorses articulations such as those stated in *Intraworld Indus. v. Girard Trust Bank*, 336 A.2d 316 (Pa.1975), *Roman Ceramics Corp. v. People's Nat. Bank*, 714 F.2d 1207 (3d Cir.1983), and similar decisions and embraces certain decisions under Section 5-114 that relied upon the phrase "fraud in the transaction." Some of these decisions have been summarized as follows in

Ground Air Transfer, Inc. v. Westate's Airlines, Inc., 899 F.2d 1269, 1272-73 (1st Cir.1990):

We have said throughout that courts may not "normally" issue an injunction because of an important exception to the general "no injunction" rule. The exception, as we also explained in Itek, 730 F.2d at 24-25, concerns "fraud" so serious as to make it obviously pointless and unjust to permit the beneficiary to obtain the money. Where the circumstances "plainly" show that the underlying contract forbids the beneficiary to call a letter of credit, *Itek*, 730 F.2d at 24; where they show that the contract deprives the beneficiary of even a "colorable" right to do so, id., at 25; where the contract and circumstances reveal that the beneficiary's demand for payment has "absolutely no basis in fact," id.; see *Dynamics Corp. of America*, 356 F.Supp. at 999; where the beneficiary's conduct has "so vitiated the entire transaction that the legitimate purposes of the independence of the issuer's obligation would no longer be served," *Itek*, 730 F.2d at 25 (quoting *Roman Ceramics Corp. v. Peoples National Bank*, 714 F.2d 1207, 1212 n.12, 1215 (3d Cir.1983) (quoting *Intraworld Indus.*, 336 A.2d at 324-25)); then a court may enjoin payment.

2. Subsection (a)(2) makes clear that the issuer may honor in the face of the applicant's claim of fraud. The subsection also makes clear what was not stated in former Section 5-114, that the issuer may dishonor and defend that dishonor by showing fraud or forgery of the kind stated in subsection (a). Because issuers may be liable for wrongful dishonor if they are unable to prove forgery or material fraud, presumably most issuers will choose to honor despite applicant's

claims of fraud or forgery unless the applicant procures an injunction. Merely because the issuer has a right to dishonor and to defend that dishonor by showing forgery or material fraud does not mean it has a duty to the applicant to dishonor. The applicant's normal recourse is to procure an injunction, if the applicant is unable to procure an injunction, it will have a claim against the issuer only in the rare case in which it can show that the issuer did not honor in good faith.

3. Whether a beneficiary can commit fraud by presenting a draft under a clean letter of credit (one calling only for a draft and no other documents) has been much debated. Under the current formulation it would be possible but difficult for there to be fraud in such a presentation. If the applicant were able to show that the beneficiary were committing material fraud on the applicant in the underlying transaction, then payment would facilitate a material fraud by the beneficiary on the applicant and honor could be enjoined. The courts should be skeptical of claims of fraud by one who has signed a "suicide" or clean credit and thus granted a beneficiary the right to draw by mere presentation of a draft.

4. The standard for injunctive relief is high, and the burden remains on the applicant to show, by evidence and not by mere allegation, that such relief is warranted. Some courts have enjoined payments on letters of credit on insufficient showing by the applicant. For example, in *Griffin Cos. v. First Nat. Bank*, 374 N.W.2d 768 (Minn.App.1985), the court enjoined payment under a standby letter of credit, basing its decision on plaintiff's allegation, rather than competent evidence, of fraud.

There are at least two ways to prohibit injunctions against honor under this section after acceptance of a draft by the issuer. First is to define honor (see Section 5-102(a)(8)) in the particular letter of credit to occur upon acceptance and without regard to later payment of the acceptance. Second is explicitly to agree that the applicant has no right to an injunction after acceptance—whether or not the acceptance constitutes honor.

5. Although the statute deals principally with injunctions against honor, it also cautions against granting "similar relief" and the same principles apply when the applicant or issuer attempts to achieve the same legal outcome by injunction against presentation (see *Ground Air Transfer, Inc. v. Westates Airlines, Inc.*, 899 F.2d 1269 (1st Cir.1990)), interpleader, declaratory judgment, or attachment. These attempts should face the same obstacles that face efforts to enjoin the issuer from paying. Expanded use of any of these devices could threaten the independence principle just as much as injunctions against honor. For that reason courts should have the same hostility to them and place the same restrictions on their use as would be applied to injunctions against honor. Courts should not allow the "sacred cow of equity to trample the tender vines of letter of credit law."

6. Section 5-109(a)(1) also protects specified third parties against the risk of fraud. By issuing a letter of credit that nominates a person to negotiate or pay, the issuer (ultimately the applicant) induces that nominated person to give value and thereby assumes the risk that a draft drawn under the letter of credit will be transferred to one with a status like that of a holder in due course who deserves to be protected against a fraud defense.

7. The "loss" to be protected against—by bond or otherwise under subsection (b)(2)—includes incidental damages. Among those are legal fees that might be incurred by the beneficiary or issuer in defending against an injunction action.

§ 5-110 Warranties.

(a) If its presentation is honored, the beneficiary warrants:

(1) to the issuer, any other person to whom presentation is made, and the applicant that there is no fraud or forgery of the kind described in Section 5-109(a); and

(2) to the applicant that the drawing does not violate any agreement between the applicant and beneficiary or any other agreement intended by them to be augmented by the letter of credit.

(b) The warranties in subsection (a) are in addition to warranties arising under Articles 3, 4, 7, and 8 because of the presentation or transfer of documents covered by any of those articles.

OFFICIAL COMMENT

1. Since the warranties in subsection (a) are not given unless a letter of credit has been honored, no breach of warranty under this subsection can be a defense to dishonor by the issuer. Any defense must be based on Section 5-108 or 5-109 and not on this section. Also, breach of the warranties by the beneficiary in subsection (a) cannot excuse the applicant's duty to reimburse.

2. The warranty in Section 5-110(a)(2) assumes that payment under the letter of credit is final. It does not run to the issuer, only to the applicant. In most cases the applicant will have a direct cause of action for breach of the underlying contract. This warranty has primary application in standby letters of credit or other circumstances where the applicant is not a party to an underlying contract with the beneficiary. It is not a warranty that the statements made on the presentation of the documents presented are truthful nor is it a warranty that the documents strictly comply under Section 5-108(a). It is a warranty that the beneficiary has performed all the acts expressly and implicitly necessary under any underlying agreement to entitle the beneficiary to honor. If, for example, an underlying sales contract authorized the beneficiary to draw only upon "due

performance" and the beneficiary drew even though it had breached the underlying contract by delivering defective goods, honor of its draw would break the warranty. By the same token, if the underlying contract authorized the beneficiary to draw only upon actual default or upon its or a third party's determination of default by the applicant and if the beneficiary drew in violation of its authorization, then upon honor of its draw the warranty would be breached. In many cases, therefore, the documents presented to the issuer will contain inaccurate statements (concerning the goods delivered or concerning default or other matters), but the breach of warranty arises not because the statements are untrue but because the beneficiary's drawing violated its express or implied obligations in the underlying transaction.

3. The damages for breach of warranty are not specified in Section 5-111. Courts may find damage analogies in Section 2-714 in Article 2 and in warranty decisions under Articles 3 and 4.

Unlike wrongful dishonor cases—where the damages usually equal the amount of the draw—the damages for breach of warranty will often be much less than the amount of the draw, sometimes zero. Assume a seller entitled to draw only on proper performance of its sales contract. Assume it breaches the sales contract in a way that gives the buyer a right to damages but no right to reject. The applicant's damages for breach of the warranty in subsection (a)(2) are limited to the damages it could recover for breach of the contract of sale. Alternatively assume an underlying agreement that authorizes a beneficiary to draw only the "amount in default." Assume a default of $200,000 and a draw of $500,000. The damages for breach of warranty would be no more than $300,000.

§ 5-111 Remedies.

(a) If an issuer wrongfully dishonors or repudiates its obligation to pay money under a letter of credit before presentation, the beneficiary, successor, or nominated person presenting on its own behalf may recover from the issuer the amount that is the subject of the dishonor or repudiation. If the issuer's obligation under the letter of credit is not for the payment of money, the claimant may obtain specific performance or, at the claimant's election, recover an amount equal to the value of performance from the issuer. In either case, the claimant may also recover incidental but not consequential damages. The claimant is not obligated to take action to avoid damages that might be due from the issuer under this subsection. If, although not obligated to do so, the claimant avoids damages, the claimant's recovery from the issuer must be reduced by the amount of damages avoided. The issuer has the burden of proving the amount of damages avoided. In the case of repudiation the claimant need not present any document.

(b) If an issuer wrongfully dishonors a draft or demand presented under a letter of credit or honors a draft or demand in breach of its obligation to the applicant, the applicant may recover damages resulting from the breach, including incidental but not consequential damages, less any amount saved as a result of the breach.

(c) If an adviser or nominated person other than a confirmer breaches an obligation under this article or an issuer breaches an obligation not covered in subsection (a) or (b), a person to whom the obligation is owed may recover damages resulting from the breach, including incidental but not consequential damages, less any amount saved as a result of the breach. To the extent of the confirmation, a confirmer has the liability of an issuer specified in this subsection and subsections (a) and (b).

(d) An issuer, nominated person, or adviser who is found liable under subsection (a), (b), or (c) shall pay interest on the amount owed thereunder from the date of wrongful dishonor or other appropriate date.

(e) Reasonable attorney's fees and other expenses of litigation must be awarded to the prevailing party in an action in which a remedy is sought under this article.

(f) Damages that would otherwise be payable by a party for breach of an obligation under this article may be liquidated by agreement or undertaking, but only in an amount or by a formula that is reasonable in light of the harm anticipated.

OFFICIAL COMMENT

1. The right to specific performance is new. The express limitation on the duty of the beneficiary to mitigate damages adopts the position of certain courts and commentators. Because the letter of credit depends upon speed and certainty of payment, it is important that the issuer not be given an incentive to dishonor. The issuer might have an incentive to dishonor if it could rely on the burden of mitigation falling on the beneficiary, (to sell goods and sue only for the difference between the price of the goods sold and the amount due under the letter of credit). Under the scheme contemplated by Section 5-111(a), the beneficiary would present the documents to the issuer. If the issuer wrongfully dishonored, the beneficiary would have no further duty to the issuer with respect to the goods covered by documents that the issuer dishonored and returned. The issuer thus takes the risk that the beneficiary will let the goods rot or be destroyed. Of course the beneficiary may have a duty of mitigation to the applicant arising from the underlying agreement, but the issuer would not have the right to assert that duty by way of defense or setoff. See Section 5-117(d). If the beneficiary sells the goods covered by dishonored documents or if the beneficiary sells a draft after acceptance but before dishonor by the issuer, the net amount so gained should be subtracted from the amount of the beneficiary's damages—at least where the damage claim against the issuer equals or exceeds the damage suffered by the beneficiary. If, on the other hand, the beneficiary suffers damages in an underlying transaction in an amount that exceeds the amount of the wrongfully

dishonored demand (e.g., where the letter of credit does not cover 100 percent of the underlying obligation), the damages avoided should not necessarily be deducted from the beneficiary's claim against the issuer. In such a case, the damages would be the lesser of (i) the amount recoverable in the absence of mitigation (that is, the amount that is subject to the dishonor or repudiation plus any incidental damages) and (ii) the damages remaining after deduction for the amount of damages actually avoided.

A beneficiary need not present documents as a condition of suit for anticipatory repudiation, but if a beneficiary could never have obtained documents necessary for a presentation conforming to the letter of credit, the beneficiary cannot recover for anticipatory repudiation of the letter of credit. *Doelger v. Battery Park Bank*, 201 A.D. 515, 194 N.Y.S. 582 (1922) and *Decor by Nikkei Int'l, Inc. v. Federal Republic of Nigeria*, 497 F.Supp. 893 (S.D.N.Y.1980), *aff'd*, 647 F.2d 300 (2d Cir.1981), *cert. denied*, 454 U.S. 1148 (1982). The last sentence of subsection (c) does not expand the liability of a confirmer to persons to whom the confirmer would not otherwise be liable under Section 5-107.

Almost all letters of credit, including those that call for an acceptance, are "obligations to pay money" as that term is used in Section 5-111(a).

2. What damages "result" from improper honor is for the courts to decide. Even though an issuer pays a beneficiary in violation of Section

5-108(a) or of its contract with the applicant, it may have no liability to an applicant. If the underlying contract has been fully performed, the applicant may not have been damaged by the issuer's breach. Such a case would occur when A contracts for goods at $100 per ton, but, upon delivery, the market value of conforming goods has decreased to $25 per ton. If the issuer pays over discrepancies, there should be no recovery by A for the price differential if the issuer's breach did not alter the applicant's obligation under the underlying contract, i.e., to pay $100 per ton for goods now worth $25 per ton. On the other hand, if the applicant intends to resell the goods and must itself satisfy the strict compliance requirements under a second letter of credit in connection with its sale, the applicant may be damaged by the issuer's payment despite discrepancies because the applicant itself may then be unable to procure honor on the letter of credit where it is the beneficiary, and may be unable to mitigate its damages by enforcing its rights against others in the underlying transaction. Note that an issuer found liable to its applicant may have recourse under Section 5-117 by subrogation to the applicant's claim against the beneficiary or other persons.

One who inaccurately advises a letter of credit breaches its obligation to the beneficiary, but may cause no damage. If the beneficiary knows the terms of the letter of credit and understands the advice to be inaccurate, the beneficiary will have suffered no damage as a result of the adviser's breach.

3. Since the confirmer has the rights and duties of an issuer, in general it has an issuer's liability, see subsection (c). The confirmer is usually a confirming bank. A confirming bank often also plays the role of an adviser. If it breaks its obligation to the beneficiary, the confirming bank may have liability as an issuer or, depending upon the obligation that was broken, as an adviser. For example, a wrongful dishonor would give it liability as an issuer under Section 5-111(a). On the other hand a confirming bank that broke its obligation to advise the credit but did not commit wrongful dishonor would be treated under Section 5-111(c).

4. Consequential damages for breach of obligations under this article are excluded in the belief that these damages can best be avoided by the beneficiary or the applicant and out of the fear that imposing consequential damages on issuers would raise the cost of the letter of credit to a level that might render it uneconomic. *A fortiori* punitive and exemplary damages are excluded, however, this section does not bar recovery of consequential or even punitive damages for breach of statutory or common law duties arising outside of this article.

5. The section does not specify a rate of interest. It leaves the setting of the rate to the court. It would be appropriate for a court to use the rate that would normally apply in that court in other situations where interest is imposed by law.

6. The court must award attorney's fees to the prevailing party, whether that party is an applicant, a beneficiary, an issuer, a nominated person, or adviser. Since the issuer may be entitled to recover its legal fees and costs from the applicant under the reimbursement agreement, allowing the issuer to recover those fees from a losing beneficiary may also protect the applicant against undeserved losses. The party entitled to attorneys' fees has been described as the "prevailing party." Sometimes it will be unclear which party "prevailed," for example, where there are multiple issues and one party wins on some and the other party wins on others. Determining which is the prevailing party is in the discretion of the court. Subsection (e) authorizes attorney's fees in all actions where a remedy is sought "under this article." It applies even when the remedy might be an injunction under Section 5-109 or when the claimed remedy is otherwise outside of Section 5-111. Neither an issuer nor a confirmer should be treated as a "losing" party when an injunction is granted to the applicant over the objection of the issuer or confirmer;

accordingly neither should be liable for fees and expenses in that case.

"Expenses of litigation" is intended to be broader than "costs." For example, expense of litigation would include travel expenses of witnesses, fees for expert witnesses, and expenses associated with taking depositions.

7. For the purposes of Section 5-111(f) "harm anticipated" must be anticipated at the time when the agreement that includes the liquidated damage clause is executed or at the time when the undertaking that includes the clause is issued. See Section 2A-504.

§ 5-112 Transfer of Letter of Credit.

(a) Except as otherwise provided in Section 5-113, unless a letter of credit provides that it is transferable, the right of a beneficiary to draw or otherwise demand performance under a letter of credit may not be transferred.

(b) Even if a letter of credit provides that it is transferable, the issuer may refuse to recognize or carry out a transfer if:

(1) the transfer would violate applicable law; or

(2) the transferor or transferee has failed to comply with any requirement stated in the letter of credit or any other requirement relating to transfer imposed by the issuer which is within the standard practice referred to in Section 5-108(e) or is otherwise reasonable under the circumstances.

OFFICIAL COMMENT

1. In order to protect the applicant's reliance on the designated beneficiary, letter of credit law traditionally has forbidden the beneficiary to convey to third parties its right to draw or demand payment under the letter of credit. Subsection (a) codifies that rule. The term "transfer" refers to the beneficiary's conveyance of that right. Absent incorporation of the UCP (which make elaborate provision for partial transfer of a commercial letter of credit) or similar trade practice and absent other express indication in the letter of credit that the term is used to mean something else, a term in the letter of credit indicating that the beneficiary has the right to transfer should be taken to mean that the beneficiary may convey to a third party its right to draw or demand payment.

Even in that case, the issuer or other person controlling the transfer may make the beneficiary's right to transfer subject to conditions, such as timely notification, payment of a fee, delivery of the letter of credit to the issuer or other person controlling the transfer, or execution of appropriate forms to document the transfer. A nominated person who is not a confirmer has no obligation to recognize a transfer.

The power to establish "requirements" does not include the right absolutely to refuse to recognize transfers under a transferable letter of credit. An issuer who wishes to retain the right to deny all transfers should not issue transferable letters of credit or should incorporate the UCP. By stating its requirements in the letter of credit an issuer may impose any requirement without regard to its conformity to practice or reasonableness. Transfer requirements of issuers and nominated persons must be made known to potential transferors and transferees to enable those parties to comply with the requirements. A common method of making such requirements known is to use a form that indicates the information that must be provided and the instructions that must be given to enable the issuer or nominated person to comply with a request to transfer.

2. The issuance of a transferable letter of credit with the concurrence of the applicant is ipso facto an agreement by the issuer and applicant to permit a beneficiary to transfer its drawing right and permit a nominated person to recognize and carry out that transfer without further notice to them. In international commerce, transferable letters of credit are often issued under circumstances in which a nominated person or adviser is expected to facilitate the transfer from the original beneficiary to a transferee and to deal with that transferee. In those circumstances it is the responsibility of the nominated person or adviser to establish procedures satisfactory to protect itself against double presentation or dispute about the right to draw under the letter of credit. Commonly such a person will control the transfer by requiring that the original letter of credit be given to it or by causing a paper copy marked as an original to be issued where the original letter of credit was electronic. By keeping possession of the original letter of credit the nominated person or adviser can minimize or entirely exclude the possibility that the original beneficiary could properly procure payment from another bank. If the letter of credit requires presentation of the original letter of credit itself, no other payment could be procured. In addition to imposing whatever requirements it considers appropriate to protect itself against double payment the person that is facilitating the transfer has a right to charge an appropriate fee for its activity.

"Transfer" of a letter of credit should be distinguished from "assignment of proceeds." The former is analogous to a novation or a substitution of beneficiaries. It contemplates not merely payment to but also performance by the transferee. For example, under the typical terms of transfer for a commercial letter of credit, a transferee could comply with a letter of credit transferred to it by signing and presenting its own draft and invoice. An assignee of proceeds, on the other hand, is wholly dependent on the presentation of a draft and invoice signed by the beneficiary.

By agreeing to the issuance of a transferable letter of credit, which is not qualified or limited, the applicant may lose control over the identity of the person whose performance will earn payment under the letter of credit.

§ 5-113 Transfer by Operation of Law.

(a) A successor of a beneficiary may consent to amendments, sign and present documents, and receive payment or other items of value in the name of the beneficiary without disclosing its status as a successor.

(b) A successor of a beneficiary may consent to amendments, sign and present documents, and receive payment or other items of value in its own name as the disclosed successor of the beneficiary. Except as otherwise provided in subsection (e), an issuer shall recognize a disclosed successor of a beneficiary as beneficiary in full substitution for its predecessor upon compliance with the requirements for recognition by the issuer of a transfer of drawing rights by operation of law under the standard practice referred to in Section 5-108(e) or, in the absence of such a practice, compliance with other reasonable procedures sufficient to protect the issuer.

(c) An issuer is not obliged to determine whether a purported successor is a successor of a beneficiary or whether the signature of a purported successor is genuine or authorized.

(d) Honor of a purported successor's apparently complying presentation under subsection (a) or (b) has the consequences specified in Section 5-108(i) even if the purported successor is not the successor of a beneficiary. Documents signed in the name of the beneficiary or of a disclosed successor by a person who is neither the beneficiary nor the successor of the beneficiary are forged documents for the purposes of Section 5-109.

(e) An issuer whose rights of reimbursement are not covered by subsection (d) or substantially similar law and any confirmer or nominated person may decline to recognize a presentation under subsection (b).

(f) A beneficiary whose name is changed after the issuance of a letter of credit has the same rights and obligations as a successor of a beneficiary under this section.

OFFICIAL COMMENT

This section affirms the result in *Pastor v. Nat. Republic Bank of Chicago*, 76 Ill.2d 139, 390 N.E.2d 894 (Ill.1979) and *Federal Deposit Insurance Co. v. Bank of Boulder*, 911 F.2d 1466 (10th Cir.1990).

An issuer's requirements for recognition of a successor's status might include presentation of a certificate of merger, a court order appointing a bankruptcy trustee or receiver, a certificate of appointment as bankruptcy trustee, or the like.

The issuer is entitled to rely upon such documents which on their face demonstrate that presentation is made by a successor of a beneficiary. It is not obliged to make an independent investigation to determine the fact of succession.

§ 5-114 Assignment of Proceeds.

(a) In this section, "proceeds of a letter of credit" means the cash, check, accepted draft, or other item of value paid or delivered upon honor or giving of value by the issuer or any nominated person under the letter of credit. The term does not include a beneficiary's drawing rights or documents presented by the beneficiary.

(b) A beneficiary may assign its right to part or all of the proceeds of a letter of credit. The beneficiary may do so before presentation as a present assignment of its right to receive proceeds contingent upon its compliance with the terms and conditions of the letter of credit.

(c) An issuer or nominated person need not recognize an assignment of proceeds of a letter of credit until it consents to the assignment.

(d) An issuer or nominated person has no obligation to give or withhold its consent to an assignment of proceeds of a letter of credit, but consent may not be unreasonably withheld if the assignee possesses and exhibits the letter of credit and presentation of the letter of credit is a condition to honor.

(e) Rights of a transferee beneficiary or nominated person are independent of the beneficiary's assignment of the proceeds of a letter of credit and are superior to the assignee's right to the proceeds.

(f) Neither the rights recognized by this section between an assignee and an issuer, transferee beneficiary, or nominated person nor the issuer's or nominated person's payment of proceeds to an assignee or a third person affect the rights between the assignee and any person other than the issuer, transferee beneficiary, or nominated person. The mode of creating and perfecting a security interest in or granting an assignment of a beneficiary's rights to proceeds is governed by Article 9 or other law. Against persons other than the issuer, transferee beneficiary, or nominated person, the rights and obligations arising upon the creation of a security interest or other assignment of a beneficiary's right to proceeds and its perfection are governed by Article 9 or other law.

OFFICIAL COMMENT

1. Subsection (b) expressly validates the beneficiary's present assignment of letter of credit proceeds if made after the credit is established but before the proceeds are realized. This section adopts the prevailing usage—"assignment of proceeds"—to an assignee. That terminology carries with it no implication, however, that an assignee acquires no interest until the proceeds are paid by the issuer. For example, an "assignment of the right to proceeds" of a letter of credit for purposes of security that meets the requirements of Section 9-203(1) would constitute the present creation of a security interest in that right. This security interest can be perfected by

possession (Section 9-305) if the letter of credit is in written form. Although subsection (a) explains the meaning of "'proceeds' of a letter of credit," it should be emphasized that those proceeds also may be Article 9 proceeds of other collateral. For example, if a seller of inventory receives a letter of credit to support the account that arises upon the sale, payments made under the letter of credit are Article 9 proceeds of the inventory, account, and any document of title covering the inventory. Thus, the secured party who had a perfected security interest in that inventory, account, or document has a perfected security interest in the proceeds collected under the letter of credit, so long as they are identifiable cash proceeds (Section 9-306(2), (3)). This perfection is continuous, regardless of whether the secured party perfected a security interest in the right to letter of credit proceeds.

2. An assignee's rights to enforce an assignment of proceeds against an issuer and the priority of the assignee's rights against a nominated person or transferee beneficiary are governed by Article 5. Those rights and that priority are stated in subsections (c), (d), and (e). Note also that Section 4-210 gives first priority to a collecting bank that has given value for a documentary draft.

3. By requiring that an issuer or nominated person consent to the assignment of proceeds of a letter of credit, subsections (c) and (d) follow more closely recognized national and international letter of credit practices than did prior law. In most circumstances, it has always been advisable for the assignee to obtain the consent of the issuer in order better to safeguard its right to the proceeds. When notice of an assignment has been received, issuers normally have required signatures on a consent form. This practice is reflected in the revision. By unconditionally consenting to such an assignment, the issuer or nominated person becomes bound, subject to the rights of the superior parties specified in subsection (e), to pay to the assignee the assigned letter of credit proceeds that the issuer or nominated person would otherwise pay to the beneficiary or another assignee.

Where the letter of credit must be presented as a condition to honor and the assignee holds and exhibits the letter of credit to the issuer or nominated person, the risk to the issuer or nominated person of having to pay twice is minimized. In such a situation, subsection (d) provides that the issuer or nominated person may not unreasonably withhold its consent to the assignment.

§ 5-115 Statute of Limitations.

An action to enforce a right or obligation arising under this article must be commenced within one year after the expiration date of the relevant letter of credit or one year after the [claim for relief] [cause of action] accrues, whichever occurs later. A [claim for relief] [cause of action] accrues when the breach occurs, regardless of the aggrieved party's lack of knowledge of the breach.

OFFICIAL COMMENT

1. This section is based upon Sections 4-111 and 2-725(2).

2. This section applies to all claims for which there are remedies under Section 5-111 and to other claims made under this article, such as claims for breach of warranty under Section 5-110. Because it covers all claims under Section 5-111, the statute of limitations applies not only to wrongful dishonor claims against the issuer but also to claims between the issuer and the applicant arising from the reimbursement agreement. These might be for reimbursement (issuer v. applicant) or for breach of the reimbursement contract by wrongful honor (applicant v. issuer).

3. The statute of limitations, like the rest of the statute, applies only to a letter of credit issued on or after the effective date and only to transactions, events, obligations, or duties arising out of or associated with such a letter. If a letter of credit was issued before the effective date and an obligation on that letter of credit was breached after the effective date, the complaining party could bring its suit within the time that would have been permitted prior to the adoption of Section 5-115 and would not be limited by the terms of Section 5-115.

§ 5-116 Choice of Law and Forum.

(a) The liability of an issuer, nominated person, or adviser for action or omission is governed by the law of the jurisdiction chosen by an agreement in the form of a record signed or otherwise authenticated by the affected parties in the manner provided in Section 5-104 or by a provision in the person's letter of credit, confirmation, or other undertaking. The jurisdiction whose law is chosen need not bear any relation to the transaction.

(b) Unless subsection (a) applies, the liability of an issuer, nominated person, or adviser for action or omission is governed by the law of the jurisdiction in which the person is located. The person is considered to be located at the address indicated in the person's undertaking. If more than one address is indicated, the person is considered to be located at the address from which the person's undertaking was issued. For the purpose of jurisdiction, choice of law, and recognition of interbranch letters of credit, but not enforcement of a judgment, all branches of a bank are considered separate juridical entities and a bank is considered to be located at the place where its relevant branch is considered to be located under this subsection.

(c) Except as otherwise provided in this subsection, the liability of an issuer, nominated person, or adviser is governed by any rules of custom or practice, such as the Uniform Customs and Practice for Documentary Credits, to which the letter of credit, confirmation, or other undertaking is expressly made subject. If (i) this article would govern the liability of an issuer, nominated person, or adviser under subsection (a) or (b), (ii) the relevant undertaking incorporates rules of custom or practice, and (iii) there is conflict between this article and those rules as applied to that undertaking, those rules govern except to the extent of any conflict with the nonvariable provisions specified in Section 5-103(c).

(d) If there is conflict between this article and Article 3, 4, 4A, or 9, this article governs.

(e) The forum for settling disputes arising out of an undertaking within this article may be chosen in the manner and with the binding effect that governing law may be chosen in accordance with subsection (a).

OFFICIAL COMMENT

1. Although it would be possible for the parties to agree otherwise, the law normally chosen by agreement under subsection (a) and that provided in the absence of agreement under subsection (b) is the substantive law of a particular jurisdiction not including the choice of law principles of that jurisdiction. Thus, two parties, an issuer and an applicant, both located in Oklahoma might choose the law of New York. Unless they agree otherwise, the section anticipates that they wish the substantive law of New York to apply to their transaction and they do not intend that a New York choice of law principle might direct a court to Oklahoma law. By the same token, the liability of an issuer located in New York is governed by New York substantive law—in the absence of agreement—even in circumstances in which

587

choice of law principles found in the common law of New York might direct one to the law of another State. Subsection (b) states the relevant choice of law principles and it should not be subordinated to some other choice of law rule. Within the States of the United States renvoi will not be a problem once every jurisdiction has enacted Section 5-116 because every jurisdiction will then have the same choice of law rule and in a particular case all choice of law rules will point to the same substantive law.

Subsection (b) does not state a choice of law rule for the "liability of an applicant." However, subsection (b) does state a choice of law rule for the liability of an issuer, nominated person, or adviser, and since some of the issues in suits by applicants against those persons involve the "liability of an issuer, nominated person, or adviser," subsection (b) states the choice of law rule for those issues. Because an issuer may have liability to a confirmer both as an issuer (Section 5-108(a), Comment 5 to Section 5-108) and as an applicant (Section 5-107(a), Comment 1 to Section 5-107, Section 5-108(i)), subsection (b) may state the choice of law rule for some but not all of the issuer's liability in a suit by a confirmer.

2. Because the confirmer or other nominated person may choose different law from that chosen by the issuer or may be located in a different jurisdiction and fail to choose law, it is possible that a confirmer or nominated person may be obligated to pay (under their law) but will not be entitled to payment from the issuer (under its law). Similarly, the rights of an unreimbursed issuer, confirmer, or nominated person against a beneficiary under Section 5-109, 5-110, or 5-117, will not necessarily be governed by the same law that applies to the issuer's or confirmer's obligation upon presentation. Because the UCP and other practice are incorporated in most international letters of credit, disputes arising from different legal obligations to honor have not been frequent. Since Section 5-108 incorporates standard practice, these problems should be further minimized—at least to the extent that the same practice is and continues to be widely followed.

3. This section does not permit what is now authorized by the nonuniform Section 5-102(4) in New York. Under the current law in New York a letter of credit that incorporates the UCP is not governed in any respect by Article 5. Under revised Section 5-116 letters of credit that incorporate the UCP or similar practice will still be subject to Article 5 in certain respects. First, incorporation of the UCP or other practice does not override the nonvariable terms of Article 5. Second, where there is no conflict between Article 5 and the relevant provision of the UCP or other practice, both apply. Third, practice provisions incorporated in a letter of credit will not be effective if they fail to comply with Section 5-103(c). Assume, for example, that a practice provision purported to free a party from any liability unless it were "grossly negligent" or that the practice generally limited the remedies that one party might have against another. Depending upon the circumstances, that disclaimer or limitation of liability might be ineffective because of Section 5-103(c).

Even though Article 5 is generally consistent with UCP 500, it is not necessarily consistent with other rules or with versions of the UCP that may be adopted after Article 5's revision, or with other practices that may develop. Rules of practice incorporated in the letter of credit or other undertaking are those in effect when the letter of credit or other undertaking is issued. Except in the unusual cases discussed in the immediately preceding paragraph, practice adopted in a letter of credit will override the rules of Article 5 and the parties to letter of credit transactions must be familiar with practice (such as future versions of the UCP) that is explicitly adopted in letters of credit.

4. In several ways Article 5 conflicts with and overrides similar matters governed by Articles 3 and 4. For example, "draft" is more broadly defined in letter of credit practice than

under Section 3-104. The time allowed for honor and the required notification of reasons for dishonor are different in letter of credit practice than in the handling of documentary and other drafts under Articles 3 and 4.

5.   Subsection (e) must be read in conjunction with existing law governing subject matter jurisdiction. If the local law restricts a court to certain subject matter jurisdiction not including letter of credit disputes, subsection (e) does not authorize parties to choose that forum. For example, the parties' agreement under Section 5-116(e) would not confer jurisdiction on a probate court to decide a letter of credit case.

If the parties choose a forum under subsection (e) and if—because of other law—that forum will not take jurisdiction, the parties' agreement or undertaking should then be construed (for the purpose of forum selection) as though it did not contain a clause choosing a particular forum. That result is necessary to avoid sentencing the parties to eternal purgatory where neither the chosen State nor the State which would have jurisdiction but for the clause will take jurisdiction—the former in disregard of the clause and the latter in honor of the clause.

§ 5-117 Subrogation of Issuer, Applicant, and Nominated Person.

(a) An issuer that honors a beneficiary's presentation is subrogated to the rights of the beneficiary to the same extent as if the issuer were a secondary obligor of the underlying obligation owed to the beneficiary and of the applicant to the same extent as if the issuer were the secondary obligor of the underlying obligation owed to the applicant.

(b) An applicant that reimburses an issuer is subrogated to the rights of the issuer against any beneficiary, presenter, or nominated person to the same extent as if the applicant were the secondary obligor of the obligations owed to the issuer and has the rights of subrogation of the issuer to the rights of the beneficiary stated in subsection (a).

(c) A nominated person who pays or gives value against a draft or demand presented under a letter of credit is subrogated to the rights of:

(1) the issuer against the applicant to the same extent as if the nominated person were a secondary obligor of the obligation owed to the issuer by the applicant;

(2) the beneficiary to the same extent as if the nominated person were a secondary obligor of the underlying obligation owed to the beneficiary; and

(3) the applicant to same extent as if the nominated person were a secondary obligor of the underlying obligation owed to the applicant.

(d) Notwithstanding any agreement or term to the contrary, the rights of subrogation stated in subsections (a) and (b) do not arise until the issuer honors the letter of credit or otherwise pays and the rights in subsection (c) do not arise until the nominated person pays or otherwise gives value. Until then, the issuer, nominated person, and the applicant do not derive under this section present or prospective rights forming the basis of a claim, defense, or excuse.

OFFICIAL COMMENT

1. By itself this section does not grant any right of subrogation. It grants only the right that would exist if the person seeking subrogation "were a secondary obligor." (The term "secondary obligor" refers to a surety, guarantor, or other person against whom or whose property an obligee has recourse with respect to the obligation of a third party. See Restatement of the Law Third, Suretyship and Guaranty § 1 (1996).) If the secondary obligor would not have a right to subrogation in the circumstances in which one is claimed under this section, none is granted by this section. In effect, the section does no more than to remove an impediment that some courts have found to subrogation because they conclude that the issuer's or other claimant's rights are "independent" of the underlying obligation. If, for example, a secondary obligor would not have a subrogation right because its payment did not fully satisfy the underlying obligation, none would be available under this section. The section indorses the position of Judge Becker in *Tudor Development Group, Inc. v. United States Fidelity and Guaranty*, 968 F.2d 357 (3rd Cir.1991).

2. To preserve the independence of the letter of credit obligation and to insure that subrogation not be used as an offensive weapon by an issuer or others, the admonition in subsection (d) must be carefully observed. Only one who has completed its performance in a letter of credit transaction can have a right to subrogation. For example, an issuer may not dishonor and then defend its dishonor or assert a setoff on the ground that it is subrogated to another person's rights. Nor may the issuer complain after honor that its subrogation rights have been impaired by any good faith dealings between the beneficiary and the applicant or any other person. Assume, for example, that the beneficiary under a standby letter of credit is a mortgagee. If the mortgagee were obliged to issue a release of the mortgage upon payment of the underlying debt (by the issuer under the letter of credit), that release might impair the issuer's rights of subrogation, but the beneficiary would have no liability to the issuer for having granted that release.

§ 7-102 Definitions and Index of Definitions.

(1) In this Article, unless the context otherwise requires:

(a) "Bailee" means the person who by a warehouse receipt, bill of lading or other document of title acknowledges possession of goods and contracts to deliver them.

(b) "Consignee" means the person named in a bill to whom or to whose order the bill promises delivery.

(c) "Consignor" means the person named in a bill as the person from whom the goods have been received for shipment.

(d) "Delivery order" means a written order to deliver goods directed to a warehouseman, carrier or other person who in the ordinary course of business issues warehouse receipts or bills of lading.

(e) "Document" means document of title as defined in the general definitions in Article 1 (Section 1-201).

(f) "Goods" means all things which are treated as movable for the purposes of a contract of storage or transportation.

(g) "Issuer" means a bailee who issues a document except that in relation to an unaccepted delivery order it means the person who orders the possessor of goods to deliver. Issuer includes any person for whom an agent or employee purports to act in issuing a document if the agent or employee has real or apparent authority to issue documents, notwithstanding that the issuer received no goods or that the goods were misdescribed or that in any other respect the agent or employee violated his instructions.

(h) "Warehouseman" is a person engaged in the business of storing goods for hire.

(2) Other definitions applying to this Article or to specified Parts thereof, and the sections in which they appear are:

"Duly negotiate". Section 7-501.

"Person entitled under the document". Section 7-403(4).

(3) Definitions in other Articles applying to this Article and the sections in which they appear are:

"Contract for sale". Section 2-106.

"Overseas". Section 2-323.

"Receipt" of goods. Section 2-103.

(4) In addition Article 1 contains general definitions and principles of construction and interpretation applicable throughout this Article.

OFFICIAL COMMENT

Purposes of Changes and New Matter:

1. "Bailee" was not defined in the old uniform acts. It is used in this Article as a blanket term to designate carriers, warehousemen and others who normally issue documents of title on the basis of goods which they have received. The definition does not, however, require actual possession of the goods. If a bailee acknowledges possession when he does not have it he is bound by sections of this Article which declare the "bailee's" obligations. (See definition of "Issuer" in this section and Sections 7-203 and 7-301 on liability in case of non-receipt.)

2. The definition of warehouse receipt contained in the general definitions section of this Act (Section 1-201) eliminates the requirement of the Uniform Warehouse Receipts Act that the issuing warehouseman be "lawfully engaged" in business. The warehouseman's compliance with applicable state regulations such as the filing of a bond has no bearing on the substantive issues dealt with in this Article. Certainly the issuer's violations of law should not diminish his responsibility on documents he has put in commercial circulation. The Uniform Warehouse Receipts Act requirement that the warehouseman be engaged "for profit" has also been eliminated in view of the existence of state operated and cooperative warehouses. But it is still essential that the business be storing goods "for hire" (Section 1-201 and this section). A person does not become a warehouseman by storing his own goods.

3. Delivery orders, which were included without qualification in the Uniform Sales Act definition of document of title, must be treated differently in this consolidation of provisions from the three uniform acts. When a delivery order has been accepted by the bailee it is for practical purposes indistinguishable from a warehouse receipt. Prior to such acceptance there is no basis for imposing obligations on the bailee other than the ordinary obligation of contract which the bailee may have assumed to the depositor of the goods.

Selected Provisions of the Uniform Commercial Code (UCC)

§ 7-304 Bills of Lading in a Set.

(1) Except where customary in overseas transportation, a bill of lading must not be issued in a set of parts. The issuer is liable for damages caused by violation of this subsection.

(2) Where a bill of lading is lawfully drawn in a set of parts, each of which is numbered and expressed to be valid only if the goods have not been delivered against any other part, the whole of the parts constitute one bill.

(3) Where a bill of lading is lawfully issued in a set of parts and different parts are negotiated to different persons, the title of the holder to whom the first due negotiation is made prevails as to both the document and the goods even though any later holder may have received the goods from the carrier in good faith and discharged the carrier's obligation by surrender of his part.

(4) Any person who negotiates or transfers a single part of a bill of lading drawn in a set is liable to holders of that part as if it were the whole set.

(5) The bailee is obliged to deliver in accordance with Part 4 of this Article against the first presented part of a bill of lading lawfully drawn in a set. Such delivery discharges the bailee's obligation on the whole bill.

OFFICIAL COMMENT

Purposes of Changes:

The statement of the legal effect of a lawfully issued set is in accord with existing commercial law relating to maritime and other overseas bills. This law has been codified in the Hague and Warsaw Conventions and in the Carriage of Goods by Sea Act, the provisions of which would ordinarily govern in situations where bills in a set are recognized by this Article.

§ 7-503 Document of Title to Goods Defeated in Certain Cases.

(1) A document of title confers no right in goods against a person who before issuance of the document had a legal interest or a perfected security interest in them and who neither

(a) delivered or entrusted them or any document of title covering them to the bailor or his nominee with actual or apparent authority to ship, store or sell or with power to obtain

593

delivery under this Article (Section 7-403) or with power of disposition under this Act (Sections 2-403 and 9-307) or other statute or rule of law; nor

(b) acquiesced in the procurement by the bailor or his nominee of any document of title.

(2) Title to goods based upon an unaccepted delivery order is subject to the rights of anyone to whom a negotiable warehouse receipt or bill of lading covering the goods has been duly negotiated. Such a title may be defeated under the next section to the same extent as the rights of the issuer or a transferee from the issuer.

(3) Title to goods based upon a bill of lading issued to a freight forwarder is subject to the rights of anyone to whom a bill issued by the freight forwarder is duly negotiated; but delivery by the carrier in accordance with Part 4 of this Article pursuant to its own bill of lading discharges the carrier's obligation to deliver.

OFFICIAL COMMENT

Purposes of Changes:

1. In general it may be said that the title of a purchaser by due negotiation prevails over almost any interest in the goods which existed prior to the procurement of the document of title if the possession of the goods by the person obtaining the document derived from any action by the prior claimant which introduced the goods into the stream of commerce or carried them along that stream. A thief of the goods cannot indeed by shipping or storing them to his own order acquire power to transfer them to a good faith purchaser. Nor can a tenant or mortgagor defeat any rights of a landlord or mortgagee which have been perfected under the local law merely by wrongfully shipping or storing a portion of the crop or other goods. However, "acquiescence" by the landlord or tenant does not require active consent under subsection (1)(b) and knowledge of the likelihood of storage or shipment with no objection or effort to control it is sufficient to defeat his rights as against one who takes by "due" negotiation of a negotiable document.

On the other hand, where goods are delivered to a factor for sale, even though the factor has made no advances and is limited in his duty to sell for cash, the goods are "entrusted" to him "with actual . . . authority . . . to sell" under subsection (1)(a), and if he procures a negotiable document of title he can transfer the owner's interest to a purchaser by due negotiation. Further, where the factor is in the business of selling, goods entrusted to him simply for safekeeping or storage may be entrusted under circumstances which give him "apparent authority to ship, store or sell" under subsection (1)(a), or power of disposition under Section 2-403, 7-205 or 9-307, or under a statute such as the earlier Factors Acts, or under a rule of law giving effect to apparent ownership. See Section 1-103.

Persons having an interest in goods also frequently deliver or entrust them to agents or servants other than factors for the purpose of shipping or warehousing or under circumstances reasonably contemplating such action. Rounding out the case law development under the prior Acts, this Act is clear that such persons assume full risk that the agent to whom the goods are so delivered may ship or store in breach of duty, take a document to his own order and then proceed to misappropriate it. This Act makes no distinction between possession or mere custody in such situations and finds no exception in the case of larceny by a bailee or the like. The safeguard in such situations lies in the requirement that a due negotiation can occur only "in the regular course of business or financing" and that the purchase be in good faith and without notice. See Section 7-501. Documents of title have no market among the commercially inexperienced and the commercially experienced do not take them without inquiry from persons known to be truck drivers or petty clerks even though such persons purport to be operating in their own names.

Again, where the seller allows a buyer to receive goods under a contract for sale, though as a "conditional delivery" or under "cash sale" terms and on explicit agreement for immediate payment, the buyer thereby acquires power to defeat the seller's interest by transfer of the goods to certain good faith

purchasers. See Section 2-403. Both in policy and under the language of subsection (1)(a) that same power must be extended to accomplish the same result if the buyer procures a negotiable document of title to the goods and duly negotiates it.

2. Under subsection (1) a delivery order issued by a person having no right in or power over the goods is ineffective unless the owner acts as provided in subsection (1)(a) or (b). Thus the rights of a transferee of a non-negotiable warehouse receipt can be defeated by a delivery order subsequently issued by the transferor only if the transferee "delivers or entrusts" to the "person procuring" the delivery order or "acquiesces" in his procurement. Similarly, a second delivery order issued by the same issuer for the same goods will ordinarily be subject to the first, both under this section and under Section 7-402. After a delivery order is validly issued but before it is accepted, it may nevertheless be defeated under subsection (2) in much the same way that the

rights of a transferee may be defeated under Section 7-504. For example, a buyer in ordinary course from the issuer may defeat the rights of the holder of a prior delivery order if the bailee receives notification of the buyer's rights before notification of the holder's rights. Section 7-504(2)(b). But an accepted delivery order has the same effect as a document issued by the bailee.

3. Under subsection (3) a bill of lading issued to a freight forwarder is subordinated to the freight forwarder's certificate, since the bill on its face gives notice of the fact that a freight forwarder is in the picture and has in all probability issued a certificate. But the carrier is protected in following the terms of its own bill of lading.

Sec. 7-504 Rights Acquired in the Absence of Due Negotiation; Effect of Diversion; Seller's Stoppage of Delivery.

(1) A transferee of a document, whether negotiable or nonnegotiable, to whom the document has been delivered but not duly negotiated, acquires the title and rights which his transferor had or had actual authority to convey.

(2) In the case of a non-negotiable document, until but not after the bailee receives notification of the transfer, the rights of the transferee may be defeated

(a) by those creditors of the transferor who could treat the sale as void under Section 2-402; or

(b) by a buyer from the transferor in ordinary course of business if the bailee has delivered the goods to the buyer or received notification of his rights; or

(c) as against the bailee by good faith dealings of the bailee with the transferor.

(3) A diversion or other change of shipping instructions by the consignor in a non-negotiable bill of lading which causes the bailee not to deliver to the consignee defeats the consignee's title to the goods if they have been delivered to a buyer in ordinary course of business and in any event defeats the consignee's rights against the bailee.

(4) Delivery pursuant to a non-negotiable document may be stopped by a seller under Section 2-705, and subject to the requirement of due notification there provided. A bailee honoring the seller's instructions is entitled to be indemnified by the seller against any resulting loss or expense.

OFFICIAL COMMENT

Purposes of Changes and New Matter:

1. Under the general principles controlling negotiable documents, it is clear that in the absence of due negotiation a transferor cannot convey greater rights than he himself has, even when the negotiation is formally perfect. This section recognizes the transferor's power to transfer rights which he himself has or has "actual authority to convey." Thus, where a negotiable document of title is being transferred the operation of the principle of estoppel is not recognized, as contrasted with situations involving the transfer of the goods themselves.

(Compare Section 2-403 on good faith purchase of goods.)

A necessary part of the price for the protection of regular dealings with negotiable documents of title is an insistence that no dealing which is in any way irregular shall be recognized as a good faith purchase of the document or of any rights pertaining to it. So, where the transfer of a negotiable document fails as a negotiation because a requisite indorsement is forged or otherwise missing, the purchaser in good faith and for value may be in the anomalous position of having less rights, in part, than if he had

596

purchased the goods themselves. True, his rights are not subject to defeat by attachment of the goods or surrender of them to his transferor [contrast subsection (2)]; but on the other hand, he cannot acquire enforceable rights to control or receive the goods over the bailee's objection merely by giving notice to the bailee. Similarly, a consignee who makes payment to his consignor against a straight bill of lading can thereby acquire the position of a good faith purchaser of goods under provisions of the Article of this Act on Sales (Section 2-403), whereas the same payment made in good faith against an unindorsed order bill would not have such effect. The appropriate remedy of a purchaser in such a situation is to regularize his status by compelling indorsement of the document (see Section 7-506).

2. As in the case of transfer—as opposed to "due negotiation"—of negotiable documents, subsection (1) empowers the transferor of a nonnegotiable document to transfer only such rights as he himself has or has "actual authority" to convey. In contrast to situations involving the goods themselves the operation of estoppel or agency principles is not here recognized to enable the transferor to convey greater rights than he actually has. Subsection (2) makes it clear, however, that the transferee of a nonnegotiable document may acquire rights greater in some respects than those of his transferor by giving notice of the transfer to the bailee.

3. Subsection (3) is in part a reiteration of the carrier's immunity from liability if it honors instructions of the consignor to divert, but there is added a provision protecting the title of the substituted consignee if the latter is a buyer in ordinary course of business. A typical situation would be where a manufacturer, having shipped a lot of standardized goods to A on nonnegotiable bill of lading, diverts the goods to customer B who pays for them. Under orthodox passage-of-title-by-appropriation doctrine A might reclaim the goods from B. However, no consideration of commercial policy supports this involvement of an innocent third party in the default of the manufacturer on his contract to A; and the common commercial practice of diverting goods in transit suggests a trade understanding in accordance with this subsection.

4. Subsection (4) gives the carrier an express right to indemnity where he honors a seller's request to stop delivery.

5. Section 1-201(27) gives the bailee protection, if due diligence is exercised, similar to that found in the third paragraph of Section 33, Uniform Bills of Lading Act, where the bailee's organization has not had time to act on a notification.

B. Uniform Foreign Money-Judgments Recognition Act

Source: National Conference of Commissioners on Uniform State Laws

Introduction

Recognition and enforcement of foreign nation judgments is affected by two uniform acts in many states. The Uniform Foreign-Money Judgments Recognition Act (Recognition Act) governs "recognition" of judgments from the courts of foreign nations. Despite being available since 1962, the fact that the Recognition Act does little to change substantive common law meant that it took until the mid-1990's before it had been adopted in a majority of states. Its most significant impact may be that it provides easier proof of reciprocity when a U.S. judgment is taken to a foreign court for recognition and enforcement.

The Uniform Enforcement of Foreign Judgments Act (Enforcement Act) deals not with foreign nation judgments, but rather with sister state judgments entitled to "full faith and credit" under Article IV of the U.S. Constitution. It is applicable to foreign nation judgments through § 3 of the Recognition Act, however, which provides that a foreign nation judgment entitled recognition under the Recognition Act "is enforceable in the same manner as the judgment of a sister state which is entitled to full faith and credit." Since enforcement is accomplished through the administrative procedures provided in the Enforcement Act, in states in which both acts are in effect, they work together to provide the substantive and procedural rules for recognition and enforcement of foreign nation judgments.

The following chart provides adoption information for both the Uniform Foreign Money-Judgments Recognition Act and the Uniform Enforcement of Foreign Judgments Act. It is current to May 1998.

598

State-by-State Enactment of the
Uniform Enforcement of Foreign Judgments Act
and the
Uniform Foreign Money-Judgments Recognition Act

an asterisk (*) denotes those states which have added a reciprocity requirement
in their adoption of the Uniform Foreign Money-Judgments Recognition Act

States and Other Jurisdictions	Uniform Enforcement of Foreign Judgments Act	Uniform Foreign Money-Judgments Recognition Act[1]
ALABAMA	ALA. CODE §§ 6-9-230 to 6-9-238	none
ALASKA	ALASKA STAT. §§ 09.30.200 to 09.30.270	ALASKA STAT. §§ 09.30.100 to 09.30.180
ARIZONA	ARIZ. REV. STAT. ANN. §§ 12-1701 to 12-1708	none
ARKANSAS	ARK. CODE ANN. §§ 16-66-601 to 16-66-608	none
CALIFORNIA	none[2]	CAL. CIV. PROC. CODE §§ 1713 to 1713.8
COLORADO	COLO. REV. STAT. §§ 13-53-101 to 13-53-108	COLO. REV. STAT. §§ 13-62-101 to 13-62-109
CONNECTICUT	CONN. GEN. STAT. ANN. §§ 52-604 to 52-609	CONN. GEN. STAT. ANN. §§ 50a-30 to 50a-38

---

[1]The following state statutes include requirements of reciprocity in the enactment of the UFMJRA: GA. CODE ANN. § 9-12-114(10); IDAHO CODE § 10-1404; MASS. GEN. LAWS ANN. ch. 235, § 23A; OHIO REV. CODE ANN. § 2329.92; TEX. CIV. PRAC. & REM. CODE ANN. § 36.005(b)(7).

[2]California has adopted its own act to deal with sister state judgments. CAL. CIV. PROC. CODE §§ 1710 to 1710.65.

DELAWARE	DEL. CODE ANN. tit. 10, §§ 4781 to 4787	DEL. CODE ANN. tit. 10, §§ 4801 to 4808
FLORIDA	FLA. STAT. ANN. §§ 55.501 to 55.509	*FLA. STAT. ANN. §§ 55.601 to 55.607
GEORGIA	GA. CODE ANN. §§ 9-12-130 to 9-12-138	*GA. CODE ANN. §§ 9-12-110 to 9-12-117
HAWAII	HAW. REV. STAT. §§ 636C-1 to 636C-8	HAW. REV. STAT. §§ 658C-1 to 658C-9
IDAHO	IDAHO CODE §§ 10-1301 to 10-1308	*IDAHO CODE §§ 10-1401 to 10-1409
ILLINOIS	735 ILL. COMP. STAT. ANN. 735 ILCS 5/12-650 to 5/12-657	735 ILL. COMP. STAT. ANN. 735 ILCS 5/12-618 to 5/12-626
INDIANA	none	none
IOWA	IOWA CODE ANN. §§ 626A.1 to 626A.8	IOWA CODE ANN. §§ 626B.1 to 626B.8
KANSAS	KAN. CIV. PROC. CODE ANN. §§ 60-3001 to 60-3008	none
KENTUCKY	KY. REV. STAT. ANN. §§ 426.950 to 426.975	none
LOUISIANA	LA. REV. STAT. ANN. §§ 13:4241 to 13:4247	none[3]
MAINE	ME. REV. STAT. ANN. tit. 14, §§ 8001 to 8088	none
MARYLAND	MD. CODE ANN., CTS. & JUD. PROC. §§ 11-801 to 11-807	MD. CODE ANN., CTS. & JUD. PROC. §§ 10-701 to 10-709

---

[3]LA. CODE CIV. PROC. ANN. art. 2541 deals with enforcement of sister state and foreign country judgments. Louisiana has not enacted the Uniform Foreign Money-Judgments Recognition Act.

MASSACHUSETTS	none	*MASS. GEN. LAWS ANN. ch. 235, § 23A
MICHIGAN	MICH. COMP. LAWS ANN. §§ 691.1171 to 691.1179	MICH. COMP. LAWS ANN. §§ 691.1151 to 691.1159
MINNESOTA	MINN. STAT. ANN. §§ 548.26 to 548.33	MINN. STAT. ANN. § 548.35
MISSISSIPPI	MISS. CODE ANN. §§ 11-7-301 to 11-7-309	none
MISSOURI	MO. ANN. STAT. § 511.760	MO. ANN. STAT. §§ 511.770 to 511.787
MONTANA	MONT. CODE ANN. §§ 25-9-501 to 25-9-508	MONT. CODE ANN. §§ 25-9-601 to 25-9-609
NEBRASKA	NEB. REV. STAT. §§ 25-1587.01 to 25-1587.09	none
NEVADA	NEV. REV. STAT. ANN. §§ 17.330 to 17.400	none
NEW HAMPSHIRE	N.H. REV. STAT. ANN. §§ 524-A:1 to 524-A:8	none[4]
NEW JERSEY	N.J. STAT. ANN. §§ 2A:49A-25 to 2A:49A-33	N.J. STAT. ANN. §§ 2A:49A-16 to 2A:49A-24
NEW MEXICO	N.M. STAT. ANN. §§ 39-4A-1 to 39-4A-6	N.M. STAT. ANN. §§ 39-4B-1 to 39-4B-9
NEW YORK	N.Y. CIV. PRAC. L. & R. §§ 5401 to 5408	N.Y. CIV. PRAC. L. & R. §§ 5301 to 5309
NORTH CAROLINA	N.C. GEN. STAT. §§ 1C-1701 to 1C-1708	*N.C. GEN. STAT. §§ 1C-1800 to 1C-1808

---

[4]N.H. REV. STAT. ANN. § 524:11 requires reciprocity to be shown for the enforcement of a Canadian federal or provincial judgment.

601

NORTH DAKOTA	N.D. CENT. CODE §§ 28-20.1-01 to 28-20.1-08	none
OHIO	OHIO REV. CODE ANN. §§ 2329.021 to 2329.027	*OHIO REV. CODE ANN. §§ 2329.90 to 2329.94
OKLAHOMA	OKLA. STAT. ANN. tit. 12, §§ 719 to 726	OKLA. STAT. ANN. tit. 12, §§ 710 to 718
OREGON	OR. REV. STAT. §§ 24.105 to 24.175	OR. REV. STAT. §§ 24.200 to 24.255
PENNSYLVANIA	42 PA. CONS. STAT. ANN. § 4306	42 PA. CONS. STAT. ANN. §§ 22001 to 22009
RHODE ISLAND	R.I. GEN. LAWS §§ 9-32-1 to 9-32-8	none
SOUTH CAROLINA	S.C. CODE ANN. §§ 15-35.900 to 15-35-960	none
SOUTH DAKOTA	S.D. CODIFIED LAWS ANN. §§ 15-16A-1 to 15-16A-10	none
TENNESSEE	TENN. CODE ANN. §§ 26-6-101 to 26-6-107	none
TEXAS	TEX. CIV. PRAC. & REM. CODE ANN. §§ 35.001 to 35.008	*TEX. CIV. PRAC. & REM. CODE ANN. §§ 36.001 to 36.008
UTAH	UTAH CODE ANN. §§ 78-22a-1 to 78-22a-8	none
VERMONT	none	none
VIRGINIA	VA. CODE ANN. §§ 8.01-465.1 to 8.01-465.5	VA. CODE ANN. §§ 8.01-465.6 to 8.01-465.13
WASHINGTON	WASH. REV. CODE ANN. §§ 6.36.010 to 6.36.045 & 6.36.130 to 6.36.910	WASH. REV. CODE ANN. §§ 6.40.010 to 6.40.915

WEST VIRGINIA	W. VA. CODE §§ 55-14-1 to 55-14-8	none
WISCONSIN	WIS. STAT. ANN. § 806.24	none
WYOMING	WYO. STAT. §§ 1-17-701 to 1-17-707	none
AMERICAN SAMOA	None	None
DISTRICT OF COLUMBIA	D.C. CODE ANN. §§ 15-351 to 15-357	D.C. CODE ANN. §§ 15-381 to 15-388
PUERTO RICO	None	None
VIRGIN ISLANDS	V.I. CODE ANN. tit. 5, §§ 551 to 558	V.I. CODE ANN. tit. 5, §§ 561 to 569
Number of jurisdictions enacting each statute:	48	30

UNIFORM FOREIGN MONEY-JUDGMENTS RECOGNITION ACT

§ 1. Definitions.

As used in this Act:

> (1) "foreign state" means any governmental unit other than the United States, or any state, district, commonwealth, territory, insular possession thereof, or the Panama Canal Zone, the Trust Territory of the Pacific Islands, or the Ryukyu Islands;

> (2) "foreign judgment" means any judgment of a foreign state granting or denying recovery of a sum of money, other than a judgment for taxes, a fine or other penalty, or a judgment for support in matrimonial or family matters.

§ 2. Applicability.

This Act applies to any foreign judgment that is final and conclusive and enforceable where rendered even though an appeal therefrom is pending or it is subject to appeal.

§ 3. Recognition and Enforcement.

Except as provided in section 4, a foreign judgment meeting the requirements of section 2 is conclusive between the parties to the extent that it grants or denies recovery of a sum of money. The foreign judgment is enforceable in the same manner as the judgment of a sister state which is entitled to full faith and credit.

§ 4. Grounds for Non-recognition.

> (a) A foreign judgment is not conclusive if

>> (1) the judgment was rendered under a system which does not provide impartial tribunals or procedures compatible with the requirements of due process of law;

>> (2) the foreign court did not have personal jurisdiction over the defendant; or

>> (3) the foreign court did not have jurisdiction over the subject matter.

> (b) A foreign judgment need not be recognized if

>> (1) the defendant in the proceedings in the foreign court did not receive notice of the proceedings in sufficient time to enable him to defend;

604

(2) the judgment was obtained by fraud;

(3) the [cause of action] [claim for relief] on which the judgment is based is repugnant to the public policy of this state;

(4) the judgment conflicts with another final and conclusive judgment;

(5) the proceeding in the foreign court was contrary to an agreement between the parties under which the dispute in question was to be settled otherwise than by proceedings in that court; or

(6) in the case of jurisdiction based only on personal service, the foreign court was a seriously inconvenient forum for the trial of the action.

§ 5. Personal Jurisdiction.

(a) The foreign judgment shall not be refused recognition for lack of personal jurisdiction if

(1) the defendant was served personally in the foreign state;

(2) the defendant voluntarily appeared in the proceedings, other than for the purpose of protecting property seized or threatened with seizure in the proceedings or of contesting the jurisdiction of the court over him;

(3) the defendant prior to the commencement of the proceedings had agreed to submit to the jurisdiction of the foreign court with respect to the subject matter involved;

(4) the defendant was domiciled in the foreign state when the proceedings were instituted, or, being a body corporate had its principal place of business, was incorporated, or had otherwise acquired corporate status, in the foreign state;

(5) the defendant had a business office in the foreign state and the proceedings in the foreign court involved a [cause of action] [claim for relief] arising out of business done by the defendant through that office in the foreign state; or

(6) the defendant operated a motor vehicle or airplane in the foreign state and the proceedings involved a [cause of action] [claim for relief] arising out of such operation.

(b) The courts of this state may recognize other bases of jurisdiction.

§ 6. Stay in Case of Appeal.

If the defendant satisfies the court either that an appeal is pending or that he is entitled and intends to appeal from the foreign judgment, the court may stay the proceedings until the appeal has been determined or until the expiration of a period of time sufficient to enable the defendant to prosecute the appeal.

§ 7. Savings Clause.

This Act does not prevent the recognition of a foreign judgment in situations not covered by this Act.

§ 8. Uniformity of Interpretation.

This Act shall be so construed as to effectuate its general purpose to make uniform the law of those states which enact it.

§ 9. Short Title.

This Act may be cited as the Uniform Foreign Money-Judgments Recognition Act.

§ 10. Repeal.

[The following Acts are repealed:

   (1)
   (2)
   (3)   .]

§ 11. Time of Taking Effect.

This Act shall take effect _____.

606

C. Uniform Enforcement of Foreign Judgments Act

Source: National Conference of Commissioners on Uniform State Laws

Introduction

The Uniform Enforcement of Foreign Judgments Act (Enforcement Act) deals not with foreign nation judgments, but rather with sister state judgments entitled to "full faith and credit" under Article IV of the U.S. Constitution. It is applicable to foreign nation judgments through § 3 of the Uniform Foreign-Money Judgments Recognition Act (Recognition Act), however, which provides that a foreign nation judgment entitled to recognition under the Recognition Act "is enforceable in the same manner as the judgment of a sister state which is entitled to full faith and credit." See the Introduction to the Recognition Act for an explanation of that Act as well as a chart showing the states in which both acts have been enacted.

UNIFORM ENFORCEMENT OF FOREIGN JUDGMENTS ACT
(1964 Revised Act)

§ 1. Definition.

In this Act "foreign judgment" means any judgment, decree, or order of a court of the United States or of any other court which is entitled to full faith and credit in this state.

§ 2. Filing and Status of Foreign Judgments.

A copy of any foreign judgment authenticated in accordance with the act of Congress or the statutes of this state may be filed in the office of the Clerk of any [District Court of any city or county] of this state. The Clerk shall treat the foreign judgment in the same manner as a judgment of the [District Court of any city or county] of this state. A judgment so filed has the same effect and is subject to the same procedures, defenses and proceedings for reopening, vacating, or staying as a judgment of a [District Court of any city or county] of this state and may be enforced or satisfied in like manner.

§ 3. Notice of Filing.

(a) At the time of the filing of the foreign judgment, the judgment creditor or his lawyer shall make and file with the Clerk of Court an affidavit setting forth the name and last known post office address of the judgment debtor, and the judgment creditor.

(b) Promptly upon the filing of the foreign judgment and the affidavit, the Clerk shall mail notice of the filing of the foreign judgment to the judgment debtor at the address given and shall make a note of the mailing in the docket. The notice shall include the name and post office address of the judgment creditor and the judgment creditor's lawyer, if any, in this state. In addition, the judgment creditor may mail a notice of the filing of the judgment to the judgment debtor and may file proof of mailing with the Clerk.

§ 4. Stay.

(a) If the judgment debtor shows the [District Court of any city or county] that an appeal from the foreign judgment is pending or will be taken, or that a stay of execution has been granted, the court shall stay enforcement of the foreign judgment until the appeal is concluded, the time for appeal expires, or the stay of execution expires or is vacated, upon proof that the judgment debtor has furnished the security for the satisfaction of the judgment required by the state in which it was rendered.

(b) If the judgment debtor shows the [District Court of any city or county] any ground upon which enforcement of a judgment of any [District Court of any city or county] of this state would

608

be stayed, the court shall stay enforcement of the foreign judgment for an appropriate period, upon requiring the same security for satisfaction of the judgment which is required in this state.

§ 5. Fees.

Any person filing a foreign judgment shall pay to the Clerk of Court _____ dollars. Fees for docketing, transcription or other enforcement proceedings shall be as provided for judgments of the [District Court of any city or county of this state].

§ 6. Optional Procedure.

The right of a judgment creditor to bring an action to enforce his judgment instead of proceeding under this Act remains unimpaired.

§ 7. Uniformity of Interpretation.

This Act shall be so interpreted and construed as to effectuate its general purpose to make uniform the law of those states which enact it.

§ 8. Short Title.

This Act may be cited as the Uniform Enforcement of Foreign Judgments Act.

§ 9. Repeal.

The following Acts and parts of Acts are repealed:

(1)
(2)
(3)

§ 10. Taking Effect.

This Act takes effect on _____.

D. Uniform Foreign-Money Claims Act

Source: National Conference of Commissioners on Uniform State Laws

Introduction

The Uniform Foreign-Money Claims Act was intended to solve common law problems arising when claims denominated in a foreign currency are brought in a U.S. court. While the official Prefatory Note claims these problems have been solved, what the Act really does is substitute a relatively rigid "payment date" rule for the common law "breach date" and "judgment date" rules. While each rule may be satisfactory in times of consistent currency fluctuation in only one direction, none is satisfactory in all circumstances. Thus, it is likely that this area of law will continue to receive criticism and commentary, and that cases under this Act will not always provide satisfactory results.

UNIFORM FOREIGN-MONEY CLAIMS ACT

PREFATORY NOTE

This Act facilitates uniform judicial determination of claims expressed in the money of foreign countries. It requires judgments and arbitration awards in these cases to be entered in the foreign money rather than in United States dollars. The debtor may pay the judgment in dollars on the basis of the rate of exchange prevailing at the time of payment.

A Uniform Act governing foreign-money claims has become desirable because:

These claims have increased greatly as a result of the growth in international trade.

Values of foreign moneys as compared to the United States dollar fluctuate more over shorter periods of time than was formerly the case.

United States jurisdictions treat recoveries on foreign-money claims differently than most of our major trading partners.

A lack of uniformity among the states in resolving foreign-money claims stimulates forum shopping and creates a lack of certainty in the law.

American courts historically follow one of two different rules in selecting a time during litigation for converting foreign money into United States dollars. These are called the "breach day rule"—the date the money should have been paid—and the "judgment date rule"—when judgment is entered. Many other countries use the "payment day rule"—when the judgment is paid. *See Miliangos v. George Frank (Textiles) Ltd.*, (1976) A.C. 1007. The merits of this approach have begun to be recognized in this country. The payment day rule is endorsed by this Act.

The three rules produce wildly disparate results in terms of making an injured person whole. This is illustrated by the following example:

An American citizen (A) owes 18,790 pounds sterling to a British corporation (BCo) suing in New York, and the pound is falling against the dollar. Due to the declining value of the pound, the three rules worked out as follows:

Date	Rate of Exchange	BCo Gets
Breach day	Pound = $2.20	$41,338
Judgment day	Pound = $1.50	$28,185
Payment day	Pound = $1.20	$22,548

A judgment of $41,338 may be entered based on the breach day rule. However, the payment in dollars was worth 34,449 pounds ($41,338 divided by $1.20) when eventually received, an excess of L15,659 over the actual loss.

611

This example is adapted from an actual case. See *Comptex v. LaBow*, 783 F.2d 333 (2d Cir. 1986). The facts are simplified.

If conversion is delayed until the date of actual payment, the creditor is recompensed with its own money or the financial equivalent in United States dollars; the debtor bears the risk of a fall in the debtor's money or reaps the benefit of a rise therein. If conversion is made at breach or judgment date, the risk of fluctuation in value of a money not of its selection falls on the creditor.

The real issue is where the risk of exchange rate fluctuation should be placed. This Act recognizes the right of the parties to agree upon the money that governs their relationship. In the absence of an agreement, the Act adopts the rule of giving the aggrieved party the amount to which it is entitled in its own money or the money in which the loss was suffered.

The principle of the Act is to restore the aggrieved party to the economic position it would have been in had the wrong not occurred. Thus, for example, if oil is spilled on the coast of France by an American ship, the loss is felt by the French in francs and a judgment of an American court for damages should reflect this fact. Courts should enter judgments in the money customarily used by the injured person.

The payment day rule, on which the Act is based, meets the reasonable expectations of the parties involved. It places the aggrieved party in the position it would have been in financially but for the wrong that gave rise to the claim. States which adopt it will align themselves with most of the major civilized countries of the world.

The Act also covers other issues that may arise in connection with foreign-money claims. These include revalorization and interest. In order to determine aliquot shares for distributions from funds created in insolvency and estate proceedings, the Act specifies use of the date the distribution proceeding was initiated for conversion of foreign money into United States dollars.

UNIFORM FOREIGN-MONEY CLAIMS ACT

SECTION 1. DEFINITIONS.

In this [Act]:

(1) "Action" means a judicial proceeding or arbitration in which a payment in money may be awarded or enforced with respect to a foreign-money claim.

(2) "Bank-offered spot rate" means the spot rate of exchange at which a bank will sell foreign money at a spot rate.

(3) "Conversion date" means the banking day next preceding the date on which money, in accordance with this [Act], is:

(i) paid to a claimant in an action or distribution proceeding;

(ii) paid to the official designated by law to enforce a judgment or award on behalf of a claimant; or

(iii) used to recoup, set-off, or counterclaim in different moneys in an action or distribution proceeding.

(4) "Distribution proceeding" means a judicial or nonjudicial proceeding for the distribution of a fund in which one or more foreign-money claims is asserted and includes an accounting, an assignment for the benefit of creditors, a foreclosure, the liquidation or rehabilitation of a corporation or other entity, and the distribution of an estate, trust, or other fund.

(5) "Foreign-money" means money other than money of the United States of America.

(6) "Foreign-money claim" means a claim upon an obligation to pay, or a claim for recovery of a loss, expressed in or measured by a foreign money.

(7) "Money" means a medium of exchange for the payment of obligations or a store of value authorized or adopted by a government or by inter-governmental agreement.

(8) "Money of the claim" means the money determined as proper pursuant to Section 4.

(9) "Person" means an individual, a corporation, government or governmental subdivision or agency, business trust, estate, trust, joint venture, partnership, association, two or more persons having a joint or common interest, or any other legal or commercial entity.

(10) "Rate of exchange" means the rate at which money of one country may be converted into money of another country in a free financial market convenient to or reasonably usable by a person obligated to pay or to state a rate of conversion. If separate rates of exchange apply to different kinds of transactions, the term means the rate applicable to the particular transaction giving rise to the foreign-money claim.

(11) "Spot rate" means the rate of exchange at which foreign money is sold by a bank or other dealer in foreign exchange for immediate or next day availability or for settlement by immediate payment in cash or equivalent, by charge to an account, or by an agreed delayed settlement not exceeding two days.

(12) "State" means a State of the United States, the District of Columbia, the Commonwealth of Puerto Rico, or a territory or insular possession subject to the jurisdiction of the United States.

COMMENT

1. "Action." A suit or arbitration may be legal or equitable in nature, but it must be based on a pecuniary claim.

2. "Bank-offered spot rate" is the rate at which a bank will sell the requisite amount of foreign money for immediate or nearly immediate use by the buyer.

3. "Conversion date." Exchange rates may fluctuate from day to day. A date must be picked for calculating the value of foreign money in terms of United States dollars. As used in the Act, "conversion date" means the day before a foreign-money claim is paid or set-off. The day refers to the time period of the place of the payor, not necessarily that of the recipient. The exchange rate prevailing at or near the close of business on the banking day before the day payment is made will be well known at the time of payment. See Comment 2 to Section 7.

4. "Distribution proceeding." In keeping with the concept underlying Section 2, the coverage of this statute is limited to judicial actions and nonjudicial proceedings which involve the creation of a fund from which pro-rata distributions are made to claimants. As provided in Section 8, a different conversion date is required where either input to or outgo from a fund involves two or more different moneys. Thus, the term includes a mortgage foreclosure proceeding, judicial or under a trust deed, distribution of property in divorce and child support proceedings, distributions in the administration of a trust or a decedent's estate, an assignment for the benefit of creditors, an equity receivership, a liquidation by a statutory successor, a voluntary dissolution of a business or a nonprofit enterprise or the like when in each case a fund must be shared among claimants and where, usually, the fund will not satisfy all claimants of the same class. An asset or a liability of the fund must also involve one or more foreign-money claims, but not all of the claims can be in the same money.

5. "Foreign money." Since only the federal government has the power to coin money and regulate the value thereof, the term "foreign" means a government other than that of the United States of America. Special Drawing Rights of the International Monetary Fund are foreign money even though the United States is a member of the Fund. Foreign governments included are all those whose moneys are, in the currency markets of the world, exchangeable for the money of other currencies even though the government is not recognized by the United States.

6. "Foreign-money claim." The term "claim" is not limited to any one party to an action or a distribution proceeding and may be asserted by a plaintiff or a defendant or by a party to an arbitration or distribution proceeding. It may be based on a foreign judgment, or sound in contract, quasi-contract, or tort.

7. "Money." The definition includes composite currencies such as European Currency Units created by agreement of the governments that are members of the European Monetary System or the Special Drawing Rights created under the auspices of the International Money Fund. These are "stores of value" used to determine the quantity of payment in some international transactions.

8. "Money of the claim." See Section 4 and the Comment thereto.

9. "Party." This combines the Uniform Commercial Code's definitions of "person" and "organization," but is limited to those who are parties to transactions or involved in events which could give rise to a foreign-money claim.

10. "Rate of Exchange." A free market rate is to be used rather than an official rate if both exist. Some countries have transactional differences in exchange rates with slightly different rates; for example, in Belgium one rate prevails for commercial and another for financial transactions. Both rates are recognized in money market transactions. The last sentence of the definition indicates that the rate appropriate to the transaction is the rate to be used.

11. "Spot rate" is the term used in the financial markets of the United States for the rate of exchange for immediate or nearly immediate transfers from one money to another, as distinguished from the rates for future options or future deliveries.

In the foreign exchange markets, as in the stock markets, quotations are either "bid" or "ask," and the spread between is where the dealer makes a profit. An "offered spot rate" is the rate at which the offeror will sell the particular money. It is, of course, higher than the rate at which that person will buy the same money. "Spot" refers to the time the trade is made, not the time for settlement, which in spot transactions is often two days after the date of the trade.

12. "State." The definition, as in other Uniform Laws, is extended to include areas given the same, or nearly the same, treatment in law as the states.

SECTION 2. SCOPE.

(a) This [Act] applies only to a foreign-money claim in an action or distribution proceeding.

(b) This [Act] applies to foreign-money issues even if other law under the conflict of laws rules of this State applies to other issues in the action or distribution proceeding.

COMMENT

Under the rules of the conflict of laws, the determination of when a foreign money is converted to United States dollars is generally considered a procedural matter for the law of the forum. Subsection (b) removes any doubt.

SECTION 3. VARIATION BY AGREEMENT.

(a) The effect of this [Act] may be varied by agreement of the parties made before or after commencement of an action or distribution proceeding or the entry of judgment.

(b) Parties to a transaction may agree upon the money to be used in a transaction giving rise to a foreign-money claim and may agree to use different moneys for different aspects of the transaction. Stating the price in a foreign money for one aspect of a transaction does not alone require the use of that money for other aspects of the transaction.

COMMENT

1. A basic policy of the Act is to preserve freedom of contract and to permit parties to resolve disputed matters by contract at any time, even as to choice of law problems. The parties may agree upon the date and time for conversion. After entry of judgment the parties may agree upon how the judgment is to be satisfied.

2. Subsection (b) covers cases where, for example, claims for petroleum may be settled in United States dollars but settlement for joint costs of exploration may be in pounds sterling. The parties also may agree on the money to be used for damages. The second sentence recognizes that a price stated in a particular money does to indicate, without more evidence, an intent that all damages from breach are to be in the same money. The principle of freedom of contract allows the parties to allocate the risks of currency fluctuations between foreign moneys as they desire. Sections 4 and 5 provide rules in the absence of special agreements by the parties for determining the money to be used. Parties may by agreement select a particular market or foreign exchange dealer to be used for exchange purposes.

SECTION 4. DETERMINING MONEY OF THE CLAIM.

(a) The money in which the parties to a transaction have agreed that payment is to be made is the proper money of the claim for payment.

(b) If the parties to a transaction have not otherwise agreed, the proper money of the claim, as in each case may be appropriate, is the money:

(1) regularly used between the parties as a matter of usage or course of dealing;

(2) used at the time of a transaction in international trade, by trade usage or common practice, for valuing or settling transactions in the particular commodity or service involved; or

(3) in which the loss was ultimately felt or will be incurred by the party claimant.

COMMENT

1. Subsection (a) uses "payment" in a broad sense not related to just the price, but to any obligation arising out of a contract to transfer money. See also Section 3(b).

2. Subsection (b) states rules to fill gaps in the agreement of the parties with rules as to the allocation of risks of fluctuations in exchange rates. The three rules will normally apply in the order stated. Prior dealings may indicate the desired money. If there are none, it is appropriate to use the money indicated by trade usage or custom for transactions of like kind. The final rule of subsection (a) is one established in English cases. See *The Despina R* and *The Folias*, (1979) A.C. 685. An example is the use of an operating account in United States dollars by a French company to buy Japanese yen for ship repairs; the loss is felt in the depletion of the dollar bank account. Appropriateness of a rule is to be determined by the judge from the facts of the case. See Section 6(d).

SECTION 5. DETERMINING AMOUNT OF THE MONEY OF CERTAIN CONTRACT CLAIMS.

(a) If an amount contracted to be paid in a foreign money is measured by a specified amount of a different money, the amount to be paid is determined on the conversion date.

(b) If an amount contracted to be paid in a foreign money is to be measured by a different money at the rate of exchange prevailing on a date before default, that rate of exchange applies only to payments made within a reasonable time after default, not exceeding 30 days. Thereafter, conversion is made at the bank-offered spot rate on the conversion date.

(c) A monetary claim is neither usurious nor unconscionable because the agreement on which it is based provides that the amount of the debtor's obligation to be paid in the debtor's money, when received by the creditor, must equal a specified amount of the foreign money of the country of the creditor. If, because of unexcused delay in payment of a judgment or award, the amount received by the creditor does not equal the amount of the foreign money specified in the agreement, the court or arbitrator shall amend the judgment or award accordingly.

COMMENT

1. Subsections (a) and (b) cover different interpretation problems. One arises where the amount of the money to be paid is measured by another money, one of which is foreign. An example is "pay 5,000 Swiss francs in pounds sterling." The issue is the time at which the rate of exchange into pounds sterling is to be applied. Subsection (a) says in a "measured by" situation with no rate specified, the rate of exchange that controls is the one prevailing at or near the close of business on the day before the day of payment. See Section 1(2), the definition of "conversion date."

2. Another problem arises when an exchange rate in effect before a default is used, as in "pay on November 30, 1989, 5,000 Swiss francs in pounds sterling at the exchange rate prevailing on June 30, 1989." In this case, the issue is how long does the specified exchange rate control in the absence of a clear expression of intent?

3. The most common application of subsection (c) will be found in international loan transactions. For example, a loan by a Japanese bank to an American company could be made with dollars purchased by yen for the purpose. The loan agreement could provide for repayment in dollars of an amount which, when received by the lender, would repurchase the amount of yen used to acquire the dollars advanced.

Inclusion of a fixed rate as of a date before default, under subsection (b), remains effective only if payment is made within a reasonable time after default, not to exceed 30 days. The 30-day limitation accords usually with the expectation of the parties. Parties may agree to a longer time.

An exemption is needed from the application of usury laws that may be interpreted to hold that the indexing of the principal amount creates additional interest. *See Aztec Properties, Inc. v. Union Planters National Bank*, 530 S.W.2d 756 (Tenn. Sup. Ct. 1975). The subsection removes all doubts as to the legal enforceability of such agreements under theories such as usury, merger in a judgment, unconscionability, or the like.

SECTION 6. ASSERTING AND DEFENDING FOREIGN-MONEY CLAIM.

(a) A person may assert a claim in a specified foreign money. If a foreign-money claim is not asserted, the claimant makes the claim in United States dollars.

(b) An opposing party may allege and prove that a claim, in whole or in part, is in a different money than that asserted by the claimant.

(c) A person may assert a defense, set-off, recoupment, or counterclaim in any money without regard to the money of other claims.

(d) The determination of the proper money of the claim is a question of law.

COMMENT

1. Subsection (a) covers not only the claim of a plaintiff but also the assertion by a defendant of a defense, set-off, or counterclaim. Subsection (b) provides that the money asserted as the money of its defenses by the defendant need not be the same as that of the plaintiff.

2. The money to be used as the money of the claim is a threshold issue to be determined, if contested, by the court after any factual issues as to expenditures, custom, usage, or course of dealing or decided. See subsection (b). If a payment is made or a debt incurred in a money other than that in which the loss was felt, the party asserting the foreign-money claim should establish the amount of the money of the claim used to procure the money of expenditure and the applicable exchange rate used.

3. Judgments may be entered in more than one money when dealings impact on more than one area. An inn-keeper in Mexico, for example, in taking in customers from many countries, should be held to foresee that treatment for injuries at the inn would occur not only in Mexico, but also in the native land of the injured party or in a third country.

SECTION 7. JUDGMENTS AND AWARDS ON FOREIGN-MONEY CLAIMS; TIMES OF MONEY CONVERSION; FORM OF JUDGMENT.

(a) Except as provided in subsection (c), a judgment or award on a foreign-money claim must be stated in an amount of the money of the claim.

(b) A judgment or award on a foreign-money claim is payable in that foreign money or, at the option of the debtor, in the amount of United States dollars which will purchase that foreign money on the conversion date at a bank-offered spot rate.

(c) Assessed costs must be entered in United States dollars.

(d) Each payment in United States dollars must be accepted and credited on a judgment or award on a foreign-money claim in the amount of the foreign money that could be purchased by the dollars at a bank-offered spot rate of exchange at or near the close of business on the conversion date for that payment.

(e) A judgment or award made in an action or distribution proceeding on both (i) a defense, set-off, recoupment, or counterclaim and (ii) the adverse party's claim, must be netted by converting the money of the smaller into the money of the larger, and by subtracting the smaller from the larger, and specify the rates of exchange used.

(f) A judgment substantially in the following form complies with subsection (a);

[IT IS ADJUDGED AND ORDERED, that Defendant __(insert name)__ pay to the Plaintiff __(insert name)__ the sum of __(insert amount in foreign money)__ plus interest on that sum at the rate of __(insert rate - see Section 9)__ percent a year, at the option of the judgment debtor, the number of United States dollars which will purchase the __(insert name of foreign money)__ with interest due, at a bank-offered spot rate at or near the close of business on the banking day next before the day of payment, together with assessed costs of __(insert amount)__ United States dollars.] [Note: States should insert their customary forms of judgment with appropriate modifications.]

(g) If a contract claim is of the type covered by Section 5(a) or (b), the judgment or award must be entered for the amount of money stated to measure the obligation to be paid in the money specified for payment or, at the option of the debtor, the number of United States dollars which will purchase the computed amount of the money of payment on the conversion date at a bank-offered spot rate.

(h) A judgment must be [filed] [docketed] [recorded] and indexed in foreign money in the same manner, and has the same effect as a lien, as other judgments. It may be discharged by payment.

COMMENT

1. Subsection (a) changes a number of statutes in the states which can be construed to require all values in legal proceedings to be expressed in United States dollars. Professor Brand, in his article in the Yale Journal of International Law, Vol. 11:139 at page 169, identified 18 states having statutes which could require all judgments to be entered in dollars. They are Arkansas, California, Idaho, Iowa, Louisiana, Maryland, Michigan, Montana, Nevada, New Jersey, New Mexico, New York, South Carolina, Tennessee, Vermont, Virginia, West Virginia, and Wisconsin. Brand, ibid. fn. 166. Hence, direct statutory authority must be given the courts in those states, and will be helpful in other states. In some states other statutes may need amendments. *See, e.g.*, Wisc. Stats. §§ 138.01, 138.02, 138.03, and 779.05.

2. Subsection (d) gives defendants the option of paying in dollars which are, at the payment date, practically the economic equivalent of the foreign money awarded. The judgment creditor should be indifferent to whether the debtor exercises the right to pay in dollars as the only difference is a small bank charge for exchanging the dollars for the foreign money. The concept of the rate of the banking day next before the payment day is taken from Section 131 of the Province of Ontario, Canada, Courts of Justice Act (Ch. 11 Ont. Stats. (1984) as recently amended). It gives the defendant and the sheriff conducting the sale the necessary conversion rate comfortably ahead of its use. Newspaper quotations are usually said to be "at or near the close of business" on the stated date, so that phrase is used in this Act.

3. Subsection (e) provides for netting the affirmative recoveries of a defendant and plaintiff, whether in the same money or in different moneys, but preserving the quantum of each for appellate purposes. The theory is that when claims are reduced to money, they become mutual debts and should be set-off, so that a person's exchange rate fluctuation risk continues only for the surplus in its money of the claim. The set-off is made by the judge or arbitrator.

4. The form of judgment in subsection (f) should be varied appropriately where the money to be paid is measured by a foreign money. See Section 5.

SECTION 8. CONVERSIONS OF FOREIGN MONEY IN DISTRIBUTION PROCEEDING.

The rate of exchange prevailing at or near the close of business on the day the distribution proceeding is initiated governs all exchanges of foreign money in a distribution proceeding. A foreign-money claimant in a distribution proceeding shall assert its claim in the named foreign money and show the amount of United States dollars resulting from a conversion as of the date the proceeding was initiated.

COMMENT

All claims must be in the same money when determining aliquot shares in a distribution proceeding. The Act requires use of the date the proceeding was initiated for applying the exchange rate to convert foreign-money claims into United States dollars. *See Re Lines Bros. Ltd.*, (1982) 2 All E.R. 99. A claim may be amended to show the proper conversion rate and the proper amount of United States dollars.

SECTION 9. PRE-JUDGMENT AND JUDGMENT INTEREST.

(a) With respect to a foreign-money claim, recovery of pre-judgment or pre-award interest and the rate of interest to be applied in the action or distribution proceeding, except as provided in subsection (b), are matters of the substantive law governing the right to recovery under the conflict-of-laws rules of this State.

(b) The court or arbitrator shall increase or decrease the amount of pre-judgment or pre-award interest otherwise payable in a judgment or award in foreign-money to the extent required by the law of this State governing a failure to make or accept an offer of settlement or offer of judgment, or conduct by a party or its attorney causing undue delay or expense.

(c) A judgment or award on a foreign-money claim bears interest at the rate applicable to judgments of this State.

COMMENT

1. As to pre-judgment interest, the Act adopts the majority rule in the United States that pre-judgment interest follows the substantive law of the case under conflict of laws rules, both as to the right to recover and the rate. English courts use a different rule, *i.e.*, the borrowing rate used by plaintiff or prevailing in the country issuing the money of the judgment. *See Helmsing Schiffarts G.M.B.H. v. Malta Drydock Corp.* (1977) 2 LLOYD'S REP. 44 (Maltese money but borrowed in West Germany; German rate); *Miliangos v. George Frank (Textiles) Ltd. (No. 2)*, (1976) 1 QB 487 at 489 (Swiss money, Swiss interest rate). Although pre-judgment interest is one form of damages, provision for pre-judgment interest is not to be taken as indicating that no other damages for delay in payment can be awarded under the substantive law applicable to the determination of damages. *Cf. Isaac Naylor & Sons, Ltd. v. New Zealand Co-operative Wool Marketing Association, Ltd.* (1981) 1 N.Z.L.R. 361 (exchange loss due to delay as additional damages).

2. Allowances of pre-judgment interest in some states depend upon a party's conduct with respect to settlement or delay of the proceeding. Subsection (b) treats these state laws as either procedural in nature or expressions of a significant policy, in either case to be governed by the law of the forum state.

3. Interest on a judgment is considered to be procedural and also goes by the law of the forum. There is a problem here in that there is great discrepancy among the states in the rates for judgment interest. When a judgment is in a foreign money, United States interest rates may result in some overcompensation or undercompensation as compared to what would be awarded in the jurisdiction issuing the foreign money. But in both the United States and in foreign countries, most jurisdictions have fixed statutory rates that do not readily respond to the inflation or deflation of the value of their money in the world market. Hence it was decided to apply the usual rules of the conflict of laws.

SECTION 10. ENFORCEMENT OF FOREIGN JUDGMENTS.

(a) If an action is brought to enforce a judgment of another jurisdiction expressed in a foreign money and the judgment is recognized in this State as enforceable, the enforcing judgment must be entered as provided in Section 7, whether or not the foreign judgment confers an option to pay in an equivalent amount of United States dollars.

(b) A foreign judgment may be [filed] [docketed] [recorded] in accordance with any rule or statute of this State providing a procedure for its recognition and enforcement.

(c) A satisfaction or partial payment made upon the foreign judgment, on proof thereof, must be credited against the amount of foreign money specified in the judgment, notwithstanding the entry of judgment in this State.

(d) A judgment entered on a foreign-money claim only in United States dollars in another state must be enforced in this State in United States dollars only.

COMMENT

1. Some states have special acts that simply cover the recognition, entry, and enforcement of foreign judgments. Common law enforcement is by action. Subsection (a) refers to the common law method; it is subject to subsection (b) which refers to statutory procedures. Subsection (c) applies to both procedures.

2. Subsection (d) avoids constitutional issues under the full faith and credit clause by requiring that judgments of sister states be enforced as entered in the sister state.

SECTION 11. DETERMINING UNITED STATES DOLLAR VALUE OF FOREIGN-MONEY CLAIMS FOR LIMITED PURPOSES.

(a) Computations under this section are for the limited purposes of the section and do not affect computation of the United States dollar equivalent of the money of the judgment for the purpose of payment.

(b) For the limited purpose of facilitating the enforcement of provisional remedies in an action, the value in United States dollars of assets to be seized or restrained pursuant to a writ of attachment, garnishment, execution, or other process, the amount of United States dollars at issue for assessing costs, or the amount of United States dollars involved for a surety bond or other court-required undertaking, must be ascertained as provided in subsections (c) and (d).

(c) A party seeking process, costs, bond, or other undertaking under subsection (b) shall compute in United States dollars the amount of the foreign money claimed from a bank-offered spot rate prevailing at or near the close of business on the banking day next preceding the filing of a request or application for the issuance of process or for the determination of costs, or an application for a bond or other court-required undertaking.

(d) A party seeking process, costs, bond, or other undertaking under subsection (b) shall file with each request or application an affidavit or certificate executed in good faith by its counsel or a bank officer, stating the market quotation used and how it was obtained, and setting forth the calculation. Affected court officials incur no liability, after a filing of the affidavit or certificate, for acting as if the judgment were in the amount of United States dollars stated in the affidavit or certificate.

COMMENT

This section protects those who must determine how much should be held subject to a levy or other collection process or what the dollar amount of a supersedeas or other surety bond should be. If the judgment debtor is damaged by a gross overstatement of the dollar amount in the affidavit or certificate of counsel for the judgment creditor or the bank officer, recovery should be against that person.

SECTION 12. EFFECT OF CURRENCY REVALORIZATION.

(a) If, after an obligation is expressed or a loss is incurred in a foreign money, the country issuing or adopting that money substitutes a new money in place of that money, the obligation or the loss is treated as if expressed or incurred in the new money at a rate of conversion the issuing country establishes for the payment of like obligations or losses denominated in the former money.

(b) If substitution under subsection (a) occurs after a judgment or award is entered on a foreign-money claim, the court or arbitrator shall amend the judgment or award by a like conversion of the former money.

COMMENT

1. Subsection (a) refers to situations in which a country authorizes the issue of a new money to take the place of the old money at a stated ratio. An example is Brazil's recent abolition of cruzieros for cruzados. The subsection mandates that foreign money claims should be subjected to the same ratio.

2. The Act takes no position on the effect of money repudiations or revalorizations so drastic as to be, in effect, confiscations. Remedy, if any, for these is usually found through diplomatic channels. Equally, the Act takes no position on the effect of exchange control laws. The effect, if any, on obligations to pay is left to other law.

SECTION 13. SUPPLEMENTARY GENERAL PRINCIPLES OF LAW.

Unless displaced by particular provisions of this [Act], the principles of law and equity, including the law merchant, and the law relative to capacity to contract, principal and agent, estoppel, fraud, misrepresentation, duress, coercion, mistake, bankruptcy, or other validating or invalidating causes supplement its provisions.

624

COMMENT

The section is taken from Section 1-103 of the Uniform Commercial Code.

SECTION 14. UNIFORMITY OF APPLICATION AND CONSTRUCTION.

This [Act] shall be applied and construed to effectuate its general purpose to make uniform the law with respect to the subject of this [Act] among states enacting it.

SECTION 15. SHORT TITLE.

This [Act] may be cited as the Uniform Foreign-Money Claims Act.

SECTION 16. SEVERABILITY CLAUSE.

If any provision of this [Act] or its application to any person or circumstance is held invalid, the invalidity does not affect other provisions or applications of this [Act] which can be given effect without the invalid provision or application, and to this end the provisions of this [Act] are severable.

SECTION 17. EFFECTIVE DATE.

This [Act] becomes effective on January 1st following its enactment.

SECTION 18. TRANSITIONAL PROVISION.

This [Act] applies to actions and distribution proceedings commenced after its effective date.

[SECTION 19. REPEALS.

The following acts and parts of acts are repealed:

(1) [Any statute requiring judgments to be entered in United States dollars.]

(2) _____.

(3) _____.]

E. ABA Model Rule for the Licensing of Foreign Legal Consultants

Source: ABA Section of International Law and Practice, Report to the House of Delegates: Model Rule for the Licensing of Legal Consultants, 28 INT'L LAW. 207 (1994).

Introduction

The ABA Model Rule for the Licensing of Foreign Legal Consultants was adopted by the ABA House of Delegates in August 1993. The text of the Model Rule as published in the *International Lawyer* is accompanied by a rather substantial and informative report of the Section of International Law and Practice. As that report explains, the Model Rule closely follows the "New York Rule" adopted in 1974 as New York Rules of Court, Rules of the Court of Appeals, Pt. 521.

AMERICAN BAR ASSOCIATION
SECTION OF INTERNATIONAL LAW AND PRACTICE
REPORT TO THE HOUSE OF DELEGATES

MODEL RULE FOR THE LICENSING OF LEGAL CONSULTANTS

§ 1. General Regulation as to Licensing

In its discretion, the [name of court] may license to practice in this State as a legal consultant, without examination, an applicant who:

(a) is a member in good standing of a recognized legal profession in a foreign country, the members of which are admitted to practice as attorneys or counselors at law or the equivalent and are subject to effective regulation and discipline by a duly constituted professional body or a public authority;

(b) for at least five of the seven years immediately preceding his or her application has been a member in good standing of such legal profession and has actually been engaged in the practice of law in the said foreign country or elsewhere substantially involving or relating to the rendering of advice or the provision of legal services concerning the law of the said foreign country;[*]

(c) possesses the good moral character and general fitness requisite for a member of the bar of this State;

(d) is at least twenty-six years of age;[**] and

(e) intends to practice as a legal consultant in this State and to maintain an office in this State for that purpose.

§ 2. Proof Required

An applicant under this Rule shall file with the clerk of the [name of court]:

(a) a certificate from the professional body or public authority in such foreign country having final jurisdiction over professional discipline, certifying as to the applicant's admission to practice and the date thereof, and as to his or her good standing as such attorney or counselor at law or the equivalent;

(b) a letter of recommendation from one of the members of the executive body of such professional body or public authority or from one of the judges of the highest law court or court of original jurisdiction of such foreign country;

(c) a duly authenticated English translation of such certificate and such letter if, in either case, it is not in English; and

---

[*]Section 1(b) is optional; it may be included as written, modified through the substitution of shorter periods than five and seven years, respectively, or omitted entirely.

[**]Section 1(d) is optional; it may be included as written, modified through the substitution of a lesser age than twenty-six years, or omitted entirely.

(d) such other evidence as to the applicant's educational and professional qualifications, good moral character and general fitness, and compliance with the requirements of Section 1 of this Rule as the [name of court] may require.

§ 3. Reciprocal Treatment of Members of the Bar of this State

In considering whether to license an applicant to practice as a legal consultant, the [name of court] may in its discretion take into account whether a member of the bar of this State would have a reasonable and practical opportunity to establish an office for the giving of legal advice to clients in the applicant's country of admission. Any member of the bar who is seeking or has sought to establish an office in that country may request the court to consider the matter, or the [name of court] may do so sua sponte.

§ 4. Scope of Practice

A person licensed to practice as a legal consultant under this Rule may render legal services in this State subject, however, to the limitations that he or she shall not:

(a) appear for a person other than himself or herself as attorney in any court, or before any magistrate or other judicial officer, in this State (other than upon admission pro hac vice pursuant to [citation of applicable rule]);

(b) prepare any instrument effecting the transfer or registration of title to real estate located in the United States of America;

(c) prepare:
   (i) any will or trust instrument effecting the disposition on death of any property located in the United States of America and owned by a resident thereof, or
   (ii) any instrument relating to the administration of a decedent's estate in the United States of America;

(d) prepare any instrument in respect of the marital or parental relations, rights or duties of a resident of the United States of America, or the custody or care of the children of such a resident;

(e) render professional legal advice on the law of this State or of the United States of America (whether rendered incident to the preparation of legal instruments or otherwise) except on the basis of advice from a person duly qualified and entitled (otherwise than by virtue of having been licensed under this Rule) to render professional legal advice in this State;

(f) be, or in any way hold himself or herself out as, a member of the bar of this State; or

(g) carry on his or her practice under, or utilize in connection with such practice, any name, title or designation other than one or more of the following:
   (i) his or her own name;
   (ii) the name of the law firm with which he or she is affiliated;
   (iii) his or her authorized title in the foreign country of his or her admission to practice, which may be used in conjunction with the name of such country; and

(iv) the title "legal consultant," which may be used in conjunction with the words "admitted to the practice of law in [name of the foreign country of his or her admission to practice]".

§ 5. Rights and Obligations

Subject to the limitations set forth in Section 4 of this Rule, a person licensed as a legal consultant under this Rule shall be considered a lawyer affiliated with the bar of this State and shall be entitled and subject to:

(a) the rights and obligations set forth in the [Rules] [Code] of Professional [Conduct] [Responsibility] of [citation] or arising from the other conditions and requirements that apply to a member of the bar of this State under the [rules of court governing members of the bar]; and

(b) the rights and obligations of a member of the bar of this State with respect to:

(i) affiliation in the same law firm with one or more members of the bar of this State, including by:

(A) employing one or more members of the bar of this State;

(B) being employed by one or more members of the bar of this State or by any partnership [or professional corporation] which includes members of the bar of this State or which maintains an office in this State; and

(C) being a partner in any partnership [or shareholder in any professional corporation] which includes members of the bar of this State or which maintains an office in this State; and

(ii) attorney-client privilege, work-product privilege and similar professional privileges.

§ 6. Disciplinary Provisions

A person licensed to practice as a legal consultant under this Rule shall be subject to professional discipline in the same manner and to the same extent as members of the bar of this State and to this end:

(a) Every person licensed to practice as a legal consultant under these Rules:

(i) shall be subject to control by the [name of court] and to censure, suspension, removal or revocation of his or her license to practice by the [name of court] and shall otherwise be governed by [citation of applicable statutory provisions]; and

(ii) shall execute and file with the [name of court], in such form and manner as such court may prescribe:

(A) his or her commitment to observe the [Rules] [Code] of Professional [Conduct] [Responsibility] of [citation] and the [rules of court governing members of the bar] to the extent applicable to the legal services authorized under Section 4 of this Rule;

(B) an undertaking or appropriate evidence of professional liability insurance, in such amount as the court may prescribe, to assure his or her proper professional conduct and responsibility;

(C) a written undertaking to notify the court of any change in such person's good standing as a member of the foreign legal profession referred to in Section 1(a) of this Rule and of any final action of the professional body or public authority referred to in Section 2(a) of this Rule imposing any disciplinary censure, suspension, or other sanction upon such person; and

(D) a duly acknowledged instrument, in writing, setting forth his or her address in this State and designating the clerk of such court as his or her agent upon whom process may be served, with like effect as if served personally upon him or her, in any action or proceeding thereafter brought against him or her and arising out of or based upon any legal services rendered or offered to be rendered by him or her within or to residents of this State, whenever after due diligence service cannot be made upon him or her at such address or at such new address in this State as he or she shall have filed in the office of such clerk by means of a duly acknowledged supplemental instrument in writing.

(b) Service of process on such clerk, pursuant to the designation filed as aforesaid, shall be made by personally delivering to and leaving with such clerk, or with a deputy or assistant authorized by him or her to receive such service, at his or her office, duplicate copies of such process together with a fee of $10. Service of process shall be complete when such clerk has been so served. Such clerk shall promptly send one of such copies to the legal consultant to whom the process is directed, by certified mail, return receipt requested, addressed to such legal consultant at the address specified by him or her as aforesaid.

§ 7. Application and Renewal Fees

An applicant for a license as a legal consultant under this Rule shall pay an application fee which shall be equal to the fee required to be paid by a person applying for admission as a member of the bar of this State under [rules of court governing admission without examination of persons admitted to practice in other States]. A person licensed as a legal consultant shall pay renewal fees which shall be equal to the fees required to be paid by a member of the bar of this State for renewal of his or her license to engage in the practice of law in this State.

§ 8. Revocation of License

In the event that the [name of court] determines that a person licensed as a legal consultant under this Rule no longer meets the requirements for license set forth in Section 1(a) or Section 1(c) of this Rule, it shall revoke the license granted to such person hereunder.

§ 9. Admission to Bar

In the event that a person licensed as a legal consultant under this Rule is subsequently admitted as a member of the bar of this State under the provisions of the Rules governing such admission, the license granted to such person hereunder shall be deemed superseded by the license granted to such person to practice law as a member of the bar of this State.

§ 10. Application for Waiver of Provisions

The [name of court] upon application, may in its discretion vary the application of or waive any provision of this Rule where strict compliance will cause undue hardship to the applicant. Such application shall be in the form of a verified petition setting forth the applicant's name age and residence address, the facts relied upon and a prayer for relief.

PART V. LAWS OF OTHER NATIONS

A. Selected Provisions of the English Sale of Goods Act

Source: Sale of Goods Act 1979 (c 54), 6 December 1979

Website information:

http://www.jus.uio.no/lm/england.sale.of.goods.act.1979/doc.html
This website contains links to the full text of the English Sale of Goods Act 1979.

Introduction

The English Sale of Goods Act 1979 (ESGA) replaced the Sale of Goods Act, 1893,[1] and parts of other statutes.[2] Representing a convenient way to consolidate and update some of the law of the intervening period, the 1979 Act is very similar to the 1893 Act, and applies retroactively to all contracts for the sale of goods made on or after 1 January 1894 (the date the original Act entered into force).[3] Because the Act is a so called "consolidating act," precedents interpreting the superseded statute are still good law.[4]

The Sale of Goods Bill was drafted in 1888 by Sir Mackenzie Chalmers. As enacted, it formed the basis for a number statutes in other common law jurisdictions, including the Uniform Sales Act (U.S.A.), which was the predecessor to the Uniform Commercial Code.[5] The ESGA was adopted with very little modification in most of the jurisdictions of the British Commonwealth, including Australia, New Zealand and India.[6]

The ESGA generally applies to all types of contracts for the sale of goods.[7] It was considered both a virtue and a fault of the 1893 Act that "virtually no distinctions were made between commercial sales and private sales, between merchants' sales and retail sales, or between sales of new

---

[1] 56 & 57 VICT. C. 71.

[2] *E.g.,* Misrepresentation Act, 1967, §4; Misrepresentation (Northern Ireland) Act, 1967, §4; Supply of Goods (Implied Terms) Act, 1973, §§1-7, 18(2).

[3] §1(1). *See* CHALMER'S SALE OF GOODS ACT, 1893 (Michael Mark, ed., 15th ed. 1967).

[4] "There is a presumption in construing a consolidating act that no alteration of the previous law was intended. . . . The presumption applies even if the language of the two provisions is not identical; but this view must yield to plain words to the contrary." BENJAMIN'S SALE OF GOODS, 7 (A. G. Guest et al. eds., 3d ed. 1987) *citing* MacConnell v. E. Prill & Co. [1916] 2 Ch. 57, 63.

[5] It is important to note the substantial differences between the U.S.A. and U.C.C. The U.C.C.—and, therefore, American law—is significantly different in many respects to the Sale of Goods Act.

[6] BENJAMIN'S SALE OF GOODS, *supra* note 4, at 4.

[7] *Id.* at 7.

633

and of second-hand goods."[8] The 1979 Act does away with the sweeping application of every provision; while it remains generally applicable to all sales of goods, the introduction into the Act of parts of other legislation (and the fact that other pieces of legislation are expressly saved by the new Act) makes particular parts of the Act applicable to one type of sale but not to others. For example, if a contract has an international element, several statutory provisions outside the context of the Act may come into play.[9] Section 62(2) saves "the rules of the common law, including the law merchant, except in so far as they are inconsistent with the provisions of this Act."

The basic scope of the Act was stated by Lord Diplock in *Ashington Piggeries Ltd. v. Christopher Hill Ltd.*:[10]

The provisions of the Act are in the main confined to statements of what promises are to be implied on the part of the buyer and the seller in respect of matters upon which the contract is silent, and to statements of the consequences of performance or non-performance of promises, whether express or implied, where the contract does not state what those consequences are to be.

Thus, Lord Diplock clearly implies that freedom of contract is an essential feature of the Act.[11]

The Act covers five broad topics: contract formation (Part I); transfer of property/title (Part II); contract performance (Part III); rights of the unpaid seller against the goods (Part IV); and, actions for breach of contract (Part V). It contains over 60 sections, most of which are not reproduced here.

---

[8]*Id.*

[9]*See id.* at 8; The Uniform Laws on International Sales Act, 1967 was enabling legislation for the two predecessors (ULF and ULIS) to the U.N. Convention on Contracts for the International Sales of Goods (CISG). The United Kingdom has not become party to the CISG; therefore, even though the Uniform Laws Act remains in force, it would presumably not be applied.

[10][1972] A.C. 441, 501.

[11]§ 55(1).

SALE OF GOODS ACT 1979 (C 54)
6 DECEMBER 1979

16. Goods must be ascertained

[Subject to section 20A below] where there is a contract for the sale of unascertained goods no property in the goods is transferred to the buyer unless and until the goods are ascertained.

ANNOTATIONS: This section derived from the Sale of Goods Act 1893, § 16. Words in square brackets added by the Sale of Goods (Amendment) Act 1995, § 1(1).

17. Property passes when intended to pass

(1) Where there is a contract for the sale of specific or ascertained goods the property in them is transferred to the buyer at such time as the parties to the contract intend it to be transferred.

(2) For the purpose of ascertaining the intention of the parties regard shall be had to the terms of the contract, the conduct of the parties and the circumstances of the case.

ANNOTATIONS: This section derived from the Sale of Goods Act 1893, § 17.

18. Rules for ascertaining intention

Unless a different intention appears, the following are rules for ascertaining the intention of the parties as to the time at which the property in the goods is to pass to the buyer.

Rule 1.—Where there is an unconditional contract for the sale of specific goods in a deliverable state the property in the goods passes to the buyer when the contract is made, and it is immaterial whether the time of payment or the time of delivery, or both, be postponed.

Rule 2.—Where there is a contract for the sale of specific goods and the seller is bound to do something to the goods for the purpose of putting them into a deliverable state, the property does not pass until the thing is done and the buyer has notice that it has been done.

Rule 3.—Where there is a contract for the sale of specific goods in a deliverable state but the seller is bound to weigh, measure, test, or do some other act or thing with reference to the goods for the purpose of ascertaining the price, the property does not pass until the act or thing is done and the buyer has notice that it has been done.

Rule 4.—When goods are delivered to the buyer on approval or on sale or return or other similar terms the property in the goods passes to the buyer:—

(a) when he signifies his approval or acceptance to the seller or does any other act adopting the transaction;

(b) if he does not signify his approval or acceptance to the seller but retains the goods without giving notice of rejection, then, if a time has been fixed for the return of the goods, on the expiration of that time, and, if no time has been fixed, on the expiration of a reasonable time.

Rule 5.—(1) Where there is a contract for the sale of unascertained or future goods by description, and goods of that description and in a deliverable state are unconditionally appropriated to the contract, either by the seller with the assent of the buyer or by the buyer with the assent of the seller, the property in the goods then passes to the buyer; and the assent may be express or implied, and may be given either before or after the appropriation is made.

(2) Where, in pursuance of the contract, the seller delivers the goods to the buyer or to a carrier or other bailee or custodier (whether named by the buyer or not) for the purpose of transmission to the buyer, and does not reserve the right of disposal, he is to be taken to have unconditionally appropriated the goods to the contract.

(3) Where there is a contract for the sale of a specified quantity of unascertained goods in a deliverable state forming part of a bulk which is identified either in the contract or by subsequent

agreement between the parties and the bulk is reduced to (or to less than) that quantity, then, if the buyer under that contract is the only buyer to whom goods are then due out of the bulk—

(a) the remaining goods are to be taken as appropriated to that contract at the time when the bulk is so reduced; and

(b) the property in those goods then passes to that buyer.

(4) Paragraph (3) above applies also (with the necessary modifications) where a bulk is reduced to (or to less than) the aggregate of the quantities due to a single buyer under separate contracts relating to that bulk and he is the only buyer to whom goods are then due out of that bulk.

ANNOTATIONS: This section derived from the Sale of Goods Act 1893, § 18. Rule 5: paras. (3), (4) added by the Sale of Goods (Amendment) Act 1995, § 1(2).

19. Reservation of right of disposal

(1) Where there is a contract for the sale of specific goods or where goods are subsequently appropriated to the contract, the seller may, by the terms of the contract or appropriation, reserve the right of disposal of the goods until certain conditions are fulfilled; and in such a case, notwithstanding the delivery of the goods to the buyer, or to a carrier or other bailee or custodier for the purpose of transmission to the buyer, the property in the goods does not pass to the buyer until the conditions imposed by the seller are fulfilled.

(2) Where goods are shipped, and by the bill of lading the goods are deliverable to the order of the seller or his agent, the seller is prima facie to be taken to reserve the right of disposal.

(3) Where the seller of goods draws on the buyer for the price, and transmits the bill of exchange and bill of lading to the buyer together to secure acceptance or payment of the bill of exchange, the buyer is bound to return the bill of lading if he does not honour the bill of exchange, and if he wrongfully retains the bill of lading the property in the goods does not pass to him.

ANNOTATIONS: This section derived from the Sale of Goods Act 1893, § 19.

20. Risk prima facie passes with property

(1) Unless otherwise agreed, the goods remain at the seller's risk until the property in them is transferred to the buyer, but when the property in them is transferred to the buyer the goods are at the buyer's risk whether delivery has been made or not.

(2) But where delivery has been delayed through the fault of either buyer or seller the goods are at the risk of the party at fault as regards any loss which might not have occurred but for such fault.

(3) Nothing in this section affects the duties or liabilities of either seller or buyer as a bailee or custodier of the goods of the other party.

ANNOTATIONS: This section derived from the Sale of Goods Act 1893, § 20.

20A. Undivided shares in goods forming part of a bulk

(1) This section applies to a contract for the sale of a specified quantity of unascertained goods if the following conditions are met—

(a) the goods or some of them form part of a bulk which is identified either in the contract or by subsequent agreement between the parties; and

(b) the buyer has paid the price for some or all of the goods which are the subject of the contract and which form part of the bulk.

(2) Where this section applies, then (unless the parties agree otherwise), as soon as the conditions specified in paragraphs (a) and (b) of subsection (1) above are met or at such later time as the parties may agree—

(a) property in an undivided share in the bulk is transferred to the buyer, and

(b) the buyer becomes an owner in common of the bulk.

(3) Subject to subsection (4) below, for the purposes of this section, the undivided share of a buyer in a bulk at any time shall be such share as the quantity of goods paid for and due to the buyer out of the bulk bears to the quantity of goods in the bulk at that time.

(4) Where the aggregate of the undivided shares of buyers in a bulk determined under subsection (3) above would at any time exceed the whole of the bulk at that time, the undivided share in the bulk of each buyer shall be reduced proportionately so that the aggregate of the undivided shares is equal to the whole bulk.

(5) Where a buyer has paid the price for only some of the goods due to him out of a bulk, any delivery to the buyer out of the bulk shall, for the purposes of this section, be ascribed in the first place to the goods in respect of which payment has been made.

(6) For the purposes of this section payment of part of the price for any goods shall be treated as payment for a corresponding part of the goods.]

ANNOTATIONS: This section was added by the Sale of Goods (Amendment) Act 1995, § 1(3).

20B. Deemed consent by co-owner to dealings in bulk goods

(1) A person who has become an owner in common of a bulk by virtue of section 20A above shall be deemed to have consented to—

(a) any delivery of goods out of the bulk to any other owner in common of the bulk, being goods which are due to him under his contract;

(b) any dealing with or removal, delivery or disposal of goods in the bulk by any other person who is an owner in common of the bulk in so far as the goods fall within that co-owner's undivided share in the bulk at the time of the dealing, removal, delivery or disposal.

(2) No cause of action shall accrue to anyone against a person by reason of that person having acted in accordance with paragraph (a) or (b) of subsection (1) above in reliance on any consent deemed to have been given under that subsection.

(3) Nothing in this section or section 20A above shall—

(a) impose an obligation on a buyer of goods out of a bulk to compensate any other buyer of goods out of that bulk for any shortfall in the goods received by that other buyer;

(b) affect any contractual arrangement between buyers of goods out of a bulk for adjustments between themselves; or

(c) affect the rights of any buyer under his contract.]

ANNOTATIONS: This section was added by the Sale of Goods (Amendment) Act 1995, s 1(3).

Part III: Effects of the Contract: Transfer of title

Part IV: Performance of the Contract

27. Duties of seller and buyer

It is the duty of the seller to deliver the goods, and of the buyer to accept and pay for them, in accordance with the terms of the contract of sale.

ANNOTATIONS: This section derived from the Sale of Goods Act 1893, § 27.

28. Payment and delivery are concurrent conditions

Unless otherwise agreed, delivery of the goods and payment of the price are concurrent conditions, that is to say, the seller must be ready and willing to give possession of the goods to the buyer in exchange for the price and the buyer must be ready and willing to pay the price in exchange for possession of the goods.

ANNOTATIONS: This section derived from the Sale of Goods Act 1893, § 28.

29. Rules about delivery

(1) Whether it is for the buyer to take possession of the goods or for the seller to send them to the buyer is a question depending in each case on the contract, express or implied, between the parties.

(2) Apart from any such contract, express or implied, the place of delivery is the seller's place of business if he has one, and if not, his residence; except that, if the contract is for the sale of specific goods, which to the knowledge of the parties when the contract is made are in some other place, then that place is the place of delivery.

(3) Where under the contract of sale the seller is bound to send the goods to the buyer, but no time for sending them is fixed, the seller is bound to send them within a reasonable time.

(4) Where the goods at the time of sale are in the possession of a third person, there is no delivery by seller to buyer unless and until the third person acknowledges to the buyer that he holds the goods on his behalf; but nothing in this section affects the operation of the issue or transfer of any document of title to goods.

(5) Demand or tender of delivery may be treated as ineffectual unless made at a reasonable hour; and what is a reasonable hour is a question of fact.

(6) Unless otherwise agreed, the expenses of and incidental to putting the goods into a deliverable state must be borne by the seller.

ANNOTATIONS: This section derived from the Sale of Goods Act 1893, § 29.

30. Delivery of wrong quantity
31. Instalment deliveries

32. Delivery to Carrier

(1) Where, in pursuance of a contract of sale, the seller is authorised or required to send the goods to the buyer, delivery of the goods to a carrier (whether named by the buyer or not) for the purpose of transmission to the buyer is prima facie deemed to be a delivery of the goods to the buyer.

(2) Unless otherwise authorised by the buyer, the seller must make such contract with the carrier on behalf of the buyer as may be reasonable having regard to the nature of the goods and the other circumstances of the case; and if the seller omits to do so, and the goods are lost or damaged in course of transit, the buyer may decline to treat the delivery to the carrier as a delivery to himself or may hold the seller responsible in damages.

(3) Unless otherwise agreed, where goods are sent by the seller to the buyer by a route involving sea transit, under circumstances in which it is usual to insure, the seller must give such notice to the buyer as may enable him to insure them during their sea transit; and if the seller fails to do so, the goods are at his risk during such sea transit.

ANNOTATIONS: This section derived from the Sale of Goods Act 1893, § 32.

33. Risk where goods are delivered at distant place

Where the seller of goods agrees to deliver them at his own risk at a place other than that where they are when sold, the buyer must nevertheless (unless otherwise agreed) take any risk of deterioration in the goods necessarily incident to the course of transit.

ANNOTATIONS: This section derived from the Sale of Goods Act 1893, § 33.

34. Buyer's right of examining the goods

... Unless otherwise agreed, when the seller tenders delivery of goods to the buyer, he is bound on request to afford the buyer a reasonable opportunity of examining the goods for the purpose of ascertaining whether they are in conformity with the contract [and, in the case of a contract for sale by sample, of comparing the bulk with the sample.]

ANNOTATIONS: This section derived from the Sale of Goods Act 1893, § 34. Words omitted repealed, and words in square brackets added, by the Sale and Supply of Goods Act 1994, §§ 2(2), 7, Sch 3.

Section 35. Acceptance

(1) The buyer is deemed to have accepted the goods [subject to subsection (2) below—

    (a) when he intimates to the seller that he has accepted them, or

    (b) when the goods have been delivered to him and he does any act in relation to them which is inconsistent with the ownership of the seller.

(2) Where goods are delivered to the buyer, and he has not previously examined them, he is not deemed to have accepted them under subsection (1) above until he has had a reasonable opportunity of examining them for the purpose—

    (a) of ascertaining whether they are in conformity with the contract, and

    (b) in the case of a contract for sale by sample, of comparing the bulk with the sample.

(3) Where the buyer deals as consumer or (in Scotland) the contract of sale is a consumer contract, the buyer cannot lose his right to rely on subsection (2) above by agreement, waiver or otherwise.

(4) The buyer is also deemed to have accepted the goods when after the lapse of a reasonable time he retains the goods without intimating to the seller that he has rejected them.

(5) The questions that are material in determining for the purposes of subsection (4) above whether a reasonable time has elapsed include whether the buyer has had a reasonable opportunity of examining the goods for the purpose mentioned in subsection (2) above.

(6) The buyer is not by virtue of this section deemed to have accepted the goods merely because—

    (a) he asks for, or agrees to, their repair by or under an arrangement with the seller, or

    (b) the goods are delivered to another under a sub-sale or other disposition.

(7) Where the contract is for the sale of goods making one or more commercial units, a buyer accepting any goods included in a unit is deemed to have accepted all the goods making the unit; and in this subsection "commercial unit" means a unit division of which would materially impair the value of the goods or the character of the unit.

Sub-§ (1) derived from the Sale of Goods Act 1893, § 35. Words in square brackets substituted by the Sale and Supply of Goods Act 1994, § 2(1).

49. Action for price

(1) Where, under a contract of sale, the property in the goods has passed to the buyer and he wrongfully neglects or refuses to pay for the goods according to the terms of the contract, the seller may maintain an action against him for the price of the goods.

(2) Where, under a contract of sale, the price is payable on a day certain irrespective of delivery and the buyer wrongfully neglects or refuses to pay such price, the seller may maintain an action for the price, although the property in the goods has not passed and the goods have not been appropriated to the contract.

(3) . . .

ANNOTATIONS: This section derived from the Sale of Goods Act 1893, § 49. Sub-s (3): applies to Scotland only.

50. Damages for non-acceptance

(1) Where the buyer wrongfully neglects or refuses to accept and pay for the goods, the seller may maintain an action against him for damages for non-acceptance.

(2) The measure of damages is the estimated loss directly and naturally resulting, in the ordinary course of events, from the buyer's breach of contract.

(3) Where there is an available market for the goods in question the measure of damages is prima facie to be ascertained by the difference between the contract price and the market or current price at the time or times when the goods ought to have been accepted or (if no time was fixed for acceptance) at the time of the refusal to accept.

ANNOTATIONS: This section derived from the Sale of Goods Act 1893, § 50.

Part VI: Actions for Breach of the Contract: Buyer's remedies

51. Damages for non-delivery

(1) Where the seller wrongfully neglects or refuses to deliver the goods to the buyer, the buyer may maintain an action against the seller for damages for non-delivery.

(2) The measure of damages is the estimated loss directly and naturally resulting, in the ordinary course of events, from the seller's breach of contract.

(3) Where there is an available market for the goods in question the measure of damages is prima facie to be ascertained by the difference between the contract price and the market or current price of the goods at the time or times when they ought to have been delivered or (if no time was fixed) at the time of the refusal to deliver.

ANNOTATIONS: This section derived from the Sale of Goods Act 1893, s 51.

52. Specific performance

(1) In any action for breach of contract to deliver specific or ascertained goods the court may, if it thinks fit, on the plaintiff's application, by its judgment or decree direct that the contract shall be performed specifically, without giving the defendant the option of retaining the goods on payment of damages.

(2) The plaintiff's application may be made at any time before judgment or decree.

(3) The judgment or decree may be unconditional, or on such terms and conditions as to damages, payment of the price and otherwise as seem just to the court.

(4) . . .

ANNOTATIONS: This section derived from the Sale of Goods Act 1893, s 52. Sub-s (4): applies to Scotland only.

53. Remedy for breach of warranty

Part VI: Actions for Breach of the Contract: Interest, etc.

54. Interest

Part VII: Supplementary

55.   Exclusion of implied terms
56.   Conflict of laws
57.   Auction sales
58.
59.   Reasonable time a question of fact
60.   Rights etc. enforceable by action

61. Interpretation

(1) In this Act, unless the context or subject matter otherwise requires—

. . . . .

"delivery" means voluntary transfer of possession from one person to another [except that in relation to sections 20A and 20B above it includes such appropriation of goods to the contract as results in property in the goods being transferred to the buyer;]

. . . . .

"property" means the general property in goods, and not merely a special property;

B. U.K. Protection of Trading Interests Act 1980

Source: Protection of Trading Interests Act 1980 (c 11) 20 March 1980

Introduction

The British Protection of Trading Interests Act 1980 is an example of "blocking legislation" enacted largely in response to the *Westinghouse Uranium Litigation* that took place in the United States in the 1970's. That litigation involved allegations of antitrust violations on the part of non-U.S. companies engaged in the mining and sale or uranium, after the world market price had increased dramatically and Westinghouse was unable to continue profitably to supply uranium for nuclear reactors it had constructed. The Act combines attacks on the process of discovery with limitations on the enforcement of foreign court damage awards.

Section 2 of the Act allows the Secretary of State to order prohibition of compliance with discovery orders issued from overseas courts, tribunals or authorities for purposes of protecting the interests of the United Kingdom, and § 3 makes failure to comply with such an order punishable by a fine. Sections 5 and 6 deal with the enforcement of multiple damages judgments in U.K. courts. Section 5 limits enforcement of a foreign award to actual damages. Section 6 provides a "clawback" remedy, allowing a U.K. citizen or business organization to recover back the excess of damages paid in foreign litigation over the amount of actual damages, thus neutralizing any foreign court award of multiple damages.

PROTECTION OF TRADING INTERESTS ACT 1980

An Act to provide protection from requirements, prohibitions and judgments imposed or given under the laws of countries outside the United Kingdom and affecting the trading or other interests of persons in the United Kingdom

1. Overseas measures affecting United Kingdom trading interests

(1) If it appears to the Secretary of State—

(a) that measures have been or are proposed to be taken by or under the law of any overseas country for regulating or controlling international trade; and

(b) that those measures, in so far as they apply or would apply to things done or to be done outside the territorial jurisdiction of that country by persons carrying on business in the United Kingdom, are damaging or threaten to damage the trading interests of the United Kingdom,

the Secretary of State may by order direct that this section shall apply to those measures either generally or in their application to such cases as may be specified in the order.

(2) The Secretary of State may by order make provision for requiring, or enabling the Secretary of State to require, a person in the United Kingdom who carries on business there to give notice to the Secretary of State of any requirement or prohibition imposed or threatened to be imposed on that person pursuant to any measures in so far as this section applies to them by virtue of an order under subsection (1) above.

(3) The Secretary of State may give to any person in the United Kingdom who carries on business there such directions for prohibiting compliance with any such requirement or prohibition as aforesaid as he considers appropriate for avoiding damage to the trading interests of the United Kingdom.

(4) The power of the Secretary of State to make orders under subsection (1) or (2) above shall be exercisable by statutory instrument subject to annulment in pursuance of a resolution of either House of Parliament.

(5) Direction under subsection (3) above may be either general or special and may prohibit compliance with any requirement or prohibition either absolutely or in such cases or subject to such conditions as to consent or otherwise as may be specified in the directions; and general directions under that subsection shall be published in such manner as appears to the Secretary of State to be appropriate.

(6) In this section "trade" includes any activity carried on in the course of a business of any description and "trading interests" shall be construed accordingly.

ANNOTATIONS: See further, in relation to the disapplication of sub-§§ (1), (3) above: the Extraterritorial US Legislation (Sanctions against Cuba, Iran and Libya) (Protection of Trading Interests) Order 1996, SI 1996 No 3171, art. 3(1).

2. Documents and information required by overseas courts and authorities

(1) If it appears to the Secretary of State—

    (a) that a requirement has been or may be imposed on a person or persons in the United Kingdom to produce to any court, tribunal or authority of an overseas country any commercial document which is not within the territorial jurisdiction of that country or to furnish any commercial information to any such court, tribunal or authority; or

    (b) that any such authority has imposed or may impose a requirement on a person or persons in the United Kingdom to publish any such document or information,

the Secretary of State may, if it appears to him that the requirement is inadmissible by virtue of subsection (2) or (3) below, give directions for prohibiting compliance with the requirement.

(2) A requirement such as is mentioned in subsection (1)(a) or (b) above is inadmissible—

    (a) if it infringes the jurisdiction of the United Kingdom or is otherwise prejudicial to the sovereignty of the United Kingdom; or

    (b) if compliance with the requirement would be prejudicial to the security of the United Kingdom or to the relations of the government of the United Kingdom with the government of any other country.

(3) A requirement such as is mentioned in subsection (1)(a) above is also inadmissible—

    (a) if it is made otherwise than for the purposes of civil or criminal proceedings which have been instituted in the overseas country; or

    (b) if it requires a person to state what documents relevant to any such proceedings are or have been in his possession, custody or power or to produce for the purposes of any such proceedings any documents other than particular documents specified in the requirement.

(4) Directions under subsection (1) above may be either general or special and may prohibit compliance with any requirement either absolutely or in such cases or subject to such conditions as to consent or otherwise as may be specified in the directions; and general directions under that subsection shall be published in such manner as appears to the Secretary of State to be appropriate.

(5) For the purposes of this section the making of a request or demand shall be treated as the imposition of a requirement if it is made in circumstances in which a requirement to the same effect could be or could have been imposed; and

(a) any request or demand for the supply of a document or information which, pursuant to the requirement of any court, tribunal or authority of an overseas country, is addressed to a person in the United Kingdom; or

(b) any requirement imposed by such a court, tribunal or authority to produce or furnish any document or information to a person specified in the requirement,

shall be treated as a requirement to produce or furnish that document or information to that court, tribunal or authority.

(6) In this section "commercial document" and "commercial information" mean respectively a document or information relating to a business of any description and "document" includes any record or device by means of which material is recorded or stored.

ANNOTATIONS: See further, in relation to the disapplication of this section: the Extraterritorial US Legislation (Sanctions against Cuba, Iran and Libya) (Protection of Trading Interests) Order 1996, SI 1996 No 3171, art. 3(1).

3. Offences under §§ 1 and 2

(1) Subject to subsection (2) below, any person who without reasonable excuse fails to comply with any requirement imposed under subsection (2) of section 1 above or knowingly contravenes any directions given under subsection (3) of that section or section 2(1) above shall be guilty of an offence and liable—

(a) on conviction on indictment, to a fine;

(b) on summary conviction, to a fine not exceeding the statutory maximum.

(2) A person who is neither a citizen of the United Kingdom and Colonies nor a body corporate incorporated in the United Kingdom shall not be guilty of an offence under subsection (1) above by reason of anything done or omitted outside the United Kingdom in contravention of directions under section 1(3) or 2(1) above.

(3) No proceedings for an offence under subsection (1) above shall be instituted in England, Wales or Northern Ireland except by the Secretary of State or with the consent of the Attorney General or, as the case may be, the Attorney General for Northern Ireland.

(4) Proceedings against any person for an offence under this section may be taken before the appropriate court in the United Kingdom having jurisdiction in the place where that person is for the time being.

(5) . . .

ANNOTATIONS: Sub-§ (5): repealed by the Statute Law (Repeals) Act 1993.

4. Restriction of Evidence (Proceedings in Other Jurisdictions) Act 1975

A court in the United Kingdom shall not make an order under section 2 of the Evidence (Proceedings in Other Jurisdictions) Act 1975 for giving effect to a request issued by or on behalf of a court or tribunal of an overseas country if it is shown that the request infringes the jurisdiction of the United Kingdom or is otherwise prejudicial to the sovereignty of the United Kingdom; and a certificate signed by or on behalf of the Secretary of State to the effect that it infringes that jurisdiction or is so prejudicial shall be conclusive evidence of that fact.

5. Restriction on enforcement of certain overseas judgments

(1) A judgment to which this section applies shall not be registered under Part II of the Administration of Justice Act 1920 or Part I of the Foreign Judgments (Reciprocal Enforcement) Act 1933 and no court in the United Kingdom shall entertain proceedings at common law for the recovery of any sum payable under such a judgment.

(2) This section applies to any judgment given by a court of an overseas country, being—

(a) a judgment for multiple damages within the meaning of subsection (3) below;

(b) a judgment based on a provision or rule of law specified or described in an order under subsection (4) below and given after the coming into force of the order; or

(c) a judgment on a claim for contribution in respect of damages awarded by a judgment falling within paragraph (a) or (b) above.

(3) In subsection (2)(a) above a judgment for multiple damages means a judgment for an amount arrived at by doubling, trebling or otherwise multiplying a sum assessed as compensation for the loss or damage sustained by the person in whose favour the judgment is given.

(4) The Secretary of State may for the purposes of subsection (2)(b) above make an order in respect of any provision or rule of law which appears to him to be concerned with the prohibition or regulation of agreements, arrangements or practices designed to restrain, distort or restrict

651

competition in the carrying on of business of any description or to be otherwise concerned with the promotion of such competition as aforesaid.

(5) The power of the Secretary of State to make orders under subsection (4) above shall be exercisable by statutory instrument subject to annulment in pursuance of a resolution of either House of Parliament.

(6) Subsection (2)(a) above applies to a judgement given before the date of the passing of this Act as well as to a judgment given on or after that date but this section does not affect any judgment which has been registered before that date under the provisions mentioned in subsection (1) above or in respect of which such proceedings as are there mentioned have been finally determined before that date.

6.   Recovery of awards of multiple damages

(1) This section applies where a court of an overseas country has given a judgment for multiple damages with the meaning of section 5(3) above against—

(a) a citizen of the United Kingdom and Colonies; or

(b) a body corporate incorporated in the United Kingdom or in a territory outside the United Kingdom for whose international relations Her Majesty's Government in the United Kingdom are responsible; or

(c) a person carrying on business in the United Kingdom,

(in this section referred to as a "qualifying defendant") and an amount on account of the damages has been paid by the qualifying defendant either to the party in whose favour the judgment was given or to another party who is entitled as against the qualifying defendant to contribution in respect of the damages.

(2) Subject to subsections (3) and (4) below, the qualifying defendant shall be entitled to recover from the party in whose favour the judgment was given so much of the amount referred to in subsection (1) above as exceeds the part attributable to compensation; and that part shall be taken to be such part of the amount as bears to the whole of it the same proportion as the sum assessed by the court that gave the judgment as compensation for the loss or damage sustained by that party bears to the whole of the damages awarded to that party.

(3) Subsection (2) above does not apply where the qualifying defendant is an individual who was ordinarily resident in the overseas country at the time when the proceedings in which the judgment was given were instituted or a body corporate which had its principal place of business there at that time.

(4) Subsection (2) above does not apply where the qualifying defendant carried on business in the overseas country and the proceedings in which the judgment was given were concerned with activities exclusively carried on in that country.

(5) A court in the United Kingdom may entertain proceedings on a claim under this section notwithstanding that the person against whom the proceedings are brought is not within the jurisdiction of the court.

(6) The reference in subsection (1) above to an amount paid by the qualifying defendant includes a reference to an amount obtained by execution against his property or against the property of a company which (directly or indirectly) is wholly owned by him; and references in that subsection and subsection (2) above to the party in whose favour the judgment was given or to a party entitled to contribution include references to any person in whom the rights of any such party have become vested by succession or assignment or otherwise.

(7) This section shall, with the necessary modifications, apply also in relation to any order which is made by a tribunal or authority of an overseas country and would, if that tribunal or authority were a court, be a judgment for multiple damages within the meaning of section 5(3) above.

(8) This section does not apply to any judgment given or order made before the passing of this Act.

ANNOTATIONS: See further, in relation to the disapplication of this section: the Extraterritorial US Legislation (Sanctions against Cuba, Iran and Libya) (Protection of Trading Interests) Order 1996, SI 1996 No 3171, art. 3(2).

7. Enforcement of overseas judgment under provision corresponding to § 6

(1) If it appears to Her Majesty that the law of an overseas country provides or will provide for the enforcement in that country of judgments given under section 6 above, Her Majesty may by Order in Council provide for the enforcement in the United Kingdom of [judgments of any description specified in the Order which are given under any provision of the law of that country relating to the recovery of sums paid or obtained pursuant to a judgment for multiple damages within the meaning of section 5(3) above, whether or not that provision corresponds to section 6 above].

[(1A) Such an Order in Council may, as respects judgments to which it relates—

(a) make different provisions for different descriptions of judgment; and

(b) impose conditions or restrictions on the enforcement of judgments of any description.]

(2) An Order under this section may apply, with or without modification, any of the provisions of the Foreign Judgments (Reciprocal Enforcement) Act 1933.

ANNOTATIONS: Amended by the Civil Jurisdiction and Judgments Act 1982, § 38.

8. Short title, interpretation, repeals and extent

(1) This Act may be cited as the Protection of Trading Interests Act 1980.

(2) In this Act "overseas country" means any country or territory outside the United Kingdom other than one for whose international relations Her Majesty's Government in the United Kingdom are responsible.

(3) References in this Act to the law or a court, tribunal or authority of an overseas country include, in the case of a federal state, references to the law or a court, tribunal or authority of any constituent part of that country.

(4) References in this Act to a claim for, or to entitlement to, contribution are references to a claim or entitlement based on an enactment or rule of law.

(5), (6) . . .

(7) This Act extends to Northern Ireland.

(8) Her Majesty may by Order in Council direct that this Act shall extend with such exceptions, adaptations and modifications, if any, as may be specified in the Order to any territory outside the United Kingdom, being a territory for the international relations of which Her Majesty's Government in the United Kingdom are responsible.

ANNOTATIONS: Sub-§§ (5), (6): repeal the Shipping Contracts and Commercial Documents Act 1964.